E. B. O'Callaghan

A List of Editions of the Holy Scriptures

And Parts thereof Printed in America Previous to 1860

E. B. O'Callaghan

A List of Editions of the Holy Scriptures
And Parts thereof Printed in America Previous to 1860

ISBN/EAN: 9783337248987

Printed in Europe, USA, Canada, Australia, Japan

Cover: Foto ©Lupo / pixelio.de

More available books at **www.hansebooks.com**

A

LIST

OF EDITIONS

OF THE

HOLY SCRIPTURES

AND PARTS THEREOF,

PRINTED IN AMERICA PREVIOUS TO 1860:

WITH

INTRODUCTION AND BIBLIOGRAPHICAL NOTES.

BY E. B. O'CALLAGHAN.

ALBANY:
MUNSELL & ROWLAND.
1861.

Entered according to Act of Congress, in the year 1861,

BY E. B. O'CALLAGHAN,

In the Clerk's Office of the District Court of the United States, for the Northern District of New York.

TO

JAMES LENOX, ESQ

NEW YORK,

THIS WORK

IS

RESPECTFULLY INSCRIBED.

INTRODUCTION.

Previous to the American Revolution this country was supplied with Bibles in the English language, chiefly from Great Britain. Publishers in the Plantations are represented as having been under the impression, that if they reprinted the work, they would be guilty of an infringement of the exclusive right possessed by certain parties in England, and expose themselves to prosecution. If we add to this, the abundant supply from abroad; the low price of English copies,[1] and, above all, the fashion which then gave, as it now gives, a preference to issues from the English press, we shall find the causes that prevented the publication of the Bible in the Old Colonies, as they are at present a bar to its publication in the remaining British Possessions on this Continent.

We might, therefore, have come down to the era of American Independence without meeting an American Bible, had not an humble Indian Missionary, as devoted as he was disinterested, translated the sacred volume for his little flock. Thus, the first edition of the Bible "that was ever printed

---

[1] In a trial in England, between John Baskett, plaintiff, and Henry Pearson, defendant, the price of the Common English Nonpareil Bible, was stated to have been in 1699, 2s. 6d., and in 1720, 21d. It fell subsequently to a shilling. No American publisher could compete against such prices.

INTRODUCTION.

in all America since the very foundations of the world,"[1] came forth most appropriately in a purely American language, a monument of the patience, piety, and zeal of the venerable ELIOT. In 1678, A Harmony of the Gospels, by the same author, followed; in 1707 a portion, and in 1708 the whole, of The Gospel of St. John, was published at Boston, in Indian and *English*, and these are all that had been accomplished in this country in the field of Biblical literature, at the commencement of the eighteenth century, if we except some metrical versions of the Psalms and detached pieces of Scripture.

COTTON MATHER was undoubtedly the first who projected the publication in America of an edition of the Bible in English. He commenced the preparation of what he called the *Biblia Americana*, about the year 1695, and having spent fifteen years in collecting and compiling notes, comments and expositions, announced, in 1710, the completion of his work, in an Advertisement at the end of one of his Tracts,[2] hoping "that the Glorious head of the Church will stir up some generous minds to forward an undertaking so confessedly worthy to be prosecuted."

But this hope was not realized. No printer could be found in the Colonies to hazard such an enterprise.

Disappointed at home, Dr. Mather determined to make an appeal abroad, and in 1713 issued another Prospectus, addressed mainly to London publishers. As the matter of the Advertisement of 1710 is included in the Prospectus of

---

[1] *Mather's Magnalia*, Book III, 197.

[2] *Bonifacius*. An Essay upon the Good, that is to be Devised and Designed, by those Who Desire to Answer the Great End of *Life*, and to Do Good while they *Live*. BOSTON in *N. England*: Printed by *B. Green*, for *Samuel Gerrish* at his Shop in Corn Hill, 1710. 16mo. This rare tract is in the Library of the Massachusetts Historical Society.

1713, we shall content ourselves with reproducing the latter only. It is entitled

A | NEW OFFER | TO THE LOVERS OF | RELIGION AND LEARNING. |

It is *Agreed* by all true Christians, and most *Certain* to them, That we are *highly Favoured* of Heaven, with a Divine *Storehouse of Truth* in our SACRED SCRIPTURES. The World has nothing in it comparable to this BOOK OF GOD, and of Life. A Book, which all the Learning under Heaven may be well employ'd, for the *Illustration* of; and is never so *well* employ'd, as when *so* employ'd. The *Illustration* of it, is indeed the most *Serviceable* and the most *Entertaining* Thing, that can be offered unto them that have any Value, and Relish or Concern for that Knowledge, which is of all the most valuable, and that would be *Wise unto the best of Purposes*.

It is a passage of the Celebrated BOYL; 'When I Consider, how much
'more to the Advantage of the Sacred Writings, and of Christian Theology
'in general, diverse Texts have been Explained, and Discoursed of, by the
'Excellent *Grotius, Masius, Mede*, and Sir *Francis Bacon*, and some other
'late great Witts (to name now no Living ones,) in their several Kinds, than
'the same Places have been handled by *Vulgar Expositors*, and other
'Divines; And when I consider, that none of these Worthies, was at once
'a great *Philosopher* and a great *Critick*; I cannot but hope, that when it
'shall please God, to stir up Persons of a *Philosophical* Genius, well fur-
'nished with *Critical Learning*, and the Principles of true *Philosophy*, and
'shall give them an hearty Concern for the Advance of His Truths, these
'Men will make *Explications* and *Discoveries* that shall be Admirable. You
'shall no more measure the Wisdom of God couched in the Bible by the
'Glosses and Systems of common Expositors,¹ than æstimate the Wisdom
'He has express'd in the Contrivance of the World, by *Magirus's* or *Eusta-
'chius's* Physicks.

This *Wise Man* was a *Prophet*, when he wrote those Lines. An Age of *Light* comes on; *Explications* and *Discoveries* are continually growing; which all that will but *shew themselves Men* cannot but imbibe with Satisfaction. The *Path of the Just One*, in His gracious Approaches towards us, causes the *Light* which opens His Oracles unto us, to *shine more and more towards the perfect Day*. Doubtless the Pagan *Longinus* pleased his Jewish Empress, the brave *Zenobia*, when she read him admiring the *High Style* of *Moses* in that stately Stroke of the Creation ; *God said, Let there be Light; And there was Light!* But how admirable is that great Work of the *most High God*, which has given effectual Order for His Church in our Day ; *Let there*

---

¹ and Preachers. *Advertisement of* 1710.

be *Light in it, and let my Oracles be Illustrated!* And, *Lo, there is Light, and the Illustrations of the Sacred Scriptures are carried on to Wonderment!* The Instruments by whom this *Light* is brought down unto us, have of late been greatly Multiplied: *God has given His Word* for it, and *Great has been the Army of those that have published it.*

Anon, We have the Admirable WITSIUS Comforting of us, with his Report, of this Importance. *Neq; profecto Officio hic suo defuerunt Illustres Animæ.*——' There have not been wanting those Illustrious Men, [*And 'Thou, my dear* Witsius, *not the least of them!*] who have observed all the ' Solid Discoveries in *Philosophy*, all the Curious Researches of *Antiquity*, or ' that has occurred in *Physick*, or in *Law*, relating to the *Sacred Scriptures*, ' and have applied it all with a signal *Dexterity* to the Illustration thereof: ' And so 'tis come to pass, that Theology, which had vast riches of its own ' before, is now also enriched with foreign *Spoils*, and appears with those 'Ornaments, which extort, even from them that are most of all disaffected ' unto it, a Confession of its most Charming Majesty.

The noble Service to Mankind, thus proposed, having been so far pursued, it is easy to imagine, that a Person of but common Abilities, [for He who now Writes may pretend unto no more;] applying himself unto it, may accomplish a very *Rich Collection of Illustrations upon the Sacred Scriptures.* An ADVERTISEMENT now comes forth, to Inform the Friends of Learning and Religion, that it is in some degree accomplished. An, *Opus Ecclesiæ*, is ready when it shall be call'd for.

No little Part of what has been Written on the great Intention of *Illustrating the Divine Oracles* has been perused. Some Hundreds of the *Latest* as well as of the *Oldest* Writers that have had any thing looking that way, have been Consulted : If not for Number enough to have built an Egyptian Pyramid, yet so many, as to render the *Extract* alone which is now made from them, a sort of *Library.*

Where small *Pamphlets*, as well as large *Volumns*, have made any valuable *Offerings* to the Service of the Sanctuary, they have not been wholly neglected. The *Names* of them, whose grateful Stores have been brought into this *Common Hive*, whether they be Dead or Living, are with all decent Ingenuity acknowledged and eternized. Not only the *Rare Thoughts* of the more Illustrious Literators, who are known for *Stars of the first Magnitude* in the Catalogue of them that have *handled the Pen of the Writer*, but also the *Hints* occurring in Books that have made no Profession of serving this Cause, and many of them very *unsuspected ones*, have been seized for it. Many Thousands of those *Fine Thoughts*, whereof sometimes *One* or *Two*, or a very *Few*, have enabled a Writer to find some Acceptance in setting up for *Authorism*, are here together set upon the Table, in order to a Feast of *Fat Things full of Marrow, of Wines in the Lees well refined.* It cannot be presumed that the

INTRODUCTION. ix

Eye of the poor Industry, which has laboured on this Design, has yet *seen every precious Thing*, yet in the more than three Lustres of years which have run since it began the Undertaking, it has often *visited the Place of Sapphires*, and *found the Dust of Gold*, which is here to be exposed unto the more Sensible and Ingenuous part of Mankind, when it shall be thought a time for it. And it may be easily supposed, that one of no more than a *Common Reach*, Conversing so much with such Things, may now and then also make a feeble Flight towards an *Illustration* of his own, that may deserve Attention. There is an *American Plant*, which alone, as *Hernandez* will with some Demonstration tell us, *Quicquid vitæ esse potest Necessarium, facile prestare potest;* it will answer all the *Necessities* of Humane Life, yea, and supply the *Delicacies* of it also. It is possible, this *American Work*, may with as Universal an Accommodation, afford what may be *Necessary*, yea, and what may be likewise *Delectable* to them, who in acquainting themselves with the *Best of Books*, and Things, would have their Studies well accommodated. The *Collection* makes Two FOLIO's of some considerable Dimensions, which now lye ready for Publication: Hoping that *Vossius's* Complaint of another Country, will not always be true of *Ours*, That one can hardly get any thing Printed, but either *Quarrels* or *Trifles; Eristica et Nugalia, quibus nihil vendibilius, ut ipsi non dissimulant Typographi.*

It has been studied, that this Work might not interfere with the large *English Annotations*, begun by the Excellent POOL, and finished by some of his Brethren. Those *Polan Annotations* have been left almost wholly unconsulted, in the Composing of this Work, that their Value and Vending may not suffer the least measure of Depreciation from it. Nor will the inestimable Performances of such as Mr. *Matthew Henry* lose the least Grain of their Esteem with the Faithful, by having this Work to wait, (if the Public please to have it so) as an *Appendix* upon them. These Composures will be singularly useful to one another.

The Work is attempted by a Person so strictly adhering to the Principles of the *Christian Religion*, professed in the *Reformed Churches*, that the Reader is perfectly released and secured from all Fear of his finding here, any dangerous *Innovations* in, or *Deviations* from, the *Faith once delivered unto the Saints*. Instead of that, he will very frequently find, that the most important Articles of our *most Holy Faith*, are here defended with *a New Force*, by setting in a *Clear Light* such Texts, as have not been observed heretofore to carry such Assertions in them, or have been encumbred with the Glosses which *Men of Corrupt Minds* have put upon them. Nevertheless, the *Attempt* is carried on, with such a *Catholick Spirit*, that it may be hoped no *Good Man*, will have any Matter of just offence given unto him. It is not a Work animated with the *Spirit of a Party;* and it may be hoped, that

B

nothing but that ungenerous and comtemptible Spirit, will cast the disdainful Eye of the *Scorner* upon it. Accordingly it is already come to pass, that very Eminent Persons, Divines of great Note, in the *Church by Law Established*, having been apprised of the Work, have generously offered their best Encouragements unto it. Numbers of the best Men among the *Dissenters* have expressed their Wishes, not without some Impatience for it. *Scotland* also invites it, expects it, requires it. In *America*, 'tis asked for, and waited for. And there may be some hope, That all *Impartial Christians*, of whatever Denomination or Subdivision in Christianity, will reckon it, *An useful Work*. For indeed *Common Sense* will say, it must needs be *so*, if the *Books*, from which the *Best Things* are fetch'd, and laid here together, were *so*. And yet, there is more than *this*, to argue for it. Briefly, Men of *every Religion*, yea, and some of *no Religion* at all, have had *Spoils* taken from them, for the Enriching of this Work; And, why should not all good Men, who embrace the *True Religion*, tho' of different Perswasions in some lesser Points of it, Unite in the Enjoyment of the Riches?

To bestow the Censure of *Pride* and *Vanity*, on the proposing of such a Work for Publication, would be therewith to Censure and Reproach all Attempts in such a way to serve the Public. Most certainly 'tis no Trespass against the Rules of *Modesty*, to give the Public a Report and a Tender, of what has been thus prepared for it; but it would look like one against the Rules of *Equity*, to call it so. Most certainly, it is a *Modest* Thing, a *Sober*, a *Proper*, and a very *Lawful* One, for an *Honest Man* to desire, that so much of a short Life, as has been spent in such a Preparation, should not be *spent in Vain*.

The Pen, which all along this Work, pays all due Acknowledgments unto those, whom the Sovereign GOD furnished and honoured with the Treasures, which are thro' their Hands come into it, *seeks not its own Honour*; And if even the small Reputation of a little *Diligence* and *Contrivance* be denied unto it, in this also it will Propound all imaginable Satisfaction. It would, if that had been possible, have kept the Authors Name under such a Reservation, that it must have been only a Retainer to *Placcius's* Treatise, *De Scriptoribus Anonymis*. It is content, that the Writer be Clouded with all possible *Obscurity;* and that it be left wholly unconsidered, whether he has ever given any Testimony of a tolerable Capacity for such a Work as this, by any *other Performances;* or, whether any considerable *Societies* in the World, have ever thought him worthy of being *Theirs*. It has nothing to object against as many *Diminutions* and *Annihilations*, as the superiour Part of Mankind may think agreeable for him. He only desires, that the Oblations which he brings from those that may be accounted *Better than himself*, (and which he might, if he had pleased, have made in the most *common Methods*,

INTRODUCTION. xi

to pass for, *His own*), may find Acceptance with the Church, to which we all owe our *All:* And that AMERICA may at length, with a Benign and Smiling Aspect of her Lady-Mother upon her, come in to do something, for an Interest that must *have these uttermost Parts of the Earth for its Possession.*

Sometimes very mean Things, have on the score of their being *Far-fetcht*, had a value set upon them, and not been look'd upon as too *Dear-bought*, when a great Price has been given for them. If a Work, which is a *Tree*, that grew on the Western side of the *Atlantic*, may on *that score* hope to be valued by good Men, in the *other Hemisphere*, there will be an accession of *this peculiar Circumstance*, that, *Gentlemen*, the *Fruits* upon it, or at least, the *Seeds* that produced them, were most of them, Originally *Your own:* And it cannot but be a Pleasure, if not a *Surprize* unto you, to find that so many of your *Best Things*, have passed over *the great and wide Sea* unto the *American Strand.* Nor will it be New or Strange, if some Things happen to be *Meliorated*, and made more *Sweet* and *Fine*, by passing over this mighty Ocean. Or, to address you under *another Figure;* The Writers whom you made much of, while you had them *at Home* with you in a more *separate Condition*, certainly, will not lose your Favour, for having *Travelled Abroad*, and now *Returned Home* in *Company;* tho' with their *Habit* and *Language* having something of an *American* Change upon it.

But, what brings this *Promiser*, that may be worthy of so much Expectation?

THIS is the TITLE of it. These Promises may be made in the *Title-Page* of it. Behold here, a *Communi Fax*, unto it.

[Here follows the Title, reprinted at page 19, *post.*]

¶ The usual Method for the Publication of such a Work, has been, first of all to Publish PROPOSALS for SUBSCRIPTIONS: For who can Dream, that such *Bulky & Costly Things*, can unassisted, make their own way into the World? But in the present Case, the Distance of the Author from *Europe*, & the Abode of the Work in *America* till it may be sent over with some hopeful Encouragement, and the uncertainty of what may be the *precise Number of Sheets* which will be needful on the Occasion, will oblige to something a little *Unusual* in the way of Proceeding.

Understanding that the Work will make *Two Volumns* in FOLIO, it is proposed, That it shall be afforded unto Subscribers, at the same Rate, that *such Books*, of the same *Quantity*, and in the same *Character*, have usually been afforded at: Which is a Rate so generally *Agreed* (and very seldom or little *Varied*,) that the venture of a more *Indefinite Subscribing* for it, need not be much scrupled at.

It shall also be insisted on, with the Booksellers, that whoever shall procure and send in *Subscriptions* for *Nine Sets* of this Work, shall have a Tenth *Gratis*.

It is therefore PROPOSED, that the Persons who are Well-wishers to a Work of this Intention and Usefulness, would send in their *Names*, affixed unto the following Declaration.

When it shall please GOD, *that the Work Entituled*, BIBLIA AMERICANA, *whereof the Public has been Advertised, in the* New Offer to the Lovers of Religion and Learning; *shall be Published, (and if it be done without unnecessary Delays) the Subscriber will take off a Sett, (namely*, The Two Volumns) *at the Price assign'd by the Booksellers, with the Advice of Three unexceptionable Ministers of the City of* London, *within the general Rate which for a Work so Circumstanced has been formerly declared Reasonable*.[1]

This Appeal met with no better success than the first. A third attempt to obtain a publisher was made in 1728, but it likewise was unsuccessful; and the Manuscript, as it came one hundred and fifty years ago from the hands of the literary Giant of New England, now sleeps forgotten and almost unknown, amid the Collections of the Massachusetts Historical Society, a reproof to the wealth and a reproach to the enterprise of the present generation.

Nearly half a century passed without a line of Scripture having been printed in this country, except, perhaps, in Psalters or Prayer Books. At length, what others with greater pretensions failed to accomplish, was effected by an humble, painstaking Immigrant, to whom the honor belongs of having given to America the first edition of the Bible in a European language.

CHRISTOPHER SAUR was born in Germany in 1693; immigrated to this country in 1724, and settled permanently in Germantown, Pa., in 1731. Being of a religious temperament and of a reflecting turn of mind, his attention was di-

---

[1] From the Tract in the Library of the American Antiquarian Society, Worcester, Mass.

rected to the destitute condition of his countrymen in respect to books, especially the Scriptures. He procured a printing press and types, and commenced the business of a publisher in 1738. In 1740 he began printing an edition of the Bible in German, and in 1743 completed the volume, which will be found fully described under that year. Mr. Saur died in 1758, before another edition of the Bible was called for. His son reprinted an edition of the work in 1763 consisting of two thousand copies, and another of three thousand copies in 1776;[1] but most of the latter were seized in the war of the Revolution and used as cartridge paper or as litter for horses. Mr. Saur's daughter succeeded, however, in rescuing the sheets of ten complete copies which she caused to be bound.[2]

Meanwhile, KNEELAND & GREEN of Boston (it is alleged), printed principally for Daniel Henchman, an edition of the Bible in the English language, in small quarto. It was carried through the press as privately as possible, and had the London imprint of the copy from which it was reprinted, viz: "London: Printed by Mark Baskett, Printer to the King's Most Excellent Majesty," in order to prevent a prosecution from those, in England and Scotland, who published the Bible by a patent from the Crown; or *Cum privilegio*, as did the English Universities at Oxford and Cambridge. "When I was an apprentice (continues Mr. Thomas), I often heard those who had assisted at the case and press in printing this Bible, make mention of the fact. The late Gov. Hancock was related to Henchman, and knew the particulars of the transaction. He possessed a copy of this impression. As it had a London imprint, at this day it can be

---

[1] *Simpson's Eminent Men of Philadelphia.*

[2] The Rev Dr. Holmes says in his *American Annals*, II, 486 (note), that Saur's edition of 1776 "was the first quarto Bible, that ever issued from an American press." He apparently was ignorant of the editions of 1743 and 1763, and had forgotten Eliot's Indian Bibles.

distinguished from an English edition of the same date, only by those who are acquainted with the niceties of typography. This Bible issued from the press about the time that the partnership of Kneeland & Green expired.[1] The edition was not large; I have been informed that it did not exceed seven or eight hundred copies.

"Not long after the time that this impression of the Bible came from the press, an edition of the New Testament, in duodecimo, was printed by Rogers and Fowle, for those at whose expense the Bible issued. Both the Bible and the Testament were well executed.... The credit of this edition of the Testament was, for the reason I have mentioned, transferred to the King's printer, in London, by the insertion of his imprint."[2] And, farther on, Mr. Thomas adds:

"During the partnership of Rogers and Fowle they printed an edition of about two thousand copies of the New Testament, 12mo., for D. Henchman, and two or three other principal booksellers, as has been already observed.

"This impression of the Testament, the first in the English language printed in this country, was, as I have been informed, completed at the press before Kneeland and Green began the edition of the Bible which has been mentioned.

"Zechariah Fowle, with whom I served my apprenticeship, as well as several others, repeatedly mentioned to me this edition of the Testament. He was at the time, a journeyman with Rogers and Fowle, and worked at the press. He informed me, that on account of the weakness of his constitution, he greatly injured his health by the performance. Privacy in the business was necessary; and as few hands were intrusted with the secret, the press work was, as he thought, very laborious. I mention these minute circumstances in proof that an edition of the Testament did issue

---

[1] 1752.

[2] *Thomas, History of Printing,* I, 305, 306.

INTRODUCTION. xv

from the office of Rogers and Fowle, because I have heard that the fact has been disputed."[1]

We have here given at length, in justice to Mr. Thomas, all he has stated on the subject of these editions, the printing of which has been not only disputed anew, but denied by Mr. Bancroft, who asserts that the Bible "was never printed here in English until the land became free," and then adds in a note:

> Thomas . . . repeats only what he heard. Himself a collector, he does not profess ever to have seen a copy of the alleged American edition of the English Bible. Search has repeatedly been made for a copy, and always without success. Six or eight hundred Bibles in quarto could hardly have been printed, bound and sold in Boston, then a small town, undiscovered. Nor would they all have disappeared. The most complete catalogues of English Bibles enumerate no one with the imprint, which was said to have been copied. Till a copy of the pretended American edition is produced, no credit can be given to the second-hand story, which is moreover at variance with the statement of Dr. Chauncey, the minister of the first Church of Boston, at the time of the pretended publication.[2]

The reader has here before him what has been said, on both sides, regarding the alleged Kneeland & Green (or Mark Baskett) Bible of 1752. Bibles near that year have been found with the following imprints:

London: Printed by Thomas Baskett, Printer to the King's Most Excellent Majesty, and by the Assigns of Robert Barker. 1751. Folio.
The Same. 1752. 12mo.
Oxford: Printed by Thomas Baskett, Printer to the University. 1752. 4to.
The Same. 1753, 1754, 1761. 4to.

---

[1] *History of Printing*, I, 324, 325.

[2] *Bancroft, History of the United States*, v, 266, 11th edition. On page xxi, *post*, will be found a letter from Dr. Chauncey on the lack of facilities for printing an edition of the Bible in Boston in 1782, but as Mr. Bancroft has omitted to indicate the source whence he derived the statement he attributes to that clergyman, we are unable to say whether the letter now published be that source.

London: Printed by Mark Baskett, Printer to the King's Most Excellent Majesty, and by the Assigns of Robert Barker. 1761. 4to.
The Same. 1763. 4to.

But as yet all efforts to discover a copy corresponding with that mentioned by Mr. Thomas, have, as far as we are aware, been unsuccessful: the titles of both Bible and Testament are, therefore, omitted in the present List.

Before taking leave of the subject it may not, perhaps, be out of place to notice a discrepancy in Mr. Thomas's account, in regard to the time that the New Testament was printed; that event having occurred, according to his statement in one place, "Not long *after* the time that the impression of the Bible came from the press," whilst in another place he says, "This impression of the Testament.... was, as I have been informed, completed at the press *before* Kneeland and Green began the edition of the Bible which has been mentioned."[1]

Whilst engaged in examining the several points connected with this matter, we were curious to know whether the Patent to Baskett did actually extend to, and include the Colonies. We accordingly endeavored to procure a copy of that to John Baskett under which we supposed that Mark Baskett held. The subjoined letters will show the result.

—— Wright, Esq. Clarendon Press, Oxford:	Agency for American Libraries, 12 Tavistock Row, Covent Garden, London, Dec. 20th, 1858.

Sir:

Can you inform me how to obtain a copy of the "Patent issued to John Baskett as King's Printer" 2 Geo. II. (Dec. 1728); if so, I shall feel greatly obliged. It is wanted for a simply literary purpose.

I am, Sir, Your Obed. Serv't,

Ask Mr. Griffiths.   EDW. ALLEN,

Can Dr. Rowden enable J. Wright to give a satisfactory reply to the inquirer?

---

[1] Compare *History of Printing*, 1, 305, 324.

SIR:
UNIVERSITY PRESS,
OXFORD, Dec. 21, 1858.

Having applied to the Registrar of the University, and also to the Keeper of the Archives, for the purpose of obtaining the desired information, I regret to say that I have done so without success, neither of the gentlemen being able to throw any light upon the mode of appointment. Could the present printers to the Queen render you any service in the enquiry? Your Obed't Servant,

JAMES WRIGHT.

AGENCY FOR AMERICAN LIBRARIES,
12 Tavistock Row, Covent Garden,
DEAR SIR: LONDON, Jan. 14th, 1859.

I have now to inform you that I cannot succeed in obtaining the Patent sought for in your enquiry of Aug. 2, '58. Enquiries had previously been made in London fruitlessly, when the enclosed note was penned to the Clarendon Press, Oxford, reply on the half sheet remaining. The Queen's Printers could not supply it, but referred to the Six Clerks' Office, they could not, but referred to the Rolls Court, where a second application was made, and a dilligent search, but to no avail, the Chief Clerk's opinion being that the Patent had been taken out, but not *registered*.

I am, &c.,

Dr. E. B. O'CALLAGHAN, Your Ob't Serv't,
New York. EDW. ALLEN.[1]

In the remaining period of Colonial dependency, we meet with only one instance of an attempt towards printing a Bible in English in this country. That attempt was made by JOHN FLEMING, a Scotch printer of Boston, who issued a Prospectus in 1770, of which the following is a copy:

The FIRST BIBLE ever printed in AMERICA. |

Proposals | for Printing by subscription, | In a most BEAUTIFUL and ELEGANT Manner | IN TWO large VOLUMES FOLIO. | The HOLY BIBLE, | containing | THE OLD AND NEW TESTAMENTS: | or a | FAMILY BIBLE, | with Annotations and Parallel Scriptures. | Containing, | I. An INTERPRETA-

---

[1] The patent to Christopher Barker and that to Reeves, Eyre and Strahan, King's printers, will be found at length in *Hansard's Typographia*, 175, 183. The latter recites the patent granted to John Baskett, 15 December, 1728.

TION of all the difficult PHRASES, and WORDS. | II. PARALLEL SCRIPTURES both as to MATTER and WORDS, with an ANNALYSIS, thereby show | ing the Frame and Contexture of the Whole. | To which is annexed, | The Reduction of Jewish Weights, Coins, and Measures, to our English Standards ; | and | A TABLE of the SCRIPTURE PROMISES. | By the late Rev. SAMUEL CLARK, M. A. |

*** This Work is recommended in the strongest Manner to every serious Christian, as best calculated for | Universal Edification, of any Book of this kind ever yet published, | By the late Worthy and Rev. GEORGE WHITEFIELD, A. M. | Subscriptions are taken in by JOHN FLEMING, at his PRINTING-OFFICE in | *Newbury-street*, nearly opposite the White-Horse Tavern, Boston. |

CONDITIONS.

I. The Text of this Bible will be printed on a *very fine new* TYPE, which, by good Judges, has been pronounced preferable, both as to SIZE and ELEGANCE, to that on which Mr. Baskervill's *celebrated Bible* is printed. (*Baskervill's Bible without Annotations cost the Subscribers four Guineas*.) The Notes will be printed on a Type somewhat smaller than the Text, though considerably *larger* than the NOTES to *any* BIBLE ever yet Published. Of both these Types the annexed two Pages are Specimens.

II. The Paper, (which is to be the *Manufacture of this Country*,) shall be the same with that on which these Proposals are printed.

N. B. A few Copies will be printed on superfine Imperial Paper, if Subscribed for.

III. In order to render the above work *easy* to the *Buyer*, it is proposed, that a NUMBER containing FIVE Sheets, or TWENTY Pages, of the same size with the annexed Specimen (sewed in a Cover) be ready to be delivered to Subscribers every Fortnight, at the Price of ONE SHILLING *Sterling* each Number. The superfine Imperial Paper, double Price.

IV. From the *splendid* Manner in which it is intended to execute this Work, it is computed it will extend to THREE HUNDRED and FIFTY SHEETS, or SEVENTY NUMBERS :— Should it exceed, the Overpluss will be DELIVERED *gratis* to the SUBSCRIBERS.—If it be comprised in fewer Numbers, our Author's *much admired* HARMONY *of the* GOSPEL, will be added to this Work.

V. In order to encourage Booksellers, Country Traders and all others to promote Subscriptions for this grand and useful Work, the Publisher will give TWO COPIES *gratis*, to such as shall collect ONE DOZEN of Subscribers, and receiving the Money from them.—Booksellers, Country Traders, &c., may be supplied with Proposals, by applying to JOHN

FLEMING, at his PRINTING-OFFICE, in *Newbury-Street*, nearly opposite the White-Horse Tavern, Boston; where Subscriptions are taken in.

VI. The Subscribers names will be printed.

N. B. The great expence with which this Work will necessarily be attended, renders it imprudent for the publisher to venture on it without the Assistance of a Subscription.— He hopes, that as it is the *first* Undertaking of the kind EVER *attempted* in AMERICA, he will meet with such Encouragement as will enable him to render this Work, as correct, elegant, and perfect, as the Importance of it demands.—Should his Expectations in this respect be answered, no *care, pains*, nor *expence* shall be spared. And he flatters himself, he shall, at the Close of the Publication, have the Honour to present to this Country, as *correct* and *beautiful* an EDITION of the Sacred Writings, with ANNOTATIONS, as has hitherto appeared in ANY PART *of the* WORLD.

⁎ This Work will be put to the Press as soon as THREE HUNDRED are subscribed for, and a Number containing FIVE Sheets, will be regularly published every Fortnight, 'till the whole is completed.

[Here follows a letter from "The late Revd. and Pious Mr. Whitefield recommendatory of Dr. Clark's edition of the Bible.][1]

This project however, failed through want of encouragement; at so low an ebb, says Dr. Miller, was the book trade in our country;[2] for books printed in London, however executed, sold better than those which were printed in America.[3]

The breaking out of the Revolution having, soon after, cut off the supply of "books printed in London," the scarcity of Bibles also came soon to be felt. Dr. PATRICK ALLISON, one of the Chaplains of Congress, and other gentlemen brought the subject before that body in a Memorial in which they urged the Printing of an edition of the Scriptures.

On the 11th September, 1777, the Committee to whom that Memorial was referred, reported;

---

[1] From the Broad Sheet in possession of George Livermore, Esq., of Boston.

[2] *Brief Retrospect*, I, 362.

[3] *History of Printing*, I, 362, 363.

The Committee to whom the Memorial of Doctor Allison and others was referred, report, "that they have conferred fully with the printers, &c., in this city, and are of opinion that the proper types for printing the bible are not to be had in this country, and that the paper cannot be procured, but with such difficulties and subject to such casualities as to render any dependance on it altogether improper: that to import types for the purpose of setting up an entire edition of the bible, and to strike of 30,000 copies, with paper, binding, &c., will cost 10.272*l*. 10*s*. 0*d*., which must be advanced by Congress to be reimbursed by the sale of the books: that in the opinion of the Committee considerable difficulties will attend the procuring the types and paper, that afterwards the risque of importing them will considerably enhance the cost, and that the calculations are subject to such uncertainty in the present state of affairs, that Congress cannot much rely on them: that the use of the bible is so universal, and its importance so great, that your Committee refer the above to the consideration of Congress, and if Congress shall not think it expedient to order the importation of types and paper, the Committee recommend that Congress will order the Committee of Congress to import 20,000 bibles from Holland, Scotland, or elsewhere, into the different ports of the States of the Union."

Whereupon it was resolved accordingly to direct said Committee to import 20,000 copies of the bible.

On this motion, New Hampshire, Massachusetts, Rhode Island, Connecticut, New Jersey, Pennsylvania and Georgia, voted in the affirmative; New York, Delaware, Maryland, Virginia, North Carolina, South Carolina in the negative.[1]

The demand could not fail to stimulate American Publishers to increased exertion. Accordingly, ROBERT AITKEN, a native of Scotland, who, a few years previous, had become a printer in Philadelphia, issued in 1777 an edition of the New Testament, the first printed in English in this country, with an American imprint. Other editions followed in each of the years immediately succeeding, and on the 21st January, 1781, Mr. Aitken announced, in a petition to Congress, that he had undertaken to print an edition of the Bible entire.

In the following year, the Rev. Dr. LYMAN, of Hatfield, Mass., addressed a letter to the Association of Congregational

---

[1] *Journal of Congress* for 1777-78, p. 387.

Ministers in Boston, urging the necessity of publishing an edition of the Holy Scriptures. This Association did not feel warranted to move in the matter, as appears by the following answer:

BOSTON, April 2, 1782.
REV. SIR:

I have communicated your letter to the Associated Ministers in this town, and they are unanimously of the opinion that the measure your Association have proposed for an impression of the Bible, will not answer, and for these reasons: All the printers in town put together have not types sufficient for such an impression; and if they had, proper paper, in quantity, is not to be procured but by sending for it to Europe. Besides, if there was a sufficiency both of type and paper, the Bibles could not possibly be sold so cheap as those that are imported from abroad. Moreover, an impression could not be completed within two years, as it must be a very large one, and would not be for the advantage either of the printers or buyers of the books, if the number was less than twenty or thirty thousand. Furthermore, there is not the least reasonable prospect the General Court would be at the expense of such an impression of the Bible, as they are so greatly in debt.

I would yet add, I have spoken with some of our printers and booksellers, who concur with the Ministers in town in their opinions upon your proposed measure; and say further, that Bibles are now imported from Holland, and more may daily be expected.

I should have written before now, but that I knew of no opportunity of sending to you, and I know of none at present, but think it proper to have a letter in readiness to be sent, whenever I can hear of a way to send it.

I am in the name of our Association here,
Your humble Servant,
Rev. WM. JOSEPH LYMAN.   CHARLES CHAUNCEY.[1]

Meanwhile Mr. Aitken's petition to Congress was referred to a Committee consisting of Messrs. Duane, McKean and Witherspoon, who reported on the 21st September, 1782,

That Mr. Aitken has at a great expense now finished an American edition of the Holy Scriptures in English; that the Committee have, from time to time, attended to his progress in the Work; that they also recommended it to the Two Chaplains of Congress to examine and give their opinion of the

---

[1] Communicated by George Livermore, Esq.

INTRODUCTION.

execution, who have accordingly reported thereon, the recommendation and report being as follows:

PHILADELPHIA, September 1st, 1782.

REVEREND GENTLEMEN:

Our knowledge of your piety and public spirit leads us without apology to recommend to your particular attention the edition of the Holy Scriptures publishing by Mr. Aitken. He undertook this expensive work at a time when from the circumstances of the War, an English edition of the Bible could not be imported, nor any opinion formed how long the obstruction might continue. On this account particularly he deserves applause and encouragement. We therefore wish you, reverend gentlemen, to examine the execution of the work, and if approved to give it the sanction of your judgment and the weight of your recommendation.

We are, with very great respect, your most obedient humble servants,
(Signed.) JAMES DUANE, Chairman,
in behalf of a Committee of Congress,
on Mr. Aitken's Memorial.

Reverend Doctor WHITE and Reverend Mr. DUFFIELD,
Chaplains of the United States in Congress Assembled.

Report.

GENTLEMEN:

Agreeably to your desire, we have paid attention to Mr. Robert Aitken's impression of the Holy Scriptures, of the old and new testament. Having selected and examined a variety of passages throughout the work, we are of opinion that it is executed with great accuracy as to the sense, and with as few gramatical and typographical errors as could be expected in an undertaking of such magnitude. Being ourselves witnesses of the demand for this invaluable book, we rejoice in the present prospect of a supply, hoping that it will prove as advantageous as it is honorable to the gentleman, who has exerted himself to furnish it at the evident risk of his private fortune.

We are, gentlemen, your very respectful and humble servants,
(Signed.) WILLIAM WHITE,
GEORGE DUFFIELD.

Honorable JAMES DUANE, Esquire, Chairman,
and the other honorable gentlemen of the Committee of
Congress on Mr. Aitken's Memorial.

Philadelphia, September 10, 1782.

Whereupon,

Resolved, That the United States in Congress assembled, highly approve the pious and laudable undertaking of Mr. Aitken, as subservient to the interest of religion as well as an instance of the progress of arts in this country, and being satisfied from the above report, of his care and accuracy in the execution of the work, they recommend this edition of the bible to the inhabitants of the United States, and hereby authorize him to publish this recommendation in the manner he shall think proper.[1]

This was the first Bible printed in this country in the English language having an American imprint. It was a small duodecimo, in two volumes, on a brevier type. The report of the Committee and of the resolution of Congress (sometimes called, in consequence, The Bible Congress[2]) are reprinted on a leaf immediately following the title page. The recommendation, however, bore no fruit. Immediately after the publication of the work, peace was proclaimed, when it was found that Bibles could be imported from Great Britain cheaper than it was possible to print them here. Mr. Aitken, therefore, not obtaining a ready sale for his edition, which had been carried on with great difficulty, was nearly ruined by the undertaking.[3] It was in view of this event that the Philadelphia Synod, on the 24th May, 1783,

Resolved, As Mr. Aitken, from laudable motives, and with great expense, hath undertaken and executed an elegant impression of the Holy Scriptures, which on account of the importation of Bibles from Europe, will be very injurious to his temporal circumstances, the Synod agree that the Committee to purchase Bibles for distribution among the Poor, purchase Aitken's Bibles and no other, and earnestly recommend it to all to purchase such in preference to any other.[4]

The habit of depending either directly or indirectly on Government or Government Agents, for a supply of the Scriptures, had hitherto served only to cripple the American

---

[1] *Journal of Congress*, New York: Patterson, 1787, VII, 468, 469.

[2] *Strickland's History of The American Bible Society*.

[3] *Brief Retrospect*, II, 387, note.

[4] *Records of the Presbyterian Church*, 1758–1788, Philadelphia, 1841, 500.

press. The Germans, as we have seen, unaided by any such patronage or recommendations, had already published several editions of the Bible; William Woodhouse of Philadelphia, equally unaided, got out, in 1790, the Christian's Complete Family Bible; and in the same year the Catholics, succeeded in putting forth a Quarto edition of the Doway Bible.

MATHEW CAREY, a native of Ireland, who, from political causes, was led to immigrate to this country, and who at this time was, we presume, the only Catholic in the Union extensively engaged in publishing, issued Proposals on the 26th January, 1789, for printing The Doway Bible by subscription, on the following

CONDITIONS:

1. This Edition will follow verbatim the Translation executed at Doway.
2. It will be printed in large Quarto, on the same kind of Type, as fine Paper, and with the same number of Pages as in the Oxford Edition of the Bible.
3. The price to Subscribers will be Six Spanish Milled Dollars; one half to be paid at the time of Subscribing; the other on delivery of the Book neatly bound.
4. As soon as 400 copies are Subscribed for, it will be put to press and completed without delay.
5. The Subscribers' names will be prefixed as Patrons of the Work.
Subscriptions received by the Rt. Rev. Dr. John Carroll, &c., &c.

These conditions were modified from time to time. As several gentlemen, unacquainted with the nature of the printing business, objected to the price of the Volume, which they conceived ought to be only four dollars, the rate at which Mr. Collins proposed to publish a Church of England Bible of the same size and on the same kind of paper and types, Mr. Carey observed, that Mr. Collins stipulated for 3000 subscribers; independent of which number, the sale of his work would ever continue extensive; as it suited every denomination of Christians but one, who alone will be purchasers of the Doway translation. To those who know that the comparative expense of an edition is reduced in a ratio with the increase of number, more need not be said; those who do not, were referred to any candid printer to determine whether a Church of England Bible with a vast subscription and an almost unlimited sale, may not be published as advantageously (to say no more) at four dollars, as a Roman Catholic edition, with a very small subscription, and a very confined sale, at six dollars.

But to obviate this objection, if eight hundred copies were subscribed for, *at any time before the publication of the volume*, the charge to subscribers was to be only five dollars, and only four, if twelve hundred.

The following Clergymen were, in addition to the different booksellers, authorized to receive subscriptions for the work: The Right Rev. Dr. John Carroll and the Rev. Charles Sewall, in Baltimore; the Rev. John Ashton, Whitemarsh, and Rev. Thos. Diggs, Mellwood, Prince George's county, Maryland; Rev. Robert Molyneux, Bohemia, Cecil county; Rev. L. Neale and Rev. —— Doyle, Port Tobacco; Rev. Ignatius Matthews, Rev. Augustus Jenkins, and Rev. John Boarman, Newtown, Charles county; Rev. Henry Pile, Newport in said county; Rev. James Walton, St. Inigo, St. Mary's county; Rev. Francis Beeston, Rev. Lawrence Graessel, and Rev. Thos. Keating, Philadelphia; Rev. James Pellentz, York county, Penna., and Rev. Mr. O'Brien, New York.[1]

The Work was announced in press in October, and on Saturday the 12th of December, 1789, the following Advertisement appeared in the *Pennsylvania Packet*, notifying the Public of the issue of *the first number*.

---

[1] The above particulars are from various advertisements on the Covers of *Carey's American Museum* in possession of John McAllister, Esq., of Philadelphia, who most politely permitted copies and extracts to be made and transmitted to us through Edward Armstrong, Esq., of that city, to whom we acknowledge our indebtedness for much valuable assistance and information.

INTRODUCTION.

This Day is Published by | M. Carey | In Front street, a few doors above Market street | Number I, of The | HOLY BIBLE. | Translated from the Latin Vulgat: Diligently compared with the Hebrew, Greek and other Editions in Divers Languages; and first published by the *English College at Doway*, Anno. 1609: Newly Revised and Corrected according to the Clementin Edition of the Scriptures; with Annotations for elucidating the principal Difficulties of Holy Writ.

Haurietis aquas in gaudio de fontibus Salvatoris.—ISAIAE xii, 3.

CONDITIONS.

I. This Work, which will contain 984 pages, will be comprised in 48 numbers, one of which will be published weekly (price one eighth of a dollar) until the whole is completed.

II. The subscribers are to be furnished with the numbers every Saturday morning at the publishers store, and are to pay for each on delivery.

III. The subscribers names will be printed. The price of the Bible to non-subscribers will be seven dollars.

⁂ As this mode of publication renders the purchase of the work easy to all classes of people, as this is the first American edition of the Doway Bible, and as Catholics equally with other religionists ought to be able "To SATISFY EVERY ONE THAT ASKETH a Reason of That Hope WHICH IS IN THEM" (1 Pet., iii, 15.) the printer flatters himself, that every Catholic family not already possessed of a Bible will favor this Work with their support.

Those gentlemen to whose laudable exertions the printer is indebted for the encouragement he has already been honored with are respectfully requested once more to employ their zeal and industry to promote the further success of an attempt which they have sanctioned with their approbation and patronage.

††† The subscription still remains open on the original plan, viz: to pay three dollars at the time of subscribing and the same sum on the delivery of the volume.[1]   4ss.

In the beginning of 1790, the name of the firm was changed to Carey, Stewart & Co. The issue in numbers was abandoned about that time, after (as we are disposed to think)

---

[1] *Pennsylvania Packet*, Dec. 19, 1789. Published once previously, viz: on Saturday, Dec. 12. E. A.

INTRODUCTION. xxvii

between 80 and 90 pages had been printed, when it was determined to publish the work in two volumes.[1]

In September of that year the printers issued the following Addresses:

TO THE SUBSCRIBERS FOR THE DOWAY TRANSLATION OF THE
VULGATE BIBLE.

Ladies and Gentlemen:

With unfeigned gratitude we return you our sincere thanks for the encouragement you have honored us with, in the prosecution of this important undertaking. The Delays though greater than were at first expected have not been greater than the extent of the work, and the tardiness of patronage at the first publication of the proposals and for a very long time afterwards, rendered inevitable. It at length draws to a conclusion, and will positively be published on the 12th day of November. Names of Subscribers will be received until the last day of October at which time the subscription list will be closed and put to press. These ladies and gentlemen therefore who are desirous to add their names to our respectable list as patrons of religion, are requested to favor us with them on or before that day.

We hope and trust that every Roman Catholic family throughout the Union, who can afford the expense, will by their encouragement of this publication, at once evince their determination to shew their reverence for the Holy Scriptures—and to prove the futility of the charge, that they are forbidden the use of the Sacred Volume.

TO THE PROTESTANTS OF THE UNITED STATES.

Ladies and Gentlemen:

We venture with some degree of confidence to solicit your patronage as well as that of the Roman Catholics for the first edition of the Doway translation of the Vulgate bible.

Many of the most learned protestant divines have produced weighty objections to particular passages in the Common Church of England translation of the Scriptures. That there are various important errors in it, is too well known to admit of controversy. The frequent demands for a new translation, bear the strongest testimony to the truth of this observation: it is therefore worthy the attention of every candid Protestant to consider whether a comparison of the present translation with his own would not enable him to

---

[1] This conclusion is arrived at from the fact that "Vol. I" does not appear on any of the signatures preceding page 89; signature Aa. The previous pages would embrace a little more than three numbers.

detect most, if not all of them—and thus to remove from his mind those doubts and difficulties which are fatal to true religion.

Liberal minded Protestants who glory in the influence of the benign sun of toleration will probably be happy in an opportunity of uniting their names with those of the Roman Catholics who have supported this work—and thus evincing that they are superior to that wretched, that contemptible prejudice which confines its benevolence within the narrow pale of one religious denomination, as is the case with bigots of every persuasion. From persons of the latter class we expect no patronage. To encourage "a Popish Bible" would in their eyes be a heinous offense. But we fondly hope, that there are few of this description here—that persons of the former character abound—and that our subscription list, by uniting together the names of members of various and hitherto hostile denominations of Christians, will afford one proof—among many that might be produced—of the rapid advances that America has made in the divine principle of toleration.

We are the public's devoted servants,

Phil., Sept. 24, 1790.   CAREY, STEWART & CO.[1]

This Work which is supposed to have been the first Quarto Bible published in English in the United States,[2] finally appeared complete on the 1st of December, 1790, on type cast expressly for it by Messrs. Baine & Co.,[3] but John Baine, the elder member of the firm, did not live to witness its final publication. He died in the preceding August.[4]

Meanwhile printers in other places were directing their attention to this department of literature. ISAAC COLLINS, a Member of the Society of Friends, originally from Delaware, but afterwards printer to the State of New Jersey and a resident of Trenton, published a New Testament in demi-Octavo, as early as 1788. In 1789, appeared the following

---

[1] *Pennsylvania Packet*, 3636, Sept. 25, 1790. E. A.

[2] It is stated in *Anderson's Annals of the English Bible*, London, 1845, and in Rev. Mr. Prime's Abridgment of that Work, New York, 1849, that Thomas' was the first Quarto Bible printed in the United States. This is altogether a mistake.

[3] Advertisement on Cover of *American Museum*, December, 1789. E. A.

[4] *History of Printing*, I, 214.

INTRODUCTION. xxix

Proposals *for publishing by Subscription,* | By ISAAC COLLINS, in *Trenton* | The HOLY BIBLE, | *Containing the* Old *and* New Testaments; *with the* Apocrypha *and* Marginal Notes.

CONDITIONS.

I. This Work, to be contained in one large volume, quarto, of nine hundred and eighty-four pages, will be reprinted, page for page, with the Oxford edition, on a beautiful new type and good paper. An Index and a Concordance will be added; and also the Scripture measures, weights and coins.

II. The price to Subscribers for the Volume, well bound, Four Spanish Dollars; One Dollar to be paid at the time of subscribing, the remainder on the delivery of the book.

III. The Work to be put to press as soon as three thousand copies shall be subscribed for and to be finished without delay.

To all whom it may concern:

Mr. Isaac Collins has, for many years last past, been and still is, Printer to the State of New Jersey: Having by this means had the more frequent opportunities to see his Work, I have had abundant proof of the accuracy and correctness of his publications, as well as of his remarkable attention to business. WIL. LIVINGSTON.
Trenton, 11th Sept., 1788.

In consequence of subscriptions received, although far short of the number proposed, and the encouragement contained in the following extracts, the Editor has ventured to begin the Work, under a hope that many more citizens of America will patronize it, especially when they are informed Downame's *Concordance,* which is annexed to Eyre and Strahan's London quarto edition of 1772, will be added, without further expense to the Subscribers;—and he has determined to risk such a number of copies as he apprehends will be sufficient to cover all the subscriptions that may be obtained.

Finding a variety of sentiments respecting the Apocrypha and Notes on the Text, the Editor informs the public, that he is desirous to comply with the wishes of every Subscriber, as well as with the directions of the Committees of different denominations on this head, Subscribers, therefore, upon timely notice, shall be supplied with books containing their Apocrypha, or Ostervald's Notes. or both, or neither—as they choose. In this situation the Editor is under the absolute necessity of throwing Ostervald's Notes at the end of the book, subject to such additional expense as shall be agreed upon by the Committee hereafter mentioned.

Meeting for Sufferings, Philad., 19th Third Month, 1789.

Proposals for printing, by subscription, an approved correct edition of the Old and New Testaments, with the Apocrypha and Marginal Notes in a neat Quarto Volume, being now submitted to the consideration of this meeting by the Printer Isaac Collins of Trenton: This undertaking being a matter of very interesting concernment, and such an edition as therein proposed appearing likely to be useful and much wanted; on a deliberate and weighty attention to these considerations, it is the united sense of the meeting, that it be recommended to the Quarterly and Monthly Meetings of Friends to encourage the Work, by appointing Committees to procure Subscriptions agreeably to the tenor of said proposals, and forwarding to this meeting lists of the Subscriptions obtained as early as may be, in order that a suitable appointment may be made for the assistance of the printer in attending to the correctness of the Work. The Clerk is directed to furnish the Printer with a copy of this minute, to be printed and distributed with the proposals.

Extract from the Minutes,

JOHN DRINKER, *Clerk.*

Extract from the Minutes of the General Assembly of the Presbyterian Church in the United States of America, Philad., May 25, 1789.

The General Assembly considering the importance of preserving faithful and correct impressions of the Holy Scriptures; and as Mr. Collins, Printer to the State of New Jersey, proposes to make an impression of the Old and New Testaments, and wishes the countenance and support of all denominations of Christians,

On motion, Resolved, *That the General Assembly of the Presbyterian Church in the United States of America, in order to give effectual encouragement to this undertaking, do hereby appoint the Rev. Mr. Joshua Hart, Mr. Judd, Dr. Alexander McWhorter, Mr. James F. Armstrong, Dr. George Duffield,*[1] *Mr. Thomas Reid, Dr. Matthew Wilson, Dr. Patrick Allison, Mr. Robert Cooper, Mr. James Finley, Mr. Moses Hoge, Mr. John Blair Smith, Mr. James McKee, Mr. Hezekiah Balch, Mr. Thomas McCaulle and Mr. David Rice, to lay Mr. Collins's proposals before their respective Presbyteries; and to recommend to them, by order of the General Assembly, that a person or persons be appointed in every congregation, vacant or supplied, to procure subscriptions; and that the Presbyteries transmit by their Commissioners to the next General Assembly the number of Subscribers.*

---

[1] This clergyman died in Philadelphia, on 2d February, 1790. He was Minister of the 3d Presbyterian Church in that city. He did not live to witness the publication of this work.

INTRODUCTION.

The General Assembly also confirm the appointment made by the Synod of New York and New Jersey, that Dr. John Witherspoon, Dr. Samuel S. Smith, and Mr. James F. Armstrong be a Committee to confer with any such Committee as may be appointed, whether from any other denomination, or from any other Synod of our denomination, to revise and correct the proof-sheets, and, if necessary, to fix upon the most correct edition of the Scriptures to be recommended to the printer from which to make his impression, and that the said Committee be ordered to agree with the printer, that Osterwald's Notes, if not inconsistent with the views of other denominations of Christians engaged in this undertaking, be printed with it, in such a manner as may best promote the publication.

The General Assembly, desirous to spread the knowledge of eternal life contained in the Holy Scriptures, earnestly recommend to all the congregations under their care to encourage this undertaking.

JAMES F. ARMSTRONG, Clerk
of the General Assembly.

Extract from the Journal of the Convention of the Protestant Episcopal Church, held in Philadelphia, August 8, 1789.

Proposals for an edition of the Holy Bible, by Mr. Isaac Collins, of Trenton, were laid before this Convention, and satisfactory information was given them as to the proposer's abilities for the execution of the work: Whereupon,

Resolved on motion of Mr. Jones, That the members of this Convention will assist Mr. Collins in the procuring of subscriptions.

Extract from the Minutes of the Baptist Association, held at Philadelphia, October 6, 1789.

This Association taking under consideration the proposals of Mr. Isaac Collins, of Trenton, in New Jersey, to print an edition of the Holy Bible in quarto after the Oxford edition; and his request to this Association to patronize the work—Being desirous to encourage so laudable a design, do appoint our brethren the Rev. Oliver Hart, Dr. Samuel Jones, Rev. Benjamin Foster and Rev. Burgiss Allison, to concur with any Committee appointed by any other denomination to revise and correct the proof-sheets, and, if necessary, to fix upon the most correct edition of the Scriptures to be recommended to the Printer, from which to make his impression. And that the same Committee be ordered to use their influence to prevent the Apocrypha, or any Notes of any kind, being printed and included in said edition, as having a dangerous tendency to corrupt the simplicity and truth of the sacred Scriptures, by being thus intimately associated with them; and, particularly, as being incompatible *with the union of people of different religious sentiments in promoting the work. And, moreover, the Association recommend to all the churches and congregations in their bounds to encourage the undertaking.*

WILLIAM VAN HORNE, *Clerk.*

The consideration, that no part of the money will be sent out of the country, it is hoped will be an additional inducement to subscribe, and of course promote the more frequent reading of this most valuable book in private families. The Editor therefore wishes to attract the attention, and obtain the countenance of people of ALL denominations in this arduous undertaking; not doubting but that, in the execution of the work, he will be able to give satisfaction, both as to its accuracy and neatness.

The CONCORDANCE will be much more correct than the London Copy, the Editor having taken the pains to examine most of the references.

*₊*A specimen of the type and paper may be seen by applying to Joseph Cruikshank, Printer and Bookseller, in Market-street, Philadelphia.

Trenton, Twelfth Month, (Dec.) 19, 1789.[1]

At the meeting of the General Assembly, 22d May, 1790, the subject of aiding Mr. Collins's project was resumed, and every person of the Assembly was recommended to promote and encourage the business of subscription in the Presbytery to which he belonged; and on 24th May, 1791, Presbyteries and members were requested to return all subscriptions, "as the impression is nearly finished."[2]

Collins's Bible, which the Rev. Dr. Miller incorrectly calls the first Quarto edition printed in the United States,[3] was published at Trenton soon after the passage of the above last mentioned resolution. In 1793, Mr. Collins issued at the same place an Octavo Bible, which Mr. Thomas pronounces to have been "a handsome and very correct edition," though he erroneously calls it the first printed at Trenton,[4] and seems to have forgotten the edition in Quarto.

---

[1] *Pennsylvania Gazette,* Jan. 27, 1790.
[2] *Minutes of General Assembly.*
[3] *Brief Retrospect,* II, 388.
[4] *History of Printing,* II, 124, 553.

INTRODUCTION. xxxiii

MASSACHUSETTS was the next to commence arrangements for the publication of an edition of the Bible, and ISAIAH THOMAS of Worcester in that State, announced one in Folio (being, as far as we are aware, the first in that form in this country) and another in Royal Quarto. The following is a copy of the Prospectus of the latter edition:

LARGE FAMILY BIBLE. |

SEARCH the SCRIPTURES, for therein are contained the Words | of Eternal Life!—They have GOD for their Author!—*Sal-* | *vation* for their End!—And *Truth*, unmixed with Error, for | their Matter! |
Proposal of *Isaiah Thomas*, | of Worcester, Massachusetts, | For PRINTING and PUBLISHING by SUBSCRIPTION, | An *American* Edition, in Large *Royal* QUARTO, | (*Ornamented with an Elegant* COPPERPLATE FRONTISPIECE) | of the | HOLY BIBLE. | containing the | Old and New TESTAMENTS, | with the | *Apocrypha*, an *Index*, *Marginal Notes* and *References*. |

Conditions.

I. It shall be printed with elegant new *Types*, already made and completed, particularly for the purpose—types large, beautiful, and suited for the accommodation of the eyes of all, especially those of the aged and infirm. See the *Specimen* annexed.

II. The *Paper* shall be fully equal in goodness, if not of a superiour quality, to the (English) Cambridge, Oxford, or London, Royal Quarto Edition.

III. The *Price* to Subscribers, handsomely bound, shall be only *Seven Dollars*, although the English Editions of the same size, and of an inferiour quality, are sold for eight and nine Dollars.

IV. To make payment easy to those who wish to be encouragers of this laudable undertaking, and to be in possession of so valuable property as a Royal Quarto Bible, and who are not able to pay for one all in Cash—from such the Publisher will receive one half of the sum, or *twenty one shillings*, in the following articles, viz. *Wheat*, *Rye*, *Indian Corn*, *Butter*, or *Pork*, if delivered at his store in *Worcester*, or at the store of himself and Company in *Boston*, by the 20th day of *December*, 1790, the remaining sum of *twenty one shillings*, to be paid in Cash, as soon as the books are ready for delivery. This proposal is made, to accommodate all, notwithstanding the sum of twenty one shillings will by no means be the proportion of Cash that each Bible bound, will cost the Publisher.

V. The work will be committed to the Press as soon as a sufficient number of Bibles are subscribed for, barely to defray half the expense of the undertaking. Notice will be given in the Newspapers, when the Bible will be put to the Press, on or before the first day of June next, and the time when it will be completed will then be mentioned.

☞ THE BOOKSELLERS in the United States, who subscribe for *twelve* or more copies in sheets, shall have them on full as generous terms as the Booksellers in England are supplied with English Editions.

To the Reverend Clergy.

THE assistance of the Reverend Clergy, of all persuasions, in this and the neighbouring States, is earnestly requested, to forward and complete so large, important and expensive an undertaking—The weight now rests entirely on the publisher of this proposal, who has already expended a very large sum for types, and other matters preparatory for the business; but he doubts not, should he be speedily favoured by having a generous number of Bibles subscribed for, to complete the work to the satisfaction of the Publick.

In order in some measure to recompense the Reverend Clergy, and all others, whose piety, goodness of heart, and regard for the manufactures of their country, may induce them to help forward so great and useful an undertaking as the one now proposed, all who subscribe for *twelve* copies, or procure *twelve* copies to be subscribed for, and will be answerable, and make payment for them, agreeably to this proposal, shall be entitled to, and receive a *thirteenth* copy, handsomely bound, for their trouble.

To CHRISTIANS *of every Denomination.*

AT a time when all descriptions of men are united to promote the political welfare of our country, by the encouragement of Agriculture and all the Arts and Sciences, printing the Bible, that sacred Book which has a nobler object—the supreme and ultimate happiness of man—cannot be thought unimportant, or uninteresting, especially as it tends to promote that Morality without which Industry, Arts and Sciences are vain. The Proposal, therefore, to publish a large quarto Bible, must be pleasing to all, more especially to the christian citizen, to whom nothing need be said as a stimulus for him to promote the good work by subscribing for one or more copies, but his being assured that due care shall be taken to have it correct and well executed—that this shall be the case, no labour or cost, within the subscriber's reach, will be wanting; for it is his ambition, should he proceed with the work, to have it completed in such a manner as shall disgrace neither himself nor his country.

It cannot be presumed that any thing need be said to *recommend the* BIBLE, that ground work of our holy Religion, to any class of citizens whatever—

if there should, nothing new can be given on the subject—we must republish the ideas of those who have gone before us.—Books are addressed to the Judgment or the Imagination—intended to touch the Passions, or please the Fancy.—The HOLY BIBLE addresses the Soul, directs to the paths of peace and happiness here, and brings to view a beautiful prospect of an hereafter—in its pages may be viewed, with awful surprise, the great and glorious works of Creation—and with pleasing admiration may be seen the Rise and Fall of Empires—the Revolutions of Kingdoms and States—the various Vicissitudes of Life in all stations—the Depravity of Human Nature, when Man is forsaken by his God—the easy transitions from Innocence to Guilt, from Virtue to Vice—the Policy of Courts, and Simplicity of Cottages—the Rage of Lust—Folly of Pride—Fate of Tyranny, and Madness of Ambition.—Here may be found Patterns for all who wish to practice the Christian and Moral Duties. St. Gregory says, "From the Patriarchs we may take the model of all virtues—Abel teaches us Innocence—Enoch, Purity of Heart—Noah, a firm Perseverance in Righteousness—Abraham, the Perfection of Piety and Faithfulness—Joseph, Chastity—Jacob, Constancy in Labour—Moses, Meekness—and Job, invincible Patience.—Salvation, the most glorious prize that man can obtain, may be perused (*sic*) with pleasure, and it may with ease be acquired, if Piety is the guide, and Faith the intercessor—the mercy of God is greater than our delinquency, and happiness eternal within our reach, if we suppress the gratification of our passions to seek it: Read, therefore, and be informed—look for, and find."

To the PUBLICK at large.

AS it is presumed that every denomination of Christians will be pleased with the intention of the proposer, so he rests assured that all will cheerfully contribute in aiding him to carry on and complete this first American Edition of a Royal Quarto Bible. He begs permission to subscribe himself,

With the greatest respect, &c.,

Worcester, November, 1789. ISAIAH THOMAS.

☞ ALL who may have SUBSCRIPTION PAPERS, are requested to return them by the first day of May next, to the Publisher in *Worcester*, or to the Bookstore of himself and Company in *Boston*.[1]

Both the editions of Mr. Thomas were finished in December, 1791, or in little more than twelve months from the time

---

[1] From the original printed Prospectus in the possession of George Brinley, Esq., of Hartford, Conn.

the prospectus was issued.[1] An 8vo. edition was published by the same house in 1793 and a 12mo. in 1797. This was known as Thomas's Standing 12mo. edition; there are some peculiarities about it noted in this Catalogue, of interest to the Bibliographer.

No copy of the Scriptures was printed in NEW YORK previous to 1790. A gentleman of literature, taste and merit, a resident of that city and well known in the political world, was engaged in 1788 in translating the sublime book of Isaiah and the other Prophets into English.[2] In 1790 HUGH GAINE published a New Testament, and ROBERT HODGE, THOMAS ALLEN and SAMUEL CAMPBELL, printers in that city, issued the following notice:

NEW-YORK, May 4th, 1790.

Brown's self-instructing Folio Family BIBLE. Embellished with a variety of elegant Copper Plates, being a genuine American Edition. The largest and cheapest ever proposed to be printed in the United States.

PROPOSALS, for Printing by Subscription, by Hodge and Campbell of New York; and will be put to Press on the 1st day of June next, THE HOLY BIBLE, containing the Old and New Testaments with the book of the Apocrypha. Illustrated with Notes and Annotations comprehending a most valuable Treasury of Divine Knowledge, With Practical References at the end of each Chapter, calculated to improve the understanding, purify the heart, promote the cause of virtue, and guide the reader to the Mansions of Eternal Bliss.

By JOHN BROWN, D. D.,
Late Minister of the Gospel at Haddington.

Conditions of Publication.

I. The whole of this extensive and valuable work, will be printed in large folio on fine paper, American manufacture, and on an excellent, large and new type, cast on purpose for this work.

II. It will be completed in forty numbers, one of which will be printed

---

[1] Advertisement to Thomas's Folio and Quarto Bibles.
[2] *New York American Magazine*, October, 1788, p. 775.

and delivered regularly every two weeks—price one Quarter of a Dollar or Twenty-five Cents.

III. Every other number will be embellished with a beautiful and elegant engraving, executed by an ingenious American Artist illustrating some remarkable transaction or incident recorded in the Holy Scriptures.

IV. That every reader may be enabled to form a proper judgment of the superiority of this work over any other Bible, the first number may be had for perusal; and if it should not meet with the approbation of the Reader, the money shall be immediately returned.

V. A correct list of the Subscribers names shall be printed and given in the last number.

VI. Gentlemen who will interest themselves in procuring Subscribers, shall receive one copy gratis, for every twelve they may obtain, and Booksellers and Printers the usual allowance.

☞ The Public may be assured, that the Editors will spare neither expence or attention in having the work carefully and correctly printed. The proof sheets shall not only be diligently revised and compared with various editions of the Holy Scriptures, but also read and corrected by clergymen of different denominations.

☞ Subscriptions received by the Publishers in New-York, and by the Printers and Booksellers on the Continent. 5—t. f.[1]

A beautiful edition of the Holy Bible, in Quarto, printed on large type and fine paper, adorned with twenty elegant copper plates, was announced at the same time by this firm; and, being desirous, like Aitken, of having the sanction of the civil authority, they petitioned the State Legislature to recommend their edition of Brown's work.

The petition was presented in the New York Senate on the 18th of March, 1790, and referred to Messrs. Duane, L'hommedieu and Van Ness, who, on the 6th of April, recommended the passage of the following concurrent resolution:

Resolved (if the House of Assembly concurr herein), That the Legislature highly approve the laudable exertions of Messrs. Hodge, Allen and Campbell, booksellers in New York, to promote the Industry and Manufactures of America by printing a correct and neat Edition of Doctor John

---

[1] *New York Journal & Patriotic Register*, August 3d, 1790.

Brown's Folio Family Bible; illustrated with short Notes and Annotations, so cautiously expressed as not to give offence to any denomination of Christians; and hope they may meet sufficient encouragement to complete their undertaking agreeably to their Memorial to the Legislature, whereby the people may be supplied with this edition much cheaper than can be imported.

The House of Assembly concurred on the same day.[1]

It is curious to remark the caution with which this resolution is drawn up. Justly doubtful of its constitutional power in the premises, the Legislature does not recommend the work, neither does it approve the project, in the words of the Old Congress, as "a pious and laudable undertaking," but as a praiseworthy effort "to promote the Industry and Manufactures of America." A singular sort of approbation, to say the least of it, when the character of the work is considered.

The publication received the commendation of the Associate Reformed Synod, and a writer of the day, under the pseudonym of *Philobiblicus*, "felicitates our Country on the undertaking of three printers of this city, who will not only have the applause of every true friend of Religion in America, but the very warm recommendation of those who know something more than common fame of the Venerable Old Man, Mr. John Brown, Minister of the Gospel of Haddington."[2]

Mr. Allen retired from the firm shortly after the passage of the above resolution, and his name is, in consequence, omitted in the imprint to the work, as it had already been dropped from the Prospectus.

The issue of the above editions was completed in the spring of 1792. They are the first Bibles that were printed in New York. In August of the same year, Hugh Gaine issued a duodecimo Bible, but the types from which it was printed

---

[1] *Journals of the New York Senate and Assembly.*

[2] *Swords' New York Magazine*, I, 278.

were imported, it is said, from Scotland, already set up in pages; they were sold eventually in 1803 to Mathew Carey of Philadelphia for *Seven thousand dollars.*

These were all the States in which editions of the Bible were published previous to 1809. A School Testament had been issued in New Haven in 1790, but as far as our enquiries have gone, no copy of the Bible was issued in Connecticut before that published by Hudson & Goodwin of Hartford, in the first mentioned year.

The advertisements of these various editions, by irresponsible persons, for as yet they appear to have been mere printers' speculations, alarmed Theologians, who at length became aware of the necessity of some steps to ensure the purity and uniformity of the text. Accordingly the subject was brought before the Congregational Ministers of Massachusetts at their Annual Convention in Boston, who on the 27th May, 1790, voted

That the Rev'd Docr. Willard, Docr. Howard, Mr. Morse, Mr. Payson and Mr. Thatcher, be a Committee, in the name and behalf of the Congregational Ministers of this Commonwealth, in convention assembled, to prepare, sign and transmit to the Congress of the United States a petition requesting the attention of that Hon'ble Body, to the subject of the several impressions of the Bible now making; representing the importance of accuracy in these impressions; and earnestly praying that they would take such measures, as the Constitution may permit, that no Edition of the Bible, or its translation be published in America without its being carefully inspected and certified to be free from error.

That the same persons be a Committee to apply to the representative Bodies of the other Denominations of Christians in America, and to request their assistance and support, in accomplishing so important and desirable an Object.

The petition was presented in the Senate of the United States, on the 10th June following, when it was ordered to lie for consideration.[1]

Agreeably to the second of the above votes, the Committee addressed a letter on the 24th June to Bishop Parker of

---

[1] *Senate Journal,* 107.

Boston, setting forth, that it was "unquestionably of the highest importance that this acknowledged fountain of truth [the Bible] be preserved pure and uncorrupted, which will not probably be the case if the matter is left wholly to printers.

We, therefore as friends and Brethren, united in promoting the same general Cause, and as jointly concerned in preserving the purity of the Holy Scriptures, do, in behalf of the Convention earnestly request the concurrence of the Episcopal clergy throughout the United States, or of their representative Body, in petitioning Congress that they would so far interpose their authority as to prevent inaccurate and spurious Editions of the Bible.

It was the wish of the Convention to have written in the first instance to your Rev'd Body and the other representative Bodies of Christians in the several States, requesting that Committees might be appointed by each to confer and unite with us in one petition and thus to concentre the whole Christian Interest in America; But to accomplish this desirable object would have taken a long time, and it was thought, the Business was of immediate importance as proposals for several editions of the Bible are now in circulation.

We take this opportunity to express our sincere desire to cultivate a friendly and christian intercourse with the ministers of your denomination, as we are firmly persuaded that such an intercourse between Christians of different Denominations and sentiments would have a happy tendency to harmonize them—to remove unreasonable prejudices—to promote a spirit of love and candour—and thus essentially serve the interest of our holy Religion. It might also have a beneficial influence on the civil affairs of our Country.

We wish you, Sir, to communicate the foregoing to the largest representative Body of the Episcopal Church in America as soon as you have an Opportunity.

Wishing prosperity to the peaceful Kingdom of our common Lord and Saviour,

We are Rev'd Sir, your Brethren in Christ,

	JOSEPH WILLARD,	
	PHILLIP PAYSON,	
	SIMEON HOWARD,	Committee.[1]
Rev'd Dr. Parker,	PETER THACHER,	
Boston.	JED'H MORSE.	

---

[1] Letter presented by Joseph Willard, Esq., to the Massachusetts Historical Society, for copy of which we are indebted to George Livermore, Esq.

INTRODUCTION.

We do not find any response to this invitation in the Journal of the Convention of the Protestant Episcopal Church. In January, 1791, the Baptist Associations of New Hampshire, Massachusetts, Rhode Island, Connecticut and Vermont renewed the application to Congress "to adopt measures to prevent the publication of any inaccurate editions of the Holy Bible.[1] An amendment had however been made to the Constitution in 1789, which enacted that "Congress shall make no law respecting an establishment of religion or prohibiting the free exercise thereof; or abridging the freedom of speech or of the press;" and all these petitions were accordingly ordered to lie on the table, as a compliance with their prayer would have undoubtedly been a violation of the above Article.

The movement seems, however to have alarmed Mr. Thomas, who addressed a letter to the Congregational Convention at its next Annual Meeting, the tenor of which may be inferred from the following answer.

BOSTON, May 26, 1791.

SIR:

Your letter addressed to the Rev'd Clergy of the Commonwealth of Massachusetts in Convention assembled, was yesterday communicated, and I am directed to return the following answer:

That the Convention highly approve of the care which you have exercised, and of the anxious desires which you express, to have the editions which you are now printing of the Holy Bible perfectly correct. That the Convention are strongly impressed with the importance of having *all* the new editions of the Bible which may be made in this country critically examined by persons duly qualified for that work; and accordingly at their last meeting they appointed a Committee to address the Honorable the Legislature of the United States on that interesting subject, and requested, that in their wisdom they would order such measures to be taken as should prevent any accidental or designed errors from being published together with the Oracles of God. Inasmuch as the Convention have requested the Legislature of the Union to interpose their wisdom and their authority for the purposes men-

---

[1] *Journal of House of Representatives*, 29, 39.

tioned above, they conceive there would be an impropriety in their appointing a Committee of their own Body to supervise the editions of the Bible which you are now making.

They most heartily wish you success in your laudable undertaking; but every kind of approbation of a work of this kind, from this body, must depend upon the accuracy and fidelity with which the work when completed shall appear to have been executed.

In the name of the Convention,
I am,
Sir,
Your most obed't,

Mr. Isaiah Thomas.   JOHN LATHROP.[1]

Meanwhile Mathew Carey of Philadelphia, who had already issued the *first* quarto Doway Bible in this country, turned his attention to getting up a Quarto edition of King James's version. Having, himself, left us the particulars of the rise and progress of that enterprise: of the difficulties he encountered and overcame, and of the success he at length achieved with his celebrated "Standing" editions, nothing remains for us but to copy his interesting Narrative:

> In 1801, I published a quarto edition of the Bible (of three thousand copies,) with various additional references, for which I paid a clergyman one thousand dollars. Price ten dollars.
>
> I had eighteen various editions to collate in the reading of the proof sheets—four London, three Cambridge, three Oxford, six Edinburg, and two American,—those of Isaac Collins and Isaiah Thomas—and found a most extraordinary number of discrepancies, some of which are incredible. In one Edinburg edition, published by Mark and Charles Kerr, 1795, among the prohibitions of incestuous marriages, one was—"*A man* may not marry his wife's mother's *brother*."
>
> Feeling deeply solicitous for the success of this undertaking, the failure of which would have almost ruined me; and fearful lest some captious hypercritic should discover any errors, which might have escaped me, notwithstanding all the care I had taken in reading the proof sheets, I prefixed to the volume a deprecatory advertisement of which I annex some extracts.

---

[1] From a copy politely communicated by S. F. Haven, Esq., of Worcester, Mass.

INTRODUCTION. xliii

"I present this edition of the BIBLE to the public, with a degree of solicitude proportioned to the magnitude of the undertaking. Having embarked therein a large property, and devoted my utmost care and attention to it, from its commencement to its completion, I find it impossible to assume that degree of stoicism necessary to regard with indifference its reception by my fellow-citizens.

"That a rigorous and severe spirit of criticism may discover grounds of censure with respect to the paper, printing, engraving, &c., &c., is, I think, highly probable. It is a very easy matter to find fault. A poor sciolist, whose circle of sciences extends no farther than the Grammatical Institute, may discern that there is a want of uniformity in the paper—that the printing is far inferior to *Baskerville's*—that the engravings are not equal to those by *Bartolozzi*, or *Heath*—that there are typographical errors in the work—and to show his taste and sagacity, may make various other objections. And when I consider the malignant pleasure many feel, in depreciating the labors, and counteracting the well founded hopes of others, I freely confess, I am disposed to approach the bar of the public with some awe and apprehension.

"But from men of this obliquity of heart, I most cheerfully avert my eye. I turn to those of liberal minds—who find more pleasure in bestowing praise, than in dealing forth censure—who are as eager to discover merit, as the envious and malicious are to decry it—who are fully conscious of, and willing to make allowance for, human imperfection—who, knowing the infant state of the arts among us, do not expect that degree of elegance and beauty, for which older and more opulent nations afford such encouragement. When I look forward to a jury of such men, sitting in judgment on this volume, I feel my spirits revive.

"That this work is wholly free from inaccuracy, I cannot pretend. In fact, I will venture to say that no work, equally voluminous, ever was so. But that there are no material errors in it, and that it is as correct as those Bibles which are brought into this country from London, Cambridge, Oxford, and Edinburgh, I fondly believe. To remove any incredulity on this subject, and to induce the reader to forgive the few trivial errors which have escaped the vigilance of the correctors of the press, I annex a small number of errata, out of hundreds which I might have selected from different British editions.

ERRATA.	CORRECT READING.
"His substance also was seven thousand sheep, and five hundred yoke of oxen, and five hundred she *ashes.*" Job, I, 3.[1]	"His substance also was seven thousand sheep, and five hundred yoke of oxen, and five hundred she *asses.*"

---

[1] *Edinburgh Quarto*, 1784.

INTRODUCTION.

"And magnified with *own* accord thine hand that fought for them." Wisdom x, 20.[1]

"Were beneath and above. Baruch II, 5.[2]

"These are the statutes between the father and his daughter, being yet in her father's house." Numb. xxx, 16.[3]

"Do not interpretations belong to God? tell me them, I pray *for* you." Gen. XL, 8.[4]

"He with *him* whom it is found, shall be my servant; and ye shall be blameless." Gen. XLIV, 10.[5]

"Behold, waters rise up out of the north, and shall be an *everflowing* flood, and shall overflow the land." Jer. XLVII, 2.[6]

"Thou shalt not build me an house to *well* in. 1 Chron. XVII, 4.[7]

"The whole land of Havilah, *whore* there is gold." Gen. II, 11.[8]

"So shall the Jews at Jerusalem bind the man that *oweth* this girdle." Acts XXI, 11.[9]

"And magnified with *one* accord thine hand which fought for them."

"Were beneath and *not* above."

"These are the statutes between the father and his daughter, being yet in her youth, in her father's house."

"Do not interpretations belong to God? tell me them, I pray you."

"He with whom it is found, shall be my servant; and ye shall be blameless."

"Behold, waters rise up out of the north, and shall be an overflowing flood, and shall overflow the land."

"Thou shalt not build me an house to dwell in."

"The whole land of Havilah, where there is gold."

"So shall the Jews at Jerusalem bind the man that owneth this girdle."

"As the proof sheets were compared with different editions, a discovery was early made, that numerous and very important variations existed between them.

"It was found that in many instances, the Oxford and Cambridge editions agreed; that they differed from the Edinburgh and London; in others, that the London and Cambridge agreed, and differed from the Oxford and Edinburgh; in others, again, that the Edinburgh varied from all the rest. This occasioned considerable difficulty. In every case, recourse was had to as many copies as could be procured, and *that* reading was uniformly preferred,

---

[1] *London Folio*, 1696.
[2] *Oxford Quarto*, 1784.
[3] *Edinburgh Common Quarto*, 1728.
[4] *Oxford Quarto*, 1784.
[5] *Cambridge Quarto*, 1769 *and* 1770.
[6] *London Folio*, 1696.
[7] *London Quarto*, 1708.
[8] *London Quarto*, 1782.
[9] *London Folio*, 1696.

which was sanctioned by the most numerous and best authorities, or which appeared most congruous with the context.

"One or two examples will suffice to illustrate the plan pursued, which has been the result of the most mature deliberation, and which, I hope will meet the approbation of the public.

"In all the Oxford, Cambridge, London, Trenton, and Worcester editions, Luke XXIII, 32, reads thus:—

"And there were also *two other malefactors* led with him to be put to death." But five respectable Edinburgh copies read,—

"And there were also *two others, malefactors*, led with him to be put to death."

"This reading was readily preferred. It was impossible that the Apostle, in speaking of his beloved Master, should have styled him a malefactor, which is the only construction whereof the first reading is susceptible. Had one of Pilate's soldiers been writing on the subject, he would have expressed himself thus. The Greek καὶ ἕτεροὶ δύο, κακοῦργοι, with a comma after δύο, admits the Edinburgh construction as perfectly correct.

"It is to be further observed, that the Latin translation of Junius and Tremellius favors this reading:—"Ducebantur autem etiam alii duo, iique facinorosi, cum eo, interimendi." *Edit. in-fol. Hanoviæ*, 1623.

"As I have touched on the subject of variations, I beg the reader's attention, while I treat on it a little more at length.

"The variations are of five kinds. 1st. Of Punctuation; 2d. Of Orthography; 3d. Where words are in one edition in Italic, as suppletory, and in Roman in another, as if they were in the original; 4th. Where the difference is merely verbal, without affecting the sense; and 5th. Where there is a variation not only in the words but in the sense.

"I. *Variations in Punctuation.*

"The variations of this class are innumerable; generally however, they are unimportant. As far as I have been able to observe, there is no edition whatever of the Bible that has an uniform system of punctuation. The same sentence, occurring in different places, in the same Bible, is by no means always punctuated in the same manner.

"I shall mention but one example of variation of this class. Gen. XXVI, 8, has eight commas in the Edinburgh, six in the Oxford, and only three in the Cambridge and London editions.

"II. *Orthographical Variations.*

"These are not so numerous as the former; but they are by no means inconsiderable. Among those that attracted most attention, in the progress of the work, were—*besides, beside; towards, toward; among, amongst;*

vallies, valleys; *champian*, champaign; *subtil*, subtile; *divers*, diverse; *aught*, ought; *born*, borne; &c., &c.

" *Diverse* and *divers* are miserably confounded together. They appear to be regarded as synonymous, which is an egregious error. *Divers* signifies many; *diverse*, different.

"III. *Variations with respect to Suppletory Verbs.*

"Those who have ever paid attention to the perusal of the Bible, know that there are numberless instances wherein words, which are well understood, but not expressed, in the original, are introduced in the English translation; all such words are generally, in the correct editions, in the Italic character, by which the reader is given to understand that they are suppletory; in most instances, the sense is complete without them. Thus:

"And they wrote *letters* by them after this manner." *Acts* xv, 23.[1]
Is in the original Greek,
"And they wrote by them after this manner."
Which conveys the same idea as the former line.

"IV. *Verbal variations, which do not affect the sense.*

"The variations of this class are incredibly numerous: and it is to be observed, that even the editions printed at any of the before-mentioned places, do not agree with each other. I subjoin some examples for the reader's inspection:—

"And Moses put of the blood upon the tip of their right ear." *Lev.* VIII, 24.[2]

"And Moses put of the blood upon the tip of their right ears."

"And all that have not fins and scales in the sea." *Lev.* XI, 10.[3]

"And all that have not fins nor scales in the sea."

"And ye shall not walk in the manners of the nations which I cast out before you." *Lev.* XX, 23.[4]

"And ye shall not walk in the manners of the nation which I cast out before you."

"V. *Variations of meaning as well as words.*

"These variations are by no means numerous. Some of them, doubtless, have arisen from the carelessness of the printers, who published the early editions, and have been servilely copied by successive editors; but others

---

[1] *Edinburgh Quarto*, 1695.
[2] *Edinburgh*, 1728 *and* 1790.
[3] *Oxford Quarto*, 1784.
[4] *Edinburgh*, 1789, 1793 *and* 1795.

INTRODUCTION. xlvii

have most probably been the result of the liberty taken by editors, of innovating upon the original translation, executed in the time of King James.

"To illustrate this idea, I shall select two examples. In many editions of the Bible, Lev. i, 6, reads—

"'And he shall *flay* the burnt offering.'

"In other editions it is—

"'And he shall *flay* the burnt offering.'

"It is obvious that the similarity between *fl* and *fl* may have led one editor into error; and that in subsequent editions the error may have been repeated.

"But we cannot in the same way account for the following variation:—

"In the Oxford Quarto editions of 1784 and 1795, and the Cambridge of 1769 and 1770, Psalm cvii, 16, reads—

"'For he hath broken the gates of brass, and cut the *gates* of iron asunder.'

"Whereas in nearly all the other editions it stands—

"'For he hath broken the gates of brass, and cut the *bars* of iron in sunder.'

"In the Cambridge Quartos of 1769 and 1770, the Octavo of 1767, and the London Quarto of 1772, Leviticus vii, 13, stands—

"'Besides the cakes, he shall offer for his offering *unleavened* bread.'

"Whereas in fourteen other editions which have been consulted, it is—

"'Besides the cakes, he shall offer for his offering leavened bread.'

"It is highly probable that *leavened bread* is the correct reading; as the marginal reference from this verse is to Amos iv, 5, which I here submit to the reader:

"'And offer a sacrifice of thanksgiving with *leaven*, and proclaim and publish the free offerings: for this liketh you, O children of Israel.'"

Soon after the publication of this edition, the success of which fully equaled my most sanguine expectations, I ventured on the publication of a standing edition of the Quarto Bible, a great undertaking for a man not long in business, of whose means a large portion was absorbed in dead stock. It was the first standing edition of the English Quarto Bible ever published. The Scotch, who had a most extensive sale for their Bibles, were wont, as I have been credibly informed, to *set up* about twenty or thirty sheets, and print off twenty thousand copies—then distribute the types, and set up as many more. Until lately, I believed that mine was the first standing Bible in Christendom. But I have recently learned that of Luther's Bible, in the German, a Quarto, and perhaps a Folio edition, had been standing in some part of Germany for probably a century.

About the time when I had the Quarto Bible set up, I purchased of Hugh

Gaine of New-York, the School Bible, for, as far as I can recollect, seven thousand dollars.[1]

In reviewing the rise and progress of Bible printing in this country, it is not our intention to trace each edition to its extinction, or to repeat here those which followed the first in rapid succession. Our design is merely to notice in this Introduction, what may be called the "pioneer" editions, referring the reader to the text for fuller and more minute information on the progress of this branch of Bibliography.

The Greek Testament was printed for the first time in these States in the year 1800. We have collected the titles of sixteen editions in the ancient and three in modern Greek, which have appeared from the American press.

An effort was made in 1810 in New Haven to publish an edition of the Bible in Hebrew, but it failed, though the Psalms had already been published at Cambridge, Mass., in that language, in the course of the previous year. The first American edition of the Hebrew Bible did not appear until 1813-14.

In 1810 the Scriptures began to be published among us in French; the first edition consisted of a Testament, with the approbation of Bishop Cheverus, of Boston. Editions in Spanish followed in 1819.

In a Catalogue of books printed in America, it would not be fair to limit our researches to the United States. We accordingly endeavored to ascertain what progress has been made in the other parts of this Continent, in the department of Biblical literature. As there are not at present any Ministers at Washington, from the Republics of Chile and Peru, our enquiries, as regards these countries, have been necessarily restricted. Ludovicus de Vera, a native of Lima,

---

[1] *New England Magazine*, VI, 230.

wrote a Commentary on the Books of Kings, which was printed in that city in Folio, in 1635, and Ferdinand de Valverde, also a native of the same place, and of the Order of St. Augustine, wrote a Life of Christ, which was published in Lima, in Quarto, in 1657. Benedict Fernandez, a Spanish Dominican, and Vicar of Mixteca, in New Spain, translated the Epistles and Gospels into the dialect of that province. Didacus de Sta. Maria, another Dominican, and Vicar of the province of Mexico (who died in 1579), was the author of a translation of the Epistles and Gospels into the Mexican tongue, or general language of the country. The Proverbs of Solomon, and other fragments of the Scriptures were translated into the same language by a Franciscan named Louis Rodriguez, and the Epistles and Gospels appointed to be read for the whole year, were rendered into the idiom of the Western Indians by Arnold Bassaccio, also a Franciscan; but the dates of these versions have not been ascertained.[1] The entire Bible is said to have been translated into the Brazilian language by an English minister, who accompanied the Dutch to the Reciff, when they acquired it from the Portuguese. This version has never been printed.[2] A Quarto edition of Scios's Spanish Bible, printed in Mexico in 1831–1835, will be found in this List.

In 1835 or 1836, Mr. William L. Mackenzie purchased from the Bible Society at New York a sett of stereotype plates, and got new title pages cast for the Old and New Testaments, substituting Toronto and his own name for the Bible Society's imprint. But he did not print an edition from these plates; they passed eventually into the hands of a Mr. Eastwood, who published a Bible from them at Toronto,

---

[1] *Biblio. Scrip. His.*

[2] *Townley's Illustrations of Bible Literature*, III, 46, 355, note.

INTRODUCTION.

in 1839 or 1840, on paper manufactured at his mill on the river Don, immediately east of that city. There was but one edition of this Eastwood Bible, after which the plates were resold in New York; it was the only Bible ever printed in Canada in the English language.[1]

The issues in Canada East are limited to an edition of the New Testament in French, with Perè du Carriere's Notes.

---

[1] As we have been unable, notwithstanding all our efforts, to find a copy of this Bible, and as its existence is already almost forgotten, we subjoin extracts from letters received on the subject.

TORONTO, Dec. 15, 1858.
Dr. E. B. O'CALLAGHAN:

DEAR SIR—I bought in 1837 and brought to Canada the plates of a complete edition of the Bible, Old and New Testament. Of these I printed specimens—say dozen of pages—and sent them around .... I think Eastwood bought the plates. I think he printed an edition ...

Yours, &c.,
W. L. MACKENZIE.

I thought I had a copy of the Bible printed by my father, but cannot find one. The edition was printed about 1839 or '40. There never was but one edition printed, after which the plates were sold in New York.

W. L. McKenzie, Esq.   D. EASTWOOD.

The Eastwood Bible was printed in Toronto. Paper made at the Don.

SOUTHAMPTON, April 8, 1859.
W. L. MACKENZIE, Esq.:

SIR—A small edition of the Bible *was* printed by my late father, but where you can procure a copy, I really cannot say.

Yours, truly,
JOHN EASTWOOD.

TORONTO, Nov. 29, 1860.
Dr. E. B. O'CALLAGHAN, Albany:

DEAR SIR— .... I bought the plates from the Bible Society, at New York in 1835 or 1836, I think. I got a new title page for the Old and also for the New Testament, substituting my name and Toronto, for that of the Bible Society and New York.   W. L. MACKENZIE.

INTRODUCTION. li

In the Gulf Provinces, a Catholic Testament has, it is said, been published in Halifax, N. S., but it has not been seen.

The Catholic Bibles published in the United States, are, with the exceptions of Archbishop Kenrick's revised edition, and the Bible and Testament edited by the Rev. Mr. McMahon, reprints of those issued in England or Ireland. They all profess, on their title pages, to be translated from the Latin Vulgate, and, with one exception, to be copied from the Doway and Rheims Testaments.

At the commencement of the Christian era, the Latin was gradually supplanting the Greek, as a general language, and, as a consequence, soon became that of the Western church, which at the first introduction of Christianity, possessed a very great number of versions of the Scriptures. One of these, known as the Old Italic, acquired a more extensive circulation on account of its clearness and fidelity. In progress of time, however, many alterations came to be made in the text by transcribers. St. Jerome, therefore, was requested by Pope Damasus, to revise it, and accordingly, towards the end of the fourth century first corrected the New Testament by the original Greek, and next translated into Latin, the books of Kings, Job, the Great and Minor Prophets, the Psalms, the books of Solomon, Esdras, Genesis, Josue, Judges, Ruth, Paralipomenon, and Esther from the Hebrew, and the books of Tobias and Judith from the Chaldaic.

He did not translate the books of Wisdom, Ecclesiasticus, Maccabees I and II, Baruch, the Epistle of Jeremias, the Deuterocanonical portions of Esther and David. These were adopted from and remain precisely as in the old, or anti-Hieronymian Vulgate. Neither are the Psalms in the present Vulgate, St. Jerome's translation, but his second correction of the old version from the κοινη of Lucian the martyr.[1]

Thus formed, the Latin Vulgate was declared authentic in the year 1546, by the Council of Trent, which ordered a standard edition to be published. One so intended was issued in 1590, by authority of Sixtus V, and was corrected under Clement VIII, in 1592. Another edition was issued with some slight changes in 1593, and this is the only recognized standard in the Catholic Church,[2] which never has made, and most probably never will make a vernacular standard.

A translation of the New Testament into English was published at Rheims in 1582, and a translation of the Old Testament into the same language, at Doway, in 1609. The English version of the Latin Vulgate is hence called the Doway Bible. It is not, however, a strict translation of the Latin, as the King James's version is of the Hebrew and Greek, but resorts occasionally to the originals.

In the course of the following century, the Doway translation was revised by Bishop Challoner of England, who issued one complete Bible and two Testaments, all differing from each other. These have been revised in turn by others, until now, in the words of Cardinal WISEMAN, "To call it any longer the Doway or Rhemish version, is an abuse of terms. It has been altered and modified till scarce any verse remains as it was originally published; and so far as

---

[1] St. Jerome made a translation of the Psalms from the Hebrew, but it was not adopted as the common version. He twice corrected the Psalters of the old Vulgate. The first edition is called the Roman Psaltery, the second the Gallican Psaltery. The latter is that printed in the Vulgate, and adopted by the church at Rome. *A General Introduction to the Sacred Scriptures.* By Rev. Joseph Dixon, D. D. Dublin, 1852. I, 159, 173, 174.

[2] *Dixon's Introduction*, I, 156 et seq.

simplicity and energy of style are concerned, the changes are in general for the worse. . . . New and often important modifications have been made in every edition, which has followed, till at length many may appear rather new versions than revisions of the old."[1]

The annexed Table will show some of the systematic variations from the Vulgate, now-a-days. We have not room to enumerate all the texts wherein these modern editions vary, not only from the Vulgate, but from each other; the text of the New Testament of Dr. Troy's Bible of 1791, differing from that of Dr. Challoner, it is said, in at least seven or eight hundred places.

These discrepancies, as well as the gross typographical errors which constantly recur, have justly excited attention, and there is, we are happy to see, every prospect that better editions will soon supersede those now issued. Dr. KENRICK, Archbishop of Baltimore, has already published an entirely new edition of the Doway Bible, and the Very Rev. Dr. NEWMAN, Superior of the Oratorians in England, has been selected, with the approbation of the Holy See, and at the request of many of the most distinguished among the Hierarchy of England and Ireland, to prepare a new English version of the Latin Vulgate.

A work which has engaged whatever leisure we have had during the last three years, is now closed. It only remains for us to acknowledge the valuable assistance we have received, both in its preparation, and whilst it was passing through the press, from JAMES LENOX and JOHN G. SHEA, Esqrs., of New York; GEORGE LIVERMORE, Esq., of Boston; GEORGE BRINLEY, Esq., of Hartford; S. F. HAVEN, Esq., of Worcester, and many other kind friends.

The volumes in the collections of these gentlemen are

---

[1] *Dublin Review*, II, 476, 477.

severally indicated in the List by the initials of their names, L. denoting those of the first named; J. G. S. of the second; G. L. the third; B. the fourth, &c.

We have appended to the whole a full and carefully digested Index, containing the names of authors and of their works; of the place where the volume was published, and that of the first publisher mentioned in the imprint, so that whoever is desirous to find a particular edition of a Bible, Testament, or other work, can easily turn to it, if in this List, if he but know the name of the publisher, or the date or place of publication.

LIST

OF

SOME OF THE ERRORS AND VARIATIONS

FOUND IN MODERN DOUAY BIBLES.

List of some of the Errors and Variations found in Modern Douay Bibles, on comparing the Text of the latter with that of the Latin Vulgate.

		VULGATE.	CAREY'S. 1790.	CUMMISKEY QUARTO.* 1825.	DOYLE'S OCTAVO.† 1836.	SADLIER'S QUARTO. 1851.	DUNIGAN'S HAYDOCK QUARTO. 1852.
Gen.	4:14	Behold thou dost cast me out this day from the face of the earth: *and from thy face I shall be hidden and shall be a vagabond and a fugitive on the earth:* every one therefore that findeth me shall kill me.	words in Italic omitted.	words in Italic omitted.	correct.	words in Italic omitted.	— words in Italic omitted.‡
	7:2	Of all clean beasts take seven and seven, the male and the female: but of the beasts which are unclean two and two; the male and the female.	ends incorrectly at the word "female," which precedes "but."	incorrect.	incorrect.	incorrect.	— incorrect.‡
	3	Of the fowls of the air also seven and seven; the male and the female: that seed may be saved upon the face of the whole earth.	begins incorrectly at *but* of V. 2.	incorrect.	incorrect.	incorrect.	— incorrect.‡
	7:21	and all men,	correct.	... and all men.	... and all men.	... and all men.	... and all men.
	9:23	But Sem	correct.	correct.	But Shem	correct.	correct.
	10: 4	Tharsis, Cetthim	correct.	correct.		correct.	Tharsis, Chettiim
	13	Nepthuim,	correct.	Nephtuim,	Nephtuim,	Nephtuim,	Nephtuim.
	15	Hethite,	correct.	Hethite.	Hethite,	Hethite.	Hethite.
	16	Gergesite,	correct.	correct.	Gergesite.		Gergesite.
	18	Amathite:	Hamathite :	Hamathite.	Hamathite;	Hamathite;	Hamathite;
	23	Hul, and Gether, and Mes.	correct.	... Hul, and Gether; and Mes. [Mes.	... Hul, and Gether; and	... Hul, and Gether; and Mes.	same as Sadlier's.
	12:19	that I might take her to me to wife?	... that I might take her	words in Italic omitted.	incorrect.	incorrect.	incorrect.
	13: 4	To the place of the altar which he had before erected in the place, ... which he had made before;	In the place, ... which he had made before;	incorrect.	incorrect.	incorrect.	incorrect.
	19: 3	and they eat,	correct,	... and they ate:	... and they ate;	... and they ate;	... and they ate;
	19	and I die.	and I die.	... and I die.	... and I die.	... and I die.	... and I die.
	23: 8	Intercede for me with Ephron	... to Ephron	incorrect.	incorrect.	incorrect.	incorrect.
	17	And the field that before was Ephron's ... was made sure	And the field that before was Ephron's ... was made sure	incorrect.	incorrect.	incorrect.	incorrect.
	24:16	To Abraham	Were made sure to Abraham				
	24:21	why standest thou without?	correct.	correct.	correct.	why standeth thou without?	correct.
	25:35	And her brother	And her brother	incorrect.	incorrect.	incorrect.	correct.
	26:30,37	the Philistines	... Palestines	incorrect.	incorrect.	Palestines	incorrect.
	31,32	the color was divers.	the color *was* divers.	incorrect.	incorrect.	the colour was divers.	incorrect.
	36: 2	Oolibama the daughter of Ana, the daughter of Sebeon	Oolibama, *the daughter of* Ana, the daughter of Sebeon	words in Italic omitted.	correct.	words in Italic omitted.	correct.
	37:10	upon the earth?	correct.	upon the earth.	correct.	... upon the earth.	correct.
	40:15	And when Joseph was come in to them	And when Joseph was come in to them	... Into them	correct.	... Into them	incorrect.
	43:32	for Joseph apart, for his brethren apart, for the	... apart	... a part, ... a part,	correct.	incorrect.	correct.
	44:15	Egyptians.	Egyptians.				
		divining?	divining?	divining.	divining.	divining.	divining.
	46:17	after Pharao thou art	after Pharao, thou art	correct.	... after Pharao thou art,	... after Pharao thou art.	correct.
	8:22	Jesuri	Jesuri	Jesuri	Jesuri	Jesuri	Jesuri
Ex.	13:9	the land of Gessen *where my people is,* the Lord brought thee out of Egypt.	words in Italic omitted.	words in Italic omitted. out of the land of Egypt.	words in Italic omitted.	words in Italic omitted.	words in Italic omitted.
	14:30	lifted up their eyes,	correct.	out of the land of Egypt.	correct.	... lifted up their eyes	correct.
	16:3	to *all* the children	... to the children	incorrect.	word in Italic omitted.	word in Italic omitted.	word in Italic omitted.
	18: 10	out of the hand of the Egyptians, and out of the hand of Pharao; who hath delivered his people out of the hand of Egypt.	... out of the hands words in Italic omitted.	... out of the hands words in Italic omitted.	And he said, Blessed is the Lord who hath delivered you out of the hand of the Egyptians, and out of the hand of Pharao, and out of the hand of the Egyptians.	incorrect.	incorrect.

* Cummiskey's Octavo, 1839, repeats the errors noted in the Quarto edition, except those in Gen. 40: 6; 1 Kgs. 4:10; 22:19; Lament 1:1 and Mat. 5:1.
† It is stated in the Approbation that this edition was most carefully collated by the Very Rev. John Power, V. G., with the Vulgate, the Douay and other approved English versions.
‡ In the edition of 1854, the texts preceded by a — are corrected; but Lev. 1: 3; 4: 4 are incorrect.

20:11	...the Lord blessed the Sabbath day,	...the seventh day, but keepeth the bed	incorrect.	incorrect.	incorrect.
21:18	...but keepeth his bed	...upon them, ... nor	incorrect.	incorrect.	incorrect.
22:25	...thou shalt not lie hard upon him ... nor oppress him	oppress them	incorrect.	incorrect.	incorrect.
27:20	...oil of the olives	...oil of the olives	correct.	correct.	Incorrect.
29:24	And thou shalt put	correct.	correct.	And thou shalt put.	
35:23	And if any man had violet, and purple, and scarlet twice dyed, fine linen and goats' hair skins, dyed red,	words in Italic omitted.	words in Italic omitted.	words in Italic omitted.	words in Italic omitted.
30:34	...be overlaid with gold, casting for them sockets of silver. And	words in Italic omitted	correct.	correct.	words in Italic omitted
Lev. 1:3	...at the door of the tabernacle of the testimony,	words in Italic omitted.	words in Italic omitted.	words in Italic omitted.	{These pages are wanting in the copy examined.
4:4	...his expiation.	...its expiation.	correct.	correct.	
4:4	...to the door of the tabernacle of the testimony,	words in Italic omitted.	words in Italic omitted.	words in Italic omitted.	
Num. 22:10	...of the priest, and	correct.	incorrect.	Incorrect.	Incorrect.
1:47	...In the tribe	...In the tribes	...In the tribes	...In the tribes	correct.
3:2	...Aleazar	...Ahiezar	...Aleazar	...Ahiezar	...Ahiezar
3:47	...sicles	...sicles	...sicles	...sicles	...sicles
3:50	...sicles	...sicles	...sicles	...sicles	...sicles
4:4	...Caath: Into the tabernacle of the covenant and the Holy of holies	...Caath:	...Caath:	...Caath:	...Caath:
	...Aaron and his sons shall enter when the camp is to set forward, and shall take down, &c.	same as Carey.	same as Carey.	same as Carey.	same as Carey.
14:14	And shall put it with all the vessels.	When the camp is to set forward, ... his sons shall go into the tabernacle of the tabernacle of Caath, In the holy of holies, and shall take down &c. And shall put it, with all the vessels.	And shall put it with all the vessels	And shall put it with all the vessels	And shall put it with all the vessels
15	These are the burdens of the sons of Caath in the tabernacle of the covenant:	These are the burdens of the sons of Caath: In the tabernacle of the covenant:	These are the burdens of the sons of Caath: In the tabernacle of the covenant:	same as Cummiskey's.	These are the burdens of the sons of Caath: In the tabernacle of the covenant:
Deut. 18:24	...oblation or tithes,	incorrect.	incorrect.	incorrect.	incorrect.
27:7	And thou shalt	word in Italic omitted.	word in Italic omitted.	word in Italic omitted.	word in Italic omitted.
30:9	And the Lord thy God will make thee abound	words in Italic omitted.	words in Italic omitted.	words in Italic omitted.	words in Italic omitted.
Jos. 7:7	...the family of Zare. Dragging that also by the hand, he found it to be Zabdi.	words in Italic omitted.	words in Italic omitted.	words in Italic omitted.	words in Italic omitted.
Judg. 5:4	...howed, the heavens and the clouds	words in Italic omitted.	words in Italic omitted.	words in Italic omitted.	words in Italic omitted.
7:1	...camp, and stood together: To the Lord and to Gideon.	words in Italic omitted.	words in Italic omitted.	words in Italic omitted.	words in Italic omitted.
11:18	...and he would not enter the bounds of Moab: For Arnon is the border of the land of Moab.	words in Italic omitted.	words in Italic omitted.	words in Italic omitted.	words in Italic omitted.
1 Kgs. 1:11	...Saph, an Ephraimite: if thou wilt look down on the affliction of thy servant,	incorrect.	incorrect.	Incorrect.	Incorrect.
4:10	...her palms had come	...her palms came	...her palms came	...her palms came	...her palms came
17:40	...struck the Philistine in the forehead; and the stone was fixed in his forehead,	words in Italic omitted.	words in Italic omitted.	correct.	words in Italic omitted.
	...the Philistine	...the Philistines	correct.	incorrect.	incorrect.
22:19	And Nobe the city of the priests	And Nobe the city of the priest	incorrect.	correct.	correct.
2 Kgs. 23:17	...and my father Saul knoweth this, which was in Jezrahel.	word in Italic omitted.	word in Italic omitted.	word in Italic omitted.	word in Italic omitted.
25:23	...the nation and its god.	...the nation and their god.	...the nation and their gods.	...the nation and their gods.	...the nation and their gods.
9:7	...and I will restore to thee all the lands which was in Jezrahel.	words in Italic omitted.	words in Italic omitted.	words in Italic omitted.	words in Italic omitted.
19:19	...By the health of thy soul, my Lord the King,	...my lord O King,	...lord my King,	...lord my King,	...my lord, O King,
19:20	...My Lord the King,	...My lord O King,	...lord my King,	...lord my King,	...my lord, O King,
20:20	...My God will throw down. (The sentence in also an oriental salutation).	...Why wilt thou throw down	incorrect.	incorrect.	incorrect.
3 Kgs. 2:2	I am under the way of all flesh:	down	incorrect.	incorrect.	incorrect.
3:9	Thou will give therefore to thy servant ... who are so numerous?	...give therefore ... which is incorrect, at end a so numerous?	...which is so numerous.	...which is so numerous.	

*The Hebrew text, Protestant version and Douay translation of 1609, have not the clause which occurs in V. 36. Kenrick.

F

List of some of the Errors, etc.—Continued.

		VULGATE.	CAREY'S. 1790.	CUMMISKEY'S QUARTO. 1825.	DOYLE'S OCTAVO. 1836.	SADLIER'S QUARTO. 1851.	DUNIGAN'S HAYDOCK QUARTO. 1825.
4 Kgs.	13: 6	... from the *sins of the house of* Jeroboam	words in Italic omitted.	words in Italic omitted.	words in Italic omitted.	words in Italic omitted.	words in Italic omitted.
	19: 23	... come up to the heights of the mountains	... gone up to the height. Carmel	incorrect. Carmel.	incorrect.... Carmel.	incorrect. Carmel.	incorrect.... Carmel.
1 Par.	11: 24	I have cut down... And	I have cut down, and	incorrect.	incorrect.	incorrect.	I have cut down, and
	16: 13	when Saul was *yet* King	word in Italic omitted.	word in Italic omitted.	word in Italic omitted.	word in Italic omitted.	word in Italic omitted.
2 Par.	32: 22	Israel his servant,	Israel his servants.	incorrect.	incorrect.	incorrect.	incorrect.
		and gave them rest on every side.	... and gave them rest on every side.	... and gave them rest on every side.			
			correct.	word in Italic omitted.			
2 Esdr.	9: 10	upon *all* the people of his land :	word in Italic omitted.	incorrect.	word in Italic omitted.	word in Italic omitted.	word in Italic omitted.
Tobias	4: 14	or in thy word :	... or in thy words :	word in Italic omitted.	incorrect.	incorrect.	incorrect.
Job	18: 4	as well as you, *neither am I inferior to you*:	words in Italic omitted.	words in Italic omitted.	words in Italic omitted.	words in Italic omitted.	words in Italic omitted.
	20: 7	The steps	The step	incorrect.	incorrect.	incorrect.	incorrect.
	22: 8	The eyes	The eye	incorrect.	incorrect.	incorrect.	incorrect.
	30: 13	doth hold it.	... hold it.	incorrect.	incorrect.	incorrect.	incorrect.
Ps.	77: 8	provoke the wrath of God,	... those who dwell therein.	... prove the wrath of God,	... prove the wrath of God,	... prove the wrath of God:	... they that
	129: 1	them that dwell therein.	... must hold	... they that dwell therein.	... they that	... they that dwell therein.	stand it?
Eccles.	11: 6	into the hands of others.	... into the hand of others.	... stand it?	incorrect.	incorrect.	incorrect.
Is.	31: 10	transgressed ; could do evil things,	... transgressed and could have done	... transgressed ; and could do	... and could	... transgressed : and could	... and could do
	2: 4	sickles ;	sickles,	correct.	correct.	correct.	correct.
	3: 3	the wisest architect	the wiser architect	word in Italic omitted.	word in Italic omitted.	word in Italic omitted.	word in Italic omitted.
	15: 3	on all its heads	on all their heads	incorrect.	incorrect.	incorrect.	incorrect.
		In its streets... on the tops of its houses, and in its streets all how!	In their streets... on their houses, and in their streets, all shall how!				
10: 14		In all its work,	In all its works,	incorrect.	incorrect.	incorrect.	incorrect.
25: 7		which he wove over all nations.	which he began over all nations.	incorrect.	incorrect.	incorrect.	incorrect.
28: 4		And the fading flower of the glory of his joy.	And the fading flower the glory of his joy, which is at the lifting up of thyself	incorrect.	incorrect.	incorrect.	incorrect.
33: 3		at the lifting up of thyself	at the lifting up of thyself	word in Italic omitted.	word in Italic omitted.	word in Italic omitted.	word in Italic omitted.
27: 12		And the virtue *of King* Ezechias	word in Italic omitted.	incorrect.	incorrect.	incorrect.	incorrect.
45: 14		my hands	my hands	correct.	correct.	correct.	correct.
46: 3		there is no God besides thee.	... beside thee.	word in Italic omitted.	word in Italic omitted.	word in Italic omitted.	word in Italic omitted.
47: 6		Hearken unto me, O house of Jacob, *and all*	the power of the flame;	incorrect.	incorrect.	incorrect.	incorrect.
57: 10		In the multitude of thy way :	... in the multitude of thy ways :	incorrect.	incorrect.	incorrect.	incorrect.
11		... nor thought in thy heart?	... nor thought on me in thy heart?	incorrect.	incorrect.	incorrect.	incorrect.
17		... wandering in the way of his heart.	... wandering in the way of his own heart.	... wandering in his own heart.	... wandering in his own heart.	... wandering in his own heart.	... his own heart.
59: 10		We have groped for the wall like the blind, and we have groped as if we had no eyes :	We have groped for the wall : and like the blind we have groped, as if we had no eyes :	incorrect.	incorrect.	incorrect.	incorrect.
16		... and the like to his enemies :	... and a reward to his enemies ;	incorrect.	incorrect.	incorrect.	incorrect.
Jer.	2: 28	Where are thy gods,	Where are the gods,	incorrect.	incorrect.	incorrect.	incorrect.
	6: 19	the fruit	the fruits	incorrect.	incorrect.	incorrect.	incorrect.
	13: 21	as *prima* a woman in labor.	word in Italic omitted.	word in Italic omitted.	word in Italic omitted.	word in Italic omitted.	word in Italic omitted.
	10: 22	*and* a great commotion	word in Italic omitted.	word in Italic omitted.	word in Italic omitted.	word in Italic omitted.	word in Italic omitted.
	24: 74	but destroy them.	... but to destroy them.	incorrect.	incorrect.	incorrect.	incorrect.
	44: 10	from *the Lord*,	... by the Lord,	incorrect.	incorrect.	incorrect.	incorrect.
		before you and *before* your fathers.	word in Italic omitted.	word in Italic omitted.	word in Italic omitted.	word in Italic omitted.	word in Italic omitted.

Lam.	1:1	... the princess of provinces	... the princess of provinces	incorrect.	correct.
	4:16	... the ancients.	... the ancient.	incorrect.	incorrect.
	5:12	The princes were hanged up by the hand;	The princes were hanged up ... the by their hand ... the ancients.	incorrect.	incorrect.
Ezek.	2:6	fear *them* not.	word in Italic omitted.	word in Italic omitted.	word in Italic omitted.
	-3:11	Thus saith the Lord *God*.	word in Italic omitted.	word in Italic omitted.	word in Italic omitted.
	7:9	And my eye shall not spare	... my eyes shall not spare	correct.	correct.
	8:18	my eye	... my eyes	incorrect.	incorrect.
	10:1	... the head of the cherubim,	... the heads of the cherubim.	incorrect.	incorrect.
	12:7	... stretched out his hand as the Lord had commanded me;	... stretched out his arm as he had commanded me was carried	incorrect.	incorrect.
		being		incorrect.	incorrect.
	24	... carried	... visions	incorrect.	incorrect.
	14:21	For thus saith the Lord *God*:	word in Italic omitted.	word in Italic omitted.	word in Italic omitted.
	16:29	... thy fornication.	thy formations.	incorrect.	incorrect.
	17:23	On the high mountain	On the high mountains	incorrect.	incorrect.
	29:6	... a staff *of* reed	... a staff of a reed	incorrect.	incorrect.
	33:10	... judgment	judgments	incorrect.	incorrect.
	35:9	Unto everlasting desolations will I deliver thee and ye shall know	I will make thee everlasting desolations; ... and thou shalt know	correct.	correct.
	37:24	they *all* shall have	word in Italic omitted.	word in Italic omitted.	word in Italic omitted.
	39:17	*that* saith the Lord *God*;	word in Italic omitted.	word in Italic omitted.	word in Italic omitted.
	25	thus *saith* the Lord *God*:	words in Italic omitted.	words in Italic omitted.	words in Italic omitted.
Dan.	9:6	*to our kings, to our princes*	... men, ye, who adore	words in Italic omitted.	words in Italic omitted.
Osee	13:2	ye men who adore calves.	calves.	... men, ye that adore	... men, ye that
Amos.	7:4	The Lord *God* called forth judgment	word in Italic omitted.	word in Italic omitted.	word in Italic omitted.
	9:1	... the lintel,	incorrect.	incorrect.	incorrect.
1 Mac	10:42	... sickles of silver,	sickles ... sicklea	... sickles of silver	... sickles
2 Mac	10:18	fled into two very strong towers	word in Italic omitted.	word in Italic omitted.	word in Italic omitted.
Matt.	5:1	And *Jesus* seeing	word in Italic omitted.	word in Italic omitted.	word in Italic omitted.
Luke	1:63	... and all these words	correct.	correct.	correct.
1 Cor.	14:4	... the church *of* God.	words in Italic omitted.	words in Italic omitted.	words in Italic omitted.

Note. In judging of the correctness or incorrectness of the above texts, for the memorandum of most of which we are indebted to our friend Mr. Sam, it is proper to remark, that we have not gone behind the Latin Vulgate, that being the standard for the other editions mentioned in this Table.

ERRATA.

Page 8, line 10 from bottom, after *omissions*, insert *and*.
" 20, " 14 from bottom, for *New Haven*, read *Worcester*.
" 33, " 2 from top, for *que*, read *qui*.
" 88, " 18, from top of, for *Famliy*, read *Family*.
" 113, erase title No. 4 on this page.
" 148, " 16, for *Wurehouse*, read *Warehouse*.
" 155, " 21, from bottom, for *Burtus*, read *Burtis*.
" 164, " 3, from top, for 6, read 8.
" 203, " 5, for 1, read 2.
" 219, " 7, for *Bloomfield's*, read *Greenfield's*.
" 309, " 10, for *Minestro*, read *Ministro*.
" 11, for *Soncto*, read *Sancto*.
" 13, for 836, read 886.
" 338, " 7, for *Achille*, read *Achilli*.
" 368, " 24, for 15, read 13.
" 385, " 1, for *Pslams*, read *Psalms*.

THE NEW
TESTAMENT
OF OUR
LORD AND SAVIOUR
JESUS CHRIST.

Translated into the

INDIAN LANGUAGE,
AND

Ordered to be Printed by the *Commissioners of the United Colonies* in *NEW-ENGLAND*,

At the Charge, and with the Consent of the

CORPORATION IN *ENGLAND*

For the Propagation of the Gospel amongst the Indians *in New-England.*

CAMBRIDG:
Printed by *Samuel Green* and *Marmaduke Johnson*.
MDCLXI.

WUSKU
WUTTESTAMENTUM

NUL-LORDUMUN

JESUS CHRIST

Nuppoquohwuſſuaeneumun.

CAMBRIDGE:
Printed by *Samuel Green* and *Marmaduke Johnſon.*
MDCLXI.

MAMUSSE
WUNNEETUPANATAMWE
UP-BIBLUM GOD
NANEESWE
NUKKONE TESTAMENT
KAH WONK
WUSKU TESTAMENT.

Ne quoſhkinnumuk naſhpe Wuttinneumoh *CHRIST*
noh oſꝏweſit

JOHN ELIOT.

C AMBRIDGE:
Printeuꝏp naſhpe *Samuel Green* kah *Marmaduke Johnſon.*
1 6 6 3.

THE
HOLY BIBLE:
CONTAINING THE
OLD TESTAMENT
AND THE *NEW*.

Tranflated into the
INDIAN LANGUAGE,
A N D
Ordered to be Printed by the *Commiffioners of the United Colonies* in N*EW-ENGLAND*,

At the Charge, and with the Confent of the
CORPORATION IN *ENGLAND*
For the *Propagation of the Gofpel amongft the* Indians in New-England.

CAMBRIDGE:
Printed by *Samuel Green* and *Marmaduke Johnfon*.
MDCLXIII.

AMERICAN BIBLES.

1661.

1. THE NEW | TESTAMENT | of our | Lord and Saviour | Jesus Christ. | Translated into the | Indian Language, | and | Ordered to be Printed by the *Commissioners of the Vnited Colonies* | in *New-England*, | At the Charge, and with the Consent of the | Corporation in England | *For the Propagation of the Gospel amongst the* Indians | in *New-England*. | (A black line across the page.) | *Cambridg:* | Printed by *Samuel Green* and *Marmaduke Johnson*. | MDCLXI. | (L.; G. L.)   sm.4

1 Blank leaf; English Title, within a border (see *Fac simile*), 1 p. verso, blank; on the upper part of the next page 2 black lines, or rules, 4½ inches in length, extend across the page nearly to the right border or edge of the paper; below these, is a head piece composed of 32 printer's flowers similar to those on the title page; then a single rule line followed by another ornamental line, as above, but with the flowers inverted, making in all *five* lines; then The Epistle Dedicatory: To | The high and Mighty | Prince, | CHARLES the SECOND, | &c. the first page of which is marked A3; the Dedication ends on verso of A⁴; at the end of the Epistle, 2 black lines one inch and a half apart, extend across the page; Indian Title, within a border (see *Fac simile*) : Wusku | Wuttestamentum | nul-lordumun | Jesus Christ | Nuppoquohwussuaeneumun. | a black line across the page; then an ornament composed of 32 printer's flowers, arranged in the shape of a Star; next, another black line across the page; Cambridge: | Printed by *Samuel Green* and *Marmaduke Johnson*. | MDCLXI. | 1 p. verso, blank; Text: Matthew to the end of Luke, sigs. A² to verso of L⁴; John to Rev. As to verso of Xx³, all in 4ˢ; at the end of the text, "Finis," between 2 black lines; a blank leaf should complete the last sig.

The size of the printed page is 6⅞ inches by 4⅜ inches, including headings, catchwords and marginal references; of the leaf, 7⅞ by 5¾ inches.

This work, which consists of 4 prelim. ff. and 126 leaves of text, was printed with new type, full faced bourgeois on a brevier body. The text is in double columns, with marginal references at the sides, and headings in Indian at the top of the pages, but there is no summary at the beginning of the chapters. Mathew, John and the Acts commence, each, with an ornamental initial letter, but the initial N of the last mentioned Book is inverted, thus, **И**. In the first three of the Gospels the name of the Evangelist is at the top of the verso, and the chap. and its number, of the recto page of the text; but in John the name of the Evangelist and number, of the chapter are at the head of each page. Each verse forms a distinct paragraph until we come to Luke XV. (verso of X*).; between the end of the Gospel, more than one, sometimes six verses are crowded occasionally into a paragraph, in order apparently to close that gospel and sig. L at the same time. The same crowding occurs again at the close of John. The 4th and 14th numbers to the chapters throughout this volume are generally, though printed IIII, not invariably, XIIII.

On comparing this Translation with the edition of 1680, we find a number of omissions in the text. These, with other errors, are noted in the following table of

ERRATA.

Matthew 4:25, "and from Judea,"
    8:5, "Jesus"
    10:19, "For it shall be given you in that same hour what ye shall speak."
    14:34, "into the land of"
         35, "of that place"
    15: headed CHHP.
    18:35, "every one his brother"
    23:16, "Whosoever shall swear by the temple, it is nothing; but"
    24:26, "Behold, he is in the desert; go not forth:"
    26:26, "Take, eat;"
Mark 2:16, "and drinketh"
    4: numbered 6, at the head of the page.
    9:25, "and enter no more into him."
    12:33, "offerings and"
Luke 1:37, numbered 47.
    3:19, reads: "and for all the other evils"
    5:36, "unto them:"
    6:12, "to pray, and"...."all night"
    8:24, "Master" not repeated.
    12:48, reads: "For unto whomsoever much is given, to him shall much be given, of him shall much be required:"
Luke 13:15, "and said,"
    15:12, "Father" not repeated.
    20:46, "and the highest seats in the synagogues,"
    21:7, "and, What sign will there be when these things shall come to pass?"
        The number of the chapter at the head of the page, is misprinted, 10.
    24:46, "from the dead"
        The number of the chapter at the head of the page, is misprinted, 15.
John 4:42, "the Christ,"
    6:69, verse numbered 59.
    10:3, "his own"
        Chapter headed, CHAp.
    13:36, verse numbered 39.
        38, numbered 48.
    18:28, reads: "Then led they Jesus from Caiphas into the hall of Pilate."
Acts 2:20, "and notable"
    6:5, "a proselyte"
    5: } numbered v, vi, at the
    6: } head of the page.
    9:10, "Behold,"

AMERICAN BIBLES.

Acts	10:14, "or unclean."	Rom.	12:20, verse marked 2 K.
	28, "or unclean."		14:10, "of Christ."
	36, "Christ"	1 Cor.	6:9, "nor adulterers,"
	12:11, "of the people"		10:16, "which we bless,"
	17, "out of the prison." The subsequent part of the verse reads: "Go shew these things to *Jewes*," instead of, "James."		14:35, "for women"
		2 Cor.	12:1, "of the Lord."
		Ephes.	2:3, "we all"
			5: headed CAAP.
		Phillip.	1:28, verse numbered 18.
	15:35, "teaching and preaching the word of the Lord,"		29 ⎫ Both these verses are run 30 ⎭ into one and numbered 29, thus making the chapter 29, instead of 30, verses.
	16:5, "and increased in number daily."		
	17:11, "daily"		
	18:25, "in the spirit,"	1 Thess.	1:9, "and true"
	19:18, "and showed"	Heb.	2:16, "he took on him"
	35, "of the Ephesians"		10:12, "sins,"
	23:14, "that we will" (eat) "nothing"		11:16, "for he hath prepared for them"
	24:1, "the governor"	Rev.	4:10, "and ever,"
	27: headed "The Acts." at the top of the page, instead of, "Chap. 27."		16: headed, CAAP.
			21:12, "of the children"

A writer in 1 *Mass. Hist. Coll.* VIII. 34, states that 1 Cor. 15:31, as here translated, countenances swearing by a creature. On comparing the text with Hosea 4:2, and, Mat. 5:34, 36, it is observed that the word "protest" in that passage, is rendered into Indian by the same verb as "swear," in the last mentioned texts.

In the running titles of the Books, Mark is printed "Marke" on the verso of E[2], E[3] and E[4]; John is printed "Iohn" above chapters 3, 19 and 20; the recto of Ll[3] is II Corinthians, instead of Chap. 1; and on the 3d page of Rev. the word is "Revelations."

Mr. ELIOT, pastor of Roxbury, Mass., commenced at the age of forty-two, the study of the Natick Indian dialect, in which this work is printed. In 1649, having made some proficiency, he expressed a desire to translate a portion of the Scriptures into that language* for the use of the Indians to whom he acted as a Missionary, and with the aid of an Indian, completed the translation of the entire Bible, including the Old and New Testament, in 1658, after a labor of eight years. This fact having been communicated to the Corporation established in London for the propagation of the Gospel among the Indians of New England,† that body expressed themselves, in a letter dated 7th May, 1659, on the subject of printing the work, in the following terms: "As to the printing of the Bible in the Indian language; mensioned in Mr. Endicott's

---

* 3 Mass. Hist. Coll., IV., 121.

† See Gov. Endicott's letter to the Corporation, dated Boston 28 Dec., 1658, in a very rare Tract, entitled: "A further Accompt of the Progresse of the Gospel amongst the Indians in New England, and of the means used effectually to advance the same. Set forth In certaine Letters sent from thence declaring a purpose of Printing the Scriptures in the Indian Tongue into which they are already Translated, &c. &c. London: Printed by M. Simmons for the Corporation of England. 1659." sm. 4to. It is in the collection of JAMES LENOX, Esq., New York.

letter; which wee vnderstand is alreddy translated into the Indian tounge; wee conceuie will not onely be acceptable vnto god; but uery proffitable to the poor heathen and will much tend to the promotion of the speritual part of this worke amongst them; and therfor wee offer it not onely as our owne but as the judgment of others that the New Testament bee first printed in the Indian language."* The printing of that part was accordingly commenced by Samuel Green, of Cambridge, the same year, when a printed sheet was sent to England as a specimen of the work.

Writing in April, 1660, the Corporation add: "We haue out of our desire to further a worke of soe great conserment hauing hopes that somthinge wilbee collected in particulare with Relation to the printing of the ould Testament, agreed with an able Printer for three years."† Marmaduke Johnson accordingly arrived in this country to superintend the printing, and possibly his arrival subsequent to the commencement of the work by Green, may account for the Gospel of John beginning with Aa; for the crowding observed in the latter part of Luke, and for the arrangement of the running title of John being different from that of the preceding part of the work. Be this as it may, this translation of the New Testament was, in the words of Gookin, "finished, printed and set forth" on the 5th September, 1661.‡ The edition was, at first, to consist of 1000, but the Corporation recommended that it should be 1500 copies. Twenty of these were ordered to be sent to England; whereof one was to be presented "well bound vp," to the King; one to the Earl of Clarendon, then lord Chancellor, and one to each of the Vice Chancellors of the Universities, "whoe have greatly Incurraged the worke;"§ and "it is our desires," add the Commissioners, "that you will take care for the printing of the preface before the New Testament with the title according to the coppies, as alsoe to send to Mr. ashurst and Mr. huchenson about twenty coppies of the New Testament to bee disposed of according to our directions and order.‖ The expence of "printing the title sheet to the New Testament" was £1.00.00; ¶ the "preface" consisted of an "Epistle Dedicatory" to his Majesty, and was in these words:

To The High and Mighty PRINCE, CHARLES the SECOND, by the Grace of God King of *England*, *Scotland*, *France* and *Ireland*, Defender of the Faith, &c. The Commiſſioners of the Vnited Colonies in New-England, wiſh increaſe of all Happineſs, &c.

Moſt Dread Soveraign,

F our weak apprehenſions have not miſled us, this Work will be no unacceptable Preſent to Your Majeſty, as having a greater Intereſt therein, then we believe is generally underſtood: which (upon this Occaſion) we conceive it our Duty to declare.

The People of theſe four Colonies (Confederate for Mutual Defence, in the time of the late Diſtractions of our dear Native Country) Your Majeſties

---

* Hazard's State Papers, II, 403.   † Ibid, 425.
‡ 1 Mass. Hist. Coll , I, 176; Hazard, II., 439.   § Hazard, II., 441.
‖ Letter to Mr. Usher, dated Plymouth, the 13th Sept., 1661, *Hazard's State Papers*, II., 446. Mr. Thomas seems to infer from it, that the Dedication accompanied only the few copies of the Testament sent to England, *Hist. of Printing*, I., 472. At page 255 same vol., he states that the Psalms in Indian Metre, accompanied the New Testament; but there is no evidence in support of that statement, in the Minutes of the Commissioners; and there is no allusion to the Psalms in the order to Mr. Usher, directing the transmission of copies of the Testament to England.   ¶ Hazard, II., 459.

natural born Subjects, by the Favour and Grant of Your Royal Father and Grandfather of Famous Memory, put themselves upon this great and hazardous Undertaking, of Planting themselves at their own Charge in these remote ends of the Earth, that without offence or provocation to our dear Brethren and Countrymen, we might enjoy that liberty to Worship God, which our own Conscience informed us, was not onely our Right, but Duty: As also that we might (if it so pleased God) be instrumental to spread the light of the Gospel, the knowledg of the Son of God our Saviour, to the poor barbarous Heathen, which by His late Majesty, in some of our Patents, is declared to be His principal aim.

These honest and pious Intentions, have, through the grace and goodness of God and our Kings, been seconded with proportionable success: for, omitting the Immunities indulged us by Your Highness Royal Predecessors, we have been greatly incouraged by Your Majesties gracious expressions of Favour and Approbation signified, unto the *Address* made by the principal of our Colonies, to which the rest do most cordially Subscribe, though wanting the like seasonable opportunity, they have been (till now) deprived of the means to Congratulate Your Majesties happy Restitution, after Your long suffering, which we implore may yet be graciously accepted, that we may be equal partakers of Your Royal Favour and Moderation; which hath been so Illustrious that (to admiration) the Animosities and different Perswasions of men have been so soon Composed, and so much cause of hope, that (unless the sins of the Nation prevent) a blessed Calm will succeed the late horrid Confusions of Church and State. And shall not we *(Dread Soveraign)* your Subjects of these Colonies, of the same Faith and Belief in all Points of Doctrine with our Countrymen, and the other Reformed Churches, (though perhaps not alike perswaded in some matters of Order, which in outward respects hath been unhappy for us) promise and assure our selves of all just favour and indulgence from a Prince so happily and graciously endowed?

The other part of our Errand hither, hath been attended with Endevours and Blessing; many of the wilde *Indians* being taught, and understanding the Doctrine of the Christian Religion, and with much affection attending such Preachers as are sent to teach them, many of their Children are instructed to Write and Reade, and some of them have proceeded further, to attain the knowledge of the Latine and Greek Tongues, and are brought up with our English youth in University-learning: There are divers of them that can and do reade some parts of the Scripture, and some Catechisms, which formerly have been Translated into their own Language, which hath occasioned the undertaking of a greater Work, *viz:* The Printing of the whole Bible, which (being Translated by a painful Labourer amongst them, who was desirous to see the Work accomplished in his dayes) hath already proceeded to the finishing of the New Testament, which we here humbly present to Your Majesty, as the first fruits and accomplishment of the Pious Design of your Royal Ancestors. The Old Testament is now under the Press, wanting and craving your Royal Favour and Assistance for the perfecting thereof.

We may not conceal, that though this Work hath been begun and prosecuted by such Instruments as God hath raised up here, yet the chief Charge and Cost, which hath supported and carried it thus far, hath been from the Charity and Piety of divers of our well-affected Countrymen in *England*; who being sensible of our inability in that respect, and studious to promote so good a Work, contributed large Sums of Money, which were to be improved according to the Direction and Order of the then-prevailing Powers, which hath been faithfully and religiously attended both there and here, according to the pious intentions of the Benefactors. And we do most humbly beseech your Majesty, that a matter of so much Devotion and Piety, tending so much to the Honour of God, may suffer no disappointment through any Legal Defect (without the fault of the Donors, or the poor *Indians*, who onely receive the benefit) but that your Majesty be graciously pleased to Establish and Confirm the same, being contrived and done (as we conceive) in the firſt year of your Majeſties Reign, as this Book was begun and now finiſhed in the firſt year of your Eſtabliſhment; which doth not onely preſage the happy ſucceſs of your Highneſs Government, but will be a perpetual Monument, that by your Majeſties Favour the Goſpel of our Lord and Saviour *Jeſus Chriſt*, was firſt made known to the *Indians*: An Honour whereof (we are aſſured) your Majeſty will not a little eſteem.

    S I R, *The ſhines of Your Royal Favour upon theſe Vndertakings, will make theſe tender Plants to flouriſh, notwithſtanding any malevolent Aſpect from thoſe that bear evil will to this* Sion, *and render Your Majeſty more Illuſtrious and Glorious to after Generations.*

      The God of Heaven long preſerve and bleſs Your Majeſty with many happy dayes, to his Glory, the good and comfort of his Church and People. Amen.

1663.

1. MAMVSSE | WUNNEETUPANATAMWE | Up-Biblum God | naneeswe | Nukkone Testament | kah wonk | Wusku Testament. | A black line extends across the page. No quoshkinnumuk nashpe Wuttinncumoh CHRIST | noh asoowesit | JOHN ELIOT. | Another black line across the page. Cambridge: | Printeuoop nashpe *Samuel Green* kah *Marmaduke Johnson.* | 1663. | *   sm. 4.

    Title, within an ornamental border, 1 f.; verso, blank; followed by a leaf, the recto of which is blank; at the top of the verso, a head piece composed of 35 printer's flowers; then *Booke Wesuongash*, &c., with the Names (in English) of the Books composing the Old Testament, and number of chapters in each; then a line consisting of 18 printer's flowers; *Wusku Testamente Bookash*. Names (in English) of the Books of the N. Test., and number of chapters in each; Text: Gen. to Mal., sigs. A. to verso of M m m m m^2, in 4s; at the end of the text, *Wohkukquohsinwog Quoshodtumwaenuog*. followed by two black lines across the page; Title to New Testament: Wusku | Wuttestamentum | Nul-lordumun | Jesus Christ | Nuppoquohwussuaeneumun. | a black line across the page; then an ornament composed of 32 printer's flowers arranged in the shape of a diamond or Star; another black line across the page. Cambridge: | Printed by *Samuel Green* and *Marmaduke Johnson*. | MDCLXI. | 1 p. verso, blank; Text: Matthevv to the end of Luke, sigs. A^2 to verso of L^4; John to Rev., As to verso of Xx^3, in 4s; at the end of the text, "Finis," between 2 black lines; a blank leaf completes sig. Xx; Psalms in Indian metre (no title page), VVame | Ketoohomae uketoohomaongash | David. | Text: 50 leaves, sigs. A. to verso of N^2; at the end of the Psalms the catch word Noowomoo, between two black lines; then one leaf containing a short Catechism in Indian; the first page is headed by an ornamental line composed of 17 printer's flowers; the second page closes by the word "Finis;" a blank leaf should complete the sig. all in 4s.

    This volume is in the same style of type as the New Testament of 1661, and is printed in double columns with marginal references at the sides. There are headings to

    * Literal Translation: The entire | Holy | Bible of God | containing | the Old Testament | and | the New Testament. | Translated by the Servant of Christ | called | John Eliot. | Cambridge: | Printed by *Samuel Green* and *Marmaduke Johnson*. | 1663.

the columns in Indian, in Italic letter, with the names of the Books and number of the Chapters at the top of the pages, in Roman, and in the centre of the verso and recto of each leaf, the marginal notes being also in Roman; there are no abstracts or summaries to the chapters. Genesis, Matthew, John, Acts and the Psalms in metre commence each with an ornamental initial letter. The printed page is 6⅜ inches by 4⅜ inches full.

It is the first edition of the Bible published in this country. The very sight of it caused the quaint Cotton Mather enthusiastically to exclaim : " Behold, ye Americans, the greatest honour that ever you were partakers of ! This .... is the only Bible that ever was printed in all America, from the very foundation of the World."

I have compared three Books of the Old Testament, in this edition, with the same Books of the edition of 1685, and found the following

ERRATA.

Genesis 1: 2, " of God " omitted.
        15, " of the heaven " not translated.
      2:23 } Both these verses are
        24 } run into one, and numbered 23.
        25, numbered 24; the chapter in consequence falls short one verse in the enumeration.
      7: 3, The syllable " oh " is repeated incorrectly in the last line.
     17:10, " among you " not translated.
        13, " with thy " not translated.
     21: is headed CHAp.
     23:17, " in all the borders round about " not translated.
     24:27, v. numbered incorrectly 28; " Abraham " omitted.
        30, " and when he heard the words of Rebekah his sister," not translated.
     26:14, " possession " is not repeated before " of herds."
     27:23, " his brother " not translated.
     31: is headed CHAp.

Genesis 32:31 } Both these verses are
        32 } run into one, making the chapter 31, instead of 32 verses.
     33:13, " men " not translated.
     41:38, " of God " omitted.
     43:28, " is in good health " not translated.
     44: 2, " the silver cup," not translated.
        3, " & " is superfluous.
        4, " kah " in the second line, superfluous.
     45:12, " the eyes of " not translated.
        16, the word for " pleased " is repeated before " his servants."
     49:28, " blessed them; every one " not translated.
Numb. 1:32, " after their families " not translated.
      8:21, " to cleanse them " not translated.
     10: 8, " the trumpets " not translated.
        19, " of the tribe " not translated.
     14: 1, reads, according to the translation: " And all the people lifted up their voices, and wept that night."
        27, " evil " not translated.

	"I have heard the murmurings of the children of Israel, which they murmured against me." also omitted.	Numb. 29: 6, "his meat-offering, and" not repeated after "burnt-offering."
Numb.	30, "Doubtless shall not" seem not to be translated. The text reads, "They come into the land" &c.	31:48, "and captains of hundreds" not translated.
		32:14, "fierce" not translated.
		36: is numbered 26, at the head of the page.
	15:39, "your own heart and" not translated.	Hosea 2: 9, "in the time thereof, and my wine" not translated.
	16:47, "Moses" omitted.	15, "out of the land" not translated.
	17: headed CAAP.	
	18: 4, "and a stranger shall not come nigh unto you." not translated.	3: 4, "many days" not translated.
		4: 9, The words for "people" and "priest" are transposed, so that the last is first in Indian.
	9, "every meat-offering of theirs," not translated.	
	13, "every one that is clean in thy house shall eat of it." not translated.	9:13, "his children" not translated.
		12:13, "Lord" not translated, or omitted.
	19: 9, "without the camp" not translated.	13:14, "the power" not translated.

In addition to the above, the headings to Exodus V. and VIII. are misprinted CAAP.; Deuteronomy XXIII. is numbered 6, and XXVIII, 14, at the head of the pages, and the name of the book, is sometimes printed "Deuteronomie," and in one place (verso of Aa) "Deuteronomie;" Job XXVIII. is marked GHAP.; XXXIX, is numbered XXIX at the head of the Chap. and XXXVIII, XXXIX, are marked 28, 29 at top of the page; the 14th Psalm is headed HSAL.; Isaiah XXXIX, is numbered 49 in the running title, and Zechariah XIV. is headed CHVP.

The New Testament accompanying this volume, is the same as that already described under 1661, less the English title page, and Epistle dedicatory; the omissions errors remaining uncorrected. The Volume consists of, Old Test., 2 prel. ff., and 414 ff.; New Test. Title p., 126 ff., and one blank leaf; Psalms 50 ff., and Catechism 1 f.; in all 594 ff.

2. THE | HOLY BIBLE: | containing the | Old Testament | and the *New*. | (A black line across the page.) Translated into the | Indian Language, | *and* | Ordered to be Printed by the *Commissioners of the Vnited Colonies* | in *New-England,* | At the Charge, and with the Consent of the | Corporation in *England* | *For the Propagation of the Gospel amongst the*

Indians | *in* New-England. | (A black line across the page.) Cambridge: | Printed by *Samuel Green* and *Marmaduke Johnson.* | MDCLXIII. | sm. 4.

1 blank leaf; then Title (within an ornamental border, See Facsimile) 1 p; verso, blank; Dedication 4 pp.; at the top of the first, two black lines extend across the page, then a head piece composed of printer's flowers and rules, as follows: the *first* line has 17 flowers; the *second* is a black rule; the *third* has 42 small flowers; the *fourth* is a black line, and the *fifth* has the same flowers as the *first*, but inverted; then follows: *To* | the high and mighty | Prince, | CHARLES the SECOND, | &c.; this page is marked A³; the "Epistle Dedicatory" terminating on verso of A⁴. Two black lines, one inch and a half apart, extend across the page below the close of this Epistle. This Dedication, with Title and peliminary blank leaf, forms one sig. in 4ˢ. The recto of the next page is blank; at the top of the verso is an ornamental line composed of 35 printer's flowers, then *Booke Wesuongash* &c. or, a List of the Books in the Old Testament with the number of chapters in each, the names of the Books being in English; next, a line composed of 18 printer's flowers; then, *Wusku Testamente Bookash*, or, a List of the Books of the New Testament and the number of chapters in each. This leaf is inserted in the manner of maps. Text: Gen. to Mal. (as in No. 1.); Title to New Testament: Wusku | Wuttestamentum | Nullordumun | Jesus Christ | Nuppoquohwussuaeneumun. | Two black lines across the page, 1⅜ inch apart. Cambridge: | Printed by *Samuel Green* and *Marmaduke Johnson.* | MDCLXI. | 1 p.; verso, blank; Text: (same as described under 1661), followed by Psalms in Indian Metre and Catechism, as in No. 1, of 1663, a blank leaf completing sig. N.

With the exceptions of the first title page and Dedication, and the absence of the "Star" on the title to the New Testament, this volume is the same as No. 1 of this year. The errors already noted in the Old and New Testaments, are continued, but those in the running titles to Luke XXI and XXIV, having been discovered whilst the work was passing through the press, are here corrected. In working off the form, however, after making these corrections, the last letter of the catchword, "waabeh," at Luke XXI, was shoved out into the margin and the word is printed "waabe h" on recto of L² in this copy. Hence the curious bibliographer will understand that, irrespective of the difference in the title pages, there are two varieties of Eliot's Indian Testament of 1661: One, with the running titles to Luke XXI and XXIV incorrect, and the catchword on L² correct; the other, vice versâ. In the copies before us, the former variety has the "Star" on the title page.

In connection with this subject, it is proper to bear in mind that there are copies of this Bible which vary from our present description in some particulars. In the volumes before us, the New Testament with the "Star" on the title page, accompanies the Old Testament with the Indian Title only, and no Dedication (supra No. 1, 1663); whilst there is no "Star" on the title page to the New Testament of the copy having the first title in English, and the Dedication, or (as it may be designated,) the "Royal" copy of the Eliot Bible. On the other hand, in the "Royal" copy belonging to JOHN ALLAN, Esq., of New York, the Bible with an English Title and Dedication, is accompanied by the New Testament with the "Star" title page. Again, the copy in the Library of the Brown University, R. I., differs from all these. It has the general title in English, (No. 2, 1663.) then the Dedication, and following that, the Indian title page (No. 1, 1663). What other varieties the binder has manufactured we know not.

AMERICAN BIBLES. [1663—

It has been already stated that Mr. ELIOT completed the immense labor of translating this Bible in 1658, but the printing of the Old Testament was not commenced until 1660. In September of that year, a sheet of Genesis was transmitted to England. "The printers doubt not but to print a sheet every weeke, and compute the whole to amount to a hundred and fifty sheets."* In September, 1661, the five books of Moses were printed;† in September, 1662, the work was about half done,‡ and completed in September, 1663.§ Three years were thus occupied in the publication of the Old Testament. The Corporation had already ordered in April, 1663, "that the Psalmes of David, in meter, shalbee printed in the Indian language." On the 18th, Sept., following, twenty copies of the Bible were ordered to be sent to England, "and as many of the Psalmes, if printed of before the shippes departure from hence." The edition, including the Psalm books, consisted of upwards of 1000 copies.‖ Three hundred and sixty-eight reams of paper were used in printing the Bible; the expence ranged from sixty to seventy shillings sterling a sheet. The cost of printing the Psalms was forty shillings a sheet, or £26, in the whole; of printing the "Epistle dedicatory" to the Bible, £1, and of "binding and clasping," two shillings and sixpence per copy.¶ JOHN RATLIFE, the book-binder, objected to this low price, and avowed in a petition to the Commissioners, "that under 3s. 4d. or 3s. 6d. per book," he could not bind them and live comfortably, "one Bible being as much as he could compleat in one day" and find the materials.**

When completed, twenty copies were ordered to be sent to the Corporation in England, with the following "Epistle Dedicatory:"

To the High and Mighty PRINCE, CHARLES the SECOND, by the Grace of God, King of *Great Britain, France* and *Ireland*, Defender of the Faith, *&c.*

The Commissioners of the United Colonies *in* New-England, *Wish all Happiness.*

Most Dread Soveraign,

S our former Prefentation of the New-Teftament was Gracioufly Accepted by Your Majefty; fo with all Humble Thankfulnefs for that Royal Favour, and with the like hope, We are bold now to Prefent the *W H O L E   B I B L E*, Tranflated into the Language of the Natives of this Country, by *A Painful Labourer in that Work*, and now *Printed* and *Finifhed*, by means of the Pious Beneficence of Your Majefties Subjects in *England:* which alfo by Your Special Favour hath been Continued and Confirmed to the intended Ufe and Advancement of fo Great and Good a Work, as is the *Propagation of the Gofpel to thefe poor Barbarians* in this (Ere-while) Unknown World.

Tranflations of Holy Scripture, *The Word of the King of Kings,* have ever been deemed not unworthy of the moft Princely Dedications: Examples whereof are extant in divers Languages. But Your Majefty is the Firft that hath Received one in this Language, or from this *American World*, or from any Parts fo Remote from *Europe* as thefe are, for ought that ever we heard of.

Publications alfo of thefe Sacred Writings to the Sons of Men (who here, and here onely, have the Myfteries of their Eternal Salvation revealed to them by the God of Heaven) is a Work that

---

* Hazard's State Papers, II., 428. † Ibid, 441. ‡ Ibid, 450. § Ibid, 474. ‖ Ibid, 494.
¶ Ibid, 489, 495. ** See his Petition in full, in N. Y. Hist. Mag., III., 248.

the Greateft Princes have Honoured themfelves by. But to Publifh and Communicate the fame to a Loft People, as remote from Knowledge and Civility, much more from Chriftianity, as they were from all Knowing, Civil and Chriftian Nations; a People without Law, without Letters, without Riches, or Means to procure any fuch thing; a People that *fate as deep in Darknefs, and in the fhadow of Death*, as (we think) any fince the Creation: This puts a Luftre upon it that is Superlative; and to have given Royal Patronage and Countenance to fuch a Publication, or to the Means thereof, will ftand among the Marks of Lafting Honour in the eyes of all that are Confiderate, even unto After-Generations.

And though there be in this Weftern World many Colonies of other Europæan Nations, yet we humbly conceive, no Prince hath had a Return of fuch a Work as'this; which may be fome Token of the Succefs of Your Majefties Plantation of *New-England*, Undertaken and Setled under the Encouragement and Security of Grants from Your Royal Father and Grandfather, of Famous Memory, and Cherifhed with late Gracious Afpects from Your Majefty. Though indeed, the prefent Poverty of thefe Plantations could not have Accomplifhed this Work, had not the forementioned Bounty of *England* lent Relief; Nor could that have Continued to ftand us in ftead, without the Influence of Your Royal Favour and Authority, whereby the *Corporation* there, *For Propagating the Gofpel among thefe Natives*, hath been Eftablifhed and Encouraged (whofe Labour of Love, Care, and Faithfulnefs in that Truft, muft ever be remembred with Honour.) Yea, when private perfons, for their private Ends, have of late fought Advantages to deprive the faid Corporation of Half the Poffeffions that had been, by Liberal Contributions, obtained for fo Religious Ends; We underftand, That by an Honourable and Righteous Decifion in Your Majefties *Court of Chancery*, their Hopes have been defeated, and the Thing Settled where it was and is. For which great Favour, and Illuftrious Fruit of Your Majefties Government, we cannot but return our moft Humble Thanks in this Publick Manner: And, as the Refult of the joynt Endeavours of Your Majefties Subjects there and here, acting under Your Royal Influence, We Prefent *You* with this Work, which upon fundry accounts is to be called *Yours*.

The Southern Colonies of the *Spanifh Nation* have fent home from this *American Continent*, much Gold and Silver, as the Fruit and End of their Difcoveries and Tranfplantations: That (we confefs) is a fcarce Commodity in this Colder Climate. But (futable to the Ends of our Undertaking) we Prefent this, and other Concomitant Fruits of our poor Endeavours to Plant and Propagate the Gofpel here; which, upon a true account, is as much better than Gold, as the Souls of men are more worth then the whole World. This is a Nobler Fruit (and indeed in the Counfels of All-difpofing Providence, was an higher intended End) of *Columbus* his Adventure. And though by his Brother's being hindred from a feafonable Application, your Famous Predeceffour and Anceftor, King *Henry* the Seventh, miffed of being fole Owner of that firft Difcovery, and of the Riches thereof; yet, if the Honour of firft Difcovering the True and Saving Knowledge of the Gofpel unto the poor *Americans*, and of Erecting the Kingdome of *JESUS CHRIST* among them, be Referved for, and do Redound unto your Majefty, and the Englifh Nation, After-ages will not reckon this Inferiour to the other. Religion is the End and Glory of Mankinde: and as it was the Profeffed End of this Plantation; fo we defire ever to keep it in our Eye as our main Defign (both as to our felves, and the Natives about us) and that our Products may be anfwerable thereunto. Give us therefore leave *(Dread Sovereign)* yet again humbly to Beg the Continuance of your Royal Favour, and of the Influences thereof, upon this poor Plantation, *The United Colonies of* N E W-E N G L A N D, for the Securing and Eftablifhment of our Civil Priviledges, and Religious Liberties hitherto Enjoyed; and, upon this Good Work of Propagating Religion to thefe Natives, that the Supports and Encouragements thereof from *England* may be ſtill Countenanced and Confirmed. May this Nurſling ſtill ſuck the Breaſt of Kings, and be foſtered by your Majeſty, as it hath been by your Royal Predeceſſors, unto the Preſervation of its main Concernments; It ſhall thrive and proſper to the Glory of God, and the Honour of your Majeſty: Neither will it be any loſs or grief unto our Lord the King, to have the Bleſſing of the Poor to come upon Him, and that from theſe Ends of the Earth.

The God by whom Kings Reign, and Princes Decree Juſtice, Bleſs Your Majeſty, and Eſtabliſh Your Throne in Righteouſneſs, in Mercy, and in Truth, to the Glory of His Name, the Good of His People, and to Your own Comfort and Rejoycing, not in this onely, but in another World.

According to Lists published in *N. Y. Historical Magazine*, II. 277; III. 87, 124, Copies of the first edition of the Eliot Bible are owned in this country, by

HARVARD UNIVERSITY,
AMERICAN ANTIQUARIAN SOCIETY,
BOSTON ATHENÆUM,
MASSACHUSETTS HISTORICAL SOCIETY,
BROWN UNIVERSITY,
LIBRARY OF THE CONGREGATIONAL CHURCH, Newport, R. I.,
LOGANIAN LIBRARY, Phila.,

AMERICAN PHILOSOPH. SOCIETY, Phila.,
JAMES LENOX, N. Y.,
JOHN ALLAN, N. Y.,
HENRY C. MURPHY, Brooklyn, N. Y.,
JOHN G. GARDNER, Gardner's Island, N.Y.
EDWARD EVERETT, Boston,
GEORGE LIVERMORE, Cambridge,
JOHN CARTER BROWN, Providence, R. I.

1678.

1: *The Harmony of the Gospels,* | IN THE HOLY | HISTORY | of the | *Humiliation* and *Sufferings* | of | Jesus Christ, | from his | INCARNATION | to his | DEATH and BURIAL. | Published by JOHN ELIOT, Teacher | of the Church in Roxbury. | Act 3, 18. *But these things which God before had shewed by the mouth | of all his Prophets, that Christ should suffer, he hath so fulfilled.* | BOSTON; | Printed by *John Foster,* in the Year 1678. (Mass. Hist. Soc. Lib.) sm 4.

Title, 1f.; verso, Imprimatur; Contents 2pp.; Text pp. 131. The printed portion of the page measures 6⅜ in. by 4 in.; the entire page 7¾ by 5¼ inches.

The following is the Imprimatur:

We having perused this Pious Discourse concerning *The* | *Sufferings of Christ,* and observed the Dilligence and | Prudence of the gracious and worthy *Author* in compiling | it; It having in the reading of it both affected and edified us, We are | perswaded through the Blessing of him that hath put it into the heart | of the Reverend Author to lay out himself this way, it will serve to | promote the Honour of Jesus Christ, and the good of Souls, and | therefore do affix our *IMPRIMATVR.*

THOMAS THACHER.   *VRIAN OAKES.*
JAMES ALLEN.   *INCREASE MATHER.*

1680.

1. VVVSKV | WUTTESTAMENTUM | Nul-lordumun | Iesus Christ | Nuppoquohwussuaeneumun. | (Two black lines across the page, seven-eighths of an inch apart.) Cambridge, | *Printed for the Right Honourable* | CORPORATION *in London, for the* | *propogation of the Gospel among the In-* | *dians in New-England* 1680. | sm. 4.

With Bible of 1685, q. v. The literal Translation of the Indian words in the title is: The New | Testament | our Lord | Jesus Christ | delivered. |

1685.

1. MAMVSSE | WUNNEETUPANATAMWE | Up-Biblum God | Naneeswe | Nukkone Testament | kah wonk | Wusku Testament. | (A black line across the page.) Ne quoshkinnumuk nashpe Wuttinneumoh Christ | noh asoowesit | *John Eliot.* | Nahohtôeu ontchetôe Printeuoomuk. | (A black line across the page.) Cambridge. | Printeuoop nashpe *Samuel Green.* MDCLXXXV. | sm. 4.

Title within a border of printer's flowers, 1 f.; verso blank; Text: Gen. to Mal. sigs. A to verso of Ppppp[1] in 4^s; below the end of the Text, *Wuhkukquorinnog Quoshodtumwatnuog* (meaning, The End of the Prophets), under which two black lines, one inch and a half apart, extend across the page; then one leaf, the recto whereof is blank, on the top of the verso, a head-piece consisting of two ornamental lines, one of 36, and the other of 44, printer's flowers; then *Booke Wesuongash*, &c. (Names of the Books and numbers of Chapter in each Book of the O. Test.), the names of the Books being in English; two ornamental lines (as above) across the page, Indian heading: *Wusku Testamente Bookash.* (Books of the New Testament), with names of the Books in English; at bottom of page, James 1 : 16, in Indian; Title to New Testament within a border of printer's flowers: VVusku | Wuttestamentum | Nul-lordumun | Iesus Christ | Nuppoquohwussuaeneumun. | (Two black lines across the page, seven-eighths of an inch apart.) Cambridge, | *Printed for the Right Honourable* | CORPORATION *in London, for the* | *propogation of the Gospel among the In-* | *dians in New-England* 1680. | 1 p.; verso, blank; Text, Mat. to Rev. sigs. A[2] to recto of Kk[2] in 4^s; at foot of the text, "Finis" between 2 black lines which extend across the page; verso of Kk[2], blank; then follow Psalms in Indian metre, without a title page but with a heading in these words: Wame | Ketoohamae uketoohomaongash | David. | surmounted by an ornamental head-piece composed of 38 printer's flowers and a broken line beneath; sigs. Kk[3] to verso of Yy[4] which closes with an *additional* metrical version of the 150th Psalm and the word "Finis.;" then Catechism in Indian, 2pp. the first having an ornamental line of 17 printer's flowers at top; the second, "Finis," at the end.*

The size of the printed page (including running title, catchword and marginal references) is 6⅜ in. by 4⅜ inches full. The volume consists of 607 leaves; viz: Old Test. 424 ff.; List of Books 1 f.; New Testament 129 ff.; Psalms 50 ff.; Catechism 1 f. and titles 2 ff. Genesis, Matthew and the Psalms commence each with an ornamental initial letter; that to Mat. is the same as in the first editions; but Genesis and Psalms have a small Roman capital in what the French call an ornamented *passe partout*. There are Italic headings to the chapters (except a few of Proverbs and some others mentioned below), and to the columns of text; the former being in English and the latter in Indian. The marginal references are in English and also in Italic; the names of the Books and numbers of the Chapters are in Roman on the verso and recto of each leaf.

The omissions in the text, and the other errors noted in the first edition of the New Testament, and of the Bible, are rectified in this edition, to the revision of which the Rev. John Cotton of Plymouth greatly contributed. But the press was, notwithstanding, corrected in a somewhat careless manner, as is demonstrated by the following

List of Errata in the brief summaries to the Chapters, and in the running titles of this Edition.

Genesis c. 5: *geneology*.
14: *battel....rescured....ttihes*.
15: no summary to this Chap.
24: } *sandeth*.
35: }
26: marked, at top of the page, 16.
28: *flone*, for, stone.
32: headed CHAF.
41: v. 47 is marked 48, and v. 48, marked 49.
49: *hurial*, for burial.
50: *suneral*, for, funeral.
Exod. 1: *Israel mnltiply*.
10: *Gf darkness...hart hardned*.
25: *Candlefleck*
27: *ole*
30: verso of L¹ is headed Chap. 30, instead of, Exodus.
39: *breast pleate*.
40: *santified*.
Lev. 2: *first frnits*.

Lev. 9: marked, at top of the page, Cpap. 9.
16: *fin-offering*, for sin-offering. ....*scape gaot*.
20: *wizads*.
23: verso of P4 is headed Chap. 23. instead of, Leviticus.
Numb. 33: v. 41 is numbered 42.
35: marked, at top of the page, 25.
Deut. 2: *flory*, for, story.
8: running title, Deuterenomy.
10: } " " Deuterinomy.
28: }
13: *stonded to death*.
21: *diisnherited*
22: *Cf humanity*.
Josh. 7: *Ifra lites....confefston*
11: headed KHAP.
12: *wutch*, for, which
17: *driveh*
Judg. 5: no headings to this Chap.

* A writer in 1 *Mass. Hist. Coll.*, VIII., 12, 33, states, that "Eliot's Indian Grammar is printed in some editions of the Indian Bibles." Such instances must be considered exceptional.

AMERICAN BIBLES.

Ruth.	3: *instrustion*	Jer.	23: *reflouration*, for, restauration.
1. Sam.	11: *reporchful*		
	13: *destress*		44: marked 45, at top of page.
	28: *reuine*	Ezek.	12: " 13, "
2. Sam.	3: *killeth*		21: " 22, "
	14: *feitch*		25: *vengence*
1. Kgs.	13: *obstinace*	Dan.	11: marked 10, at top of page.
	19: marked, at top of page, 29.	Hos.	11: *ingratiude*
	20: " " " 21.	Joel	1: running title, Joel, instead of Chap. 1.
	22: verso of Yy², headed Chap. 22. instead of, I. Kings.	Zeph.	2: *Philiftians*
2. Kgs.	1: marked at top of the page, II. Kings, instead of Chap. 1.	Zach.	3: *Vnter*, for *vnder*.
		Mat.	7: running title, Matthew. *Wise huilter*, for, *Wise builder*.
	2: *Jardon*		
1. Chron.	6: *priest*		10: headed, BHAP.
	10: *kingness*		14: headed, CHPA XIIII.
2. Chron.	2: *buillding*		21: *Driveth the buyeres*
	24: marked, at top of page, 14.		28: headed, CHPA
Neh.	5: *morgage....reftitution;*	Mark	9: v. 23 numbered 33.
	7: *of them them which*		16: *three woman*.
Esth.	4: } no summaries to these 5: } chapters.	Luke	1: v. 64 numbered 74.
			11: *cafteth out a dumb devil*.
Job	16: } marked at top of the page, 17: } 16, I7.		14: *Teacheth*
			15: *peices of Silvar*.
Ps.	81: *dudy*		16: *porable....Pharifees*.
	85: *codinuance*		22: headed CAHP.
	99: *of forefathers*, for, *of their forefathers,...holy bill*, for, *holy hill*.	John	1: *Humvnity*
			6: *heareers*
			7: *tabernables*.
	126: *selebrating*		9: headed CAHP.
Prov.	7: *an enzample*		16: *trihulation*
	22: marked CAAP.	Acts	2: *appearene of the eloven tongues*.
Eccl.	10: *Obsarvations*		
	12: *antodote*		10: headed CAHP. v. 37, numbered 38; v. 42, numbered 32; v. 44, numbered 34.
Is.	10: *tyrans*		
	14: *triumhant....* Chap. printed, CAAP.		
	23: *Therc*, for, *Their*		11: *The Gospel peached*
	26: *softlen e*		13: *Gentiles beleve. The Jews hlaspheme*.
	49: number of Chap. omitted at top of the page.		14: *creeple*, Chap. numbered 15, at top of the page.
	56: *invigheth*		16: v. 27 numbered 37.
	59: marked, CAAP.		20: *pracheth*
	61: *forusaodness*.		21: *Jerusdlem*,
	65: *stat of the new Jernsalem*		25: numbered 15, at top of the page.
Jer.	21: marked 20 at top of the page.		

Acts	26: v. 19, numbered 18.	Jam.	4: *coveteousness....judgmet*
Rom.	Wut-pistleum, printed WutepistIeum.		5: *odversity,*—Chapter headed BHAP.
	4: *ritghteousness*	2 Pet.	1: *kuowing*
	10: *rtghteeusness....beliver*	1 John	5: headed CAAP.—no summary to Chap.
	11: *Isral.*		
	13: *drnnkenness*, for, drunkenness	2 } John 3 }	no summaries.
	16: *sandeth*	Jude	1: *profossion of the faih.... teabbers...borrible*, for horrible....*assistanc.*
1. Cor.	WutepistIeum.		
	1: *folutation*		
	2: *praching*	Rev.	1: *comming*
	7: *matriage,*		2: headed, CHAP*t.....augels, os....foundwant ig*
	10: *diviles.*		
	15: *prvveth*		4: *Tbe....Elder*, for, Elders..
	16: numbered 26, at top of the page.		6. *Ths*, for The....*heasts*
			5: *woathy....redetmed*
2. Cor.	9: *bouutifull*		6: *propheecy*
Ephes.	1: *adoptiou....onr*		7: *Servents....othor....washtd rhe throne*
	6: no summary to Chapter.		
1. Thes.	2: } running title, Theffalo- 3: } nians.		8: *iueense....sainrs*
			9: *first....angsls.*
	4: *resnrrecttion....judgment.*		10: headed, CAAP.
2. Thes.	3: *idleneness*		12: *travileth...delvired....wildernese....persecuteth*
1. Tim.	3: *rhings*		
	6: *Servents*		17: *hend, fitteth....punushment*
2. Tim.	3: } no summaries to these 4: } Chapters.		19: headed, CHAP*t......bleud ....marrage*
Titus	3: headed, BHAB.	Psalm	44: headed, ISAL.
Heb.	2: *onght....npon*	in	103: headed, ɟSAL.
	4: headed CAAP.	Metre.	104: headed, PSHL.
	9: *sacrsices*		
	13: *charits,*		

N. B. The ¶ at the close of each of the preceding Epistles, is omitted in this Volume.

Jam. 1: *under*
3: *peaceahle,*

NOTE. This edition contains 2 versions of the 100th, 130th, 131st, 133d, 134th, and 150th Psalms. The 1st Psalm only is headed in full "Psalm"—all the rest "Psal." The running titles are very incorrect.

The proposition to print this second edition was submitted by Mr. ELIOT to the Commissioners of the New England Colonies on the 20th March, 1678-9; but after some debate, it was judged most expedient to refer the determination of the matter to the next meeting.* The printing was commenced, we presume, the following year, and, as in the instance of the first edition, with the New Testament; for we find Mr. Eliot informing Mr. Boyle, Nov. 4, 1680, that they were on the 19th chap. of the Acts, and he intended, when they had "impressed the New Testament," to proceed with

* Hazard's State Papers, II, 539, 540.

the "preparing and impressing the Old."* The progress of the work seems, however, to have been slow. Writing in March 168¾ Mr. Eliot says: We have but one man (viz. the Indian printer) that is able to compose the sheets, and correct the press, with understanding. One tenth part or near of the Bible work is done. We are in Leviticus. On the 22d April, 1684, he again writes: We have but few hands, one Englishman and a boy and one Indian.† The work was completed in October of the following year. The edition was 2000.

Prince's copy of this Bible, in the New England Library, has on the second leaf the following Dedication, to which public attention has already been directed by GEO. LIVERMORE, Esq., of Boston, who has had it printed in facsimile.

TO THE HONOURABLE
Robert Boyle Efq:
GOVERNOUR, And to the COMPANY, for the Propagation of The Gofpel to the *Indians* in *New-England*, and Parts adjacent in *America*.

Honourable S^{rs}.

There are more than thirty years paffed fince the Charitable and Pious Collections were made throughout the Kingdom of England, for the Propagation of the Gofpel to the Indians, *Natives of His MAJESTIES Territories in* America; *and near the fame time: Since by His late* MAJESTIES *favour of ever bleffed Memory, the Affair was erected into an Honourable Corporation by Charter under the Broad Seal of* England; *in all which time our felves and thofe that were before us, that have been Your Stewards, and managed Your Truft here, are witneffes of Your earneft and fincere endeavours, that that good Work might profper and flourifh; not only by the good management of the Eftate committed to You, but by Your own Charitable and Honourable Additions thereto; whereof this fecond Edition of the HOLY BIBLE in their own Language, much corrected and amended, we hope will be an everlafting witnefs; for wherefoever this Gofpel fhall be Preached, this alfo that you have done, fhall be fpoken of for a Memorial of you; and as it hath, fo it fhall be our ftudious defire and endeavour, that the fuccefs amongft the Indians here, in reducing them into a civil and holy life, may in fome meafure anfwer the great and neceffary Expences thereabouts: And our humble Prayer to Almighty God, that You may have the glorious Reward of your Service, both in this and in a better World.*

We are Your Honours moft Humble and Faithful Servants,

Bofton Octob. 23. *William Stoughton.*
1685.   *Jofeph Dudley.*
     Peter Bulkley.
     Thomas Hinckley.

Though the purpose for which this Translation was originally undertaken has failed, and the immediate expectations of its patrons have been disappointed, the labors of the pious Missionary have answered an important end which he, perhaps, never anticipated. In connection with his Grammar, this rare volume affords invaluable aid in the study of Indian philology; and furnishes the means of acquiring an insight into the structure and character of the Algonquin language, which otherwise would have been forever lost to the learned.‡ It is, says Duponceau, "a rich and

---
* 1 Mass. Hist. Coll., III, 180. † 1 Mass. Hist. Coll., III, 181, 186. ‡ Francis's Life of Eliot, 238.

valuable mine; a complete grammar and dictionary might, with labor and perseverance, be extracted from it; for there is hardly a mode or figure of speech, which is not to be found somewhere in the sacred writings. Every copy of it, that is yet extant, ought to be preserved with the greatest care, as it is hardly to be hoped that it will ever be entirely reprinted." *

According to Lists in *N. Y. Historical Magazine*, II, 277; III, 157, Copies of this edition are owned in this country, by

NEW YORK STATE LIBRARY,	PHILADELPHIA LIBRARY,
HISTORICAL SOCIETY, New York,	AMERICAN PHILOSOPHICAL SOCIETY, Philadelphia,
HARVARD UNIVERSITY,	
AMERICAN ANTIQUARIAN SOCIETY,	YALE COLLEGE,
NEW ENGLAND LIBRARY, Boston,	JAMES LENOX, New York,
BOSTON ATHENÆUM,	GEORGE W. PRATT, New York,
MASSACHUSETTS HISTORICAL SOCIETY,	EDWARD EVERETT, Boston,
ANDOVER THEOLOGICAL SEMINARY,	GEORGE LIVERMORE, Cambridge,
TOWN OF NATICK,	JOHN CARTER BROWN, Providence,
BOWDOIN COLLEGE, Maine,	GEORGE BRINLEY, Hartford.

Copies, the dates of which are not ascertained, are owned by
CONGREGATIONAL LIBRARY ASSOCIATION, Boston,
REV. DR. ALLEN, Northampton, Mass.

1707.

1. ST. JOHN. Chapter I, v. 1–28. (In Indian and English on opposite pages.) Boston: N. E. Re-printed by *B. Green*, 1707. (L.) 12.

This portion of Scripture forms 4 pp. (2 in Indian and 2 in English) at the end of a Tract (also printed in Indian and English) entitled, A Discourse Concerning the Institution and Observation of the Lord's Day, delivered in Boston, 4 d. 1 m. 1703. By Rev. Cotton Mather. The Indian translation is by Rev. Experience Mayhew.

1709.

1. THE | GOSPEL | According to JOHN, | In Columns of *Indian* and *English*. | Search the Scriptures, &c. | Boston, N. E. | Printed by *B. Green*, and *J. Printer*, for the | Honourable COMPANY for the Propa- | gation of the Gospel in *New-England*, &c. | 1709. | (B.; G. L.; L.) 12.

This Gospel forms 101 pp. of The Massachuset Psalter, by the Rev. Experience Mayhew of Martha's Vineyard, who was employed by the Commissioners of the society for the propagation of the gospel among the N. E. Indians, to make a new version of the Psalms and the Gospel of John: he executed the work in collateral columns, English and Indian, with great accuracy. 2 *Mass. Hist. Coll*, III, 68.

* 2 Mass. Hist. Coll., IX, ix.

1710, 1713.

1. BIBLIA AMERICANA. The SACRED SCRIPTURES of the OLD and NEW Testament; Exhibited, in the *Order of Time*, wherein the several and successive Occurrences, may direct the Placing and Reading of them: Which Exhibition alone, will do the service of a *Valuable Commentary*. With,

I. A proper Notice taken of those Instances, wherein the most Polite and Pious Masters in Philology, have expressed their wishes to see the *Common Translation* Amended and Refined. II. A Rich Collection of ANTIQUITIES, which the studious Researches of Inquisitive and Judicious Men in the later Ages, have recovered ; for a sweet Reflection of *Light* from thence upon the Heavenly *Oracles;* Especially those wherein the *Idolatry*, the *Oeconomicks*, the *Politicks*, the *Agriculture*, the *Architecture*, the *Art of War*, the *Music*, the *Habits*, and the *Diets* in the former Ages, may be referr'd unto. III. The Laws of the *Israelitish Nation* in these *Pandects of Heaven*, interpreted ; and the *Original* and *Intention* thereof, rescued from the Mis-interpretations, that some famous writers have put upon them. With a particular History of the City JERUSALEM, under its wondrous Vicissitudes, from the days of *Melchizedeck*, down to Ours ; and a Relation of the present & wretched Condition, in which it waits, the *Time to favour the set Time to come on*. IV. The TYPES of the Bible, accommodated with their *Antitypes:* And this Glorious Book of God, now appearing a Field, that yields a marvellous Mixture of Holy *Profit* and *Pleasure*, in those Paragraphs of it, which have sometimes appeared the least Fruitful with Instruction. V. *Golden Treasures*, and *more to be desired than such*, fetch'd out of those very *unpromising Heaps*, the TALMUDS, and other *Jewish Writings;* not only to illustrate the *Oracles* once *committed* unto the *distinguished Nation;* but also to demonstrate the Truths of *Christianity*. VI. NATURAL PHILOSOPHY call'd in to serve *Scriptural Religion*. The fairest *Hypotheses* of those *Grand Revolutions*, the *Making*, the *Drowning*, and the *Burning* of the WORLD, offered. The *Astronomical* Affairs, the *Meteors*, the *Minerals*, the *Vegetables*, the *Animals*, the *Diseases*, the *Anatomical* Curiosities, and what relates to the *Invisible World* of Good or Evil Spirits, mention'd in these immortal Pages, represented with the *Best Thoughts of our Times* upon them. To all which there is added, *The Christian Virtuoso*, with a Commentary of the more Modern and Certain Philosophy on, *His Work which men behold;* Embellished with the Discoveries which *our Days at Length* have made of Things wherein the Glorious GOD of Nature calls for our *Wonders* & our *Praises*. VII. The CHRONOLOGY of this admirable Book, every where cleared, from all its Difficulties ; and the *Clock of Time* set right, in its whole motion, from the Beginning which *He that Inhabits Eternity* gave unto it. Besides the most Accurate *Harmony of the Gospel*, that has yet been offered among them that *know the Joyful Sound*. VIII. The GEOGRAPHY of it *Survey'd;* The Scituation especially of *Paradise*, & of *Palestine* laid out : With an Account how the *whole Earth* has been Peopled : And many Notable and Enlightning Things contributed unto this Work, by *Travellers* of unspotted Veracity, by whose *Running to and fro Knowledge has been increased*. IX. A Sort of *Twenty ninth Chapter of the* ACTS ; Or, An elaborate and entertaining History, of what has befallen the *Israelitish Nation*, in every Place, from the Birth of our great REDEEMER to *this very Day:* And the present Condition of that Nation, the Reliques of the *Ten*, as well as of the *Two Tribes* (and of their Ancient *Sects*,) yet existing in the several parts of the World, where they are now dispersed, at *this Time*, when their approaching Recovery from their sad and long Dispersion is hoped for. X. The HISTORIES of all Ages, brought in, to show how the *Prophecies* of this Invaluable Book, have had their most punctual Accomplishment, and strongly established *Conjectures*, (yet made with all due Modesty,) on such as yet *remain to be accomplished:* In the prosecution whereof, the Reader finds an entire *Body of Church-History*, brought into his Possession. XI. The true Doctrine of the CHILIAD, which more opens & breaks in upon the more considerate Enquirers, *as the Day approaches*, brought in as a *Key* to very much of the Wealth, which the Church of GOD enjoys in this *Book of the Kingdom*. Whereto are added, the most *unexceptionable Thoughts* of the ablest Writers on the *Apocalypse;* defecated from the more Arbitrary and less Defensible Conceits, of *overdoing Students* in the Prophecies. XII. Some *Essays* to Illustrate the *Scriptures* from EXPERIMENTAL PIETY, or the Observations of *Christian Experience*. With many of the *Excellent Things*, observed in and extracted from the *Holy Scriptures that make Wise unto Salvation*, especially by the *North-British Expositors*, who with a penetrating and peculiar Search after Hints for *Christian Practice*, have been found worthy to *Open* many *Books* of the Bible. And many Thousands of curious Notes, found scattered and shining, in the Writings both of the *Ancients* and the *Moderns*, laid here together, in a grateful Amassment of them.

All done with a most Religious & Inviolate and Perpetual Regard unto the *Principles of Religion*, which are the Life of the *Reformed Churches*.

By the Blessing of CHRIST on the Labours of an *American*. In Two VOLUMES.

In 1710, the Rev. Cotton Mather, author of the above Work, issued Proposals for its publication. These proposals are to be found, Mr. LIVERMORE informs me, at the end of one of Mr. Mather's Tracts, entitled, Bonifacius, or, Essays to do Good. Boston, 1710. Not meeting, then, with the desired encouragement, the author turned his attention again to the subject in 1713, as appears by his Diary, from which S. F. HAVEN, Esq. of New Haven, politely furnishes the following extract:

"*December*. It seems now high time for me to come into action & do what my hand finds to do that y^e *Biblia Americana* may be brought forth into the World. Let me therefore publish a sheet entitled *A New Offer to ye Lovers of Religion & Learning*, therein giving an account of the work, & so an opportunity for subscriptions towards ye encouragement of it; and not only spread Copies of that Offer through this country but also send them to Europe."

Proposals were issued a third time, after Mr. Mather's death, in 1728, but no printer could be found to hazard the undertaking; and the manuscript, as it came from the author's pen, is now in the Library of the Massachusetts Historical Society, in Six Volumes Folio.

The title page above printed is borrowed from, *A New Offer to the Lovers of Religion and Learning*, a copy of which is in the Library of the American Antiquarian Society, Worcester, Mass.

1715.

1. GENESIS. Chapters I, II, III, in Mohawk. Printed by
William Bradford in *New York*, 1715. (L.)   sm.4.

This portion of the Scriptures is contained in a volume entitled: The Morning and Evening Prayer, &c. Translated into the *Mahaque Indian* Language by *Lawrence Claesse*, Interpreter to *William Andrews*, Missionary to the Indians, &c.

1. THE GOSPEL of St. MATTHEW, Chapter I, v. 18-23; Chapters II and V, with various detached sentences from the New Testament.

In the Mohawk language, in the above mentioned Book of Common Prayer.

1718.

1. EXODUS. Chapter XV, v. 1-18; Chapter XX, v. 2-17; Chapter XXIV, v. 6, 7; DEUTERONOMY, Chapter XXXII, v. 3-43; 1 SAMUEL, Chapter II, v. 1-10; ECCLESIASTES, Chapters XI, v. 9, 10, and XII, v. 1-14; CANTICLES, Chapters I, II, VIII (several verses); ISAIAH, Chapter XII, v. 1-6; Chapter XXVI, v. 1-21; Chapter LVI, v. 1-7; LVIII, v. 13, 14, in blank lyric verse. (In *Psalterium Americanum*.) Boston: N. E. Printed by S. Kneeland, for B. Eliot, S. Gerrish, D. Henchman, and J. Edwards, and Sold at their Shops. 1718. (N. Y. State Library; L.; B.; G. L.)   16.

1. ST. MATTHEW. Chapter VI, 9-13; Chapter V, 3-13; Chapter XI, 4, 5; LUKE, II, 10, 11, 14, 24-32; Chapter XII, 33, 34; ROMANS, Chapter V, 6-11; Chapter VIII, 30-32; 1 CORINTHIANS, XI, 23-26; EPHESIANS, Chapter I, 3, 4; Chapter II, 4-6; Chapter V, 21, 23-25, 28, 33; HEBREWS, Chapter XII, 5-7, 10, 11, and sundry other texts of the New Testament, in blank lyric verse. (In *Psalterium Americanum*, as above.) Boston: S. Kneeland.   16.

1742.

1. THE SONG OF SONGS, which is SOLOMON'S: First Turn'd, then Paraphras'd in *English* Verse. 15th Edition. Boston: Printed by *Tho. Fleet*, for D. Henchman in Cornhill. 1742. (B.) 24.

In a volume entitled SPIRITUAL SONGS, and attributed to Rev. John Mason, A. M. *Cotton's Editions of the Bible*, 8vo, 1852, p. 76.

1743.

1. BIBLIA, | Das ist: | Die | Heilige Schrift | Altes und Neues | Testaments, | Nach der Deutschen Uebersetzung | D. Martin Luthers, | Mit jedes Capitels kurtzen Summarien, auch | beygefügten vielen und richtigen Parllelen; | Nebst einem Anhang | Des britten und vierten Buchs Esrä und des | britten Buchs der Maccabäer. | (An ornamental line across the page.) Germantown: | Gedruckt bey Christoph Saur, 1743. | (L.; G. L.) 4.

Title, 1 p.; verso, blank; Vorrede, 1 p. having an ornamental head piece at the top consisting of four lines, the first composed of 36 printer's flowers, then two rows of stars, and the fourth line the same as the first, but the flowers inverted ; Verzeichnisz aller Bücher | Des Alten und Neuen Testaments. | 1 p. This list is accompanied by an Index indicating the number of the page at which each Book commences. Text: Gen. to Mal., pp. 1–805 ; Apocrypha (in similar type), pp. 806 to the Prayer of Manasses, which ends on the upper part of p. 949 ; the 3d and 4th Books of Ezra, and 4th Book of Maccabees (in smaller type), pp. 949–995, filling one-third of that p. "Ende des dritten Buchs der Maccabaer, und des Anhangs des alten Testaments." Beneath, a Seraph's head and wings; the remainder of p. 995 and its verso are blank. Sigs. A to Kkkkkk² in 4ˢ. Das Neue | Testament | Unsers | HErrn und Heylandes | JEsu Christi. | Verteutscht | Von | Dr. Martin Luther. | Mit | Jedes Capitels kurtzen | Sumarien, | Auch beygefügten vielen richtigen | Parallelen. | (An ornamental line across the page.) Germantown: | Gedruckt und zu finden bey Christoph Saur, 1743. | 1 p. verso, Verzeuchnisz der Bücher des Neuen Testaments; Text: Mat. to Rev. pp. 3–277; at the end of Rev.: Der Offenbarung S. Johannis, und des Neuen Testaments Ende, beneath which, another Seraph's head and wings. Register der Episteln und Evangelium, 3 pp., not numbered; "Ende," on last p.; Kurtzer Begriff. | Von den Heiligen Schrifften und deren | Uebersetzungen. Mit etlichen Anmer- | ckungen. | 4 pp. in double columns. Sigs. A² to Mm, all in 4ˢ except the last, which is in 6ˢ.

This is the first Bible printed in this country in a European language. The 1st, 4th, 6th, 8th, 11th and 14th lines of the first or general title, are printed in red, the others in black ; the title to the New Testament is in black ink ; an ornamental head piece, 1⅞ inches wide, extends across the page at the beginning of Genesis, and there is another ornamental head piece at the commencement of Matthew ; the other pp. have each two black lines at the top, between which are printed the name of the Book, the number of the Chapters on the page and brief summary of the contents. The text is reprinted from the 34th Halle edition of Luther's Bible, more than 100 errors in which were corrected. It is in double columns, and the parallel references are at the end of their respective verses. The signature letters to the Old Testament are in German, to the New Testament in Roman, characters. The covers of the Volume are wood boards, each three-eighths of an inch thick, covered with calf; each board being further protected by five brass rivets and two clasps. The edition consisted of about 1000 copies, and the price of the Book was two dollars and a half.

The types with which this Volume was printed, were imported from Germany. Twelve copies of the Volume were in return sent to Europe. Mr. Lenox saw, in 1856, what may have been one of those copies, in the City Library of Frankfort on the Main. It was as fresh and in as good order as if it had just left the hands of the binder, and was supposed to have been a present from Saur to Hainrich Ehrenfried Luther, from whom he had received or purchased the type. Mr. Luther presented it to the above library, as appears from an inscription pasted on the inside of the cover, and which is in these words:

Sanctum Hunc Codicem
in
India Occidentali
nullo plane Exemplo
et
Nec Anglico, nec Batavo, nec alio quovis idiomate
antehac
Nuper vero Germanico
Primum
Et quidem Typis Officinæ suæ
favente numine
Excusum
Splendidæ Hujus Civitatis
Bibliothecæ
Dono Dat
H. E. Luther J. N. D et C. W. A.
Francofurti quod ad Manum est
Kalendis Junii. MDCCXLIV.

2. THE SONG OF SONGS, which is SOLOMON'S: First Turn'd, then Paraphras'd in *English* Verse. 16th Edition. Boston: Printed by Green, Bushell and Allen, for D. Henchman in Cornhil. 1743.   (G. L.; B.)   24.

In a volume entitled *Spiritual Songs*. See 1742.

1745.

1. **Das Neue | Testament** | ünsers | Herrn und Heylandes | Jesu Christi, | Verteuscht | Von | D. Martin Luther | Mit | Jedes Capitels Kürtzen | Sümarien. | Auch beygefügten vielen richtigen | Parallelen. | Germantown | Gedrückt und zu finden by Christoph Saur, 1745. | 8.

Title (printed in red and black lines), 1 p.; verso, blank; Vorrede, signed C. S. 1 p.; Verzeüchniss der Bücher &c. 1 p.; Text: Mat. to Rev. pp, 1–592; Register der Episteln und Evangelien, &c., 3 pp.; Episteln und Evangelien der Apostel-Tage, &c., 1 p.; sigs. A to verso of Pp² in 8ˢ. Text in double columns; references in Roman.

This is the *first* edition of the New Testament, printed in German, in this country, by the son of the Christopher Saür, who published the 4to Bible, Germantown, 1743, and retired from business in 1744.

1752.

1. THE SONGS of MOSES, Exodus, Chap. XV, Deuteronomy, Chap. XXXII; The SONG of DEBORAH, Judges, Chap. V; PROVERBS, Chap. VIII (abridged); and parts of ISAIAH, Chap. II, IX, XLV, LIII, LV, paraphrased in verse. By John Barnard, Pastor of a Church in *Marblehead*. Boston: N. E. Printed by J. Draper, for T. Leverett, in *Cornhill*. 1752.   (N. Y. State Library.)   12.

In Barnard's New Version of the Psalms of David.

2. THE SONG of MARY; The SONG of ZACHARIAS; The ANGEL'S MESSAGE and SONG; The SONG of SIMEON, Luke, Chap. I, II; and The SONG of JOHN the Divine, Rev. I, v. 5, 6, paraphrased in verse.   8.

Also in the last mentioned work.

1755.

1. **Das Neue | Testament** | &c., as in No. 1, 1745. Germanton | Gedruckt und zu finden bey Christoph Saur, 1755. | 8.

Title (in red and black lines), 1 f.; verso, blank; Vorrede, signed C. S. 1 p.; Verzeuchniss, 1 p.; Text: Mat. to Rev. pp. 1–562; Registers, 4 pp. sigs. A to verso of Nn³ in 8ˢ. Text in double columns; references in Roman.

This is represented as the *second* edition of Saur's Testament.

1760.

1. **Das Neue Testament,** &c., as in No. 1, 1745. Germanton |
Gebruckt und zu finden bey Christoph Saur, 1760. | 12.

1763.

1. BIBLIA, | Das ist: | Die | **Heilige Schrift** | Altes und Neues |
Testaments, | &c., as in No. 1, of 1743. Germantown: |
Gebruckt bey Christoph Saur, 1763. | (L.)   4.

Title, 1 f.; verso, blank; Vorrede, 1 p. (This is different from that of 1743, and is signed "Chr. Saur," and dated Germantown, den 8ten December 1763.) Verzeichnisz aller Bücher, &c., 1 p.; Text: Gen. to Mal. pp. 1–805; Apocrypha to Manasses' prayer (in smaller type), pp. 806–949; 3d and 4th books of Ezra and 3d book of Maccabees pp. 849–992; sigs. A to Iiiiii⁴ in 4ˢ; Title to the New Test. same as that to the ed. of 1743, 1 p.; Verzeichnisz, &c., 1 p.; Text: Mat. to Rev. pp. 3–277; Register 3 unnumbered pp.; sigs. A to Mm⁴, in 4ˢ.

The type of the general title is set closer than that of the 1st edition; some of the letters in the title of the New Test. differ in size from those used on the corresponding title of the ed. of 1743; the type of pp. 987–992, containing a part of the last chapter of 4th Ezra and the whole of 3d Mac., is smaller than the other part of the Apocrypha. The sigs. to the Old Test. are in Black letter; those to the New Test. in Roman. This volume is entirely reprinted. The titles are printed entirely in black.

1. **Das Neue | Testament |** Unsers | Herrn und Heylandes | JEsu
Christi, | Verteutscht | Von | D. Martin Luther. | Mit | Jedes
Capitels kurzen | Summarien. | Auch beygefügten vielen richtigen |
Parallelen. | Germantown, | Gebruckt und zu finden bey Christoph
Saur, 1763. | (L.)   12.

Title, 1 f.; verso, blank; Vorrede, 1 p. signed, C. S.; Verzeichnisz, 1 p.; Text: Mat. to Rev. pp. 1–679; Register der Episteln, &c., 4 pp., not numbered; sigs. A to Jf⁶ in 12ˢ.

This is the *fourth* edition of Saur's Testament. Printed in double columns.

1764.

1. THE PROVERBS of SOLOMON. (In The New-England Psalter.)
Boston: | Printed by D. and J. Kneeland, opposite | the
Probate-Office, in *Queen-Street*, for | Wharton and Bowes.
1764. | (Conn. Hist. Soc.)   sm. 8.

4

26   AMERICAN BIBLES.   [1765—

1. ST. MATTHEW. Chapters V, VI, VII, or, Christ's Sermon on the Mount. (In The New-England Psalter.) Boston: Printed by D. and J. Kneeland, opposite the Probate-Office, in *Queen-Street*, for Wharton and Bowes. 1764. (Conn. Hist. Soc.)   sm. 8.

1765.

1. VERBUM | SEMPITERNUM. | The Third Edition | With Amendments. | Boston: Printed | for, and sold by | N. Proctor, | near Scarlet's Wharffe. | n. d. (G. L.) 142.

The 1st title is without any date; but on that of the New Testament, "Salvator Mundi." 1765. This is an exact reprint of the Third London edition of The Thumb Bible of 1693.

1766.

1. ST. MATTHEW. Chapter VI, 9–13. (In, An Essay on the Lord's Prayer. By Samuel Mather, A. M., Pastor of a Church in *Boston, New-England*.) Boston: Printed by Kneeland and Adams, in Milk-Street, for Wharton and Bowes, in Corn-hill. MDCCLXVI. (Mass. Hist. Soc.) 8.

The following is the Author's version of the Prayer: "Our Father, *who art in the Heavens; sanctified* be thy Name; Thy Kingdom come; Thy Will be done, *as in Heaven, so upon the Earth;* Give us to *Day* that our Bread, *the supersubstantial;* And forgive us *our Debts,* as we forgive *them who are our Debtors:* And *introduce us not into afflictive Trial;* but deliver us *from the wicked One: Because* thine is the Kingdom and the Power and the Glory *for the Ages:* Amen!" The *Italics* are the Author's.

1768.

1. THE PROVERBS OF SOLOMON. (In The New-England Psalter.) Boston: | Printed by Edes and Gill, in Queen-Street, | M,DCC,LXVIII. | (B.)   sm. 8.

1. ST. MATTHEW. Chapters V, VI and VII. (In The New-England Psalter.) Boston: Edes and Gill. 1768. (B.) sm. 8.

1769.

1. GENESIS. Chapters I, II, III. In a volume entitled: The Order for Morning and Evening Prayer, &c., collected and translated into the Mohawk Language under the direction

of the late Rev. Mr. *William Andrews*, the late Rev. Dr. *Henry Barclay*, and the Rev. Mr. *John Oglivie:* formerly Missionaries....to the *Mohawk Indians.* Printed in the year M,DCC,LXIX. (N. Y. Hist. Soc.)   8.

1. 𝔇𝔞𝔰 𝔑𝔢𝔲𝔢 | 𝔗𝔢𝔣𝔱𝔞𝔪𝔢𝔫𝔱 | &c., as in No. 1, 1763. Sechste Auflage. | Germantown | Gedruckt und zu finden bey Christoph Saur, 1769. | 12.

Title, 1 f. ; verso, blank ; Vorrede, signed C. S. 1 p.; Verzeichniss, 1 p.; Text: Mat. to Rev. pp. 5–529 ; Registers, 3 pp.; sigs. A3 to verso of 3²; references in German characters.

This is the *sixth* edition of Saur's Testament.

2. THE GOSPEL of ST. MATTHEW. Chapter I, v. 18–23; Chapters II and V, with various detached sentences from the New Testament. Printed in the year M,DCC,LXIX.   8.

In Mohawk Book of Common Prayer, supra, No. 1, 1769.

1770.

1. GENESIS. Chapter I, v. 1–26; Printed by John Fleeming at his Printing Office in *Newbury-Street*, nearly opposite the White-Horse Tavern, Boston. n. d.   (G. L.)   fol.

This portion of the Scriptures accompanied Proposals issued by the above printer for republishing the Rev. Samuel Clarke's edition of the Bible. It was announced as "the *first* Undertaking of the kind EVER *attempted* in America." The project fell through for want of encouragement.

2. THE PROVERBS of SOLOMON. (In The New-England Psalter.) Boston: | Printed by D. Kneeland, in *Queen-Street*, | for Thomas Leverett in *Cornhill.* 1770. | (L.)   12.

1. ST. MATTHEW. Chapters V, VI and VII. (In The New-England Psalter.) Boston: D. Kneeland, for Thomas Leverett. 1770.   (L.)   12.

1771.

1. THE PROVERBS of SOLOMON. (In The New-England Psalter.) Boston: | Printed and Sold by William | McAlpine in *Marlborough-* | *Street.* MDCCLXXI. | (B.)   12.

28　　　　　AMERICAN BIBLES.　　　[1775—

1. St. Matthew. Chapters V, VI and VII. (In the New-England Psalter.) Boston: William McAlpine. 1771. (B.) 12.

1775.

1. Biblia, | Das ist: | Die ganze | **Heilige Schrift** | Alten und Neuen Testaments, | Nach der teuschen Uebersetzung | D. Martin Luthers, | Mit vorgesetztem kurtzen | Inhalt eines jeden Capitels, | wie auch mit richtigen | Summarien und vielen Schriftstellen | auf das allersorgfaltigste versehen, | Nach denen bewahrtesten und neusten Ausgaben | mit grossem Fleisse ausgefertiget. | Sammt einer Vorrede | von | Herrn D. Johann Gottlieb Faber, | Herzogl. Wurtemb. Oberhofprediger, Consistorials | Rath, General-Superintendenten und Abbten | des Klosters Atelberg. | Philadelphia, | zu finden bey Ernst Ludwig Baisch, | in der zweyten Strasse nahe bey der Rees-Strasse. 1775. |　　　(B.)　　　8.

Title, 1 f.; verso, blank; Vorrede, dated Stuttgart, 20 Nov. 1773, and signed by D. Johann Gottlieb Faber, 14 ff.; Die Bucher des alten Testaments, 1 p.; Bucher Apocrypha und des Neuen Test., 1 p.; making, with title, 16 ff.; sigs.)(to)(^{8} in 8^s; Text: Gen. to Mal. pp. 1-768; Apocrypha, pp. 769-909, verso of 909 blank; sigs. A to recto of Ll7; Die | Heilige Schrift, | Neuen | Testaments, | Unsers | HErrn JEsu Christi, | Nach der teutschen Uebersetzung | D. Martin Luthers, | Mit kurtzem | Inhalt eines jeden Capitels, | Und | beygefügten vielen richtigen und mit Fleiss nach gesehenen | Schrift-Stellen, | Samt aller Sonn-und Fest-Tage | Evangelien und Episteln, | Auf das allersorgfältigste eingerichtet und | aufgefertiget. | Reuttlingen, | Bey Johan Georg Fleischhauer, 1773. | 1 p. verso, Verzeichniss der Bücher ; .Text: Mat. to Rev. pp. 3-265; Anweizung, 3 pp.; Episteln, 1 p. "Ende." Sigs. [A2 to recto of [R7] followed by one blank leaf; sigs. all in 8^s.

This Bible was imported probably in sheets from Germany, where the first title page is considered also to have been printed on a slip, for a portion of the edition sent to this country. It will be observed that the Imprint announces cautiously, that the book is "to be found," &c.

1. **Das Neue** | **Testament** | Unsers | HERRN JESU Christi, | Nach der Deutschen Uebersetzung | D. Martin Luthers, | mit kurzem | Inhalt eines jeden Capitels, | und vollstandiger | Anweisung gleicher Schrift-Stellen. | Wie auch | aller Sonn- und Fest-tagigen | Evangelien und Episteln. | Sechste Auflage. | Germantown, | gedruckt und zu finden bey Christoph Saur, 1775. |　　　(G. L.)　　　8.

Title, 1 p.; verso, blank; Vorrede, signed C. S., 1 p.; Verzeichniss, 1 p.; Text: Mat. to Rev., pp. 5-529; Registers, 3 pp,; sigs. A3 to verso of Ll2 in 8^s.

This is represented, incorrectly, as the *sixth* edition of Saur's Testament. It is actually the *seventh*. See next Title.

2. **Das Neue | Testament** | Unsers | Herrn und Heylandes | Jesu Christi | Nach der deutschen Uebersetzung | D. Martin Luthers, | mit kurtzem | Inhalt eines jeden Capitels, | und vollstandiger | Anweisung gleicher Schrift-Stellen. | Wie auch | aller Sonn-und Fest-tagigen | Evangelien und Episteln, | Siebente Auflage. | Germantown, | Gedruckt und zu finden bey Christoph Saur, 1775. | 8.

Title, 1 f.; verso, blank; Vorrede, signed C. S. 1 p.; Verzeuchniss, 1 p.; Text: Mat. to Rev. pp. 5-529; Registers, 3 pp.; sigs A to Ll² in 8ˢ; text in double columns; references in German characters.

This is the *seventh* edition of Saur's New Test. In some copies the preface reads as of the 6th edition, but this was corrected on being discovered. It will be observed that the title page differs from those of the previous editions.

1776.

1. BIBLIA, | Das ist: | Die Ganze Göttliche | **Heilige Schrift** | Alten und Neuen | Testaments | nach der Deutschen Uebersetzung | D. Martin Luthers; | Mit jedes Capitels kurzen Summarien, auch | beygefügten vielen und richtigen Parallelen: | Nebst einem Anhang | Des dritten und vierten Buchs Ezrä, und des | dritten Buchs Maccabäer | (A single line drawn across.) Dritte Auflage | (Double lines across.) Germantown: | Gedruckt und zu finden bey Christoph Saur, 1776. | (L.; G. L.)   4.

Title, 1 f.; verso blank; Vorrede, signed Chr. Saur, but no date, 1 p. It is almost word for word the same as that in 2d ed.—the 2d ed. being referred to in that, and the 3d in this; Verzeichnisz aller Bücher 1 p.; Text: pp. 1-805; Apocrypha, p. 806 to Prayer of Manasseh ⅔ of page 949; Anhang, being 3d and 4th books Ezra and 3d book Maccabees, in smaller type, rest of 949-992; type again reduced on pages 986-992; sigs. A to Ziiiii⁴ in 4ˢ; Das Neue | Testament | unsers | Herrn und Heylandes | JEsu Christi | nach der Deutschen Uebersetzung | Dr. Martin Luthers. | Mit kurzem | Inhalt eines jeden Capitels | und vollständiger | Anweisung gleicher Schrift-Stellen. | Wie auch | aller Sonn-und Fest-tägigen | Evangelien und Episteln. | (A single line across.) Dritte Auflage. | (Double lines across.) Germantown. | Gedruckt und zu finden bey Christoph Saur, 1776. | 1 p. verso, Die Bücher | des | Neuen Testaments. | 1 p.; Text: Mat. to Rev. pp. 3-277; Register, 3 pp., not numbered; sigs. A² to Mm⁴ in 4ˢ.

This edition consisted of 3,000 copies. The revolutionary war broke out about the time it was issued, and after the battle of Germantown, Saur, to preserve the residue of his property, and in the supposition that American Independence could not be maintained, went into Philadelphia and resided there whilst the British held possession of that city. His estate was subsequently confiscated in consequence, and his books sold. The principal part of this third edition of the Germantown Bible in sheets was thus destroyed, having been used for cartridge paper. *Thomas' Hist. Printing*, II, 83, 84.

1777.

1. THE NEW | TESTAMENT | Of our Lord and Saviour | Jesus Christ: | Newly Translated out of the | Original Greek; | And with the former | Translations | Diligently compared and revised. | Appointed to be read in Churches. | Philadelphia: | Printed and Sold by | R. Aitken, | Printer and Bookseller, | *Front Street.* | 1777. | Spectamur+agendo. |
(L.) 12.

The Imprint is an ornamental wood cut of an irregular form, having for a crest: A Bird with an olive branch in its bill. The letters are in white on a black ground. Supporters: Two children. Motto on a dark scroll: Spectamur + agendo. The whole title is surrounded by 2 lines. On verso of title, The Order of the Books of the *New Testament*, with their Names, and the Numbers of their Chapters; Text: Mat. to Rev. pp. 3-353; sigs. A² to Gg³ in 6ˢ. On verso of p. 353, Books Printed and Sold at R. Aitken's Printing-Office, opposite the London Coffee-House, Front-street. No headings.

The following Errors occur in this Edition: "For whosoever shall be ashamed of me, and of my works," *Luke*, 9:26; "For there is no man that dost any thing in secret," *John*, 7:4; "I have heard their groning," *Acts*, 7:34; "Take heed unto thyself, and unto thy doctrine;" 1 *Tim.*, 4:16. The Chap. is numbered XI, instead of X, on p. 99, and the number is omitted at the head of p. 273.

2. Evangelia und Episteln | Auf alle Sonntage, | Wie auch, auf die hohe Feste, andere Feyer=und | Apostel=Tage durchs ganze Jahr. | (In the Vollstandiges Marburger Gesangbuch.) Germantown: | Gedruckt und zu finden bey Christoph Saur, 1777. | (B.) 8.

1778.

1. NEW TESTAMENT. Philadelphia: Printed and Sold by R. Aitken, Printer and Bookseller. 1778. 12.
Not seen; advertised in *Penn. Packet*, 10 Nov., 1778.

1779.

1. NEW TESTAMENT. Philadelphia: R. Aitken. 1779. 12.
A School edition.

1780.

1. NEW TESTAMENT. Philadelphia: Francis Bailey, Market Street. 1780.
Not seen; *Penn. Gazette*, 2595, March 8, 1780.

2. NEW TESTAMENT. Philadelphia: Hall & Sellers. 1780.
Not seen; *Penn. Gazette*, 2608, June 7, 1780.

1781.

1. THE NEW | TESTAMENT | Of our Lord and Saviour | Jesus Christ: | Newly Translated out of the | Original Greek; | And with the former | Translations | Diligently compared and revised. | (Vignette engraved on wood.) Philadelphia: | Printed and Sold by R. Aitken, Bookseller, | opposite the Coffee-House, Front-Street. | M.DCC.LXXXI. | 12.
With Bible of 1782; for collation, see that Vol.

1782.

1. THE | HOLY BIBLE, | Containing the Old and New | Testaments: | Newly translated out of the | Original Tongues; | And with the former | Translations | Diligently compared and revised. | (Arms of the State of Pennsylvania: Escutcheon—a Ship, a Plough and 3 Sheaves of Wheat; Crest—an Eagle; Supporters—Horses rampant, and behind each, a stalk of Indian Corn; Motto—*Virtue, Liberty and Independence:* | Philadelphia: | Printed and Sold by R. Aitken, at Pope's | Head, Three Doors above the Coffee | House, in Market street. | M.DCC.LXXXII. | (L.) 12.

Title (within double lines), 1 f.; verso, blank; Proceedings in Congress, 1¼ pp.; Names and Order of all the Books of the O. & N. Test. ¾ p.; Text: Gen. to Mal. (not paged), sigs. A² to verso of Aaa⁵ in 12ˢ; The New | Testament | Of our Lord and Saviour | Jesus Christ: | Newly Translated out of the | Original Greek; | And with the former | Translations | Diligently compared and revised. | (Vignette: A hat, flute, &c.) Philadelphia: | Printed and Sold by R. Aitken, Bookseller, | opposite the Coffee-House, Front-Street. | M.DCC.LXXXI. | 1 p.; verso, Names and Order of the Books of the N. T.; below, Initials, R. A. in large scrip letter; Text: Mat. to. Rev. (not paged); sigs. A² to recto of Dd⁶ in 6ˢ.

This is the *first* Bible printed in English in this country, with an American imprint. Hosea VI, is numbered, Chap. VII, and 1 Tim. 4:16, is incorrect. The size of the printed page is 5⅝ in. long by 3¼ in. wide; of the page, 6 in. by 3¼.

2. THE | HOLY BIBLE | Abridged: | or, the | History of the | Old and New Testament | illustrated | with Notes, and adorned with Cuts, | For the Use of Children. | Suffer

little Children, &c. | Boston: | Printed by Robert
Hodge, for Nathaniel | Coverly, in Newbury-Street. |
n. d.   (B.; G. L.)   sm. 18.

Pp. 107; sigs. A to C¹⁸ in 18ˢ. A number of coarse wood cuts are printed in with the text.

1783.

1. **Das Neue | Testament** | unsers | Herrn und Heylandes | JEsu
Christi, | nach der Deutschen Ueberſetzung | D. Martin Luthers. |
Mit | Kurzem Inhalt eines jeden Capitels, | und | Vollſtändiger An-
weizung gleicher Schriftſtellen. | Wie auch | aller Sonn-und Feſt-
tägigen | Evangelien und Epiſteln. | Philadelphia: | Gedruckt bey
Melchior Steiner, in der Rees- | ſtraſſe, nahe bey der Dritten-ſtraſſe.
1783. | (L.)   8.

Title, 1 f.; verso, blank (no Verzeichnisz); Text: pp. 1–537; Anweizung, 1 p. not numbered; sig. A to L1⁶ in 8ˢ. Two leaves to complete Ll wanting; text in double columns.

1784.

1. THE PROVERBS of SOLOMON. (With The Psalter.) Boston: |
Printed and Sold by Benjamin Edes & Sons, | In Cornhill. |
MDCCLXXXIV. | (G. L.)   8.

1. Christ's Sermon on the Mount, contained in the Vth, VIth
and VIIth Chapters of St. Matthew's Gospel. (With The
Psalter.) Boston: | Printed and Sold by Benjamin Edes &
Sons, | In Cornhill. | MDCCLXXXIV. | (G. L.)   8.

1786.

1. THE | NEW TESTAMENT | of Our | Lord and Saviour |
Jesus Christ: | Translated out of the | Original Greek; |
And with the | former Translations | diligently com-
pared and revised. | (An ornament in printer's flowers.)
Philadelphia: | Printed for J. Cruikshank, F. Bailey,
Young, | Stewart, and McCullock, and J. Dobson. |
M.DCC.LXXXVI. | (L.)   12.

Title (within a neat line border), 1 f.; verso, Order of the books; Text: Mat. to Rev. sigs. A² to verso of O¹², in 12ˢ. 1 Tim. 4: 16, incorrect.

1787.

1. SELECTÆ | e Veteri | Testamento | Historiæ. | Ad usum Eorum que Latinæ Linguæ Ru- | dimentis imbuuntur. | Nova Editio, | Prioribus multo emendatior. | Philadelphia: | Excuderunt Prichard et Hall, vico vulgariter dicto Market | Street, et J. James, vico Chesnut-Street. | M.DCC.LXXXVII. | (N. Y. State Library.) 12.

This work was originally composed by a former professor of the University of Paris, at the suggestion of M. Rollin. It contains extracts of some of the Historical parts of the Old Testament, and the Histories of Joseph and Tobias, entire. *Preface.*

2. THE PROVERBS of SOLOMON. (With The Psalter.) Boston: | Printed and Sold by John Norman in Marshal's- | Lane, near the Boston-Stone. | MDCCLXXXVII. | (B.) 8.

1. Christ's Sermon on the Mount, Contained in the Vth, VIth, and VIIth Chapters of St. Mathew's Gospel. (With The Psalter.) Boston: Printed and Sold by John Norman, (as above.) MDCCLXXXVII. (B.) 8.

1788.

1. A Curious | HIEROGLYPHICK BIBLE; | or, | Select Passages | in the | Old and New Testaments, | represented with | Emblematical figures, | for the | Amusement of Youth: | Designed chiefly | To familiarize tender Age, in a pleasing and diverting | Manner, with early Ideas of the Holy Scriptures. | To which are subjoined, | A short Account of the Lives of the Evangelists, and | other Pieces. | Illustrated with nearly Five Hundred Cuts. | The First Worcester Edition. | Printed at Worcester, Massachusetts, | By Isaiah Thomas, | And sold, Wholesale and Retail, at his bookstore. | MDCCLXXXVIII. | (G. L.) 24.

1. THE NEW | TESTAMENT | of our | Lord and Saviour | Jesus Christ: | Translated out of the | Original Greek; | And with the | former Translations | Diligently Com-

pared and Revised. | Appointed to be read in Church-
es. | Trenton : | Printed and Sold By Isaac Collins. |
M.DCC.LXXXVIII. | (L.; G. L.)   8.

<small>Title, 1 f. ; verso, Names and Order, &c. Text : Mat. to Rev. (not paged), sigs. A³ (misprint for A²) to recto of Kkk⁴ in 4ˢ . 1 Tim. 4: 16, incorrect.</small>

2. THE NEW | TESTAMENT | Of our Lord and Saviour | Jesus
Christ, | Newly translated out of the | Original Greek; |
And with the former | Translations | Diligently Compared
and Revised. | (A line across.) Appointed to be Read in
Churches. | (Another line across; then an Ornament in
printer's flowers, followed by a third line across.) Eliza-
beth-town: | Printed and Sold by Shepard Kollock. |
M,DCC,LXXXVIII. | (G. L.)   12.

<small>Title (within ornamental line), 1 f.; verso, the Order of the Books; Text: Mat. to Rev.-(not paged) sig. A (which includes title), to verso of Ii⁶ on which there are six lines of text, the remainder of the page being occupied by a Table of Kindred; sigs. in 6ˢ ; no heading. Mat. 7:6, reads "least they trample them ;" 20:1, "For the kingdom of heaven"</small>

1789.

1. GENESIS. Chapter III, and part of IV. Worcester: Isaiah
Thomas. November, 1789. (Mass. Hist. Soc.; B.)   fol.

<small>This is a specimen accompanying a sheet of Proposals issued by Mr. Thomas for publishing by subscription, his 4to edition of the Bible.</small>

1790.

1. THE | HOLY BIBLE, | translated from the | Latin Vulgate : |
Diligently compared with the | Hebrew, Greek, and other
editions, | in divers languages; | And first published by |
the English College at Doway, Anno 1609. | Newly
revised, and corrected, according to | the Clementine
edition of the Scriptures. | With Annotations for elucidat-
ing | the principal difficulties of Holy Writ. | Haurietis
aquas in gaudio de fontibus Salvatoris. Isaiae xii. 3. |
Philadelphia: | Printed and Sold by Carey, Stewart, and
Co. | M.DCC.XC. | (L.; J. G. S.; G. L.)   4.

<small>Two Volumes bound in one. Title, 1 f. ; verso, Order of the Books of the O. and N. Test.; Approbations, 2 pp.; Subscribers' names, pp. v-viii, p. v having at foot, "Vol. I," and (sig.) b; Text: Gen. to Prov. pp. 1-487; sigs. B to Aa; [Here the number</small>

of the Vol. begins to be also printed on the sigs. of the text;] Bb to 6H², on recto of which is, End of the First Volume; verso of 487, blank, followed by two blank leaves. Vol. II. (no title) Ecclesiastes to Mac. pp. 1–280, then *[281, 282]*, *[283, 284]*, sigs. A. to 3E, Ff, 3G to 3L, 6M, 3N, 3O, 6P, 3Q, to 4A, [4B]*; at foot of p. 284]*, "N. B. The third and fourth book of Machabees—as also the third and fourth book of Esdras (which some call the first and second of Esdras), and the prayer of Manasses—are here omitted; because they have never been received by the church." New Testament (no title) Text : Mat. to Apocalypse, pp. 281–484; sigs. 4B to 4V, then X, Y, Z, 5A to 5Y, Z, 6A to 6F², on verso of which the text ends; Table of References, pp. 485, 486; Chronological Table, pp. 486–488; Order and Distribution of the Psalms, pp. 488, 489; a Table of the Epistles and Gospels p. 490; sigs. 6G. and 6H¹, followed by a blank leaf; sigs. all in 2ˢ. The heading on p. 245, of Vol. I. is "Chap. XXIII." instead of XXII.; on p. 356 of Vol. II., "St. Luke," instead of St. John ; on p. 472, "*Of St.* John," instead of, The Apocalypse.

This is the first American edition of the Douay and Rheims versions of the Scriptures, and is supposed to be the first *quarto* Bible, published in English in the United States. It was originally advertised to be issued in 48 weekly numbers, the first of which appeared Dec. 19, 1789. About twenty sheets were issued in that form, when the plan seems to have been abandoned when the work was finally published on the 1st of December, 1790. The types for the work were cast in the foundry of John Baine, Philadelphia. The text is reprinted from Challoner's 2d edition of the Bible, 1763–4, 5 Vols. 12. The annotations are at the foot of the pages.

2. THE CHRISTIAN'S NEW AND COMPLETE FAMILY BIBLE. Philadelphia: Published by William Woodhouse. 1790.

This edition has not been seen. It was published in numbers, and the above title is extracted from the advertisements in the *Penn. Packet*, Nov. 15, 1788, and Jan. 3, 1789, when Nos. 1 and 10 appeared (*E. A.*), and *Penn. Gaz.*, May 26, 1790, which last is as follows:

"This day is published, and to be sold by all the booksellers, The Christian's New and Complete Family Bible, No. 77. The Old and New Testaments being now entirely printed off, subscribers are requested to send for their numbers as quick as possible. The Apocrypha will soon be ready for delivery. Agreeable to the proposals the work was to be comprised in 75 numbers; however, it will considerably exceed that quantity; but all above No. 75 shall be delivered *gratis* to subscribers, the number of whom is nearly 1000." (*Copied by Mr. McAllister.*) Paul Wright, D. D., Vicar of Oakley, was the editor of a work bearing a somewhat similar title to this.

3. HOLY BIBLE: Philadelphia: | Printed by W. Young, Bookseller and Stationer, | the corner of Second and Chesnut-Streets. | M.DCC.XC. | (L.)   12.

Text: Gen. to Mal. (not paged), sigs. A to Cc¹²; verso, Tables of Kindred and Time; Title to New Test. within a border; 1 p. verso, blank; Text: Mat. to Rev. sigs. Dd² to Ll⁹, all in 12ˢ. This edition was advertised in the *Penn. Packet*, Jan. 27, 1789, as a School Bible, about to be published. (*E. A.*) It appeared in the course of the following year, price five eighths of a dollar. The copy examined wants the first Title, and is in other respects imperfect. The imprint described is that on the title to the New Testament. 1 Tim. 4: 16, is incorrect.

4. THE | HOLY BIBLE | Abridged: | or, the | History | of the | Old and New Testament. | Illustrated with Notes, and adorned with | Cuts. | For the Use of Children. | *To which is added,* | A Compleat Abstract | of the | Old and New Testament, | With the Apocrypha, | In Easy Verse. | Suffer little children, &c. | New York : | *Printed by* Hodge, Allen and Campbell, | *And Sold at their respective Bookstores.* | M,DCC,XC. | · (L.; B.; G. L.)   24.

Frontispiece, Adam and Eve 1 f.; Title 1 f.; Contents 5 pp.; Advertisement of Books, 3 pp., among them the folio and 4to Bibles printed by H. & C.; Text pp. 13, 180; sigs. B to P⁶ in 6ˢ. The wood cuts are coarse; "Adam and Eve," was by Maverick in his ninth year, who was afterwards an engraver of merit, and honorably mentioned by Trumbull for his plate of "The Holy Family" in Collins's Bible of 1807.

1. THE NEW | TESTAMENT | of our | Lord and Saviour | Jesus Christ, | Newly translated out of the | Original Greek: | And with the | former Translations | Diligently Compared and Revised. | (A line across the page.) Appointed to be Read in Churches. | Π. C. | (within an ornamental circle and two lines.) New-York: | Printed and sold by Hugh Gaine, at his Book-Store and | Printing-Office, at the Bible, in Hanover-Square. | M,DCC,XC. | (G. L.; B.) 12.

Title, within double lines, 1 f.; verso, The Order of the Books; Text: Mat. to Rev. not paged) sigs. A² to recto of O¹²; at foot of the text, "Finis," under which a line composed of 9 printer's flowers, a *, and 8 printer's flowers; on verso of O¹², A Table of Kindred; sigs. in 12ˢ ; short headings to columns and chapters.

Errors: The catchword at foot of recto of C³, is "3" instead of "7"; and at foot of C⁵, is "say," instead of "I say"; in Acts 8:9, "sorcercy" is printed for "sorcery"; the catchword at foot of K² is omitted; and in Philippians 4:15, the word is printed, "begginning."

2. THE NEW | TESTAMENT | of our | Lord and Savior | Jesus Christ, | translated out of the | Original Greek : | and with the | former Translations | diligently compared and revised, | By his Majesty's Special Command. | Appointed to be read in Churches. | New-Haven: | Printed by A. Morse, | M.DCC.XC. | 12.

Title, 1 f.; verso, The Order *of all* the Books *of the* New Testament, *with their proper* Names *and* Number *of* Chapters; Text: Mat. to Rev. sigs. A² to recto of Mm² which

—1790.] AMERICAN BIBLES. 37

is followed by a blank leaf to complete the half sig.; the text ending on recto of Mm²; sigs. in 6ˢ. The title page is within a single heavy line; pages are not numbered; and the columns are of irregular length, some being longer than others.

The Errors in this volume are innumerable. Some of them are designated in the following List of

ERRATA.

Mat.	5:30, fot it is profitable;	Luke	24:28, they drew nigh unto the village whether they went:
	8:24, but he was a-asleep;		
	9:14, we and the Prarisees;		
	14: 3, his bother Philip's wife	John	1:25, Why baptized thou then
	18:15, If thy brocher shall trespass against the,		2: 6, there were set there six water-pots
Mark	1:20, and they left their fa-Zebedee (the catch word "ther" is not carried over.)		10, and when men have well dunk,
			3:33, He that hath receiveth his testimony
	3:17, Boanerges, which is, The Sons of thuder.		5:17, My Father worketh hirtherto,
	5:13, the herd ran voilently		31, my winess is not true.
	14: 2, not on the feast-day, least		32, another that beareth watness
	30, thou shalt deny me thirce.		7: 4, For there no man that doeth any thing in secret,
	64, ye heave hared the blasphemy;		
Luke	1: 8, defore God,		5, nither did his brethren
	9, his lot was to burnt incense,		7, but me it, hateth,
			9, he abode flill
	17, and the disobedient to the wisdmo of the just:		14, and tought.
			45, Then came the ossicers
	2: 9, the Angle of the Lord		8:42, if God were your Father he would love me:
	48, have sought the sorrowing.		
			49, ye dishonor me
	5:30, their scribes and Pharisees murmred		10: 7, Then faid Jesus
			12:28, and will glirify it again.
	16:29, let them here them.		14:17, neither knownth him:
	17: 4, trun again to thee, saying, I repent!		21:18, When thou wast young, thou girdestd thyself,
	18:24, how heardly	Acts	5:27, and the high priest skaed them,
	19: 4, fycamore-tree		
	23:17, for of neceffity		7:43, the tabernacles of Molech,
	32, And there were also, two other, malefactor,		8: 9, which before time in the same city used sorcercy,
	38, a superscription also was writted over him		16:30, the word "said" is omitted in the text, though it forms the catchword of the previous page.
	24:14, which had hapopened.		
	21, But we trusteth		

Acts 22: 5, As also doth the high priest bear we witness, 22, they gave him audience
Rom. 16:23, Gaius mine host....saluteteh you.
1 Cor. 2:10, the Spirit searcheth all things,
2 Cor. 11:29, who is offended and I burnt not?
Gal. 4:27, For it is witten, Rejoice, thou barran
Ephes. 4:32, And be ye king one to another,
Philip. 2: 8, And being sound in fashion
Coloss. 4:10, Aristarchus, my fellow prisoner, salute you, and Marcus, sister's son to Banabas,
1 Tim. 4:16, Take heed unto thyself, and unto thy doctrine;
Philem. 1: 8, that which is convenient,
Rev. 11:11, and great fear feel upon them
12: 6, that they should seed her there
20: 4, And I saw thrones, and they set upon them.... which had not worshipped the best,

1791.

1. THE | Holy Bible, | containing the | Old and New | Testaments : | With the | Apocrypha. | Translated | Out of the Original Tongues, | and | with the former Translations diligently Compared and Revised, | By the Special Command of King James I, of *England*. | With an | Index. | *Appointed to be read in Churches.* | Vol. I. | United States of America. | Printed at the Press in Worcester, Massachusetts, | By Isaiah Thomas. | Sold by him in Worcester; and by him and Company, at Faust's Statue, No. 45, Newbury Street, Boston. | M.DCC.XCI. | (L.; Am. Antiq. Soc.; G. L.) fol.

Vol. I. Title, 1 f.; verso, blank; Directions to Binder and list of Plates, 1 f ; verso, blank; The printer's Address, To Christians of every Denomination, dated Worcester, Massachusetts, December, 1791, pp. 1, 2; To the Publick, including the Address of the Translators to King James (in Italic) p. 3, and part of p. 4; on remainder of which is, Names and Order of Books. These 4 pp. form sig. A (not marked); Text: Gen. to end of Prov. pp. 5—460; B to 2 Z. in 2^s , making 48 forms ; then 49 A to 115 T ; Vol. II. Title (as above) 1 f. verso blank ; Text : Ecclesiastes to Malachi, pp. 461-635 ; at foot of p. 635, (under a festoon) *The End of the Prophets.* | Printed at Worcester, Massachusetts, by Isaiah | Thomas. MDCCXCI. | verso of 635, blank; sigs. 116 U to 159 P, in 2^s; Apocrypha, pp. 637-786; at foot of p. 786 (within an ornamental cut). This Folio Edition of the Bible, and one in Royal | Quarto, were printed by Isaiah Thomas, at | Worcester, *Massachusetts*, in the year MDCCXCI. | sigs. 160 Q to 197 E^1 in 2^s. The New | Testament | of | Our | Lord and Saviour | Jesus Christ, | Translated | Out of the Original Greek, | and | with the former Translations diligently compared and revised, | By the Special Command of King James I, of England. | Together with an | Index | to the | Holy Bible. | *Appointed to be read in Churches.* | (Imprint as above.) 1 p. verso, blank (being counted as pp. 787, 788 and as sig. 197 E².) Text: Mat. to Rev. pp. 789-991; sigs. 198 F to 248 H in 2s; verso of 991, blank; Index, pp. 993—1008; sigs. 249 I to 252 M in 2s; Table of Weights, Measures, Coins, &c. pp. 1009, 1010; Tables of Time, Offices and Conditions, p. 1011; Table of Kindred, p. 1012; sig. 253 N; at the bottom of p. 1012, is the catchword "An," indicating that "An Alphabetical Table of Proper Names," ought to follow (as in the 4to ed. *post*); but it is wanting in those copies we have seen.

The following is a list of the Engravings in this Bible, with the Engravers' names:

1. Frontispiece to Old Test., illustrating the Triumph of the Gospel throughout the world,..Engraved by *Sam'l Hill*.
2. The Creation...*J. H. Seymour*.
3. Adam and Eve in a state of Innocence............................*J. Norman*.
4. Expulsion of Adam and Eve from Paradise........................*Jos. Seymour*.
5. Noah and his family entering the Ark.
6. Abraham's Faith ....*Jos. Seymour*.
7. Moses in the Bulrushes...*J. Seymour*.
8. Pharaoh and his Host drowned.
9. The Amalekites defeated by Joshua..............................*J. Seymour*.
10. The Ark of the Covenant.......................................*J. Seymour*.
11. Falling of the walls of Jericho................................*J. Seymour*.
12. The Battle of Ai..*Jos. Seymour*.
13. Gideon's sacrifice consumed...................................*J. Seymour*.
14. The fugitive Sechemites burnt and suffocated..................*S. Hill*.
15. Samson slaying the Philistines................................*Sam'l Hill*.
16. Samson carrying off the gates of Gaza.
17. The Philistines cutting off the heads of Saul and of his sons........*Sam'l Hill*.
18. Abner assassinated..*S. Hill*.
19. Solomon's Temple.
20. Solomon receiving the Queen of Sheba..........................*J. Seymour*.
21. Elijah raising the Widow's son................................*J. Seymour*.
22. Elijah carried up to Heaven...................................*J. Seymour*.
23. Benhadad stifled. ....*J. Seymour*.
24. Destruction of the Temple of Baal.............................*J. Norman*.
25. Zachariah stoned to death.....................................*J. H. Seymour*.
26. Manasseh in chains..*J. Seymour*.
27. Plan of Jerusalem...*J. Norman*.
28. Daniel in the Lions' den......................................*J. Seymour*.
29. Emblematical representation of the Old and New Dispensations (Frontispiece to Apocrypha).
30. Queen Esther fainting...*J. Norman*.
31. Susanna surprised by the Elders...............................*Jos. H. Seymour*.
32. Judas Maccabeus defeats the Samaritan army....................*J. H. Seymour*.
33. The first and second Adam.....................................*Jos. H. Seymour*.
34. Christ baptised...*Seymour*.
35. John the Baptist's head brought to Herodias...................*J. Seymour*.
36. A Woman healed of a bloody issue.

37. Christ restoring Bartimeus to sight..................................*J. Seymour.*
38. Mary Magdalene...*J. H. Seymour.*
39. The Woman of Samaria...*J. Seymour.*
40. Christ curing the Impotent Man at the pool of Bethesda..............*J. Seymour.*
41. Martha..*J. Seymour.*
42. The Crucifixion (after Rubens)...................................*J. Seymour.*
43. Joseph of Arimathea taking our Saviour's body from the cross....*Jos. H. Seymour.*
44. The Ascension..*Sam'l Hill*, Boston.
45. St. Paul..*J. Seymour.*
46. Paul before Felix..*J. Norman.*
47. Paul shaking the Viper from his hand....................*Doolittle*, N. Haven.
48. Hominum Salvator...*J. Seymour.*
49. St. John the Evangelist..*J. Seymour.*
50. Michael and the Devil......................................*Jos. H. Seymour.*

On the top of each of the plates in the body of the work is inscribed—"Engraved for Thomas's Edition of the Bible." On the frontispiece to the O. Test. the words are—"Engraved for Thomas's Folio Edition of the Holy Bible;" at the foot—"Published by Isaiah Thomas, at Worcester, 1791;" and on that to the N. Testament—"Worcester, Engraved for Thomas's Folio Edition of the Bible, November, 1791;" on a scroll at the foot—"The Wages of Sin is Death, but the Gift of God is Eternal Life through Jesus Christ our Lord.—*Rom.* vi, 23."

In addition to the plates above enumerated, there is a wood cut at the head of each division of the vol. That before Genesis represents Eve giving Adam the apple; that to the Apocrypha, Judith giving the head of Holofernes to her maid; and that to the New Testament, the Crucifixion.

Previous to printing this edition of the Scriptures, Mr. Thomas, the editor, furnished himself with nearly thirty copies of the Bible, printed at different times and places; from these he selected the most correct, by which to revise the whole of this work. Every sheet of the text, before its commitment to the press, was carefully examined by the clergymen of Worcester [the Rev. Aaron Bancroft, D. D., and the Rev. Samuel Austin, D. D.], and by other capable persons, and compared with not less than eight different copies. Each book commences with an ornamental Initial letter, and each of the chapters is preceded by a brief abstract of its contents.

Other copies of the work have been issued in one volume, and with two title pages only, one to the Old and the other to the New Testament, and without any directions to the binder or list of plates.

2. THE | HOLY BIBLE, | containing the | Old and New Testaments: | together with the | Apocrypha: | Translated out of the | Original Tongues, | and | with the former Translations diligently compared and revised, | By the Special Command of King James I, of England. | With | Marginal Notes and References. | To which are added, an | Index, | and an | Alphabetical Table | of all the Names in the Old and New Testaments, with their Significations. | *United*

States of America. | Printed at the Press in Worcester, Massachusetts, | By Isaiah Thomas. | Sold by him in Worcester; and by him and Company, at Faust's Statue, No. 45, Newbury Street, Boston. | MDCCXCI. | (L.; Am. Antiq. Soc.; G. L.)   .   4.

Title, 1 f. ; verso, blank ; The printer's Address, To Christians of every Denomination, pp. 3, 4; To the Publick, including Address of Translators to King James (in Ital.), pp. 5 and part of 6 ; on remainder of p. 6, Names and Order of all the Books ; The | Old Testament, | translated | out of the | Original Hebrew, | and | with the former Translations diligently compared and revised. | Together with the | Apocrypha. | Done by the | Special Command of his Majesty King James I, of *England.* | (A line in Hebrew.) United States of America. | Printed at the Press in Worcester, Massachusetts, | By Isaiah Thomas. | Sold by him in Worcester. Sold also by said Thomas, and Andrews, | at Faust's Statue, No. 45, Newbury Street, Boston, | MDCCXCI. | 1 p. (within parallel rules.) verso, *The Property of* (within an ornamental circle.)   These 4 ff. make one sig. Text : Gen. to Mal. pp. 9–824 ; at foot of p. 824, End of the Prophets ; sigs. A to Z, then 25-A to 103-K in 4^s ; Apocrypha, pp. 825–1014 ; at foot of 1014, End of the Apocrypha, in a circular wreath ; Printed at Worcester, by Isaiah Thomas, | MDCCXCI. | beneath a festoon and within an ornamental wreath; sigs. 104-L to 127-K^3 followed by one blank leaf to complete sig. The | New Testament | of our | Lord and Saviour | Jesus Christ. | Translated | out of the | Original Greek : | and with the former Translations diligently | compared and revised, | by the Special Command of his Majesty King James I, of England. | (A Greek Text, 2 lines.) United States of America. | Printed at the Press in Worcester, Massachusetts, | By Isaiah Thomas. | Sold by him in Worcester. Sold also by said Thomas, and Andrews, | at Faust's Statue, No. 45, Newbury Street, Boston. | MDCCXCI. | (within parallel rules.) Marked at foot 128 L ; Text : Mat. to Rev. pp. 1020–1276 ; at foot of 1276, The End, and, on an ornamental slab : This Royal Quarto Edition of the Bible, | and likewise one in Folio, With Fifty Copper | plates, were printed by Isaiah Thomas, | at Worcester, *Massachusetts,* MDCCXCI. | Sig. 128-L^2 to 160-U^2 ; Index pp. 1277–1297; at foot of 1297, End of Index ; Tables of Scripture measures, &c., pp. 1298–1300 ; at foot of 1300, Table of Time ; Table of Offices, p. 1301 ; Table of Kindred, p. 1302 ; sigs. 160-U^3 to 163-Z^3 ; Alphabetical Table of Proper Names, pp. 1303–1310 ; at foot of 1310, The End.   Sigs. 163-Z^4 to 164-A^3 , all in 4^s.

This edition was issued also in two volumes, and differs materially in its typographical composition from that in folio, by the same publisher. Parallel rules divide the columns of the text, which are embraced on the outer side by single lines. It has, also, marginal notes and references, " all examined and compared with the Text by the Minister of Holden,"—the Rev. Joseph Avery—and running head-lines of contents at the head of the columns. None of these are in the folio edition. On the other hand, this Quarto wants the woodcuts at the head of each of the divisions of the Volume, and has ornamental Initial letters at the beginning of these divisions only, instead of each book. According to Isaiah Thomas's Catalogue of Books for Sale at the Worcester Bookstore, 1801, in the possession of Mr. BRINLEY, this Bible was issued in three different styles, viz : with 48 copper plates and Concordance ; without plates or Concordance ; and with Concordance. The copy before us has no Concordance, and only two engravings; these are printed from the plates of the folio edition, on quarto paper, or reduced to that size. The following is a copy of the title page to the Concordance mentioned in the 1st and 3d of the above varieties: A | Brief Concordance | to the | Holy Scriptures | of the | Old and New Testaments : | By which All or Most of the Principal Texts of Scripture | may be easily found out. | Revised and Corrected | By John Brown | Late Minister of the Gospel at Haddington in Scotland. | Printed at Worcester, Massachusetts, | By Isaiah Thomas. | Sold at his Bookstore in Worcester, and by him and | Company in Boston. | MDCCXCI. | 4to.

3. THE | HOLY BIBLE, | containing the | Old and New | Testaments: | translated out of the | Original Tongues: | And with the former | Translations | Diligently compared and revised. | Trenton: | Printed and sold by Isaac Collins. | M.DCC.XCI. | (L.)   4.

Title, within heavy double black lines, 1 f.; verso, blank; "To the Reader" 2 pp.; Account of dates and times, &c., 1 p.; verso, blank; Names and Order of Books of O. and N. Test., 1 p.; verso, blank; making sig. A. Text: (not paged) Gen. to Mal. sigs. B to 4 R^2; verso, blank. Apocrypha: A to U, followed by two blank leaves to complete sig. The New | Testament | of our | Lord and Saviour | Jesus Christ, | translated out of the | Original Greek: | And with the former | Translations | Diligently compared and revised. | Trenton: | Printed and Sold by Isaac Collins. | M.DCC.XCI. | 1 p.; verso, blank. Text: Mat. to Rev. ‡A^2 to verso of ‡Dd^3; Index, Table of Time, Tables of Measure, Table of Offices, Table of Kindred, ‡Dd^4 to ‡Hh^2. A Brief | Concordance | or | Table | to the | Bible | of the | Last Translation: | Serving for the more easy finding out of the most useful Places | therein contained. | Carefully Perused and Enlarged by John Downame, B. A. | Psalm cxix, 105, *Thy Word is a Lamp*, &c. | Trenton: | Printed and Sold by Isaac Collins. | Title, 1 p.; verso, To the Reader; A to I^4; sigs. all in 4^s.

This is the *first* Bible printed in New Jersey. Proposals for its publication were issued as early as 1788. The Dedication to King James is omitted, and in its place is printed an Address "To the Reader," by Rev. John Witherspoon, D. D. Some copies have Ostervald's Practical Comments on the Books of the Old and New Testaments, with separate Title page: Trenton: Isaac Collins, 1791. But the Baptist Association having objected to these and to the Apocrypha, they are left out in some copies. The work is sometimes met in two volumes.

4. THE | HOLY BIBLE | containing the | Old and New | Testaments: Translated out of the | Original Tongues; | and with the | former Translations | diligently compared and revised. | Philadelphia: | Printed by W. Young, No. 52 Second, | The Corner of Chesnut-Street. | M,DCC,XCI. | (L.)   18.

Vol. I. Title (within a wood-cut border), 1 f.; verso, blank; To the Reader, beginning, "The Providence of God," &c., 1½ pp,; Names and Order of the Books, ½ p. Text: (pp. not numbered,) Gen. to Prov. 21:14: sigs. A^2 to Mm^{12}, in 12^s and

6ˢ alternately; Vol. II, Title (as above) 1 f.; verso, blank; Text: Prov. 21:15 to Mal.; sigs. Nn to verso of Ddd², in 12ˢ and 6ˢ alternately. The New | Testament | of our | Lord and Saviour | Jesus Christ, | translated out of the | Original Greek | and with the | former Translations | diligently compared and revised. | Philadelphia: | Printed by W. Young, No. 52, Second, | The Corner of Chesnut-Street. | M.DCC.XCII. | marked at foot, Ddd², 1 f.; verso, blank; Mat. to Rev. Ddd³ to verso of Ttt⁸, in 12ˢ and G³; Tables of Kindred and Time, Days of the Week, Watches, 1 p.; Tables of Weights, &c., 1 p.; The Scotch version of the Psalms in metre, no title page nor pagination; sigs. A to recto of E⁵ in 12 and 6ˢ; Table to find any Psalm, 2 pp.; verso of E⁵ and recto of E⁶; on verso of E⁶, Philadelphia: | Printed by William Young, No. 52, Second | Street, the Corner of Chesnut-Street. | M,DCC,XCIII. |

1. NEW TESTAMENT. Philadelphia: Published by John Mc-Cullock. circ. 1791.   12.
   A School edition. (Mr. McA.)

2. THE NEW | TESTAMENT | of our | Lord and Saviour | Jesus Christ, | newly Translated out of the | Original Greek; | and with the former | Translations | diligently compared and revised. | (An ornament composed of printer's flowers.) Newbury-port: | Printed and Sold by John Mycall. n. d.   .   (B.; G. L.)   12.
   Title (within ornamental lines), 1 f.; verso, The Order of the Books;. Text: Mat. to Rev. (not paged), sigs A² to recto of Cc⁵; "To benefit the English Scholar, here follows an alphabetical etymological Explanation of many names of PERSONS, PLACES, &c., which are mentioned in the NEW TESTAMENT," verso of Cc⁵ to verso of Cc⁶. Sigs. in 6ˢ. The running title on the verso of I⁵, is "Chap. XXI," instead of "S. Luke;" and on the recto of I⁶, "S. Luke," instead of "Chap. XXII." 1 Tim. 4: 16, "Take heed unto thyself, and unto thy doctrine."
   Mycall carried on the printing business in Newburyport, from about 1777 to 1797. See, *Thomas's Hist. of Printing*, I, 399.

1792.

1. THE | SELF-INTERPRETING BIBLE: | Containing, | The Sacred Text | of the | Old and New | Testaments. | Translated from the Original Tongues, and with the former Translations | Diligently Compared and Revised. | To which are annexed, | Marginal References and Illustrations, | An exact Summary of the several Books, | A Paraphrase on the most obscure or important Parts, | An Analysis of the Contents of each Chapter, | Explanatory Notes, | and Evangelical Reflections. | (An ornamental line across part

of the page.) By the late | Reverend John Brown, | Minister of the Gospel at Haddington. | (Four Texts of Scripture: John 5: 39, Acts 10: 43, Heb. 9: 16, Rev. 13: 8, follow between two lines which extend across the page.) | New-York: | Printed by Hodge and Campbell, | And Sold at their respective Book Stores. | M.DCC.XCII. | (L.) fol.

Title (within an ornamental border), 1 f.; verso, blank. The Author's Address, 1 p.; To the Reader, beginning, "The Providence of God," 1 p.; An | Introduction | to | the Right Understanding of the Oracles of God. | 18 ff.; sigs. a to verso of i^2; Appendix of Weights, Measures and Times mentioned in Scripture, Table of Offices, Names and Order of Books; Tables of Kindred, 2 ff.; sig. k; in 2^s. Text: Gen. to Mal. (not paged), sigs. A to verso of 8 A^2; Apocrypha (in smaller type and without notes or explanations), sigs. A to verso of T^1 followed by a blank leaf which completes the sig. The | New | Testament, | of | Our Lord and Saviour | Jesus Christ: | To which are annexed, | Marginal References and Illustrations, | An exact Summary of the several Books, | A Paraphrase on the most Obscure or Important Parts, | An Analysis of the Contents of each Chapter, | Explanatory Notes, | and Evangelical Reflections. | (An ornamental line partly across the page.) By the late | Reverend John Brown, | Minister of the Gospel at Haddington. | (3 Texts of Scripture, between two lines.) New-York: | Printed by Hodge and Campbell, | and Sold at their respective Book-Stores. | M.DCC.XCII. | (within an ornamented border), 1 p.; verso, blank. Text: Mat. to Rev,, sigs. A^2 to verso of 3 X^2; Alphabetical Table of Proper Names, 2 ff.; sig. *, "The End;" List of Subscribers (headed by GEORGE WASHINGTON, Esq., President of the United States of America), 4 ff.; sigs. [1] and [2]; on last leaf, an acknowledgment of thanks for the support and encouragement received, dated New York, 1st April, 1792, and signed by the Publishers. All the sigs. are in 2^s. In some copies, the List of Subscribers is in the fore part of the Vol., inserted between "To the Reader," and "The Introduction."

The following is a list of the Engravings, and names of the Engravers:

Frontispiece: America, with the "Constitution" in her hand, receiving the Bible; The Goddess of Liberty on one side; behind America a Pedestal with the Names of Washington, Montgomery, Greene, Franklin, Warren, Adams, Mercer, Putnam, Jay, Clinton, Gates, Morris and Fayette inscribed thereon. The whole surmounted by the arms of the State of New York....*Dunlap, delint.*

1. Adam giving Names......................................*A. Godwin.* 1790.
2. Moses before the burning bush..........................*C. Tiebout.* 1790.
3. Sampson Killing the Lion.................................*Tiebout.* 1790.
4. Ruth..*Maverick.*
5. David and Bathsheba....................................*Doolittle.*
6. Elijah and Elisha......................................*Tiebout.*
7. Solomon's Temple......................................*Rollinson.*
8. Queen Esther fainting.
9. David playing on the harp.............................*Doolittle.*
10. Vision of the Cherubims.................*Rollinson.* N. York, 1791.
11. Daniel in the Lion's den..............................*Doolittle.*

12. Jonah under the gourd..*Rollinson.*
Front. to N. T.: An accurate Map of the Holy Land..............*Rollinson.* 1790.
13. The flight into Egypt.......................................*Doolittle.* N. H.
14. Christ restoring Bartimeus to Sight........................*Doolittle.* N. H.
15. The Angel appearing to Mary..................................*Doolittle.*
16. The Impotent man healed............................*Rollinson.* N. York, '92.
17. Paul shaking off the viper..........................*Rollinson.* N. York, '92.
18. The Angel presenting the Book......................*Rollinson* N. York, 1792.

All are marked, "Engraved for the American Edition of Brown's Family Bible." These plates are arranged in a different order in some copies.

This is the earliest edition of the Bible composed and printed in the State of New York. It was published in forty numbers, the first of which appeared in the Spring of 1790. It was two years passing through the press.

2. THE | HOLY BIBLE | containing the Old and New Testaments: | Newly translated out of the | Original Tongues, | and with the former | Translations | diligently compared and revised. | Search the Scriptures, &c. | To Him give all the Prophets, &c. | Where a testament is, &c. | The Lamb slain, &c. | New York: | Printed by Hodge and Campbell, | and Sold at their respective Bookstores. | M.DCC.XCII. | (Am. Bible Soc.)   4.

Title (within ornamental lines), 1 f.; verso, blank; To the Reader;* verso, Names and Order of Books, 1 f.; Text: Gen. to Mal. (not paged); sigs. A to 4R⁴ in 4ˢ. The whole of Mal. is contained in the last page and half, and is in smaller type than the other portion of the O. T.; Apocrypha (in type like that of Malachi); sigs. A to verso of Q⁴ in 4ˢ. The | New | Testament | of | Our Lord and Saviour | Jesus Christ, | Newly Translated out of the | Original Greek, | and with the | former Translations | diligently compared and revised. | New York: | Printed by Hodge and Campbell, | and Sold at their respective Bookstores. | M.DCC.XCII. | 1 p.; verso, blank; Text: Mat. to Rev. sigs. A² to verso of Ff², in 4ˢ; Index of the Holy Bible, sigs. a to ⅔d of the recto of g; Tables of Measures, Weights, Coins, Kindred, Time, Offices, the rest of recto of g to recto of h; Alphab. Table of Proper Names, verso of h to i², all in 2ˢ; Psalms of David in Metre (Scotch version) pp. 1-49; sigs. †A to recto of †N¹, in 2ˢ.

In an advertisement of Books by Hodge and Campbell affixed to The Holy Bible Abridged (*supra* p. 36), this edition is announced with 20 elegant copper plates. But there are no plates in this copy.

3. THE | HOLY BIBLE, | containing | The Old and New | Testaments: | Translated out of the | Original Tongues; | And with the former | Translations | diligently compared and revised. | II. G. | (With a double line above and

* The upper portion of the page is torn off in the copy examined.

below.) New-York: | Printed and sold by Hugh Gaine, at his Book-Store and | Printing-Office, at the Bible, in Hanover-Square. | M,DCC,XCII. | (L.)   12.

<small>Title (within a double line), 1 f.; verso, blank; The Names and Order of all the Books of the O. and N. Test. 1 p ; Account of the Dates or Time of writing the Books of the New Testament, 1 p.; Text: Gen. to Mal. A³ to Cc¹²; verso of Cc¹², Tables of Kindred and of Time, 1 p.; The New Testament, &c. (same imprint), 1 p.; verso, blank; Text: Mat. to Rev. Dd² to Ll¹²; verso, A Table of Offices and Conditions of Men.</small>

<small>This Bible is printed in Ruby type, and is said to have been imported by Gaine, already set up in pages.</small>

4. HOLY BIBLE. Philadelphia: Printed by William Young, Bookseller and Stationer, No. 52 Second, the corner of Chesnut Street. 1792.   18.

<small>Carey's *American Museum* for February, 1792. See *supra*, No. 4, 1791.</small>

1. NEW TESTAMENT. Philadelphia: Published by Wm. Young, No. 52 Second, the corner of Chesnut Streets. 1792. 18.

1793.

1. THE | HOLY BIBLE, | containing the | Old and New Testaments: | Together with the | Apocrypha: | Translated out of the | 𝔒𝔯𝔦𝔤𝔦𝔫𝔞𝔩 𝔗𝔬𝔫𝔤𝔲𝔢𝔰, | and | with the Former Translations diligently | Compared and Revised, | by the | Special Command of King James I, of England. | 𝔘𝔫𝔦𝔱𝔢𝔡 𝔖𝔱𝔞𝔱𝔢𝔰 𝔬𝔣 𝔄𝔪𝔢𝔯𝔦𝔠𝔞. | Printed in Worcester, Massachusetts, | By Isaiah Thomas. | Sold by him in Worcester. Sold also by said Thomas, and | Andrews, at Faust's Statue, No. 45, Newbury Street, Boston; | and by said Thomas, and Co. in Walpole, Newhampshire. | MDCCXCIII. | 8.

<small>Title (within ornamental rules), 1 f.; verso, blank; Advertisement to the Folio and Quarto Editions, To Christians of every Denomination. "*N. B. This* Octavo Edition *was carefully copied from the* Folio *and* Quarto *Editions above mentioned*. ISAIAH THOMAS having made preparation therefor, is now putting to Press two other Editions of the Bible, viz: one in Demy Quarto, the other in Duodecimo, or the Common School Bible, which will be completed with all speed.... Both Editions will be printed on beautiful New Types, cast particularly for the purpose." To the Publick and Address of the Translators to King James; Names and order of all the Books, 2 pp.; sig. ✢2; The | 𝔒𝔩𝔡 𝔗𝔢𝔰𝔱𝔞𝔪𝔢𝔫𝔱, | Translated | out of the | Original Hebrew, | and | with the Former Translations diligently | Compared and Revised, | together with the | Apocrypha. | Done by the | Special Command of his Majesty King James I, of England. |</small>

(Gen. ii, 17, in Hebrew, within an ornamental cut.) Printed at Worcester, Massachusetts, | by Isaiah Thomas. | Sold by him in Worcester. Sold also by said Thomas, and Andrews, | at Faust's Statue, No. 45, Newbury Street, Boston; and by said Thomas, | and Co. in Walpole, Newhampshire. | MDCCXCIII. | (within double rules), 1 p.; verso, *The Property of*   , within a circular wreath; Text: Gen. to Mal., pp. 7-735; at foot of 735, The End of the Prophets. | then a double line across the page; Printed at Worcester, Massachusetts, by Isaiah Thomas, MDCCXCIII. | Another double line across the page; on verso of 735, Tables of Scripture Measures, Weights and Money, and of Time; sigs. *4 to 45Z³, in 8ˢ; Apocrypha (not paged), sig. A to verso of Y⁴, in 4ˢ; The | New Testament | of our | Lord and Saviour | Jesus Christ. | Translated | out of the | Original Greek. | And with the Former Translations diligently | Compared and Revised, | by the Special Command of his Majesty King James I, of England. | (2 lines of Greek within an ornamental cut.) Printed at Worcester, Massachusetts, | by Isaiah Thomas. | Sold by him in Worcester. Sold also by said Thomas, and Andrews, | at Faust's Statue, No. 45, Newbury Street, Boston; and by said Thomas, | and Co. in Walpole, Newhampshire. | MDCCXCIII. | 1 p. (within parallel rules), marked at foot, 46A; verso, blank; Text: Mat. to Rev. pp. 739-959; Table of Offices and Conditions of Men, p. 960; sigs. 46A² to 590³ in 8ˢ.

An Edition of this Bible has also been published without Apocrypha. (L.)

2. The | Holy Bible | containing the | Old and New | Testaments. | Translated out of the | Original Tongues; | And with the former | Translations | diligently compared and revised. | Trenton: | Printed and Sold by Isaac Collins. | M.DCC.XCIII. | (L.; G. L.)   8.

Title, 1 f.; verso, blank; Names and Order of Books, (A²); Account of the dates and times of writing the Books of the N. T., 2 pp.; To the Reader, beginning, "As the Dedication of the English Translation," &c., 2 pp.; Text: (not paged) Gen. to Mal. A⁴ to verso of 5P⁴ in 4ˢ; The New | Testament | of our | Lord and Saviour | Jesus Christ, | Translated out of the | Original Greek | and with the | former Translations | diligently compared and revised. | Trenton: | Printed and Sold by Isaac Collins. | M.DCC.XCIV. | 1 p.; verso, blank; Text: Mat. to Rev. 5Q² to verso of 7B², in 4ˢ; Tables of Measures, Weights and Kindred, Time, Days, Hours, Watches, 1 p.; Tables of Offices and Conditions, 1 p. sig. 7B³, followed by a blank leaf to complete the sig. The title pages are within double lines. The address to the Reader is by the Rev. Dr. Witherspoon.

1794.

1. A New | Hieroglyphical Bible | For the Amusement & Instruction of Children; | Being | A Selection | of the most useful Lessons; | and | most interesting Narratives; | (Scripturally Arranged) From Genesis to Revelations. | Embellished with | Familiar Figures & Striking Emblems | Neatly Engraved | To the whole is Added a Sketch of the

life of | Our Blessed Saviour, | The Holy Apostles &c. | Recommended by the Rev⁴. Rowland Hill M. A. | Boston: | Printed for W. Norman, Book & Chartseller. | n. d.   (L.; B.; G. L.)   12.

Pp. 144. A Mr. Thompson, was the author of this volume; the recommendation is dated May 12, 1794.

2. ISAIAH. | A | New Translation; | By the late Robert Lowth, D. D. | Bishop of London. | To which is added, | A plain, concise and particular Explanation | of each Chapter. | Extracted chiefly from "A Treatise on the Prophets," | By John Smith, D. D. | Minister of the Gospel at Campbleton, Scotland. | In the Summary Explanation, | perfixed to each Chapter, the | Time and Occasion when the Prophecy was written; the | peculiar Style of ISAIAH; the Beauty and Sublimity of | particular Passages; the Allusions to ancient Customs and | Manners; 'the Connexion and Scope of the several Parts | of the Prophecy, and the Events in which the Predictions | seem to have had their Accomplishment, are occasionally | ascertained and illustrated: The whole forming an agree- | able and instructive Exposition of this Seraphic Prophet, | equally removed from dull and tedious Criticisms, and | from general and foreign Observations. | Albany: | Printed by Charles R. and George Webster, | No. 2, Pearl-Street. | M.DCC.XCIV. | (N. Y. State Lib.; G. L.; Conn. Hist. Soc.)   12.

Title, 1 f.; verso, blank; pp. 231; sigs. A, including title, to recto of Dd⁴, in 4ˢ.

3. DANIEL. REVELATIONS. Remarks | on the | Book of Daniel, | and on the | Revelations. | = | Whereby it appears, | That Daniel had visions of eight great tem- | poral monarchies: That the three last of | Daniel being future when John wrote, he only | has visions of the three last great temporal | powers. | That the prophetic periods of Daniel and John, | all terminate in 2520 years from the first of | Cyrus, and 1890 from the birth of Christ, | so far as temporal powers are concerned. | That the end of temporal powers, designates an | end of mankind in the flesh; the com-

mence- | ment of the millenium; the resurrection of | the Just, and the restitution of all things. | = | Revelations III. | "Because thou hast kept the word of my patience, I will | also keep thee from the hour of temptation, that cometh | upon all the world, to try them that dwell upon the | earth: Behold I come quickly: Hold fast that which thou | hast, that no man take thy crown." | = | New-York, printed at Greenleaf's Press, | April 19, A. D. 1794. | 8.

Title, 1 f.; verso, blank; The Book of Daniel, pp. 1-28; Revelations begin at p. 272, but the text is not printed like that of Daniel, but with remarks intercalated; the volume ends on p. 503; Errata, 2 pp.; the signatures run from A to S^3. (J. G. S.)

1. THE NEW | TESTAMENT | of our | Lord and Saviour | Jesus Christ, | translated out of the | Original Greek: | And with the | former Translations | diligently Compared and Revised. | **Appointed to be read in Churches.** | (Vignette, American Eagle.) Printed at Boston, | by Alexander Young and Thomas Minns, | for J. Boyle, B. Larkin, J. White, Thomas and Andrews, | D. West, E. Larkin, W. P. Blake, and J. West. | Sold by them at their respective Book Stores. | MDCCXCIV. | (Am. Antiq. Soc.) 12.

Title, 1 f.; verso, Order of Books; Text: Mat. to Rev. (not paged); sigs. A^2 to Z^5; Table of Kindred Z^6; verso, blank; sigs. in 6^s.

2. NEW TESTAMENT: Trenton: Printed and Sold by Isaac Collins. M.DCC.XCIV. 8.

With Bible, *supra* No. 2, 1793.

3. EXPOSITORY NOTES, | with | Practical Observations | upon the | New Testament | of | Our Lord and Saviour | Jesus Christ. | Wherein the whole of the | Sacred Text is recited, the Sense explained, | and the | instructive Example of the blessed Jesus, and his Apostles, | to our Imitation recommended. | By William Burkitt, M. A. | Late vicar and lecturer of Dedham, in Essex. | New-Haven: | Printed by Abel Morse, for the Rev. David Austin of Elizabeth-town. | M,DCC,XCIV. | (Conn. Hist. Soc.) 4.

Pp. 1168.

4. APOCALYPSE. An | Attempt | to translate the prophetic part | of the | *Apocalypse of St. John* | into familiar language, | by divesting it of the Metaphors in which it is involved. | By James Winthrop, Esq. | And he turned, &c., Luke x, 23, 24. | I Jesus have sent, &c., Rev. xxii, 16. | Printed in BOSTON, for the Author, | By Belknap and Hall, | Sold at their Office, No. 8, Dock Square. | MDCCXCIV. | (Harvard Coll.; B.)   8.

Pp. 79. The author was for some years chief justice of the court of common pleas in Massachusetts. He died in 1821.

1795.

1. JOB. A | Paraphrase | on | Some Parts | of | the Book | of | Job. | Printed by Samuel Hall, No. 53, Cornhill, Boston. | 1795. | (B.)   8.

Pp. 39. RICHARD DEVENS, the author of this Metrical Paraphrase, was a native of Charlestown (Mass.), and educated at Princeton College, where he subsequently filled the chair of Mathematics. His reason forsook him at the early age of twenty-four years. *Preface.*

2. ISAIAH. A | Paraphrase | on | Eight Chapters | of the | Prophet Isaiah: | Wherein it is attempted to express the Sense of the | Prophet, in proper English Style. | Whoso readeth, let him understand. | Printed at Worcester, Massachusetts, | by Isaiah Thomas, | and Sold at the Worcester Bookstore. | 1795. | (L.; Am. Antiq. Soc.)   8.

Mock Title: Paraphrase | on | Eight Chapters | of | Isaiah. | 1 f.; verso, blank; Title, 1 f.; verso, blank; Explanation of the Terms and Phrases used by the Prophet, pp: 5-10; Text: pp. 11-41; sigs., including both Titles, A to F¹. The chapters paraphrased are 41-48.

1. Das Neue | Testament | unfers | HErrn und Heylandes | JEfu Chrifti, | nach der Deutfchen Ueberfetzung | D. Martin Luthers. | Mit Kurzem | Inhalt eines jeden Capitels, | und | volftändiger Anweifung gleicher Schriftftellen. | Wie auch | aller Sonn=und Feft= tägigen | Evangelien und Epifteln. | Zweyte Auflage. | German= taun: | Gedruckt bey Michael Billmeyer, 1795. | (L.)   12.

Title, 1 f.; verso, blank; Verzeichnitz der Bücher, &c., 1 p. sig. A²; verso, blank; Text: pp. 5-537; Anweisung, &c., 5 pp. not numbered; sigs. A³ to verso of L⁷, in 8ˢ; text in double columns.

1796.

1. THE | HOLY BIBLE, | Containing the | Old and New Testaments, | Translated out of the | Original Tongues | and | With the Former Translations | Diligently Compared and Revised. | And the | Apocrypha: |·With | Marginal References. | Philadelphia: | Printed for Berriman & Co. by Jacob R. Berriman. | M.DCC.XCVI. | (L.)   fol.

Title, 1 f. ; verso, blank; Names and Order of Books, 1 p.; verso, blank; Text: Gen. to Mal., sigs.· B to recto of 6E^1; verso, blank; Apocrypha, sigs. 6E^2 to recto of 7I^2; verso, blank; The | New Testament | of our | Lord and Saviour | Jesus Christ, | translated out of the | Original Greek: | And | *With the former Translations diligently Compared and Revised:* | With | Marginal References. | Philadelphia: | Printed for Berriman & Co. By Jacob R. Berriman. | MDCCXCVI. | 1 p.; verso, blank; Text: Mat. to Rev. 7K^2 to recto of 8Z^2; verso, blank; Index, 11½ pp.¦ Tables of Time, Measure, Coins, &c., 2 pp.; Tables of Offices and Kindred, ⅔ p.; List of Subscribers, 2 pp., making 8 ff.; sigs 9A to verso of 9D^2; all in 2^s.

The following is a List of Engravings:

1. Front., Adam and Eve in Paradise; 2. Map of the Garden of Eden; 3. Parting of Lot and Abraham; 4. Hagar in the Wilderness; 5. The Egyptian Midwives drowning the Male Children of the Hebrews; 6. Map of The Holy Land; 7. Gideon's Sacrifice; 8. Sampson slaying the Philistines; 9. Delilah cutting off Sampson's hair; 10. The Triumph of David; 11. David presenting Uriah with the letter to Joab; 12. Nathan rebuking David; 13. Elias carried up to Heaven; 14. The Temple of Solomon; 15. Daniel in the Lions' Den; 16. Judas Maccabeus defeats the Samarian Army; 17. He betrayed him with a Kiss; 18. Paul presiding at Athens. No. 1, was engraved by F. Shallus, and has on it: Philadelphia Published by Berriman & Co. 1796. Nos. 2, 6, 14, were engraved by A. Anderson; 4, 5, 7, 9, 15, by C. Tiebout, N. Y.; 8, 17 and 18, by Rollinson, N. Y.; 10 and 16, by A. Doolittle, New Haven. The designs of 7, 8, 13, 14 and 16, are copied exactly from those of Thomas's edition of the Bible, but the Ornaments are very different; that of 15 also, but in counter proof, the Ornaments being likewise entirely different.

2. HOLY BIBLE: and the Apocrypha, with Marginal References. Philadelphia: Printed for Berriman and Co., by Jacob R. Berriman. n. d.   (L.)   fol.

The Collation of this volume agrees with that preceding, but there are no plates. The titles of both copies are essentially different. In the first, the words " Holy - Bible," are in ornamented capitals; in the second, in plain caps.; "Old and New Testaments" in Roman in the first; in the second, in Black letter; the title to the New Testament has been also reprinted. The type used in it is smaller and very different, and the words: " *With the Former Translations* | Diligently Compared and Revised." | are now in two lines, the first only being in Italics. The Imprint as on the O. T. title.

3. THE | HOLY BIBLE | Abridged: | or, the | History | of the Old and New Testament. | Illustrated with Notes, and adorned | with Cuts, | For the Use of Childrens. | *Suffer little children to come unto me, and | forbid them not.* LUKE, xviii, 16. | The Second WORCESTER Edition. | Worcester, (Massachusetts) | From the Press of | Thomas, Son & Thomas, | and sold at their Bookstore. | MDCCXCVI. | (B.) 32.

Pp. 171, in 8ˢ ; BOOKS *for the Instruction and Amusement of Children, which will make them wise and happy, printed and Sold by* THOMAS, SON *and* THOMAS, Worcester. 3 pp. Frontispiece: Adam and Eve tempted, engraved on wood; with a number of other woodcuts printed with the text.

1. THE FOUR GOSPELS, translated from the Greek, with preliminary Dissertations, and Notes Critical and Explanatory. By George Campbell, D. D., F. R. S. Philadelphia: Thomas Dobson. 1796. (Rev. Dr. Jenks, Boston.) 4.

2. First American Edition. | EXPOSITORY NOTES, | with | Practical Observations | on the | New Testament | of our | Lord and Savior | Jesus-Christ | where-in | The Sacred Text is at Large Recited, the Sense Explained and the Instructive Example | of the Blessed Jesus, and his Holy Apostles, to our Imitation Recommended. | The whole Designed to Encourage the Reading of the Scriptures in Private Families, | and to Render the Daily Perusal of them Profitable and Delightful. (A double rule across the page.) By William Burkitt, M. A. | Late vicar and lecturer of Dedham, in Essex. | (Another double rule across the page.) From the Twentieth European edition carefully corrected. | (A black line across the page.) | New-York: | Printed by T. Dunning and W. W. Hyer, No. 21, Gold Street. | = | 1796. | (Mrs. Ferris, Miami.) fol.

3. EXPOSITORY NOTES, with Practical Observations on the New Testament of our Lord and Saviour Jesus Christ &c. By William Burkitt M. A. 1st American from the 20th European Edition. Philadelphia: Printed by William W.

Woodward, *Chesnut Street*, No. 16. *Franklin's Head.*
1796. (Seminary of St. Sulpice, Balt.; L.) fol.

<small>This copy of Burkitt's Notes agrees entirely with the preceding, except in the Imprint on the Title page. It consists of 2 ff. and 631 pp.</small>

1797.

1. THE | HOLY BIBLE, | containing the | Old and New Testaments: | Translated out of the | 𝕺riginal 𝕿ongues, | and | with the former Translations | diligently Compared and Revised, | by the | Special Command of King James I, of *England.* | A text of Hebrew, Gen. ii:7. | 𝖀nited 𝕾tates of 𝕮olumbia. | Printed at Worcester, Massachusetts, | By Isaiah Thomas. | Sold by him in Worcester, by Wholesale, Bound or in Sheets. | Sold also by said Thomas and Andrews in Boston, and by the | Booksellers in the United States of Columbia. | 1797. | (Am. Antiq. Soc.; G. L.) 12.

<small>Title (within rules), 1 f.; verso, blank; Advertisement, To Christians of every denomination; To the Publick, 2 pp.; Names and Order of Books, at foot of 2d p.; Text: Gen. to Mal. (not paged), sigs. A³ to Cc⁹; verso of Cc³, Tables of Measures, Weights, Money and Time; The | New Testament | of our | Lord and Saviour | Jesus Christ. | Translated out of the Original Greek, | And with the former Translations, | diligently Compared and Revised, by the Special Com- | mand of his Majesty King James I, of England. | Two lines of Greek text; Imprint and date as above; 1 p.; verso, blank; Text: Mat. to Rev., Cc⁵ to Kk¹², in 12ª.

When Thomas published his 8vo Bible in 1793, he announced two other editions, viz: "One in Demy Quarto, the other in Duodecimo, or the Common School Bible, to be printed on the beautiful New Types cast particularly for the purpose." The latter was not issued until this year. It is called "Thomas' Standing 12mo Edition," as the types were kept undistributed, or "standing," ready for the press. It contains an error in Acts, 6:3, where the text reads: "whom ye may appoint over this business."</small>

1. THE | NEW TESTAMENT | of our | Lord and Saviour | Jesus Christ, | Newly translated out of the | Original Greek: | And with the former | Translations | Diligently Compared and Revised. | Lancaster, | Printed by J. Bailey and W. & R. Dickson in Kingstreet, 1797. | (E. A.) 12.

<small>Title (within double lines), 1 f.; verso, The Order of the Books; Text: Mat. to Rev., sigs. A² to verso of N⁶, in 12ª.</small>

2. NEW TESTAMENT: New Haven: Published by Edward O'Brien; also Sold wholesale and retail by John Turner, Philadelphia. 1797. (Mr. McA.) 12.

3. ST. MATTHEW. Chapters V, 1–20; VI, 19–34; VII, 1–12; St. Paul's Epistle to the Romans, Chapter XII; To the Colossians, Chapter III; St. James's Epistle, Chapter I. (N. Y. Hist. Soc.)   8.

These portions of the New Testament are contained in a Volume entitled, "Catholic Liturgy, or Forms of Prayer," printed in Boston, by Isaiah Thomas, 1797.

1798.

1. THE | *HOLY BIBLE*, | containing | 𝕿𝖍𝖊 𝕺𝖑𝖉 𝖆𝖓𝖉 𝕹𝖊𝖜 𝕿𝖊𝖘𝖙𝖆𝖒𝖊𝖓𝖙𝖘: | Together with the | Apocrypha; | Translated out of the | Original Tongues: | And with the Former Translations, | 𝕯𝖎𝖑𝖎𝖌𝖊𝖓𝖙𝖑𝖞 𝕮𝖔𝖒𝖕𝖆𝖗𝖊𝖉 𝖆𝖓𝖉 𝕽𝖊𝖛𝖎𝖘𝖊𝖉. | Vignette: Holy Bible open, surrounded by rays of Light, encircled with 15 stars and supported by the American Eagle. 𝕻𝖍𝖎𝖑𝖆𝖉𝖊𝖑𝖕𝖍𝖎𝖆: | Printed for John Thompson & Abraham Small, | [from the Hot-press of John Thompson.] | M.DCC.XCVIII. | (L.; G. L.)   fol.

Title, 1 f.; verso, blank; The Names and Order of the Books, 1 p.; verso, blank; Text: Gen. to the end of Psalms (not paged), sigs. B. to verso of 7 N¹, in 2ˢ; Title and Imprint (as above) repeated with the addition of "Volume II," beneath the Vignette; 1 p.; verso, blank; Text: Prov. to Mal. sigs. 7 N² to recto of 10 F¹; verso, blank; in 2ˢ; Apocrypha, sigs. A to recto of Ll²; verso, blank; then 2 blank ff.; 𝕿𝖍𝖊 𝕹𝖊𝖜 𝕿𝖊𝖘𝖙𝖆𝖒𝖊𝖓𝖙 | of our | Lord and Saviour | Jesus Christ, | Translated out of | The Original Greek: | and with the | former Translations, | 𝕯𝖎𝖑𝖎𝖌𝖊𝖓𝖙𝖑𝖞 𝕮𝖔𝖒𝖕𝖆𝖗𝖊𝖉 𝖆𝖓𝖉 𝕽𝖊𝖛𝖎𝖘𝖊𝖉. | (Vignette as in first title.) 𝕻𝖍𝖎𝖑𝖆𝖉𝖊𝖑𝖕𝖍𝖎𝖆, | Printed for John Thompson & Abraham Small, ⊦[from the Hot-press of John Thompson.] | M.DCC.XCVIII. | 1 p.; verso, blank; Text: Mat. to Rev. sigs. A to verso of 3 Q²; Index, 9 pp.; Table of Scripture Measures, Weights, Coins; Tables of Offices; of Time; of Kindred, 3 pp. sigs. 3 R to verso of 3 T²; sigs. in 2ˢ.

This is the first hot-pressed edition of the Bible printed in America; it was issued originally in 40 numbers, commencing June, 1796, at half a dollar a number. Hence the division into volumes is altogether arbitrary. The text is from the Cambridge ed. published by John Baskerville, and is without notes of any kind. There are brief headings to each chapter The work is accompanied by a Frontispiece, engraved by Lawson, at foot of which are the words, *Published by J. Thompson and Ab*ᵐ. *Small for the Hot-pressed Bible. Philadelphia, Nov*ʳ *1798*. The Apocrypha is entirely in Italics. Some copies have 2 pp. of Subscribers' Names at the end.

2. HOLY BIBLE: 𝖀𝖓𝖎𝖙𝖊𝖉 𝕾𝖙𝖆𝖙𝖊𝖘 𝖔𝖋 𝕮𝖔𝖑𝖚𝖒𝖇𝖎𝖆. Printed at Worcester, Massachusetts, By Isaiah Thomas. Sold by him in Worcester, by Wholesale, Bound, or in Sheets. Sold also by said Thomas and Andrews in Boston, and by the

Booksellers in the United States of Columbia. 1798.
(Am. Antiq. Soc.; L.; B.; G. L.)   12.

<small>This is Thomas's "standing" Edition of 1797, (q. v.) with new date to title pages only. The error in Acts 6:3, is continued.</small>

1. NEW TESTAMENT | of our | Lord and Saviour, | Jesus Christ: | Translated from the Greek. | *Appointed to be read by Children.* | Hartford: | Printed by John Babcock. | 1798. | (Conn. Hist. Soc.)   24.

<small>Pp. 69. This is an ill-written paraphrase or narrative, adhering not much to Biblical phraseology. It is illustrated by coarse wood-cuts, and has a few Hymns and an advertisement of the printer at the end.</small>

2. BURKITT'S EXPOSITORY NOTES on the New Testament. New Haven: Tiebout and O'Brien. circ. 1798.   4.
<small>Not seen.</small>

1799.

1. HOLY BIBLE. **United States of Columbia.** Printed at Worcester, Massachusetts, By Isaiah Thomas. Sold by him in Worcester, by Wholesale, Bound, or in Sheets. Sold also by said Thomas and Andrews in Boston, and by the Booksellers in the United States of Columbia. 1799. (L.; Am. Antiq. Soc.)   12.

<small>Thomas's "standing" Edition of 1797 (q. v.), with a new title page. The error in Acts 6:3, is continued.</small>

1. NEW TESTAMENT; Philadelphia: Printed by Charles Cist, No. 104, North Second Street, near Race Street. M.DCC.XCIX. | (L.)   12.
<small>Not paged; sigs. A to U⁶ in 6s; 1 Tim. 4:16, "thy doctrine."</small>

2. THE | FOUR GOSPELS, | Translated from the Greek. | With | Preliminary Dissertations, | and | Notes Critical and Explanatory. | By George Campbell, D. D., F. R. S. Edinburgh; | Principal of Marischal College, Aberdeen. | ΜΟΝΗ ΘΥΤΕΟΝ ΤΗ ΑΛΗΘΕΙΑ. | Philadelphia: | Printed by A. Bartram. | 1799. | (N. Y. State Lib.)   4.

<small>Title, 1 f.; verso, blank; Ded. pp. (iii not marked) iv; Contents, pp. ϛ-viii; these 4 ff. are without any sig. mark; Pref., pp. i-xvi; sigs. A, B in 4s; Pre-</small>

liminary Dissertations, pp. 1-260; sigs. C to Mm²; Pref. to Matthew's Gospel, pp. 261-276; then 275, 276, 277; verso of 277, blank; Contents, pp. 279-282; sigs. Nn to Pp, all in 4ˢ; Gosp. of Mat., pp. 285-333; verso of 333, blank; (p. 295 is numbered 195) sigs. Qq to 3 C, then 4 D to recto of 4 E¹, all in 2ˢ except the last sig.; Pref. to Mark's Gospel, pp. 335-340; sig. 4 E² to 4 E⁴; Contents, pp. 341, 342; Gosp. of Mark, pp. 343, 373; verso of 373, blank; sigs. 4 F. to 4 O¹ in 2ˢ; Pref. to Luke's Gosp., pp. 375-383; 384 blank; Contents, 385-388; sigs. 4 O² to 4 P in 4ˢ; Gosp. of Luke, pp. 389-440; sigs. 4 Q to 5 E in 2ˢ; Pref. to John's Gosp., pp. 441-446; Contents, pp. 447-450; Gospel of John, pp. 451-488; sigs. 5 F to 5 L, then M to Q, 5 R, all in 2ˢ; Notes Critical and Explanatory (mock title), 1 p.; verso, Advertisement; Notes, pp. 3-196; sigs. A to E in 4ˢ, F to Xx in 2ˢ; Index of Texts, Index of Greek words and Phrases (not paged), Yy to 3 B in 2ˢ.

Thomas Dobson of Philadelphia, printed an edition of Campbell's Gospels (*supra*, p. 52). The Title page of this volume is inserted.

2. Die | Geschichte | von der | Martenwoche, Auferstehung | und | Himmelfahrt | unsers | Herrn und Heilandes | Jesu Christi. | Uebersetzt in die Aruwackische Sprache, | und erklärend umschrieben. | Philadelphia: | Gedruckt bey Carl Cist, 1799. | (B.) 8.

1 leaf; recto, blank; verso, Title, as above; Indian Title: Wadaijahun | Wuussada-goanti | Wappussida-goanti | baddia | JESUS CHRISTUS | Amonaigaddunnua, heikann, akkarraddi gid- | dunnia baddia, waijàlukkùduwa, ùssondàgan, | laggùnnegunnua hitti ullugga waria ku, wu- | wussá-wa, laggujunnua baddia aijùmuniru uk- | kunna munta adiabù, duhu garda: bibiti gunnu | Evangelistinu, nari hiddia muttu MATTHÆUS, | MARCUS, LUCAS, JOHANNES, matti aïbussia | guba Wamun abbullidin, | naddikin ullukkudi | ròn, Jesus umattinni hinna guba je. | Philadelphia mùn 1799. | Assabbadahùgan duhu gárda hiddia muttu wijua uk- | kunna: Ein Tausend, Sieben Hundert, und Neun | und Neunzig wijua tabbugoawa, Wadaijabùn | Wappussida goanti Jesus Christus elontin apaddi gid- | din benna guba dannuhu hidda. | 1 p.; verso, blank; Text: pp. 1-213; sigs. A to recto of Dd³ in 4ˢ; a blank leaf completes the last sig.

This is a History of the Passion, Resurrection and Ascension of the Savior, translated into the language of the Arawaks (a tribe of Indians in Guiana), by the Rev. Johannes Jacob Gottlob Fischer, a Missionary to those parts.

1800.

1. H KAINH | ΔΙΑΘΗΚΗ. | Novum | Testamentum. | Juxta Exemplar Joannis Millii ac- | curatissime impressum. | (A figure in printer's flowers.) Editio prima Americana. | Wigorniæ, Massachusettensi: | Excudebat Isaias Thomas, Jun. | Singulatim et Numerose eo vendita Officinæ suæ. | April—1800. | (L.; B.; G. L.) 12.

Title, 1 f.; verso, blank; A Chronological Table of the Books of the New Testament (in English), signed, Caleb Alexander, 1 p.; verso, blank; Text: pp. 5-478, followed

by a list of Books printed and sold by Isaiah Thomas, Jun., 1 p.; verso, Advertisement of said Thomas, dated Worcester, December 25, 1802. Sigs. A to Rr⁶ in 6ˢ .
This is the *first* edition of the New Testament printed in Greek in this country.

1801.

1. THE | HOLY BIBLE | containing | 𝕮𝖍𝖊 𝕺𝖑𝖉 𝖆𝖓𝖉 𝕹𝖊𝖜 𝕿𝖊𝖘𝖙𝖆-
𝖒𝖊𝖓𝖙𝖘, | with the | Apocrypha: | Translated out of the |
Original Tongues, | and with the | former Translations |
diligently Compared and Revised. | Correctly copied from
Collins's Quarto Edition. | (Wood-cut of Adam and Eve
in Paradise.) New-York: | Printed for William Durell,
Bookseller, No. 106, Maiden Lane. | By George F. Hop-
kins, at Washington's-Head. | 1801. | (L.; B.)   fol.

Title, 1 f.; verso, blank; To the Reader (Dr. Witherspoon's Preface), 1 p.; Names and Order of the Books; Account of Dates of writing the Books of the N. Test., 1 p.; Text: Gen. to Mal., pp. [5–319, then 318,] [319, 320]–[701; sigs. A³ to 4 Q⁴ in 4ˢ; Apocrypha, pp. [703–868]: sigs. 4 R to 5 N³ in 4ˢ; The New | Testament | of our | Lord and Saviour | Jesus Christ, | Translated out of the | Original Greek: | And with the | Former Translations | Diligently Compared and Revised. | Correctly copied from Collins's Quarto Bible. | New York: | Printed for William Durell, Bookseller, No. 106, Maiden Lane. | 1801. [1 p.; verso, blank; Text: Mat. to Rev., pp. [3–118] ; sigs. A to Ff in 2ˢ; then pp. [119, 120], sig. Gg, 1 f.; pp. [121–136], sigs. Aa, Bb, in 4ˢ; pp. [137, 138], [139, 140], sigs. Cc and Cc²; pp. [141–212], sigs. Dd to Mm, in 4ˢ. (Sigs. Gg and Cc are in much smaller type than the other parts of the text.)

The following are the plates in this volume, and the Engravers' names:
1. Adam and Eve, *Scoles*, sc.; 2. Moses on Mount Sinai, *J. J.*, sc.; 3. Aaron the High Priest; 4. Balek and the Princes of Moab; 5. David and Goliah; 6. Naaman the Syrian; all by *Scoles ;* 7. Job in deep distress (no Engraver's name); 8. David at his early devotion, *Scoles ;* 9. Jonah sitting under his gourd, *Anderson ;* 10. The Kingdom of Christ, Is. 2:1–9, *Scoles ;* 11. The Wise Men worshipping the Infant ; 12. Christ rebuking the Pharisees; 13. Stephen before the Council, *Gilbert Fox ;* 14. St. John in the Island of Patmos, *J. J.*; 15. The Church in distress, *Scoles.* The plates are all copied from Heptinstall's Imperial 4to edition, 1794, 1795.

The Old Testament and Apocrypha were published in 14 parts; the New Testament probably in 4: but there is no indication of any division. A misprint occurs in *Acts,* 10:26: "Saying stand up," for, "saying, Stand up:"

2. HOLY BIBLE: Philadelphia: Printed for Mathew Carey, No.
118 Market Street. October 20, 1801.   4.

Title (wanting); Preface, 2 ff.; Subscribers' Names, 2 ff.; Text: Gen. to Mal. not paged, sigs. B to recto of 4F⁴; on verso, This Bible is the Property of   (within an ornamental border, surmounted by two vases); Apocrypha (in smaller type), not paged, sigs. A, B, then [C] to verso of [R]³ ; The | New Testament | of our |

Lord and Saviour | Jesus Christ, | Translated out of the | Original Greek ; | And with
the | former Translations | diligently compared and revised. | By the Special Com-
mand of King James I, of England. | 𝔓𝔥𝔦𝔩𝔞𝔡𝔢𝔩𝔭𝔥𝔦𝔞 : | Printed for Mathew Carey, No.
118, Market Street. | October 20, 1801. | 1 p. ; verso, blank ; Family Record, 2 ff. ;
Mat. to Rev., sigs. 4G to recto of 5G^2 ; at the end of the text of the New Testament,
A wood cut representing a stunted tree, and in the background, a castellated building
on the margin of a river ; verso, blank ; Index, sigs. [*aaa*], [*bbb*]^4 ; remainder of the
volume wanting. All the sigs. are in 4^s except 5G.

The following is a list of the Engravings in this volume and of the Engravers'
names :

1. Abel offering Sacrifice..................................Engraved by *C. Tiebout.*
2. Judgment of Solomon..*Tanner.*
3. David playing on the Harp..*C. Tiebout.*
4. Shepherds worshipping the Infant.....................*C. Tiebout.* 1800.
5. The Master of the Vineyard chiding the dissatisfied Laborer............*Tanner.*
6. The Resurrection..*C. Tiebout.*
7. The Good Samaritan, (Etched by James Akin)......................*C. Tiebout.*
8. The Woman of Samaria...*B. Tanner.*
9. He that is without Sin among you, let him first cast a Stone at her........*Tanner.*

Each of the plates has at foot ; "Phil^a (or Philadelphia), Published by M. Carey,
No. 118, Market St.," except Nos. 2, 5 and 9, which have simply, "Published by M.
Carey," and 7 and 8, which have no imprint.

The following errors occur in this volume :

Exodus	12 : 22, and on the two	*for*	and the two
	23, and the two		and on the two
	37, Ramses		Rameses
Deut.	9 : 2, of Anakims		of the Anakims
	34 : at top, Chap. XXXIV		Deuteronomy.
2 Sam.	21 : at top, pnt to death		put to death
1 Kings	1 : 26, 32, } Jehoida		Jehoiada
	8 : 59, cause of		cause of
2 Kings (note)	3 : 24, it even in		in it even
1 Chron.	1 : 21, Ual		Uzal
	6 : 54, of the		of the
2 Chron.	3 : 2, year of		year of
	4 : 6, offering		offering
(note)	5 : 11, found		found
(note)	22 : 10, Kngs		Kings
Job	12 : 18, gir deth thei		girdeth their
(note)	37 : 22, Cold		Gold
Psalm (note)	7 : 11, righteons		righteous
(note)	84 : 10, threshold		threshold
Isaiah	50 : 2, for thirst		for thirst
	64 : at top, CHRST		CHRIST
Jerem.	2 : 12, horrb ly		horribly
1 Esdras	2 : 16, Beltethmus		Beeltethmus
Judith	2 : 19, forth		forth

—1801.]   AMERICAN BIBLES.   59

    Baruch   4: 1, fore ver   for ever
    Susan (note)   54, lentish tree   lentisk tree
    1 Mac. top at 2:   instructetb   instructeth

    The first title to this volume is wanting in the copy examined, but is supposed to correspond with the following:

3. THE | HOLY BIBLE, | containing the | *Old and New Testaments:* | together with the | Apocrypha: | 𝕿𝖗𝖆𝖓𝖘𝖑𝖆𝖙𝖊𝖉 𝖔𝖚𝖙 𝖔𝖋 𝖙𝖍𝖊 𝕺𝖗𝖎𝖌𝖎𝖓𝖆𝖑 𝕿𝖔𝖓𝖌𝖚𝖊𝖘, | and | with the former Translations diligently compared and revised, | *By the Special Command of* King James I, *of* England. | With | marginal notes and references. | To which are added, | An Index; | An Alphabetical Table | of all the Names in the Old and New Testaments, with their Significations; | and | Tables of Scripture Weights, Measures, and Coins. | Embellished with a | Map of Palestine, and nine Historical Engravings. | Philadelphia: | Printed for Mathew Carey, No. 118 Market Street, | By Joseph Charless. | October 20, 1801. | (L.)   4.

    Title, 1 f.; verso, Names and Order of all the Books; Subscribers' Names, 2 ff.; Preface, 2 ff.; These 4 ff. are marked A. The subsequent matter then corresponds with that of the volume immediately preceding, until we reach the End of the New Testament. Here the wood cut is removed, and its place supplied by a table of "ERRATA," enumerating the several errors found in the preceding copy, except those at the top of Deut. XXXIV. and of 2 Sam. XXI, but with an additional one in John 6:31, "Isw ritten" for, "is written ;" A Family Record, 1 p. occupies the blank in the preceding edition, on verso of 5G^2; Index, sigs. [*aaa*] to [*ddd*]^1, 12 ff.; Tables of Offices; of Scripture Measures, [*ddd*]^1 to verso of [*ddd*]^2, 2 ff.; Alphabetical Table, [*ddd*]^3 to verso of [*eee*]^2, 4 ff.; on foot of the verso, Table of Time; Chronological Catalogue of the Apostles, 3 pp. [*eee*]^3 to recto of [*eee*]^4; on verso of [*eee*]^4, Chronological Index of Years and Times, 2 ff.; Cowper's Portrait of an Apostolic Preacher; Table of Kindred; Clergyman's Address to Married Persons; The Old and New Testament dissected; Judea, Palestine & the Holy Land, sigs. [*fff*] to [*fff*]^2, 2 ff.; two blank leaves complete the sig.; all in 4^s. The Engravings are the same as those last enumerated, with the addition of "Map of Palestine."

4. THE | HOLY BIBLE, | containing | the Old and New Testaments: | Translated out of the | Original Tongues; | and with the | former Translations | diligently compared and revised. | New York: | Printed by M. L. & W. A. Davis, | For Gaine & Ten Eyck, S. Campbell, John Reid, John Broome & Son, E. Duyckinck, | T. & J. Swords, T. S. Arden, P. A. Mesier, S. Stevens, and T. B. Jansen & Co. | 1801. | (G. L.)   4.

60 AMERICAN BIBLES. [1801—

Title, 1 f.; verso, blank; Names and Order of the Books of the Old and New Testaments. 1 p.; verso, blank; Text: Gen. to Mal. not paged, sigs. A³ to verso of 4H²; Apocrypha, 4H³ to verso of 5C¹; The | New Testament | of our | Lord and Saviour | Jesus Christ, | translated out of the | Original Greek; | and with | the former Translations | diligently compared and revised. | 𝔑𝔢𝔴 𝔜𝔬𝔯𝔨: | Printed by M. L. & W. A. Davis, | For Gaine & Ten Eyck, S. Campbell, John Reid, John Broome & Son, E. Duyckinck, T. & J. Swords, | T. S. Arden, P. A. Mesier, S. Stephens, and T. B. Jansen & Co. | 1801. | 1 p.; verso, blank; Text: Mat. to Rev., 5C³ to verso of 6D²; Index, 6D³ to verso of 6F³, one blank leaf completing the sig., all which are in 4ˢ.
This copy contains the Apocrypha, though not mentioned in the Title page.

5. HOLY BIBLE: Printed at Boston, Massachusetts, | By I. Thomas and E. T. Andrews. | Sold by them wholesale and retail: Also by I. Thomas in *Worcester;* | Thomas, Andrews & Penniman, *Albany;* Thomas, | Andrews & Butler, Baltimore; and by all the | principal Booksellers in the *United States.* | 1801. | (Am. Antiq. Soc.)   12.

Title, 1 f.; verso, blank; Names and Order of Books, 1 p.; Account of Dates, 1 p. The text is the same as that of the edition, No. 1 of 1797; the types of that "standing" edition having been removed from Worcester to Boston. The error in Acts 6 : 3, is continued.

1. THE | 𝔑𝔢𝔴 𝔗𝔢𝔰𝔱𝔞𝔪𝔢𝔫𝔱 | of | our Lord and Saviour | Jesus Christ, | Translated out of | 𝔗𝔥𝔢 𝔒𝔯𝔦𝔤𝔦𝔫𝔞𝔩 𝔊𝔯𝔢𝔢𝔨 | and with | the Former Translations | diligently Compared and Revised. | Correctly copied from Collins's Quarto Edition. | New York: | Printed for William Durell, Bookseller, No. 106, Maiden Lane. | 1801. | (L.)   fol.

This is the New Test. accompanying Durell's Folio Bible of this year; the title only is reprinted; and this copy has two plates. The misprint in Acts 10 : 26; "Saying stand up," for, "saying, Stand up," is continued.

2. THE NEW | TESTAMENT | of our | Lord and Saviour | Jesus Christ, | Newly translated out of the | Original Greek : | And with the | former Translations | Diligently Compared and Revised. | Appointed to be Read in Churches. | *B. G.* | New-York: | Printed and Sold by Benjamin Gomez, | Book-seller and Stationer, | No. 97, Maiden Lane. | 1801. | (L.)   12.

Title, 1 f.; verso, Order of the Books, &c.; Text: Mat. to Rev., sigs. A² to recto of O¹²; verso, Table of Kindred. The title is within heavy rules; pages not numbered; Headings to Chapters and Columns.
Gomez was a Jew, and supplied the trade with this edition. (*Mr. Bradford.*) It agrees with that published by Hugh Gaine in 1790, errors included.

3. THE NEW | TESTAMENT | of our | Lord and Saviour | Jesus Christ, | newly translated out of the | Original Greek; | and with the former | Translations | diligently compared and revised. | Newbury-port: | Printed and Sold by Parker and Robinson. | n. d.   (B.)   12.

<small>The body of this volume agrees with that printed by Mycall; (No. 2, *supra*, 1791.)</small>

4. NEW TESTAMENT: Philadelphia: Published by Thomas Dobson. 1801.   12.

<small>Not seen; mentioned in *Portfolio*, 4to I, 51.</small>

5. NEW TESTAMENT: Printed at Worcester, Massachusetts, by Isaiah Thomas. Sold by him in Worcester. Sold also by said Thomas and Andrews, at Faust's Statue, No. 45, Newbury Street, Boston; and by said Thomas and Thomas in Walpole, New-Hampshire. 1801.   8.

<small>With Bible of 1802; q. v.</small>

6. THE | NEW AND COMPLETE | LIFE | of our | blessed Lord and Saviour | Jesus Christ, &c. | With the Lives, Acts, and Sufferings | of his | Holy Apostles, Evangelists, Disciples, &c. | and of other eminent and primitive Christians. | By Paul Wright, D. D. | Vicar of Oakley, &c. | Embellished with Engravings. | New York: | Printed by Lazarus Beach: | Published and sold by William Durell, Bookseller, | No. 106 Maiden Lane. | n. d.   (L.)   fol.

<small>Title, 1 f.; verso, blank; Preface, 1 f.; Text: pp. 5–380; sigs. B to 4Y, in 2*. The Engravings are as follow:

1. Frontispiece from Is. 6: 1–9......................................Engraved by *Scoles*.
2. Christ baptized...*Doolittle*, New Haven.
3. Woman of Samaria, (marked No. xxxix).........................*J. Seymour*.
4. Woman healed of a bloody issue, (marked No. xxxvi).
5. Martha, (marked xlii, engraved for Durell's edition of the Bible).....*J. Seymour*.
6. Lazarus and The Rich Man.
7. Tribute money.
8. Judas casting down the money in the Temple..........................*Scoles*.
9. Christ sent back to Pilate.
10. Christ crowned with thorns..*Scoles*.
11. The Crucifixion, (after Rubens; marked xlii.)......................*J. Seymour*.
12. The Ascension, (marked No. 44; engraved for Durell's edition of the Bible)..*Sam'l Hill*, Boston.</small>

This volume was originally published in 16 parts, and Nos. 2, 3, 4, 5, 11 and 12 of the engravings are from Thomas's Bible of 1791, though the references to it on the coppers are entirely obliterated, except from Nos. 5 and 12, where Thomas's name only is erased and Durell's inserted. No. 1 is from Durell's Bible, and No. 2 seems to have been reëngraved. Dr. Wright styles himself in the Preface, Author of the New and Complete Christian's Family Bible, with Notes.

1802.

1. THE | HOLY BIBLE: | containing the | Old and New Testaments: | Together with the | Apocrypha: | *Translated out of the Original Tongues*, | and | with the former Translations diligently compared and revised. | *By the Special Command of King James I. of England.* | With | Marginal Notes and References. | To which are added, | An Index; | An Alphabetical Table | of all the Names in the Old and New Testaments, with their Significations; | Tables of Scripture Weights, Measures and Coins; | John Brown's Concordance, &c. &c. &c. | Embellished with | Six Maps, and Twenty four Historical Engravings. | Philadelphia: | Printed for Mathew Carey, *No.* 118, Market-Street. | October 27th, 1802. | (L.) 4.

Title, 1 f.; verso, blank; Second Title: The | Old Testament, | Translated | out of | the Original Hebrew, | and | *With the Former Translations diligently compared and revised.* | Together with the | Apocrypha. | Done by the | Special Command of his Majesty, King James I. of England. | Philadelphia: | Printed for Mathew Carey, *No.* 118, Market-Street. | October 27th, 1802. | 1 p.; verso, Names and Order of all the Books, 1 p., making one sig. in 2^s; Subscribers' Names, 5 ff.; sigs. *a* to c^1, in 2^s; Text: Gen. to Mal., pp. 1–591; sigs. B to recto of $4F^4$, in 4^s; at foot of p. 591, is: Joseph Charless, | Printer, | Philadelphia. | 1 p. 592, Family Record; Apocrypha (in smaller type), pp. 593–726, sigs. [A] to verso of $[R]^3$, in 4^s; Family Record, 2 ff., the last of which is marked, [g]; The | New Testament | of our | Lord and Saviour | Jesus Christ, | translated | out of the Original Greek; | and | with the former Translations | diligently compared and revised, | By the Special Command of King James I. of England. | Philadelphia: | Printed for Mathew Carey, *No.* 118, Market-Street. | October 27, 1802. | 1 p.; verso, blank, completing $4F^4_s$; Text: Mat. to Rev., pp. 727–913; sigs. 4 G to $5 G^2$; at bottom of p. 913, This Book was purchased | *Anno Domini* | By | ; p. 914, Family Record; Table of Passages, &c., 1 f., 5 H; Index, 12 ff., [*aaa*] to [*ccc*]; Tables of Offices and of Scripture Weights, &c., 2 ff.; Alphabetical Table of Names; Chronological Catalogue; Index of years, from Adam to Christ, 6 ff. [*ddd*] to [*eee*]; Portrait of an Apostolic Preacher, from Cowper; Table of Kindred; Clergyman's address to Married persons; The Old and New Test. dissected, 1 f.; Judea, Palestine or the Holy Land, 1 f.; Concise View of the Evidences of the Christian Religion, by J. Fletcher, 2 ff.; sig. [*fff*], all in 4^s; A | Brief | Concordance | to | The Holy Scriptures | of the | Old and New Testaments, | by which | All, or Most, | of | *The Principal Texts of Scripture* | may be easily found out. | Revised and Corrected. | By John Brown, | *Late Minister of the Gospel at Haddington in Scotland.* | Search the Scriptures, &c. | Philadelphia : | Published by Mathew Carey, No. 118, Market Street. | Thomas S. Manning, Printer. | 1802. | 1 p.; verso, To the Reader; Text, pp. 3-118; sigs. A² to P³; List of the Engravings, 1 p., P⁴.

The following is a list of the Plates which accompany this edition:

No. 1. The Finding of Moses.
2 A. Journeyings of the Children of Israel.
2 B. Adam, Eve, Cain and Abel.
3. Map of Canaan.
4. Hagar and Ismael in the desert.
5. Abraham going to offer up Isaac.
6. Isaac blessing Jacob.
7. The Plague of Hail.
8. The fall of Manna.
9. Map of Palestine.
10. Map of the Assyrian and other Empires.
11. Sampson destroying the Philistines, with the jaw-bone of an Ass.
12. Minor Prophets.
13. Land of Moriah.
14. Adoration of the Infant by the Magi.
15. Flight into Egypt.
16. Massacre of the Innocents.

No. 17. Broad is the way that leadeth to destruction.
18. Christ appeasing the storm.
19.   casting out devils.
20.   curing the lunatic.
21.   presenting the child to his disciples.
22.   laying his hand on the children.
23.   healing the man sick of the palsy.
24.   teaching the doctors in the temple.
25.   restoring the blind man to sight.
26.   betrayed by Judas.
27.   exhibited to the Jews by Pilate.
28.   his body embalmed.
29. (see 2 B, above).
30. Map of the travels of the Apostles.

The error in 2 Kings, 3: 24 (note), of the edition of 1801, is continued in this volume.

2. THE | HOLY BIBLE, | containing the | Old and New Testaments : | Together with the | Apocrypha: | Translated out of the | Original Tongues, | and | with the Former Translations diligently | compared and revised, | by the | special Command of King James I. of England. | Second Worcester Edition. | United States of America. | Printed in Worcester, Massachusetts, | for Isaiah Thomas, | Sold by him in Worcester. Sold also by said Thomas & Andrews, | at *Faust's Statue*, No. 45, Newbury Street, Boston; by Thomas and | Thomas, in Walpole, *Newhampshire;* by Thomas, Andrews and | Butler, in Baltimore, and by Thomas, Andrews & Penni- | man, in Albany, | MDCCCII. | (Am. Antiq. Soc.)   8.

This edition is not an exact reprint of the Thomas 8vo Bible of 1793, though there is considerable correspondence in the Old Testaments of both. The words, "Together with the Apocrypha," follow "The Old Testament" on the title page to the latter, and there is no Imprint at the "End of the Prophets." The New Testament seems to have been originally a separate book, and many variations or modifications are observable in the typographical composition. The Imprint on the title of that division is: Printed at Worcester, Massachusetts, by Isaiah Thomas, Jun. | for Isaiah Thomas. | Sold by him in Worcester. Sold also by said Thomas and Andrews, at Faust's | Statue, No. 45, Newbury Street, Boston; and by said Thomas and Thomas in | Walpole, Newhampshire. | 1801. |

The following Errors are found in this edition:

The last line of 2 Sam. 6:22 is printed: "spok en of, of them shall I behad in honour." 1 Cor. 15:42 reads, "So also is the resurrection of the dead. It is sown in corruption; it is raised in corruption." (S. F. H.)

3. HOLY BIBLE: 𝔚𝔥𝔦𝔱𝔢𝔥𝔞𝔩𝔩: Printed for Wm. Young, Bank Street, *the first house at the right hand from Chesnut Street*, Philadelphia. 1802. (L.) 8.

With the Scotch Psalms in Metre—Philadelphia: Mathew Carey, No. 122 Chesnut Street, 1805. Whitehall is a hamlet in the neighborhood of Philadelphia.

4. HOLY BIBLE: Worcester: Isaiah Thomas. 1802. (L.) 12.

This is another copy of Thomas's "standing" 12mo of 1797, with a new title page.

5. ISAIAH. A Paraphrase on Four Chapters of the Prophet Isaiah: In which it is attempted to express the Sense of the Prophet in proper English style. By the Author of the Paraphrase on the Eight Chapters of Isaiah. Northampton: Printed by William Butler. 1802. (Am. Antiq. Soc.) 8.

The Chapters paraphrased are 49-52.

1. THE NEW | TESTAMENT | of our | Lord and Saviour Jesus Christ, | translated out of the | Original Greek: | And with the | former Translations | diligently compared and revised. | Philadelphia: Printed for | Benjamin Johnson No. 31 High Street, and | Jacob Johnson No. 147 High-Street. | 1802. | (G. L.) 8.

Title (within parallel rules), 1 f.; verso, Order of the Books; Text: Mat. to Rev., not paged, sigs. A^2 to Yy, in 4^s; short headings to chapters and columns; the name of the Books, or Evangelist, is printed at the head of the verso pages, and number of the chapter on the rectos, throughout the gospels; this order is inverted from the beginning of Acts to 1 Cor., vii, viii; in this last instance, the chapter and its number are at the top of both verso and recto pp.; after which, the usual order, observed when printing the running titles in the gospels, is again resumed and continued to the close.

2. NEW TESTAMENT: 𝕬ppointed to be read in 𝕮hurches. | Printed at Worcester, | by Isaiah Thomas, Jun. | Sold Wholesale and Retail, at his Printing Office, and by | the various Booksellers in the United States: | September 1802. | (Am. Antiq. Soc.)   12.

Title (within ornamental rules), 1 f.; verso, Order of Books; Text (not paged), A to Cc; verso of Cc⁶, Table of Kindred; sigs. in 6ˢ.

3. THE | NEW TESTAMENT | of our Lord and Saviour | Jesus Christ, | Translated out of the | Original Greek; | And with the former | Translations | diligently compared and revised. | Appointed to be read in Churches. | Wilmington: (Del.) | Printed and Sold by Peter Brynberg. | 1802. | (L.)   12.

Title, 1 f.; verso, Order of Books; Text, pp. 3-279; sig. A to recto of Z² in 6ˢ; verso of Z², Books printed and sold wholesale and retail by Peter Brynberg, Wilmington, (Del.)

1803.

1. THE | HOLY BIBLE: | containing the | Old and New Testaments: | Together with the | Apocrypha: | *Translated out of the Original Tongues*, | and | with the former Translations diligently compared and revised. | *By the Special Command of King James I. of England.* | With marginal Notes and References. | To which are added, | An Index; | An Alphabetical Table | of all the Names in the Old and New Testaments, with their Significations; | Tables of Scripture Weights, Measures, and Coins; | John Brown's Concordance, &c. &c. &c. | Embellished with Ten Maps, and Twenty Historical Engravings. | Philadelphia: | Printed by John Adams and William Hancock, | for Mathew Carey, *No.* 122, Market-Street. | November 7th, 1803. | 4.

Title, 1 f.; verso, blank; second title: The | Old Testament, | Translated | out of | the Original Hebrew, | and | *with the former Translations diligently compared and revised.* | Together with the | Apocrypha. | Done by the | Special Command of his Majesty King James I. of England. | Philadelphia: | Printed for Mathew Carey, *No.* 122, Market-Street. | November 7th, 1803. | 1 p.; Names and Order of all the Books; Index of Articles annexed to this edition; List of Maps and Engravings, 1 p.; Text: Gen. to Mal., pp. 1-674 (p. 61 being printed 65); sigs. A to verso of UU¹, and in 8g.

(1) to 43 (27, the fig. to DD, is omitted) : Table of Offices, p. [675]; on verso of [675], THIS BIBLE *is the Property of*   , within a square border; Family Rec., pp. [677]-]680], sigs. UU² to UU⁴ ; all in 8ˢ except the last; Apocrypha (in smaller type), pp. 681-831 (p. 682 being printed 632); A Chronological Index of years and times; Analysis of the O. & N. T., p. 832; sigs. 2 X to verso of 3 Q⁴ , and in fig. 43 (*bis*, or error for 45), then 46 to 63 in 4ˢ ; The | New Testament | of our | Lord and Saviour | Jesus Christ, | translated | out of the Original Greek; | and | with the former Translations | diligently compared and revised, | By the Special Command of King James I. of England. | Third Philadelphia Edition. | Philadelphia: | Printed for Mathew Carey, No. 118, Market-Street. | July 25, 1803. | In the left corner at bottom, 64, 1 p.; verso, blank; Text: Mat. to Rev., pp. 835-840; then 839, 842, 843, 842, 843, 846, 847, 846, 849, 850-1046; sig. 3 R (which incl. title) to verso of 4 U³ , and in fig. 64 to 90³ ; in 4ˢ ; Judea, Palestine or the Holy Land, p. [1047], 1048, 4 U⁴ ; Index, pp. 1049-1066; at foot of 1066, Table of Time; Alphabetical Table of Names, pp. 1067-1073; at foot of 1073, Table of Kindred; Fletcher's Concise View, pp. 1074-1076 ; Table of Scripture Measures, Weights and Coins, from foot of p. 1076-1078 ; Table of Passages, pp. 1079, 1080; sigs. 4 X to verso of 5 A⁴ , and in figures 91-94; at foot of 1080, The End. | T. S. Manning, Printer, *No.* 143, *N. Third Street, Philadelphia.* | A Brief Concordance, &c. By John Brown, *Late Minister*, &c. Philadelphia : | Published by Mathew Carey, No. 118, Market-Street. | T. Kirk, Printer. | 1803. | 1 p.; verso, blank; To the Reader, 1 p.; verso, blank; Text, pp. 5-72, sigs. A³ to verso of I⁴ , in 4ˢ ; near the foot of p. 72, End of the Concordance. Below is pasted a slip of printed paper with the following words :

"The Reader is requested with his pen to correct the following ERRATA :

Page.	Chap.	Verso.				
102	26	16	Note	For	*upon him*	read *upon you*
268	3	28	Note		*of them*	*of him*
286	19	6	Note		*bolst*	*bolster*
466	137	7	Note		*made bare*	*make bare*
467	140	11	Note		*man, violence*	*man of violence*
540	3	19	Note		*soon after*	*from after*
576	47	3			And the	At the
594	11	19			them heart	them an heart
758	17	16			fleshy	fleshly
996	1	21			For me	For to me
1052	Col. 1	last line			swor amount,d	sword, amount "

List of Engravings and names of the Engravers :
1. Journeyings of the Children of Israel ....Engraved by *Weston*.
2. Noah building the ark..*Henry W. Weston*.
3. Map of Canaan ....*F. Shallus*.
4. Map of Egypt ....*Jas Poupard*.
5. Map of Places in Books of Moses...................................*F. Shallus*.
6. Dresses of the High Priest & Levites..............................*W. H Jr*.
7. Map of Canaan from the time of Joshua.
8. Map of Purveyorships.. ....*F. Shallus*.
9. Samuel anointing David.
10. Map of Solomon's Dominions..................................... *F. Shallus*.
11. Map of the Assyrian & other Empires............................*Shallus*.

12. Job receiving intelligence of his misfortunes.
13. Job in his prosperity, (Etch'd by *G. Fox*)..................... *W. Harrison, Jun.*
14. Map of Moriah... *Draper.*
15. The Hypocrite taking the mote out of his neighbor's eye.
16. Christ curing the Leper.
17. John the Baptist sending his disciples to Jesus Christ................. *Tiebout.*
18. The Labourers receiving their Hire............................ *W. Harrison, Junr.*
19. The Jews presenting the Coin to Christ.
20. The Last Supper. .... *Tiebout.*
21. The Good Samaritan.
22. The Shepherd carrying the lost sheep...................... *W. Harrison, Junr.*
23. The Prodigal Son received by his father......................... *W. Harrison.*
24. The Miracle at the pool of Bethesda....................................... *Tiebout.*
25. The Woman caught in Adultery.
26. The Jews demanding of Jesus if he were the Messiah................... *Tiebout.*
27. The Resurrection of Lazarus.. *Tiebout.*
28. The Crucifixion.. *W. Harrison, Junr.*
29. Map of the Travels of the Apostles......................... *W. Harrison, Junr.*
30. The Conversion of Cornelius the Centurion............................. *Tanner.*

The engravings are not inserted in the volume in the above order, which is copied from the printed list. Some copies of this edition are without plates.

2. THE | HOLY BIBLE: | containing the | Old and New Testaments: | Together with the | Apocrypha: | *Translated out of the Original Tongues,* | and | with the former Translations diligently compared and revised, | *by the Special Command of King James I. of England.* | With | Marginal Notes and References. | To which are added, | An Index; | an Alphabetical Table | of all the Names in the Old and New Testaments, with their Significations; | Tables of Scripture weights, Measures and Coins. | Philadelphia: | Printed by John Adams, | for Mathew Carey, *No.* 122, Market-Street. | Nov. 9th, 1803. | 4.

Title, 1 f.; verso, blank; second title: The | Old Testament, | translated | out of | the Original Hebrew, | and | *With the former Translations diligently compared and revised.* | Done by the | Special Command of his Majesty King James I. of England. | Fourth Philadelphia Edition. | Philadelphia: | Printed by John Adams, | for Mathew Carey, *No.* 122, Market-Street. | Nov. 9th, 1803. | 1 p.; verso, blank: Text: Gen. to Leviticus 4:23, pp. 1-80; sigs. A. to E, inc., in 8^s; Lev. 4:23 to 16:1, pp. 81-88, *89, *90, *91, *92, sig. F in 6^s; Lev. 16:1 to II Samuel, 9:10, pp. 81 (*bis*)-216, sigs. M to Z_2E in 4^s; II Samuel, 9:11 to 18:33, pp. 217-224, and 2 pp. not numbered; sig. 2 F in 5^s; II Samuel, 19:1 to end of Mal., pp. 225-591; sigs. 2 G to recto of 4 F, in 4^s; verso of p. 591 and the following leaf, Fam. Rec.; Apocrypha, in smaller type, pp. 593-726, sigs. [A] to verso of [R]^3; New Testament, title (as in the preceding edition); Fourth Philadelphia Edition. | Printed from the last Oxford edition. | Philadelphia: | Printed by William Hancock, | for Mathew Carey, No. 122, Market-Street. | M.DCCC.IV. | 1 p.; verso, blank; Text: Mat. to Rev., pp. 727-913; sigs. 4 G to recto of 5 G², in 4ˢ; at the end of the text on p. 913, 𝕿𝖍𝖎𝖘 𝕭𝖔𝖔𝖐 𝖜𝖆𝖘 𝖕𝖚𝖗=𝖈𝖍𝖆𝖘𝖊𝖉, | *Anno Domini* | By   within an oblong ornamented border; verso of p 913, Family Record; Index to Bible (not paged), sigs. [*aaa*] to recto of [*eee*]², in 2ˢ; Alphabetical Table of Names, verso of [*eee*]² to verso of [*ggg*]¹, in 2ˢ; at foot of [*ggg*]¹, Table of Time; Catalogue of the Apostles and their successors, recto of [*ggg*]² to top of [*hhh*]¹, followed by Chronol. Index of Years; on verso of [*hhh*]¹, Cowper's Portrait of an Apostolical Preacher; Table of Kindred; A Clergyman's Address to Married persons; Old and New Test. dissected; Account of Judea, [*hhh*]² to top of [*iii*]¹, followed by Fletcher's Concise View, which is continued to ₫ds of recto of [*iii*]²; at foot, Table of Scripture Weights, Measures and Coins, continued on verso, and concluded on recto of [*kkk*]¹; verso of [*kkk*]¹, Table of Offices, and Table of Passages in O. T. quoted by Christ in the New Test., continued on recto, and concluded on verso of the sig., at bottom of which is, End of the Appendix; Psalms of David in metre (Scotch version), without a title, pp. 1-36; then 33-36 (*bis*), sigs. A to I; then I (*bis*) all in 2ˢ.

This Bible is evidently made up of odd signatures that remained over from other editions, and now connected by reprinting other portions of the text. The first 80 pp. are from the edition of November 7th, 1803; the page is 9⅜ by 6¼ inches, including the catchword but exclusive of the head lines and marginal references, and the columns are divided by double or parallel rules; the next sig., pp. 81–*92, is recomposed; the page is 9 in. in length by 6¼ in width, and the matter which is contained in a little more than 11½ pp. of the ed. of Nov. 7, is made to cover 12 pp., the spacing at the heads of the chapters being in this, wider than in the part preceding it. From p. 81 (*bis*) to 176, agrees exactly with the Carey ed. of 1802; the page is 9⅝ × 6⅞ in.; the columns are separated by *single* rules, and the numerals marking the pages and verses, which are in small pica type in the previous part, are in this changed to type the face of which is long primer on a small pica body. From p. 177-216, the numerals are again small pica, though the size of the page and the single rule between the columns are continued. From p. 217 to the end of sig. 2F, the text is recomposed; the double or parallel rule is reintroduced; the length of the page varies from 9 to 7½ in.; its width is 6¼ in., and the heads of the chapters are " blanked out," so that the matter, which in the ed. of the 7th Nov., fills eight pages, is here spread over ten. The small pica numerals continue from p. 217 as far as p. 297, inc.; from p. 297-308, the smaller numerals are again used, but from 309 to the end of Malachi, they are in small pica. From p. 225 to the end of Mal., the p. is 9¼ by 6⅜ in., and the columns are divided by the single rule.

3. THE | HOLY BIBLE, | containing | the Old and New Testaments: | Translated out of the | Original Tongues; | and | with the | former Translations | diligently Compared and Revised. | New York: | Printed by Sage and Clough, | For S. Campbell, E. Duyckinck, T. & J. Swords, P. A.. Mesier, T. S. Arden, and | McDermot & Thompson. | 1803. | (L.)   4.

—1803.] AMERICAN BIBLES. 69

Title, 1 f.; verso, blank; Names and Order of the Books, 1 p.; verso, blank; Text:
Gen. to Mal. (not paged), sigs. A³ to verso of 4 H²; Apocrypha (in smaller type),
sigs. A to verso of Q²; The | New Testament | of our | Lord and Saviour | Jesus
Christ, | translated | out of the Original Greek, | and | with the former Translations |
diligently Compared and Revised. | New York: | Printed by Sage and Clough, | For
S. Campbell, E. Duyckinck, T. & J. Swords, P. A. Mesier, T. S. Arden and | Sage &
Thompson. | 1803. | 1 p.; verso, blank; Mat. to Rev., 4 I¹ and ² (2 ff.), then 4 K to
verso of 5 K²; Index, A to B. All the signatures are in 4ˢ.

4. The | Holy Bible, | containing the | Old and New Testa-
ments: | Together with the | Apocrypha: | 𝕮𝖗𝖆𝖓𝖘𝖑𝖆𝖙𝖊𝖉 𝖔𝖚𝖙
of the 𝕺𝖗𝖎𝖌𝖎𝖓𝖆𝖑 𝕮𝖔𝖓𝖌𝖚𝖊𝖘, | and | with the former Transla-
tions diligently Compared and Revised, | By the Special
Command of King James I. of England. | With | Mar-
ginal Notes and References. | To which are added, | An
Index; | An Alphabetical Table | of all the Names in the
Old and New Testaments, with their Significations; |
and | Tables of Scripture Weights, Measures, and Coins. |
Also, | Brown's Concordance. | Embellished with a | Map
of Palestine, and Nine Historical Engravings. | 𝕮𝖍𝖆𝖗𝖑𝖊𝖘-
𝖙𝖔𝖜𝖓, (*Massachusetts*,) | Printed by and for Samuel Ethe-
ridge; | and for J. White & Co. Thomas & Andrews;
West & Greenleaf; | E. Larkin; and J. West, Boston. |
1803. | (G. L.)   4.

Title, 1 f.; verso, The Names and Order of all the Books of the O. & N. T.; Etheridge's Preface, dated September 15th, 1803, and Summary History of the Bible, 2
pp., making with 1 blank leaf and frontispiece, sig. A; Text: Gen. to Mal. (not paged),
sigs. B to recto of 4 F⁴; on verso of 4 F⁴, This | Bible | is the Property of |
within a ruled square and a circular wreath; Apocrypha, in smaller type, sigs. A to
verso of R³; below the text, The End of | the | Apocrypha. | within a ruled square
and circular wreath, as above; The | New Testament | of our | Lord and Saviour
Jesus Christ, | translated out of the | Original Greek: | And with | the former Trans-
lations diligently compared | and revised. | By the Special Command of King James I.
of England | S. E. | 𝕮𝖍𝖆𝖗𝖑𝖊𝖘𝖙𝖔𝖜𝖓: (*Massachusetts*.) | Printed and Sold by Samuel
Etheridge. | 1803. | 1 p.; verso, blank; Text, Mat. to Rev., 4 G to recto of 5 G²; at
the end of the text is printed (within a circular wreath), This Edition of the | Bible |
was Published in Charlestown, | by | 𝕾. 𝕰𝖙𝖍𝖊𝖗𝖎𝖉𝖌𝖊. | 1803. | 5 G is completed by 5
pp. of Family Record. An Index, sigs. [aaa] to the top of recto of [ddd]¹; Tables of
Offices; of Scripture measures, &c.; An Alphabetical Table of Names; Table of Time;
Catalogue of the Apostles and their Successors; Index of years from Adam to Christ;
Cowper's Portrait of An Apostolic Preacher; Table of Kindred; A Clergyman's Ad-
dress to Married persons; The Old and New Testament dissected; Judea, Palestine or
the Holy land; sigs. [ddd] to verso of [fff]², all in 4ˢ. A | Brief Concordance | to

the | Holy Scriptures | of the | Old and New Testaments: | By which All, or Most, of the principal Texts of Scripture | may be easily found out. | Revised and Corrected. | By John Brown, | Late Minister of the Gospel at Haddington, in Scotland. | Search the Scriptures, &c. | The Bereans were more noble, &c. | 𝕮𝖍𝖆𝖗𝖑𝖊𝖘𝖙𝖔𝖜𝖓: (*Massachusetts*.) | Printed and Sold by Samuel Etheridge. | 1803. | 1 p.; verso, To the Reader; Text: sigs. A to Z, in 2^s. Beneath the word, Finis: Printing | in its various branches, executed with | neatness and dispatch. | By Samuel Etheridge, | 𝕮𝖍𝖆𝖗𝖑𝖊𝖘𝖙𝖔𝖜𝖓. | in an ornamental square and circle, as already described.

The following are the Engravings, with the names of the Engravers:
1. Cain and Abel offering sacrifice. ....*James Hill*.
2. Judgment of Solomon...*James Hill*.
3. David playing on the Harp. ....*James Hill*.
4. Shepherds adoring the Infant.................................*E. G. Gridley*.
5. The Master of the Vineyard chiding the dissatisfied Laborer...........*Doolittle*.
6. The Resurrection..*James Hill*.
7. The Good Samaritan...*James Hill*.
8. The Woman of Samaria..*James Hill*.
9. The Adultress dismissed by the Savior..........................*James Hill*.
10. Map of Palestine.

Each of these Engravings has at foot: Charlestown: (Massachusetts.) Published by S. Etheridge, except No. 5, which has only the words, Published by S. Etheridge. The Subjects are the same as those of Carey's 4to of 1801, from which this volume seems to have been set up; but the errors in the Carey are corrected except the note to Job, 37:22, which is still misprinted, "Cold."

5. THE | HOLY BIBLE, | containing | The Old and New | Testaments: | Translated out of the | Original Tongues; | and with the former | Translations | diligently compared and revised. | Seventh Philadelphia Edition. | Philadelphia: | Printed for Mathew Carey, | No. 118, High-Street. | Robert Cochran, printer. | 1803. | (L.)   12.

Title, 1 f.; verso, blank; Names and Order of the Books, 1 p.; Account of the Dates or Time of writing the Books of the New Testament, 1 p.; Text: Gen. to Mal. (not paged), sigs. A^3 to Cc^{12}; verso of Cc^{12}, Tables of Kindred and of Time; Title to New Test.: Printed for Mathew Carey, | No. 118, High-Street, | Philadelphia. | 1802. | 1 p.; verso, blank; Text: Mat. to Rev., sigs. Dd^2 to recto of Ll^{12}; verso, Table of Offices. The titles are within ornamental lines.

Mr. Carey purchased the standing types of the Hugh Gaine Bible of 1792, which this edition mainly resembles.

6. HOLY BIBLE: Eighth Philadelphia Edition. Philadelphia: Printed for Mathew Carey, No. 118 High Street. Robert Cochrane, Printer. 1803.   (L.)   12.

Agrees with the preceding, No. 5.

7. HOLY BIBLE: Printed at Boston, Massachusetts, | By I. Thomas and E. T. Andrews. | Sold by them wholesale and retail: | Also by I. Thomas in *Worcester;* Thomas, Andrews & Butler, Baltimore; and by all | the principal Book-Sellers in the *United States.* | 1803. | (L.)   12.

<small>This is Thomas's "Standing" Edition of 1797, with new titles; but each book has a blank head line not in that copy. The error in Acts, 6:3 is continued.</small>

8. THE | SONG OF SONGS | which is by | Solomon. | A new Translation | with | a Commentary and Notes | by T. Williams. | Philadelphia: | Printed by Wm. W. Woodward, | No. 52, South Second, corner of Chesnut Street. | 1803. | (L.; G. L.)   8.

9. ISAIAH. A Paraphrase on Nine Chapters of the Prophet Isaiah. By the Author of the Paraphrase on the Eight Chapters of Isaiah. Northampton: Printed and Sold by William Butler, 1803.   (Am. Antiq. Soc.)   8.

<small>The chapters here paraphrased are 52–60.</small>

10. ISAIAH. A | Paraphrase | on | the six last Chapters | of the | Prophet Isaiah: | *In which it is attempted to express the* Sense *of the* | Prophet, *in proper* English Style. | By the Author of the | Paraphrase, on Eight Chapters of Isaiah, | (lately published.) | Whoso Readeth, let him Understand. | Northampton: | Printed & Sold by William Butler. | 1803. | (Am. Antiq. Soc.)   8.

1. **Das Neue | Testament** | unsers | Herrn und Heilandes | Jesu Christi, | nach der Deutschen Uebersetzung | D. Martin Luthers. | Mit kurzem | Inhalt eines jeden Capitels, | und vollständiger Anweisung gleicher Schriftstellen. | Wie auch | aller Sonn=und Festagigen | Evangelien und Episteln. | Dritte Auflage. | Germantaun, | Gedruckt bey Michael Billmeyer, 1803. | 12.

<small>Title, 1 f.; verso, blank; Verzeichnisz, 1 p.; verso, blank; Text: Mat. to Rev., pp. 5–537; Anweisung, 5 pp., not numbered; sigs. A³ to Q¹⁷, followed by a blank page; sigs. in 8ˢ. Text in double columns, with references under the respective verses. See 2d edition; *Supra*, p. 50.</small>

2. NEW TESTAMENT. Charlestown: Printed and Sold by Samuel Etheridge. 1803.   (G. L.)   12.

1804.

1. THE | HOLY BIBLE: | containing the | Old and New Testaments: | Together with the | Apocrypha: | *Translated out of the Original Tongues*, | and | with the former Translations diligently compared and revised. | *By the Special Command of King James I. of England.* | With | Marginal Notes and references. | To which are added, | An Index; | An Alphabetical Table | of all the Names in the Old and New Testaments, with their Significations; | Tables of Scripture Weights, Measures, and Coins, | John Brown's Concordance, &c. &c. &c. Fourth Philadelphia edition. | Printed from the last Oxford edition, and page for page with that of Isaac Collins. | Embellished with | Ten Maps and Twenty Historical Engravings. | Philadelphia: | Printed by John Adams, | For Mathew Carey, *No.* 122, Market-Street. | July 25th, 1804. | (L.) 4.

Title, 1 f.; verso, blank; The | Old Testament, | translated | out of | the Original Hebrew, | and | *with the former Translations diligently compared and revised.* | Done by the | Special Command of his Majesty King James I. of England. | Fourth Philadelphia edition. | Philadelphia: | Printed by John Adams, | for Mathew Carey, *No.* 122, Market-Street. | July 25th, 1804. | 1 p.; verso, Names and Order of all the Books; Index to the various Articles annexed to this edition; List of Maps and Plates; Text: Gen. to Mal., pp. 1–674; sigs. A to UU^1, and in numbers, 1 to 43, in 8^s; Table of Offices, p. 675; Chronological Index, Analysis of O. & N. Test., p. 676; sig. UU^2; Family Record, pp. 677–680; sig. [VV] in 2^s; Apocrypha, pp. 681–834; then [829] [830] [831] [832] [833] [834]; sigs. 2 X to 3 R; in numbers, 43 (*bis*) to 64, in 4^s; The | New Testament | of our | Lord and Saviour | Jesus Christ, | translated | out of the Original Greek; | and | with the former Translations | diligently compared and revised, | By the Special Command of King James I. of England. | Fourth Philadelphia edition. | Printed from the last Oxford edition. | Philadelphia: | Printed by William Hancock, | for Mathew Carey, No. 122, Market-Street | M.DCCCIV. | marked on the left side, "64;" 1 p.; verso, blank; Text: Mat. to Rev., pp. 835–1046; sigs. (including title page) 3 R *bis* (not marked) to 4 U^3; in numbers, 64 (*bis*) to 90^3; Judea, Palestine, &c., pp. 1047, 1048; Index, pp. 1049–1066; at foot of p. 1066, A Table of Time; An Alphabetical Table, pp. 1067–1073; at foot of p. 1073, A Table of Kindred; Fletcher's Concise View, pp. 1074–1076; Tables of Scripture Measures, pp. 1076–1078; Table of Passages, pp. 1079, 1080; sigs. 4 U^4 to 5 A^4; in numbers, 90^4 to 94; all in 4^s; A | Brief | Concordance | to | The Holy Scriptures | of the | Old and New Testaments, | by which | All, or Most, | of | the principal texts of Scripture | may be easily found out. | By John Brown, | *Late Minister of the Gospel, at Haddington, in Scotland.* | Search the Scriptures, &c. | Revised and Corrected. | Philadelphia: | Published by Mathew Carey, No. 118, Market-Street. | T. Kirk, Printer. | 1804. | 1 p.;

verso, blank; To the Reader, 1 p.; verso, blank; Text, pp. 5-72; sig. (including title and prelim. f.) A to 1, in 4ˢ.

The Maps in this edition are: 1. Journeyings of the Children of Israel; 2. Map of Canaan; 3. Map of Egypt; 4. Map of the Places mentioned in the five books of Moses; 5. Map of Palestine; 6. Map of the Purveyorships; 7. Map of the Assyrian, Median, Persian, and Babylonian Empires; 8. Map of the Dominions of Solomon; 9. The Plan of Jerusalem & Land of Moriah; 10. Travels of the Apostles.

The Historical Engravings and names of the Engravers are:
1. Joseph discovering himself to his brethren........................... *Tiebout*.
2. Samuel preaching repentance to the Jews.
3. Obadiah concealing the Prophets...................................... *Tiebout*.
4. Fourth Vision of Daniel... *Tiebout*.
5. St. Mathew.. *C. Tiebout*.
6. The Magi offering gifts to the Saviour............................... *Tiebout*.
7. John the Baptist preaching in the Wilderness.
8. Christ curing the Centurion's servant........................... *C. Tiebout*.
9. Christ calling the Twelve apostles.
10. The disciples shewing the Temple to our Saviour................ *C. Tiebout*.
11. The punishment of the useless servant.............................. *Tiebout*.
12. Judas treating with the Scribes and Pharisees..................... *Tiebout*.
13. St. Mark.. *C. Tiebout*.
14. Christ healing the Woman who touched his garment............... *C. Tiebout*.
15. St. Luke.. *Tiebout*.
16. The Annunciation... *C. Tiebout*.
17. The cure of the Ten Lepers....................................... *Tiebout*.
18. St. John... *C. Tiebout*.
19. Our Saviour washing the disciples' feet........................... *Tiebout*.
20. The lame man cured by St. Peter............................. *C. Tiebout*.

All these are marked: Engraved for M. Carey's Family bible; some with the year 1804, also.

In 1803, Mr. Carey determined to publish a new edition of the Bible in 4to, and to keep the types "standing." This is one of those "standing" editions.

2. THE HOLY BIBLE, containing the Old and New Testaments according to the authorized versions; with original Notes, practical Observations and copious marginal References. By Thomas Scott, Rector of Aston Sandford, Bucks. Philadelphia: Printed and published by W. Woodward. 1804. 4 vols.   4.

This is the *first* American edition of Scott's Family Bible. It was published by subscription. *Philadelphia Literary Magazine*, II, 319; *N. Y. Am. Rev.*, II, 497, 498.

3. THE | HOLY BIBLE: | containing | the Old and New Testaments; | Translated out of the Original Tongues, | and | with the former Translations, | diligently compared and revised. | In Four Volumes. | Vol. I. | Philadelphia: |

74   AMERICAN BIBLES.   [1804—

Published by Benjamin Johnson, | No. 31, Market Street. | And H. Caritat New York. | Robert Carr, Printer. | 1804. | 8.

Title, 1 f.; verso, blank; Contents, 2 pp.; Text: Gen. to end of Ruth (not paged); sigs. B to recto of 3 N⁴ in 4ˢ; at the foot of the last page: Printed by Robert Carr, | No. 10, Church Alley. | ; Vol. II, Title as above; Philadelphia: | Published by Benjamin Johnson, No. 31, Market-Street, | and Abraham O. Stansbury, New York. Robert Carr, Printer. 1804; 1 f.; verso, blank; Contents, 4 pp.; Text: I Samuel to Psalm CL; sigs. B to verso of 4 A⁴, at foot of which is: Printed by Robert Carr, | No. 10, Church-Street. | ; Vol. III, Title as above; Philadelphia: Published by Benjamin Johnson, | No. 31, Market-Street. Robert Carr, Printer. 1804. | 1 f.; verso, blank; Contents, 3 pp.; Text: Proverbs to Mal.; sigs. A⁴ to verso of 3 M¹, at foot of which is: Printed by Robert Carr, | No. 10, Church-Street. | 3 blank ff. make up the last sig.; The New Testament, &c. Philadelphia: Printed for | Benjamin Johnson No. 31, High-Street, and | Jacob Johnson No. 147, High-Street. | 1802. | 1 f.; verso, The Order of all the Books of the New Testament; Text: Mat. to Rev.; sigs. A² to Yy; all in 4ˢ.

The text in Vols. I, II, III, is in two columns, "leaded," 42 lines long each; the columns being divided by a double line. The last Vol. is not numbered on the title page, which is included within double lines with ornamental corners, but is marked, "Vol. IV." on the back; The columns are divided by a single rule, and are 49 lines long and not leaded. The Old Testament has no headings, except a brief one in small caps, at the beginning of each chapter. The New Testament has italic headings to each column and chapter.

4. THE | HOLY BIBLE: | containing | The Old and New Testaments; | Translated out of the Original Tongues, | and | with the former Translations, | diligently compared and revised. | In Four Volumes. | Vol. I. | Philadelphia: | Published by Benjamin Johnson | No. 31 Market Street. | Robert Carr, Printer. | 1804. | (L.; H.; G. L.; E. A.)   8.

The titles and imprints of the four volumes agree. The matter of Vols. I, II, III, is as described in the copy immediately preceding. Vol. IV: title and imprint as above, 1 p.; verso, blank; Contents, 4 pp.; Text: Mat. to Rev.; sigs. B to recto of 3 M³; 3 M⁴, blank; Family Record, 2 ff. Each Vol. terminates with the printer's address, as described in No. 3, Church *Street* being substituted for Church *Alley* in Vols. II, III and IV. Brief headings to chapters.

5. HOLY BIBLE. · Boston: | Printed for Thomas & Andrews | by J. T. Buckingham. | Sold, wholesale & retail, at their Book Store, No. 45, New- | bury-Street, and by the principal Book | sellers in the United States. | 1804. | (L.; B.) 12.

Apparently the same as Thomas's edition of 1803, with new title pages. The error in Acts 6:3, is continued.

6. Selectæ e Veteri Testamento Historiæ. Philadelphia. 1804.
(Brown Univ.) 12.
See No. 1, 1787.

1. NEW TESTAMENT. Wilmington: Printed and Sold by Bonsal and Niles—also Sold at their Book Store, 192 Market Street, Baltimore. 1804. (L.) 12.
See New Test., No. 3, 1802.

1805.

1. THE | HOLY BIBLE, | translated from the | Latin Vulgat: | Diligently Compared | with the Hebrew, Greek, and other editions | in divers Languages. | The | Old Testament, | first published by | the English College at Doway, A. D. 1609. | And | The New Testament, | first published by | the English College at Rhemes, A. D. 1582. | With | Annotations, References, and an Historical and Chronological Index. | First American, from the Fifth Dublin edition. | Newly revised and corrected according to the Clementin edition of the Scriptures. | Philadelphia : | Published by Mathew Carey, | No. 122, Market-Street. | Oct. 15, M.DCCC.V. | . (Rt. Rev. Bishop McCloskey.) 4.

Title. 1 f. ; verso, blank; Subscribers' Names, 2 pp., forming, with title, one sig. in 2ˢ ; Hist. & Chronol. Index to the Old Test. (within rules), sig. *a**, *b**, 4 ff. in 2ˢ ; on verso of last leaf, The Order of the Books of the O. T., and List of Plates in this Bible. This List is pasted over "The Directions for placing the Plates" mentioned in the edition on the next page. Text: Gen. to 2 Mac., pp. 1–384; then *385, 386*, *387, 388*, 385–568, 573–772 ; sigs. B to D, then [E] to [3 C], then *[3 D]*, [3 D] to [4 C], all in 4ˢ ; then [4 D] in 2ˢ , [4 E] to [5 E] in 4ˢ , and 5 F in 2ˢ ; The | New Testament | of | our Lord and Saviour | Jesus Christ, | translated from the | Latin Vulgat: | Diligently compared with the Original Greek: | and first published by | The English College at Rhemes, A. D 1582. | With | Annotations, References, and an Historical and Chronological Index. | First American, from the Fifth Dublin Edition, | Newly revised and corrected according to the Clementin edition of the Scriptures. | Philadephia : | (*sic*) Published by Mathew Carey. | No. 118, Market-Street. | 1805. | 1 p. ; verso, blank ; Admonition, Letter of Pope Pius the Sixth and A Prayer, 1 p.; Decree of the Council of Trent and Order of the Books of the New Testament, 1 p.; Text: Mat. to Apocal., pp. 1–40, *41–48*, 41–57, verso of 57 marked 70, then 71–214 ; sigs. B to F, then *G*, G to M, all in 4ˢ , then N in 2ˢ (no O), P to 2 E³ ; Hist. & Chronol. Index to New Test., 2 pp., 2 E⁴ ; Table of References, Table of Epist. and Gosp., 2 ff., followed by two blank leaves to complete 2 F in 4ˢ .

76   AMERICAN BIBLES.   [1805—

The plates are:
1. Scheme of the Lives of the Patriarchs.
2. Samuel anointing David..*Tanner.*
3. Judgment of Solomon.
4. The Angel appearing to Elijah.
5. Map of Syria & Asyria.
6. The Shepherds in the Stable with our Saviour (marked, Page 46. *Front.* to N. T.).
7. Land of Moriah..*Bower.*
8. Last Supper...*Tanner.*
9. Our Saviour in the Temple......................................*Tiebout.*
10. Miracle of Bethesda..*Tiebout.*
11. Travels of the Apostles..*Bower.*

2. HOLY BIBLE, translated from the Latin Vulgat: &c. (as in the preceding title). Philadelphia: Published by Mathew Carey, No. 122, Market Street. Oct. 15, M,DCCC,V. (Georgetown Coll.; Sem. St. Sulpice, Balt.; L.)   4.

Title, 1 f.; verso, blank; Subscribers' Names, 2 pp.; Admonition and Prayer, 1 p.; Decree of the Council of Trent, and Order of the Books of the New Test., 1 p., supposed to form, with a blank leaf, sig. A; Text: Gen. to 2 Mac. (as in No. 1); then title to New Testament (also as in No. 1), 1 p.; verso, blank; Approbation, &c., 1 f.; (sig. A in 2ˢ;) Text (as in No. 1); Hist. and Chronol. Index to the Old Test., 4 ff.; sigs. *a**, *b** in 2ˢ; on verso of last leaf, Order of the Books of the Old Test., and Directions for placing the Plates; Index to New Testament, 1 f., 2 E⁴; Table of References, 1 f.; Table of Epistles and Gospels, 1 f.; sig. 2 F in 2ˢ.

The following is a list of the plates accompanying this edition:

1. Map of Palestine (*Front.* to O. T.).
2. The Land of Moriah.
3. The Evangelist St. Mathew.
4. St. John in the Wilderness.
5. Christ healing the Centurion.
6. The Evangelist St. Mark.
7. St. Luke.
8. Shepherds visiting the infant Jesus & his Mother.
9. Jesus cleansing the 10 lepers.
10. The Evangelist St. John.
11. Jesus washing his disciples' feet.
12. Map of the Travels of the Apostles.
13. St. Peter healing the Cripple.

The expression, "First American from the Fifth Dublin edition," meaning only the first American edition of Dr. Troy's Bible (1791), has led many to suppose this the first American Catholic Bible. *Bibliog. Account of Catholic Bibles, &c., printed in the United States.* By J. G. Shea; p. 11. This, however, is an erroneous supposition. See *supra,* p. 34.

3. THE | HOLY BIBLE: | containing the | Old and New Testaments: | Together with the | Apocrypha: | *Translated out of the Original Tongues,* | and | With the former Translations diligently Compared and Revised, | *By the Special Command of King James I. of England.* | With | marginal Notes and References. | To which are added, | An Index; | An Alphabetical Table | of all the Names in the Old and

New Testaments with their Significations; | Tables of Scripture Weights, Measures, and Coins, &c. &c. | Embellished with | Three Maps and Twenty-seven Historical Engravings. | Philadelphia: | Printed and Published | by Mathew Carey, *No.* 122, Market-Street. | May 8th, 1805. | (L.) 4.

Title, 1 f.; verso, blank; The | Old Testament, | translated | out of | The Original Hebrew, | and | *With the former Translations diligently compared and revised.* | Together with the | Apocrypha. | Done by the | Special Command of his Majesty King James I. of England. | Philadelphia: | Printed and published | By Mathew Carey, *No.* 122, Market-Street. | May 8th, 1805. | 1 p.; verso, Names and Order of Books; Index to articles annexed to this Edition. List of Maps & Engravings, 2 pp.; Text: Gen. to Mal., pp. 1–674; sigs. A to UU^1, in numbers 1–43^1, in 8^s; Table of Offices and Conditions of men, p. [675]; Chronol. Index, and Analysis, p. 676, sig. UU^2; Family Record, pp. 677–680; Apocrypha, pp. 681–834; then [829] [830] [831] [832] [833] [834] *bis.*; sigs. 2 X to 3 R^4, in numbers 45 (no number 44) to 64, in 4^s; New Testament: Tenth Philadelphia Edition. Printed from the last Oxford edition. Philadelphia: Printed by Mathew Carey, No. 122, Market-Street. M.DCCCVI. (marked in the left corner, 64) 1 p.; verso, blank; Text: Mat. to Rev., pp. 835–1046; sigs. (3 R^2 *bis*, not marked), to 4 U^3, and in numbers 64–90; Judea, Palestine & the Holy Land, p. [1047], 4 U^4; Index, pp. 1049–1066; 4 X to 4 Z^1; at foot of p. 1066, Table of Time; Alphabetical Table, pp. 1067–1073; 4 Z^2 to 5 A^1; at foot of p. 1073, Table of Kindred; Fletcher's Concise View, pp. 1074–1076; verso of 5 A^1 to verso of 5 A^2; Tables of Scripture measures, weights, &c., pp. 1076–1078; Table of passages, pp. 1079, 1080; 5 A^3 and 5 A^4; the numbers from the close of Rev. to the end are 90^4–94; sigs. all in 4^s.

The Engravings are:
1. The Journeyings of the Children of Israel.
2. The Finding of Moses..*C. Tiebout.*
3. The first family.
4. Canaan..*F. Shallus.*
5. Hagar in the desert.
6. Abraham offering up Isaac.....................................*Jones.*
7. Isaac blessing Jacob..*W. Harrison, Junr.*
8. The Plague of Hail..*W. Harrison, Junr.*
9. The fall of the Manna.
10. Sampson destroying the Philistines.........................*W. Harrison, Junr.*
11. David playing on the Harp....................................*C. Tiebout.*
12. The Minor Prophets.
13. Map of Palestine.
14. Land of Moriah.
15. Adoration by the Wise Men.
16. Flight into Egypt.
17. Massacre of the Innocents....................................*W. Harrison, Junr.*
18. The Broad way to destruction................................*C. Tiebout.*
19. Christ stilling the Storm......................................*Weston.*

20. Christ curing the men possessed of devils (entitled in the list, incorrectly, Christ healing the Leper).
21. Christ curing the lunatic.
22. Christ presenting the Child to his disciples.
23. Christ laying his hand on the Children.
24. The labourers receiving their hire.................................... *Tanner.*
25. Christ healing the man sick of the palsy.
26. Christ teaching the doctors.
27. The Good Samaritan... *C. Tiebout.*
28. The Woman of Samaria....... ....*B. Tanner.*
29. Christ giving Sight to the blind man.
30. Christ presented to the Jews crowned with thorns.

The above plates had already appeared in some of Carey's 4tos. The text, &c., is from the "standing" types.

4. THE | HOLY BIBLE: | containing the | Old and New Testaments: | together with the | Apocrypha: | *Translated out of the Original Tongues,* | and | With the former Translations diligently compared and revised. | *By the Special Command of King James I. of England.* | With | Marginal Notes and References. | To which are added, | An Index; | An Alphabetical Table | of all the Names in the Old and New Testaments, with their Significations; | Tables of Scripture Weights, Measures, and Coins, &c. &c. | Embellished with | A Map of Palestine, and a Map of the Travels of the Apostles. | Philadelphia: | Printed and published | By Mathew Carey, *No.* 122, Market-Street. | August 19th, 1805. | (L.)   4.

Title, 1 f. (in the left corner, "No. 6."); verso, blank; title to Old Testament, same as in No. 3, except date, which is August 19th, 1805, 1 p.; verso, Names and Order of books; Index of articles annexed. The pagination signatures, and articles annexed, are the same as the preceding edition, with the following exceptions: Each sig. of the O. T. and Apocrypha, is marked "7" in addition to its appropriate number and letter. The New Testament title has: Seventh Philadelphia edition, printed from the last Oxford edition. Philadelphia, &c. (as above), M.DCCCV. And the Volume contains, Brown's Concordance: New-York: | Published by William Durell, Bookseller, No. 106, Maiden-Lane, | T. Kirk, Printer. | 1803.' | , though not announced on the title.

The Finding of Moses forms a frontispiece to this Vol., but it is not mentioned on the title; and instead of the Map of the Travels of the Apostles, The Journeyings of the Children of Israel, is given.

5. BIBLIA, | Das ist: | Die ganze Göttliche | **Heilige Schrift** | Alten und Neuen | Testaments, | nach der Deutschen Uebersetzung | D. Martin Luthers: | Mit jedes Capitels kurzen Summarien, auch |

—1805.] AMERICAN BIBLES. 79

beygefügten vielen und richtigen Parallelen: | Nebst einem Anhang | Des dritten und vierten Buchs Esrä, | und des dritten Buchs der Maccabäer. | Erste Auflage. | Reading, | Gedruckt und zu finden bey Gottlob Jungmann, | 1805. | (L.)   4.

Title, 1 f.; verso, blank; Vorrede, 1¼ pp., signed Gottlob Jungman; Wahrhafte und gewisse Jahrzahl aller Zeiten und Jahre | von Adam an bis auf Jesum Christum, und bis auf das Jahr 1806, &c., 2 pp. and a small portion of the 3d p.; Register der furnehmsten Glaubens-und Lebens-Puncten Christlicher Lehre, &c., remainder of 3d and 4th pp., and 9¼ following ff.; Zeit Register, 4¼ ff.; Register zur Erläuterung einiger Werter und Gebräuche, &c.. 6 ff.; sigs. B in 2ˢ; C to M¹ in 1ˢ; M², N to Q in 2ˢ, R¹; Diese Bible ist gekauft worden in Jahr unsers Herrn, | und gehört | within ornamented lines, 1 p.; Verzeichniß aller Bücher, 1 p., R²; Text: Gen. to Mal., pp. 1–805; Apocrypha, pp. 806–949; and rest of Prayer of Manasseh, ½ p.; Anhang (containing 3d and 4th Books of Ezra and 3d Book of Maccabees), rest of 949–1008; sigs. A to Llll⁴ in 4ˢ; Family Rec., 2 ff; Das Neue | Testament | unsers | Herrn und Heylandes | Jesu Christi, | nach der deutschen Uebersetzung | Dr. Martin Luthers, | mit kurzem | Inhalt eines jeden Capitels, | und vollständiger | Anweisung gleicher Schrift-Stellen. | Wie auch | aller Sonn-und Fest-tagigen | Evangelien und Episteln. | Erste Auflage. | Reading | Gedruckt und zu finden bey Gottlob Jungmann. | 1805. | 1 p.; Die Bücher | des | Neuen Testaments | 1 p.; Text: Mat. to Rev.; pp. 3–276 and half of 277; Register der Episteln, &c., the rest of p. 277 and 3 following pages (not numbered); sigs. A² to Ll⁴ in 4ˢ; then Mm, Nn in 2ˢ.

6. THE | HOLY BIBLE, | containing the | Old and New Testaments, | together with the | Apocrypha: | Translated | out of the Original Tongues, | and | With the Former Translations *diligently compared* | *and revised.* | Morris-Town: | Printed by Mann and Douglass, | *For themselves; for J. Tiebout....S. Stephens....S. Gould & Co....Ronalds & Lou- | don....Sage & Thompson....D. D. Smith....C. Flanagan....J. Harrison....G. & R.* | *Waite....T. Kirk....C. Brown....D. Longworth....R. M'Gill....G. Sinclair,* New- | York. *Daniel Brewer, Jun.,* Taunton (Massa.). *S. Kollock,* Elizabeth-Town. | *J. Oram,* Trenton (N. Jersey). 1805. | (L.; G. L.)   8.

Title, 1 f.; verso, blank; Index of the Names and Order of all the Books, &c., 1 p.; verso, The Property of   (within an oblong ornament); Text: Gen. to Mal., pp. 5–737; verso of 737, Tables of Scripture Measures, &c.; sigs. A (not marked) to Zz, then A 3 to verso of U 4³; Apocrypha, pp. 739–914; sigs. U 4⁴ to verso of S 5³; New Testament title: Morris-Town: | Printed and Sold by Mann and Douglass. | 1805. | 1 p.; verso, blank; sig. S 5⁴; Text: Mat. to Rev., pp. 917 to the top of 1141; A Table of Offices and Conditions of Men, remainder of p. 1141, and half of 1142; then "Finis," sigs. T 5 to verso of Y 6¹; three blank leaves complete the sig.; all in 4ˢ. The running title to p. 636 is, Chap. lii, instead of, Jeremiah.

7. HOLY BIBLE. Boston: | Printed for Thomas & Andrews | By J. T. Buckingham. | Sold, wholesale and retail, at their Bookstore, No. 45 New- | bury-Street, and by the principal Book- | sellers in the United States. | 1805. | (L.) 12.

The same as the edition of 1804.

8. A | SHORT and PLAIN | EXPOSITION | of the | Old Testament, | with | devotional | and | practical Reflections, | for the | use of Families. | By the late | Reverend Job Orton, S. T. P. | Published from the Author's manuscripts, | by Robert Gentleman. | First American, from the second London edition. | Vol. I — VI. | Charlestown: | Printed and sold by Samuel Etheridge. | 1805. (Conn. Hist. Soc.; Sem. St. Sulpice, Balt.) 8.

Vol. 6 has, "1806."

9. THE LIFE of JOSEPH, the Son of Israel. In Eight Books. Briefly designed to allure young minds to a love of the Sacred Scriptures. By John Macgowan. Printed at Greenfield, Massachusetts: By John Denio. 1805. (B.) 12.

This work is recommended to the public by William Rogers, D. D., Professor of English, &c., in the college and Academy of Philadelphia, Jan. 1, 1791. The following extract from p. 32, will enable the reader to judge of the author's style : "As Phœbus approached the northeast verge of this dusky world, and fair Aurora purpled the sky, the messengers set out by different ways," &c.

1. THE | NEW TESTAMENT | of | our Lord and Saviour, | Jesus Christ, | translated from the | Latin Vulgat: | Diligently compared with the Original Greek: | and first published by | The English College at Rhemes. A. D. 1582. | With | Annotations, References, and an Historical and Chronological Index. | First American, from the fifth Dublin edition, | Newly revised and corrected according to the Clementin edition of the Scriptures. | Philadelphia: | Published by Mathew Carey, | No. 118, Market-Street. | 1805. | (G. L.) 4.

This is the New Testament described in connection with Carey's Douay Bible of this year (*supra*, No. 1). It was, however, issued previously to the Bible.

2. THE | NEW TESTAMENT | of our | Lord and Saviour | Jesus Christ, | newly translated out of the | Original Greek: | And with the | former Translations | Diligently Compared and Revised. | Appointed to be Read in Churches. | New York: | Printed and Sold by E. Duyckinck, No. 110 Pearl-Street, | and P. A. Mesier, No. 107 Pearl-Street. | 1805. | (L.) 12.

Title, within double lines, 1 f.; verso, The Order of the Books; Text: Mat. to Rev. (not paged); sigs. A^2 to recto of O^{12}; at foot of the text, "Finis," under which is a line composed of 9 printer's flowers, a * and 8 printer's flowers; on verso of O^{12}, A Table of Kindred. Short headings to columns and chapters. Sigs. in 12^s.

Errors: Mat. 17:18 reads, "And Jesus rebuked the devil, and .... the child was cured from that very four (or four)." The catchword on recto of C^3, is "3" instead of "7"; the heading to recto of D^7, reads: *How we must love our enemies;* Acts 8:9, sorcery is printed, "sorcercy"; sig. H^2 is marked, 2 H; the catchword to recto of H^4, is "James," instead of "Jews"; II Cor., 7:8, reads: "for I perceive that the same epistle hath made you sorry, though *it were* but for a reason," instead of "season"; in v. 11 of the same chapter, the words, "yea, what fear," are omitted; Philippians 4:15 reads: "in the begginning," and in the heading to the last column on the same page, the word "*bounty*" is left out. Besides these errors, a number of catchwords are omitted.

On a close examination of the volume, it appears to have been set up from Hugh Gaine's Testament (*supra,* p. 36; No. 1, 1790), with which it agrees, with the exception of the title page and II Cor., 7:11, and a few minor errors.

3. NEW TESTAMENT: Brooklyn: Printed by T. Kirk for Campbell and Mitchell, Sage and Thompson, S. Stansbury, D. Smith and B. Dornin, Booksellers, New York. 1805. (L.) 12

Title, 1 f.; verso, Order of the Books; Text, sigs. A^2 to recto of Y^4; verso of Y^4, Table of Kindred; sigs. in 6^s.

4. THE | NEW TESTAMENT | of our Lord and Saviour | Jesus Christ, | Translated out of the | Original Greek: | And with the former | Translations | Diligently compared and revised. | Appointed to be Read in Churches. | Wilmington (Del): | Printed and Sold by Peter Brynberg. | 1805. | (L.) 12.

Title, 1 f.; verso, Order of Books; Text: Mat. to Rev.; A^2 to A^4, B to Z^2 in 6^s; on verso of Z^2, Books Printed by Peter Brynberg, Wilmington, Del.

1806.

1. SELF-INTERPRETING BIBLE: With the Apocrypha; Marginal References and Illustrations, &c. *By the late Reverend John Brown*, &c. Second American Edition. New York: Printed by Sage & Clough, for Robt. McDermut, No. 248, and J. & T. Ronalds, No. 188 Pearl Street, April 1806. (L.; G. L.) fol.

This volume agrees with the edition of 1792, *supra* p. 43, Except in the imprints on the title pages; that on the New Testament title is: New York: Printed by Hopkins and Seymour, for Robt. McDermut (as above). The plates are 24 in number, from the coppers of Thomas's ed. No. 1, 1791, *supra* p. 38, with the references to that edition erased, the numbers, however, generally remaining. These numbers are V, IX, XI, O (Thomas's XII), XVII, XVIII, XXII, O (Thomas's XXIII), XXIV, XXV, XXVI, I (Thomas's frontispiece to O. T.), XXX, XXXII, XXXV, XXXVIII, XXXVII, XLIX, XL, XLIII, XLV, XLVII, O (XXXIII, or Thomas's frontisp. to Apocrypha and New Test.), L. The subjects of these plates will be ascertained by comparing these numbers with the corresponding ones on pp. 39, 40 (*supra*).

2. THE | HOLY BIBLE: | Containing the | Old and New Testaments: | Together with the | Apocrypha: | *Translated out of the original Tongues,* | and | with the former Translations diligently compared and revised, | *By the Special Command of King James I. of England.* | With | Marginal Notes and References. | To which are added, | An Index; | An Alphabetical Table | of all the Names in the Old and New Testaments, with their Significations; | Tables of Scripture Weights, Measures and Coins; | John Brown's Concordance, &c., &c., &c. | Embellished with Ten Maps and Twenty Historical Engravings. | Philadelphia: | Printed and published | by Mathew Carey, No. 122, Market Street. | 1806. | (L.; B.) 4

This volume agrees with Carey's edition of July 25, 1804, except: I. The sig. to Family Record is 1; II. The numeral accompanying sig. 2 X is 45 (not 43), and there is no 44; III. The following is the Title to the New Testament: The | New Testament, | of our | Lord and Saviour | Jesus Christ, | Translated | out of the Original Greek; | and | with the former Translations | diligently comared (*sic*) and revised, by the Special command of King James I. of England. | Philadelphia: | Printed by Mathew Carey, No. 122, Market-street. | M.DCCC.VI. | No. 64 in left corner; IV. The words "Old and New Testaments," on the title to Brown's Concordance, are in black letter, and the words following the author's name are in Pearl caps; the imprint being—Brooklyn, Printed by Thomas Kirk, 1807.

—1806.] AMERICAN BIBLES. 83

The following is a list of the Maps and Plates:
1. Journeyings of the Children of Israel.
2. Noah building the Ark.
3. Map of Canaan.
4. Map of Egypt.
5. Map of places mentioned in the five books of Moses.
6. Dresses of the High Priests and Levites.................................. *W. H^n, J^r*.
7. Map of Canaan from the time of Joshua.
8. Samuel anointing David.
9. Map of the Purveyorships.
10. Map of Solomon's dominions.
11. Map of the Assyrian and other Empires.
12. Job receiving intelligence of his Misfortunes.
13. Job's wife tantalizing him................................. *W. Harrison, Junr*.
14. Map of Moriah.
15. The Hypocrite taking the Mote out of his Neighbor's eye.
16. Christ curing the Leper... *W. Harrison, J^r*.
17. John the Baptist sending his disciples to Christ......................... *Tiebout*.
18. The Laborers receiving their hire................................ *W. Harrison, Junr*.
19. The Jews presenting the coin to Christ.
20. The Last Supper.. *Tiebout*.
21. The Good Samaritan.
22. The Shepherd carrying the lost sheep..................... *W. Harrison, Junr*.
23. The Prodigal Son received by his father........................... *W. Harrison*.
24. The Miracle at the pool of Bethesda............................ *Tiebout*.
25. The Woman caught in adultery.
26. The Jews demanding of Jesus if he were the Messiah................. *Tiebout*.
27. The Resurrection of Lazarus... *Tiebout*.
28. The Crucifixion... *W. Harrison, Junr*.
29. Map of the Travels of the Apostles.
30. Conversion of the Centurion.. *Tanner*.

It is to be observed that other issues of this, which in some instances is called The Tenth Philadelphia edition, vary in the number of Plates; one has the same Maps and Engravings as the edition of July 25, 1804, *supra*, p. 72; and another, only the Maps. The New Testament title is sometimes found with the date, 1807.

3. HOLY BIBLE: Philadelphia: Printed by Mathew Carey, No. 122, High Street. 1806. (L.) 12.

Title, 1 f.; verso, This Bible | is the Property of | (within an oblong ornament composed of printer's flowers). The Text agrees with that of Hugh Gaine (No. 3, 1792.), and with Carey's 12mo (No. 5, 1803), except that there are no catchwords.

4. HOLY BIBLE: Philadelphia: Printed by and for W. W. Woodward, No. 52, Second, the Corner of Chesnut Street. 1806. (L.; B.) 12.

Text not paged; sigs. A to Ss, in 12s; verso of Ss, Table of Offices, followed by a blank leaf—With Scotch Psalms; same printer. The Vol. resembles very much the Scotch editions of the Bible of the same size.

5. HOLY BIBLE: Boston: | Printed for Thomas & Andrews | by J. T. Buckingham. | Sold at their Bookstore No. 45, Newbury Street, and by | the principal Booksellers in the United States. | 1806. | (B.)   12

See *supra*, No. 6 of 1805.

6. A | PRACTICAL EXPOSITION | on the | CXXXth Psalm. | Wherein | the nature of the forgiveness of sin is decla- | red, the truth and reality of it asserted, | and | the case of a soul destroyed with the guilt | of sin, and relieved by a discovery of | forgiveness with God, is at large dis- | coursed. | By John Owen, D. D. | John, v. 39, Search the scriptures. | Salem, (N. Y.) | Printed by Dodd & Rumsey, 1806. | (J. G. S.)   12.

419 pp; sigs. in 12s.

1. NEW TESTAMENT. Tenth Philadelphia Edition. Philadelphia: Printed for Mathew Carey. 1806.   4.

With Bible of 1805.

2. NEW TESTAMENT: Hartford: Printed by Lincoln and Gleason. 1806.   (B.)   12.

The type on which this Testament was printed, was cast expressly for it, in Philadelphia; set up in Hartford, and distributed as fast as each form was worked off. The edition was 10,000.

3. Η ΚΑΙΝΗ | ΔΙΑΘΗΚΗ. | Novum | Testamentum, | cum versione Latinâ | Ariæ Montani, | in quo tum selecti versiculi 1900, quibus omnes Novi | Testamenti voces continentur, Asteriscis | notantur; | tum omnes & singulæ voces, | semel vel sæpius occurrentes, | peculiari notâ distinguuntur. | Auctore | Johanne Leusden, professore. | Editio prima Americana: | qua plurima Londiniensis Errata, diligentissime animad- | versa, corriguntur: | Curâ Johannis Watts. | Philadelphiæ: | Ex Officina Classica: | Impensis S. F. Bradford. | 1806. | (B.; G. L.)   12.

Mock title, 1 f.; verso, blank; title, 1 p.; verso, blank; Leusden's Pref., pp. 5–8; Text, pp. 1–561; sigs. A to recto of 3 B⁴, in 6s; on p. 561, "Finis," and "Excudebat J. Watts." Text, in Greek and Latin, in parallel columns.

4. H KAINH | ΔΙΑΘΗΚΗ. | Novum | Testamentum | Græcum. | In quo tum selecti versiculi 1900, quibus omnes Novi | Testamenti voces continentur, Astericis | notantur; | tum omnes & singulæ voces, semel vel sæpius occurrentes, | peculiari notâ distinguuntur. | (Wood-cut vignette.) Editio secunda Americana; | qua plurima Londinensis errata, diligentissime animad- | versa, corriguntur: | Curâ Johannis Watts. | Philadelphiæ: | Ex Officina Classica: | Impensis S. F. Bradford. | 1806. | (L.)   12.

Mock title, 1 p.; verso, blank; title, 1 p.; verso, blank; Text, pp. 1-286; sigs. A to verso of Aa⁵, in 6ˢ, followed by a blank leaf; on p. 286, "Finis," and "Excudebat J. Watts." Text in double columns.

1807.

1. THE | HOLY BIBLE, | Containing the | Old and New Testaments: | Together with the | Apocrypha: | Translated out of the Original Tongues, | and | with the former Translations Diligently compared and revised | By the Special Command of King James I. of England. | With marginal Notes and References. | To which are added, | An Index; | An Alphabetical Table | of all the Names in the Old and New Testaments, with their Significations; | And | Tables of Scripture Weights, Measures and Coins. | Also, | Brown's Concordance. | Edinburgh, | Printed for W. Swan et S. Allinson, New York; | And Sold at Paris, by Truchy, Bookseller, 18 Boulevart des Italiens. | 1807. | (L.)   .   4.

Title, 1 f.; verso, blank; Names & Order of Books and Summary History of the Bible, 1 f.; Text: Gen. to Mal.; sigs. B to recto of 4 F⁴, in 4ˢ; verso of 4 F⁴, blank; Apocrypha, in smaller type, A to R³, in 4ˢ; verso of R³, blank; Title to New Test., R⁴; The | New Testament | of our | Lord and Saviour Jesus Christ | Translated out of the | Original Greek: | And with | the former Translations diligently Compared and Revised. | By the Special Command of King James I. of England. | Edinburgh: | Printed for W. Swan & S. Allinson, New York: | And Sold by them, and by the principal Booksellers in the United States. | 1807. | 1 p.; Text: Mat. to Rev.; 4 G to recto of 5 G², in 4ˢ; verso of 5 G², and the two next leaves of the signature, form a Family Record; Title to Brown's Concordance, same date and imprint as the N. T., verso; To the Reader, 1 f.; Text, A² to M⁴, in 4ˢ; Index to Bible, [aaa] to [ccc], in 4ˢ; 12 ff.; Tables of offices, weights, measures, coins, 2 ff.; Alphabet: Table of Proper Names & Table of times, 4 ff.; Chronol: Catalogue of the Apostles & their Successors, Chronol: Index of years, from Adam to Christ, 2 ff.; Portrait of Apostolic

Preacher, from Cowper; Table of Kindred; A Clergyman's Address to Married persons, at the Altar; Old & New Test. dissected; Account of Judea; 2 ff.=10 ff.; [ddd] to [fff]², in 4ˢ.

The general appearance of the volume is that of an English or Scotch Bible; but the title pages have a French or Dutch air. The contents and the wording of the first title, resemble Carey's edition.

2. THE | HOLY BIBLE: | Containing the | Old and New Testaments: | Together with the | Apocrypha: | *Translated out of the Original Tongues,* | and | with the former Translations diligently compared and revised; | With | Marginal Notes and References, and the Explanatory Notes of Ostervald. | To which are added, | An Index; | An Alphabetical Table | of all the Names in the Old and New Testaments, with their Significations; | Tables of Scripture Weights, Measures, and Coins: | John Brown's Concordance, &c. &c. &c. | Embellished with Maps, and a number of Elegant Historical Engravings. | New-York: | Printed and Sold by Collins, Perkins, and Co. | 1807. | (L.; Conn. Hist. Soc.)   4.

Title, 1 f.; verso, blank; Adv. to the Second Edition, 1 p.; verso, blank; To the Reader (Dr. Witherspoon's Address), 2 pp.; Account of Dates and Time, and List of Maps and Engr., 1 p.; Names and Order of Books, &c., 1 p., making sig. A; Text: Gen. to Mal. (not paged); sigs. B to recto of 4 R², in 4ˢ; verso of 4 R², blank; Family Record, two leaves; at foot of O. T., "The End of the Prophets;" Apocrypha, sigs. A* to verso of U*⁴, in 4ˢ; Practical | Observations | on the | Old and New | Testaments, | Illustrating the Chapters, a very few excepted, in their Order. | With | Arguments to the different Books. | *By the Reverend Mr.* Ostervald, | *Professor of Divinity.* | And one of the Ministers of the Church at Neufchatel in Switzerland. | New York: | Printed and Sold by Collins, Perkins & Co. | 1806. | 1 p; verso, blank; Text: sigs. A² to verso of U², in 4ˢ; The | New Testament | of our | Lord and Saviour | Jesus Christ, | Translated | out of the Original Greek: | And | with the former Translations | diligently Compared and Revised. | Collins's Second Edition. | New York: | Printed and Sold by Collins, Perkins, & Co. | 1806. | 1 p.; verso blank; Text: Mat. to Rev. ‡ A² to ‡ Dd³; Index, ‡ Dd⁴ to recto of ‡ Gg⁴. At foot of ‡ Gg⁴ a Table of Time; verso of ‡ Gg⁴, Tables of Scripture Weights, Measures, &c., which ends on ‡ Hh², on which page is a Table of Offices, &c.; verso, Table of Kindred. Alphabetical Table, ‡ Ii, all in 4ˢ; A | Brief | Concordance | to | The Holy Scriptures | of the | 𝕺𝖑𝖉 𝖆𝖓𝖉 𝕹𝖊𝖜 𝕿𝖊𝖘𝖙𝖆𝖒𝖊𝖓𝖙𝖘, | by which | All, or Most, | of | the Principal Texts of Scripture | may be easily found out. | By John Brown, | late Minister of the Gospel, at Haddington, in Scotland. | Search the Scriptures, &c. | The Bereans were more noble, &c. | Revised and Corrected. | New York: | Published by Collins, Perkins, and Co., No. 189, Pearl-street. | T. Kirk, Printer, Brooklyn. | 1806. | 1 p.; verso, blank. To the Reader, 1 p.; verso, blank; Text: pp. 5-72; sig. (including Title and To the Reader), A-I; all in 4ˢ.

—1807.]   AMERICAN BIBLES.   87

List of Engravings: (all having at the top, "Engraved for Collins's Quarto Bible, Second Edition;" and at foot, "New York: Published by Collins, Perkins & Co., 1807.")

1. Providence (Frontis. after Caracci)...... ....Engraved by *G. Fairman.*
2. Finding of Moses ....*W. S. Leney.*
3. Moses presenting the Tables............................... *Tanner & Levey.*
4. Map of Cannan.......................... ....*Scoles.*
5. Elijah raising the Widow's Son............ ....*W. S. Leney.*
6. The Holy Family (Front. to N. T. after A. Caracci)..............*Peter Maverick.*
7. St. Matthew ....*W. S. Leney.*
8. St. Mark........... ....*Scoles.*
9. St. Luke..*W. S. Leney.*
10. St. John the Evangelist ....*A. Anderson.*
11. Map of the Country travelled by the Apostles, &c......................*Tanner.*
12. St. Paul...................... ....*Tiebout.*

For the accommodation of purchasers this Bible was issued in eight different styles: 1. With Concordance; 2. With Concordance and Plates; 3. With Concordance and Apocrypha; 4. With Concordance, Apocrypha and Plates; 5. With Concordance and Ostervald's Notes; 6. With Concordance, Ostervald's Notes and Plates; 7. With Concordance, Apocrypha and Ostervald's Notes; and 8. With Concordance, Apocrypha, Ostervald's Notes and Plates.

3. The | Holy Bible | Containing the | Old and New Testaments: | Translated out of | the Original Tongues, | and | With the former Translations | Diligently Compared and Revised. | With those copious marginal References, | known by the name of | Canne's Notes. | Philadelphia: | Published by Jacob Johnson, No. 147, and | Kimber, Conrad and Co., No. 93 | Market Street. | 1807. | (L.)   8.

Title, 1 f.; verso, blank; Names and Order of Books, 1 p. (the Apoc. included in this enumeration, but the text not in the volume); Tables of Weights, Moneys, Time, &c., 1 p.; Text: Gen. to Rev.; B to 6 H⁴, in 4ˢ; Table of Offices, &c., 1 p.; Table of Passages in the O. T. quoted in the New Test., 2¾ pp ; Table of Kindred, rest of the page, making 4 pp. (6 I¹ & ²); at the bottom: Printed | By Kimber, Conrad & Co. |

Canne was a Brownist. His references appeared originally in 1644, and are said to be generally very judicious and apposite. The later editions, which pass under the name of Canne's Bible, are full of errors, and crowded with references which do not belong to the original author. *Bohn's Lowndes,* I, 187.

4. Holy Bible, &c.   Printed by Mathew Carey, No. 122 High Street, Philadelphia, 1807.   (L.)   12.

See No. 5, 1803.

88   AMERICAN BIBLES.   [1807—

1. NEW TESTAMENT. Philadelphia: Printed by Matthew Carey, No. 122 Market Street. 1807.   4.
With Bible No. 2 of 1806.

2. NEW TESTAMENT: New York: Printed and Sold by E. Duyckinck, No. 110 Pearl-Street, and P. A. Mesier, No. 107 Pearl-Street. 1807.   (L.)   12.
This is the edition of Duyckinck's New Test. of 1805, with a new title page. The errors are continued.

3. **Das Neue | Testament** | unsers | HErrn und Heilandes | JEsu Christi, | nach der Deutschen Uebersetzung | D. Martin Luthers. | mit kurzem | Inhalt eines jeden Capitels, | und | vollständiger Unweisung gleicher Schriftstellen. | Wie auch | aller Sonn=und Festtägigen | Evängelien und Episteln. | Vierte Auflage. | Germantaun. | Gedruckt bey Michael Billmeyer, 1807. | (L.)   12.
Title, 1 f.; verso, blank; Verzeichniss, 1 p.; verso, blank; Text: pp. 5–537; Registers, 5 pp., not numbered; sigs. A3 to Ll7, in 8s, followed by a blank leaf. For 2d and 3d editions of this Testament, see *supra*, pp. 50 and 71.

4. THE | FAMLIY EXPOSITOR; | or, | a Paraphrase | and | Version of the New Testament; | With | Critical Notes, | and | a Practical Improvement of each Section. | In Six Volumes. | Volume First, containing the Former Part of | The History of our Lord Jesus Christ, | as recorded by the Four Evangelists, | Disposed in the Order of an Harmony. | By P. Doddridge, D. D. | To which is prefixed, | A life of the Author, | By Andrew Kippis, D. D., F. R. S. and S.A. | Ει δε τις υπο τευων μη πασχη των λογων, υπο μονων αν των εν αδε δικαςηριων | υπευθυνθειη.—Simplic. in Epictet. Proem. | **Etheridge's Edition,** | from the Eighth London Edition. | Sold by him at Washington Head Bookstore. Sold also by said | Etheridge and Company, in Boston. | S. Etheridge, Printer, Charlestown, Massachusetts. | 1807. | (Am. Antiq. Soc.) 8.
Title, 1 f.; verso, blank; Life, pp. iii–cxiv; sigs. 1 to verso of 14⁴, in 4s; Dedication, 4 pp.; Preface, 8 pp.; Tables of Chapters and Sections, 3 pp.; Directions for Reading, 1 p.; sigs. 15, 16 in 4s; Text: pp. 21–492; sigs. C to verso of 3 N⁴, in 4s; Vol. II: Title as above, except the line: Volume Second, containing the Latter part of, | 1 p.; verso, blank; Pref. pp. iii–vi; Tables of Chapters and Sections, 3 pp.; sigs., including title, 1, in 4s, and 2¹; Text: pp. 1–636; Table for finding any verse, 6 pp.; sigs. 2² to verso of 82², in 4s; Vol. III: Title as above, except: Volume

Third. | Containing the Acts of the Apostles: | With additional Notes | on the Harmony of the Evangelists; | And | Two Dissertations—First, on Sir Isaac Newton's System of the | Harmony.—Second, on the Inspiration of the | New Testament. | With a Proper Index to the Whole. | By P. Doddridge, D. D., | a Greek quotation from the Gospel of John, imprint as above, 1 p.; verso, blank; Preface, pp.iii-xi; Postscript, pp, xii-xvi; sigs. 1, 2, including title, in 4^s; Text: pp. 1–403; Appendix No. 1, pp. 404–414; Postscript, p. 415; Appendix No. 2, pp. 416–439; Postscript, pp. 440–443; Advertisement to Appendix 3, pp. 444, 445; Table, pp. 446–465; Additional Note relating to the Time when the Hist. Books of the New Test. were written, pp. 466–468; sigs. 3 to verso of 61^4, in 4^s; Vol. IV: Title as above, except: Volume Fourth. | Containing the Epistle of Paul the Apostle to the | Romans, | and | His First and Second Epistles to the | Corinthians. | By P. Doddridge, D. D. | a Greek quotation from Origen; imprint as before, except 4th line, which reads: Etheridge and Bliss, in Boston, 1 p.; verso, blank; Preface, pp. iii-v; verso of p. v, blank; Half title: The | Family Expositor; | or, | a Paraphrase | on | The Epistle of Paul the Apostle to | the | Romans; | with | Critical Notes, and a practical Improvement | on each Section. | 1 p.; verso, blank; 4 ff.; sig. 1; Gen. Introd., pp. 1–6; Text: (Epist. to the Rom.) pp. 7–182; Half title to 1st Epist. to Cor. 1 p.; verso, blank; Introduction, pp. 185–192; Text: pp. 193–372; Half title to 2d Epist. to Cor. 1 p.; verso, blank; Introd., pp. 375–380; Text: pp. 381–484; sigs. 2 to verso of 62^2 in 4^s; N. B. The notice of Kippis's Life is omitted on the Titles of the 3d and 4th Vols.; Vol. V: Title as before, except: Volume Fifth. | Containing the Epistles of Paul the Apostle |

To the Galatians,
Ephesians,
Philippians,
Colossians,
I. Thessalonians,

II. Thessalonians,
I. Timothy,
II. Timothy,
Titus,
Philemon.

By P. Doddridge, D. D. | To which is prefixed, | A Life of the Author, | By Andrew Kippis, D. D., F. R. S., and S. A. | Latin quotation. | 𝔈𝔱𝔥𝔢𝔯𝔦𝔡𝔤𝔢'𝔰 𝔈𝔡𝔦𝔱𝔦𝔬𝔫, | From the Eighth London Edition. | Sold by him at Washington Head Bookstore. Sold also by said | Etheridge and Bliss, in Boston. | S. Etheridge, printer, Charlestown, Massachusetts. | 1808. | 1 p.; verso, blank; Half title to Epist. to Gal., 1 p.; verso, blank; Introd., pp. 1–9; verso of p. 9, blank; sigs. 1 to verso of 2^1 in 4^s; Text: pp. 11–86; Half title to Ephes., 1 p.; verso, blank; Introd., pp. 89–97; verso, blank; Text: pp. 99–183; verso of 183, blank; Half title to Philipp., 1 p.; verso, blank; Introd., pp. 187–192; Text: pp. 193–237; verso of 237, blank; Half title to Coloss., 1 p.; verso, blank; Introd., pp. 241–244; Text: pp. 245–283; verso, blank; Half title to I Thes., 1 p.; verso, blank; Introd., pp. 287–292; Text: pp. 293–327; verso, blank; Half title to II. Thess., 1 p.; verso, blank; Introd., pp. 331–334; Text: pp. 335–352; Half title to 1 Tim., 1 p.; verso, blank; Introd., pp. 355–366; Text: pp. 367–417; verso, blank; Half title to II Tim., 1 p.; verso, blank; Introd., pp. 423–425; verso, blank; Text: pp. 427–459; verso, blank; Half title to Titus, 1 p.; verso, blank; Introd., pp. 463–467; verso, blank; Text: pp. 469–487; verso, blank; Half title to Philemon, 1 p.; verso, blank; Introd., pp. 491–494; Text: pp. 495–502; followed by a leaf containing, Advertisements of Books for Sale by S. Etheridge; sigs. 2 to 63^4, in 4^s; Vol. VI: Title as before, except: Volume Sixth. | Containing | The Epistles of Paul the Apostle | to the | Hebrews—James—I Peter—II Peter—I John—II John | III John—Jude—Revelation. | By P. Doddridge, D. D. | &c., as in Vol. V; Greek quotation from Origen; date, 1808, 1 p.; verso, blank; Advertisement by the Editor, pp. iii-vi; Half title to Heb., 1 p.; verso, blank; Introd., pp. 3-8; Text: pp. 9-126; Half title to James, 1 p.; verso, blank; Introd., pp. 129-134; Text: pp. 135-173; verso, blank; Half title to I Peter, 1 p.; verso, blank; Introd., pp. 177-181; verso, blank; Text: pp. 183-227; verso, blank; Half title to II Peter, 1 p.; verso, blank; Introd., pp. 231-234; Text: pp. 235-268; Half title to I John, 1 p.; verso, blank; Introd., pp. 271-273; verso, blank; Text: pp. 275-319; verso, blank; Half title to II John, 1 p.; verso, blank; Introd. to 2d and 3d Epist., pp. 323, 324; Text: pp. 325-329; verso, blank; Half title to III John, 1 p.; verso, blank; Text: pp. 333-338; Half title to Jude, 1 p.; verso, blank; Introd., pp. 341, 342; Text: pp. 343-354: Half title to Rev., 1 p.; verso, blank; Introd., pp. 357-365; verso, blank; Text: pp. 367-516; sigs. (including title p.) 1 to verso of 66^1, in 4^s ; Index to Greek words and phrases, sigs. 66^2 to verso of 67^4, in 4^s ; General Index, sigs. 68 to verso of 79^4, in 4^s ; on last p., Finis, Charlestown (Mass.) | Printed and Published by S. Etheridge, | July, 1808. |

5. THE | FAMILY EXPOSITOR | Abridged: | according to the plan of its Author, | the Rev. P. Doddridge, D. D. | In Two volumes. | By S. Palmer. | To which are prefixed, | Memoirs of Doctor Doddridge. | First American edition. | Hartford: | Printed by Lincoln & Gleason. | 1807. | (Conn. Hist. Soc.)   8.

6. THE | GENERAL HISTORY | of the | Christian Church, | from her Birth | to her | Final triumphant State in Heaven : | chiefly deduced from the Apocalypse of St. John, | the Apostle and Evangelist. | The Fourth edition. | With a few additional Remarks and Elucidations, | by the Author, | Sig. Pastorini. | Apocal. i: 3. | New York: | Printed by Hopkins & Seymour, | for Bernard Dornin, Bookseller, | 136, Pearl-street. | 1807. | 12.

Title, 1 f.; verso, blank; Editor's address, pp. iii-viii; Introd., pp. ix-xxii; Table of Contents, pp. xxiii, xxiv; Text, pp. 1-418; The Apocalypse, pp. 419-456; Subscribers' names, pp. i-viii; verso of viii, Announcement of New Works, dated Dec., 1807. The Apocalypse in this edition is according to Challoner's text, 1749. (J. G. S) Dr. Charles Walmesly, afterwards Vicar Apostolic of the Western district of England, and Titular Bishop of Rama, was the author of this work. It appeared originally in 1771, and has been published in French, Latin, German and Italian.

1808.

1. HOLY BIBLE: Philadelphia: Printed and Published by Mathew Carey, No. 122 Market Street. 1808. (L.) 4.

Title wanting; imprint borrowed from the next title page; The | Old Testament, | Translated | out of | the Original Hebrew, | and | *With the former Translations diligently compared and revised.* | Done by the | Special Command of his Majesty King James I. of England. | Philadelphia: | Printed and Published | by Mathew Carey, No. 122, Market Street. | 1808. | 1 p.; verso, names and order of the books of the O. and N. Test., and Index of various Articles; Text: Gen. to Mal., pp. 1-674; sigs. A to verso of UU^1, and in figures 1 to 43^1, in 8^s; Table of Offices, p. [675]; Chronological Index and Analysis, p. 676; Family Record, 2 ff.; The | New Testament, | of our | Lord and Saviour | Jesus Christ, | translated | out of the Original Greek: | And | with the former Translations | diligently compared and revised. | *By the special Command of King James I. of England.* | Philadelphia: | Printed by Mathew Carey, No. 122, Market Street. | 1809. | 1 p.; verso, blank; Text: Mat. to Rev., pp. 835-1046 (1st leaf of Mat. marked (26.3); sigs. 3 R (not marked) to verso of $4 U^3$; in numbers 65-90^3, in 4^s; Account of Judea, pp. 1047, 1048; Index, Tables, Fletcher's Concise View, pp. 1049-1080; sigs $4 U^4$ to $5 A^4$; in numbers 90^4 to 94^4; in 4^s.

2. THE | HOLY BIBLE, | containing | The Old and New Covenant, | commonly called | the Old and New Testament: | Translated | from the Greek. | By Charles Thomson, | *Late Secretary to the Congress of the United States.* | Philadelphia: | Printed by Jane Aitken, No. 71, | North Third Street. | 1808. | 4 vols. (N. Y. State Lib.; L.) 8.

Vol. I. Gen. Title, 1 f.; verso, Certificate of Copyright; Title to O. T.: The | Old Covenant, | commonly called | The Old Testament: | Translated from | The Septuagint. | By Charles Thomson, | *Late Secretary to the Congress of the United States.* | Vol. I. | (same Imprint as on Gen. T.) 1 f.; verso, blank; Text: Gen. to 31: Samuel, sigs. A to recto of $3 S^2$; verso, blank. Vol. II. (Same titles and imprint as in I.) Text: II Samuel to 150th Psalm, sigs. A to recto of $3 P^3$; verso, blank. Vol. III. (Titles, &c., as in I.) Text: Proverbs to Malachi, sigs. A to verso of $3 I^3$. At the end of last page of O. T. a Note; Adv. to Reader and Errata, $3 I^4$; verso, blank. Vol. IV. with double titles, as in the other volumes; New Test. Text: Mat. to Rev.; A to $3 N^2$. Sigs. all in 4^s. This is the first translation of the Septuagint into English.

He (Charles Thomson) told me that he was first induced to study Greek from having bought a part of the Septuagint at an auction in this city (Philadelphia). He had bought it for a mere trifle, and without knowing what it was, save that the crier said it was outlandish letters. When he had mastered it enough to understand it, his anxiety became great to see the whole; but he could find no copy. Strange to tell, in the interval of two years, passing the same store, and chancing to look in, he then saw the remainder actually crying off for a few pence, and he bought it! I used to tell him that the translation which he afterwards made should have had these facts set at the front of the work as a preface; for that great work, the first of the kind in the English language, strangely enough, was ushered into the world without any preface. *Watson's Annals of Philadelphia*, 1850, I, 568.

3. HOLY BIBLE: Boston: | Printed for Thomas & Andrews, | by J. T. Buckingham. | Sold, wholesale and retail, at their Bookstore, No. 45 New- | bury-Street, and by the principal Book- | sellers in the United States. | 1808. | (L.; B.) 12.

Same as the edition of 1803.

4. HOLY BIBLE: Philadelphia: Printed by Mathew Carey, No. 122 High Street. 1808. (L.; B.; G. L.) 12

The signatures of this edition correspond to those of Carey's 12mo Bible, already recorded. In 1 Tim., 4:16, however, the text reads, "thy doctrine," in this edition, whereas it is correct in the others.

5. THE OLD AND NEW TESTAMENTS, digested and illustrated by way of Question and Answer, from the Writings of the most eminent Historians and Commentators. First American edition. Baltimore: 1808. (Catal. Am. Bib. Soc.) 8.

1. NEW TESTAMENT: Whitehall, Printed for Wm. Young, Bank Street, The first house at the right hand from Chesnut Street, Philadelphia. 1808. (L.) 12.

2. NEW TESTAMENT: New York: Printed and sold by E. Duyckinck, No. 110 Pearl-Street, and P. A. Mesier, No. 107 Pearl-Street. 1808. (B.) 12.

This is the edition No. 2 of 1805 (q. v.), with a new title page. The errors noted there are continued.

3. THE | ACTS of the Days | of | the Son of Man, | from the Passion Week | to | his Ascension. | Philadelphia: | Printed by Conrad Zentler, | North Second Street, near Sassafras Street. | 1808. | (L.) 12.

Title, 1 f.; verso, blank; Text: pp. 3–72; sigs. A^2 to verso of F^6, in 6^s. This is a Harmony, from the Gospels and 1st Chapter of Acts, of the last days of the Savior's life.

1809.

1. THE | HOLY BIBLE: | Containing the | *Old and New Testaments:* | Together with the | Apocrypha: | *Translated out of the Original Tongues,* | and | With the former Translations diligently compared and revised, | By the Special Command of his Majesty King James I. of England. | With | Marginal Notes and References. | To which are added, | An Index; | An Alphabetical Table | of all the names in the Old and New Testaments, with their Significations; | Tables of Scripture Weights, Measures and Coins; | John Brown's Concordance, &c., &c., &c. | Philadelphia: | Published by Johnson and Warner. | Printed by M. Carey. | 1809. | (L.) 4.

Title, 1 f.; verso, blank; Second Title: The | Old Testament, | translated | out of | the Original Hebrew, | and | *with the former Translations diligently compared and revised.* | Together with the | Apocrypha. | Done | by the Special Command of King James 1. of England. | Philadelphia: | Published by Johnson and Warner. | 1809. | 1 p.; verso, The names and order of all the books; Index to the various articles annexed; Text: Gen. to Mal., pp. 1-674; sig. 1 A to 43 UU¹ in 8ˢ; Table of Offices, p. [675]; Chron. Index and Analysis, p. 676, UU²; Family Record, sig. 1, pp. [677]-[680]; in 2ˢ; Apocrypha, pp. 681-834, then [829], [830], [831], [832], [833], [834]; sigs. 45 XX to 64, 3R, in 4ˢ; There is no 44; New Testament title: Philadelphia: Printed by Mathew Carey, No. 122 Market-Street. 1809. 1 p.; verso, blank; Text: Mat. to Rev., pp. 835-1046; sig. (64, 3 R *bis*, not marked) to 90 4 U³; 1st page of Mat. marked (26. 3); Judea, &c., pp. 1047, 1048, 4 U⁴; Index, pp. 1049-1066; sigs. 91 4 X to 93 4 Z¹; at foot of p. 1066, Table of Time; Table of Names, pp. 1067-1073; sigs. 4 Z² to 94 5 A; at foot of p. 1073, Table of Kindred; Fletcher's Concise View, pp. 1074-1076; Tables of Scripture Measures, &c., from foot of p. 1076-1078; Table of Passages, pp. 1079, 1080; verso of 5 A¹ to verso of 5 A⁴; all in 4ˢ. The Concordance has been removed from this Copy.

The volume is embellished with a Frontispiece and Nineteen Engravings, taken (except Nos. 3 and 7) from Thomas's folio Bible, with the references to his edition erased. The following is the list of these plates and the names of the Engravers:

Plan of Jerusalem, (Frontispiece)..*J. Norman.*
1. The Creation..*J. H. Seymour.*
2. Adam and Eve in a state of Innocence.
3. Cain slaying his brother...*G. Love.*
4. Expulsion of Adam and Eve from Paradise.....................*Jos^h Seymour.*
5. Abraham's faith..*Jos. Seymour.*
6. Moses in the bulrushes...*J. Seymour.*
7. Moses and Aaron expostulating with Pharaoh...................*Negalle.*
8. Pharaoh and his host drowned..*Love.*

9. The Ark... *J. Seymour.*
10. Gideon's offering consumed.
11. The fugitive Shechemites burnt.................................. *G. Love.*
12. Samson slaying the Philistines.................................. *Sam¹ Hill.*
13. Sampson carrying off the gates of Gaza......................... *G. Love.*
14. Solomon receiving the visit of the Queen of Sheba............. *J. Seymour.*
15. Elijah raising the Widow's Son .... *J. Seymour.*
16. Daniel in the Lions' den .... *J. Seymour.*
17. Susanna surprised by the Elders......................... *Jos^h H. Seymour.*
18. Paul before Felix... *J. Norman.*
19. Hominum Salvator .... *J. Seymour.*

2. THE | HOLY BIBLE | containing the | *Old and New Testaments:* | Together with the | Apocrypha | *Translated out of the Original Tongues* | and | With the former Translations diligently compared and revised, | By the Special Command of his Majesty King James I. of England. | With | Marginal Notes and References. | To which are added, | An Index | An Alphabetical Table | of all the Names in the Old and New Testaments, with their Significations. | Tables of Scripture Weights, Measures and Coins, | John Brown's Concordance, &c. &c. &c. | Embellished with Ten Maps. | Philadelphia: | Printed and Published by Mathew Carey | No. 122 Market Street. | 1809. | (L.)   4.

Title, 1 f.; verso, blank; second title, The | Old Testament. | translated | out of | The Original Hebrew, | and | With the former Translations diligently compared and revised, | Together with the | Apocrypha. | Done by the | By the Special Command of King James I. of England. | Philadelphia: | Printed and Published by Mathew Carey, No. 122, Market Street. | 1809. | The list of Maps is added on the verso of the title to the Old Test.; the imprint of the title to the New Test. corresponds to that on the title page of the Old. The volume agrees in other respects with the preceding edition. Brown's Concordance—Philadelphia: Printed and Published by Mathew Carey, No. 122 Market Street. M.DCCC.X., 1 p.; To the Reader, 1 p.; verso, blank; Text, pp. 5–70; A³ to I³, in 4ˢ. The first page of Mat. is marked at bottom (28–3). The Maps are the same as those in Carey's 4to of July 25th, 1804.

3. THE | HOLY BIBLE: | Containing the | *Old and New Testaments:* | Together with the | Apocrypha: | *Translated out of the Original Tongues,* | and | With the former Translations diligently compared and revised, | With | Marginal Notes and References. | Philadelphia: | Published by Kimber and Conrad, No. 93, Market-Street, | Printed by M. Carey. 1809. | (L.)   4.

—1809.] AMERICAN BIBLES. 95

Title, 1 f.; verso, blank; Names and Order of all the Books, 1 p.; verso, blank; Text, &c., as in the two preceding editions. Imprint to the New Test. title, as above. The volume ends with Revelations, on p. 1046. There are no articles annexed.

In a printed list of Lincoln & Edmands, Booksellers, Boston, of this year, the following editions of Carey's 4to Bible are offered for sale: 1. Without Apocrypha; 2. With Apocrypha; 3. With Apocrypha and 30 plates; 4. With Concordance and 30 plates; 5. With Apocrypha, Concordance and 2 maps; 6. With Apocrypha, Concordance and 30 plates; 7. With Apocrypha, Concordance and 30 maps and plates.

4. THE | HOLY BIBLE | containing | the Old and New Testaments: | Translated | out of the Original Tongues, | and | With the former Translations | diligently compared and revised. | Boston: | Printed by Greenough and Stebbins, | for Hastings, Etheridge and Bliss, E. Larkin, Thomas and Andrews, | D. West, Andrews and Cummings, Manning and Loring, | J. West and Co. and O. C. Greenleaf. | 1809. | (L.; G. L.) 8.

Title, 1 f.; verso, a wood-cut border, and within, The Property of   ; To the Reader (Dr. Witherspoon's Preface), 2 pp.; Account of Times of writing, &c., 1 p.; Names and Order of Books, including Apocrypha, 1 p.; (The Apocrypha, however, is not included in this volume.) Text: Gen. to Mal., pp. 7-735; sigs. 1^4 to recto of 92^4; Tables of Measures, Weights, Money and Time, 1 p.; Title to N. Test. (imprint as above), 1 p.; verso, blank; Text: Mat. to Rev., pp. 739-959; sigs. 93^2 to recto of 120^4; verso of 120^4, Table of Offices, 1 p.; sigs. in 4^s.

1 Tim., 4:16, reads: thy doctrine.

5. HOLY BIBLE: Boston: Printed by Greenough and Stebbins. 1809.   (L.; G. L.)   12.

Acts, 6:3, reads: whom ye may appoint.

6. THE | HOLY BIBLE, | containing the | Old and New | Testaments: | Translated out of | 𝕿𝖍𝖊 𝕺𝖗𝖎𝖌𝖎𝖓𝖆𝖑 𝕿𝖔𝖓𝖌𝖚𝖊𝖘. | And with | the former Translations diligently | compared and revised. | H. & G. | (Between double lines.) Hartford, Connecticut. | Printed and sold by Hudson & Goodwin. | 1809. | (L.; B.)   12.

Title, 1 f.; verso, blank; Dedication of the Translators to King James; The Names and Order of the Books of the Old and New Test. 2 pp.; Text: Gen. to Mal., sigs. A (which includes Tit. and 2 prel. pp.) to recto of Cc^{12}; verso of Cc^{12}, Table of Kindred and Table of Time. The | New Testament | of our | Lord and Saviour | Jesus Christ, | translated out of | the Original Greek; | and with | the former Translations diligently | compared and revised. | Hartford, Connecticut. | Printed and sold by Hudson & Goodwin. | 1809. | 1 p.; verso, blank; Text: Mat. to Rev.; Dd^2 to recto of Ll^{12}; verso of Ll^{12}, Table of Offices; sigs in 12^s; pages not numbered. Headings to chapters and columns. 1 Tim., 4: 16, reads: Take heed unto thyself, and unto thy doctrine.

"NEW SCHOOL BIBLE. ☞ Hudson and Goodwin have the satisfaction to announce to the public that they have this day completed their *first edition of the School* BIBLE. The type is entirely new, imported at a heavy expense, and the paper is of so good a quality that it is asserted with confidence to be the best of the kind offered for sale in this country."—*Connecticut Courant*, 18 October, 1809.

This is supposed to be the earliest edition of the Bible printed in Connecticut. "It was set up in Nonpareil, small 12mo, making, I believe, 68 forms (34 sheets), put in chases, corrected, and shipped from the foundry of Wilson and Sons, Glasgow, to Hudson and Goodwin at a cost, as I have understood, of 6000 crowns...... The type was sold for old metal about the year 1837."—*P. Canfield, Hartford.*

In some copies the date on the title to the New Testament is 1810.

7. ספר תהלים | Liber Psalmorum | Hebraïce | cum | notis selectis | ex editione | Francisci Hare S. T. P. | Episcopi Cicestrensis: | et cum | selecta lectionum varietate | ex ed. vet. Test. Heb. | Benj. Kennicott, S. T. P. | = | Cantabrigiæ Nov-Anglorum | Typis Academicis | Excudebant Hilliard et Metcalf. | 1809. | (J. G. S.)   12.

Title, 1 f.; verso blank; Text, 1–495; verso, blank; sigs. B to I; I² should be on p. 89, but it has A²; p. 97 is I again; K to recto of Ss¹. The Hebrew text is above, with the various readings below; under them the Latin translation, and under that the notes in two columns.

8. SACRED EXTRACTS | from | the Scriptures | of the | Old and New Testaments. | For the more convenient attainment of a knowledge of | the Inspired Writings, | For the use of Schools and Families. | And that from a child thou hast known the holy scriptures, which are able to make | thee wise unto salvation through faith which is in Christ Jesus. | 2 Timothy, iii, 15. | Boston: | Printed by Thomas B. Wait and Company, | Court Street. | 1809. | (Mass. Hist. Soc.)   12.

Title, 1 f.; verso, Certificate of Copyright; From the Preface to the London Edition, 1 p.; Contents of the English Edition, 2 pp.; Advertisement, 1 p.; Table of Chapters of which the whole or part is contained in this edition, 2 pp.; Sacred Extracts, pp. 1–460.

1. THE | NEW TESTAMENT, | in an | Improved Version, | upon the basis of | Archbishop Newcome's New Translation | with | A Corrected Text, | and | Notes critical and explanatory. | Published by a Society for Promoting Christian

Knowledge and | the Practice of Virtue by the distribution of Books. | No offence can justly be taken for this new labour; nothing prejudicing any other man's | judgement by this doing; nor yet professing this so absolute a translation, as that hereafter | might follow no other who might see that which as yet was not understood. | *Archbishop Parker's Preface to the Bishops' Bible.* | From the London edition. | Boston: | Printed by Thomas B. Wait and Company, Court-Street. | For W. Wells. | 1809. | (N. Y. State Lib.; L.; G. L.) 8.

Title, 1 f.; verso, blank; Introduction, pp. iii–xxx; Contents, 2 pp.; sigs. A to verso of D^4; Text (in paragraphs), pp. 1–612; sigs. 1 to verso of 77^2, in 4^s.

This version is avowedly made to support the modern socinian scheme; for though the late learned Archbishop Newcome's name is specified in the title page, as a kind of model, his authority is disregarded whenever it militates against the creed of the anonymous editors.—*Horne.* The Introduction and most of the Notes were written by the Rev. Thomas Belsham. See *Belsham on the Epistle of St. Paul,* I, 9. note.

2. NEW TESTAMENT: [Appointed to be read in Churches and Families.] | Philadelphia: | Published and Sold by Solomon Wiatt, | No. 368, North Second Street. | *Dickinson, Printer.* | 1809. | (L.)   12.

Title, 1 p.; verso, Notice and Order of Books; Text, A^2 to recto of Z^2, in 6^s. The notice on the verso of the title page, states that: "This book is not to be sold, but given away." The expense was defrayed by a legacy of $1000, left by JOHN HANCOCK of Burlington, N. J., for the gratuitous distribution of the New Testament and other religious books, among the poor.

3. THE | NEW TESTAMENT | of our | Lord and Saviour | Jesus Christ, | translated out of the | Original Greek, | and with the | former Translations, | diligently | Compared and Revised. | Philadelphia: | Published by Benjamin Johnson, | No. 249 High Street. | 1809. | (L.)   12.

Title, 1 f.; verso, Order of the Books; Text: pp. 3–347; sigs. A^2 to recto of Ff^6, in 6^s.

4. H KAINH | ΔΙΑΘΗΚΗ. | Novum Testamentum | Græcè | ex recensione | Jo. Jac. Griesbachii, | cum | selectâ Lectionum Varietate. | Tomus Primus. | Lipsiæ, G. J. Göschen. 1805. | Cantabrigiæ Nov-Anglorum. | 1809. | Typis Academicis; | Sumptibus W. Wells et W. Hilliard. | (G. L.) 8.

98   AMERICAN BIBLES.   [1810—

Title, 1 f.; verso, blank; V. V. | Spectassimis | Universitatis Harvardiensis | Præsidi et Sociis | Hanc | ΤΗΣ ΚΑΙΝΗΣ ΔΙΑΘΗΚΗΣ | Editionem | eorum | Hortatu et Auxilio | excusum, | summâ cum observatiâ | D. D. D. | W. W. | W. H., | 1 p.; verso, blank; Griesbach's Preface, pp. vii-x; Conspectus potiorum observationum criticarum et regularum, ad quas nostrum discrepantibus lectionibus judicium conformavimus, pp. xi-xxiv; Text: pp. 1-275; Tomus Secundus, title and pp. 277-615.

This edition contains the text, together with a selection of the principal various readings, and an extract from the Prolegomena of the second edition.—*Horne.*

5. AN | ENGLISH HARMONY | of | the Four Evangelists, | generally | disposed after the manner of the Greek | of | William Newcome, | Archbishop of Armagh: | With a Map of Palestine, divided according to the Twelve Tribes. | Explanatory Notes, and Indexes. | Philadelphia: | Published by Kimber and Conrad, | No. 93, Market-Street. | Brown & Merritt, Printers, No. 24, Church-alley. | 1809. | (N. Y. State Lib.)   8.

Title, 1 f.; verso, blank; Pref., iii-v; p. vi blank; Contents, pp. vii-xiii; p. xiv, blank; Text: pp. 1-434; Notes and Illustrations, pp. 435-474; Index, 1 p.; Table, pp. 472 (not marked), 473, 474, 475, 476; sigs. (including Title) A to G, then K to 3 Q in 4'; a blank leaf completing the last sig.; 3 E is marked 3 C.

6. AN | Appendix | to the | New Testament. | By James Winthrop, Esq. | The judgment was set and the books were opened. | DAN. vii: 10. | Cambridge: | Printed by Hilliard and Metcalf. | 1809. | (B.; G. L.; Harv. Coll.)   12.

This is a reprint in one volume of the Translation of the Apocalypse and other tracts, already published separately and at different dates by the Author; pp. 211.

1810.

1. HOLY BIBLE: With Apocrypha, Index, Tables, Brown's Concordance, &c. &c. &c. Embellished with Ten Maps and Twenty Historical engravings. Philadelphia: Printed and Published by Mathew Carey, No. 122 Market-Street. 1810.   (L.)   4.

Printed from the same types as the edition of 1809. The first sig. to Apocrypha, is 45 XX; the first p. of Mat. is marked (29-1), and the Concordance is dated, M.DCCC.X. The maps are the same as in the edition of 1804.

The Engravings are:
1. Joseph discovering himself to his brethren...........................*Tiebout.*
2. Samuel preaching repentance.
3. Obadiah concealing the Prophets.

4. Fourth vision of Daniel.. *Tiebout.*
5. St. Mathew... *C. Tiebout.*
6. Magi offering gifts.. *Tiebout.*
7. John the Baptist in the Wilderness.
8. Christ curing the Centurion's servant............................. *C. Tiebout.*
9. Christ calling the Twelve Apostles.
10. The Disciples shewing the Temple............................... *C. Tiebout.*
11. Punishment of the useless servant.............................. *Tiebout.*
12. Judas treating with the Scribes & Pharisees...................... *Tiebout.*
13. St. Mark... *C. Tiebout.*
14. Christ healing the woman who touched his garment.
15. St. Luke... *Tiebout.*
16. Annunciation.. *C. Tiebout.*
17. Cure of the Ten Lepers.. *Tiebout.*
18. St. John.
19. Our Savior washing the disciples' feet.
20. The Lame man cured by St. Peter.

These engravings already appeared in Carey's 4to edition of July 25, 1804. Some are marked, "Engraved for M. Carey's Family Bible;" in other instances the words "Family Bible," are erased, and "Philad^a" or "Philadelphia" substituted, with the date 1805, the former date being also erased. Tiebout's name is likewise erased from several of the plates.

2. THE | HOLY BIBLE, | containing the | Old and New Testaments, | Translated out of the | Original Tongues, | and | With the former Translations diligently | Compared and Revised; | With the learned and excellent | Preface of the Rev. Thomas Scott, D. D., | Author of the Commentary on the Bible, &c. | Illustrated with Maps. | New York: | Published by Williams and Whiting, | Theological and Classical Booksellers, No. 118, Pearl Street. | J. Seymour, Printer. | 1810. | (L.)   8.

Title, 1 f.; verso, blank; Preface, pp. iii-xx; Introduction to the O. T., &c., pp. xxi, xxii; sigs. (including title) A to C³, in 4ˢ; Text: Gen. to Mal.; sigs. C⁴ to verso of 5 T², in 4ˢ; Fam. Rec., 2 ff.; The | New Testament | of our | Lord and Savior Jesus Christ, | Translated out of the | Original Greek, | and | With the former Translations diligently | Compared and Revised; | With the learned and excellent | Preface of the Rev. Thomas Scott, D. D., | Author of the Commentary on the Bible, &c. | Illustrated with Maps. | New York : | Published by Whiting and Watson, | Theological and Classical Booksellers, No. 96, Broadway. | J. Seymour, Printer. | 1812. | 1 p.; verso, Names and Order of all the Books of the N. T.; Introduction to the N. T., 3 pp.; Text: Mat. (on verso of A³) to Rev.; sigs. A to about the middle of recto of 2 N⁴, in 4ˢ; below, Names and Order of the Books of the Old and New Test., the remainder of the page; Tables of Weights and Measures; of Money; of Kindred and affinity, verso of 2 N⁴. No pagination.

This Vol. is without maps, notwithstanding the announcement on the title pages.

It has an engraved Frontispiece — Mercy and Truth — Angelica Kauffman, R. A. Pinx. P. *Maverick*, Newark, N. J., sculp. (below) Charlestown, Mass**tts**, Published by S. Etheridge, Jun**r** . It is sometimes found with the addition, at the end, of: A | Brief | Concordance | To the | Holy Scriptures | of | The 𝔒𝔩𝔡 𝔞𝔫𝔡 𝔑𝔢𝔴 Testaments, | by which All, or Most, | of the | Principal Text of Scripture | may be easily found out. | By John Brown, | *Late Minister of the Gospel at Haddington, in Scotland.* | Search the Scriptures, &c. | Revised and Corrected. | New York : | Published by Whiting and Watson, | Theological and Classical Booksellers, No. 96, Broadway. | *Thomas Kirk, Printer.* | 1812. | 1 p.; verso, blank; To the Reader, 1 p.; verso, blank; Text: pp. 5-92; sigs. A to verso of L⁴, in 4ˢ .

3. THE | HOLY BIBLE, | containing the | Old and New Testaments, | with | original Notes, practical Observations, | and | copious References. | By Thomas Scott, | Rector of Aston Sandford, Bucks, and Chaplain to the Lock Hospital. | In Six Volumes. | Vol. I. | A new American, from the last London edition, | improved by a more conspicuous insertion and arrangement of the | marginal References, | on an original Plan of the present Publishers. | New-York : | Published by Williams and Whiting, | Theological and Classical Booksellers, No. 118, Pearl Street. | J. Seymour, printer. | 1810. | (Conn. Hist. Soc.) 8.

Vol. 2 has in imprint, " Whiting and Watson, No. 96, Broadway. 1811." Otherwise, same title as Vol. 1, exactly.

Vol. 3, same as Vol. 2.

Vol. 4, "   "   except date, which is 1812.

Vols. 5 and 6, same as Vol. 4.

An edition of Scott's Commentary, or Family Bible, had already been published in this country in 1804. See No. 2, p. 73.

4. HOLY BIBLE: Philadelphia: | Printed by and for William W. Woodward, | No. 52 Second, corner of Chesnut Street. | 1810. | (L.)   12.

Title, 1 f.; verso, blank; To the Reader; Names and Order of the Books. 2 pp.; Text: Gen. to Mal. (not paged); sigs. A² to 3 L⁶, in 6ˢ; then 3 M, 3 N, 3 O in 1ˢ, ending on verso of 3 O¹; New Testament title; imprint: Philadelphia: | Printed by W. W. Woodward, No. 52, corner of Second and | Chesnut-Streets. | 1811. | 1 p.; verso, blank; Text: Mat. to Rev.; sigs. A to verso of S³; Memoranda, 3 ff. to complete the sig.; all in 6ˢ .

5. HOLY BIBLE. Philadelphia: Printed by Mathew Carey, No. 122, Market Street. 1810.   (N. Y. State Lib.; L.)   12.

This edition agrees in every respect, with No. 3, 1806, *supra*.

—1810.] AMERICAN BIBLES. 101

6. HOLY BIBLE. Boston: | Printed by Greenough and Stebbins, | *and sold by them, at their Office, Suffolk Buildings, Congress Street, and* | *by the principal Booksellers in the United States.* | 1810. | (L.; G. L.)   12.

The same as the edition, No. 5, of 1809. 1 Tim. 4: 16, incorrect.

7. HOLY BIBLE. Hartford, Connecticut. Printed by Hudson & Goodwin. 1810. (L.; B.) 12.

The same as No. 6, of 1809, supra, p. 95. With: A Dictionary of the Bible, or an Explanation of the proper Names and difficult words with other particulars, &c. First American edition from the second London edition enlarged. Printed at the Press of and for Isaiah Thomas, Junr, &c., Worcester, January 1st, 1798. At the end, an Advertisement or Card and List of Books, dated March 18, 1798.

8. GENESIS. Chapters I and part of II. (In Hebrew.) New Haven: Printed by Mills Day. March 20, 1810. 8.

This is a specimen of a Hebrew Bible, and consists of 2 pp. which accompanied a Prospectus for the work, issued by Mr. Day. It is the opinion of well informed gentlemen, that the book was never issued.

9. WISDOM IN MINIATURE, | or the | *Young Gentleman and Lady's* | Magazine, | being a Collection of Sentences | Divine and Moral. | (A Text from Proverbs.) Adorned with Cuts. | From Sidney Press | (J. Cooke & Co.), New-Haven. | 1810. | (L.)   32.

A school book, containing extracts chiefly from Proverbs and Ecclesiasticus; pp. 30; advertisement, page 31.

1. THE | NEW TESTAMENT | of our | Lord and Saviour | Jesus Christ. | Translated out of | 𝕮𝖍𝖊 𝕺𝖗𝖎𝖌𝖎𝖓𝖆𝖑 𝕲𝖗𝖊𝖊𝖐, | and | with the former Translations | *Diligently Compared and Revised.* | Baltimore: | Published and sold by John Hagerty, | No. 12, Light-Street. | Brook W. Sower, Printer. | 1810. | (B.)   12.

Title, 1 f.; verso, blank; Text (not paged) sigs. A^2 to Q, in 6^s; no heading to columns or chapters; references at foot of the pages; 1 Tim., 4: 16, incorrect.

2. THE | NEW TESTAMENT | of our Lord and Saviour | Jesus Christ: | Translated out of the Original Greek | and | with the former Translations Diligently | Compared and Revised. | The first American, from the | Cambridge

Stereotype Edition. | New York: | Printed for Williams and Whiting, and the | New York Bible Society: | Sold at Their Bible Warehouse, | 118 Pearl Street. | 1810. | (G. L.) 12.

Title. 1 f.; verso, Order of Books, and Paul & Thomas, printers; pages not numbered; sigs. 2 to 27*; brief headings to chapters and columns.

3. THE NEW | TESTAMENT | of our | Lord and Saviour | Jesus Christ | Newly Translated out of the | Original Greek, | and with the | former Translations | Diligently Compared and Revised. | Appointed to be read in Churches. | Brookfield, Massachusetts, | Printed by E. Merriam & Co., | For the Booksellers. | MDCCCX. | (G. L.)   12.

Title (within a plain border of 2 lines), 1 f.; verso, The Order of the Books of the New Testament, &c. &c.; Text, not paged; sigs. A to O⁶; brief headings to chapters and columns; Acts, 6:3, reads: whom ye may appoint.

4. LE NOUVEAU | TESTAMENT | de Notre | Seigneur Jésus-Christ, | en Français, | Sur la Vulgate. | Traduction de L. M. de Sacy. | Revue sur les Meilleures éditions. | Vol. I (or II). | Boston: | De l'imprimerie de J. T. Buckingham. | 1810. | (L.; J. G. S.; G. L.)   8.

Vol. I: Mock Title, 1 f.; verso, blank; Title, 1 f.; verso, blank; Avis, 3 pp., the last numbered vii; verso, Prière avant la lecture de l'Ecriture-Sainte; Text: Mat. to Acts, pp. 9–403, followed by Errata at foot of p. 403; sigs. 2 to recto of 51², in 4ˢ. Vol. II: Mock Title and verso, Title and verso, 2 ff.; Text, pp. 5–326, followed by Approbation; then 1 p., Errata; sigs. 2 to 41⁴, in 4ˢ.

The following is a copy of the Approbation:

J'ai lu attentivement, et comparé avec la Vulgate cette | nouvelle édition du Nouveau Testament, imprimée à Boston, | par J. T. Buckingham. Elle est fidèle; le langage en est | pur; et elle ne contient rien qui ne soit entièrement conforme | à la foi Catholique, Apostolique et Romaine.

+JEAN *Evêque de Boston.*

Boston, 22 *Décembre*, 1810.

The Text is in paragraphs, without notes, but with an introduction to each book concluding with a pious aspiration.

The version of the New Testament by Le Maistre de Sacy and others, appeared at Mons in 1667, but was condemned as containing the doctrines of the Jansenists. A corrected edition accordingly appeared the same year, and subsequent editions omitting or correcting the censured portions were well received. Le Maistre de Sacy, in 1672–95, published a version of the whole Bible, which was modified subsequently by Calmet and others. His edition of the New Testament published at Paris in 1759, with approbation, has been taken as a standard and was probably followed in this, although we can not say so positively. Having been compared by Bishop CHEVERUS with the Vulgate and approved by him, 'tis to be presumed that it is after the standard edition.—See further, *Dictionnaire de Bibliographie Catholique*, Ch. XI and XII.

5. A NEW | LITERAL TRANSLATION | from the Original Greek | of all the | Apostolical Epistles | with | a Commentary and Notes, | Philological, Critical, Explanatory and Practical. | To which is added, | A History of the Life of the Apostle Paul. | By James Macknight, D. D., | Author of a Harmony of the Gospels, &c. | In Six volumes. | To which is prefixed, | An Account of the Life of the Author. | Boston: | Published by W. Wells and T. B. Wait & Co. | T. B. Wait & Co., printers. | 1810. | (Am. Antiq. Soc.) 8.

1st Vol. contains: Memoir, Gen. Preface, Preliminary Essays, Romans. 2d Vol. contains: 1st and 2d Corinthians. 3d Vol. contains: Galatians, Ephesians, Philippians, Colossians. 4th Vol. contains: Thessalonians, 1st and 2d Timothy, 1st and 2d Titus, Philemon. 5th Vol. contains: Hebrews, James, 1st and 2d Peter. 6th Vol. contains: John, 1st, 2d and 3d Jude, Supplement to Essay IV, Essay VIII, Life of Apostle Paul, To which are added Proofs and Illustrations.

1811.

1. THE | HOLY BIBLE: | Containing the | *Old and New Testaments:* | Translated out of the Original Tongues, | and with the former Translations diligently compared and revised, | by the | Special Command of his Majesty King James I. of England. | With marginal Notes and References. | To which are added, | An Index; | An Alphabetical Table | of all the Names in the Old and New Testaments, with their Significations; | and Tables of Scripture Weights, Measures and Coins. | Philadelphia: | Printed and published by Mathew Carey, | No. 122, Market-Street. | 1811. | (L.; G. L.) 4.

Title, 1 f.; verso, blank; second title: The | Old Testament, | translated | out of | The Original Hebrew, | and | with the former Translations diligently compared and revised. | Done | by the Special Command of King James I. of England. | Philadelphia: | Printed and published by Mathew Carey, No. 122, Market-Street. | 1811. | 1 p.; verso, Names and Order of all the Books; Index to the various Articles annexed to this edition; Text: Gen. to Mal., pp. 1-674; sigs. 1.A to 43.UU^1, in 6^s; Table of Offices, p. 675; Index of years and times, and Analysis of O. & N. T., p. 676, UU^2; Family Record, pp. 677-680 (marked), 86.4R; The | New Testament | of our | Lord and Saviour | Jesus Christ, | translated | out of the Original Greek; | and | with the former Translations | diligently compared and revised, | *By the Special Command of*

King James I. of England. | Philadelphia: | Printed and published by Mathew Carey, No. 122, Market-Street. | 1811. | 1 p. (marked in the left corner, "107"); Text: Mat. to Rev., pp. 835-1046; sig. 5 R (which includes title) to 6 S^3, and in numbers 107-133; p. 835 is marked at foot (35-1), and we supply the mark 5 R though the first sig. is not marked by any letter, only by "107;" the following sig. is marked 108 5 Q; Judea, Palestine, &c., pp. 1047, 1048, 6 S^4; Index, pp. 1049-1066, 6 T to 6 X,^{1}, in numbers 134-136^1; at foot of p. 1066, Table of Time; Alphabetical Table, pp. 1067-1073, 6 X^2 to 6 Y^1; at foot of p. 1073, Table of Kindred; Fletcher's Concise View, pp. 1074-1076; Tables of Scripture measures, &c., pp. 1076-1078; Table of Passages, pp. 1079, 1080; verso of 6 Y^2 to verso of 6 Y^4, in numbers 136^2 to 137^4, in 4^s. The hiatus from p. 680 to p. 835, is caused by the omission of the Apocrypha.

2. THE | HOLY BIBLE, | containing the | Old and New Testament: | the Text | carefully printed from the most correct copies of the present | authorized Translation. | Including the | marginal Readings and parallel Texts. | With a Commentary and critical Notes, | designed as a help to a better understanding of | the Sacred Writings. | By Adam Clarke, L.L. D. | Volume I-VI. | For whatever things were written aforetime, were written for our learning; that we, | through patience and comfort of the scriptures, might have hope. Rom. xv. 4. | New-York: | published by Ezra Sargeant, No. 86 Broadway, | opposite Trinity Church. | 1811. | (Conn. Hist. Soc.; G. L.)   4.

Vol. 2 has, before "New-York," and in a separate line, | "Third Edition." | Also, for second line of imprint, "Published by Daniel Hitt and Abraham Paul, 182 Waterstreet, corner of Burling-Slip. | Abraham Paul, printer. | 1821." Also, the word "the" is transferred from 3d to 4th line of title; the colon after line 4 is made a period; as is the comma after "notes" in line 10; "the" before "sacred" in line 12 is placed at the end of line 11; after "LL. D." is added, "F. S. A."

Vol. 3, same as vol. 2, except that after "F. S. A." is "M. R. I. A.;" the edition is not designated; and the imprint has but three lines, the 2d and 3d being "Printed and published by Abraham Paul, No. 72 Nassau-street. | 1825." Vol. 4, as vol. 3.

Vol. 5 has a different title page, viz.: "The | New Testament | of our | Lord and Saviour Jesus Christ. | The text | carefully printed from the most correct copies of the present | authorized version. | With the marginal readings, | a collection of parallel texts, and copious summaries to each chapter. | With | a commentary and critical notes. | Designed as a help to a better understanding of | the sacred writings. | By Adam Clarke, LL. D., F. S. A. | Volume I. | New-York: | published by Daniel Hitt and Abraham Paul, | 182 Water-street, corner of Burling-slip. | Abraham Paul, Printer. | 1818. | Vol. 6 same as vol. 5, except " Vol. II." instead of ".Vol. I."

This work was advertised in New York before it appeared in London. The American copyright bears date 11 May, 1810, and in that, and in the prospectus, the Title was set forth as follows: The | Holy Scriptures | of the | Old and New Testaments. | The Text | taken from the most correct copies of the present | Authorized Version: | With all the Marginal Readings; an ample collection of parallel texts; and copious Summaries to each chapter. | The Date of every Transaction through the whole of the Old and New Testaments, as far as it has been ascer- | tained by the best Chronologers, will be marked in the A. M. or years from the Creation, collated throughout with the | years of the Julian period; and in the A. a. C. and A. D., or years *before* and *after* Christ. | With | a Commentary and Critical notes. | In this work | the whole of the Text has been collated with the *Hebrew* and *Greek* originals, and all the *Ancient* versions: | The most *difficult words* analyzed and explained: The most important *Readings* in the *Hebrew* collections of Kennicott | and De Rossi, and in the *Greek* collections of Mill, Wetstein and Griesbach, noticed: The *peculiar customs* of | the Jews and neighbouring Nations, so frequently alluded to by the *Prophets, Evangelists,* and *Apostles,* explained from the | best *Asiatic Authorities:* the *great doctrines* of the Law and Gospel *defined, illustrated* and *defended;* and | the Whole *applied* to the important purposes | of | Practical Christianity and Vital Godliness. | Designed as a help to a better understanding of the Sacred Writings. | By Adam Clarke, LL. D. | New York: | Printed for Ezra Sargeant, | No. 86 Broadway, opposite Trinity Church. | *Prospectus in N. Y. Hist. Soc. Lib.*

The work was advertised to be issued in parts at one dollar and fifty cents each, but before it was completed, it appears to have passed out of the hands of the original publisher. It is the *first* American edition of Clarke's Commentaries.

3. HOLY BIBLE: With Original and Practical Observations, and Copious Marginal References. By Thomas Scott, D. D., Rector of Aston Sandford, Bucks, and Chaplain to the Lock Hospital. Woodward's Second American, from the Second London Edition, improved and enlarged. Philadelphia: Printed for and published by William W. Woodward, corner of Second and Chesnut Streets. Sold also by William Barlas, New York; D. Mallory & Co., Boston; and by the Booksellers in different Parts of the United States. Dickinson, Printer. 1811–1813. Five Volumes.   (Brown Univ.)   4.

4. HOLY BIBLE: Philadelphia: Printed by Mathew Carey, No. 122 Market Street. 1811.   (L.)   12.

5. HOLY BIBLE: With Apocrypha. Boston: Thomas & Andrews &c. Greenhough and Stebbins, Printers. 1811. (L.) 12.

Contains Dr. Witherspoon's Preface to Collins's ed. of 1807, and an Account of Judea; 1 Tim. 4: 16, is incorrect.

6. THE | HOLY BIBLE | 𝔄𝔟𝔯𝔦𝔡𝔤𝔢𝔡: | Containing the | History | of | The New Testament. | For the Use Childrens. | *Suffer*

little Children, &c. | Greenfield: | Printed by John Denio. |
1811. | (B.) 24.
Pp. 36.

7. BIBLE | HISTORY. | New York: | Printed and Sold | By S.
Wood, | No. 357 Pearl Street. | 1811. | (L.) 142.

Title, 1 f.; verso, blank; Pref., pp. 3-11; Text, pp. 12-254; sigs. A to Q, in 8ˢ, including a frontispiece. Wood-cuts are interspersed throughout.

1. NEW TESTAMENT; Translated out of the Latin Vulgate;
Philadelphia: Printed by Mathew Carey, No. 122 Market-
Street. 1811. 4.

11 Plates. (J. G. S.)

2. NEW TESTAMENT: Appointed to be read in Churches and
Families. | Philadelphia: | Published and Sold by Benja-
min C. Buzby, | No. 2 North Third-Street. | Sweeny &
M'Kenzie, Printers. | 1811. | (B.) 12.

Title, 1 f.; verso, order of the Books ; Text, not paged; sigs. A² to verso of Ff⁰, in 4ˢ and 8ˢ alternately; short headings to columns and chapters.

Acts, 6:3, reads: whom ye may appoint over this business; 1 Tim., 4:16, Take heed unto thyself and unto thy doctrine:

3. NEW TESTAMENT: Philadelphia: Printed by and for William
W. Woodward, No. 52, Second, Corner of Chesnut Street.
1811. 12.

With Bibles of 1810 and 1813. q. v.

4. NEW TESTAMENT. Baltimore: Published and Sold by John
Hagerty, No. 12 Light Street. Brook W. Sower, Printer.
1811. (L.) 18.

Same as the edition of 1810.

5. THE | FOUR GOSPELS, | translated from the Greek. | With |
preliminary Dissertations, | and | Notes critical and ex-
planatory. | By George Campbell, D. D., F. R. S., Edin-
burgh. | Principal of the Marischal College, Aberdeen. |
In Four Volumes. | With the Author's last corrections. |
Μονη Θυτσον τη αληϑεια. | Boston: | Published by W. Wells,
and Thomas B. Wait & Co. | T. B. Wait & Co., printers. |
1811. | (Harvard Coll. ; Conn. Hist. Soc.) 8

1812.

1. THE | HOLY BIBLE: | Containing the | *Old and New Testaments:* | Together with the | Apocrypha. | Translated out of the Original Tongues, | and with the former Translations diligently compared and revised, | by the | Special Command of his Majesty King James I. of England. | With marginal Notes and References. | To which are added, | An Index; | An Alphabetical Table | of all the names in the Old and New Testaments, with their Significations; | And Tables of Scripture Weights, Measures and Coins; | John Brown's Concordance, &c., &c. | Embellished with Twenty-five Engravings. | Philadelphia: | Printed and published by Mathew Carey, | No. 122 Market-street. | 1812. | (L.)   4.

Title, 1 f.; verso, blank; title to Old Test., same imprint, 1 p.; verso, Names and Order of Books; Index of various articles annexed; List of Engravings; Text: Gen. to Mal., pp. 1–674; p. 161 marked 164; sigs. A to verso of 4 Q; and in numbers (1) to (85), in 4ˢ; Table of Offices, p. 675; Index of years, and Analysis of Old and New Test., p. 676; sig. 4 Q²; Family Record, pp. [677]-[680]; sig 4 R numbered 86, in 2ˢ: Apocrypha, pp. 681–834, and then [829] to [834]; sigs. 4 S to recto of 5 O; in numbers (87)-(106) in 4ˢ; Title to New Test., same imprint; numbered on the left corner [107], Mat. to Rev. pp. 835–1046; sigs. 5 P to verso of 6 S³, in numbers, [107]-(133); 1st page of Mat. marked at foot (40.4); Account of Judea, pp. 1047, 1048; sig. 6 S⁴; Index, pp. 1049–1066; at foot of p. 1066, Table of Time; Table of Proper Names, pp. 1067–1073; at foot of p. 1073, Table of Kindred; Fletcher's Concise View, pp. 1074–1076; Table of Scripture Weights, Measures, &c., pp. 1076–1078; Table of Passages, pp. 1079, 1080; sigs. 6 T to recto of 6 Y⁴ and in numbers (134)-(137); all in 4ˢ; Title to Brown's Concordance: Philadelphia: | Printed and Published by Mathew Carey, | No. 122 Market-Street, | M.DCCC.XI. | 1 p.; verso, blank; To the Reader, 1 p.; verso, blank; Text: pp. 5–72; sigs, A³ to I in 4ˢ.

List of Engravings in this edition:

1. Journeyings of the Children of Israel.
2. Scheme of the Lives of the Patriarchs............................... *J. Bower.*
3. Map of Canaan .... *F. Shallus.*
4. The Lord appearing to Isaac.
5. Map of Egypt (name erased).
6. Map of the Places recorded in the books of Moses (name erased).
7. Map of Canaan from Joshua to the Babylonian captivity.
8. Samuel anointing David... *Tanner.*
9. Solomon's judgment.
10. Map of the Purveyorships.. .... *F. Shallus.*
11. Map of the Assyrian and other Empires.

12. Elijah raising the widow's son.
13. The Angel appearing to Elijah.
14. Map of Solomon's dominions. .... *F. Shallus.*
15. David playing on the harp.
16. Map of Moriah and plan of Jerusalem.
17. John baptizing our Saviour.
·18. The Adoration of the Wise Men.
19. The Last Supper ....*Tanner.*
20. Our Saviour in the Temple............................. ......*Tiebout.*
21. John the Baptist sending his disciples to our Saviour.................*Tiebout.*
22. The Miracle at the pool of Bethesda............................... .....*Tiebout.*
23. The Woman caught in Adultery.
24. Jews Interrogating our Saviour..................................*B. Tanner.*
25. Map of the Travels of the Apostles.

The design of the Historical Engravings in this volume, is different from those in the standing edition. Nos. 2, 8, 9, 13, 19, 20, 22 and 25 already appeared in Carey's Doway Bible, No. 2, 1805.

This Bible was published without the Apocrypha; also, Embellished with A Scheme of the Lives of the Patriarchs, and a Map of the Travels of the Apostles. In such editions, the general title is altered accordingly.

The following errors occur, for the first time, in the text: Leviticus, 19 : 12, *the God ;* for, thy God : Esther, 1 : 8, *to* the King—for, so the King.

. 2. THE | HOLY BIBLE: | Containing the | *Old and New Testaments:* | Together with the | Apocrypha. | Translated out of the Original Tongues, | and with the former Translations diligently compared and revised, | By the | Special Command of his Majesty King James I. of England. | With Marginal Notes and References. | To which are added, | An Index; | An Alphabetical Table | of all the Names in the Old and New Testaments, with their Significations; | And Tables of Scripture Weights, Measures, and Coins. | Windsor: | Published by Merrifield and Cochran. | Sold Wholesale and Retail by them at the Sign of the Bible. | Sold also by I. Thomas, Worcester; J. West & Co., Boston; | I. Thomas & Co., Walpole, N. H., and S. Swift, Middlebury, Vt. | John Cunningham, Printer. | MDCCCXII. | 4.

Title, 1 f.; verso, blank ; The | Old Testament, | translated | out of | The Original Hebrew, | and | with former Translations diligently compared and revised. | Together with the Apocrypha: | Done | by the Special Command of King James I. of England. | Windsor : | Published by Merrifield and Cochran. | Sold wholesale and retail by them at the sign of the Bible. | Sold also by I. Thomas, Worcester; J. West & Co, Boston; |

I. Thomas & Co., Walpole, N. H., and S. Swift, Middlebury, Vt. | MDCCCXII. | 1 p.; verso, Names and order of all the books of the O. and N. Test. 1 p. making sig A in 2^s ; Text: Gen. to end of Mal. pp. 5-617; sig. B (not marked) to K, then M to recto of Hhhh^3 in 4^s , except S which is in 6^s and T in 2^s ; verso of 617, blank; Apocrypha, pp. 619-762; sig. Hhhh^4 to verso of Bbbbb^3 ; The | New Testament | of our | Lord and Saviour | Jesus Christ, | translated out of the original Greek; | and | with the former Translations | diligently compared and revised, | By the Special Command of King James I. of England. | Windsor: | Published by Merrifield and Cochran. | Sold wholesale and retail by them at the sign of the Bible. | Sold also by E. Goodale, Hallowell; J. West & Co. | Boston; I. Thomas & Co., Walpole, N. H. | and S. Swift, Middlebury, Vt. | MDCCCXII. | 1 p.; verso, blank; (Bbbbb^4 not marked); Text: Mat. to Rev., pp. 765-956; sigs. Ccccc to verso of Cccccc^4 in 4^s ; Family Record, pp. [959], [960]; A Clergyman's address to Married persons; Analysis of the O. and N. Test., p. 961; a Chronological Index of years, &c., p. 962, sig. Dddddd^1; Summary History of the Bible (in smaller type), pp. 963, 964, Dddddd^2; An Index to the Holy Bible (also in smaller type, not paged), 9 ff.; sigs. A to verso of C^2 ; [The last sig. letter is omitted]; Alphabetical table, C^3 to D^2 ; Table of weights and measures occupying the lower half of D^2 ; verso, Table of Kindred and Table of Time.

List of Engravings:
Elijah raising the Widow's Son.....................*Isaac Eddy*. Weathersfield, Vt.
St. Mark..*Isaac Eddy*. Weathersfield, Vt.
The Resurrection...................................*James Hill*.
The Holy Family....................................*Isaac Eddy*. Weathersfield, Vt.
St. John the Evangelist............................*Isaac Eddy*. Weathersfield, Vt.
St. Luke...*Isaac Eddy*. Weathersfield, Vt.
St. Paul...*Isaac Eddy*. Weathersfield, Vt.

These Engravings are exceedingly coarse; each plate, except that of The Resurrection, is surmounted with the words: First Vermont Edition; having at the bottom: Windsor: Published by Merrifield and Cochran, 1812. At the top of The Resurrection are the words: Vermont First Edition. Page 74 is headed Exodus, instead of Leviticus; page 117, Joshua, instead of Judges; page 313, I Chronicles, instead of II Chronicles; page 347, S. Jonn, instead of S. John; page 906, Ephesians instead of Galatians. And the Epistles to the Ephesians and Philippians are entitled: The Epistle of Paul, the Aposle, &c. There are brief headings to columns, and full headings to the chapters.

3. The | Holy Bible: | Containing | The Old and New Testaments; | together with the | Apocrypha: | Translated | out of the Original Tongues, | and | with the former Translations | diligently compared and revised. | *First New York Edition.* | New York: | Published by E. Duyckinck, Smith and Forman, Collins and Co., | J. Tiebout, S. A. Burtus, B. Crane. | *George Long, Printer.* | 1812. | (L.) 8.

Title, 1 f.; verso, "The property of," within an oblong of printer's ornaments; To the Reader, 2 p.; (Dr. Witherspoon's Preface, from Collins's Bible of 1807; Account of dates, &c., 1 p.; Names and Order, 1 p.; Text: pp. 7-735, (misprinted 765);

Tables of Measures, Weights, Money and Time, 1 p.; sigs., including title page, &c., 1 to verso of 92⁴ in 4ˢ; Apocrypha not paged; sigs. 1* to verso of 21*⁴; N. T. title agrees, 1 p.; verso, blank; Mat. to Rev., pp. 739-959; sigs. (incl. title) 73 to recto of 120⁴ in 4ˢ; verso of 120⁴ Table of Offices, &c. There are 4 wood cuts, including, front. to O. and N. Test.

4. THE | HOLY BIBLE, | containing the | Old and New Testaments: | Translated | out of the Original Tongues, | and | With the former Translations | diligently Compared and Revised. | Stereotype Edition. | Stereotyped for the | Bible Society at Philadelphia. | By T. Rutt, *Shacklewell, London.* | 1812. | (L.)   12.

Title, 1 p.; verso, blank; Names and Order; Account of dates or Time, 1 p.; verso, blank; Text: Gen. to Mal., pp. 5-633; verso, Tables of Measures, Weights, and Money and Time; sigs. A³ to verso of Dd⁵ in 12ˢ; New Test. title, 1 p.; verso, blank; Text: Mat. to Rev., pp. 1-192; sigs. *B to verso of *I¹² in 12ˢ.

This is the first Bible printed in the United States from Stereotype plates. They were imported from England by the Phil. Bible Society.

5. HOLY BIBLE. First American Diamond Edition. | Baltimore: | Published and Sold by John Hagerty, | No. 12, Light Street. | B. W. Sower & Co., printers. | 1812. | (B.; L.)   12.

With Synopsis of the Holy Bible, 7 pp. In some instances the imprint to the New Test. title has, Brook W. Sower, printer. 1811.

6. HOLY BIBLE: Philadelphia: | Printed by Mathew Carey, | No. 122 Market-Street. | 1812. | (L.)   12.

7. THE HOLY BIBLE. | Boston: | Printed for Thomas and Andrews, West and Richardson, | and West and Blake. | *W. Greenough, Printer.* | 1812. | (Harvard Coll.)   12.

8. HOLY BIBLE: Hartford, Connecticut: Printed and Sold by Hudson & Goodwin. 1812.   (B.; Conn. Hist. Soc.)   12.

1. THE | NEW TESTAMENT | of our | Lord and Saviour Jesus Christ, | translated out of the | Original Greek; | and | with the former Translations | diligently compared and revised: | with the learned and excellent | General Preface, | the | valuable preliminary Remarks to the several

books, | and the | most copious marginal References | of | *Dr. Scott's Family Bible,* | to which are added, | An Index; | An Alphabetical Table | of all the Names in the Old and New Testaments, with their Significations; | Tables of Scripture Weights, Measures, Coins, &c. &c. &c. | Illustrated with Maps. | New York: | Published by Whiting and Watson, | Theological and Classical Booksellers, No. 90, Broadway. | J. Seymour, Printer. | 1812. | 4.

With Bible of 1813. q. v.

2. NEW TESTAMENT. New York: Published by Whiting and Watson, Theological and Classical Booksellers. 1812. 8.

3. NEW TESTAMENT. New York: Whiting and Watson. 1812. 12.

4. NEW TESTAMENT. New York: Whiting and Watson. 1812. 32.

The Testaments, Nos. 2, 3, 4, have not been seen. They are from a list of books on the cover of a pamphlet printed by W. & W., New York. 1812.

5. NEW TESTAMENT. Philadelphia: Printed by Mathew Carey, No. 122 Market Street. 1812. 12.

6. NEW TESTAMENT: Appointed to be Read in Churches. | New York: | Printed and Sold by E. Duyckinck, No. 102, Pearl Street. | 1812. | (G. L.) 12.

3. **Das | Neue | Testament** | unsers | HErrn und Heilandes | JEsu Christi, | nach der Deutschen Uebersetzung | D. Martin Luthers. | Mit kurzem | Inhalt eines jeden Capitels, | und | volständiger Anweisung gleicher Schriftstellen. | Wie auch | aller Sonn- und Festtägigen | Evangelien und Episteln. | Vierte Auflage. | Lancaster: | Gedruckt bey Wilhelm Hamilton. | 1812. | (L.) 12.

Title, 1 f.; verso, blank; Verzeichniss, &c., 1 p.; verso, blank; Text: pp. 5-572; Anweisung, &c., 5 pp., not numbered; sigs. A (not marked) to recto of Bbb^5, in 6^s.

This year Messrs. Delaplaine and Murray, Draper, Fairman & Co., Philadelphia, advertised to print a Splendid hot pressed Edition of Macklin's celebrated Bible, with 200 Engravings, 50 numbers Roy. 4to; 1 No. every 6 weeks, at $3.50 each number.—*Analectic Magazine* for 1812, p. 184. The project was not executed.

1813.

1. HOLY BIBLE: With the Apocrypha, Marginal Notes and References, Index, Tables, and Brown's Concordance, &c. Embellished with Twenty-five Maps and Engravings. Philadelphia: Printed and published by Mathew Carey, No. 122, Market Street. 1813. . (L.) 4.

<small>This is a continuation of Carey's 4to edition of 1812 Page 161 is numbered 164, and the errors in Leviticus, 18 : 12, and Esther, 1 : 8, are repeated. The plates are the same as already enumerated in the edition of 1812. The imprint to Brown's Concordance is: Brooklyn : | Printed by Thomas Kirk, Main Street. | 1812. | Title, 1 f.; verso, blank; To the Reader, 1 f.; verso, blank; Text; pp. 5–62; sigs. A to N, in 2^s, then O, in 3^s. Another copy of this edition is without the Apocrypha.</small>

2. THE | HOLY BIBLE: | Containing the | Old and New Testaments: | Together with the | Apocrypha; | and | Arguments prefixed to the different Books: | With moral and theological | Observations illustrating each Chapter. | Composed by | the Reverend Mr. Ostervald, | professor of Divinity, and one of the Ministers of the Church at Neufchatel in Swisserland. | Translated at the desire of, and recommended by, | The Society for Propagating Christian Knowledge. | To which are added, | An Index; | An Alphabetical Table | of all the Names in the Old and New Testaments, with their Significations; | Brown's Concordance, &c., &c., &c. | Embellished with Maps, and a Number of Elegant Historical Engravings. | New York: | Published by Evert Duyckinck, John Tiebout, G. & R. Waite, and Websters & Skinners of Albany. | George Long, Printer. | 1813. | (L.) 4.

<small>Title, 1 f.; verso, blank; Preliminary Discourse, pp. iii-viii; at foot of p. viii Names and Order of Books of the O. & N. T., forming with Title, sig. A; Text : Gen. to Mal. (not paged); sigs. A to verso of 4 U^4, Apocrypha, in smaller type, A* to verso of M*^{2}, Family Record, 2 ff.; The New Testament Title : Imprint as above; 1 p.; verso, blank; Text: Mat. to Rev., sigs. (including Title) 4 X to verso of 6 B^4; Index, 6 C to 6 D^3, 7 ff.; Table of Kindred, Table of Time, Table of Offices, 6 D^4, 2 pp.; all the sigs. are in 4^s except M* of Apocrypha, which is in 2^s; Brown's Brief Concordance; New York: | Published by Evert Duyckinck, Smith & Forman, John Tiebout, G. & R. Waite, | and Websters & Skinners of Albany. | George Long, Printer. | 1813. | 1 p.; verso, blank; To the Reader, 1 f.; verso, blank; Text: pp. 5–72; sig. B to S in 2^s. Ostervald's Observations are at the foot of the respective pages.</small>

The following is a list of the Engravings:

Moses on Mount Sinai (Front.)..*Scoles*.
Journeyings of the Children of Israel.................................*Scoles*.
Ahab in Naboth's Vineyard.. *A. Anderson*.
The Scribe reading the Law to King Josiah........................*A. Anderson*.
Job in deep distress...*Scoles*.
David at his early devotions...*Scoles*.
The Wise Men worshiping Christ......................................*Scoles*.
Jesus in the Cornfield reproving the Pharisees.......................*Scoles*.
Jesus conversing with his Disciples after Supper.................*A. Anderson*.
Map of the Country traveled by the Apostles......................*A. Anderson*.
St. John in the Isle of Patmos...*Scoles*.

The designs of these Engravings are the same as in Hepinstall's London 4to.

3. THE | HOLY BIBLE, | containing | 𝔈𝔥𝔢 𝔒𝔩𝔡 𝔞𝔫𝔡 𝔑𝔢𝔴 𝔗𝔢𝔰𝔱𝔞-
𝔪𝔢𝔫𝔱𝔰, | translated out of the | Original Tongues, | and
with the | former Translations diligently compared and
revised. | To which are now first added, the | learned and
excellent general Preface, | the | valuable preliminary
Remarks to the several Books; | and the | copious mar-
ginal References | of | Dr. Scott's Family Bible. | To-
gether with | An Index; | An Alphabetical Table, | of all
the Names in the Old and New Testaments, with their
Significations, | Tables of Scripture Weights, Measures,
and Coins; | and | Brown's Concordance. | Illustrated
with Maps. | New York: | Published by Whiting and
Watson, Theological and Classical Booksellers. | J. Sey-
mour, Printer. | 1813. | (L.)   4.

Title, 1 f.; verso, blank; Pref. 11¼ pp.; To the Reader, signed T. Scott; Note by the Publishers; Introd. to the O. Test., &c., 2 pp.; sigs. A, B, in 4^s; Text: Gen. to Mal.; sigs. C to 5 H^4, in 4^s; New Testament title with the imprint: New York: | Published by Whiting and Watson, | Theological and Classical Booksellers, No. 96, Broadway. | J. Seymour, Printer. | 1812. |; verso, Names and Order of the Books of the New Test., 1 f.; Introd. to New Test., 1 f.; sig. 5 I^2; Text: Mat. to Rev.; sigs. 5 I^3 to recto of 6 X^2, in 4^s; verso of 6 X^2, blank; Index, 13 ff.; *A to *D^1, in 4^s; Tables of Measures, Weights, Time, States and Offices; Proper Names; Kindred and Affinity; 5 ff.; *D^2 to verso of *F^2, in 4^s.

4. HOLY BIBLE: Charlestown, Mass.: Published by Saml. Etheridge, Junr. 1813.   4.

Not seen; its publication inferred from having found A Biblical Map of the Land of Canaan, shewing the situation of the principal places mentioned in the Histories of Joshua & the Judges, with the above imprint on it.

5. BIBLIA, | Das ist: | Die Ganze Göttliche | **Heilige Schrift,** | Alten und Neuen Testaments, | nach der deutschen Uebersetzung | Dr. Martin Luthers. | Mit jedes Capitels kurzen Summarien, auch beygefüghten vielen | und richtigen Paralellen. | Nebst schicklichen Nutzanwendungen | zu den fünf Büchern Mosis, bem Hohenlied Salomonis und den Offenbarung S. Johannis. | Die erste Auflage. | Somerset: Gedruckt und zu finden bey Friedrich Goeb. | 1813. | (L.) 4.

Title, 1 f.; verso, blank; Vorrede, signed by Goeb and dated Somerset (Penn.), the 26th June, 1813, 1 p.; Verzeichniß, &c., 1 p.; Text: Gen. to Mal.; pp. 1-527; 528, blank; sigs. in numbers, 1 and 2, each one leaf, 3 to 68^2, in 4^s; Apocrypha, in smaller type, pp. 1-66; sigs. A to verso of R^1, in 2^s; Das | Neue Testament | unsers | Herrn und Heilandes | Jesu Christi, | verdeutscht | von | Dr. Martin Luther. | Mit schicklicher Einleitung zur Offenbarung S. Johannis, und völliger Anweisung gleicher Schriftstellen. | Die Erste Auflage. | Somerset: Gedruckt und zu finden bey Friedrich Goeb. | 1813. |, 1 p.; Verzeichniß, &c., 1 p.; Text: Mat. to Rev.; pp. 1-169; 170, blank; Anweisung, &c., 2 pp., unnumbered; sigs. in numbers, 1 to 20, in 4^s; 21 in 6^s.

F. GOEB, the printer, was a clergyman. He established a small printing office, and published the first ed. of the Bible in Western Pennsylvania. The Preface, the Remarks prefixed to each chapter of the 5 Books of Moses, and the Commentary to the Song of Solomon, are said to have been written by him. There are no comments or remarks on the Revelations, though announced on both title pages.

6. HOLY BIBLE: With Original and Practical Observations and Copious Marginal References. By Thomas Scott, D. D., In Six Vols. New York: Published by Whiting and Watson, Theological and Classical Booksellers. J. Seymour, Printer. 1813. 8.

A reissue of the edition of 1810. See *Supra*, p. 100.

7. HOLY BIBLE: Philadelphia: | Printed by and for William W. Woodward | No. 52 Second, corner of Chesnut-street. | 1813. | (L.) 12.

The same as Bible No. 4 of 1810, with The | Psalms of David | in metre: | translated and diligently compared | with | the Original Text | and | former translations. | More plain, smooth and agreeable to the Text | than any heretofore | Allowed by the authority of the General Assembly of the Kirk | of Scotland, and appointed to be sung in | Congregations and Families. | Philadelphia: | Printed by W. W. Woodward, No. 52, corner of Second and | Chesnut streets. | 1811. | Sigs. A. to F^4; sigs. in 6^s. Text not paged. There are copies of this edition without the Psalms, in some of which the new Test. is dated, 1815.

8. HOLY BIBLE: Boston: | Printed for Thomas and Andrews, West and Richardson, | and West and Blake. | *W. Greenough, Printer.* | 1813. | (B.) 12.

<small>Title, 1 f.; verso, The Property of (within an ornamental border); Names and Order, 1 p.; Account of Dates, 1 p. The sigs. of the text (not paged) agree with Thomas's 12mo of 1797. No catch words; Acts, 6 : 3, correct.</small>

9. HOLY BIBLE: | Hartford, Connecticut. | Printed by | Hudson & Goodwin. | 1813. | (B.) 12.

<small>Imprint to New Test. title: Printed and sold by | &c., as above.</small>

10. AN | ABRIDGEMENT | of the | Holy Scriptures. | By the Rev. Mr. Sellon, | late Minister of St. James's, Clerkenwell. | *From a child thou hast known the Holy Scriptures,* | *which are able to make thee wise unto Salvation, through* | *Faith which is in Christ Jesus.* | Hartford: | Printed and sold by Hale and Hosmer. | 1813. | (B.) 12.

<small>Pp. 215.</small>

11. THE HOLY BIBLE abridged; or the History of the Old and New Testament. For the use of children. Adorned with cuts. Suffer little Children, &c. Barnard, V^t. Published by Joseph Dix, 1813. J. H. Carpenter, printer. (L.) 24.

<small>Pp. 124.</small>

1. THE | NEW TESTAMENT | of our | Lord and Saviour | Jesus Christ | Translated out of the Original Greek, | and with the | former Translations | Diligently compared and revised. | Philadelphia: | Published by Benjamin Johnson, | No. 455 Market Street. | J. Bouvier, Printer. | 1813. | (L.) 12.

<small>Title, 1 f.; verso, This book is the property of, and order of books; Text: Mat. to Rev., A² to Z⁶ in 6ˢ ; Finis on recto of Z⁶.</small>

2. THE | NEW TESTAMENT | of our | Lord and Saviour | Jesus Christ, | translated out of the Original Greek, | and with the | former Translations diligently compared and revised. | Boston: | published by | E. Larkin, 47 Cornhill, and Lincoln & Edmands, 53 Cornhill. | 1813. | Lincoln & Edmands, printers. | (Conn. Hist. Soc.) 8.

<small>Unpaged.</small>

3. NEW TESTAMENT: Boston: | Printed for Thomas and Andrews, West and Richardson | and West and Blake. | W. *Greenough, Printer.* | 1813. | (B.) 12.

4. THE | NEW TESTAMENT | of | Our Lord and Saviour | Jesus Christ: | Translated out of | the Original Greek; | and | With the former Translations diligently | compared and revised. | The second American | Edition, from the | Cambridge Stereotype Edition; | carefully revised and corrected, by the Rev. John McDonald, | of Albany. | Albany: | Printed and sold by H. C. Southwick. | Sold, also, wholesale and retail, by S. Wood, | New York. | 1813. | (N. Y. State Lib.) 12.

Title, 1 f.; verso, Order of the Books; Text: Mat. to Rev., sigs. 1 to verso of 28⁵ (including title page) in 6ˢ. A blank leaf completes the last sig. The pp. are not numbered. Brief headings: 1 Tim. 4: 16, incorrect.

The type of this Testament was kept standing for several years; it is advertised in Albany Register of July 12, 1816.

5. NEW TESTAMENT: Appointed to be read in Churches. | New York: | Printed for and sold by Evert Duyckinck, | No. 102 Pearl Street. | 1813. | (L.) 12.

Title, 1 f.; verso, Order of Books; G. Long, Printer; pp. 334; Sigs. agree with those of the Duyckinck's Test. No. 2 of 1805.

6. NEW TESTAMENT. Philadelphia: Jonathan Pounder. 1813. (Seminary St. Sulpice, Balt.) 24.

7. EVANGELICAL HISTORY: | or | a Narrative | of the | Life, Doctrines and Miracles | of | Jesus Christ, | Our Blessed Lord and Saviour, | and of His Holy Apostles: | Containing the | Four Gospels and the Acts: | with a general Introduction, · | and | Prefatory Remarks to each Book | and | Notes, Didactic, Explanatory and Critical. | Designed chiefly for those who have not leisure to peruse | the larger works of Voluminous Commentators. | By Alden Bradford. | And many other Miracles Jesus in fact performed, which are | not written in this book. But these are written that ye may | believe that Jesus is the Christ, the SON OF GOD; and that be- | lieving ye may have life through his name.

John xx: 20.* | Boston: Published by Bradford & Read. | and for sale by J. Brewer, Providence; | A Sherman, Jr., New | Bedford; J. Avery, Plymouth; J. Dabney, Salem; J. | Babson, Wiscasset; E. Goodale, Hallowell; Var- | ney & Co., Dover; E. Foley, Philadel- | phia; Eastburn, Kirk & Co., New York. | 1813. | (G. L.)   12

Pp. 526, sigs. 1 to *44.

1813. Messrs. Delaplaine, Parker, Kimber & Richardson issue proposals for printing an edition of the Bible, 2 Vols. Roy. 8vo, 60 plates; The subjects to be chosen by Rembrandt Peale and Thomas Sully, and to be engraved by our most eminent artists. *Analectic Magazine* for 1813, p. 350.

Mr. Peale knows nothing about this work, and is of opinion that it has never been published in whole or in parts.

1814.

1. THE | HOLY BIBLE, | containing | *The Old and New Testaments,* | Together with the | Apocrypha: | *Translated out of the Original Tongues,* | and with the | former Translations diligently compared and revised; | With | Marginal Notes and References. | To which are added, | An Index; | An Alphabetical Table | of all the Names in the Old and New Testaments, with their Significations; | Tables of Scripture Weights, Measures and Coins: | John Brown's Concordance, &c. | New York: | Printed and sold by Collins & Co. | Sold also by the Principal Booksellers in the United States. | 1814. | (L.; G. L.)   4.

This edition, though recomposed, agrees, in the sigs. of the Old and New Testaments, with that of the 2d edition, 1807, as far as ‡ Dd^3; but "The Advertisement" has been rewritten, and in this edition is shorter than in that to the second. The words at the close of Malachi are, "End of the Old Testament." The Apocrypha is in the same type as the rest of the volume; sigs. A* to U* in 4^s. The Title to the New Testament corresponds with that of 1807, except the words "Collins's Third Edition" on this, and the imprint, which is, New York: | Printed and sold by Collins & Co. | 1814. | The matter after the New Testament is as follows: Index, Dd^4 to verso of Gg^2; at foot of Gg^2, Table of Time; Table of Scripture Measures, &c., Gg^{3,4}; Table of Offices and Table of Kindred, Gg^4; Alphabetical Index, Hh, in 4^s, 4 ff.; Brown's Brief Concordance. New York: | Published by Collins & Co., No. 189 Pearl Street. | 1814. | Title, 1 f.; verso, blank; To the Reader, 1 f.; verso, blank; Text: pp. 5-72, sig. B to S in 2^s.

* Error, should be verses 30 and 31.

Engravings:
The Murder of Abel..*P. Maverick.*
The Deluge...*Boyd.*
Joseph interpreting Pharaoh's Dream ....*Boyd.*
Jacob blessing the sons of Joseph ....*Furman.*
Map of the Journeyings of the Children of Israel.
Map of Palestine.
Elisha restores the Shunammite's Son to Life...............*P. Maverick,* Newark.
The Virgin Mary and Child ....*D. Edwin.*
Simeon's Benediction ....*W. Harrison.*
The Good Samaritan...*Kearney.*
The Prodigal Son..*W. Harrison.*
Map of St. Paul's Travels.
This edition has been also issued without Apocrypha.

2. THE | HOLY BIBLE: | containing the | Old and New Testaments, | together with the | Apocrypha: | Translated out of the Original Tongues, | and with the former translations diligently compared and revised, | *By the Special Command of his Majesty, King James I. of England.* | With Marginal Notes and References. | To which are added, | An Index; | An Alphabetical Table | of all the Names in the Old and New Testaments, with their Significations; | and Tables of Scripture Weights, Measures, and Coins: | Brown's Concordance, &c., &c., &c. | Embellished with Twenty-five Engravings. | Philadelphia: | Printed and published by M. Carey, | No. 121 Chesnut street. | 1814. | (L.) 4

This copy agrees with Carey's 4to of 1812. The imprint to N. T. same as above, but in 3 lines; the errors in Leviticus 19: 12, and Esther 1: 8 are continued. Page 161 is correct.

The plates are as follows:
1. Shepherds adoring our Saviour (Front.).
2. Journeyings of the Children of Israel.
3. Scheme of the lives of the Patriarchs.
4. Map of the Land of Canaan..*Bower.*
5. The Lord appearing to Isaac.
6. Map of Egypt.
7. Map of places mentioned in the books of Moses.
8. Map of Canaan.
9. Samuel anointing David.
10. Solomon's judgment.
11. Map of the Assyrian and other empires.
12. Elijah raising the Widow's Son.

13. The Angel appearing to Elijah.
14. Map of Solomon's dominions.
15. Map of Moriah (Front. to N. T.)............... .... Bower.
16. Adoration of the Wise Men.
17. Flight into Egypt.
18. Baptism of our Saviour.
19. Last Supper..................... .... Tanner.
20. The Annunciation.
21. Our Saviour in the Temple........................... ....Tiebout.
22. John the Baptist sending his disciples to our Saviour................... Tiebout.
23. The Miracle at the pool of Bethesda (marked at top, "Frontispiece, Plate 1.")... Tiebout.
24. The Jews interrogating our Saviour.......................... ....B. Tanner.
25. Map of the Travels of the Apostles.

The names of the engravers are erased from all the plates except where they are affixed above.

This Bible has also been issued without Apocrypha, Concordance and Plates.

3. HOLY BIBLE: With original and practical Observations, &c. By Thomas Scott, D. D., &c. In five Volumes. 4th American edition. New York: Dodge and Sayre. 1814– 1816. [Mr. Hastie.] 4.

4. HOLY BIBLE: With the References, Introductions and general Preface of Dr. Thomas Scott. Philadelphia: Printed for and Published by William W. Woodward, corner of Second and Chesnut Streets. Griggs & Dickinsons, printers. 1814. (L.) 8.

5. HOLY BIBLE: Philadelphia: Printed by Mathew Carey, No. 121 Chesnut Street. 1814. (L.) 12.

6. HOLY BIBLE: Hartford: Printed by Hudson and Goodwin. 1814. (B.) 12.

The same as the edition of 1809; but the script letters H and G are not on the title page; the imprint to the New Testament title is: Hartford, Connecticut. | Printed and sold by | Hudson & Goodwin. | 1814. |

7. HOLY BIBLE: Boston: | Printed for Thomas & Andrews, West and Richardson, | and West and Blake. | W. Greenough, Printer. | 1814. | (B.) 12.

This appears to be the same as the edition of 1801 and 1802, except that it has no catch words.

8. תורה נביאים וכתובים | Biblia Hebraica, | Secundum ultimam Editionem | Jos. Athiae, | a | Johanne Leusden | Denuo recognitam, | Recensita variisque notis Latinis illustrata | ab | Everardo Van Der Hooght, | V. D. M. | Editio Prima Americana, sine punctis | Masorethicis. | Tom. I. | Philadelphæ : | Cura et Impensis Thomæ Dobson edita ex Ædibus Lapideis. | Typis Gulielmi Fry. | MDCCCXIV. | (L. ; J. G. S.) 8

Half title, 1 p.; verso, blank; title 1 p.; verso, blank; 1 blank page; Notice in English, dated February, 1814; Preface by Van der Hooght, 8 pp.; sigs. a to a⁴; Text: Genesis to Deut., ff. 1-159; sigs. A to recto of 2 R³ in 4ᵃ; verso of 2 R³, numerus Versuum, Sectionum, &c. in Pentateucho, 1 p.; half title to Prophetæ Anteriores, 1 p.; verso, blank; full title, 1 p.; verso, blank, 2 ff; Text : Joshua to Kings ff. 161-296 ; at end of text on 296, Numerus, &c.; sigs. 2 S to recto of 4 E⁴ in 4ᵃ.

Tom. II., Half title 1 p.; verso, blank ; title 1 p., agrees with 1st vol. except Tom. II. verso, blank, 2 ff; Half title to Prophetæ Posteriores (Jesaia to Malachia), 1 p.; verso, blank. Text : ff. 2-142, numerus, &c., foot of 142 and ends on verso of that p.; sigs. including Half title, † A to † 2 N² verso, in 4ᵃ. Half title to Hagiographa, (Psalms, &c.-2 Chron.), 1 p.; verso, blank; Text: ff. 144-312. Sig. † 2 N⁴ to † 4 I⁴ (verso) in 4ᵃ.

The Hebrew Bible, or Old Testament, contains twenty-four books, which are divided into three classes : תורה Torah, which contains the five books of Moses. נביאים Neviim, which is again divided into the *former* prophets, which comprehend the four books called Joshua, Judges, Samuel and Kings; and the *letter* prophets, containing likewise four books, namely, Isaiah, Jeremiah, Ezekiel, and the twelve minor prophets, which are considered as one book. כתובים Kethuvim, containing eleven books, namely, Psalms, Prov., Job, Cant., Ruth, Lam., Eccl., Esther, Daniel, Ezra, Neh. and Chro. *N. B.*—Ezra and Neh. are considered as one book.

In 1812 Mr. Horwitz had proposed the publication of this edition of the Hebrew Bible, the first proposal of the kind in the United States; early in 1813 he transferred his right and list of subscribers to Mr. Thos. Dobson, who published, soon afterwards, the 1st volume ; the title pages and preface were furnished with the 2d vol.; with which they are bound in some instances.

9. A | COMPENDIUM | of the | Religious Doctrines, Religious and Moral | Precepts, Historical and Descrip- | tive Beauties | of the Bible; | with | a Separate Moral Selection from the | Apocrypha; | being | a Transcript of the received Text: | Intended for the use of Families, but more par- | ticularly as a Reading Book for Schools. | By Rodolphus Dickinson, Esq., | *Author of Law Tracts, Geographical Publica-* | *tions, &c.* | Greenfield, Mass. | Published at the Compiler's Office. | *Horace Graves, Printer.* | 1814. | (B.) 12.
Pp. 250.

10. The | History | of the Holy Bible, | interspersed with | Moral and Instructive Reflections, | Chiefly taken from the | Holy Fathers. | From the French. By J. Reeve. | In two Volumes. | Vol. I. | New-York: | Printed by J. Seymour, No. 49 John Street. | 1814. | 12.

Title, 1 f.; verso, blank; Contents, pp. iii, iv; Preface, dated Exeter, 1780, pp. v–viii; Text: pp. 13–220; sigs. B to verso of T² in 6ˢ ; Vol. II., Title (as above, except "Vol. II."), 1 p.; verso, blank; Cont., 1 p.; verso, blank; Text: pp. 13–159; verso, blank; Subscribers' Names, pp. 161–163 ; sigs. B to recto of O⁴ in 6ˢ .

The | History | of the | New Testament, | interspersed with | Instructive and Moral Reflections, | chiefly taken from the | Holy Fathers. | From the French, by J. Reeve. | New-York: | Printed by J. Seymour, No. 49 John Street. | 1814. | 12

Title, 1 f.; verso, blank ; Cont., 2 pp.; Text: pp. 13–172; Subscribers' Names, pp. 173–175, sigs. B to P⁴ ; two blank leaves complete the sig. in 6ˢ .

This work is based on *L'Histoire du Vieux et du Nouveau Testament*, by M. Louis Isaac le Maistre de Sacy, who wrote under the pseudonym of Sieur de Royaumont. But as he had in some of his reflections "studiously flattered his friends of Port-Royal" (the Jansenists) and been partially severe in others on the Dignitaries of the Church, and in many of his passages had given such a turn to the thought and expression of the Fathers, as was more calculated to support an enthusiastic system of Theology than to promote the interest of piety, an alteration was therefore judged expedient."—*Preface*.

1. The | New Testament | of our | Lord and Saviour | Jesus Christ, | translated | out of the original Greek; | and | with the former Translations | diligently compared and revised. | Collins's third Edition. | New York: | Printed and Sold by Collins & Co. | 1814. | 4.

With Brown's Concordance, 40 pages.

2. The | New Testament | of | our Lord and Saviour | Jesus Christ | with an | Introduction | giving an account of | Jewish and other sects; | with Notes | illustrating obscure Passages | and explaining | obsolete Words and Phrases; | for the use of | Schools, Academies, and Private Families. | By J. A. Cummings, | Author of Ancient and Modern Geography. | Boston: | Published and Sold by Cummings and Hilliard, | No. 1, Cornhill. | Andover: Flagg and Gould, printers. | 1814. | (Boston Athenæum; Harvard Coll. Lib.)   12.

3. NEW TESTAMENT: Newburyport: | Printed by William B. Allen & Co. | Sold Wholesale and Retail by H. G. Allen, Haverhill, Mass., and | by the various Booksellers in New England. | 1814. | (Am. Antiq. Soc.; Conn. Hist. Soc.)   12.

<small>Sigs. A to O⁸ in 12ˢ ; Text not paged.</small>

4. **Das Neue | Testament** | unſers | HErrn und Heilandes | JEſu Chriſti, | Nach der Deutſchen Ueberſetzung | Dr. Martin Luthers. | Mit kurzem | Inhalt eines jeden Capitels, | und | vollſtändiger Anweiſung gleicher Schriftſtellen. | Wie auch | aller Sonn- und Feſttägigen | Evangelien und Epiſteln. | Die erſte Auflage. | Somerſet: | Gedruckt und zu finden bey Friedrick Goeb. | 1814. | (B.; L.)   12.

<small>Title, 1 f.; verso, blank; Verzeichniss, 1 p.; verso, blank; Text: pp. 5-537; Register, 3 pp., not numbered; Sigs. A² to verso of Uu⁶ in 6ˢ .</small>

5. Η ΚΑΙΝΗ | ΔΙΑΘΗΚΗ. | Novum Testamentum, | Juxta Exemplar Joannis Millii | accuratissime Impressum. | (The wood cut found in Thomas's larger Bibles, viz: two figures supporting the Bible, in front of drapery and a Greek text below). Bostoniæ: | Excudebat Esaias Thomas, Jun. | Typis Watson & Bangs. | 1814. | (L.)   12

<small>Title, 1 p.; verso, blank; Chronol. Table of the Books of the New Test., 1 p.; verso, blank; Text in 2 cols., 5-478; sig. 1³ to verso of 40 ⁵ in 6ˢ followed by a blank leaf.</small>

6. A | HARMONY in Greek | of the | Gospels, | with notes, | by William Newcome, D. D. | Dublin, 1778: | reprinted from the | text and select various readings | of | Griesbach, | by the junior class in the | Theological Seminary | at Andover, | under the superintendance of | Moses Stuart, | associate professor of Sacred Literature in said | Seminary. | Andover: | Printed by Flagg and Gould. | 1814. | (Conn. Hist. Soc.)   8.

<small>Title, 1 f.; verso, copyright; Advertisement, p. iii; Explanation of the marks prefixed to the various readings, p. iv.; A table for finding any passage of the Gospels, pp. v-viii; Contents, pp. ix-xvi; Preface to the original edition, pp. i-xii; Text, pp. 13-424; Notes, pp. 1-188. Signatures (first four leaves) not marked, 1 to 54, then a to i, then k to u, then w, x, y and z⅓, the latter being only two leaves; all in 4s.</small>

1815.

1. THE | HOLY BIBLE: | Containing the | Old and New Testaments, | together with the | Apocrypha: | Translated out of the Original Tongues, | and with the former Translations diligently compared and revised, | *By the special Command of his Majesty, King James I. of England.* | With Marginal Notes and References. | To which are added, | An Index; | An Alphabetical Table of all the Names in the Old and New Testaments, with their Significations: | and Tables of Scripture Weights, Measures and Coins. | Embellished with Twenty-five Maps and Historical Engravings. | Philadelphia: | Printed and published by M. Carey, | No. 121 Chesnut Street. | 1815. | (L.) 4.

This edition agrees with Carey's 4to of 1812, (with 25 engravings) less the Concordance. The 1st page of Mat. is marked at foot (62.4); Index, p. 1050, is marked at foot 1. (62.3); p. 1058, 1. (62.3)*, p. 1066, 2. (62.3); p. 1074, also 2. (62.3). The errors in Leviticus and Esther, already noted, are continued.

The following is a list of the engravings:
1. Journeyings of the Children of Israel (reëngraved.)
2. Map of the Garden of Eden.
3. Scheme of the Lives of the Patriarchs.
4. Map of the Land of Canaan,..*Shallus.*
5. Map of the Countries peopled by the descendants of Ham.
6. Map of Egypt.
7. Ark of the Covenant..*J. Bower.*
8. Moses consecrating Aaron and his Sons.............................*J. Y.*
9. Joshua's spies in Jericho...*J. Bower.*
10. Samson betrayed by Delilah.
11. Jerusalem..*J. Bower.*
12. Temple of Solomon...*J. Bower.*
13. Map of the Assyrian and other empires.
14. Map of Solomon's Dominions.
15. The Tomb of Jonathan...*J. Bower.*
16. Map of Moriah.
17. Massacre of the Innocents...*J. Y.*
18. Judas casting away the Thirty pieces of Silver.
19. Shepherds in the Stable with our Saviour........................*J. Y.*
20. Christ raising the Widow's son....................................*J. Y.*
21. Lazarus at the gate of Dives......................................*A. Doolittle.*
22. Miracle at the pool of Bethesda.
23. St. Thomas putting his finger in the side of the Saviour.......*J. Y.*
24. Travels of the Apostles...*Bower.*
25. The Dragon chained..*J. Y.*

Nos. 2, 7, 8, 9, 10, 11, 12, 15, 18, 19, 20, 21, 23 and 25 are new engravings.

2. HOLY BIBLE: With the Apocrypha. Philadelphia: Printed and Published by M. Carey, No. 121 Chesnut Street. 1815. (L.) 4.

<small>The same as the preceding, except, I. The omission on the Title page of the words "Embellished with Twenty-five Maps and Historical Engravings." II. The omission of the List of Engravings on verso of 2d title. III. The date to the New Test. Title is 1816. IV. 1st page of Mat. is marked at foot (65.1); p. 1066 is marked at foot, 2. (65.1); p. 1074, 2 (65.4). V. No plates.</small>

3. HOLY BIBLE: Philadelphia: Printed and Published by M. Carey, No. 121 Chesnut Street. 1815. (L.) 4.

<small>Same as No. 1, except, I. No Apocrypha. II. 1st page of Mat. marked at foot (61.1); pp. 1050 and 1066 marked at foot, 2 (61.6); p. 1058, 2 (61.3); p. 1074, 2 (61.2). III. Has, A | Brief | Concordance | to the | Holy Scriptures, | of the | Old and New Testaments | &c. By John Brown, &c. Brooklyn: | Printed by Thomas Kirk, Main Street. | 1812. |</small>

4. HOLY BIBLE: With the Apocrypha. New York: Printed and sold by Collins & Co. Sold also by the Principal Booksellers in the United States. 1815. (L.) 4

<small>This is the *fourth* edition of Collins's 4to Bible; its contents correspond with that already described, No. 1 of 1814. The titles to the New Test. and Concordance are, however, dated 1814. It is accompanied by the same plates and maps.</small>

5. THE | HOLY BIBLE: | Containing | the Old and New Testaments: | Together with | The Apocrypha: | Translated out of | the Original Tongues, | and | with the former Translations | diligently compared and revised. | First Brookfield edition. | Brookfield: | Printed by E. Merriam and Co. | 1815. | (B.; G. L.) 8

<small>Title, 1 f.; verso, The property of   within an oblong ornament; To the Reader (Dr. Witherspoon's Preface), | 2 pp.; Account of the dates or time of writing the Books of the New Testament, 1 p.; The names and order of all the Books in the O. and N. Test. and Apocrypha, 1 p.; Text: Gen. to Mal. pp. 7–735; sigs. 1* to recto of 92⁴; verso, Tables of Scripture Measures, Weights, Money and Time; Family Record, 2 ff.; Apocrypha (not paged), sigs. 1* to verso of 21*⁴; The New Testament, &c. *First Brookfield Edition.* | Brookfield: | Printed by E. Merriam & Co. | 1815. | 1 p. verso, blank; Text: Mat. to Rev. pp. 739–959; sigs. 93² to recto of 120⁴; verso, Table of Offices; sigs. all in 4ˢ. 1 Tim. 4:16 incorrect.</small>

<small>This Bible was printed in the years 1814 and 1815. The edition consisted of 12,000 copies, consuming 1,800 reams of paper. Ebenezer Merriam, the publisher, was born in 1777; served his apprenticeship to Isaiah Thomas and died in West Brookfield, Mass., 1st November, 1858.—*Springfield Republican.*</small>

6. HOLY BIBLE: Second New York Edition. | New York : |
Published by E. Duyckinck, Collins & Co., T. & J. Swords,
Peter A. | Mesier, Samuel A. Burtis, T. A. Ronalds, |
and G. & R. Waite. | G. Long, Print. | 1815. | (Mrs. Peter
Ferris, Miamis.)   8.

The above imprint is borrowed from the title to the New Test., that of the Old Test.
being lost. The first edition is described, *supra*, p. 109, No. 3.

7. THE | HOLY BIBLE, | containing the | Old and New Testa-
ments: | Translated out of | the Original Tongues; | and |
with the former Translations | diligently compared and
revised, | By the Special Command of King James I. of
England. | Walpole, (N. H.) | Published by Anson Whip-
ple. | 1815. | (G. L.; Am. Antiq. Soc.; L.)   8.

Title, 1 f. ; verso, The Property of........ within an oblong ornament ; To the Publick, 1¼ pp.; account of dates, ¼ p.; Names and order of Books, 1 p. ; Tables of Scripture
Measures, Weights, Money, and Time, 1 p.; Text : Gen. to Mal. pp. 7–735 ; sigs. A.,
(which includes title and 2 prel. ff.) to 4 U⁴ in 4ˢ ; verso, blank; Apocrypha, not paged,
sigs. A to verso of X⁴ in 4ˢ ; New Test. title, 1 f.; verso, blank; Text : Mat. to Rev.,
pp. 739–959 ; verso, Table of Offices ; sigs. 4 Y (not marked) to 5 Z⁴ in 4ˢ.
This edition was printed at Walpole, N. H., by A. Whipple & Co., from a Press
owned by I. Thomas.—*Ms. note in the vol. belonging to the Am. Antiq. Soc.*
About 1810, Cheever Felch, afterwards a chaplain in the U. S. Navy, commenced
setting in type and printing at Walpole, N. H., a Bible for Mr. Whipple, Isaiah
Thomas's son-in-law. It was of octavo form, on Bourgeois (English or Scotch) type
and consisted of an edition of 8,000 copies, on coarse paper. Felch, however, prosecuted the work no farther than to the close of the 26th chapter of Deuteronomy,
when it was suspended till about the year 1813. The composition was then recom-
menced by Charles Kendall, who, in about 18 months completed the work, except the
Apocrypha, which was set up by a man named Brown.—*Statement furnished by Mr.
Kendall, through G. M. Davison, Esq., Saratoga Springs.*

8. THE | HOLY BIBLE, | containing the | Old and New Testa-
ments: | Translated out of | the Original Tongues, | and
with | the former Translations diligently compared | and
revised. | New-York : | Stereotyped and Printed by D. &
G. Bruce, | No. 27 William-street. | 1815. | (Seminary
St. Sulpice, Balt.)   12..

Title, 1 f.; verso, This first American Stereotype Bible has been copied from the
Edinburgh edition | printed under the revision of the General Assembly of the Kirk of
Scotland, and care- | fully compared with the Cambridge, Oxford, Hartford and New
York editions. | D. & G. BRUCE. | *New York, June*, 1815. | Names and order of the
Books of the O. and N. Test.; Text : Gen. to Mal., pp. 3–525 ; sigs. A² to recto of

Y¹¹; verso, Table of Offices and Table of Time; The | New Testament | of our | Lord and Saviour | Jesus Christ, | translated out of | the Original Greek; | and with | the former Translations diligently | compared and revised. | New York : | Stereotyped and printed by D. & G. Bruce, | No. 27 William-street. | 1815. | marked p. 527; sig. Y¹²; verso, Table of Kindred ; Text: pp. 529–684; sigs. Z to verso of Ff⁶ in 12ˢ . Brief headings to chapters and columns.

This is the first Bible printed from stereotype plates cast in the United States. It is in nonpareil type. DAVID BRUCE, to whose perseverance it owes its existence, died in Brooklyn, N. Y., 15th March, 1857, aged 87 years.

9. THE | HOLY BIBLE, | containing the | Old and New Testament: | Translated | out of the Original Tongues, | and | with the former Translations | diligently compared and revised. | Newburyport: | Published by Wm. B. Allen & Co. | And for sale wholesale and retail, bound or in sheets, by them at | The Newburyport Bookstore. | 1815. | (L.; B.) 12.

Title, 1 f.; verso, Names and Order; Text: Gen. to Mal., pp. 3–550; sigs. (including title) A to verso of Xx⁵ in 6ˢ; New Test. title, 1 p; Revelation ends on p. 720, sigs. Yy to verso of Mmm⁶ in 6ˢ .

10. THE | HOLY BIBLE, | containing the Old and New Testaments; | Translated | out of the Original Tongues, | and | with the former Translations | diligently compared and revised. | Boston : | Published by Munroe, Francis and Parker, | No. 4, Cornhill. | 1815. | (L.)   12.

Agrees with the preceding edition; Tables of Measures, Weights, Money and of Time (p. 551); verso, Chronol. Index of Years and Times from Adam to Christ; New Test. title, 1 p. verso, Account of Dates and Times, Analysis; Text as in the last mentioned edition.

These two Bibles are no doubt from the same types. The imprints only differ.

11. HOLY BIBLE. Hartford: Printed by Hudson and Goodwin. 1815.   (L.; B.)   12.

In every respect a reprint of the edition of 1809, except the titles and imprint. The letters H & G are omitted from the title of the Old Test.

12. LA SAINTE BIBLE, | Contenant | Le Vieux et le Nouveau | Testament: | Imprimée sur l'édition stéréotype de Londres, | Et selon l'édition de Paris, de l'année 1805: | Revue et corrigée avec soin | D'après les textes Hébreu et Grec. | À New York : Imprimée aux frais et sous l'inspection | de la Société établie dans cette Ville | sous le

—1815] AMERICAN BIBLES. 127

titre de | "The New York Bible Society." | Chez J. Seymour, imprimeur, John-street, No. 49. | 1815. | (N. Y. Soc. Lib.) 12.

Title, 1 p.; verso, blank; nom de tous les livres, 1 p.; verso, blank; Texte: Gen. à Mal. p. 3-798; sigs. A³ to verso of 3 X³ in 6ˢ; Title, Le | Nouveau Testament | De | Notre Seigneur | Jésus Christ. | Imprimé sur l'édition de Paris de l'année 1805. | Same imprint as above, 1 p.; verso, Les Noms, &c.; Texte: Mat. à Rev., pp. 3-246; sigs. including title, 3 X⁴ to verso of 4 S⁶ in 6ˢ.

The Paris edition of 1805, from which this is copied, was reprinted for The British and Foreign Bible Society, London, in 1807.

13. ISAIAH: a new translation: with a preliminary Dissertation and Notes. By Robert Lowth, D. D., Bishop of London. Boston: Printed and published by Joseph T. Buckingham, Winter Street. 1815. (Brown Univ.) 8.

1. NEW TESTAMENT: With Original Notes and Practical Observations. By Thomas Scott, &c. Fifth American edition. Boston: Samuel S. Armstrong. 1815. 2 vols. 8.

With Scott's Family Bible of 1816.

2. NEW TESTAMENT. Stereotyped by D. & G. Bruce, No. 27 William Street. 1815. (L.) 8.

3. THE NEW | TESTAMENT | of our | Lord and Saviour | Jesus Christ, | translated out of | 𝕿𝖍𝖊 𝕺𝖗𝖎𝖌𝖎𝖓𝖆𝖑 𝕲𝖗𝖊𝖊𝖐; | and with the | former translations | diligently compared and revised. | H & G | Hartford: | Printed by Hudson and Goodwin. | 1815. | 12.

Title, 1 f.; verso, The Order of the Books; Text: pp. 1-334; sigs. A² to verso of O¹² in 12ˢ.

Acts 6 : 3 and I Tim. 4 : 16 incorrect.

4. NEW TESTAMENT. Philadelphia. Printed by Wm. W. Woodward. 1815. 18.

With Bible of 1813.

5. 𝕯𝖆𝖘 𝕹𝖊𝖚𝖊 | 𝕿𝖊𝖘𝖙𝖆𝖒𝖊𝖓𝖙 | unſers | HErrn und Heilandes | JEſu Chriſti, | nach der Deutſchen Ueberſetzung | D. Martin Luthers. | mit kurzem | Inhalt eines jeden Capitels, | und | vollſtändiger Anweiſung gleicher Schriftſtellen. | Wie auch | aller Sonn=und Feſtä=

gigen | Evangelien und Epistelu. | Siebente auflage. | Philadel=
phia: | Gedruckt bey G. und D. Billmeyer, 1815. | (L.) 12.

<small>Title, 1 f.; verso, blank; Verzeichniss, 1 p.; verso, blank; Text: pp. 5–537; An-
weizung, 3 pp. not numbered; sigs. A³ to verso of Z⁶ in 12ª; double columns</small>

6. A Synopsis | of | the Four Evangelists, | or, | a regular
History | of the | Conception, Birth, Doctrine, Miracles,
Death, Resur- | rection and Ascension | of | Jesus Christ |
in | the Words of the Evangelists. | By Charles Thom-
son. | Philadelphia: | Published for the Author. | Wm.
McCullogh, Printer. | 1815. | (L.) 8.

<small>Title, 1 f.; verso, Certificate of copyright; Pref., 2 pp.; Text: pp. 1–200; sigs. A.
to Bb⁴ in 4ª; Notes critical and explanatory and 3¼ pp. of Appendix, pp. 1–50; sigs.
A to G¹ in 4ª; Index, 4 pp. G² & ³.</small>

1816.

1. [Collins's Stereotype Edition.] | The | Holy Bible: | Con-
taining | The Old and New Testaments: | Together with
the | Apocrypha: | Translated out of the Original
Tongues, | and with | the former Translations | diligently
compared and revised; | with | Canne's Marginal Notes
and References. | To which are added, | An Index; | An
Alphabetical Table | of all the Names in the Old and New
Testaments, with their Significations; | Table of Scripture
Weights, Measures, and Coins; | John Brown's Concord-
ance, &c. | *Embellished with Maps and elegant Historical En-
gravings.* | Stereotyped by B. & J. Collins, New York. |
New York: | Printed and Sold by Collins and Co. | Sold
also by the principal Booksellers in the United States. |
1816. | (Amer. Bib. Soc.) 4.

<small>Title, 1 f.; verso, blank; Adv. to the Stereotype Edition, dated New York, 1816,
1 f.; verso, blank; To the Reader (Dr. Witherspoon's Pref.), 2 pp.; Account of the
dates and times, 1 p.; The names and order of all the Books, 1 p.; making, with title,
sig. A, not marked; Text: Gen. to Mal., pp. (9)–(663); sigs. B to recto of 4 R ²; p.
684 blank; Family Record, 2 ff.; Apocrypha, pp. (1)–(160); sigs. A* to U*⁴. [Collins's
Stereotype Edition.] | The | New Testament | of our | Lord and Saviour | Jesus
Christ, | Translated | out of the Original Greek, | and | With the former Trans-
lations | diligently Compared and Revised; | Stereotyped by B. & J. Collins, New
York. | New York: | Printed and Sold by Collins & Co. | 1816. | 1 p.; verso, blank;
Text: Mat. to Rev., pp. (687)–(898); sigs. ‡A² to ‡Dd³; Index, pp. (899)–(916); at
foot of p. (916), Table of Time; sigs. ‡Dd⁴ to verso of Ff⁴; Table of Scripture Weights,</small>

&c., pp. (917)-(919); at foot of p. (919), Table of Offices; Table of Kindred, Index of Years and Times, p. 920; sigs. Gg. to Gg^2; Alphabetical Table, pp. (921)-(927), sigs. Gg^3 to Hh^2; verso of Hh^2 blank; Judea, Palestine or the Holy Land, pp. (929), (930), not marked; Table of passages, pp. (931), (932); sig. Hh^3, Hh^4; [Stereotype Edition.] A Brief Concordance, &c. By John Brown, late Minister of the Gospel at Haddington, in Scotland. Search the Scriptures, &c. New York: Published by Collins and Co., No. 189 Pearl-Street. 1815. 1 f.; verso, To the Reader; Text: pp. 3-56; sig. A^2 to verso of G^4; sigs. in 4s except 4 R, which is in 2s.

The following are the engravings in this edition:
1. The Murder of Abel. Frontispiece to O. T..... A. Sacchi, pinx.; *P. Maverick*, sc.
2. The Deluge...Poussin, pinx.; *Boyd*, sc.
3. Hagar in the Wilderness. (Wood cut.)
4. The Creation. (Wood cut.)
5. Joseph interpreting Pharaoh's dream......Guercino, pinx.; *Boyd & Maverick*, sc.
6. Joseph's Brethren offering their presents.......................*B. Tanner*, sc.
7. Jacob blessing the sons of Joseph....Rembrandt, pinx.; *Fairman & Maverick*, sc.
8. Map of Canaan, Palestine, Judea or the Holy Land..................*Hooker* sc.
9. Balaam. (Wood cut.)
10. Map of Journeyings of the Children of Israel......................*Hooker*, sc.
11. Sampson slayeth a Lyon. (Wood cut.)
12. Elisha restoreth the Shunamite's son to Life.. West, pinx.; *P. Maverick*, Newark, sc.
13. The Virgin and Child. Front to N. T....Raphael, pinx.; *Edwin & Maverick*, sc.
14. The Wise men's offering. Above, Bassano...................*Plocher*, sc.
15. John the Baptist in the Wilderness.......... ......Raphael, pinx.; *Boyd*, sc.
16. The Three Maries at the Sepulchre............Annibal Caracci, pinx.; *Boyd*, sc.
17. John the Baptist, baptizing......................Poussin, pinx.; *Kearney*, sc.
18. Jerusalem, with the neighboring country.
19. The Good Samaritan...............Rembrandt, pinx.; *Kearney & Maverick*, sc.
20. Jesus with the two Disciples at Emmaus.........Titian, pinx.; *W. Harrison*, sc.
21. Thomas's Incredulity..............................Rubens, pinx.; *Boyd*, sc.
22. Map of St. Paul's Travels. (Size of page.)
23. St. Paul. (Engraved for Collins's Quarto Bible, 4th ed.)...*Tiebout & Maverick*, sc.
24. Map of St. Paul's Travels. (Large folding Map.)..................*Robinson*, sc.

Plates Nos. 1, 2, 5, 7, 12, 13, 19, 20 have inscribed above, "Engraved for Collins's Quarto Bible, Fourth Edition, 1816." Nos. 4, 6, 8, 10, 15, 16, 17, 18, 21, 22, "Engraved for Collins's Quarto Bible, Stereotype Edition."

This is the *first* 4to edition of the Bible stereotyped by Collins, and the 5th of his quartos, including the Trenton edition. The Circular announcing the proposed publication of this Bible is dated "New York, First Month, 1815." To stereotype this work the publishers had employed John Watts, who introduced the art into the United States about the year 1813, after having received complete instruction in the business from his brother, Richard Watts, and from Andrew Wilson, of London. It is printed in small pica, and was issued on superfine, and on coarse paper, in the following styles: 1. The Old and New Testaments, alone; 2. The same, with Apocrypha; 3. With Apocrypha and Concordance; 4. With Concordance; 5. With Ostervald's Notes; 6. With Ostervald's Notes and Concordance; 7. With Ostervald's Notes, Apocrypha and Concordance. Any of the superfine copies could be furnished, with 12 maps and plates, for one dollar and fifty cents extra; and those on coarse paper, with 20 maps and plates, at an extra charge of one dollar; the prices ranging from $3.50 to $18.50, according to the paper and binding. See Circular in *N. Y. Hist. Soc. Lib.*

2. HOLY BIBLE: With Apocrypha, Marginal Notes and References, Index, an Alphabetical list of Names, Tables of Scripture Weights, Measures and Coins, Brown's Concordance, &c., &c. Embellished with Seventy Maps and Historical Engravings. Philadelphia: Printed and published by M. Carey, No. 121 Chesnut street. 1816. (L.) 4

This copy agrees in matter and pagination with the edition of 1812 and intermediate editions, though it has the appearance of being recomposed. The errors in Leviticus and Esther already mentioned are continued. The imprint to the title of the New Test. is as above ; in that to the Concordance, Mr. Carey's christian name is in full.

The following are the Engravings :
1. Table of births &c. of the Patriarchs (Front.)........................*J. Bower.*
2. Map of the Garden of Eden, &c.
3. Noah building the Ark.
4. Countries peopled by the descendants of Ham.
5. Countries peopled by the descendants of Shem.
6. Scheme of the lives of the Patriarchs.
7. Map of Canaan.
8. Abraham and the three Angels.
9. Esau selling his birthright...*I. L. F , sc.*
10. The Lord appearing to Isaac.
11. Map of Egypt.
12. Moses in the bulrushes.
13. Countries mentioned in the books of Moses.
14. Journeyings of the Children of Israel.
15. Golden Altar and Golden Candlestick.
16. The Altar and the Laver ....*J. Y.*
17. Dresses of the High Priests.
18. Consecration of Aaron.
19. Naomi and her daughters-in-law.
20. The Marriage of Boaz and Ruth..*J. Y.*
21. Dagon falling before the Ark...*J. Y.*
22. Samuel anointing David.
23. Judgment of Solomon.
24. Map of the Purveyorships, &c.
25. Jerusalem ....*J. Bower.*
26. Temple of Solomon ....*J. Bower.*
27. Map of Syria, Assyria, &c.
28. Elijah raising the Widow's Son.
29. Angel appearing to Elijah.
30. Elisha multiplying the Widow's oil.
31. Map of the dominions of Solomon.

32. David playing on the harp.
33. Daniel's second vision.
34. Daniel's fourth vision .... "Engraved for M. Carey's Family Bible." *Tiebout.*
35. Manasseh in chains.
36. The tomb of Jonathan.
37. Land of Moriah.
38. St. Matthew.
39. The Magi offering presents.
40. Flight into Egypt.
41. John Baptist baptizing our Saviour.
42. Decapitation of John Baptist ....*J. Yeager.*
43. The unjust Steward..... ....*J. Y.*
44. Our Saviour blessing Little Children.
45. The Labourers receiving their hire................................*Robinson.*
46. Our Saviour before Pilate.
47. Crowning with thorns...*J. L. .F*
48. The Angel and devout women at the Sepulchre.
49. St. Mark..*J. Y.*
50. Our Saviour curing a diseased woman..............................*Warnick.*
51. St. Luke.
52. The Annunciation.
53. Zacharias writing his son's name.
54. Our Saviour in the manger................. ....*W. W.*
55. Our Saviour in the Temple.
56. John Baptist sending his disciples to Christ.
57. Our Saviour asleep in the storm................................*J. Y.*
58. The good Samaritan.
59. St. John.
60. The Miracle at the Pool of Bethesda.............................*Tiebout.*
61. Jews interrogating our Saviour..................................*B. Tanner.*
62. Incredulity of St. Thomas.................................*J. Y.*
63. Map of the Travels of the Apostles.
64. The sick cured by the shadow of Peter.
65. St. Peter's vision of the unclean animals............ ....*W.*
66. Conversion of the Centurion.
67. St. Paul striking Barjesus with blindness.
68. John's vision of the four seals.
69. Vision of the beast.
70. Vision of the dragon chained................................*J. L. Frederick.*

This Bible was published originally at $12.50, $15 and $18. A second hand copy was lately sold at $20.

3. HOLY BIBLE, containing the Old and New Testaments. Philadelphia: Printed and Published by M. Carey, No. 121 Chesnut Street. 1816. 4.

This edition, without the Apocrypha, was published on "coarse paper, not lettered," at $3.75; on "common paper filleted," at $4.25; on "common paper, lettered and filleted," at $4.50; on fine paper, $6.00. *Carey's Advertisement.*

4. HOLY BIBLE and Psalms. Philadelphia: M. Carey, No. 121 Chesnut Street. 1816. 4.

On coarse paper, not lettered ; $4.00. *Carey's Advertisement.*

5. Holy Bible, and Apocrypha. Philadelphia: M. Carey, No. 121 Chesnut Street. 1816. 4.

On coarse paper, not lettered, $4.25; on coarse paper, lettered and filleted, $4.50; on common paper, filleted, $4.75; on common paper, lettered and filleted, $5.00; on fine paper, $6.50; on superf. paper, bound in sheep, $8.00. *Carey's Advertisement.*

6. Holy Bible, with Apocrypha and Psalms. Philadelphia: M. Carey, No. 121 Chesnut Street. 1816. 4.

On coarse paper, not lettered, $4.50; on coarse paper, lettered and filleted, $4.75; on fine paper, $6.75. *Carey's Advertisement.*

7. Holy Bible, with Apocrypha and eleven plates. Philadelphia: M. Carey, No. 121 Chesnut Street. 1816. 4.

On coarse paper, lettered and filleted, $5.00; on common paper, lettered and filleted, $5.50. *Carey's Advertisement.*

The designs of the plates are the same as Nos. 6, 7, 25, 26, 37, 54, 63, 65, 67 and 68 enumerated in the edition with seventy maps and engravings, No. 2 of this year; but the engravings are inferior. Nos. 54, 65, 67 and 68 are marked J. Y.

8. Holy Bible, with Apocrypha, eleven Plates and Psalms. Philadelphia: M. Carey, No. 121 Chesnut Street. 1816. 4.

On coarse paper, lettered and filleted, $5.25; on common paper, 11 plates and Psalms, $5.75. *Carey's Advertisement.*

9. HOLY BIBLE, with Apocrypha and 25 Plates. Philadelphia: M. Carey, No. 121 Chesnut Street. 1816. 4.

On coarse paper, lettered and filleted, $5.50; on common paper, lettered and filleted, $6.25. *Carey's Advertisement.*

10. HOLY BIBLE, with Apocrypha, 25 plates and Psalms. Philadelphia: M. Carey, No. 121 Chesnut Street. 1816. 4.

On common paper, lettered and filleted, $6.50. *Carey's Advertisement.*

11. HOLY BIBLE, with Concordance. Philadelphia: M. Carey, No. 121 Chesnut Street. 1816. 4.

On coarse paper, lettered and filleted, $4.75. *Carey's Advertisement.*

12. HOLY BIBLE, with Apocrypha and Concordance. Philadelphia: M. Carey, No. 121 Chesnut Street. 1816. 4.

On coarse paper, lettered and filleted, $5.25. *Carey's Advertisement.*

13. Holy Bible, with Apocrypha, Concordance and 2 Maps. Philadelphia: M. Carey, No. 121 Chesnut Street. 1816. 4.

On common paper, lettered and filleted, $6; on fine paper, $7.50. *Carey's Adv.*

14. HOLY BIBLE, with Apocrypha, Concordance, 2 Maps and Psalms. Philadelphia: M. Carey, No. 121 Chesnut Street. 1816. 4.

On fine paper, $7.75. *Carey's Advertisement.*

15. HOLY BIBLE, with Apocrypha, Concordance and 10 Maps. Philadelphia: M. Carey, No. 121 Chesnut Street. 1816. 4.

On common paper, lettered and filleted, $7; on fine paper, $8; on superfine paper, sheep, $9.25. *Carey's Advertisement.*

16. HOLY BIBLE, with Apocrypha, Concordance, 10 Maps and Psalms. Philadelphia: M. Carey, No. 121 Chesnut Street. 1816. 4.

On common paper, lettered and filleted, $7.25; on superfine paper, sheep, $9.50. *Carey's Advertisement.*

17. HOLY BIBLE, with Apocrypha, Concordance and 25 Maps and Plates. Philadelphia: M. Carey. No. 121 Chesnut Street. 1816. 4.

On coarse paper, lettered and filleted, $6.25; on fine paper, $8.50; on superfine paper, sheep, $10; on superfine paper, plain calf, 11.50; in Morocco gilt or calf extra, $13. *Carey's Advertisement.*

18. HOLY BIBLE, with Apocrypha, Concordance, 25 Plates and Psalms. Philadelphia: M. Carey, No. 121 Chesnut Street. 1816. 4.

On fine paper, $8.75; on superfine paper, sheep, $10.25. *Carey's Advertisement.*

19. Holy Bible, with Apocrypha, Concordance, 25 Maps and Plates, and Ostervald's Notes. Philadelphia: M. Carey, No. 121 Chesnut Street. 1816. 4.

On coarse paper, lettered and filleted, $7; on fine paper, $9.50; on superfine paper, sheep, $11. *Carey's Advertisement.*

20. Holy Bible, with Apocrypha, Concordance and 100 Plates.
Philadelphia: M. Carey, No. 121 Chesnut Street. 1816. 4.

On superfine paper, sheep, $16; calf, $17; calf extra or Morocco gilt, $18; Morocco gilt and gilt edges, $20. *Carey's Advertisement.*

21. Exposition of the Old and New Testaments. By Mathew Henry. 6 vols. Philadelphia. Hogan & Towers. 1816.

This is said to be the 1st American edition of what is known as Henry's Commentary.

22. HOLY BIBLE: With Original Notes and Practical Observations. By Thomas Scott. In six Volumes. Fifth American Edition. Boston: Published by Samuel T. Armstrong. 1816. (Harvard Coll.) 8.

The first four volumes contain the Old Testament; the other two volumes the New Testament, which is dated 1815. This work is known as Armstrong's First edition of Scott's Commentary.

23. THE | HOLY BIBLE: | containing | The Old and New Testaments: | Together with the | Apocrypha: | Translated out of the Original Tongues, | and with the | former Translations diligently compared and revised. | Stereotyped by B. & J. Collins, New York. | Albany: | Printed and published by E. F. Backus. | 1816. | (N. Y. State Lib.; L.) 8.

Title, 1 f.; verso, blank; Address to the Reader (Dr. Witherspoon's Pref. to Collins's Bible); Names and order of all the books, 2 pp.; Text: Gen. to Mal. pp. (5)-(756); sigs. A (which incl. t. and pr. f.) to verso of Bbb^2; Apocrypha pp. (1)-(181); sigs. A to M^3; verso of 181, blank; then 1 blank leaf, to complete a half sig.; [*Stereotype Edition.*] The | New Testament | of | our Lord and Saviour | Jesus Christ: | translated | out of the original Greek; | and with the | former Translations | diligently | compared and revised. | Stereotyped by B. & J. Collins, New York. | Albany: | Printed and published by E. F. Backus. | 1816. | 1 p.; verso, blank; Text: Mat. to Rev., pp. 3–234; sigs. A^2 to verso of Q^1. The sigs. are in 8^s, except those otherwise noted above, and sig. P of the New Test., which is a 4.

24. HOLY BIBLE: Boston: Printed for Lincoln and Edmands; Sold at their Bible Warehouse, No. 53, Cornhill. *W. Greenough, Printer.* 1816. 12.

25. HOLY BIBLE: Hartford: Printed by Hudson and Goodwin. 1816. (B.) 12.

A continuation of the edition of 1809 with a different imprint. New Testament dated 1815.

26. The | Holy Bible, | containing the | Old and New Testaments: | Translated out of | the original Tongues, | and with the | former Translations diligently compared and revised. | New-York: | Stereotyped by E. & J. White | For "The New-York Bible Society," and | "The Auxiliary New York Bible Society." | 1816. | (L. ; G. L.)   12.

Title, 1 f.; verso, Names and Order ; Text : Gen. to Mal. pp. 3–832; sigs., including title, A to verso of 2 M⁸ in 12ˢ ; N. T. title : The | New Testament | of our | Lord and Saviour | Jesus Christ : | Translated out of | the Original Greek | and with the | former Translations diligently compared and revised. | New York : | Published by the American Bible Society. | *Stereotyped by E. & J. White.* | 1816. | Verso, Tables of Measures, Weights and Money, and Time ; Text : pp. 3–254; sigs., including title, 2 M⁹ (not marked) to verso of 2 Z³ in 12ˢ.

These stereotype plates belonged to the N. Y. Bible Society. The American Bible Society was instituted in 1816, and either purchased or borrowed the plates until they could get others. The imprint of the American Bible Society is met now, for the first time, on the title page of the New Testament of this edition.

27. Holy Bible: New-York Stereotype edition. | New-York : | Stereotyped by E. and J. White, | For the Auxiliary New York Bible and | Common Prayer-Book Society. | Instituted in the year 1816. | 1816. | 12.

28. The | Holy Bible, | containing the | Old and New Testaments : | Translated out of | the Original Tongues ; | and with | the former Translations diligently compared | and revised. | New York : | Printed and Published By   W. Mercein, | No. 93 Gold-street. | 1816. | (L.)   12.

This is the Bruces' Stereotype Bible, No. 8, of 1815, with Mercein's imprint and a new date. The verso of the Title page contains the notice of D. & G. Bruce, dated June, 1815.

29. Holy Bible: Philadelphia : | Printed by Mathew Carey, | No. 122 Chesnut-street. | 1816. | (L.)   12.

The imprint to the New Testament title is : Whitehall : | Printed for William Young, Bank street, | *The first house from the right hand from Chesnut street.* | Philadelphia. | 1808. | verso, a wreath and This Book is the Property of |

30. Holy Bible: Philadelphia: Printed by W. W. Woodward, No. 52 South Second, corner of Chesnut Street, 1816.   12.

136   AMERICAN BIBLES.   [1816—

1. NEW TESTAMENT: Translated from the Latin Vulgate. Philadelphia: M. Carey, No. 122 Chesnut Street. 1816.   4.

<small>It contains the same number of plates as one of the issues of 1805. *Carey's Advertisement.*</small>

2. THE | NEW TESTAMENT | of our Lord and Saviour | Jesus Christ: | Translated | 𝕺ut of the 𝕺riginal 𝕲reek | and · | with the former translations | diligently compared and revised. | Stereotyped for the Bible Society at Philadelphia. | *By T. Rutt, Shackleville, London.* | 1816. | (L.)   8.

<small>Title, verso, Names, &c.; Text: Mat. to Rev., pp. 3–303; verso, Measures, Weights and Time; sigs. (including title) A to verso of T⁵ in 8ˢ.</small>

3. NEW TESTAMENT. Philadelphia: M. Carey, No. 122 Chesnut Street. 1816.   12.

<small>A school edition, with Psalms. *Carey's Advertisement.*</small>

4. THE | NEW TESTAMENT | of our | Lord and Saviour | Jesus Christ, | translated out of the original Greek; | and with the | former Translations | diligently compared and revised. | Stereotyped by B. & J. Collins. | Hartford, Conn. | Printed and sold by Sheldon & Goodrich. | 1816. | (B.) 12.

<small>Title, (headed *Stereotype Edition*,) 1 f.; verso, The Order of all the Books; Text: Mat. to Rev., pp. 3–290; sigs. A to verso of Bb¹. Sigs. in 6ˢ. Short headings to chapters; none to columns.</small>

5. NEW TESTAMENT: Appointed to be read in Churches. Stereotyped by D. & G. Bruce, New York. Philadelphia: Printed by Thomas Desilver, No. 220 Market Street. 1816.   (L.)   12.

<small>Title 1 f.; verso, Order of Books; Text: pp. 3–335; sigs. A² to O¹²; verso of O¹², Table of Kindred.</small>

6. THE | NEW TESTAMENT | of | our Lord and Saviour | Jesus Christ, | translated | out of the Original Greek; | and | with the former Translations | diligently | compared and revised. | Windsor, Vt. | Printed by Jesse Cochran | And sold wholesale and retail, at his Bookstore, and by the principal | Booksellers in New-England. | 1816. | 12.

<small>Title, 1 f.; verso, The Order of the Books; Text: not paged; sigs. A. (which includes title page) to Dd. Brief headings to chapters and columns.</small>

7. NEW TESTAMENT. New Ipswich, N. H.: Printed and published by Simeon Ide. Date unknown. 12.

Not seen. Mr. Ide, having purchased a small Ramage press and a font of bourgeois type which had already been pretty well worn on an edition of Shakespeare, placed them in the blacksmith's shop on his father's farm, and undertook to print an edition of the New Testament in duodecimo form. By the assistance of a sister, about twelve years old, in setting type, it was accomplished in about six months. That this, his first publication, might be as free from errors as possible, he engaged the Rev. Dr. Payson, of Rindge, to read the proof sheets. As there was only type enough to set twelve pages at a time, he walked to his house, a distance of four miles, twice a week, to read proofs with him; and to give greater currency to the edition, he prevailed on Dr. Payson to allow him to insert on the title page, "Revised and corrected by Rev. S. Payson, D. D." Some of the Doctor's friends having got the impression that he had been making a new Translation of the Testament, it gave him no little uneasiness. To relieve him of this, Mr. Ide printed the words "First New Ipswich edition," and pasted the slip over the obnoxious line. An edition of 5000 was worked off, and 1000 copies, in full binding, were sold to the New Hampshire Bible Society, for $280, which was less than cost, in order to raise money to purchase paper. The others were retailed at fifty cents a copy. *Kidder and Gould's History of New Ipswich.* Boston, 1852, p. 237.

1817.

1. HOLY BIBLE: with Canne's Marginal Notes and References; an Index; Tables of Names, Scripture Weights, Measures and Coins; John Brown's Concordance, &c., *Embellished with Maps and Elegant Historical Engravings.* Stereotyped by B. & J. Collins, New York. New York: Printed and sold by Collins & Co. Sold also by the principal Booksellers in the United States. 1817. (N. Y. S. Lib.; L.) 4.

This is the *second* edition of Collins's stereotyped 4to, and the 5th of his quartos including the Trenton edition. The collation agrees with No. 1, 1816, except that the Family Record follows the Apocrypha, and the dates of the New Testament and of the Concordance are 1816.

The following is a List of the Engravings:

1. The Last Supper, after Leonardi da Vinci. Front. (Engraved for Collins & Co.'s Stereotype Quarto Bible.).............. *Tanner, Vallance, Kearney & Co.*
2. The Creation. (Woodcut, Engraved for Collins & Co.'s Quarto Bible, Stereotype edition.)
3. The dismissal of Hagar and Ismael. (Engraved for Collins & Co.'s Stereotype Quarto Bible. 1816.)........................ .... *Gimbrede.*
4. Hagar in the Wilderness. (Wood cut.) (Above, *Mola.*)
5. Isaac blessing Jacob. (Wood cut.) (Above, *Coning.*)
6. Joseph's brethren offering the presents. (Engraved for Collins & Co.'s Quarto Bible, Stereotype edition.)....................................... *B. Tanner.*
7. Map of Canaan. (Engraved for Collins's Bible, Stereotype edition.)...... *Hooker.*

138   AMERICAN BIBLES.   [1817—

8. Balaam. (Wood cut.) (Above, *Craig*.)
9. Map of the Journeyings of the Children of Israel. (Engraved for Collins's Bible, Stereotype edition.)..................................*Hooker*.
10. Nathan reproving David. (Wood cut.) (Above, *Raphael*, but supposed to be after West.)
11. Elijah's burnt Sacrifice. (Wood cut.) (Above, *Lebrun*.)
12. David. (Wood cut.) (Above, *Domenichino*.)
13. Daniel in the Lion's den. (Wood cut.) (Above, *Northcote*.)
14. Jonah preaching to the Ninevites. (Wood cut) (Above, *B. Picart*.)
15. Mariæ Virginis. (Engraved for Collins & Co.'s Stereotype Quarto Bible, 1816. Hans Holbein, pinx..................................*T. Gimbrede*, N. Y.
16. John the Baptist in the Wilderness. After Raphael. (Engraved for Collins & Co.'s Quarto Bible, Stereotype edition.) ....*Boyd*.
17. Christ walking on the Sea. (Wood cut.) (Above, *Craig*.)
18. Jerusalem. (Engraved for Collins's Bible, Stereotype edition.)
19. Crowning with Thorns. (Wood cut.) (Above, *L. Caracci*.)
20. Touch me not. (Wood cut.) (Above, *Pietro da Collona*.)
21. Thomas's Incredulity. After Rubens. (Engraved for Collins & Co.'s Quarto Bible, Stereotype edition.)..................................*Boyd*.
22. Small Map of St. Paul's Travels.

2. HOLY BIBLE. New York: Stereotyped by E. & J. White for the American Bible Society. 1817. (Am. Bib. Soc. Cat.)   Long Primer. 8.

3. HOLY BIBLE: New York: Stereotyed by E. & J. White for the American Bible Society. 1817. (Rev. Dr. Brigham.)   Brevier. 12.

4. HOLY BIBLE: New York: Stereotyped by D. & G. Bruce for the American Bible Society. 1817. (Rev. Dr. Brigham.)   Minion. 12.

5. HOLY BIBLE: Stereotype edition. Stereotyped by B. & J. Collins. New York: Printed and sold by Collins & Co., No. 189 Pearl Street. 1817.   12.

Title, 1 f.; verso, blank; To the Reader; Names and Order of Books, 2 pp; Text: Gen. to Mal., pp. 5–690; New Test. Stereotyped (as above). New York: Published by Collins and Hannay, No. 230 Pearl street. J. & J. Harper, Printers. 1818. Title, 1 p.; verso, blank; Text: Mat. to Rev., pp. 3–210.

6. Stereotype edition. | THE | HOLY BIBLE, | containing the | Old and New Testaments: | Translated | out of the

Original Tongues, | and | with the former Translations | diligently compared and revised. | Stereotyped by B. & J. Collins, New York. | Albany: | Printed by Websters and Skinners, | at their Bookstore, corner of State | and Pearl Streets. | 1817. | 12.

<small>Title, 1 f.· verso, blank; Names and Order of all the Books; Account of the dates or time, &c., 1 p.; verso, blank; Text: Gen. to Mal., pp. 5–605; p. 606, Table of Scripture Measures; sigs. A. to verso of Cc³, including 2 prel. ff.; New Test. title, imprint: Albany: | Printed by Websters and Skinners, | at their Bookstore, corner of State and Pearl Streets, | 1818. | 1 p., verso, blank; Text: Mat. to Rev., pp. 609–792. Sigs. Cc⁵ to verso of Kk¹², all in 12ˢ.

There is another edition of this Bible, dated and paged as above, but with a double set of signatures; one, as above, in 12ˢ, and another set, A to Sss in 6ˢ; the title page to the N. Test. being marked under the date (1818), Ccc², showing that it was worked in 6ˢ. I Tim. 4: 16, is incorrect in all these editions.</small>

7. HOLY BIBLE. Philadelphia: Printed for M. Carey & Son., No. 121 Chesnut street. 1817.   (L.)   12.

<small>The imprint to title of the N. T. is: Mathew Carey & Son, No. 126 Chesnut Street, 1817. This copy is accompanied by the Scotch Psalms. Philadelphia: Wm. Young. M.DCC.XC.</small>

8. HOLY BIBLE. Philadelphia: Printed by Mathew Carey, No. 121 Chesnut street. 1817.   (L.)   12.

<small>The imprint on the title to N. T. is: Whitehall, Printed for Wm. Young, Bank Street, *The first house on the right hand from Chesnut Street.* Philadelphia, 1808. The sigs. run consecutively on.</small>

9. HOLY BIBLE. Hartford: Hudson and Goodwin, 1817. (B.) 12.

<small>The edition of 1809 with a different imprint.</small>

10. HOLY BIBLE. Boston: | Printed for Lincoln and Edmands. | *Sold at their Bible Warehouse, No. 53 Cornhill.* | *Sold also by Collins & Co., New York.* | *W. Greenough, Printer.* | 1817. | (L.)   12.

<small>Title, 1 f.; verso, The Property of   ; Names and order, 1 p.; Account of dates, 1 p.; Text: Gen. to Mal., sigs. A³ to recto of Cc³ in 12ˢ; verso, table of Measures, Weights and Time; Title to New Test., 1 p.; verso, blank; Cc⁴; Mat. to Rev., sigs. Cc⁵ to verso of Kk¹² in 12ˢ.</small>

11. A | SHORT | BIBLICAL CATECHISM, | Containing Questions | historical, doctrinal, practical and experimental. | Designed

to promote an intimate acquaintance with the | Inspired
Volume. | By Hervey Wilbur, A. M. | *"Search the Scriptures."* JESUS CHRIST. | "Let the word of Christ dwell in
you richly in | all wisdom." "For whatsoever things
were | written aforetime were written for our learn- | ing;
that we, through patience and comfort of | the Scriptures,
might have hope." PAUL. | Ninth Edition, | *In which the
first sets of references are quoted.* | Greenfield, Mass. | Printed
by Denio and Phelps. | 1817. | And sold by them at their
Bookstore, wholesale | and retail. | 12.

<small>This volume consists of pp. 198 in 6ᵃ ; the Answers to the several Questions are composed of texts of Scripture quoted literally. On the verso of the title is a certificate of copyright, from which it appears that the *fourth* Edition was published in 1813.</small>

1. NEW TESTAMENT: With Original Notes and Practical Observations. By Thomas Scott....Sixth American (Armstrong's Second) Edition. Boston: Samuel T. Armstrong.
1817.   8.

<small>Vols. 5 and 6 of Scott's Commentary. Boston, 1818.</small>

2. NEW TESTAMENT. Stereotype edition. New York: Stereotyped by E. & J. White for the American Bible Society.
1817.   (L.)   8.

<small>Title, 1 f.; verso, blank; Text: pp. 3–215; It belongs to an edition of the Bible. See Bible No. 6. *post*, 1818.</small>

3. THE | NEW TESTAMENT | of | our Lord and Saviour | Jesus
Christ, | translated out of the | Latin Vulgate : | Diligently
compared | with the original Greek : | And first puplished
(*sic*) by the | English College of Rhemes, | Anno 1582 : |
With annotations. | Newly revised and corrected according
to the Clementin | edition of the Scriptures. | Georgetown,
D. C. | Printed by W. Duffy, Bookseller and Stationer. |
1817. | (Georgetown Coll.; Sem. St. Sulpice, Balt. ; L.) 12.

<small>Title, 1 f. ; verso, blank; Admonition, 1 p ; Letter of Pope Pius VI., p. [4]; Approbations, pp. 5 and [6] ; on p. 6, the following :</small>

<small>GEORGETOWN, February 20, 1817.
Having had this edition of the NEW TESTAMENT | printed in Georgetown, by WM. DUFFY, examined ; it has | been found strictly conformable to the Dublin Edition of | the same work printed in 1811, and also that printed 1814. | Hence I permit it to be published, | LEONARD, Archbishop of Baltimore.</small>

Text: Mat. to Apocal., pp. 1–507; verso of 507, N. B. In the following Table, the titles of the books and order of the psalms are quoted as they are set down in the Protestant Bible. Table of Controversies, pp. 509–513; Table of Epist. and Gosp., [514]–516. Sigs. including title and 2 prel. pp., A to verso of Vv³ in 6ˢ ; List of Subscribers, 7 pp. ; verso of 7th p., Catalogue of Books for sale by William Duffy, and the following Notice : W. DUFFY, *has now in the Press, a splendid edition of the* DOWAY BIBLE, *in quarto, illustrated with Plates by the first artists in America, which will be delivered to subscribers at* $10, *elegantly bound*. There are brief headings to the chapters, and notes at foot of the pages.

The projected edition of the Bible mentioned above was, we are informed, never published.

4. THE | NEW TESTAMENT | of | Our Lord and Saviour | Jesus Christ: | Translated | out of the original Greek. | And | with the former Translations | diligently | compared and revised. | Hartford : | Printed by George Goodwin & Sons. | 1817. (B.) 12.

Title, 1 f. ; verso, The Order of the Books; Text: Mat. to Rev., pp. 1–334; sigs. A² to verso of O¹², in 12ˢ . 1 Timothy, 4 : 16 incorrect.

5. NEW TESTAMENT : Stereotyped by B. & J. Collins. Hartford, Conn. Published by Sheldon and Goodrich. 1817. 12.

With Bible of S. G. Goodrich, 1818.

1818.

1. HOLY BIBLE: With Apocrypha, Marginal Notes and References, Index, Alphabetical Table of Names, Tables of Scripture Weights, Measures and Coins, Brown's Concordance, &c., &c., Embellished with one hundred Maps and Historical Engravings. Philadelphia: Printed and published by M. Carey & Son, No. 126 Chesnut Street. 1818. (L.) 4.

The matter and pagination agree with Carey's edition of 1812. The imprint to N. Test. is the same as above. In that to the Concordance the christian name of Mr. Carey is in full. The error in Leviticus 19: 12 is continued, but Esther 1: 8 is correct.

The engravings already enumerated in Carey's 4ᵗᵒ Bible of 1816, except No. 47, are republished in this edition, together with the following :

Cain killing Abel.	The vocation of St. Matthew.
Figure of the Ark.	Scribes and Pharisees.
Brazen Serpent in the Wilderness. *J. L. F.*	Visiting the sick.
Balaam striking his Ass.	Woman pouring ointment on our Savior's head.
Death of Moses.	

David assaulted by Saul.
The Molten sea.
Great famine at the Siege of Samaria.
Jezabel cast out of the window.
Idolatry destroyed by Hezekiah.
Jehoiakim delivered from Captivity.
Jehoiakim casting the Books of Baruch into the fire.
Jeremiah taken out of prison.
Daniel's third Vision.
Judith putting Holofernes' head into a bag.
Peter taking the money of tribute from the fish's mouth.

Pilate causes Jesus to be scourged.
Visit of the Virgin Mary to Elizabeth.
Warnick.
Anne prophecying about the Infant Jesus.
The Virgin Mary presenting the Infant Jesus.
Woman washing our Savior's feet.
Jesus driving the money changers.
Jews stoning our Savior.
Ananias struck dead.
The Conversion of St. Paul.
St. Peter delivered from prison.
Apparition of Christ to St. John.

2. HOLY BIBLE, with Apocrypha, &c., as in No. 1. Embellished with eleven Maps and Historical Engravings. Philadelphia: Printed and published by M. Carey & Son, No. 126 Chesnut Street. 1818. (L.) 4.

The contents and pagination agree with Carey's edition of 1812. The imprint to N. Test. is: Philadelphia: Published by H. C. Carey & I. Lea, No. 126 Chesnut Street. 1822. The imprint to the Concordance is: Philadelphia: Printed and published by Matthew Carey & Son, No. 126 Chesnut Street. 1821. Title, 1 f.; verso, blank; To the Reader, 1 p., verso, blank; Text, pp. 5–72; sig. A³ to I.

Leviticus 19 : 12, is incorrect; Esther 1 : 8, correct.

The engravings, of which the following is a list, are on wood:

1. Journeyings of the Children of Israel.
2. Moses in the bulrushes.
3. Pharaoh's sorcerers turning the rods into serpents.
4. Daniel interpreting for Belshazzar.
5. Daniel in the Lions' den.
6. Land of Moriah.
7. Magi offering presents.
8. John baptizing Jesus Christ.
9. The Annunciation.
10. Virgin Mary's visit to Elizabeth.
11. Travels of the Apostles.

3. THE HOLY BIBLE, including the Old and New Testaments and the Apocrypha, according to the Authorized Version; with Notes, Explanatory and Practical, taken principally from the most eminent writers of the United Church of England and Ireland; Together with Introductions, Tables and Indexes. Prepared and arranged by the Rev. George D'Oyley, B. D., and the Rev. Richard Mant, D. D., Domestic Chaplains to his Grace the Lord Archbishop of Canterbury. Under the direction of the Society for Promoting Christian Knowlege. For the use of Families. The first American edition, with Additional Notes, selected and arranged by John Henry Hobart, D. D., Bishop of the

Protestant Episcopal Church in the State of New York. Vols. I. II. New York: Printed and Published by T. and J. Swords, No. 160 Pearl street. 1818. (N. Y. Soc. Lib.) 4.

<small>This work is in two volumes. Vol. I. contains Gen. to Isaiah; Vol. II. Jeremiah to Revelations. It has the same imprint as I. except the year, which is 1820. The work is not paged and is supposed to have been originally issued in numbers, each of the signatures having also the No. of the Vol. to which it belongs.</small>

4. HOLY BIBLE: With Original Notes and Practical Observations. By Thomas Scott, Rector, &c. | In six Volumes. | Sixth American (Armstrong's Second) Edition. | Boston: | Published by Samuel T. Armstrong, | Theological Printer and Bookseller, No. 50, Cornhill. | 1818. | (Harvard Coll.; Am. Antiq. Soc.) 8.

<small>Vols. 5 and 6 contain the New Testament and are dated in one copy, 1817, in another 1820.</small>

5. THE | HOLY BIBLE, | containing | the Old and New | Testaments: | Translated out of the | Original Tongues, | and with the former | Translations | diligently compared and revised. | Philadelphia: | Printed by M. Carey & Son, | No. 126 Chesnut-Street. | 1818. | 12.

<small>Title, 1 f.; verso, This Bible | is the Property of | within an oblong of ornamental lines; Names and Order of the Books, 1 p.; verso, Account of the Dates or Time; Text: Gen. to Mal., sig. A. (which includes T. and prel. leaf) to Cc^{12}, and in numbers 1 (not marked) to (26); verso of Cc^{12}, Table of Kindred and Table of Time; New Testament title, imprint: Philadelphia: | Printed by Mathew Carey & Son, | No. 126, Chesnut-Street. | 1818. | 1 p., verso, blank; Text: Mat. to Rev., sigs. Dd to Ll^{12}, and in figures 27 (not marked) to (34); (Ff. Gg, Ii, Kk have no figure marks); verso of Ll^{12}, Table of Offices and Conditions of Men.

Though at first view this edition would seem to be a Carey's 12mo of 1808, with only new Title pages, yet the text has evidently been recomposed. Like the editions of 1812, 1814 and 1817, there are no head lines to the columns. In many places the short s is used where the long f is found in the other edition; and there are no signature figures to the edition of 1808. Again, the verso of the page bearing the signature mark has at foot figures which are wanting in the ed. of 1808; thus, the verso of sigs. B to G is marked at foot 78-6, the last mentioned sig. having in addition G^2 on the verso; the verso of H has H^2, and 78-6 is on foot of the following p.; the verso of I is marked 78-4; of K, 78-1; of L, 78-3; of M, 78-2; of N, 78-5; of O, O^2, 78-1; of P, P^2 (78-2); of Q, 78-5; of R (78-1); of X, 78-2; of Y (87-5); of Z, 78-4; of Aa (78-3); of Bb (78-6); of Cc (78-2); at foot of the 1st p. of Mat. is 78-5; on verso of Ee (78-1); of Ff 78-3; of Gg (78-4); of Hh (78-3); of Ii (78-1); Kk (78-4), and of Ll, 78-6. In Exodus 19: 11, "Sinai" is printed "Sinia:"</small>

(an error to be found also in the editions of 1814 and 1817) and in 1 Kgs. 4: 29, "the sea shore," is printed "thes ea shore."

6. HOLY BIBLE. Stereotype edition. New York: Stereotyped by E. and J. White, for the American Bible Society. 1818.   (L.)   8.

Third edition. Daniel D. Fanshaw, Printer, No. 20 Sloat Lane. Pp. 3–705 and 3–215.

7. HOLY BIBLE: Stereotyped by B. & J. Collins. | New York: | Published by Collins and Hannay, | No. 230 Pearl Street. | J. & J. Harper, Printers. | 1818. | (L.)   12.

Title, 1 f.; verso, blank; To the Reader; Names and Order of the Books, 2 pp.; Text: Gen. to Mal., pp. 5–690; New Test. t., same impr., 1 p.; verso, blank; Text: Mat. to Rev., pp. 3–210.
Some copies of this edition are accompanied by the Psalms of David in metre; Scotch version; same imprint.

8. HOLY BIBLE: Stereotyped by B. & J. Collins, New York. Albany: Printed by Websters & Skinners, at their Bookstore, corner of State and Pearl Streets. 1818.   12.

See No. 6 of 1817.

9. HOLY BIBLE. Stereotype edition. Stereotyped by B. & J. Collins. Boston: Published by R. P. & C. Williams, No. 2, Cornhill Square, *opposite the South West corner of the Old State House.* 1818.   (L.; G. L.)   12.

Title, 1 f.; verso, blank; To the Reader, and Names and Order, pp. 3, 4; Text: Gen. to Mal., pp. 5–690; sigs. A^3 to recto of 3 M^3; New Test. t., 1 p.; verso, blank; Mat. to Rev., pp. 3–210; sigs. A^2 to verso of S^3; sigs. in 6^s; Has an engraved frontispiece.
It will be observed that this edition agrees with No. 5 of 1817 and with No. 7 *supra*.

10. HOLY BIBLE: Brattleborough, Vt.: Printed by J. Holbrooke. 1818.   12.

Stereotype edition. E. A.

11. HOLY BIBLE: Hartford, Connecticut: Printed and sold by Hudson and Goodwin. 1818.   (B.)   12.

12. HOLY BIBLE: Stereotyped by B. and J. Collins. Hartford, Connecticut: Published by S. G. Goodrich, 1818. (L.; B.) 12.

The same as No. 9, *supra*, with an engraved frontispiece. The imprint on the N. T. title is: Hartford, Conn^t. Published by Sheldon and Goodrich. 1817. Other copies of this issue have the words "Stereotype Edition" at the head of the title pages.

13. A New | Hieroglyphical | Bible | For | *the Amusement and Instruction of* | Children | &c. Embellished with | nearly Two hundred Emblems | &c. With sketch of the Life of our Blessed Saviour and the Holy Apostles &c. | Hartford: | Published by Cooke and Hale | 8 rods north of the State House. | 1818. | Hamlen & Newton Printers. | (L.)   12.

14. A Catechism of the Bible: in which all the most important events, characters and circumstances recorded in the Scriptures of the Old and New Testaments are noticed and illustrated by way of question and answer. By the Rev. Menzies Rayner, Rector of the Episcopal Churches in Huntington (Conn.). New Haven: Flagg and Gray, Printers. 1818.   12.

1. New Testament: Stereotyped by B. and J. Collins, New York. Boston: Published by West and Richardson, No. 75 Cornhill. J. H. A. Frost, Printer. 1818.   12.
With Bible of 1820.

2. New Testament: Stereotyped by B. & J. Collins. Boston. Published by R. P. and C. Williams, No. 2 Cornhill Square, *opposite the south west corner of the Old State House.* 1818.   (L.)   12.
Has the same engraved frontispiece as the Bible, *supra*, No. 9. The text is from the same plates.

3. New Testament: Hartford, Connecticut. Sold by Oliver D. Cooke and Sons. 1818.   (L.)   24.
Title, 1 f.; verso, blank; Names and Order, 1 p.; verso, blank; Text: pp. 3–321; sigs. A³ to recto of Dd⁵ in 6s. See No. 2 of 1821.

4. New Testament: Hartford, | Printed and Sold by Samuel G. Goodrich. | 1818. | (G. L.)   12.
Pp. 321.

5. NEW TESTAMENT: Stereotyped by B. and J. Collins, New-York. Keene, (N. H.): S. A. Morrison & Co. 1818. (Harvard Coll.) 12.

6. Nene | Karighyoston | Tsinihorighhoten ne | Saint John. | New-York: | Printed for the American Bible Society. | *D. Fanshaw, Printer.* | 1818. | (N. Y. State Lib.) 18.

<small>1 p.; recto, blank; verso, title as above; then, English title: The | Gospel | according to | St. John. | (In the Mohawk language.) | Imprint, as above, 1 p.; verso, Text: pp. 2-116; The text is printed in Indian and English on opposite pages which have the corresponding numbers. On verso of 116 is list of Errata. Sigs. in 6s.</small>

7. NEK | NECHENENAWACHGISSITSCHIK | BAMBILAK | naga | Geschicchauchsitpanna | Johanessa | elekhangup. | Gischitak Ellenicchsink, | untschi C. F. Dencke. | New York: | Printed for the American Bible Society. | *D. Fanshaw, Printer.* | 1818. | 12.

<small>1 leaf; recto, blank; verso, Title, as above; then, The | Three Epistles | of the | Apostle John. | Translated into the Delaware Indian, | by C. F. Dencke. | Imprint, as above; 1 p. verso, Text in Indian: 1-21; On the opposite page, the Text in English, the pp. of which are marked also 1-31; sigs. A to recto of D¹ in 6s.</small>

1819.

1. BIBLIA, | Das ist: | Die ganze | Heilige Schrift | Alten und Neuen Testaments. | Nach der Deutschen Uebersetzung | von | Doctor Martin Luther. | Mit lehrreichen Vorreden und vielen nützlichen und seltenen | Registern versehen. | Nebst dem dritten Buch der Maccabäer, und Zugabe des dritten und vierten Buchs Esra. | Imgleichen | Eine kurz gefaßte Biblische Geschichte | und Lebensbeschreibung Doctor Martin Luthers. | Laßt das Buch dieses Geseßes nicht von deinem Munde kommen &c. Josua Cap. 1. V. 8. | Lancaster, [Penn.] | Gedruckt und im verlage des Johann Bär. | 1819. (L.) fol.

<small>Title 1 f.; verso, blank; Vorrede, 1 f.; Subschreibenten, Verzeichniss, 5 pp.; 1 blank p.; Kurzgefaßte Geschichte | des | Alten and Neuen Testamentes. | pp 1-100; sigs. A to 3 in 2s; Wahrhafte Beschreibung | Von der Geburt, dem Leben und Tod | Des Seligen Martin Luther | &c. pp. 1-8; Vorrede | auf das Alte Testament | von Doctor Martin Luther, | pp. 9-12; August Herman Frankens | Kurzen Unterricht | wie man die Heilige Schrift zu seiner wayren Erbauung lesen solle. | 2 pp., not numbered; Verzeichniß | Aller Bucher | der Alten und Neuen Testaments. | 1 p.; Verzeichniß | der Bücher des Alten Testaments | bis auf die Propheten | 1 p; sigs. A to D in 2s; Text: Gen. to Mal, pp. 1-644; sigs. A to verso of Ffff² in 4s; Apocrypha in smaller type, pp. 645-738; sigs.</small>

—1819.]   AMERICAN BIBLES.   147

Ffff³ to verso of Ssss¹ in 4ˢ ; Anhang (3 and 4 Ezra and 3d Jude) in smaller type, pp. 1-26; sigs in numbers 1 to verso of 7¹ in 2ˢ ; Title to N. T : Das | Neue Testament | unsers | Herrn und Heilandes | Jesu Christi. | Verdeutschet | durch | Doctor Martin Luther. | Lancaster, [Penn.]: | Gedruckt, und im Verlage bey Johann Bär. | 1819. | 1 p., verso, blank; Vorrede | Auf das Neue Testament, von Doctor Martin Luther. | p. 3 [A]² ; and part of 4 Verzeichnis der Bücher der Neuen Testament, | rest of page 4; Text: Mat. to Rev., pp. 5-227; Sonn-und Festtägliche Episteln und Evangelien, | 1 p. not numbered; sig. [A³] to verso of [Dd]² in 4ˢ ; Register | ueber die Namen in der Heiligen Schrift, | pp. 1-76; Register | Zur Erklärung einiger dunkeln——Wörter und Gebräuche, &c , pp. 77-82; Verzeichnis | Der Erb-und Stuhlfolge der Jüdischen Hohenpriester, | &c., pp. 83-86; Zeit Register, pp. 87-92. Ende. Sigs. A to 3 in 2ˢ .

Engraved frontispieces; that to the Old Test., Moses with the Tables of the Law ; to the New Test., The Adoration of the Shepherds ; both engraved by J. Henry.

2. HOLY BIBLE: With Apocrypha, Marginal Notes and References. To which are added, An Index, An Alphabetical Table of Names, Table of Scripture Weights, Measures and Coins. Embellished with twenty-five Maps and Historical Engravings. Philadelphia: Printed and published by M. Carey & Son, No. 126 Chesnut Street. 1819. (L.) 4.

This is another issue of the edition of 1812, with Esther 1: 8, correct; the error in Leviticus being continued.

The Maps and Engravings are selections from previous issues, and consist of Nos. 6, 7, 10, 11, 13, 14, 22, 25, 26, 27, 31, 37, 40, 52, 55, 56, 60, 63 of the edition of 1816, with 75 plates, and of The Brazen Serpent ; Idolatry destroyed ; Burning of the Books of Baruch ; Woman anointing our Savior ; Visit of the Virgin to Elizabeth ; Mary presenting Jesus ; and The Expulsion of the Money Changers, from the ed. of 1818, with 100 plates.

Brown's Concordance, though not announced on the title, accompanies this volume, with the imprint as above, but Mathew Carey & Son. 1818.

3. HOLY BIBLE: With Apocrypha, Canne's Marginal Notes, Index, Tables of Names, Weights, Measures and Coins, Brown's Concordance, &c. *Embellished with Maps and Elegant Historical Engravings.* Stereotyped by B. & J. Collins, New York. New York: Printed and sold by Collins and Co. Sold also by the principal Booksellers in the United States. 1819.   (L.)   4.

This is another issue of Collins's stereotyped 4to Bible already described.

4. HOLY BIBLE: Stereotype edition. New York: Stereotyped by E. and J. White, For "The American Bible Society." 1819.   8.

148   AMERICAN BIBLES.   [1819—

7th edition. D. Fanshaw, printer, No. 20 Sloat Lane. Text: Gen. to Mal., pp, 3–705; verso, Tables of Weights, &c. Sigs. 1 to verso of 45¹ in 8ˢ. Mat. to Rev. pp. 3–315; sigs. 45² to recto of 58⁵ in 8ˢ.

5. HOLY BIBLE: Stereotyped | for the American Bible Society | by D. & G. Bruce. | *Printed by D. Fanshaw, No. 20, Sloat Lane,* | New York. | 1819. | (L.)   12.

Title, 1 l.; verso, Names and Order of the Books; Text: Gen. to Mal., pp. 3–637; sigs. 1² to recto of 27⁷; verso, Table of Measures, Weights and Money, and of Time; New Test. title: imprint—Stereotyped for the American Bible Society by D. & G. Bruce, New York. 1819. 1 p., verso, blank; Text, pp. 641–837; sigs. 27⁹ to recto of 35¹¹ all in 12ˢ. 17th edition.

6. THE | HOLY BIBLE, | containing the | Old and New Testaments: | Translated | out of the Original tongues | and | with the former Translations | diligently compared and revised. | Boston : | Printed for Lincoln and Edmands. | *Sold at their Bible Warehouse,* No. 53 Cornhill | Sold also by Collins & Co., New York. | W. Greenough, Printer. | 1819. | (L.; B; G. L.)   12.

The imprint of the New Testament is the same except that "Sold also by Collins & Co., New York" is left out and the date is 1817. See *supra,* No 10 of that year, for collation.

7. HOLY BIBLE: Hartford, Conn.: Printed and sold by Hudson and Goodwin. 1819.   (L.; B.)   12.
See 1809.

8. HOLY BIBLE: Philadelphia: Printed by and for Wm. W. Woodward, No. 52 South Second Street, corner of Chesnut Street. Will. Will. Woodward, Printer. 1819.   12.
Same as the edition of 1806.

9. HOLY BIBLE: Printed for the Kentucky Auxiliary Bible Society. Lexington. 1819.   12.

10. CRITICAL and EXPLANATORY | NOTES, | on many passages in the | New Testament, | which to common readers are hard to be understood. | Also, | an Illustration | of the | Genuine beauty and force of several other passages. | By Ezekiel J. Chapman, A. M., | Pastor of a Church of Christians in

Bristol, N. Y. | Canandaigua: | Printed by James D.
Bemis. | 1819. | (Boston Athenæum.)   8.
Pp. 208.

In the Preface to "The Christian Monitor," a Prayer Book published by W. H. Creagh, New York, 1819, the Rev. Wm. Taylor, the Compiler, says:

"I beg leave to announce to the Roman Catholics of this country my intention of causing to be published in this city an edition of the DOWAY translation of the Scriptures, with approved Notes selected and translated from unexceptionable commentators and expositors. A Prospectus in a few days will be circulated to obtain a sufficient number of subscribers."

This project was not executed. *Shea's Catalogue of Catholic Bibles.*

1. NEW TESTAMENT. Stereotyped by D. & G. Bruce, New York.
   1819.   (Rev. Dr. Brigham.)   Bourgeois. 12.

2. NEW TESTAMENT: New York: Published by the American Bible Society. Daniel Fanshaw, Printer, 20 Sloat Lane. *Stereotyped by E. & J. White.* 1819.   12.

3. NEW TESTAMENT: Hartford: | Printed and Sold by Samuel G. Goodrich. | 1819. | (L.)   12.
   Engraved Frontispiece. Pp., 321.

4. THE | NEW TESTAMENT | of | our Lord and Saviour | Jesus Christ: | Translated out of | the Original Greek; | and | with the former Translations diligently | compared and revised. | The second American, | from the | Cambridge Stereotype edition; | Carefully revised and corrected. | Utica: | Printed and published by William Williams, | No. 60 Genesee Street. | 1819. | (Judson J. Hopkins; B.) 12.

Title, 1 f.; verso, Order of the Books; Text: pp. 3-334, sigs. A² to Dd⁵ in 6ˢ. The last sig. is completed by a blank leaf.

This resembles the Albany edition revised by the Rev. John McDonald, and printed by H. C. Southwick, 1813; but the numbers of the pages are inserted, and the sig. marks altered. The paging is very irregular; pp. 5, 6, 10, 27, 31, 38, 52, 53, 62, 87, 89, 115, 116, 137, 158, 198, 200, 206, 213, 250, 257, 311 have no numbers; p. 110 is marked 101; 324 is marked 234, and the signature marks are sometimes on one part, and at other times on a different part of the pages.

5. EL | NUEVO TESTAMENTO | de neustro Señor Jesu Christo, | traducido | de la Biblia Vulgata Latina | en Espanol | por el Rmo. P. Felipe Scio de S. Miguel, | Obispo electo de Segovia. | Reimpreso | literal y diligentemente, | conforme a la Segunda edicion hecha en Madrid, Año de 1797, | Revista y Corregida por su mismo Traductor. | JESUS les dixo: *Errais, no sabiendo las Escrituras.* | S. Mat. Cap. xxii. V. 29. | Nueva York: | Edicion esteriotipa, por Elihu White. | A costa de la Sociedad Americana de la Biblia. | Año de 1819. | (Am. Bib. Soc.)   12.

<small>Title, 1 f.; verso, blank; Orden de los Libros, 1 p.; verso, blank; Text: pp. 5–376; sigs. 1 (which includes Title and 1 prel. f.) to verso of 16⁶ in 12°.</small>

6. Das | Neue Testament | unsers | Herrn und Heilandes | Jesu Christi, | Nach der Deutschen Uebersetzung | D. Martin Luthers. | Mit kurzem | Inhalt eines jeden Capitels, | und | vollständiger Anweisung gleicher Schriftstellen. | Wie auch | aller Sonn-und Festtägigen | Evangelien und Episteln. | Achte Auflage. | Germantaun: | Gedruckt bey M. Billmeyer, 1819. | (Am. Bib. Soc.)   12

<small>Title, 1 f.; verso, blank; Verzeichniss, 1 p; verso, blank; Text: Gen. to Rev. pp. 5–537; Anweizung, 3 pp. not numbered. Sigs. A² to Z⁶; sigs. in 12°. The text is in double columns; the references follow their respective verses.</small>

1820.

1. SELF INTERPRETING BIBLE: New York: Printed and Published by S. Walker, 148 Cherry Street. Aug. 23, 1820. fol.

<small>Not seen. See *post*, No. 1, of 1822.</small>

2. HOLY BIBLE: New York: | Published by the American Bible Society. | *Stereotyped by E. & J. White.* | 1820. | (N. Y. Soc. Lib.)   12.

<small>Title, 1 f.; verso, (20*th Edition.*); Names and Order; at foot, Fanshaw, *Printer*, 20 Sloat Lane; Text: Gen. to Mal.; 3–832; N. Test. Title: New York: | Published by the American Bible Society. | Daniel Fanshaw, Printer, 20 Sloat Lane. | *Stereotyped by E. & J. White.* | 1819. | 1 p; verso, Table of Scripture Measures, &c., and of Time; Text: Mat. to Rev., pp. 3–254; sigs. run through from 1 to verso of 46³ in 12°.
We have seen the 35th edition also of this volume.</small>

3. HOLY BIBLE: Boston: Printed for Lincoln and Edmands. *Sold at their Bible Warehouse.* No. 53 Cornhill. Sold also by Collins & Co., New York. W. Greenhough, Printer, 1820. 12.

See No. 6 of 1819, and No. 10 of 1817.

4. HOLY BIBLE: Stereotyped by B. & J. Collins, New York. Boston: Printed by John H. A. Frost, Congress Street, for West, Richardson and Lord, No. 75 Cornhill. 1820. (L.) 12.

Title to New Test. dated 1818.

5. LA SAINTE BIBLE, | Qui contient | Le Vieux et le Nouveau | Testament: | Imprimée sur l'édition de Paris | de l'année 1805. | Edition Stéréotype. | Revue et Corrigée | avec soin d'après les textes Hébreu et Grec. | À New York: | Imprimé avec des planches solides, | aux frais de la Société Biblique Américaine. | Par Daniel Fanshaw. | 1820. | (N. Y. Soc. Lib.) 12.

Title, 1 p.; verso, Nom de tous les livres; Texte: Gen. à Mal, pp. 3-789; one p. blank; sigs., including title page, 1 to recto of 33^{11}, in 12^s; Le | Nouveau Testament | de | Notre Seigneur | Jesus Christ. | Imprimé sur l'édition de Paris de l'année 1805. | Edition Stéréotype. | Revue et corrigée avec soin d'après le texte Grec. | À New York. | Imprimé avec des planches solides par D. Fanshaw. | Aux frais de | La Société Biblique Américaine. | 1820. | Title, 1 p.; verso, Les Noms, &c., sig. 33^{12}; Texte: Mat. à Rev., pp. 3-207; sigs. 34 to recto of 44^7, in 12^s; at the bottom of p. 207: Fin. | Imprimé avec des planches, &c., as in title, but without the date; verso of 44^7, blank.

1. A | TRANSLATION | OF THE | NEW TESTAMENT: | by | Gilbert Wakefield, B. A. | From the Second London edition. | Cambridge: | Printed at the University Press, | by Hilliard and Metcalf. | 1820. | (N. Y. State Lib.) 8.

Title, 1 f.; verso, blank; Adv. to this first American edition, 1 p.; verso, Errata; Dedication pp. v, vi; Pref. pp. vii-xii; these 8 pp. are marked sig. b; Text: Mat. to Rev. pp. 1-450; sigs. 1 to 57^1 in 4^s; one blank leaf; Notes 1 f.; verso, blank; Text: pp. 3-163; sigs. 1^2 to 21, two blank leaves completing the sig. in 4^s.

2. THE | NEW TESTAMENT | of our | Lord and Saviour | Jesus Christ, | translated out of | the Original Greek; | and with | the former Translations | Diligently Compared and Revised. | Leicester: | Printed by Hori Brown. | 1820. | (G. L.) 12.

Title, 1 f.; verso, The Order of the Books of the New Testament, with their proper names, and number of their chapters; Text: Mat. to Rev., pp. 3-336; sigs. A. to Dd². Errors: Acts, 6: 3, "ye" instead of "we" 1 Tim., 4: 16, "thy" instead of "the"

3. NEW TESTAMENT: Stereotyped by B. & J. Collins. | Philadelphia: | Printed for the Booksellers. | 1820. | (L.) 12.

Title, 1 f.; verso, Order of Books; Text: Mat to Rev., pp. 3-290; sigs. A² to N¹ in 12ˢ; Table of Kindred, N²; verso, blank.

4. NEW TESTAMENT: Stereotyped | for "The American Bible Society" | By D. & G. Bruce. | Printed by Daniel Fanshaw, 20 Sloat Lane. | New York: | 1820. | (N. Y. Soc. Lib.) 12.
Pp. 312.

5. NEW TESTAMENT: Stereotype edition. | New York: | Printed by Daniel Fanshaw. | Stereotyped by A. Chandler & Co. | For "The American Bible Society." | 1820. | (N. Y. Soc. Lib.) 12.

5th edition; pp. 352.

1821.

1. THE | HOLY BIBLE: | Containing the | Old and New Testaments: | Translated out of the Original Tongues, | and with the former Translations diligently compared and revised. | With | Cannes's Marginal Notes and References. | Together with | The Apocrypha. | To which are added, | An Index: | And an Alphabetical Table of all the Names in the Old and New Testaments, | with their Significations. | Also, | Tables of Scripture Weights, Measures and Coins. | Stereotyped for Collins and Co. by B. & J. Collins. | New York: | Published by Collins and Co., No. 189 Pearl-Street. | Sold also by the principal Booksellers in the United States. | J. & J. Harper, Printers, No. 230 Pearl-Street. | 1821. | (L.) 4.

Title, 1 f.; verso, blank; Adv. to the stereotype ed., dated New-York, 1819, 1 f.; verso, blank; To the Reader, 1 p; The Books of the O. and N. Test., Account of the Dates or Time, &c., 1 p. Text, Gen. to Mal., pp. 9-744. sigs. B. to 5 A. Apocrypha (in smaller type), pp. 1-136. Sig. A to S¹. New Testament—New-York: | Printed and sold by Collins & Co. | No. 189 Pearl street. | Sold also by the principal Booksellers in the United States. | 1821. | 1 p.; verso, blank; Text: Mat. to Rev., pp. 747–

974; sigs. (including Title), 5 B to 6 G³; Index, pp. 975-994; at foot of p. 994, Table of Time; Tables of Scripture Weights, &c., pp. 995-997, at foot of p. 997, Table of Offices; Table of Kindred, Chronol. Index, p. 998 and part of p. 999; An Alphabetical Table of Names, pp. 999-1006; Judea, &c., pp. 1007, 1008, at foot of p. 1008, Analysis of O. and N. Test.; An Account of the Lives, Sufferings and Martyrdom of the Apostles and Evangelists, pp. 1009, 1010; sigs. 6 G⁴ to 6 M¹; Brown's Concordance. New-York: Published by Collins and Co., No. 189, Pearl-street. 1819. Title, 1 p ; verso, To the Reader; Text: pp. 3-56; sigs. A² to G; all the sigs in 4s.

The following are the Engravings:
Frontispiece.
The Deluge. Engraved for Collins's Quarto Bible, fourth edition, 1816.........*Boyd*.
Joseph interpreting Pharaoh's dream. Engraved for Collins's Quarto Bible,
    fourth edition...*Boyd & Maverick*.
Joseph's brethren offering their Present. Engraved for Collins & Co's
    Quarto Bible, stereotype edition ....*B. Tanner*.
Map of the Journeyings, &c. Engraved for Collins's Bible, stereotype
    edition ....*Hooker*.
Map of Palestine. Engraved for Collins's Bible, stereotype edition..........*Hooker*.
Jerusalem. Engraved for Collins's Bible, stereotype edition.
Elijah restores the Shunamite's son to life. Engraved for Collins's
    Quarto Bible, fourth edition, 1816..........................*P. Maverick*, Newark.
Mariæ Virginis. Engraved for Collins & Co's stereotype Quarto Bible,
    1816..*T. Gimbrede*, N. Y.
John the Baptist. Engraved for Collins & Co's Quarto Bible, stereotype
    edition...*Kearny*.
The Three Maries at the Sepulchre. Engraved for Collins & Co's Quarto
    Bible, stereotype edition....................................*Boyd*.
The Good Samaritan. Engraved for Collins's Quarto Bible, fourth edition,
    1816...*Kearny & Maverick*.
Map of St. Paul's Travels. Engraved for Collins's Bible, stereotype edition.

2. HOLY BIBLE. Stereotyped by E. and J. White for the American Bible Society. New York. 1821. (Am. Bib. Soc.) 8.

3. HOLY BIBLE. Printed by the New York Auxiliary Bible and Common Prayer Book Society. New York. 1821. 12.

4. HOLY BIBLE. Stereotyped by D. and G. Bruce. New York, 1821. (L.) 12.
Pp. 839; sigs. A to recto of Mm¹¹ in 12s.

5. THE | HOLY BIBLE, | containing the | Old and New Testaments: | Translated from the | Original Tongues, | And with the | former Translations | diligently compared and revised. | Stereotyped by B. & J. Collins. | New York: |

. Published by Collins and Hannay, | No. 230 Pearl Street. | J. & J. Harper, Printers. | 1821. | 12.

<small>Title (with the words, Stereotype Edition, on top) 1 f ; verso, blank ; To the Reader, and Names and Order of Books, 2 pp. ; Text : pp. 5–690, 210, in 6ˢ. The sig. marks to the O. T. are letters ; to the New, figures ; date to New Test. title, 1818 (in some copies the date is 1820), with : The | Psalms of David | in metre : | Translated and diligently compared with the | Original Text, | and | former Translations. | More plain, smooth, and agreeable to the | Text, than any heretofore. | Allowed by the Authority of the General Assembly of the | Kirk of Scotland, and appointed to be sung in | Congregations and Families. | Stereotyped by B. & J. Collins, New York. | New York : | Published by Collins & Hannay, | No. 230 Pearl-street. | n. d., 1 p. ; verso, blank ; Text : 33 ff., not paged.</small>

6. HOLY BIBLE: Stereotyped by E. & J. White for the American Bible Society. New York. 1821.   12.

7. THE | HOLY BIBLE, | containing the | Old and New Testaments; | Translated | out of the Original Tongues, | and | with the former translations | diligently compared and revised. | Lunenburg, (Mass.) | Printed and sold by W. Greenough. | 1821. | (B.)   12.

<small>Title, 1 f.; verso, blank ; Names and Order of all the Books, 1 f.; verso, blank ; Text : Gen. to Mal , pp. 5–605 ; A³ to recto of Cc³ ; verso, Table of Scripture Measures, Weights and Money, Table of Time ; New Testament title, 1 f ; verso, Account of the Dates or Time of writing the Books of the New Testament ; Mat. to Rev. pp. 609–792. sigs. Cc⁵ to Kk¹².
This ed. corresponds with the 12mo of Websters & Skinners, Albany, 1817, q. v.</small>

8. HOLY BIBLE: Hartford: Printed by Hudson and Goodwin. 1821.   (B.)   12.

<small>The edition of 1809 continued.</small>

9. LESSONS | for Schools | taken from the | Holy Scriptures, | in the words of the text, | without note or comment. | In three parts. | Philadelphia: | Published by Kimber & Sharpless, | No. 93 Market Street. | 1821. | 16.

<small>Pp. 244. (Gowans.)</small>

1. NEW TESTAMENT: Hartford: Printed by George Goodwin and Sons. 1821.   (B.)   12.

<small>Text : pp. 1–334 (p. 326 marked 226) ; sigs. A² to verso of O¹² in 12ˢ. Short headings to columns and chapters. I Tim. 4 : 16 incorrect.</small>

2. NEW TESTAMENT: Fifteenth Edition: | Hartford: | Printed and Sold by Samuel G. Goodrich. | 1821. | (L.) 18.

Pp. 321. Sigs. A to recto of Dd⁵ in 6ˢ. See No. 3 of 1818.

3. THE NEW TESTAMENT of Our Lord and Saviour Jesus Christ. Translated out of the Original Greek; and with the former translations diligently compared and revised. Stereotyped by B. & J. Collins, New York. Providence (R. I.): Printed and published by Miller and Hutchens, No. 1, Market Square (up stairs). 1821. (Mr. Bartlett.) 12.

Pp. 312.

4. NEW TESTAMENT: The Second American from the Cambridge Stereotype edition. Utica: Printed and published by William Williams, No. 60, Genesee Street. 1821. 12.

Same as the edition of 1819. *Supra*, p. 149.

5. NEW TESTAMENT: New York: Stereotyped by D. & G. Bruce. 1821. 12.

6. THE | NEW TESTAMENT | of our | Lord and Saviour | Jesus Christ, | translated | out of the Original Greek; | And | with the former Translations | diligently compared and revised. | New York: | Published and Sold by James A. Burtus, 19 Peck Slip, | Corner of Water-Street. | *Gray & Bunce, Printers, 347 Pearl-Street, Franklin Square.* | 1821. | (L.) 12.

Title, 1 p.; verso, Order of Books; Text: pp. (3)-(312); sigs. A to verso of N¹², in 12s; Brief Headings to chapters.

7. THE | HISTORY | of our | Lord and Saviour | Jesus Christ: | Comprehending all that the | Four Evangelists | have recorded concerning Him; | All their relations being brought together in one Narration, | so that no Circumstance is omitted, but that inestimable | History is continued in one Series, in the very words of | Scripture. | By the Rev. Samuel Lieberkuhn, M. A. | Translated into the | Delaware Indian Language | by the | Rev. David Zeisberger, | Missionary of the United Brethren. | New York: | Printed by Daniel Fanshaw, No. 20 Slote Lane. | 1821. | (B.) 12.

Pp. viii. and 222. Zeisberger's Translation of Lieberkuhn's Harmony of the Gospel, was printed only for the use of the Missionaries and is not to be purchased. *Du Ponceau's Preface to Zeisberger's Delaware Grammar,* p. 93.

1822.

1. THE HOLY BIBLE: | Containing the | Old and New Testaments, | with | References and Illustrations; | An | exact Summary of the several Books; | A | Paraphrase | on the most obscure or important parts; | an | Analysis of the contents of each chapter; | to which are annexed, | an extensive Introduction, | explanatory Notes, evangelical Reflections, &c. | By the | late Rev. John Brown, | Minister of the Gospel at Haddington. | Embellished with a series of beautiful engravings. | New York: | Printed and Published by T. Kinnersley, 148 Cherry-street; | and sold by appointed agents in all cities and principal towns in the United States. | 1822. | (Conn. Hist. Soc.; Am. and For. Bib. Soc., N. Y.)   fol.

After two blank ff., a copperplate engraving filling the verso of 3d leaf: Moses seated near an altar, his right hand resting on a double tablet, with the words: " Unto Him | ye shall | listen." | Deuteronomy | Chap. 18. Vers. 15. | Above is a Sun, Christ holding a Cross, and two Cherubims with crown of thorns and the nails. At foot, " N. York, pub'd by S. Walker, 148 Cherry St. 1821." On recto of next fol , an engraved Title : The | Self Interpreting | Bible, | with an Evangelical Commentary | by the late Revd John Brown, | Minister of the Gospel | at | Huddington | containing marginal References and Reflections | Embellished with Elegant Engravings. | New York | Printed and published by S. Walker, 148 Cherry street | 1820. | With an oval Vignette (Adam naming the Beasts;) Engraved by J. Palmer Alb*r* from an original painting by B. West Esq.; verso, blank; Printed Title (as above) 1 f ; verso, blank; Introduction, pp. i–ii, sigs. *a* to *n* in 2⁵ ; Names and Order, p. lii ; To the Reader, 1 f. ; Calculation of No. of Books, 1 f. ; Text: Gen. to Mal., pp. 3–876 ; sigs. (including To the Reader) B. to 10 N. in 2ˢ (110 numbers) ; Apocrypha (mock title), 1 f ; verso, blank ; Text: pp. 1–158, sigs. B to Ss¹ (10 numbers) ; New Test. title, same imprint, 1 f. ; verso, blank ; Text : Mat. to Rev., pp. 877–1216 ; sigs. 10 O to 14 F, in 2ˢ (numbers 110 to 152) ; Collection of Similes, pp. 1217–1221 ; Table of Scripture Measures, &c., p. 1222 ; Table of Offices, 1 p.; sigs. 14 G and 14 H.

Engravings:

Adam and Eve weeping over dead Abel (Front.)...................*Chs. T. Harrison.*
Tower of Babel. Published by T. Kinnersly, Jan. 30, 1818.
Isaac & Rebecca..*Neagle.*
Joseph cast into the pit..*J. Neagle.*
Plague of Blood..*J. Neagle.*
Moses smiting the rock...*J. Neagle.*

Moses on Mount Sinai...*J. B. Neagle.*
The Golden Calf ....*T. Brown.*
Levites receiving the Sacred Treasures....................................*Neagle.*
Feast of Tabernacles....................... ....*Neagle*, Phil.
Death of Sisera.
Samson slaying the lion.
Philistines sending back the Ark................................. *T. Kelly*, Boston.
David's Victory over Goliah.................................... *T. Kelly*, Boston.
Witch of Endor...*Neagle.*
Solomon's Temple.
Ahasuerus & Esther ....*Kelly*, Boston.
Triumph of Mordecai..*Neagle.*
Daniel in the Lions' den.
Map of Jerusalem.
Christ's temptation..*J. Palmer.*
Last Supper (Da Vinci)..*J. Neagle*, Phil.
Taking from the cross..*J. Palmer.*
Christ bearing the Cross...*J. B. Neagle.*
The Ascension. ....*J. Brown.*
Christ in the garden (with Mary)...*J. B. Neagle.*
Peter and John healing the Lame...*Neagle.*
St. Paul's conversion...*Palmer.*

The above work was printed in 162 numbers; 152 of which were taken up by the Old and New Testaments; and 10 by the Apocrypha, the latter being furnished to subscribers at their option.

2. Daniel D. Smith's Stereotype Edition. | The Holy Bible, | containing the | Old and New Testaments, | Translated out of the Original Tongues | and with | the former Translations diligently compared and revised. | With | Canne's Marginal Notes and References. | To which are added, | An Index; | An Alphabetical Table | of all the Names in the Old and New Testaments, with their Significations; | Tables of Scripture Weights, Measures, and Coins, &c. | Stereotyped by E. White, New-York. | New-York: | Published and Sold by Daniel D. Smith, | at the Franklin Juvenile book and stationary store, No. 190 Greenwich Street, | also by the principal booksellers in the United States. | 1822. | 4.

3. THE | HOLY BIBLE, | containing the | Old and New Testaments: | Translated out of the Original Tongues, | and with | the former Translations diligently compared and re-

vised. | With Canne's Marginal Notes and references. | To which are added, | an Index; | an Alphabetical Table | of all the Names in the Old and New Testaments, with their Significations; | Tables of Scripture Weights, Measures and Coins, &c. | Cooperstown, (N. Y.) | Stereotyped, printed and published by H. & E. Phinney, | and sold by them at their Book-Store, and by the Booksellers generally | in the United States. | 1822. | 4.

Title 1 f.; verso, blank; Names and Order of all the books, 1 p.; verso, blank; To the Reader (Witherspoon's Pref.), p. 3; Contents, pp. 4–8; Text: Gen. to Mal., pp. 9–574; Table of Passages; Index of Years and Times; Table of Time and Offices, p. 575; sigs. B to 3 W^4; Family Record, 2 ff; Title to New Test., 1 p.; verso, Account of the dates or time; Text: Mat. to Rev. pp. 579–754; sigs. 3 X^2–4 U^1; Index, pp. 755–762; 4 U^2 to 4 V^1, Tables of Measures, Weights, &c, p. 763; Analysis of the O. and N. Test., Table of Kindred, Judea, or Palestine, p. 764; Alphabetical Table, pp. 765–768, 4 V^2 to 4 V^4. No Apocrypha. Sigs. in 4s.

H. & E. PHINNEY commenced printing 4to Bibles Aug. 1st, 1822, and published from that time to the winter of 1848, when their establishment was destroyed by fire, 138 editions, or 154,000 copies, averaging about 6,000 per annum. About 100,000 of them contained the Apocrypha, and 14,750 had Brown's Concordance. Only 500 copies were printed in 1822, and 4,475 for the first half of 1848; this will show the ratio of increase from the beginning. The stereotype plates were made by H. & E. P., at Cooperstown. The proofs were read with the greatest care, the text having been compared with other editions, and a premium offered to the men in the establishment for the discovery of errors, even after the plates were cast.—*Letter of E. Phinney, Esq.*

4. HOLY BIBLE: *Stereotyped by D. & G. Bruce, New York.* Albany: Printed and published by E. & E. Hosford. 1822. 12.

Title, 1 f.; verso, Names and order of the Books; Text: pp. 3–637. Sigs. A to recto of Mm in 12^s.

5. HOLY BIBLE: Hartford: Printed by Hudson and Goodwin. 1822. (B.) 12.

6. HOLY BIBLE: Second Stereotype edition. | New York: | Published by E. Bliss & E. White. | 1822. | 24.

Title, 1 f.; verso, A. Paul, printer; The Translators to King James, pp. 3, 4; Names and Order of the Books of O. and N. Test., also on p. 4; Text: Gen. to Mal., pp. 5–704; sigs. A to recto of Gg^1; N. Test. title. 1 p.; verso, blank; Text: Mat. to Rev., pp. 3–216; Sigs. 1–9; all in 12.

Foot notes on passages in the text are interspersed throughout this Volume. The title page to the New Test. has at foot: "Ch. i. v. i. This title of the book was put to it by the Evangelist himself." This note ought to be at foot of the first page of Matthew.

BERNARD DORNIN, a Catholic publisher, announced this year his intention to publish early in the ensuing winter two editions of the Doway Bible, with superb engravings; one in folio and the other in quarto, in order to accommodate purchasers. He never carried out his plan. *Shea's Catalogue of Catholic Bibles*, p. 12.

1. NEW TESTAMENT: Philadelphia: Published by H. C. Carey and I. Lea, No. 126, Chesnut Street. 1822. 4.
   With Carey & Son's Bible of 1818.

2. NEW TESTAMENT: Appointed to be read in Churches. | Philadelphia, | Printed for the Booksellers. | 1822. | (L.) 12.
   Pp. 335; Sigs. A to recto of O^{12}; verso, Table of Kindred; sigs. in 12^s.

3. NEW TESTAMENT: Stereotyped | For "The American Bible Society" | By D. & G. Bruce. | New York | 1822. | 12.
   Pp. 201.

4. THE PRONOUNCING TESTAMENT. | The | New Testament | of our | Lord and Saviour, &c. To which is applied, in numerous words, the orthoepy of the Critical Pronouncing Dictionary; also, the Classical Pronunciation of the Proper Names as they stand in the Text—scrupulously adopted from "A Key to the Classical Pronunciation of Greek, Latin, and Scripture Proper Names. By John Walker, author of the Critical Pronouncing Dictionary, &c." By which "the Proper Names are accented and divided into syllables exactly as they ought to be pronounced, according to rules drawn from analogy and the best usage." To which is prefixed, An Explanatory Key. By Israel Alger, Jun., A. M., Teacher of Youth, Author of Elements of Orthography, and the New Practical Book-Keeper. Boston: Printed and published by Lincoln & Edmands, No. 53 Cornhill. 1822. 12.
   First edition.

5. NEW TESTAMENT: Stereotyped by J. Howe, New York. Printed at Treadwell's power press, Boston. Boston: 1822. (Am. Bib. Soc.) 12.

6. NEW TESTAMENT: Hartford: Printed by George Goodwin and Sons. 1822. (B.) 12.

<small>This is the edition of 1821, with a new Title page only. P. 326 is marked 226, and 1 Tim. 4 : 16 is incorrect.</small>

7. NEW TESTAMENT: Utica: Printed and published by William Williams, No. 60, Genesee street. 1822. (B.) 12.

<small>See *supra* No. 4 of 1821.</small>

8. Η ΚΑΙΝΗ | ΔΙΑΘΗΚΗ. | The | New Testament, | in | Greek and English; | The Greek according to Griesbach; the English upon the basis of the | Fourth London edition of the Improved Version, with an at- | tempt to further improvement from the translations | of Campbell, Wakefield, Scarlett, Mac- | Knight and Thomson. | In Two Volumes. | By Abner Kneeland, | Minister of the First Independent Church of Christ, called Universalist, | in Philadelphia. | Philadelphia: | Published by the Editor, No. 9, North Second Street, and sold by him—also | by Abm. Small, No. 165 Chesnut Street; and by the | principal booksellers in the city. | William Fry, Printer. | 1822. | 8.

<small>Pp. 360 and 452. (*Gowans*.)</small>

9. Η ΚΑΙΝΗ | ΔΙΑΘΗΚΗ | Novum Testamentum | Græce | ex recensione | Jo. Jac. Griesbachii | omissa | Selecta Lectionum varietate ejus | Lipsiæ G. J. Goschen. 1805. | Cantabrigiæ Nov-Anglorum | 1809. | Philadelphiæ : | Cura et Impensis Abneri Kneeland edita. | Typis W. Fry. | 1822. | (B.) 12.

<small>Title, 1 f. ; verso, Certificate of Copyright ; Preface (in English), dated Philadelphia, May 1, 1822. Signed Abner Kneeland, 2 pp; Text: pp. 5–340 ; sigs. 1 (which includes Text and Pref) to verso of 29^2; Errata, pp. 341–344; sigs. 29^3 to verso of 29^1 in 6^s.

Having determined to publish the New Testament in Greek and English, the editor was solicited to publish his improved translation by itself, which could be easily done by changing the forms, while the matter was thus in type ; and this circumstance suggested the thought of publishing the Greek Testament also in the same manner.— *Preface*.</small>

10. EL NUEVO TESTAMENTO....traducido de la Biblia Vulgata Latina en Español, por el Rmo. P. Felip Scio....conforme a la Segunda edicion hecha en Madrid, Año de 1797. Nueva-York: Edicion esteriotipa, por Elihu White. A costa de la Sociedad Americana de la Biblia. Año de 1822. (Am. Bib. Soc.) 12.

The text of this edition is from the same plates as that of 1819.

6. Das | Neue Testament | unsers | Herrn und Heilandes | Jesu Christi, | Nach der Deutschen Uebersetzung | D. Martin Luthers. | Mit kurzem | Inhalt eines jeden Capitels, | und | vollständiger Anweisung gleicher Schriftstellen. | Wie auch | aller Sonn=und Festtägigen | Evangelien und Episteln. | Achte Auflage. | Germantaun: | Gedruckt bey M. Billmeyer, 1822. | (Am. Bib. Soc.) 12

1823.

1. THE | HOLY BIBLE | Containing the | Old and New Testaments: | Translated out of the Original Tongues, | And with the former Translations diligently compared and revised. | With Canne's Marginal Notes and References. | Together with | The Apocrypha. | To which are added, | An Index: | and an Alphabetical Table of all the Names in the Old and New Testaments | with their Significations. | Also, | Tables of Scripture Weights, Measures and Coins. | Kimber & Sharpless Stereotype Edition. | Philadelphia: | Published by Kimber and Sharpless, | No. 50 North Fourth-Street, | n. d. (L.) 4.

Title, 1 f.; verso, Names and Order, Account of dates; Contents, pp. (1)–(6); Text: Gen. to Mal., pp. 8–744; sigs. 2 to 93^4, in 4^s; Apocrypha, in smaller type, pp. 1–138; sigs; A. to R^1 in 4^s; Fam. Rec., 2 ff.; The | New Testament | of our | Lord and Saviour | Jesus Christ; | translated out of the Original Greek: | And with the former Translations diligently compared and revised. | Stereotyped by B. & J. Collins, | New York. | Philadelphia: | Published by Kimber & Sharpless, | No 50 North Fourth-Street. | 1 p.; verso blank; Text: Mat. to Rev., pp. 747–974; Index, pp. 975–994; Table of Time also on p. 994; Tables of Weights, Measures, &c., Offices, Kindred, pp. 995–998; Chronol. Index, pp. 998–999; Alphabetical Table of Names, pp. 999–1006; Judea, Palestine, &c., pp. 1007 and part of 1008; Analysis, remainder of p. 1008; sigs. 94 to 126^4 in 4^s; Psalms of David in Metre, no title, pp. 1–18; sigs. A to C^1 in

162   AMERICAN BIBLES.   [1823—

4s ; [Kimber and Sharpless Stereotype Edition.] | A brief | Concordance | to the | Holy Scriptures | of the | Old and New Testaments: | &c., by John Brown, &c., | Revised and Corrected. | Stereotyped by J. Howe. | Philadelphia: | Published by Kimber and Sharpless, No. 50 North 4th-Street. | 1 p., to the Reader, 1. p.; Text, pp. 3-54; sigs. 98 to 104³ in 4s .

The following are the Engravings in this Bible :
1. The Last Supper. Front. to O. T. L. Da Vinci, pinx.: Engraved by *J. B. Neagle.*
2. Moses receiving the Law (Vignette) .... Westall.   *Heath.*
3. The murder of Abel ....,........A. Sacchi, pinx.   *F. Kearney.*
4. The Deluge ....Poussin.   *F. Kearney.*
5. The Dismissal of Hagar......................Guercino.   *Gimbrede.*
6. Joseph interpreting Pharaoh's Dream ....*Boyd & Maverick.*
7. Joseph's brethren offering their presents................. ....*D. Tanner.*
8. Jacob blessing the sons of Joseph.............Rembrandt. *Fairman & Maverick.*
9. Elisha raising the Shunamite's son .... West.   *P. Maverick*, Newark.
10. The peaceable kingdom of Christ.... ....Westall.   *Tanner, Vallance.*
11. The vision of the Horses.................... ...Westall.   *Kearney & Co., Heath.*
12. Journeyings of Israel. } 2 Maps.
13. Palestine.   }
14. Tobit and the Angel ....Westall. *Tanner, Vallance & Co.*
15. Judith and Holofernes.......................Westall. *Tanner, Vallance & Co.*
16. Mariæ Virginis. Front. to N. T..............Holbein, pinx.   *J. Neagle.*
17. The angels appearing to the shepherds (Vignette) Westall.   *Heath.*
18. The angel appearing to Joseph ....Westall.   *Heath.*
19. The Annunciation..........................Westall.   *Tanner.*
20. The adoration of the Shepherds..............Westall.   *Heath.*
21. Christ with the Doctors.....................Westall.   *Heath.*
22. Christ raising the widow's son........Westall. *Tanner, Vallance, Kearney & Co.*
23. The good Samaritan........................Rembrandt. *Kearney & Maverick.*
24. Christ's agony ....Westall.   *Heath.*
25. The entombing of Christ....................Westall.   *Heath.*
26. Christ instructing Nicodemus .. ..Westall.   *Heath.*
27. Christ appearing to Mary Magdalen ....Westall.   *B. Tanner.*
28. Thomas's Incredulity........................Rubens.   *Haines.*
29. St. Paul ....*Tiebout & Maverick.*
30. Travels of St. Paul (Map) . ...*Haines.*

Nos. 3, 4, 5, 6, 7, 8, 9, 10, 23, 28, 29 have at the top—Kimber and Sharpless' Quarto Bible. Stereotype Edition.

The *first* edition of this Bible was printed in 1823. The stereotype plates of the Old Testament were cast by Elihu White of New York; those of the New, by B. & J. Collins. Kimber and Sharpless continued the publication of large and numerous editions until 1844, when they sold the plates to Jasper Harding of Philadelphia. In some copies the engravings are on wood.

2. HOLY BIBLE: Stereotyped by D. & G. Bruce. | Philadelphia. | 1823. | 12.

Pp. 837. Imprint to New Test. title: New York. 1821.

3. HOLY BIBLE: Stereotype edition. New York: Stereotyped
by E. and J. White, for "The American Bible Society."
1823. 12.
Pp. 706, 215 (Gowans).

4. THE BIBLE CLASS TEXT BOOK; or Bible Catechism, contain-
ing Questions.... To promote an intimate acquaintance
with the Inspired Volume. By Hervey Wilbur, A. M.
Twelfth Edition. Boston: Published by Cummings &
Hilliard, No. 1, Cornhill. Stereotyped by T. H. and C.
Carter, Boston. 1823. (L.) 12.
Engraved Title, 1 f.; Pref. and Recom., i-x; Text: pp. 11-132.

5. SCRIPTURE LESSONS: being a New Selection from the Old and
New Testaments, for the use of Schools. In three parts.
Boston: Published by W. B. Fowles, No. 45, Cornhill.
True and Green, Printers. 1823. (L.) 12.
Pp. 242.

1. NEW TESTAMENT: With References and a Key sheet of Questions historical, doctrinal and practical. By Hervey Wilbur. Boston: Published by Cummings, Hilliard & Co.
1823. 12.

2. PRONOUNCING TESTAMENT. Boston: Printed and published
by Lincoln and Edmands, No. 53 Cornhill. Stereotyped
by T. H. & C. Carter. 1823. 12.
See No. 4 of 1822.

3. NEW TESTAMENT; Stereotyped by B. and J. Collins, N.
York. Concord, (N. H.): Printed and published by Luther
Roby. And sold at his Bookstore wholesale and retail.
1823. (L.) 12.
Title (marked at head of page), *Roby's Stereotype Edition*, 1 f.; verso, Order of
of books; Text: Mat. to Rev., pp. 3–380; p. 381, Table of kindred; sigs. A² to recto
of Ii⁵, in 6ˢ.

4. THE NEW TESTAMENT: translated from the original Greek,
according to Griesbach; with an attempt to further improvement from the translations of Campbell, Wakefield,

Scarlett, Macknight and Thomson. By Abner Kneeland. Philadelphia, 1823. 8.

See No. 6 of 1822.

5. NEW TESTAMENT. By A. Paul for the American Bible Society, New York. 1823. (Amer. Bib. Soc.) 12.

6. NEW TESTAMENT: Stereotyped by J. Howe, New York. | New 𝔜ork: | Printed and sold by Johnstone and Van Norden. | 1823. | (L.) 12.
Pp. 288.

6. THE NEW TESTAMENT | of | our Lord and Saviour | Jesus Christ, | translated | 𝔒ut of the 𝔒riginal 𝔊reek: | And | with the former Translations | diligently Compared and Revised. | Hartford: | Printed and Sold by George Goodwin. | 1823. | (R. G. Tallcott; L.) 16.

Frontispiece, Christ instructing Nicodemus, R. Westall, pinx. *O. Pelton*, sc. Engraved title: Vignette from Luke 2:9, 1 p.; verso, blank; Printed title, 1 p.; verso, Order of the Books; Text: pp. 3–412; Contents, pp. 413–416; sigs. A (which includes printed title) to Bb⁸, in 8ᵃ. Brief headings to columns and chapters.

1 Tim., 4:16 reads: Take heed unto thyself and unto thy doctrine.

1824.

1. THE | HOLY BIBLE: | Containing the | Old and New Testaments: | Translated out of the Original Tongues, | and with the former Translations diligently compared and revised. | With | Canne's Marginal Notes and References. | Together with | The Apocrypha. | To which are added, | An Index: | and an Alphabetical Table of all the Names in the Old and New Testaments, | with their Significations. | Also, | Tables of Scripture Weights, Measures and Coins. | Stereotyped for Collins & Co. by B. & J. Collins. | Boston: | Published by C. Ewer & T. Bedlington. | J. H. A. Frost, Printer. | 1824. | (L.) 4.

Title, 1 f.; verso, blank; Advertisement to the (Collins) stereotype edition, dated New York, 1819, 1 p.; verso, blank; To the Reader (Witherspoon's Pref.) 1 p.; verso, The Books of the Old and New Test.; Account of dates, 1 p.; verso, blank; Then follow, Text: Gen. to Mal., and Apocrypha, the same as in Collins & Co.'s 4ᵗᵒ, New York, 1821; Family Record, 2 ff.; New Test. Title, imprint as above, 1

—1824.] AMERICAN BIBLES. 165

p.; verso, blank; Text, and appended matter in Collins & Co's ster. ed. of 1821, (*supra*) as far as p. 1010 (6 M¹); Psalms in metre, pp. 1-39; p. 40, blank; sigs. A to K in 2ˢ; Brief Concordance. Stereotyped by B. & J. Collins. Boston: Published by C. Ewer & T. Bedlington. 1827. Same as in Collins & Co's 4ᵗᵒ ed. of 1821. 2 frontispieces engraved on wood, and 16 plates.

This ed. is from the same, or duplicate, plates of the Collins Bible of 1821, with the introductory matter differently arranged and the Psalms in metre added. Other copies correspond with the Collins edition and have not the Psalms. In these the Concordance is dated 1824.

2. HOLY BIBLE: Cooperstown, (N. Y.) Stereotyped, printed and published by H. & E. Phinney, and sold by them at their Bookstore, and by the Booksellers generally in the United States. 1824. 4.

3. THE | HOLY BIBLE, | translated from | the Latin Vulgate: | Diligently compared | with the Hebrew, Greek, and other editions, | in divers languages. | The | Old Testament, | first published by | The English College at Doway, A. D. 1609. | And | 𝕿𝖍𝖊 𝕹𝖊𝖜 𝕿𝖊𝖘𝖙𝖆𝖒𝖊𝖓𝖙, | first published by | The English College at Rhemes, A. D. 1582. | With | Annotations, References, and an Historical and Chronological Index. | First Stereotype, from the Fifth Dublin Edition. | Newly revised and corrected according to the Clementin edition of the Scriptures. | 𝕻𝖍𝖎𝖑𝖆𝖉𝖊𝖑𝖕𝖍𝖎𝖆: | Published by Eugene Cummiskey. | Stereotyped by J. Howe. | 1824. | (Sem. St. Sulpice, Balt.) 8.

Engraved frontispiece (Jesus, Mary and Joseph). Title, 1 f.; verso, blank; Admonition, Letter of Pius VI., A Prayer, 1 p.; verso, Decree of the Council of Trent, and Books of the Old Test.; Text; Gen. to Esther, pp. 5-335; verso of 335, blank; sigs. A (which includes title and 2 prel ff.) to recto of 2 T⁴; Job to the end of II Mac., pp. 1-444; sigs. A. to verso of 3 K²; The | New Testament | of our | Lord and Saviour | Jesus Christ, | translated from | 𝕿𝖍𝖊 𝕷𝖆𝖙𝖎𝖓 𝖁𝖚𝖑𝖌𝖆𝖙: | Diligently compared with the Original Greek : | and first published by | the English College at Rhemes, A. D. 1582. | With | Annotations and References and a Historical and Chronological Index, | From the fifth Dublin Edition, | Newly revised and corrected according to the Clementin edition of the Scriptures. | 𝕻𝖍𝖎𝖑𝖆𝖉𝖊𝖑𝖕𝖍𝖎𝖆: | Published by Eugene Cummiskey. | Stereotyped by J. Howe. | 1824. | 1 p.; verso, blank; Admonition, Letter of Pius VI, and Prayer, 1 p.; verso, Approbation of Dr. Troy, and order of Books of New Test.; Text : Mat. to Apocal. pp. 5-189; sigs., including title and prel. pp.; A to recto of 2 A³ ; Table of Reference, pp. 190, 191 ; Table of Epist. and Gosp., 1 p. not numbered; verso of 2 A³ and 2 A⁴ ; Historical and Chronological Index to New Testament, 2 pp., not marked ; Index to Old Testament, paged at top, 1 to 10; p. 9 is marked at bottom *A. Sigs. all in 4ˢ.

4. HOLY BIBLE: translated from the Latin Vulgate: First American, from the Fifth Dublin Edition. Philadelphia: Eugene Cummiskey. Stereotyped by J. Howe. 1824. (L.) 8.

<small>This differs in various respects from the preceding. The engraved frontis. of the O. T. is Moses in the bulrushes, and is dated 1827; That of the N. T. has no date, but the title page is 1831. This copy has approbations of Dr. Troy on the verso of both titles and that of the Bishop of Philadelphia accompanies the N. T. The edition preceding has neither.</small>

5. LA | BIBLIA SAGRADA, | a saber: | El Antiguo y el Nuevo Testamento, | traducidos de la | Vulgata Latina | en Español, | por el Rmo. P. Felipe Scio de S. Miguel, | Obispo electo de Segovia. | Nueva Edicion, | a costa de la Sociedad Americana de la Biblia, | conforme a la Segunda, que revista y corregida publico su mismo traductor | el Año de 1797 en Madrid. | Jesus.respondió: Escudriñad las Escrituras. | S. Juan, cap. v. ver. 39. | Nueva-York: | Edicion estereotipica por A. Chandler. 1824. | 8.

<small>Title, 1 f.; verso, Orden des libros; Text: Gen to Mal., pp. 3-928; sigs 1 to 58; El | Nuevo Testamento, | traducido de la | Vulgata Latina | en Español, | por el Rmo. P. Filipe Scio de S. Miguel, | de las escuelas pias, Obispo electo de Segovia. | Nueva edicion, | a costa de la Sociedad Americana de la Biblia, | quen la ha hecho cotejar con la que revista y corrigeda publicó su traductor | el año de 1797 en Madrid. | Nueva-York: | Edicion estereotipica por A Chandler. | 1824. | 1 p.; verso, Orden de los libros; Text: pp. 3-251; sigs. 1-16. No notes. *Shea's Catalogue of Catholic Bibles*, p. 12.</small>

6. HOLY BIBLE: Stereotyped | for the American Bible Society | By D. & G. Bruce. | Printed by A. Paul, 72 Nassau-Street, | New York. | 1824. | 12.

<small>Title, 1 f.; verso, [64th Edition.] Names and Order; Text: Gen. to Mal. pp. 3-637; Table of Scripture Measures, Weights and Money; Table of Time, p. 638; sigs. A² to C which is also marked 3, then the sigs. run 4 to verso of 27⁷ in figures only; New Test. Title, imprint: Stereotyped | for the American Bible Society | By D. & G. Bruce. | New York, | 1824. | 1 p.; verso, blank; (sig. 27⁸) Text: Mat. to Rev., pp. 641-837; 27⁹ to recto of 35¹¹; all in 12s. No headings to columns or chapters.</small>

7. HOLY BIBLE. Stereotyped by A. Chandler, New York, 1824. (Rev. Dr. Brigham.) 24.

8. HOLY BIBLE: Stereotyped by B. and J. Collins, New York. | Albany: | Printed by Websters and Skinners, | at their Bookstore, corner of State | and Pearl Streets. | 1824. | 12.

This is a continuation of the edition of 1817, with new Titles only. 1 Tim. 4: 16 incorrect.

9. THE | HOLY BIBLE, | containing the | Old and New Testaments: | Translated out of the | Original Tongues, | and with the | former Translations | diligently compared and revised. | Stereotyped by B. & J. Collins, New-York. | Hartford: | Published by Silas Andrus. | Johnstone & Van Norden, Printers. | 1824. | (B.) 12.

Engraved Title (same imprint), 1 f.; Printed Title, 1 f.; verso, blank; To the Reader and Names and Order, 2 pp.; Text: Gen. to Mal., pp. 5–690; sigs. A^3 to recto of Ff^9; New Test. Title, 1 p.; verso, blank; Text: Mat. to Rev., pp. 3–210; sigs. Ff^{10} to Pp^6 in 12^s. Front. to Old Test., Moses receiving the Law.

Some copies of this edition have, on the engraved title page, the following imprint: Hartford: Published by Silas Andrus and Johnstone and Van Norden, New York; and on the printed title, Hartford: Published by Silas Andrus.

10. HOLY BIBLE: Hartford: Printed by Hudson and Goodwin. 1824. (B.) 12.

The edition of 1809 continued.

11. HOLY BIBLE: Philadelphia: | H. C. Cary and I. Lea, Chesnut street. | 1824. | (L.) 12.

12. THE | HOLY BIBLE, | containing | The Old Testament, | and | The New; | Translated out of | 𝔈𝔥𝔢 𝔒𝔯𝔦𝔤𝔦𝔫𝔞𝔩 𝔗𝔬𝔫𝔤𝔲𝔢𝔰; | and with the | former Translations diligently | Compared and Revised. | Stereotyped by J. Howe.... Philadelphia. | New-York: | Published by Daniel D. Smith, | No. 190, Greenwich-Street. | 1824. |. 24.

Title, 1 f.; verso, blank; Contents, pp. 3–x; at foot of p. x, The Books of the Old Testament; Text: Gen. to Mal., pp. 11–743; verso, blank; sigs. A (including title and 4 prel. ff.) to recto of Hh^{12}; New Test. Title, same imprint, 1 p.; verso, blank; Contents, pp. 3–v; verso, The Books of the New Test; Text: Mat. to Rev., pp. 7–238; sigs. A (including title and 2 prel. ff.) to verso of K^{11}, followed by 1 blank leaf; sigs in 12^s.

168   AMERICAN BIBLES.   [1824—

13. ERRATA | OF THE PROTESTANT BIBLE: | or the | Truth | of the | English Translations | examined: | in a Treatise, showing some of the errors that are to be found in the English | translations of the Sacred Scriptures, used by Protestants against such points | of religious doctrine as are the subject of controversy between them and the | Members of the Catholic Church. | *In which also,* | from their mistranslating the twenty-third verse of the fourteenth chapter of | the Acts of the Apostles, the consecration of Doctor Matthew Parker, the first | Protestant Archbishop of Canterbury, is occasionally considered. | By Thomas Ward, | Author of the celebrated poem, entitled "England's Reformation." | For I testify, &c. Rev. xxii: 18, 19. | A New Edition, carefully revised and corrected. | London, Printed in the year 1688: | and | Philadelphia | Re-printed for Eugene Cummisky (*sic*), No. 182 North Fourth Street. | 1824. | 8.

Title, 1 f.; verso, blank; Life of Mr. Ward, pp. iii, iv; Pref. pp. v-xvi; Text: pp. 1-95. Sigs. 1 to 12, in 4s .

1. THE | NEW TESTAMENT | of our | Lord and Saviour | Jesus Christ, | Translated from | 𝕮𝖍𝖊 𝕷𝖆𝖙𝖎𝖓 𝖁𝖚𝖑𝖌𝖆𝖙𝖊: | Diligently compared with the Original Greek: | and first published by | The English College at Rhemes, A. D., 1582. | with | Annotations, References, and a Historical and Chronological Index. | From the Fifth Dublin Edition. | Newly revised and corrected according to the Clementin edition of the Scriptures. | 𝕻𝖍𝖎𝖑𝖆𝖉𝖊𝖑𝖕𝖍𝖎𝖆: | Published by Eugene Cummiskey. | Stereotyped by J. Howe. | 1824. | (L.)   8.

This is the New Testament to Cummiskey's 8vo Bible, *supra*, p.   published separately. It has Dr. Troy's approbation on verso of the Title; and that of Dr. Conwell, Bishop of Philadelphia, on the verso of 2d leaf. An engraved frontispiece, Jesus, Mary and Joseph, accompanies the Vol.

2. NEW TESTAMENT: Stereotype Edition. | New York: | Stereotyped by A. Chandler, | For "The American Bible Society." | 1824. | (L.)   8.

Pp. 429. On verso of Title—3d Edition. A. Paul, Printer.

3. NEW TESTAMENT: Stereotype edition. Stereotyped by B. & J. Collins, New York. Bridgeport, Con. Printed and published by Josiah B. Baldwin. 1824. 12.

Pp. 290; Table of Kindred, 1 p. Sigs. A to Bb² in 6ˢ.

4. 𝕽𝖊𝖛𝖎𝖘𝖊𝖉 𝕿𝖊𝖘𝖙𝖆𝖒𝖊𝖓𝖙. | The | New Testament | of | 𝕺𝖚𝖗 𝕷𝖔𝖗𝖉 𝖆𝖓𝖉 𝕾𝖆𝖛𝖎𝖔𝖚𝖗 | Jesus Christ; | In which | the Text of the Common Version | is divided into paragraphs, the Punctuation in many | cases altered, and some words, not in | the Original, expunged. | Stereotyped by T. H. Carter & Co. | 𝕭𝖔𝖘𝖙𝖔𝖓. | Published by Cummings, Hilliard & Co. | No 1, Cornhill. | 1824. | (L.)   12.

Title, 1 f.; verso, Certificate of Copyright; Preface, dated May 15, 1824, 2 pp.; Text: pp. 3–297. This work is copyrighted by John H. Wilkins.

5. THE | NEW TESTAMENT, | of | our Lord and Saviour | Jesus Christ, | Translated from the | Original tongues; | and with the | former Translations | Diligently compared and revised. | Stereotyped by B. and J. Collins. | Hartford: Published by Silas Andrus. | 1824. | (L.)   18.

Pp. 210.

6. NEW TESTAMENT: Stereotyped for | the Bible Society of Philadelphia. | 1824. | (L.)   18.

7. THE | NEW TESTAMENT, | by way of | Question and Answer; | with | Illustrations taken from the Holy Fathers | and most approved Interpreters. | By the Rev. John Power, | of St. Peter's Church. | "Intenti estote ad Scripturas: codices vestri sumus." Apply your minds | seriously to the Scriptures: we are your books.—*St. Augustin, Sermon* 227. | New-York: | Published by James Cunningham, | No. 95 *Maiden Lane*. | 1824. | 12.

Title, 1 f.; verso, Certificate of Copyright, dated 11 Sept. 1824; Preface, pp. iii-xi; verso, blank; Text: pp. 2–364; List of the Sovereign Pontiffs, and Constitution of the Catholic Church, a folding leaf; Subscribers' names, pp. 365–380.

The pith of the New Testament is, as it were, brought into a focus, and the difficulties that occur therein especially in the Gospels are solved, I trust, satisfactorily. *Preface.*

1825.

1. THE | HOLY BIBLE, | translated from | *The Latin Vulgate:* | Diligently compared | with the Hebrew, Greek, and other editions in divers Languages. | The | Old Testament, | first published by the English College at Douay, A. D. 1609. | and | The New Testament, | first published by the English College at Rheims, A. D. 1582. | With Useful Notes, | *Critical, Historical, Controversial, and Explanatory.* | Selected | from the most eminent Commentators, and the most able and judicious Critics. | By the Rev. Geo. Leo Haydock, | and other Divines. | *Haurietis aquas, &c.* | *Da mihi intellectum,* &c. | Embellished with Twenty Superb Engravings. | Philadelphia : | Printed and published by Eugene Cummiskey. | 1825. | fol.

Title, 1 f.; verso, blank; Advertisement, Approbations, 1 p.; Admonition, Letter of Pius VI., A Prayer, Decree of the Council of Trent, 1 p.; Decree (concluded), Short Sketch of the principal Epochs, Approbation of Cummiskey's quarto and octavo editions of the Bible, signed † Henry Conwell, Bishop of Philadelphia, dated 13th December, 1824, with a N. B. Approbation of this folio edition, p. vii.; Preface, p. vi. (not marked)–ix; on verso of last p., Names and Order of the Books of the O. & N. T. These 4 ff. are marked B*, C.; Text: Gen. to Ecclesiastes, pp. 13-812, sigs. D* to Z, then A², 2 B to 9 U¹; (p. 29 is printed 26; 215 is printed 213, and 664 is printed 666; p. 774 is blank; and at p. 365, chap. XXII is marked XXVII. at the top of the column; Solomon's Canticles to 1 Mac., p. 3–409; verso of 409, blank; (p. 319 is marked 419, and at p. 166 the chap. is printed XXXII at the top of the page instead of XXXI; sigs. B to 5 L; each of these sigs. is also marked, Vol. II.; Historical and Chronol. Index, 2 ff., not paged ; sig. 5 M.; Fam. Rec. 1 f.; The | New Testament | of | our Lord and Saviour | Jesus Christ ; | first published by the English College at Rheims, A. D. 1582. | Translated from | 𝔗𝔥𝔢 𝔏𝔞𝔱𝔦𝔫 𝔙𝔲𝔩𝔤𝔞𝔱𝔢. | Diligently compared | with the original Text, and other editions in divers languages ; | With | Useful Notes, | Critical, Historical, Controversial, and Explanatory, | selected | from the most eminent Commentators, and the most able and judicious Critics. | Enriched with Superb Engravings. | *Haurietis aquas,* &c. | *Da mihi intellectum,* &c. | All things that are read in the Holy Scriptures, &c. | 2 lines from *S. Aug. tract,* 2. | 𝔓𝔥𝔦𝔩𝔞𝔡𝔢𝔩𝔭𝔥𝔦𝔞 : | Printed and Published by Eugene Cummiskey, at his Catholic Publication Warehouse, | South-east corner of Walnut and Fourth streets. | 1825. | 1 p.; verso, blank; Gen. Pref. to N. Test. pp. iii-xii ; sigs. (*A, not marked, which includes title) to *C ; Text : Mat. to Apocal., pp. 1–112, then 119, 120, 121, 122, 123, 124, * 119, *120, *121, *122, *123, *124, 125-367; sigs. * D to *5 C.; on verso of p. 367, Directions to the Binder, Eugene Cummiskey's Catalogue of Catholic Standard Stereotype Publications for the year 1824-5; Historical and Chron. Index to N. Test., 1 f.; Useful Table of References, 2 ff.; Table of Epist. and Gosp.; 1 f.; Sigs. *5 D. *5 E.; Theological History in Miniature, 1 folding page; verso, blank; Subscribers' names, 3 pp. (not numbered). All the signatures are in 2ˢ.

List of engravings:
1. Jewish High Priest; front to O. T. ..... W. M. Craig, del.; engraved by *G. B. Ellis*.
2. Tower of Babel........................Schenchzer, del.;   *Neagle*, sc.
3. Joseph sold to the Ishmaelites..............Marillier, pinx.;   *T. Kelly*, Boston.
4. Moses in the Burning Bush................ ....*P. E. Hamm*.
5. Plague of Blood........................ ....*Neagle*.
6. Moses smiting the rock..,...*Neagle*.
7. Philistines sending back the Ark...........W. M. Craig, del.; *T. Kelly*, Boston.
8. David and Goliah........................Corbould, del.;   *T. Kelly*, Boston.
9. The Witch of Endor......................West, pinx.;   *Neagle*.
10. Solomon's Temple.
11. Job's Temptation..... ....*W. Woodruff*, Philadelphia.
12. Daniel's Vision.................................*W. Woodruff*, Philadelphia.
13. Christ giving the Keys to Peter; front to N. T....W. M. Craig, del.; *J. B. Neagle*.
14. The Wise Men offering.. ....*W. Woodruff*.
15. Judas taking the price of blood.....................*W. Woodruff*, Philadelphia.
16. Little children brought to Christ....................*W. Woodruff*, Philadelphia.
17. Christ before the Doctors...................Monsiau, del.;   *J. B. Neagle*.
18. The Prodigal Son...... ....*Neagle*.
19. Woman of Samaria..*Neagle*.
20. View of Jerusalem................... .. ....W. M. Craig, del.; *T. Kelly*, Boston.

Nos. 2, 5, 6, 7, 8, 9, 10 are to be found also in Kinnersley's edition of Brown's Self-Interpreting Bible, folio, 1822.

This Cummiskey Bible is a reprint of Haydock's folio, Manchester, 1811–1814, (J. G. S.) It was published originally in 120 weekly numbers of 16 pages each, at twenty-five cents a number. The publication was commenced in 1823, (as I infer from the advertisement accompanying No. 20, which appeared at the close of that year) and was completed in 1825. The date on the back of the volume is: Philadelphia, 1826. The price of the work, bound, was $35, and the edition consisted of One thousand copies. It was not stereotyped.

Other copies are without plates, or date on back. Plate No. 20 is found in many Bibles—as to design.

2. THE | HOLY BIBLE, | translated from | 𝔗𝔥𝔢 𝔏𝔞𝔱𝔦𝔫 𝔙𝔲𝔩𝔤𝔞𝔱: | Diligently | compared with the Hebrew, Greek, and other Editions, | in divers languages. | The | Old Testament, | first published by | the English College at Doway, A. D. 1609. | And | the New Testament, | first published by | the English College at Rhemes, A. D. 1582. | With | Annotations, References, and a Historical and Chronological Index. | First Stereotype, from the fifth Dublin Edition. | Newly revised and corrected according to the Clementin

edition of the Scriptures. | 𝔓𝔥𝔦𝔩𝔞𝔡𝔢𝔩𝔭𝔥𝔦𝔞 : | Published by
Eugene Cummiskey. | Stereotyped by Hammond Wallis, |
New-York. | 1825. | (Georgetown Coll.) 4.

Title, 1 f.; verso, blank; Admonition, Letter of Pius VI., a Prayer, 1 p.; Translation of the Decree of the Council of Trent, Order of the Books of the Old Testament, 1 p.; Text: Gen. to II Mac., pp. 9–789; verso of p. 789, blank; sigs. B to recto of 5 G3, in 4s; sig. K is marked, incorrectly, I; Fam. Rec. 2 ff.; The | New Testament | of our | Lord and Saviour Jesus Christ, | translated from | 𝔗𝔥𝔢 𝔏𝔞𝔱𝔦𝔫 𝔙𝔲𝔩𝔤𝔞𝔱 : | diligently compared with the Original Greek : | And first published | by the English College at Rhemes, A. D. 1582. | With | Annotations, References, and a Historical and Chronological Index. | First Stereotype, from the fifth Dublin Edition. | Newly revised and corrected according to the Clementin edition of the Scriptures. | 𝔓𝔥𝔦𝔩𝔞𝔡𝔢𝔩𝔭𝔥𝔦𝔞 : | Published by Eugene Cummiskey. | Stereotyped by Hammond Wallis, | *New-York.* | 1825. | 1 p.; verso, blank; Admonition, Letter of Pius VI., a Prayer, 1 p.; Approbation of Cummiskey's 4to and 8vo editions by Bishop Conwell, dated 13th December, 1824; Approbation of the O. T. by the University of Doway; Approbation of the N. T. by the University of Rhemes; The Order of the Books of the N. T., 1 p.; Text: Mat. to Apocal., pp. 5–222; sigs. A (which includes Title and 1 prel. leaf) to verso of Ee3; Table of Epistles and Gospels, pp. 223, 224; Table of References, pp. 225, 226; Hist. and Chronol. Index to N. T., pp. 227, 228; sigs. Ee⁴ to Ff² followed by an Historical and Chronol. Index to O. T., marked at foot *1 (2 not marked) 3–7; verso of 7, blank; These 4 ff. ought, properly, to precede Genesis, but are bound in here; Subscribers' names, 1 f.

The edition of this Bible consisted of 1200 copies. The vol. is accompanied by ten engravings, viz: Nos. 1, 2, 4, 11, 12, 13, 14, 15, 16, 17, of Cummiskey's folio, *supra* p. 170.

3. HOLY BIBLE: With Apocrypha, Marginal Notes and References, Index, Tables of Names, Weights, Measures and Coins. Embellished with Eleven Maps and Historical Engravings. Philadelphia: H. C. Carey & I. Lea—Chesnut street. 1825. (L.) 4.

This is another issue of Carey's 4to Bible of 1812. Leviticus, 19:12, incorrect; Esther, 1:8, correct. The maps are on copper, the other illustrations on wood.

4. Daniel D. Smith's Stereotype Edition. | THE | HOLY BIBLE, | containing | The Old and New Testaments, | together with the | Apocrypha : | Translated out of the Original Tongues, | and with | the former Translations diligently compared and revised. | With | Canne's Marginal Notes and References : | And a concise Table of Contents of the Books of the Old and | New Testaments. | Stereotyped by

J. Howe, Philadelphia. | New York : | Published and sold by Daniel D. Smith, | at the Franklin Juvenile Book and Stationery Store, No. 190 Greenwich street, | also by the principal Booksellers in the United States. | 1825. | (L.) 8.

Engraved title : The | Old Testament | illustrated with Engravings | from the Designs of | Richard Westall Esqr | R. A. | Vignette, Moses receiving the Law; Exodus, Chap. XXXI, Ver. 18; verso, blank ; Printed title, 1 f. as above; verso, Names and Order of the Books, including those of the Apocrypha; then the above printed title repeated (less the words "together with the Apocrypha"), same imprint, 1 p.; verso, Names and Order of the Books of the Old and New Test. (Apocrypha omitted); To the Reader, 2 pp., not numbered; Contents, pp. 5–10 ; Text: Gen. to Mal., pp. 11–619; verso, Tables of Scripture Measures, Weights, Money and of Time; sigs. A to verso of 2 O^6, in 8^s, except 2 O; and in figures, 1 to verso of 78^2 in 4^s; (these signatures include the 2d printed Title page, To the Reader and the Table of Contents only ; the 1st title p. being inserted); Apocrypha, printed solid, in chapters, without division of verses, though these are numbered, pp. 1–109 ; verso, blank; sigs. A* to recto of G*^{7} in 8^s, and in figures 1* to recto of 14*^{3} in 4^s; Engraved Title : The New Test.; Vignette: The Angel appearing to the Shepherds, St. Luke, Chap. II, v. 8 and 9; Printed title, imprint as above, 1 p.; verso, Account of the Dates; Text: pp. 623–811; sigs. 2 P (not marked) to recto of 3A^8 in 8^s; and in figures, 78^3 to recto of 102^2 in 4^s; verso, blank; Psalms in metre (no title p.), pp. 1–39; sigs. A to recto of C^4 in 8^s; verso, blank; A Brief | Concordance | to the | Holy Scriptures | of the | Old and New Testaments : | By which | All, or Most, of the principal Texts of Scripture | may be easily found out. | By John Brown, | Late Minister of the Gospel at Haddington, in Scotland. | Search the Scriptures, &c. | The Bereans, &c. | Revised and corrected. | Stereotyped by J. Howe, Philadelphia. | New York: | Published by Daniel D. Smith, No. 191 Greenwich street. | 1825. | 1 p.; verso, To the Reader. Text, pp. 3–136; sigs. A to verso of I^4 in 8^s.

Engravings :
    Jacob and Esau. Frontispiece to Old Testament.
    David and Bathsheba.
    Jeremiah foretelling the Siege of Jerusalem.
    Christ and Nicodemus. Frontispiece to New Testament.
    The Angel appearing to Joseph in a dream.
    The Annunciation. All engraved by Wm. D. Smith.
This Bible has also been published without Apocrypha or Psalms.

5. THE PRONOUNCING BIBLE. | The | Holy Bible, | containing | The Old and New Testaments ; | Translated | out of the Original Tongues, | and with the | former Translations diligently compared and revised. | (Vignette : Moses striking the rock.) Exodus, xvii: 6. | The proper Names of which, and numerous other words, being accurately | accented in the Text, and divided into syllables, as they

ought to be | pronounced, according to the Orthoepy of John Walker, as | contained in his critical pronouncing Dictionary and | Key to the Classical pronunciation of Greek, | Latin, and Scripture proper Names. | By Israel Alger, Jun. A. M. | **Boston**: | Printed and published by Lincoln and Edmands, | No. 59, Washington-street, (53, Cornhill.) Stereotyped by T. H. Carter & Co. | 1825. | (L; Conn. Hist. Soc.)   8.

Engr. Title, 1 f; Title, 1 f.; verso, Certificate of Copyright, dated 4th April, 1825; Advertisement of the Editor; Explanatory Key, and Books of the O. and N. Test., pp. iii, iv; Text: Gen. to Mal., pp. 5–714; sigs. A³ to verso of Ooo⁴ in 6ˢ, and 1³ to verso of 46¹ in 8ˢ; Fam. Rec. 1 f.; blank, 1 f.; New Testament, &c. (Vignette: Christ sending forth his disciples.) Luke, ix, 1–7. | To the proper Names of which, and other words, accents are applied; | indicating the standard pronunciation. | By Israel Alger, Jun., A. M. | **Boston**: | Printed and published by Lincoln & Edmands, | No. 59 Washington Street. | *Stereotyped by S. Walker & Co.*, | 1 p.; verso, Tables of Measures and of Offices; Text: Mat. to Rev., pp. 3–218; sigs. A* to verso of T*¹ in 6ˢ, and 1* to verso of 14*⁵ in 8ˢ; Recommendations, pp. 219, 220. Engraved frontispieces to Old and New Testaments.

6. HOLY BIBLE: Stereotyped by B. and J. Collins, N. York. | Lunenburg, Mass. | Published by Edmund Cushing. | 1825. | (L.)   12.

This edition corresponds, except in the imprints, with Bible No. 7, *supra* p. 154, and with Websters and Skinners' editions, No. 6, 1817, and No. 8, 1824. At the top of each of the title pages are the words **Stereotype Edition**. 1 Tim. 4: 16 is incorrect.

7. THE | OLD AND NEW TESTAMENTS | having | a rich and comprehensive assembly of | Half a Million | Parallel and Illustrative Passages | from those esteemed authors | Canne, Browne, Blaney, and Scott, | with those from the | Latin Vulgate, | the French and German Bibles. | The whole arranged in Scripture order, and presenting, in a portable pocket volume, | A complete Library of Divinity. | Bonus Textuarius est bonus Theologus. | Philadelphia: | Printed for Thomas Wardle. | M.DCCC.XXV. | 12.

Mock Title: The English Version | of the | Polyglott Bible, | with | the Scripture Harmony, | or | Concordance of Parallel Passages. | &c., &c. | 1 f.; verso, Advertisement; Printed Title (as above), 1 p.; verso, blank; Præfatio | in | Biblia Polyglotta, | 2 pp.; Pref. to the English version | of the | Polyglot Bible. | 5 pp.; verso, Order of

Books, 1 p.; mock Title, repeated, 1 p.; verso, Genesis, ch. I to ch. II, v. 4. The Text of Moses called Genesis; at foot, figure 1. (Here I would remark that the References are between the columns, and that each fol. is interleaved with References. Each verse is treated thus: (ex. gr.). The last verse in 2d col. on recto of p. 2 is v, 20, ch. III of Genesis which is reflected on the opposite p., thus: v. 20, Eve; Heb. Chavah; That is, Living; ch. 2: 20, 23–5–29–16–11–29, 32. . 35. 18; Ex. 2. 10; 1 Sa. 1: 20; Mat. 1, 21, 23; Ac. 17: 26; Ga. 3: 26, 1 Pe. 3: 6.); Text: Gen. to Mal., pp. 1–585; The | New Testament | having | an extensive | selection of appropriate References; | both | parallel and illustrative, | from Canne, | Brown, | Blaney and Scott, | and the Latin Vulgate, the French and German Bible. | Philadelphia: | Printed for Thomas Wardle. | M.DCCC.XXV. | 1 p.; verso, blank; mock title: The English version, &c., *ut supra*, 1 p.; verso, References as in Old Test. (being interleaved); Text: Mat. to Rev., pp. 1 to 188, ending on verso and facing page of references. The pp. of references are similarly paged with the Text. *Edw. Armstrong.*

8. JOB. Ten Chapters | of | **The Book of Job,** | rendered from the | Common Translation, | into Verse. | By Abraham Rowley. | Ye have heard, &c., *James, Chap.* 5, v. 11. | The pencil of the Holy Ghost hath laboured more in describing the afflictions of Job, than | the felicities of Solomon. *Lord Bacon.* | Boston: | Printed by J. H. A. Frost, | Congress-street. | 1825. | (B.)   8.

Pp. 24: The preface is dated March 20, 1826.

1. NEW TESTAMENT: New York: Daniel D. Smith. 1825. (L.) 4.

2. NEW TESTAMENT, &c. From which is selected, | an | Extensive Vocabulary, | comprising the Proper Names and all other important | words, which occur in the | New Testament. | The words are arranged in Columns, and placed over the | chapters respectively from which they are select- | ed: and are divided, defined, and pronounced, | according to the authorities of the | celebrated John Walker. | *The words in the Vocabulary, and their correspondent words in the Text,* | *are marked with characters of reference.* | To which is prefixed | Walker's Explanatory Key, | governing the Vocabulary. | *Embellished with several Engravings of Sacred characters.* | By Jeremiah Goodrich. | Albany: | Published and sold wholesale and retail by S. Shaw, | *Proprietor of the copy right for the United States.* | 1825. | 12.

Title, 1 f.; verso, Certificate of Copyright, dated 12 Oct., 1824; Cont., pp. 3–5; on part of p. 5, Analysis of the Old and New Test.; verso of p. 5, Books of the New

Test. ; a Table of Simple and Dipthongal vowels; Text: Mat. to Rev., pp. 7-333 (pp. 332, 333 not marked); sigs. A⁴ to recto of Dd³ in 6ˢ.
   This is called, The Definition Testament. It has observations at the head of each of the books, borrowed from a Testament published in Edinburgh by the Rev. William Brown, and woodcuts. 1 Tim. 4: 16 is incorrect.

3. Stereotype Edition. | The | New | Testament | of our | Lord and Saviour Jesus Christ: | Translated out of | The Original Greek; | and with the former translations diligently | compared and revised. | Stereotyped by T. H. & C. Carter, Boston. | Newbury: | Published by White & Reed. | 1825. | David Watson, Printer. Woodstock. | 12.
   This is a Vermont edition.

4. New Testament. Stereotype Edition. New York: Stereotyped by A. Chandler and Co., for the American Bible Society. 1825.   12.
   42d edition, pp. 352.

5. The | Four Gospels | of the | New Testament | In Greek, | From the Text of Griesbach: | with | a Lexicon in English | of | all the Words Contained in them. | Designed | for the Use of Schools. | Boston: | Cummings, Hilliard, and Company, Washington Street. | 1825. | (G. L.)   8.

1826.

1. Self Interpreting Bible: By the late Rev. John Brown, Minister of the Gospel at Haddington. With Engravings. New York: Printed and published by T. Kinnersley, opposite the Manhattan Bank, Broadway. 1826.   fol.
   A reissue of the edition of 1822, in 162 numbers.

2. Holy Bible, translated from 𝔱𝔥𝔢 𝔏𝔞𝔱𝔦𝔫 𝔙𝔲𝔩𝔤𝔞𝔱𝔢 : With Annotations, References, Indexes, &c. 𝔓𝔥𝔦𝔩𝔞𝔡𝔢𝔩𝔭𝔥𝔦𝔞 : Published by Eugene Cummiskey. Stereotyped by Hammond Wallis, *New York.* 1826.   (L.)   4.
   This is Cummiskey's Catholic Bible, No. 2, of 1825, q. v., with the date altered. Sig. K is correctly marked. The Hist. and Chron. Index to the Old Testament, at the

end of the vol., runs from p. 229-235; verso of 235, blank; no List of Subscribers; The sigs. of New Test., and additional matter, run from A³ to Gg². The engravings are Nos. 1, 2, 4, 11, 12, 13, 14, 15, 16, 17 of the Cummiskey folio, No. 1, 1825.
The edition was 1000 copies.

3. THE | COLLATERAL BIBLE | or, | a Key | to the | Holy Scriptures : | In which all the corresponding texts are brought together into one view, and | arranged in a familiar and easy manner. | By William McCorkle, | assisted by the Rev. Ezra Stiles Ely, D. D., and the Rev. Gregory T. Bedell, A. M. | (7 texts from Scripture.) | Philadelphia : | Printed by Samuel F. Bradford, | and by | E. Bliss and E. White, New York. | J. Harding, Printer. | 1826. | (L.) 4.

Vol. I. Title 1 f.; verso, Copyright certificate, dated 9 June, 1824. The Hebrew Scriptures—Genesis, &c. The Greek Scriptures—Mat., &c. Mills's Chronology of the New Test., 1 p.; Account of Translations and Tables, 4 pages; Genealogy of Christ, with Observations, 1 p.; Preface, 2 pp.; (excluding title), 4 ff. [iii] to [x]; sig. A*; Text in 3 columns : Gen. to Ruth, pp. 1-809; sigs. A to 4H⁴ in 4°; then 4I in 5; Title to Vol. II, as in 1st vol. down to "manner," then, By the Rev. Ezra Stiles Ely, D. D., Pastor of the Third Presbyterian Church, | And | the Rev. Gregory T. Bedell, A. M., Rector of St. Andrew's Church. | Texts of Scripture. | Vol. II. | Philadelphia : | Published by John Laval and Samuel F. Bradford. | J. Harding, Printer. | 1828. | 1 p.; verso, Copyright cert., as before; Text: Ruth to Psalms, inclusive, pp. 1-1013; A to 6M³ in 4°; Title to Vol. III, as in Vol. 2, except that 7th line ends with "arranged." Below texts, Vol III; imprint and verso the same; Text: Proverbs to Malachi, pp. 3-731; sigs. A² to 4 Z² in 4°.

The plan of the work is to print the parallel texts in full at the end of each verse. The work was not continued beyond the Old Testament. The New Testament, on a similar plan, was printed in England, in 1825, in 8vo, under the Title of Scientia Biblica. Bagster published in 1854, what he calls a Commentary wholly Biblical, on the same plan.

4. THE | HOLY BIBLE | containing the | Old and New Testaments : | Translated out of | the Original Tongues : | And with the former Translations | **Diligently Compared and Revised** : | With References and various Readings. | In Two Volumes. | Vol. I. | Boston : | Printed and published by S. Walker, | Washington-street. | Stereotyped at the Boston Type and Stereotype Foundry, | late T. H. Carter & Co. | n. d. 4.

Engraved Title, 1 f.; then printed Title, 1 f.; verso, blank; Names and Order of the Books, 1 p.; verso, A Guide to a regular perusal of the Holy Scriptures; Text: Gen. to Song of Solomon, pp. 1-787; sigs. B to recto of 5 K² in 4°; verso, blank; Engraved

Title, 1 f.; Printed Title, as above, except Vol. II. 1 p.; verso, blank; Text, Isaiah to Mal., pp. 3–277; sigs. A² to recto of 2 M³ in 4s; verso, blank; Apocrypha, in smaller type, pp. 1–139, sigs. A to recto of S² in 4º; verso, blank; Fam. Rec., 2 ff.; New Test. Title, same Imprint, except, Stereotyped by James Conner, New York, 1 p.; verso, blank; Text: Mat. to Rev., pp. 281–600; sigs. 2N to verso of 4F⁴ in 4s. Bound in with Genesis is a separate folding page, with this title: The Intention of the present Table is to shew, at one view, which of the Patriarchs were contemporary with each other, *and consequently how easy it was to hand down from* Adam *to* Isaac (*a period of* 2158 *years*) *the particulars of the* Creation *and* Fall of Man.

Engravings:
Moses pointing to Christ. Unto Him ye shall listen (Front.) W. M. Craig, del;
T. *Kelly*, sc.
Finding of Moses...................................Stothard, del.; R. *Campbell*, sc.
David's Victory over Goliah..................Corbould, pinx.; T. *Kelly*, Boston, sc.
The Philistines sending back the Ark.........M. Craig, del.; *Neagle*, sc.
Ahasuerus and Esther...T. *Kelly*, sc.
Ecce Homo. (Front to Vol. II.).............................J. B. *Neagle*, sc.
Belshazzar's Impious Feast.........................J. B. *Neagle*, Philadelphia, sc.
Last Supper. (Front to N. Test.)....Da Vinci, pinx.; J. B. *Neagle*, Philadelphia, sc.
Simeon's Benediction..R. *Campbell*, sc.

Some of these engravings are dated 1826, and appeared previously in an edition of Brown's Self-Interpreting Bible, which Walker owned.

The present Bible was issued in 116 numbers, exclusive of the Apocrypha, which was issued separately.

5. PRONOUNCING BIBLE: **Boston**: Lincoln & Edmands. 1826. 12.
The same as No. 5 of 1825, with new title pages.

6. HOLY BIBLE: Stereotyped at the Boston Type and Stereotype Foundry, | late T. H. Carter & Co. | Boston : | Published by Hilliard, Gray, Little, and Wilkins, Munroe & Francis, | Richardson & Lord, Lincoln & Edmands, Crocker & Brewster, T. Bed- | lington, R. P. & C. Williams, Charles Ewer, Thomas Wells, and Josiah | Loring. | *Printed at Treadwell's Power-Press.* | 1826. | (I.) 8.

Title, 1 f.; verso, The Books of the O. and N. Testaments; Text: Gen. to Mal., pp. 3–687; sigs. 1² to recto of 86¹ in 4º; verso, Tables of Scripture Measures, Weights and Money, and of Time; Apocrypha (not mentioned in the title nor in the Table of the Books), pp. 1–134; sigs. 1 to verso of 17³; Contents of the Books of the O. and N. Test., pp. i–ix. There is no New Testament in the copy before us, which, notwithstanding appears perfect; that portion, it is hence inferred, formed, if published, a distinct volume.

7. THE | REFERENCE BIBLE, | containing an accurate copy | of the common English Version | of | The Old and New Testaments: | With References and a key sheet of Questions, Geographi- | cal, Historical, Doctrinal, Practical, and Experimental; | Accompanied with valuable chronological Harmonies of | both Testaments; correct and elegant Maps, and highly | useful Tables of Scripture Names, Scripture Geography, | Scripture Chronology, Scripture References, &c. | *The whole designed to facilitate* | The acquisition of Scriptural knowledge | In Bible Classes, Sunday schools, Common schools, | and Private Families. | By Hervey Wilbur, A. M. | Vol. I. | Fourth Edition. | Boston: | Published by Cummings, Hilliard, & Co. and Crocker | & Brewster; Also by the American Sun- | day school Union, Philadelphia. | *Power Press.—J. G. Rogers & Co.* | 1826. | (L.) 12.

Engraved Title, 1 f.; Printed title (as above), 1 f.; verso, Certificate of Copyright, dated 18th August, 1825; Advertisement; Key, 1 p.; verso, Names and Order of the Books, and Hints; Text: Gen. to Ecclesiastes, pp. 3–736; sigs. A (which includes the Key sheet) to verso of Qqq² in 6ˢ; Key repeated, 1 folding leaf (inserted); Vol. II. Title (as above), 1 p.; verso, Key (as in Vol. I); Text: Song of Solomon to Mal., pp. 737–1003; sigs. Qqq³ to recto of Pppp⁴ in 6ˢ; Contents of O. T., pp. 1004–1012; verso of Pppp⁴ to verso of Qqqq².

8. HOLY BIBLE. Stereotype edition. | Stereotyped by B. & J. Collins, N. York. | Lunenburg, Mass. | Published by Edmund Cushing. | 1826. | (J. G. S.) 12.

Same as the ed. of 1825, with New Testament of that year. 1 Tim. 4:16 is incorrect.

9. HOLY BIBLE: Lunenburg, (Mass.) Printed and sold by W. Greenough and Son. 1826. (L.) 12.

Same as Bible, No. 7 of 1821. 1 Tim. 4:16, is incorrect.

10. HOLY BIBLE: Stereotyped | for the American Bible Society | by D. & G. Bruce. | A. Paul, Printer. | New York, | 1826. | (L.) 12.

[87th Edition.]; pp. 837; sigs. in 12ˢ.

11. HOLY BIBLE: Stereotyped by B. & J. Collins, New York. Hartford: Published by Silas Andrus. Johnstone and Van Norden, Printers. 1826. (B.) 12.

12. HOLY BIBLE: Hartford: Printed by Hudson and Goodwin. 1826. (B.) 12.

Continuation of the Bible of 1809.

1. THE | NEW TESTAMENT | of | our Lord and Saviour | Jesus Christ: | With References and a key sheet of Questions, | Geographical, Historical, Doctrinal, | Practical, and Experimental: | Designed to | Facilitate the acquisition of Scriptural knowledge, | in Bible classes, Sunday schools, Common schools | and Private Families. | By Hervey Wilbur, A. M. | Stereotyped by S. Walker & Co., Boston. | Boston: | Published by Cummings, Hilliard, & Co., and Crocker | & Brewster; also by the American Sun- | day School Union, Philadelphia. | 1826. | (Sem. St. Sulpice, Balt.) 12.

Title 1 p.; verso, blank; Remarks, 1 p.; verso, blank; Text: Mat. to Rev., pp. 5-321; at foot of p. 321, A Table of St. Paul's Apostolic Journeys; sigs. A (including Title and Rem.) to recto of Dd⁵; Contents of N. T., pp. 322-324; remainder of sig. Dd; Useful Tables | of | Scripture Names, Scripture Geography, | Scripture Chronology, and Scrip- | ture References. | Including | Valuable Harmonies of the Scriptures, | by Rev. G. Townsend and S. F. Jarvis, D. D | Prepared to | Accompany the Reference Bible. | By Hervey Wilbur, A. M. | Boston: | Imprint, as above, 1 p.; Note; Walker's Key to the Vowel Accents; An Alphabetical Table of all the Proper Names, pp. 3-27; Etymological Table, foot of p. 27 and p. 28; Gen. View of Sacred Geography, by J. E. Worcester, pp. 29 and part of 30; Geographical Vocabulary, remainder of p. 30-50; A Chronological Harmony of the Old Test., pp, 51-76; Harmony of the Four Gospels, pp. 77-83; Chronol. Table; Table of References, 3 pp. not numbered; sigs. 1 to verso of 7⁷; Miscellaneous Table and Key, 1 folding sheet, inserted.

In Vol. I. Map of the Journeyings of the Children of Israel; Map of Canaan. In Vol. II. Canaan adapted to the Gospel History; Travels and Voyages of St. Paul. The general Titles in both volumes, and the last leaf of Vol. II. containing "Table of References," are inserted. Other copies of this work have only two maps.

2. NEW TESTAMENT: Stereotype edition. Hartford: Published by Silas Andrus. Stereotyped by A. Chandler. 1826. 12.

Front, and Engr. title with the following Imprint: Hartford: Published by Silas Andrus, and Johnstone and Van Norden. New York. 1824. Pp. 251.

3. THE | NEW TESTAMENT | of our | Lord and Saviour | Jesus Christ; | Translated out of | the Original Greek | and with | the former translations diligently com- | pared and

revised. | Stereotyped by Hammond Wallis, New York. | Windsor, (Vt.) | Printed and sold by Simeon Ide. | 1826. | (B.)   12.
Pp. 372; double lines around the title page.

4. NEW TESTAMENT: Stereotype edition. New York: Stereotyped by A. Chandler & Co. For "The American Bible Society." 1826.   12.
55th ed., pp. 352. Sigs. in 12ˢ.

5. LE NOUVEAU TESTAMENT | de | Notre Seigneur | Jesus Christ. | Imprimé sur l'édition de Paris, de l'année 1805. | Edition Stéréotype. | Revue et corrigée avec soin d'après le Texte Grec. | A New York, | Imprimé avec des Planches solides par A. Paul, | aux frais de | La Societé Biblique Americaine. | 1826. | (Am. Bib. Soc.)   12.
Title, 1 f.; verso, Les Noms des Livres; at foot, 1st *Edition*; Texte: pp. 3–207; at foot of last p., Imprimé avec des planches solides par A. Paul, | aux frais de | La Société Biblique Americaina. | Sigs. 34 to recto of 42^7 in 12ˢ.

6. THE | NEW TESTAMENT | of our | Lord and Saviour | Jesus Christ, | translated out of | the original Greek; | and with the | former translations diligently | compared and revised. | New-York: | Printed by Samuel Marks. | 1826. | (L.)   12.
Text: pp. 3–192, in paragraphs; sigs. 1–16 in 6ˢ. An engraved frontispiece.

7. NEW TESTAMENT: Elizabethtown, (N. J.) Published and sold by Mervin Hale. 1826.   (B.)   12.

1827.

1. BIBLIA, | Das ist: | Die | ganze | **Heilige Schrift** | des | Alten und Neuen | Testaments, | Nach dem deutschen Übersetzung | D. Martin Luthers; | Mit eines jeden Capitels kurzen Summarien, | auch beygefügten vielen aufs neue berichtigen Parallelen, | und 40 vortrefflichen bildlichen Vorstellungen versehen. | In Stereotypen verfertight, von J. Howe. | Philadelphia: | Gedruckt und zu haben bey Kimber und Scharpless Buchhändler. | Nro. 50, in der Nord-Viertenstrasse. | n. d.   (L.)   4.

Title, 1 f.; verso, Verzeichniß aller Bücher, &c.; Uebersicht des Inhalts | aller Bücher, &c., pp. 3–8; Text: Gen. to Mal., pp. (9)–(614); Apocrypha (in smaller type to prayer of Manasseh), pp. (615)–(722); Anhang, (containing 3d and 4th Books of Ezra, and 3d Book Maccabees, in smaller type), pp. (723)–(754); Fam. Rec., 2 ff. (not paged nor included in sig.). Das | Neue Testament | unsers Herrn und Heilandes | Jesu Christi, | verdeutscht | von | D. Martin Luther. | In Stereotypen, verfestigt von J. Howe. | Philadelphia: | Gedruckt und zu haben bey Kimber und Scharpless, Buchhandler, | Nro. 50, in der Nord-Viertenstrasse. | n. d., 1 p.; verso, blank; Text: Mat.'to Rev., pp. (757)–(961); Anweisung, pp. (962)–(964); Register | der vornehmsten Hauptartikel Biblischer Lehre, &c., pp. (965)–(975); verso, blank; Die Zerstörung Jerusalems, &c., pp. (977)–(992); sigs. B to 6 I⁴ in 4⁸.

This is the *first* edition of Kimber & Sharpless's German Bible. It was continued to be issued by them until 1851.

2. HOLY BIBLE: With Canne's Marginal Notes and References, Apocrypha, Index and Tables. Stereotyped for Collins & Co. by B. & J. Collins. Boston: Published by C. Ewer and T. Bedlington. 1827. (L.) 4.

For collation, &c., of this edition, see No. 1, of 1824.

3. HOLY BIBLE: Utica, N. Y.: Published by William Williams. 1827. 4.

This is Phinney's edition, No. 3 of 1822, *supra* p. 157, with a different imprint only.

4. SCOTT'S FAMILY BIBLE: Stereotype Edition in Five Volumes. New York: Published by J. P. Havens. 1827. 4.

Not seen. Mentioned in the *Magazine* of the *Ref. Dutch Church*, I, 31.

5. THE | HOLY BIBLE, | containing the | Old and New Testaments, | according to the authorized version; | with | Explanatory Notes, practical Observations, | and | copious Marginal References. | By | Thomas Scott, | Rector of Aston Sandford, Bucks. | Stereotype Edition, | from the Fifth London Edition, with the Author's last corrections and improvements. | Boston: | Samuel T. Armstrong, | and Crocker and Brewster. | New York: J. Leavitt. | *Stereotyped by T. H. Carter & Co., Boston Type and Stereotype Foundry.* | 1827. | [In six Volumes.] 8.

Vol. I. Title 1 f.; verso, Names and Order of Books of the O. and N. Test.; Preface, pp. 3–25; Postscript and adv., pp. 25, 26; Introd. to O. T., p. 27; Text: Gen.

to Judges, pp. 28-756; sigs. in numbers, 1 to verso of 95²; Vol. II. title, 1 f.; verso, blank; Text: Ruth to Esther, pp. 3-652; Epitome of the Hist. of the Jews, pp. 653, 654; sigs. 1 to 82, a blank leaf completing the last sig.; Vol. III. title, 1 f.; verso, blank; Text: Job to Sol.'s song, pp. 3-654; sigs. 1 to 82, a blank leaf completing last sig ; Vol. IV. title, 1 f.; verso, blank; Text: Isaiah to Mal., pp. 3-904; sigs. 1 to 113; Vol. V. title, 1 f.; verso, blank; Introduction to N. T., pp. 3-6; Text: Mat. to Acts, pp 7-775; sigs. 1 to 97; Vol. VI, title, 1 f.; verso blank; Text: Rom. to Rev., pp. 3-791; Retrospective view, pp. 792, 793; Table of Measures, &c., pp. 793, 794; Table of States, Offices, &c., pp 795, 796; Chron. Table, pp. 797-807; sigs. 1 to 101, all in 4°, the title of each volume being included in sig. 1.

A portrait of Dr. Scott, engraved by Hoogland, accompanies this work, having, in addition to the names of the Boston and New York publishers, that of John P. Haven, New York.

Eight editions of Scott's Family Bible, consisting of 25,250 copies, were printed in the United States of America, from 1808 to 1819. *Horne.*

6. HOLY BIBLE, translated from the Latin Vulgate: Philadelphia: Printed and published by Eugene Cummiskey. 1827.　　　　　　　　(L.)　　　　　　　　8.

A continuation of the edition of 1824.

7. HOLY BIBLE: With Canne's Marginal Notes and References, &c. Stereotyped by J. Howe, Philadelphia. New York: Published and sold by Daniel D. Smith, at the Juvenile Book and Stationery Store, No. 190, Greenwich Street. Also by the principal Booksellers in the United States. 1827.　　　　　　　　8.

This is a reissue of the Bible No. 4 of 1825, with new Title pages only.

8. HOLY BIBLE. *Stereotyped by D. & G. Bruce, New York.* New York: *Printed and Published by Daniel D. Smith*, No. 190, Greenwich street. 1827.　　　　　　　　12.

Pp. 837. Sigs. run to recto of Mm11 in 12°.

9. HOLY BIBLE. Stereotyped | For the American Bible Society | By D. & G. Bruce. | Printed by A. Paul, 72 Nassau Street, | New-York. | 1827. |　　　　　　　　12.

Pp. 837. No headings to columns or chapters. These two Bibles (Nos. 8 and 9) are from the same, or duplicate, plates.

10. HOLY BIBLE. New York: Stereotyped for the American
Bible Society by A. Chandler. Printed by A. Paul.
1827.   12.
    Pp. 824, 251.

11. THE | HOLY BIBLE, | containing | The Old Testament, |
and | The New; | Translated out of | 𝔗𝔥𝔢 𝔒𝔯𝔦𝔤𝔦𝔫𝔞𝔩
𝔗𝔬𝔫𝔤𝔲𝔢𝔰; | and with the | former Translations diligently |
compared and revised. | Third stereotype edition. | New
York: Published by White, Gallaher & White. | 1827. |
(L.)   24.

    Title, 1 f.; verso, blank; Address of the Translators to James I, p. 3 and part of 4;
Names and Order of the Books, remainder of p. 4; Text: Gen. to Mal., pp. 3–704;
sigs. A³ to verso of Gg⁴; New Test. title, 1 p.; verso, blank; Text: Mat. to Rev.,
pp. 3–216; sigs. 1 to verso of 9¹² in 12ˢ. Engraved frontispiece to Old and New
Testaments.

12. Holbrook and Fessenden's Stereotype Edition. | THE |
HOLY BIBLE, | containing the | Old and New Testaments: |
Translated out of | the Original Tongue; (*sic*) | And
with | the former Translations diligently compared and |
revised. | Brattleborough, Vt. | Printed and published
by | Holbrook and Fessenden, 1827. | (B.)   12.

    Title, 1 f.; verso, " This first American Stereotype Bible has been copied from the
Edinburgh edition, printed under the revision of the General Assembly of the Kirk of
Scotland, and carefully compared with the Cambridge, Oxford, Hartford and New
York editions. D. & G. BRUCE. *New York, June*, 1815." and Names and Order of the
Books; Text: Gen. to Mal., pp. 3–525; Tables of Offices and of Time, p. 526; New
Testament title (no imprint), 1 p.; verso, Table of Kindred; Mat. to Rev. pp. 529 to
684; sigs. A (which includes Title) to verso of Ff⁶ in 12ˢ. Short headings to columns
and chapters.
    This Vol. agrees with Bruce's 1st stereotyped Bible (No. 8, of 1815.) In Bruce's ed.,
however, figures 2–6 accompany the sig. letters on the first half of the form; in
this, the letters and numbers are omitted, except on fol. 5 of the sig. In other respects, they are alike; in both, Chap. XXXVII of Genesis is marked XXXII, at top of
the page.

13. HOLY BIBLE. Stereotyped by J. Howe, Philadelphia.
Hartford: Published by Silas Andrus. Sold also by the
Booksellers generally. 1827.   12.
    Pp. 655; Contents, 656–651; Psalms in metre.

14. HOLY BIBLE: Hartford: Published by Silas Andrus. 1827. 18.

15. Job. The Book of Job: An Amended Version; with an Introduction and Notes, by George R. Noyes. Cambridge: Hilliard and Brown. 1827. 8.

1. NEW TESTAMENT: Stereotyped by David Hills. | Boston: | Printed by F. Ingraham and J. Putnam. | 1827. | (L.) 8.

In paragraphs; the chapter, book and verse to which the first line belongs, are noted at the top of each page. The sections, which are nearly the same with Griesbach, are taken from an edition of the Bible, published by John Reeves, Esq., London, 1802. The heads of those sections are omitted. The punctuation of Knapp's Greek Testament is mostly followed. The Advertisement is signed B. G., and dated, Boston, July 27, 1827. The volume contains pp. 499, and Names and Order of the Books on the verso of last page.

2. NEW TESTAMENT: With an | Introduction | giving | An Account of Jewish and other Sects; | with | Notes | illustrating obscure Passages, and explaining obsolete | Words and Phrases; | for the use of | Schools, Academies, and private Families. | By J. A. Cummings, | Author of Ancient and Modern Geography. | Second Edition, | revised and improved. | Stereotyped at the Boston Type and Stereotype Foundry. | Boston: | Hilliard, Gray, Little, and Wilkins. | 1827. | (L.) 12.

Title 1 f; verso, Certificate of copyright, dated 5th January, 1827; Introd., pp. 3–6; Order of Books also on p. 6; Pref. Remarks, 1 p.; Text: pp. 8–305; Table of Offices, p. 306; Table of Measures, Weights and Money, p. 307; and of Time, p. 308; sigs. 1 to verso of 26⁴ in 6ˢ; 3 Maps.

3. NEW TESTAMENT: With References and a Key sheet of Questions, &c. *Designed to* facilitate the Acquisition of Scriptural Knowledge in Bible Classes, &c. By Hervey Wilbur, A. M. Boston: Hilliard, Gray, Little and Wilkins. 1827. *Stereotyped at the Boston Type and Stereotype Foundry.* (L.) 12.

On verso of Title is Certificate of copyright, dated 13 Nov., 1822; then a page of Recommendations, on verso of which is Order of Books and Hints. Text, &c., same as No. 1 of 1826, to p. 324; Key, a folding leaf; Useful Tables, &c., By Hervey Wilbur. Boston: Hilliard, Gray, Little, and Wilkins. *Printed at Treadwell's Power-Press.* 1827. 1 p.; verso, Adv. and Walker's Key to Vowel Accents; Tables, pp. 3–18.

4. NEW TESTAMENT. *Stereotyped by Baker and Greele, Boston.* |
New York: | Printed for the American Bible Society, | By
Abraham Paul. | 1827. | (L.)   12.

<small>2d Edition, pp. 315. The Am. Antiq. Soc. possesses a copy of the 5th edition of this Testament, printed for the Am. Bib. Soc. by D. Fanshaw; same date.</small>

5. NEW TESTAMENT. New York: Stereotyped by A. Chandler
& Co. For the American Bible Society. 1827. (L.) 12.
<small>78th edition.</small>

6. NEW TESTAMENT. Stereotyped by J. Howe, Philadelphia.
New York: Published by E. Bliss. 1827.   12.

<small>Front. "Paul's sight restored." Title, with Vignette, The Angel appearing to the Shepherds; both engr. by S. Maverick. Printed title, 1 f.; verso, Order of Books; Text: Mat. to Rev., pp. 3-252; sig. A includes title and is in 8ˢ; B in 4ˢ, C in 12 (No D), E in 8, F in 4ˢ, G in 8, H in 4ˢ, and so on alternately to X, which is in 6ˢ.</small>

7. NEW TESTAMENT: Arranged in paragraphs, such as the
Sense requires; the division of the chapters and verses
being noted in the margin. By James Nourse, Student in
the Theological Seminary, Princeton, N. J. New York:
Published by G. & C. Carvill. 1827.   (L.)   12.

<small>This work was printed at Princeton, by D. A. Borrenstein. It has Notes, Index and a Harmony at the end. It contains pp. 373 and xxiii.</small>

8. THE | NEW TESTAMENT | of our | Lord and Saviour | Jesus
Christ: | Translated out of | the Original Greek; | and
with the | former Translations diligently compared | and
revised. | Stereotype edition. | Hartford: | Published by
Silas Andrus. | Stereotyped by A. Chandler. | 1827. |
(B.)   12.

<small>Title, 1 f.; verso, blank; Text: Gen. to Rev., pp. 3-251; sigs. A² to recto of L⁶. Short headings to chapters and columns.</small>

9. Η ΚΑΙΝΗ | ΔΙΑΘΗΚΗ. | Novum | Testamentum | Græcum. |
Ad exemplar | Roberti Stephani accuratissime editum. |
Cura P. Wilson, LL.D. | Coll. Columb. Neo-Eboracen.

Prof. Emer. | Stereotypis Hammondi Wallis, Novi Eboraci. | Hartfordiæ: | Apud Oliverum D. Cooke et Filios. | 1827. | (B.) 12.

Title, 1 f.; verso blank; Text: pp. 3–369; sigs. A² to recto of Q⁵ in 12ˢ.

10. NEW TESTAMENT: Exeter, N. H. Published by J. & B. Williams. 1827. 12.

Pp. (299); verso of 299, Table of Kindred; sigs. in 6ˢ.

11. NEW TESTAMENT. Lowel, Ms.: Published by Thomas Billings. 1827. (L.) 24.

Text, pp. 3–330; An account of the Lives, Sufferings and Martyrdom of the Apostles and Evangelists, pp. 331–335, verso, Table of Kindred.

12. NEW TESTAMENT: Brattleborough, Vt. Published by Holbrook & Fessenden. n. d. (L.) 24.

From the same types as the preceding, No. 11. It has a frontispiece, title page, and 4 plates, all engraved on wood.

13. APOCALYPSE of St. John; Being a New Interpretation, by George Croly. New York: 1827. (Am. Antiq. Soc.) 12.

1828.

1. HOLY BIBLE. Boston: Published by C. Ewer and T. Bedlington. 1828. 4.

Same as No. 2, of 1827.

2. HOLY BIBLE: With Marginal Notes and References, Apocrypha, Index, Tables of Names, &c. Lunenburg, Mass. Published and sold by Edmund Cushing. 1828. (L.) 4.

This Bible is from the same, or duplicate, plates of Collins's Stereotype edition of 1816, except the last leaf, which is blank in this issue. The title to the New Test. has, added: By B. & J. Collins, New York.

The following engravings illustrate this volume:
1. Adam naming the Creation, ... *F. & J. Andrews*, sc., Lancaster, Mass.
2. Noah building an altar.
3. Abraham's servant meeting Rebekah.
4. The Mother of Moses leaving her child in the bulrushes. Drawn by Westall;
Engr by *Chas. Heath*.

5. Ruth gleaning. By Westall..................................Engr. by *Chas. Heath.*
6. In the same hour came forth fingers of a man's hand.
7. Daniel in the Lion's den. By Westall....................Engr. by *Chas. Heath.*
8. Christ raising the Widow's son. (Front to N. T.) By Westall. Engr. by *Chas. Heath.*
9. Now Jacob's Well was there.
Nos. 2, 3, 6 and 9 are on wood.

8. HOLY BIBLE: With | Canne's Marginal References, | An | Index, | also | References and a Key sheet of Questions, | geographical, historical, doctrinal, practical, and experimental; accompanied with valuable chronologi- | cal Harmonies of both Testaments, and highly useful Tables of Scripture Names, Scripture Geography, | Scripture Chronology, Scripture References, &c. The whole designed to facilitate the acquisition of | Scriptural Knowledge in Bible Classes, Sunday Schools, Common Schools, and private Families. | By Hervey Wilbur, A. M. | The Text corrected according to the Standard | of the | American Bible Society. | Stereotyped by James Conner, New-York. | New-York: | Printed and published by Henry C. Sleight, 142 Nassau street. | Sold by—John F. Haven, J. Leavitt, G. & C. Carvill, E. Bliss, White, Gallaher & White, Collins & Hannay, S. Wood & Sons, Collins & Co., G. Long, E. Duyckinck, | and W. B. Gilley, New York—Central Sabbath School Union, Albany—Hastings & Tracy, and W. Williams, Utica—E. Peck & Co., Rochester—American Sunday | School Union, and Towar & Hogan, Philadelphia—Plaskitt & Co., and Cushing & Jewitt, Baltimore—Hilliard, Gray & Co., Crocker & Brewster, Lincoln & Ed- | munds, (*sic*) and Benjamin Perkins & Co., Boston—H. Howe, New Haven—Robinson & Co., Hartford—Shirley & Hyde, and James Adams, Jun., Portland—Child | & Co., Portsmouth—Whipple & Lawrence, Salem—W. Bigelow, Brooklyn, (N. Y.) | 1828. | (L.)   4.

Title, 1 f.; verso, Copyright, dated 18th August, 1825, Massachusetts; List of Books, including Apocrypha, which is not in this copy; below, Hints. Pref. to Reference Bible, 1 p.; To the Reader; Remarks and Key, 1 p.; verso, Guide to a regular perusal of the Holy Scriptures, by Wm. Stones, and Proper Lessons; Text: Gen. to Mal., pp. 5–527; sigs. 2 to recto of 132^2 in 2^s, and A^3 to recto of $3U^4$ in $4s$; on verso of p. 527, Stones' Guide, &c., repeated; Fam. Rec., 2 ff.; Title to N. Test., same imprint, 1 p.; verso, Remarks and Key repeated; Text: Mat. to Rev., pp. 3-163; sigs. 133 to verso of 174² in 2ˢ; and 3X to verso of 48⁴ in 4ˢ; Index and Tables, pp. 1-10, sigs. 177 to 179¹ in 2ˢ, and 4U, 4X¹; Title to Useful Tables, Imprint, as above, 1 p.; verso, Walker's Key to Accents; Text: pp. 13-31; p. 32, Key and Remarks, repeated; sigs. 179² to verso of 184², and 4X² to 4Z⁴; 4 Maps.

The Text is not precisely according to the standard set forth on the Title page, for 1 Tim. 4: 16 reads: Take heed unto thyself and unto thy doctrine. This error having been discovered, is avoided in the 12mo. editions of Wilbur's Reference Bible.

4. HOLY BIBLE: With | Canne's Marginal References. | Also | An Index, | A Table of Texts, | and what has never before been added, | An Account of | The Lives and Martyrdom of the Apostles and Evangelists. | With Plates. | The Text corrected according to the Standard | of the | American Bible Society. | Stereotyped by James Conner, New York. | Brattleborough, Vt. | Printed and published by Holbrook and Fessenden | 1828. | (L.) 4.

This volume is accompanied by 9 large Woodcuts. The Text is printed from the same plates as Wilbur's Reference Bible, immediately preceding. Mr. Kendall says that it was the second quarto Bible printed in Vermont. The error in 1 Tim. 4: 16, noticed above, is continued.

5. HOLY BIBLE: With Canne's Marginal Notes and References, Index, Tables, &c. Cooperstown, (N. Y.) Stereotyped, printed and published by H. & E. Phinney, and sold by them at their Book-store, and by Booksellers generally in the United States. 1828. (L.) 4.

2 Woodcuts; no Apoc. See *supra*, 1822, for the *first* edition.

6. HOLY BIBLE: With | Marginal Notes and References. | To which are added, | An Index; | An Alphabetical Table of all the Names in the Old and New Testaments, with their Significations; | Tables of Scripture Weights, Measures and Coins. | John Brown's Concordance, &c., &c. | Embellished with Maps and Historical Engravings. | Philadelphia: | McCarty & Davis, No. 171 Market-street. | I. Ashmead & Co., Printers. | 1828. | (J. G. S.) 4.

This is Carey's 4ᵗᵒ Bible of 1812, with new Title pages, Fletcher's Concise View being omitted. Leviticus, 19: 12 is incorrect. Esther, 1: 8, correct.

The engravings are:
1. Journeyings of the Children of Israel.
2. Dresses of the High Priests.

3. Marriage of Boaz and Ruth.
4. Judgment of Solomon.
5. Jeremiah taken from the dungeon of Ebedmelech.
6. John baptizing Jesus.
7. Our Savior and his Apostles in the storm.
8. The sick cured by the Shadow of Peter.
9. The Dragon chained.

The names of the engravers are erased from the plates, except No. 1, which has *J. Bower*, and No. 9, which has *J. L. Frederick*.

7. HOLY BIBLE, translated from the Latin Vulgat: With Annotations, References, &c. Philadelphia: Published by Eugene Cummiskey. Stereotyped by J. Howe. 1828. 8.

The Bible of 1824, with new Title pages. Edition consisted of 550 copies.

8. HOLY BIBLE: Printed for the Bible Society by the American Sunday School Union. Philadelphia. 1828. (Am. Bib. Soc. Cat.) 12.

9. HOLY BIBLE: Brattleborough, Vt. Printed and Published by Holbrook and Fessenden, 1828. (L.) 12.

A reissue of No. 12, of 1827, which see. The error at the top of the page at Gen. Chap. XXXVII, is continued.

10. HOLY BIBLE: Stereotype Edition. New York: Stereotyped by James Conner, for the American Bible Society. 1828. 12.

Pp. 486, 162.

11. HOLY BIBLE: New York: Published by the American Bible Society. Stereotyped by E. & J. White. 1828. 12.

41st edition, pp. 832 and 254.

12. HOLY BIBLE: New York: Stereotyped by A. Chandler for the American Bible Society. 1828. Nonpareil 12.

13. HOLY BIBLE: New York Stereotype Edition. New York: Stereotyped by E. & J. White, for the Auxiliary New York Bible and Common Prayer Society. Instituted in 1816. 1828. 12.

14. HOLY BIBLE: Published by the Methodist Book Concern.
New York: 1828. 12.

15. HOLY BIBLE: Hartford: Printed by Hudson and Goodwin.
1828. (B.) 12.
See 1809.

16. THE | HOLY BIBLE, | containing the | Old and New Testaments : | Translated out of the original tongues, | and with | the former translations | diligently compared and revised. | Hartford: | Published by Hudson and Skinner. | 1828. | (B.) 12.

Title, 1 f.; verso, blank; Names and Order, 1 f.; verso, blank; no paging; "End of Old Testament." On verso of last leaf, Table of Kindred and Affinity, and Table of Time, &c. Title to N. Testament, same date; "End of the New Testament." On verso of last leaf, "A Table of Offices," &c.; Finis.

17. HOLY BIBLE: Stereotyped by J. Howe . . . Philadelphia. Hartford: Published by Silas Andrus. Sold also by the Booksellers generally. 1828. (L.) 12.

The same as No. 13 of 1827, less the Psalms in metre. 2 engravings: David playing on the Harp, and Moses receiving the Law. *C. Pelton*, sc.

18. HOLY BIBLE: Stereotyped by B. and J. Collins, New York. Hartford: Published by Silas Andrus. 1828. (L.) 24.

With Dr. Witherspoon's Preface to Collins's Bible. Text: pp. 690, 210. Engraved Front. and Title. 1 Tim. 4: 16, "thy doctrine."

19. THE | HOLY BIBLE, | containing | The Old Testament | and | The New; | Translated out of | 𝕮𝖍𝖊 𝕺𝖗𝖎𝖌𝖎𝖓𝖆𝖑 𝕿𝖔𝖓𝖌𝖚𝖊𝖘, | and with the | former Translations diligently | compared and revised. | Stereotyped by J. Howe, Philadelphia. | New York: | Published by Daniel D. Smith, | No. 190 Greenwich St. | 1828. | (L.) 24.

Title, 1 p.; verso, Names and Order of the Books; Text: Gen. to Mal., pp. (3) to (615); 616, blank; New Test. title, same imprint, 1 p.; verso, Books of the N. T.; Text: (3) to (192); sigs. in 6^s.

The text of this edition is printed in two columns, but in paragraphs, each paragraph embracing several verses, numbered as usual. There is an engraved Title and Front. to each Test.

1. THE | NEW TESTAMENT | in the | Common Version, | conformed to | 𝔊𝔯𝔦𝔢𝔰𝔟𝔞𝔠𝔥'𝔰 𝔖𝔱𝔞𝔫𝔡𝔞𝔯𝔡 𝔗𝔢𝔵𝔱. | Boston: | Press of the Boston Daily Advertiser. | William L. Lewis, Printer. | 1828. | (Harv. Univ.; N. Y. State Lib.; L.)   8.

Title, 1 f.; verso, Certificate of Copyright, dated 7th July, 1828. Advertisement (by the Editor), pp. 3-8; Text: Mat. to end of Acts (not paged), sigs. A to verso of EE³ in 4ˢ; Romans to Rev., sigs. 1 to verso of 21³ in 4ˢ; last leaf of sig. blank.

JOHN GORHAM PALFREY, afterwards Dexter professor of Sacred Literature in Harvard, is the editor of this volume. He has exactly reprinted the common version, except in places where the Greek text, from which that version was made, is now understood to have been faulty.

2. NEW TESTAMENT: Philadelphia: Towar & Hogan, 255 Market Street. 1828.   8.

3. NEW TESTAMENT: *Stereotyped by L. Johnson.* Philadelphia: American Sunday School Union, No. 146 Chesnut street. 1828.   (L.)   12.

4. NEW TESTAMENT: *Twelfth Edition.* With References and a Key sheet of questions, &c., for Bible Classes, &c. By Hervey Wilbur. Amherst, Mass.: Published by J. S. & C. Adams. 1828.   (L.)   12.

5. NEW TESTAMENT; | Stereotyped by Hammond Wallis, New York. | Windsor, (Vt.) | Printed and sold by Simeon Ide. | 1828. | (Harvard Univ.)   12.

Same as the ed. No. 3, of 1826; pp. 372.

6. NEW TESTAMENT: Stereotype edition. New York. Stereotyped by James Conner for "The American Bible Society." 1828.   12.

D. Fanshaw, printer. 31st ed.

7. NEW TESTAMENT: 𝔑𝔢𝔴 𝔜𝔬𝔯𝔨: Published by Henry C. Sleight, 142 Nassau street. 1828.   12.

With Bible of 1829.

8. PRONOUNCING TESTAMENT: Boston: Printed and Published by Lincoln & Edmands, No. 53, Cornhill. Sold also by Cushing & Jewett, Baltimore; Abraham Small, Philadel-

phia; John P. Haven, New-York; and by Booksellers generally in the United States. *Stereotyped by T. H. & C. Carter, Boston.* 1828.   (L.)   12.

<small>This is another issue of Alger's Testament, already noticed; see No. 4, 1822.</small>

9. NEW TESTAMENT: Stereotyped by Baker & Greele, Boston. Boston: Timothy Bedlington; and William Greenough, Lunenburgh. 1828.   (Conn. Hist. Soc. Lib.)   18.

<small>Pp. 315. See No. 4, of 1827.</small>

10. NEW TESTAMENT, translated from the Latin Vulgat. Philadelphia: Published by Eugene Cummiskey. 1828.   16.

<small>Mr. Cummiskey represents the edition to have been 1250 copies. See *post* p. 199, No. 4 of 1829.</small>

11. NEW TESTAMENT. H. Adams. Philadelphia. 1828.   32.

<small>With Tower and Hogan's Bible of 1829.</small>

12. Das | Neue Testament | unsers | Herrn und Heilandes | Jesu Christi. | Nach der Uebersetzung | Doctor Martin Luthers. | Mit kurzem | Inhalt eines jeden Capitels, | und | vollständiger Anweisung gleicher Schriftstellen. | Wie auch | aller Sonn= und Festa= gigen | Episteln und Evangelien. | Philadelphia, | Herausgegeben von Georg W. Mentz, Buchhändler, | Nro. 71, in der Rehs=Straße. | 1828. | Stereotypirt von J. Howe. | (Am. Bib. Soc.)   12.

<small>Title, 1 f.; verso, Verzeichniß; Uebersicht des Inhalts aller Bücher, pp. iii-vi; Text: pp. 7-500; Verzeichniß, pp. 501-504; sigs. 1 (which includes Title and 2 prel. ff.) to verso of 21^{12} in 12^s.</small>

13. THE SACRED WRITINGS of the Apostles and Evangelists of Jesus Christ, commonly styled the New Testament. Translated from the Original Greek, by George Campbell, James MacKnight, and Philip Doddridge, *Doctors of the Church of Scotland.* With prefaces to the Historical and Epistolary Books, and an Appendix, containing Critical Notes and various Translations of difficult passages. Second Edition. Bethany, Brooke Co., Va. Printed and published by Alexander Campbell. 1828. (N. Y. State Lib.)   12.

194   AMERICAN BIBLES.   [1829—

Title, 1 f.; verso, Copyright, dated 3d February, 1826; Gen. Pref., pp. iii-xiv; Pref. to Gospels, pp. xvi-xxiii; Hints to Readers, pp. xxiv-xxx; Introd. to Acts, pp. xxxi-xxxiv; Pref. to Epist., pp. xxxv-xlvii; Pref. hints, pp. xlvii-lix; Text: Mat. to Rev., pp. 61-389; Appendix, pp. 390-456.

ALEXANDER CAMPBELL, the editor and publisher of this Volume was originally a Presbyterian, but withdrew from that Church in 1812, and became a Baptist. He was finally excluded from the fellowship of the Baptist Churches, on account of his peculiar views on Baptismal Regeneration, and founded a religious sect called "Disciples of Christ"—popularly known as Campbellites. Dr. Doddridge was a Congregationalist, not a Presbyterian.

14. A Practical HARMONY of the FOUR GOSPELS, arranged according to the most approved Harmonies, in the words of the authorised Version, and accompanied with Notes. By Joseph Muenscher. Northampton: 1828.   12.

Not seen. Mentioned in Doyle's Catalogue.

15. ST. PAUL's EPISTLE to the Hebrews. A new Translation with a Commentary, by the Rev. Moses Stuart, M. A. Andover, Mass. 1828.   8.

1829.

1. SELF INTERPRETING BIBLE: By the late Rev. John Brown, Minister of the Gospel at Haddington. With Engravings. New York: Printed and published by T. Kinnersley, *at the junction of Broadway and the Bowery.* And sold by appointed Agents in all the Cities and principal Towns in the United States. 1829.   fol.

2. HOLY BIBLE: With Canne's Marginal Notes and References. Together with the Apocrypha. To which are added, An Index: and Tables of Scripture Weights, Measures and Coins. Stereotyped by James Conner, New York. Hartford (Conn.): Printed and published by Silas Andrus. 1829.   fol.

Title, 1 f.; verso, Order of the Books and Account of the Dates, &c. To the Reader (Dr. Witherspoon's Preface), 1 p.; Account of the Lives, Sufferings, &c., of the Evangelists and Apostles, 1 p.; Text: Gen. to Mal., pp. 5-555, sigs. 2-139 in 2^s; p. 556 blank; Apocrypha, in smaller type, pp. 1-82, sigs. A to X^1; Family Record, 2 ff.; New Testament title, 1 f.; verso, blank; Text: Mat. to Rev., pp. 3-174; sigs. (including

Title), 1–441; Index and Table of Measures, pp. 1–11; sigs. A. to C. all in 2s, except X of Apocrypha and 44 of N. T.

It contains a frontispiece to each Testament: Jacob and Rachel, engr. by *V. Balch,* and The Ascension, by *J. G. Kellogg.*

Mr. Conner manufactured the Stereotype plates of this Bible as a speculation. Mr. Andrus purchased them readily for *five thousand dollars,* the price first asked. It is said to be the *first* folio ed. of the Bible stereotyped in the United States. *N. Y. Printer.*

3. HOLY BIBLE: Lunenburgh, Mass.: Published and sold by Edmund Cushing. 1829. (Mr. Hastie.) 4.

Same as No. 2 of 1828.

4. HOLY BIBLE: Cooperstown, (N. Y.) Stereotyped, printed and published by H. & E. Phinney, and sold by them. at their Bookstore, and by the Booksellers generally in the United States. 1829. 4.

5. THE | HOLY BIBLE: | Containing the | Old and New Testaments: | Translated out of the original tongues, | and with the former Translations diligently compared and revised. | with | Canne's Marginal Notes and References. | Together With | the Apochrypha. | To which are added | An Index: | And an Alphabetical Table of all the Names in the Old and New Testaments, | with their significations, | also | Tables of Scripture Weights, Measures and Coins. | Stereotyped by B. & J. Collins, New York. | Philadelphia | Published by Kimber & Sharpless, | No. 8, South Fourth Street. | 1829. (G. L.) 4.

See No. 1 of 1823.

6. HENRY'S COMMENTARY. Philadelphia: Towar and Hogan. 1829. 8.

Stereotype Edition. 3 vols., published in Jan., 1829. *Mag. Ref. D. Ch.,* III, 317.

An Edition of Henry's Commentary, edited by Burder and Hughes, was published in Philadelphia, 6 vols. 8vo., in 1829, with a Preface by Dr. A. Alexander. It is called the *first* American edition in *Cat. Am. Bib. Soc.,* p. 86. It is probably a reissue of the edition of 1816. See No. 21, *supra* p. 134.

7. HOLY BIBLE: Stereotype edition. New York: Published by the *Auxiliary New York Bible Society and Common Prayer*

Book Society (instituted in the year 1816), and to be had at their Depository, Protestant Episcopal Press Buildings, No. 46 Lumber-Street, in the rear of Trinity Church. *Printed at the New-York Protestant Episcopal Press,* No. 8 Rector Street. 1829. 8.

8. HOLY BIBLE: Stereotype edition. New York: Stereotyped by E. & J. White, for the American Bible Society. 1829. (Am. Antiq. Soc.) 8.
<small>34th edition. D. Fanshaw, printer; pp. 3–705 and 215; sigs. in 8°.</small>

9. HOLY BIBLE: Stereotype Edition. New-York: Stereotyped by A. Chandler, For "The American Bible Society." 1829. (L.; G. L.) 12.
<small>10th *Edition*. D. Fanshaw, Printer. Pp. 824, 251.</small>

10. HOLY BIBLE: Stereotyped | For the American Bible Society | by D. & G. Bruce. | *D. Fanshaw, Printer.* | New York. | 1829. | (L.) 12.
<small>[154th Edition;] pp. 837.</small>

11. HOLY BIBLE: Stereotype edition. New York: Stereotyped by James Conner, for the American Bible Society. 1829. 12.
<small>32d Edition; also 42d Edition; pp. 486, 162. D. Fanshaw, Printer.</small>

12. HOLY BIBLE: Stereotype Edition. New York: Printed by D. Fanshaw, for the American Bible Society. 1829. Min. 12.
<small>This is the first of the Bible Society's 12mos, with full contents to chapters.</small>

13. SLEIGHT'S EDITION. Holy Bible: Stereotyped by James Conner. New-York: Printed and published by Henry C. Sleight, No. 8 Marble Buildings, Chatham Square. 1829. (L.; B.) 12.
<small>On verso of Title, 1st *Edition*. Names and Order of all the Books, and Table of Time; Text: pp. 3–486; N. Test. title, 1 p.; verso, blank; Text: pp. 3–162.
Another copy of this Bible has the following Imprint: New York: Printed by Henry C. Sleight, and Published at the American Tract Society's House, *No.* 142 *Nassau-street*. 1829. With New Test., dated 1828.</small>

14. HOLY BIBLE: Hartford: Printed by Hudson and Goodwin.
1829. (B.) 12.

15. HOLY BIBLE: Hartford: | Published by Hudson and Skinner. | 1829. | (L.; B.) 12.

This volume is not paged, and has not the Dedication to King James. On verso of title to O. T., The property of   in an oblong; Names and Order on recto of 2d leaf; verso, blank; Tables of Kindred and Time on verso of last leaf of O. T., and Table of Offices on verso of last leaf of N. T. Hudson & Goodwin's editions of 1809 and 1810 have the Dedication, filling the whole of recto and part of verso of the leaf following the title; the rest of the verso has Names and Order; Tables on last pp. of O, and N. T., as in 1829. In other respects they seem to agree.
In the present Volume 1 Tim. 4:16 is incorrect.

16. HOLY BIBLE: Stereotyped by J. Howe, Philadelphia. Hartford: Published by Silas Andrus. Sold also by the Booksellers generally. 1829. 12.

Text: pp. 655; Cont. 656-681; verso of 681, blank; followed by 1 blank leaf; Psalms in Metre, pp. 661-720; 2 front. to O. T.; several wood cuts in N. T., 2 on a page.

17. HOLY BIBLE: Stereotype Edition. Boston: Published by Charles Ewer, No. 141 Washington street. 1829. (L.) 18.

Pp. 624 and 251.

18. HOLY BIBLE, containing the Old Testament and the New. Stereotyped by J. Howe, Philad. Philadelphia: Towar & Hogan, 255 Market-St. 1829. 32.

Pp. 852, 259. Engraved Titles to O. and N. T., with Imprint: Philadelphia: Published by Henry Adams. 1828. Imprint to New Test.: H. Adams, Philadelphia. 1828.

19. LA | BIBLIA SAGRADA, | a Saber: | El Antiguo y el Nuevo Testamento, | traducidos de la | Vulgata Latina | en Español, | por el Rmo. P. Felipe Scio de S. Miguel, | Obispo electo de Segovia. | Nueva Edicion, | a costa de la Sociedad Americana de la Biblia, | Jesus respondió: *Escudriñad las Escrituras.*-S. Juan, Cap. v. Ver. 39. | Nueva-York: | Edicion estereotipica por A. Chandler. | 1829. | (L.) 8.

Title, 1 f.; verso, Edicion V. Orden de los Libros; D. Fanshaw, Imprimador; Text: Gen. to Mal., pp. 3-440, then 463-468, 447, 448, 475-592, 567-580, 663-755, 671-684,

773-816, 729-744, 837-874, 783; verso, blank; sigs. A² to Dd in 8ˢ; then Ee in 5ˢ; Gg in 6ˢ; Hh to Oo in 8ˢ; Pp in 12ˢ; followed by Uu to Zz in 8ˢ; then Aaa, which consists of 7 ff.; Bbb (not marked); Ccc, Ddd in 8ˢ; Eee in 8⁴; Fff in 6ˢ (not marked); Ggg in 8ˢ; Hhh in 6ˢ; El | Nuevo Testamento, | traducido de la | Vulgata Latina, | en Español, | por el Rmo. P. Felipe scio de S. Miguel, | de las Escuelas pias, Obispo electo de Segovia. | Nueva Edicion, | a costa de la Sociedad Americana de la Biblia, | Quien la ha hecho cotejar con la que revista y corregida publicó su traductor | el ano de 1797 en Madrid. | Nueva-York : | Edicion Esterotipica por A. Chandler. | 1826. | 1 p.; verso, Orden de los Libros ; Text : Mat. to Apocal., pp. 3–251; sigs A² to recto of Q⁵, in 8ₛ. There is a double set of sigs. in figures, but these run very irregularly.

The irregularity in the paging and signatures of the Old Testament induces us to conclude that that portion of this Bible is made up of odd signatures of different editions. The type of the inserted leaves is greatly spread, or spaced very open.

Though this professes to be a Translation from the Latin Vulgate, and therefore a Catholic Bible, it is only just to state that it does not contain the 1st and 2d Books of Maccabees, which accompany all Catholic Bibles, having been inserted in the List of Sacred Books by the Council of Trent.

1. NEW TESTAMENT: Arranged in paragraphs, such as the Sense requires; the division of the chapters and verses being noted in the margin for Reference. By James Nourse, A. M. Philadelphia : Published by the Sunday School Union. *Stereotyped by J. Howe.* 1829.   (L.)   8.

Though this work appeared in 1827 (see *supra*, p. 186), the copyright and preface to this second edition are dated April, 1829. Two pp. of recommendations of the Plan of the work, dated, mostly, 1826, precede the title. The Text contains pp. 3–272.

I Tim. 4: 16 reads : Take heed unto thyself and unto thy doctrine.

2. THE | NEW TESTAMENT | of our | Lord and Saviour | Jesus Christ, | Translated out of the | Latin Vulgate ; | Dilligently compared with the Original Greek ; | and first Published By the | English College of Rhemes, Anno, 1582. | Newly Revised and Corrected according to the Clementine | Edition of the Scriptures ; | with Annotations, | to clear up the Principal difficulties of Holy Writ. | *As approved by the* Right Reverend John Dubois, | *Catholic Bishop of New-York.* | The Law of the Lord is unspotted, converting souls: the testimony of the Lord is faithful, giving wisdom to little ones.—Ps. xviii, 8. | Stereotype Edition. | Utica : | Printed for the Proprietors, by William Williams, No. 60, Genesee Street. | 1829. | (L. ; G. L.)   12.

Title, 1 f.; verso, Approbation dated 7 Sept. 1828 ; and notice of copyright, dated 13 Sept. 1828 ; Table of Controversies, 3 pp.; Table of Epistles and Gospels, 3 pp.; Chronol. Table, 3 pp.: Table of Books, 1 p.; 6 ff., making, including title, sig. 1; Text; pp. 13–344; sigs. 1 to verso of 29⁴.

This is the *first* Edition of what is called The Devereux Testament, from the fact that the late Nicholas Devereux, Esq., of Utica, owned the stereotype plates from which the volume was printed.

An error occurs in *James*, 5:17, where the text reads—Elias was a man possible like unto us.

3. NEW TESTAMENT: Translated from the Latin Vulgate. With Annotations, References, and an Historical and Chronological Index. Philadelphia: Published by Eugene Cummiskey. 1829. 12.

Not seen. Mr. Cummiskey informed me that the edition of this Testament consisted of 1250 copies.

4. THE | NEW TESTAMENT | of our | Lord and Saviour Jesus Christ, | translated from | the Latin Vulgat: | diligently | compared with the Original Greek: | and first published by the | English College at Rhemes, A. D. 1582. | With | Annotations, References, | and | A Historical and Chronological Index. | From the fifth Dublin Edition. | Newly revised and corrected according to the | Clementin Edition of the Scriptures. | Stereotyped by J. Conner, New-York. | Philadelphia: | Published by Eugene Cummiskey. | 1829. | (Georgetown Coll.; Mount St. Mary's Coll.; G. L.) 16.

On the verso of Title is—Published by Permission, The Order of the Books, and Note. Then, Admonition; Letter of Pope Pius the Sixth, and A Prayer, pp. 3, 4; Text, pp. 5 to one-third of 406; Table of References, remainder of p. 406–409; Table of Epistles and Gospels, pp. 410–412; Subscribers' Names, 1 p.; Cummiskey's Catalogue of Catholic Publications for 1827, 8, 3 pp. Sigs. 1 (including Title and 1 prel. f.) to verso of 13¹⁶ in 16s.

The size of this Pocket Testament is 4½ by 2¾ inches. The edition consisted of 1250 copies. Each of the Gospels is headed, The Holy Gospel of Jesus Christ, &c., and each of the Books is preceded by a brief account of its author and his work. No headings to columns; brief summaries to chapters.

5. NEW TESTAMENT: With References and a Key sheet of Questions. By Hervey Wilbur, A. M. Belchertown: Published by S. Wilson, And sold by the principal Booksellers in the United States. 1829. 12.

Stereotyped edition. See 1823.

6. NEW TESTAMENT: Stereotyped by J. Howe, Philadelphia. Hartford: Published by Silas Andrus. Sold also by the Booksellers generally. 1829. (L.) 12.

Pp. 503–655; the pagination shows that it is a part of Bible No. 13, 1827.

7. NEW TESTAMENT. New York: Printed by A. Chandler. 1829. (L.) 12.

8. NEW TESTAMENT. Stereotype edition. New York: Stereotyped by A. Chandler & Co., For "The American Bible Society." 1829. (L.) 18.

Pp. 352. D. Fanshaw, Printer.

9. NEW TESTAMENT. Stereotype edition. New York: Stereotyped by James Conner, For "The American Bible Society." 1829. 18.

52d Edition; pp. 237. D. Fanshaw, Printer.

10. NEW TESTAMENT: Elizabethtown, (N. J.) Printed and published by J. Sanderson. 1829. (L.) 18.

Pp. 330. Lives, Sufferings and Martyrdom of the Apostles and Evangelists, pp. 331–335; verso, Table of Kindred.

11. NEW TESTAMENT: Stereotyped by James Conner, New-York. Philadelphia: Printed and published by Daniel Neall. 1829. (L.) 18.

Title, 1 f.; verso, blank; Text: pp. 3–226; sigs. in 6s; in the head line on p. 3 the words: *The Gospel according*, are out.

12. NEW TESTAMENT: Stereotyped by James Conner, New-York. Concord, (N. H.) Printed and published by Horatio Hill & Co. n. d. 18.

Same as No. 11, immediately preceding, except the Imprint and verso of title, which has Order of the Books. The head line of p. 3 is perfect.

13. THE | MONOTESSARON: | or | the Gospel History | according to | The Four Evangelists : | Harmonized and Chronologically arranged | in a | New Translation | From the Greek Text of Griesbach. | Illustrated by selections from

the most eminent Commentators, An | cient and Modern, and by a great variety of original Notes | and Dissertations, exhibiting the latest improvements | in Biblical science and criticism. | By the Rev. John S. Thompson of the Universities of Glascow and Edinburgh, Professor of | Languages and "Systematical Theology." | The Holy Scriptures are able to make thee wise unto salvation through Faith in Christ Jesus.—2 Tim. ii, 15. | How can I understand unless some one guide me?—Acts viii, 31. | The unlearned wrest the Scripture to their own destruction.— 2 Peter iii, 16. | Baltimore: | Printed for the Author. | 1829. | (G. L.)   8.

Pp. 408. Mr. Thompson was pastor of the Universalist Church in Charlestown, Massachusetts. . . . His opinions are what are usually called Arian. *Magazine of the Reformed Dutch Church*, IV. 151, 152.

14. ANNOTATIONS | on the | New Testament: | Compiled from the best critical Authorities, | and designed for popular use. | By J. P. Dabney. | Part I. | The Historical Books. | Cambridge: | Hilliard and Brown. | 1829. | (L.)   12.

On verso of Title, Certificate of Copyright, dated 10th August, 1829; Preface, pp. iii-viii; Table of Works used in this publication, pp. ix-x; Table of Contractions, 1 p.; Errata, 1 p.; Text: pp. 1-560; sigs. in.. 6ˢ; p. 13 is marked 12. In the copy before us p. 80 terminates on verso of sig. 7⁶ with the Annotation on v. 43 of Mark xv; the next p. is marked 85 and begins on recto of 8¹ with the words, *Since the world began*, Luke 1: 70. Though the sigs. are perfect, 4 pp. seem to be wanting.

15. NE Raorihwadogenti ne Shonwayaner Yesus Keristus Jenihorihoten ne Royatadogenti Mark &c. New York: Printed by McElrath and Bangs for the New York District Bible Society. 1829.   12.

Pp. 239. This is a reprint of Brant's Translation of the Gospel of St. Mark into the Mohawk language, published in 1787, by the Society for Propagating the Gospel in Foreign Parts.

16. NE | *Hoiwiyosdosheh Noyohdadogehdih* | ne | Saint Luke, | nenonodowohga nigawenohdah. | New-York: | Printed for the American Bible Society. | D. Fanshaw, Printer. | 1829. | 18.

Opposite title: The Gospel | according to Saint Luke, | translated | into the Seneca Tongue, | By T. S. Harris. | Imprint as above. The English text in this version is on the right hand page.

17. CHRIST'S SERMON ON THE MOUNT: In the Seneca Tongue. New-York: American Bible Society. 1829. 18.

1830.

1. HOLY BIBLE: Cooperstown, N. Y. Stereotyped, printed and published by H. & E. Phinney, and sold by them at their Bookstore and by the Booksellers generally, in the United States. 1830. 4.

Same as edition of 1822. New Test. Title dated 1829.

2. THE | HOLY BIBLE, | containing | The Old and New Testaments; | Translated | out of the Original Tongues | And with | The former Translations diligently Compared and Revised. | Stereotyped by L. Johnson, Philadelphia. | Philadelphia: | Towar & Hogan, No. 255 Market street. | New York—John P. Haven; Boston—Pierce & Williams; Charleston, (S. C.) | Ebenezer Thayer; | Pittsburgh— Robert Patterson and John D. Davis; Cincinnati—N. & G. Guilford. | 1830. | (L.; Friends' Assoc., Phil.)   8.

Title, 1 f.; verso, The Names and Orders of all the Books of the O. and N. T. and the Apoc., &c.; Text: Gen. to Mal., pp. 3–750; sig. A² to verso of 5B³ in 4s; 1 f. blank, to complete the sig.; Fam. Rec., 4 ff. The | New Testament | of our | Lord and Saviour Jesus Christ | Translated | out of the original Greek: | And with | The former Translations diligently compared and Revised. | Stereotyped by L. Johnson, Philadelphia. | Philadelphia: | Published and sold by Towar & Hogan, | No. 255 Market street. | 1828. | 1 p.; verso, The Names and Order of all the Books; Text: Mat. to Rev., p. 3–238; sigs. A² to verso of Gg³; 1 f. blank;·| A Brief | Concordance | to the Holy Scripture | of the | Old and New Testaments : | By which | All, or Most, of the Principal texts of Scripture may be easily found out. | By John Brown, | late Minister of the Gospel at Haddington, in Scotland. | Search the Scriptures: for they testify of me.—John, V, 39. The Bereans were more noble—in that they searched the | Scriptures daily.—Acts, XVII, 11. | Revised and Corrected. | Philadelphia : | Published by Towar and Hogan, No. 255 Market-street. | Stereotyped by L. Johnson. | 1830. | verso, To the Reader; Text : pp. 3–85 recto; sig. A³ to S2; sigs. in 4s.

This edition has also been published without Concordance.

3. HOLY BIBLE: Stereotyped by L. Johnson, Philadelphia. 𝔓𝔥𝔦𝔩𝔞𝔡𝔢𝔩𝔭𝔥𝔦𝔞: Towar, J. & D. M. Hogan; and Hogan & Co. Pittsburgh. C. Sherman & Co., Printers. 1830. (L.; Friends' Assoc., Phil.) 8.

From the same plates as No. 1, but the imprint on the title to the N. Test. agrees with the above.

This also has been issued less the Concordance.

4. LA BIBLIA SAGRADA, | a saber: | El Antiguo y el Nuevo Testamento, | traducidos de la | Vulgata Latina | en Español, | por el Rmo. P. Felipe Scio de S. Miguel, | Obispo electo de Segovia. | 𝔑𝔲𝔢𝔳𝔞 𝔈𝔡𝔦𝔠𝔦𝔬𝔫, | a costa de la Sociedad Americana de la Biblia, | Jesus respondiò: *Escudriñad las Escrituras.* | S. Juan, Cap. v, Ver. 39. | Nueva-York: | Edicion estereotipica por A. Chandler. | 1830. | (L.) 8.

Title, 1 f.; verso, Edicion V; Orden de los Libros; D. Fanshaw, Imprimador; Text: Gen. to Mal., pp. 3–763; Title to New Test., same imprint, 1 p.; verso, Orden de los Libros; Text: Mat. to Apocal., pp. 3–261.

The 1st and 2d Books of Maccabees are omitted also in this edition.

5. HOLY BIBLE: New York. Published by the American Bible Society. 1830. Brevier 8.

From stereotype plates obtained from the Baltimore Bible Society. *Rev. Dr. Brigham.*

6. HOLY BIBLE: Stereotyped by Baker and Greele, For The American Bible Society. New York. 1830. (Am. Bib. Soc. Cat.) 8.

7. HOLY BIBLE: Stereotype Edition. New York: Stereotyped by A. Chandler for the American Bible Society. 1830. (L.) Nonpareil 12.

96th and 100th editions. *D. Fanshaw, Printer.* Pp. 669; short heading to columns and chapters.

8. HOLY BIBLE: Philadelphia: Published by George W. Mentz & Son, No. 53 North Third Street. 1830. (L.) 12.

This appears to be Carey's 12mo. Bible of 1818, with the imprints only changed.

9. **Die Bibel,** | ober | Die Ganze | **Heilege Schrift** | des | Alten und Neuen | Testaments. | Nach Dr. Martin Luthers Uebersetzung. | Text of Joshua 1:8. | Philadelphia, | Herausgegeben von Georg W. Mentz und Sohn, Buchhandler, | Nro. 53, in der Nord-Drittenstraße. | .1830. | Stereotypirt von J. Howe, Philadelphia. | (Am. Bib. Soc.) 12.

Title, 1 f.; verso, Verzeichniß; Text: Gen. to Mal., pp. 3–900; sigs. 1² to verso of 75s; Das | Neue Testament | unsers | Herrn und Heilandes | Jesu Christi. | Nach Dr. Martin Luthers Uebersetzung, | Vignette of the Savior praying, beneath which the words, Unser Vater in Himmel. | Philadelphia, | Herausgegeben von Georg W. Mentz und Sohn, Buchhandler, | Nro. 53, in der Nord-Drittenstraße. | 1830. | Stereotypirt von J. Howe, Philadelphia. | 1 p.; verso, Verzeichniß; Text: Mat. to Rev., pp. 3–308; Anweisung, pp. 309–311; sigs. 1² to recto of 26⁶; sigs. in 6s.

10. HOLY BIBLE: Stereotype Edition. Stereotyped by B. and J. Collins, New-York. Boston: Richardson, Lord and Holbrook. 1830. (B.; Harvard Univ.) 12.

Title, 1 f.; prel. matter (containing Account of dates, &c., and on reverse Names and Order of books, &c.), "Old Testament," p. 5, a. 3, to p. 605, The End of the Prophets; on the reverse of last leaf Table of Measures, &c. New Testament, p. 609 to 792, Finis. No catchwords.

11. HOLY BIBLE: Stereotype edition. Claremont Manufacturing Company's Power Press; Claremont, New Hampshire. n. d. 12.

Gen. to Mal., pp. 3–486; sigs. A to X³; N. T., pp. 3–162; sig. X* to 2D¹².

12. HOLY BIBLE: Hartford: Printed by Hudson and Goodwin. 1830. (B.) 12.

13. HOLY BIBLE: Hartford: Hudson and Skinner. 1830. (B.) 12.
See No. 15 of 1829.

14. HOLY BIBLE: containing the Old Testament and the New; translated out of **The Original Tongues,** and with the former Translations diligently compared and revised. Stereotyped by J. Howe . . . Philad. Hartford, *Ct.* Published by Silas Andrus. 1830. 24.

Engraved Frontisp. and 2 plates—Manoah's Sacrifice; engr. by *J. G. Kellogg;* and Samson betrayed by Delilah (on steel), and the following on wood: Adam and Eve driven out of Paradise; Murder of Abel; Noah leaving the Ark; Hagar in the Desert; Joseph cast into a Pit; The Return of the Spies; The fall of Jericho; Samson killing the Lion; Death of Samson, Elijah and the Prophets of Baal; The Man of Sorrows; Jonah thrown ashore,—in the O. Test. The Flight into Egypt; Simon and Andrew called,—in the New Test. Title, 1 f.; verso, blank; Contents, pp. 3-10; Text: Gen. to Mal., pp. 11-729; Mat. to Rev., 3-222.

15. HOLY BIBLE: Woodstock, Vt. R. Colton & G. W. Seeley. 1830. (G. L.) 24.

1. NEW TESTAMENT: Philadelphia: McCarty & Davis. 1830. 4.
With Bible of 1831.

2. NEW TESTAMENT: Stereotyped by H. & H. Wallis, New-York. | Philadelphia: Printed and published by Wm. F. Geddes. | At the Office of the Philadelphian, 59 Locust street. | 1830. | (L.) 12.
Pp. 201; Brief headings to chapters.

3. Das | Neue Testament | unsers | Herrn und Heilandes | Jesu Christi. | Nach der Uebersetzung | Doctor Martin Luthers. | Mit kurzem | Inhalt eines jeden Capitels, | und | vollständiger Anweisung gleicher Schriftstellen. | Wie auch | aller Sonn- und Festagigen | Episteln und Evangelien. | Philadelphia, | Herausgegeben von Georg W. Mentz, Buchhändler, | Nro. 71, in der Rehs-Straße. | 1830. | Stereotypirt von J. Howe. | (Am. Bib. Soc.) 12.
Title, 1 f.; verso, Verzeichniß; Uebersicht des Inhalts aller Bücher, pp. iii-vi; Text: pp. 7-500; Verzeichniß, pp. 501-504; sigs. 1 (which includes Title and 2 prel. ff.) to verso of 21^{12} in 12^s.

4. PRONOUNCING TESTAMENT: | Boston: | Printed and Published by Lincoln & Edmands, No. 53, Cornhill. | Sold also by Cushing & Jewett, Baltimore; Abraham Small, Philadelphia; John P. Haven, | New-York; and by Booksellers generally in the United States. | *Stereotyped by T. H. & C. Carter, Boston.* | 1830. | (L.) 12.
See No. 4 of 1822, *supra*, p. 159.

5. THE | NEW TESTAMENT | in the | Common Version, | conformed to | Griesbach's Standard Greek Text. | Third Edition. | Boston: | Gray and Bowen. | 1830. | (L.; G. L.) 12.

Title, 1 f.; verso, Certificate of Copyright, dated 7th July, 1828. Preface, pp. iii–viii; Text: Mat. to Rev., pp. 9–491; sigs. 1 to verso of 41⁶ in 6ˢ. See No. 1 of 1828. *Supra*, p. 192.

6. NEW TESTAMENT: New York: Stereotyped for the American Bible Society. 1830. Long Primer 12.

7. NEW TESTAMENT: New-York: Stereotyped by James Conner For the American Bible Society. 1830. Nonpareil 18.

8. THE SACRED WRITINGS | of the | Apostles and Evangelists | of | Jesus Christ, | Commonly Styled the | New Testament. | Translated from the | Original Greek, | by Doctors George Campbell, James Macknight, | and | Philip Doddridge, &c. | By A. Campbell. | Second Edition. | Bethany, Virginia. | 1830. | 12.

For the character of this work, see p. 194.

9. THE | GOSPEL OF ST. JOHN, | in Greek and English, | interlined and literally translated; | with a transposition of the words into their due Order | of Construction; | and A | Dictionary, | defining and parsing them; | principally designed for the use of Schools. | By E. Friederici. | New York: | Published for the Author, by G. F. Bunce, | 224 *Cherry-street.* | 1830. | (L.) 12.

10. A MANUAL. | The | Apostolic Epistles; | with Amendments | in conformity to | the Dutch Version. | New York: | Published by the Translator. | Sold by Booksellers generally. | 1830. (L.) 12.

Title, 1 f.; verso, blank; paged at foot 189 to 296. Signatures in 6ˢ, commence on 3d folio, or page 193, with R, and run to Bb 4 leaves. Without note or comment. Size of page, about 6¾ by 3¾ inches over all headings and sigs.

This translation is from the pen of the late Judge BENSON, whose principal object was to give the proper translation of the words *charity* and *bishop*, in accordance with the Dutch Version. This he does by substituting *love* for *charity*, and *overseer* for *bishop* wherever they occur. The pagination and signatures probably agreed with those of some copy of the Testament in general use, as the Judge did not extend his translation any further. *J. Carson Brevoort.*

1831.

1. HOLY BIBLE: Together with the | Apocrypha: | Translated out of the Original Tongues, | and with the former Translations diligently compared and revised, | By the Special Command of His Majesty King James I. of England. | With marginal Notes and References. | To which are added | An Index; | An Alphabetical Table of all the Names in the Old and New Testaments, with their significations; | Tables of Scripture Weights, Measures, and Coins. | Embellished with Maps and Historical Engravings. | Philadelphia | McCarty & Davis—No. 171 Market Street. | *I. Ashmead & Co., Printers* | 1831. | (L.) 4.

From the plates of Carey's 4to Bible of 1812, Fletcher's Concise View being omitted; Leviticus 19:12 is incorrect; Esther 1:8 correct. (See No. 6 of 1828.) The New Test. is dated 1830, and The Psalms in Metre, without a separate Title, are at the end of the vol. Pp. 1-24.

Engr. Front. to O. T. Marriage of Boaz and Ruth; all the other engravings are on wood.

2. HOLY BIBLE: with Canne's Marginal Notes and References, Apocrypha, Index, Tables of Names, Weights, Measures and Coins. Stereotyped by B. & J. Collins. Boston: Published by Langdon Coffin, 31 Washington Street. 1831. (L.) 4.

This volume agrees with Collins & Co.'s 4to edition of 1821, q. v. for collation; and is, we presume, from the same stereotype plates. It contains Brown's Concordance, stereotyped by B. & J. Collins, with Imprint as above, but dated 1830. The printed title to the vol. is preceded by an engraved frontispiece, "The Creation," with a partially cancelled inscription, of which these words only are legible: "Engraved for & Co.'s Edition 1825;" and an engraved (inserted) Title page: The | Holy Bible | containing the | Old and New Testaments | ornamented with engravings. | (above a circular engraving) Our Saviour washing his disciples' feet; John xiii, 8, 10. The two upper corners of the page contains drapery, in festoons; the lower right hand corner, a Censor and the Tables of the Law; the lower left hand corner, a Cross, Cup, Crown of Thorns and two Nails; all the foregoing is included within an engraved square, outside of which at the bottom is the inscription, Our Saviour, &c., and — Boston Edition, Published by Langdon Coffin. Engraved by J. B. Neagle. The volume is further embellished with the following wood cuts:

1, Elijah and the Angel; 2, Nehemiah; 3, In the Same Hour, Dan. 5:5; 4, Daniel in the Lion's Den (Northcote's design); 5, The Repentance of Judas; 6, Good Samaritan; 7, The Resurrection; 8, Touch me not; and an engraved front. to N. Test.

The Plague of Blood, in an ornamental frame, with the Tables of the Law, above. This is an old engraving by Neagle (but without his name), and is from the Old Testament. See No. 1 of 1822, *supra*, p. 156. 1 Tim., 4:16, is incorrect.

3. HOLY BIBLE: with Marginal Notes, Apocrypha, Index, &c. Lunenburg, Mass. Published and Sold by Edmund Cushing. 1831. 4.

Engraved front. to Old Test., Abraham's Servant meeting Rebekah; and several illustrations, all on wood. See No. 2, 1828.

4. HOLY BIBLE: Cooperstown (N. Y.), stereotyped, printed and published by H. & E. Phinney, and sold by them at their Bookstore, and by the Booksellers generally in the United States. 1831. 4.

5. HOLY BIBLE, translated from the Latin Vulgat: with Annotations, References, Index, &c. Philadelphia: Published by Eugene Cummiskey. Stereotyped by J. Howe. 1831. 8.

This edition consisted of 500 copies. It is from the plates of 1824.

6. HOLY BIBLE: With References. Stereotype edition. | Philadelphia: | Published by | The Bible Association of Friends in America. 1831. (L.) 8.

Pp. 1061; verso of 1061, Table of Offices (Bagster's), pp. i-xxxiii; verso, blank; Table of Scripture Measures, Weights, and Greek Money reduced to Federal Money, and Time, 1 p.; verso blank, followed by a blank leaf; Title to Concordance (no imprint), 1 p.; verso, To the Reader; Text, pp. 3-92.

7. HOLY BIBLE (Scott's): From the 5th London edition. 6 vols. Boston: 1830-1831. (Brown Univ.) 8.

8. HOLY BIBLE: In Two Volumes. Vol. I. Boston: Published by Gray and Bowen. 1831. (L.) 8.

On verso of Title: Boston Press. Francis Jenks, Proprietor — Stephen Foster, Printer. Then, Contents of Vol. I, 1 p.; verso, blank; Text: Gen. to Psalms, pp. 1-915; sigs. 1 to recto of 115²; 2d Vol., Title and Imprint as above, except, Vol. II, verso, as above; Contents of Vol. II, 1 p.; verso, blank; Text: Proverbs to Mal., pp. 1-400; The New Testament, &c. (Mock Title, no imprint), 1 p.; verso, blank; Text: Mat. to Rev., pp. 403-805; sigs. 1* to recto of 101*³; all in 4s.

Front. to Vol. I, Garden of Eden (from the original painting by Thomas Cole, engraved by James Smillie; Front. to Vol. II, Mary Magdalen Reading the Scriptures (Correggio), engraved by Geo. W. Hatch.

9. HOLY BIBLE: Stereotype edition. | Stereotyped by T. Rutt, London. | And printed | for the American Bible Society, | By D. Fanshaw, Printer, New York. 1831. | (L.)   8.

5th edition, pp. 968. The stereotype plates of this edition were cast in London, and bought from the Baltimore Bible Society. It was the first 8vo Bible printed by the Society with headings to columns and full contents to chapters. It also shows the amendments made by collations since 1816. See No. 12, p. 196.

10. HOLY BIBLE: 37th Edition. New York: Stereotyped by E. & J. White for the American Bible Society. 1831. (L.)   8.

Headings to columns; but no contents to chapters.

11. HOLY BIBLE: Stereotype edition. New-York: Printed by D. Fanshaw, for the American Bible Society. 1831. Nonp. 12.

112th edition, pp. 660. Headings to columns and chapters.

12. HOLY BIBLE: Stereotype Edition. New York: Printed by D. Fanshaw, for the American Bible Society. 1831. Min. 12.

18th edition, pp. 852. Brief headings to columns; contents to each chapter.

13. HOLY BIBLE: New York: Published by the Auxiliary New York Bible and Common Prayer Book Society Depository. No. 46, Lumber Street. 1831.   12.

14. THE ENGLISH VERSION of the POLYGLOTT BIBLE: With the Marginal readings: Together with a Copious and Original Selection of References to parallel and illustrative Passages. Exhibited in a manner hitherto unattempted. Stereotyped by L. Johnson. Philadelphia: Published by Key & Meilke, No. 181 Market Street. 1831.   (L.)   12.

With Preface to the English version signed 𝕰. 𝕮. pp. iii-viii; Text: pp. 587, 190; engraved front. and Titles to both Testaments.

15. HOLY BIBLE: 𝔓𝔥𝔦𝔩𝔞𝔡𝔢𝔩𝔭𝔥𝔦𝔞: Published by G. W. Mentz & Son, No. 53 North 3d St. Stereotyped by L. Johnson, 1831.   (L.)   12.

Pp. 599, 1,179.

16. HOLY BIBLE, containing the Old Testament and the New. Stereotyped by J. Howe, Philadelphia. Pittsburgh: Published by H. Holdship & Son. J. B. Butler, Print. 1831. 12.

Pp. 743, 238 ; with Psalms in Metre.

17. HOLY BIBLE: (Boston stereotype edition.) Boston: Published by Waitt and Dow, and Sold at their Bookstore in Charlestown, Mass., and by Lincoln & Edmands, 59 Washington Street. MD.CCC.XXXI. (L.) 12.

Pp. 426, 162 ; 2 small woodcuts on 1 p. to the O. T., and 2 also on 1 p. to N. T.

18. HOLY BIBLE: Boston, Mass. Printed and Published by George Clark. 1831. (L.) 12.

Same as the Brattleboro' Bible, No. 12, 1827. See Remarks to that edition.

19. HOLY BIBLE: Hartford: Hudson & Skinner. 1831. (B.) 12.

See No. 15 of 1829.

20. HOLY BIBLE: Hartford: Printed by Hudson and Goodwin. 1831. (B.) 12.

21. HOLY BIBLE: Stereotyped by J. Howe, Philadelphia. Hartford: Published by Silas Andrus, Sold also by the Booksellers generally. 1831. (L.) 12.

Pp. 655 ; 2 plates, and 24 woodcuts arranged on 12 leaves.

22. HOLY BIBLE: Concord, N. H. Published by Moses G. Atwood. 1831. (L.) 12.

Title, 1 f.; verso blank; Account of Dates, 1 p.; verso Names of Books; Gen. to Mal., pp. 5–605 ; sig. A³ to recto of Cc³; verso, blank ; recto of next leaf, blank; verso, Tables of Measures, Weights, Money and Time; no title to New Test.; Mat. to Rev., pp. 509–792; sigs. Cc⁵ to verso of Kk¹².

This is a wretchedly printed book. The text is from the same plates as Websters & Skinners' Albany edition of 1817. 1 Tim. 4:16 is incorrect.

1. NEW TESTAMENT: Translated from the Latin Vulgat: Philadelphia; Published by Eugene Cummiskey. 1831. 8.

This is the New Testament part of the Cummiskey Bible of 1824, published separately. Edition 500 copies.

2. NEW TESTAMENT: Published by the Association of Friends in America. Philadelphia: 1831.   8.

3. NEW TESTAMENT: Stereotype edition. Boston, Published by Stimpson and Clapp. 1831.   (L.)   8.
This is a reissue of the paragraph Testament, No. 1 of 1827, with a new Title page. See *supra*, p. 185.

4. THE | NEW TESTAMENT | of our | Lord and Saviour Jesus Christ, | translated from the | Latin Vulgate. | Diligently compared with the Original Greek : | First published by | the English College at Rheims, A. D. | 1582: | With | Annotations, References, and an Historical | and Chronological Index. | F. L. | in ornamented or fancy letters. Baltimore: | Published by Fielding Lucas, Jr. No. 138, Market Street. n. d.   (L.)   12.
Title, 1 f. ; verso, Approbation, signed JAMES, Archbishop of Baltimore. A Prayer; The Books of the New Testament ; Text : pp. 13–344; sigs. 2 to verso of 29⁴ in 6ˢ ; Table of References, pp. 345–347; Tables of Epistles and Gospels, pp. 348–350 ; a Chronological Table, pp. 351–353 ; sigs. 1² to recto of 1⁶, verso, blank.

Mr. Cummiskey informs me that he sold the plates of his 12mo Testament (*See supra*, p. 199), to Mr. Lucas, in 1830 or 1831. I have not been able to find a copy of the Cummiskey 12mo, and am therefore unable to say how far that volume agrees with this ; but on comparing it with the Devereux Testament of 1829 (*supra*, p. 198), the text of both appears to be identical ; even the error in James, 5 : 17, is common to one and the other. The preliminary matter of the Devereux Testament, included on pp. ii–xi, is, in the Lucas edition, transferred to the end of the volume, where the " Table of Controversies " is entitled " Table of References." In consequence of this transfer, pp. iii–xii, are not enumerated in the Lucas Testament before the text, which begins immediately after the Title leaf and abruptly with p. 13. If, as is represented, this volume is printed from the plates of Cummiskey's 12mo Testament, then it and the Devereux Testament are from duplicate plates manufactured by James Conner, N. Y.

5. THE | NEW TESTAMENT | of our | Lord and Saviour Jesus Christ; | Translated out of the | Original Greek, and with the former Translations | diligently compared and revised. | To which are added | Explanatory Notes ; | embracing | A Historical and Geographical Account of the Places mentioned in | the New Testament; and Biographical Notices of Individu- | als; also Definitions of Terms, References, &c. | With an Outline of Jewish History ; | and a | Histo-

rical and Geographical Sketch of | Palestine. | Prepared for the Instruction of Youth. | (Vignette.) *The Last Supper.* | Whoso readeth let him understand. | By J. Olney, | Author of a "Practical System of Geography," "National Preceptor," &c. | Hartford: | Published by Silas Andrus. | 1831. | (L.)   12.

Pp. 378. Map of Palestine; Map of the places mentioned in the New Testament.

6. NEW TESTAMENT: By J. Olney, author &c. Published by | Silas Andrus, Hartford, Conn.—Luke Loomis & Co., Pittsburg, Penn.— | A. B. Roff, Cincinnati, Ohio.— | J. S. Kellogg, Mobile, Ala. | 1831. | (L.)   12.

2 Maps. In all respects the same as the preceding, except the Imprint.

7. NEW TESTAMENT: Stereotype edition. Stereotyped by James Conner, New York. Pittsburgh, *Pa.* Published by Luke Loomis & Co. Wood street. Sixth Edition. 1831.   12.

Verso of Title, Order of the Books; Text: pp. 3–226; Catalogue of Proper Names, 3 pp., the last two of which are marked 53, 54 at top; Contents, 3 pp.; the last two marked 61, 62 at top; short headings to columns and chapters.

8. NEW TESTAMENT: New York: Published by R. Schoyer. Ludwig & Tolefree, Printers. 1831.   (J. G. S.)   12.

Title, 1 f.; verso, The Order of all the Books; Text: Mat. to Rev., pp. 3–315. Sigs. A to Dd^2; verso of p. 315, A Table of Kindred. Sigs in 6^s.

There are no headings either to the columns or chapters throughout this edition, until we come to II Peter, c. 3, when there are short headings to each chapter, as far as Jude inclusive, when they again disappear.

9. POCKET REFERENCE TESTAMENT. | The | New Testament, | of our | Lord and Saviour Jesus Christ; | With | Original Selections of References to Parallel | and Illustrative Passages; | and | Marginal Readings: | Together with other valuable additions; | the whole designed to facilitate the acquisition | of Scripture Knowledge | in Bible classes, Sunday Schools, &c. | Stereotyped by L. Johnson. | Baltimore: | Published by Armstrong & Plaskitt, No. 134 and | Plaskitt & Co., No. 254 Market Street. | 1831. | 24.

Pp. 281.

10. The | New Testament | of our | Lord and Saviour | Jesus Christ, | 𝔗ranslated from the 𝔏atin 𝔙ulgat : | with | Annotations and References. | Baltimore : | Published by F. Lucas, Jr. | No. 138 Market Street. | n. d. (Amer. Bib. Soc.) 32.

Title, 1 p., enclosed within double rules; verso, Approbation of the Archbishop of Baltimore, Order of Books and Note; then Admonition and other matter, as in Cummiskey's 32mo (No. 4 on p. 199), with which this agrees except in the signature marks, which are in letters in this edition—A (not marked) to verso of 2 C⁶ and run in 8ˢ.

Mr. Cummiskey has informed me that he sold the plates of his 32mo Testament to Mr. Lucas in 1830 or 1831.

11. Polyglott New Testament: With Marginal Readings, illustrated with numerous Engravings. New York: Published by J. C. Riker, Franklin Building. 1831. 32.

12. New Testament: Exeter, N. H. Published by James Derby. *Stereotyped by the Publisher.* 1831. (L.) 32.

13. New Testament: Stereotyped by Henry Wallis & Luther Roby...Concord, N. H. Claremont, N. H.: Claremont Manufacturing Co. (n. d.) 48.

14. El | Nuevo Testamento | traducido | de la Biblia Vulgata Latina | en Español | por el Rmo. P. Felipe Scio de S. Miguel, | Obispo electo de Segovia. | Reimpreso conforme a la Segunda edicion hecha en Madrid, Año de 1797, | Nueva York: | Edicion esteriotipa. | A costa de la Sociedad Americana de la Biblia. | Año de 1831. | (Am. Bib. Soc.) .12.

15. Nouveau Testament: Edition stereotype. A Nouveau York: Par la Societé Biblique. 1831. (L.) 12.

16. Critical and Explanatory Notes on many passages of Scripture, which to common readers are hard to be understood. By Ezekiel I. Chapman. Utica: 1831. (Doyle.) 12.

17. Ne Raorihwadogenti ne Shongwayaner Jesus Keristus Jenihorihoten ne Royatadogenhti Matthew, &c. Printed by McElrath and Bangs for the Young Men's Auxiliary Methodist Bible Society. New York, 1831.   12.

This is a translation of the Gospel according to St. Matthew into the Mohawk Language. The English text is on the left hand page. *Am. Bib. Soc. Cat.*, p. 27.

1832.

1. The | Holy Bible | translated from | the Latin Vulgate : | diligently compared with | the Hebrew, Greek, and other editions, in various languages. | The Old Testament was first published by the English College at Doway, A. D. 1609 : | and the New Testament, by the English College at Rheimes, A. D. 1582. | With | Annotations, by the Rev. Dr. Challoner : Together with References, and an | Historical and Chronological Index. | Revised and corrected according to the Clementine edition of the Scriptures. | Baltimore : | Published by Fielding Lucas, Jr. | No. 138, Market Street. | n. d.   (L.)   4.

Title, 1 f. ; verso, blank ; Approbation of the Old Testament, Approbation of the New Testament, Translation of the Decree of the Council of Trent, 1 p. Letter of Pope Pius VI, Admonition and Prayer, List of the Books of the Old Testament, 1 p. ; Text : Gen. to 2 Mac. pp. 9–789 ; Sigs. B to 5 G^3; verso of 5 G^3, blank ; 5 G^4 blank ; Fam. Record, 2 ff ; Title to New Testament (imprint as above) 1 p. verso, blank ; Admonition, Letter of Pius VI. and Prayer, 1 p. ; Approbation of New Test. ; List of Books of the New Testament and Note, 1 p. ; Text : Mat. to Apocal. pp. 5–222 ; sigs. A^3 to verso of Ee^3; Table of Epistles and Gospels, pp. 223, 224 ; sig. Ee^4 ; Table of Reference, pp. 225, 226 ; Hist. and Chron. Index to New Test., pp. 227, 228 ; to Old Test., pp. 229–235 ; sigs. Ff to Gg.^{2} all in 4s.

This edition is from the plates of Cummiskey's 4to which Mr. Lucas purchased in 1830 or 1831. It omits the Approbation of the Bishop of Philadelphia, but agrees in other respects.

2. Holy Bible : With Apocrypha, Marginal Notes and References, Index and Tables. Embellished with Maps and Historical Engravings. Philadelphia: McCarty and Davis, No. 171 Market Street. I. Ashmead & Co., printers. 1832.   (L.)   4.

A reissue of Carey's 4to Bible, same as the editions of 1828 and 1831, less Apocrypha, Concordance and Psalms. Two woodcuts to O. & N. Test. : Leviticus 19 : 12 is incorrect ; Esther 1 : 8 correct.

3. HOLY BIBLE: Cooperstown (N. Y.), Stereotyped, printed and published by H. & E. Phinney, and sold by them at their Bookstore, and by the Booksellers generally in the United States. 1832.   4.

4. HOLY BIBLE: Stereotyped at the Boston Type and Stereotype Foundry, late J. H. Carter & Co. Boston: Nathan Hale, Sampson and Clapp, Hilliard, Gray, Little and Wilkins, Richardson, Lord and Holbrook, Lincoln and Edmands, Crocker and Brewster, Munroe and Francis, and R. P. and C. Williams. Hale's Steam Press. 1832. (L.) 8.

Text of O. Test., pp. 681, 1; Apocrypha (in smaller type), pp. 1–134; Text of N. Test. pp. 3–212; Contents, pp. i–xii.

5. HOLY BIBLE: Boston: J. A. Ballard. 1832. (Sem. St. Sulpice, Baltimore, Md.)   8.

6. SCOTT'S FAMILY BIBLE: with Brown's Concordance. Stereotyped by J. Pell & Brother, New York. New York: Collins and Hannay. W. E. Dean, Printer. M.DCCC.XXXII. 3 volumes.   8.

7. Daniel D. Smith's Stereotype Edition. HOLY BIBLE: With Canne's Marginal Notes and References and a concise Table of contents of the Books of the Old and New Testaments. Stereotyped by J. Howe, Philadelphia. New York: Published and sold by Daniel D. Smith at the Franklin Juvenile Book and Stationery Store, No. 190 Greenwich Street: also by the principal Booksellers in the United States. 1832.   (L.)   8.

It has an engraved frontispiece by Westall, and Collins's Preface. In other respects seems to be a reprint of the edition of 1825.

8. HOLY BIBLE translated from the Latin Vulgat: With Annotations, References and Indexes. Philadelphia: Published by Eugene Cummiskey. Stereotyped by J. Howe. 1832. 8.

Edition 500 copies.

9. La | Biblia Sagrada, | a Saber : | El Antiguo y el Nuevo Testamento, | traducidos de la | Vulgata Latina | en Español, | por el Rmo. P. Felipe Scio de S. Miguel, | Obispo electo de Segovia. | 𝔑𝔲𝔢𝔳𝔞 𝔈𝔡𝔦𝔠𝔦𝔬𝔫, | a costa de la Sociedad Americana de la Biblia, | Jesus respondió: *Escudriñad las Escrituras*.–S. Juan, Cap. v. Ver. 39. | Nueva-York : | Edicion estereotipica por A. Chandler. | 1832. | 8.

10. Holy Bible : Philadelphia : Published by Jas. B. Smith & Co., No. 610 Chestnut St. n. d.   12.
<small>Stereotype edition, pp. 436, 162.</small>

11. English Version of the Polyglott Bible. Stereotyped by L. Johnson. Philadelphia : Key, Meilke and Biddle, 181 Market Street. 1832.   12.
<small>Pp. 587, 190. See 1831.</small>

12. English Version of the Polyglott Bible. Stereotyped by L. Johnson. Philadelphia. Published by Edward C. Mielke, No. 381 Market Street. 1832. (Mr. McA.) 12.
<small>Same as No. 10; with Psalms in metre—Philadelphia: Key & Mielke, No. 181 Market Street. *Stereotyped by L. Johnson.* 1831, pp. 64.</small>

13. Holy Bible : Stereotyped by B. &. J. Collins, New York. Concord, N. H. Published by Moses G. Atwood. 1832. (L.)   12.
<small>See No. 22 of 1831.</small>

14. Holy Bible : Stereotyped edition. | Middletown, Con. | Published by William H. Niles. | Stereotyped by A. Chandler. | 1832. | 12.
<small>Title, 1 f.; verso, Names and Order of the Books; Text: pp. 3–824 and 251 in 12^s, printed in half sheets.</small>

15. Holy Bible : Hartford, Ct. : Silas Andrus. 1832.   12.
<small>Pp. 660 with Contents. The title to the New Test. of the copy examined, is on the verso, and Names and Order of the Books on the recto of the leaf, shewing that it is a new title p. inserted.</small>

16. HOLY BIBLE, containing the Old Testament and the New. Hartford: *Ct.* Published by Silas Andrus. 1832.   24.
Pp. 729, 222; Contents, 223–225; Psalms in metre, pp. 70.

17. HOLY BIBLE: Hartford: Printed by Hudson and Goodwin. 1832.   (B.)   12.

18. HOLY BIBLE: Hartford: Hudson & Skinner. 1832. (B.) 12.

19. POCKET REFERENCE BIBLE. | The | English Version | of the | Polyglott Bible, | containing the | 𝔒𝔩𝔡 𝔞𝔫𝔡 𝔑𝔢𝔴-𝔗𝔢𝔰𝔱𝔞𝔪𝔢𝔫𝔱𝔰; | with | Original Selections of References to Parallel | and Illustrative Passages; | and | Marginal Readings: | Together with other valuable additions: The | whole designed to facilitate the acquisition | of Scripture Knowledge | in Bible Classes, Sunday Schools, &c. | Stereotyped by L. Johnson. | Baltimore: | Published by Armstrong & Plaskitt, No. 134, and | Plaskitt & Co. No. 254 Market Street. | 1832. | (L.)   24.
Title, 1 f.; verso, blank; Order of the Books of the O. Test. and Chronol. Order, marked p. ii; verso, blank; Pref. pp. iii–viii; Gen. to Mal. pp. 3–891; Table exhibiting Chronol. of our Saviour's Life, p. 892; Contents of Books of O. T. pp. 893-900; Table of Offices, pp. 901, 902; Scripture Names with their signification, pp. 903-914; Discourses, Parables and Miracles of Jesus in Chronol. Order, pp. 915, 916; Harmony of the Gospels, pp. 917-919; Table of Scripture Measures, Weights, Money and Time, part of p. 919 and p. 920. Title to N. Test. Imprint as above, 1 p.; verso, Order of Books; Mat. to Rev. pp. 3–277; verso, blank; Contents, pp. 279–281; Proper Lessons for Sunday Mornings, p. 282.

20. HOLY BIBLE, containing the Old Testament and the New. Seventh Stereotype edition. New-York: Published by N. and J. White, 108 Pearl-street. 1832.   (L.)   24.
Engraved front. to Old and New Test.; Address of the Translators; Text: pp. 704, 216.
This is a continuation of the Bible published by White, Gallaher & White in 1827. See *supra* p. 184.

21. HOLY BIBLE: Philadelphia: Alexander Towar, also Hogan & Thompson 139½ Market Street. *Stereotyped by L. Johnson.* 1832.   (L.)   32.
Pp. 819 and 256. With engraved frontispiece and title page: Imprint, Towar & Hogan: dated in some copies 1629; in others 1834.

22. A Harmony of the Kings and Prophets, or an Arrangement of the History contained in the Books of Kings and Chronicles, together with the Writings of the Prophets, arranged in Chronological Order as they were delivered, commencing with the Revolt of the Ten Tribes, and closing with the Prophecies of Malachi. By Stephen Merrell. Kittery (Maine). 1832. (Horne.) 8.

1. New Testament: With an Introduction and Notes. By J. A. Cummings. Second Edition revised and improved. Boston: Hilliard, Gray, Little and Wilkins. 1832. 4 maps. (L.) 12.
Pp. 305. Copyright dated 5 Jany., 1827.

2. New Testament: Stereotype Edition. New York: Printed for the American Bible Society. 1832. 12.
27th edition.

3. New Testament: Stereotyped by Hammond Wallis, New York. Windsor (Vt.) Printed and sold by Simeon Ide. 1832. 12.
Pp 372. See 1828.

4. New Testament: Elizabethtown, N. J. Published by B. F. Brookfield. Stereotyped by L. Johnson. 1832. 32.
Pp. 344.

5. New Testament: Philadelphia: Published by Jos. B. Smith & Co., No. 610 Chestnut Street. n. d. 32.
Pp. 344.

6. New Testament: Philadelphia: Alexander Towar. Also, Hogan & Thompson, 139½ Market Street. *Stereotyped by L. Johnson.* 1832. 32.
Pp. 256. Engr. front and title; on the latter: Philadelphia, R. W. Pomeroy, 1832. This is the New Test. of No. 21, p. 217, published separately.

7. New Testament: Cooperstown: H. & E. Phinney. 1832. 32.
Pp. 340; Contents, pp. 341-344.

8. Η ΚΑΙΝΗ ΔΙΑΘΗΚΗ. The New Testament: With short explanatory Notes, and numerous References to illustrative and parallel passages, printed in a centre column. *Illustrated with Maps.* New York: Published by Jonathan Leavitt, 182 Broadway. Boston: Crocker and Brewster, 47 Washington-street. M.DCCC.XXXII. (L.) 32.

This is called the Polymicrian Testament; it is on the plan of Bloomfield's Greek Test. published in London in 1829. The Title is preceded by an engraved page containing the words "New Testament" in 48 different languages. The work is stereotyped by James Conner; D. Fanshaw, Printer. The following is a list of the Maps: Tetrarchies of Palestine; Jerusalem; St. Paul's Travels and Countries referred to in the Acts; Map of Canaan; The World. There are headings to each column. 4 prel. ff. and pp. 546.

9. THE GOSPEL OF MATTHEW, the ACTS of the Apostles, &c., with Hymns translated into the Cherokee Language by S. A. Worcester and E. Boudinot. American Board of Commissioners for Foreign Missions. New Echota. 1832. (Cat. Am. Bib. Soc.) 24.

10. A PRACTICAL EXPOSITION of the Gospel of St. LUKE in the form of Lectures; intended to assist the Practice of domestic Instruction and devotion. By John Bird Sumner D. D. Bishop of Chester, Author of a Practical Exposition of St. Matthew and St. Mark. First American edition. New York: Protestant Episcopal Press. M.D.CCC.XXXII. 8.

1833.

1. SELF INTERPRETING BIBLE: By the late Rev. John Brown, minister of the Gospel at Haddington. With a series of beautiful Engravings. New York: Printed and published by T. Kinnersley, Thirty-fifth street, Eighth Avenue, and sold by appointed agents in all the cities and principal towns in the United States. 1833. fol.

Another issue of the edition of 1822. q. v. The engraved title page is dated 1826.

2. STEREOTYPE EDITION. HOLY BIBLE: Together with the Apocrypha: Canne's Marginal Notes and References. To which are added, an Index; Tables of Names, Scripture Weights, Measures, and Coins. Saratoga Springs: Printed and published, wholesale and retail, | by G. M. Davison. | 1833. | (Mr. Davison.) 4.

<small>This edition is identical with that printed in Cooperstown by H. & E. Phinney. It is accompanied by a few wood cuts. Mr. Davison continued the issues of this Bible for two or three years and then sold the plates to S. & W. Ward of New York.</small>

3. HOLY BIBLE: With Canne's Marginal References; together with the Apocrypha and Index. Also, References and a Key sheet of Questions, Geographical, Historical, Doctrinal, Practical and Experimental; accompanied with valuable Chronological Harmonies of both Testaments; correct and elegant Maps and highly useful Tables of Scripture Names, Scripture Geography, Scripture Chronology, Scripture References, &c., &c., &c. By Hervey Wilbur, A. M. The Text corrected according to the standard of the American Bible Society. Stereotyped by James Conner, New York: Published by N. and J. White, No. 108 Pearl street. 1833. (E. A.) 4.

<small>This is a reissue of Wilbur's Reference Bible already described *supra*, p. 188. The Apocrypha contains pp. 1-78.</small>

4. HOLY BIBLE: With Apocrypha, Canne's Marginal References, Index, &c. The Text corrected according to the standard of the American Bible Society. Stereotyped by James Conner, New York. Brattlebro, Vt. Published by Peck and Wood. 1833. (L.) 4.

<small>This is another issue from the plates of Wilbur's Reference Bible, *supra* p. 188. It has a wood cut front., and 7 plates, but no Apocrypha.. I. Tim. 4:16 is incorrect.</small>

5. THE | HOLY BIBLE, | translated from the | Latin Vulgate: | diligently compared with the Hebrew, Greek, and other | editions, in divers Languages; | The | Old Testament, | first published by the | English College, at Douay, A. D. 1609; | and The | New Testament, | first published by The | English College, at Rheims, A. D. 1582. | With | Annota-

tions, References, | and | An Historical and Chronological Index. | From the last London and Dublin editions. | The whole revised and diligently compared with the Latin Vulgate. | Published with the approbation of the Right Rev. John Dubois, Catholic Bishop of N. Y. | New York: | Published by John Doyle, No. 12, Liberty street. | Stereotyped by Conner & Cooke. | 1833. | (L.; N. Y. State Lib.) 8.

Title, 1 f.; verso, Approbations, the Names and Order of all the Books of O. and N. Test., A short sketch of the Principal Epochs, note; Admonition, Letter of Pius the Sixth, A Prayer before reading the Scriptures, Translation of Decree of the Council of Trent, 1 p.; Catalogue of the Sacred Books, &c., 1 p.; Text: Gen. to II Maccab., pp. 5-752, sigs. 1 to 94, followed by four pages (interleaved) for Family Record, ruled with black lines, each page embraced within double ruled lines. New Testament (imprint as above) title, 1 f.; verso, The Books of the New Test.; the Sum of the N. T.; the Sum of the Four Gospels, marked 954 (for 754). Text: Mat. to Apoc., pp. 755-959; sigs. 95 to 120¼; verso, A Table of all the Epist. and Gosp.; Hist. and Chronol. Index to the Old Test., pp. 961-964; to the New Test., pp. 965, 966; Tables of Weights, &c., and of Time, at foot of p. 966; Table of References, pp. 967, 968; Table of Offices and Conditions of Men, at foot of p. 968. *Printed by* WM. PEARSON, 60 *Cliff St.* sigs. 121, all in 4ˢ. Both title pages are included within sigs 1 and 95.

The engravings are:

1. Abraham offering Isaac. Drawn by J. Thurston; engraved by *W. D. Smith.* Frontispiece.
2. Universal Peace, p. 533. Drawn by Westall; engraved by *W. D. Smith.*
3. Christ Tempted. Front. to N. T. Drawn by H. Corbould; engraved by *W. D. Smith.*
4. Christ's Agony, p. 795. Drawn by Corbould; engraved by *W. D. Smith.*

This is the first edition of Doyle's Catholic Bible. The Parallel References are printed at the foot, instead of at the side of the Text. It was published at prices ranging from $2.50 to $5. The cheaper copies have a wood cut of the Tower of Babel as a frontispiece; a wood cut of Solomon's Temple, and plates 2 and 4 *supra.* A transposition of lines occurs on p. 43, the latter part of v. 29 and the entire of v. 30 of chap. xlix- being inserted between the first line of v. 17 and the 18th verse.

Approbations of the Rt. Rev. Dr. Dubois and of the Rt. Rev. the Bishop of Charleston are printed on the reverse of the title.

6. THE | COTTAGE BIBLE, | and Family Expositor; | containing the | Old and New Testaments, | with | Practical Expositions and Explanatory Notes. | By Thomas Williams, | author of "The Age of Infidelity," in answer to Paine; a new Translation of Solomon's Song; an Historic Defence | of Experimental Religion; a Dictionary of all Religions, Religious Denominations, &c., &c. | To which are added, | The References and Marginal Readings | of the

Polyglott Bible, | together with Original Notes, and Selections from | Bagster's Comprehensive Bible, and other Standard works, | introductory and concluding Remarks on each Book of the Old and New Testaments, | and | A Valuable Chronological Index. | The whole carefully revised, | and adapted to the use of Sunday Schools, Bible Classes, | and Christians generally. | 𝔈𝔪𝔟𝔢𝔩𝔩𝔦𝔰𝔥𝔢𝔡 𝔴𝔦𝔱𝔥 𝔐𝔞𝔭𝔰 𝔞𝔫𝔡 𝔈𝔫𝔤𝔯𝔞𝔳𝔦𝔫𝔤𝔰. | Edited by Rev. William Patton. | Understandest thou what thou readest? &c.—*Acts* viii, 30, 31. | They read in the book, &c.—*Nehemiah* viii, 8. | Complete in Two Volumes. Vol. I. | New York: | Conner and Cooke, Franklin Buildings. | 1833. | 8.

Title, 1 f.; verso, Names and Order of the Books; The Chronological Order with abbreviations used in the References; Tables of Jewish Money, Weights and Measures; Notice of Copyright, 1833; Stereotyped by Conner & Cooke. H. Mason, Print. Preface to the London Edition; Preface to the Amer. Edition, dated New York, 1833; List of Authors consulted; Directions to the Reader, pp. 3, 4; Introduction, pp. 5-10; Text: Gen. to Solomon's Song, pp. 11-736; sigs. 1 to 92 in 4s, including Title and prel. pp.   Vol. II. Title as above, with Vol. II instead of Vol. I, 1 f.; verso, blank; Text: Isaiah to Mal., pp. 737-990; sigs 93 to 124³; Historical Connexion, pp. 991-994; on p. 994, Chronological Table; Genealogical Table of the Patriarchs, 1 p.; verso, blank; Fam. Rec. 2 ff. Cottage Bible. | The | New Testament | of our | Lord and Saviour Jesus Christ, | according to the | Authorized Version, | with | Practical Expositions, &c., as above, 1 f.; verso, blank; Introd. to N. Test., pp. 1003 to 1004 ; Text: Mat. to Rev., pp. 1005-1420; sigs. 126 to 178²; Index to the principal Notes, pp. 1421-1431; Chronological Index, pp. 1431-1440; sigs. 178³ to 180, in 4s; References in the centre of the pp.

The engravings are the same as in Conner & Cooke's 12mo, 1833, *post*, No. 9, except the wood cut entitled Massacre of the Innocents, which is omitted. Each vol. is accompanied by three maps.

The stereotype plates of the above Bible were sold by Mr. Conner to D. F. Robinson of Hartford, Ct., who published the work for several years. He sold them to Mr. Sumner of Hartford; now they are the property of Case, Lockwood & Co. of that city. *W. P.*

7. HOLY BIBLE: Stereotype Edition. New York: Stereotyped by A. Chandler, For the American Bible Society. 1833. D. Fanshaw, printer, 117 Nassau street.   (L.)   Sm. pica 8.

First edition, pp. 1214, with references.

8. HOLY BIBLE: With amendments of the language, by Noah Webster, LL. D.   New Haven: Published by Durrie and

Peck. Sold by Hezekiah Howe & Co. and A. H. Maltby, New Haven; and by N. & J. White, New York. 1833. (L.; N. Y. State Lib.; G. L.) 8.

First edition. Preface dated September, 1833. Pp. xvi, 907. The text is mainly from Collins' 4to edition, from which the error in 1 Tim. 4:16 is copied. The copy in the State Library has at the end of the vol. a slip containing Corrections in this edition. Mistranslations and Misprints corrected, in which it is stated that in "Job, xvii, 13, in the French Copy published by the American Bible Society, *thee* is used for *me.*"

9. THE | HOLY BIBLE; | containing the | Old and New Testaments, | according to the | Authorized Version; | with | Introductory and concluding Remarks | to—each Book of the Old and New Testaments; | and | the References and marginal readings | of the | Polyglott Bible, | with numerous additions from | Bagster's Comprehensive Bible; | and | A valuable chronological Index. | 𝔈𝔪𝔟𝔢𝔩𝔩𝔦𝔰𝔥𝔢𝔡 𝔴𝔦𝔱𝔥 𝔖𝔱𝔢𝔢𝔩 𝔈𝔫𝔤𝔯𝔞𝔳𝔦𝔫𝔤𝔰. | New York: | Conner & Cooke, Franklin Buildings. | 1833. | 12.

Title, 1 f.; verso, Names and Order of all the Books; Notice of copyright, 1833, by James Conner and William R. Cooke. Sleight & Van Norden, Print. Advertisement, 2 pp.; Introduction, pp. 3-11. Tables of Moneys, Weights and Measures; Table of Offices, foot of p. 11 and p. 12; sigs. (including Title) A to B[1]; Historical connexion, pp. 13-18; Introd. to N. T., pp. 19, 20; Introd. and conclud. Remarks on each Book of the O. and N. T., pp. 21-70; sigs. B[2] to F in 6s. Text: Gen. to Mal., pp. 3-716; p. 668 is marked 558; sig. 1[2] to 60[4]; New Testament &c. First Edition. Imprint as above; 1 p.; verso, blank (sig. 60[5]); Text: Mat. to Rev., pp. 719-937; verso, blank; sigs. 60[6] to 79[1]. Chron. Index, pp. 939-961; sigs. 79[2] to 81[1], followed by 3 blank leaves. Sigs. in 6s.

Engravings:
Scripture Genealogy, from Adam to Christ.................Milan del., *Dick* sc.
Jacob's Dream..(woodcut *J. A. Adams*).
Sampson carrying off the Gates of Gaza.................Lucas pinx., *Smellie* sc.
Elisha restoring the Widow's Son..................Painted by West, *Longacre* sc.
Christ blessing the bread; Front. to N. T..........Carlo Dolci pinx., *F. Kearny* sc.
Massacre of the Innocents.............................(woodcut by *Adams*).
Christ blessing little children........................West pinx., *F. Kearny* sc.
The Crucifixion. ....J. Martin pinx., *W. Keenan* sc.

Being desirous that the Polyglott Bible should appear with a few wood engravings, Mr. Conner secured the services of J. A. Adams, Esq., to execute them in the highest and most finished style of the art. All the arrangements completed, he had the satisfaction of publishing a splendid edition of the Bible as an annual New Year's present. *N. Y. Printer.*

This edition is known as The Bible Annual, and the copy before us is endorsed "Annual 1834."

10. HOLY BIBLE: Hartford: Published by Gilman and McKillip. 1833. 12.

Title, 1 f.; verso, The Property of ———— Names and Order, 1 p.; verso, blank; Text: Gen. to Mal. (not paged); sigs. A to Cc¹²; verso, Tables of Kindred and Time. New Test., Hartford: published by Hudson & Skinner. 1 f.; verso, blank; Text: Mat. to Rev.; sigs. Dd to Ll; last p., Table of Offices.

11. HOLY BIBLE: Stereotyped by J. Howe......Philadelphia. Hartford, Ct. Published by Andrus & Judd. 1833. 12.

A reprint, seemingly, of Silas Andrus's 12mo of 1828, with new title pages, but without plates.

12. HOLY BIBLE: Stereotype edition. Hartford: Published by Andrus & Judd. 1833. 12 or 24.

Stereotyped by A. Chandler, pp. 824, 251 in 6s; 2 steel engr. in front of O. T.

13. HOLY BIBLE: Stereotyped by James Conner. Elizabethtown, N. J.: Printed and published by Edward Sanderson. 1833. 12.

14. **Die Bibel,** | oder | Die Ganze | **Heilege Schrift** | des | Alten und Neuen | Testaments. | Nach Dr. Martin Luther's Uebersetzung. | Zwölfte Auflage | Stereotypirt von J. Howe, Philadelphia. | Philadelphia, | Gedruckt für die Amerikanische Bibel-Gesellschaft, | bey Georg W. Mentz und Sohn, Buchhändler, | Nro. 53, in der Nord-Drittenstrasse. | 1833. | (L.)   12.

Title, 1 p.; Verzeichniss, 1 p.; Text: Gen. to Mal. pp. 3–828; sigs. A² to 3T⁶ in 6s. Title to N. T., Das | Neue Testament | unsers | Herrn und Heilandes | Jesu Christi. | Nach Dr. Martin Luthers Uebersetzung. | Stereotypirt von J. Howe, Philadelphia. | Philadelphia, | as above, 1833. | 1 p.; verso, Verzeichniss der Bücher, &c., 1 p.; Text: Mat. to Rev., pp. 3–269. Verzeichniss der Episteln, &c., 270–273; sigs. A² to X⁵, in 6s; a blank leaf completes the last sig.

15. HOLY BIBLE, containing the Old Testament and the New. Seventh stereotype edition. New York: Published by N. & J. White, 108 *Pearl-street*. 1833. 24.

Same as No. 11 of 1827, and No. 20 of 1832.

1. A | NEW AND CORRECTED VERSION | of | The New Testament; | or, a | minute revision, and professed Translation | of the original | Histories, Memoirs, Letters, Prophecies, | and other productions of the | Evangelists and Apostles; | To which | are subjoined, a few, generally brief, critical, explanatory, and | practical Notes. | By Rodolphus Dickinson, | a Presbyter of the Protestant Episcopal Church in the United States; and Rector of St. | Paul's parish, District of Pendleton, South Carolina. | Boston: | Published by Lilly, Wait, Colman, & Holden. | 1833. | (L.; G. L.) 8.

Mock Title, Dickinson's | Corrected Version | of the | Christian Scriptures, 1 p.; verso, blank; Portrait, Schaver pinx., Eddy sculp.; below, Rodolphus Dickinson, Pastor of the Episcopal Parish, Montague, Massachusetts. Then, Title, 1 p ; verso, extract of Copyright, dated 1831; Dedication, dated Deerfield, Franklin Co., Massachusetts, January 1, 1833, pp. v, vi; Preface, pp. vii–xviii; References, 1 p.; verso, blank; Divisions, 1 p.; verso, blank; Subdivisions, pp. xxiii–xl; Text: pp. 41–381; verso of 381, blank; Appendix, pp. 383–499; verso, Names of Subscribers; sigs. 1 to verso of 63^2 in 4^s.

Mr. Dickinson has *reformed* the titles of the several books of the New Testament, substituting for those generally received such as the following: *History by Matthew ; Luke's History of Apostolic and Ecclesiastical Transactions ; John's General Address to Christians ; John's Letter to an Eminent Christian Woman ; John's Letters, Visions, and Prophecies.* Whether there is not a ridiculous affectation in all this, let our readers judge. This work is announced on the title-page as a *professed* translation. By this we are, it is presumed, to understand, that it is not an *actual* translation, but a concoction of materials in the vernacular tongue, designed to pass as a new translation. And we are very willing to believe it a professed translation ; for a pretty thorough examination has failed to shew us the faintest traces of a critic's hand. Where ill-chosen and ill-arranged phraseology has not made the work utterly unintelligible, the sense is generally the same with that of the received version, with here and there a modification borrowed from Campbell or Macknight......Apart from its literary execution, this *professed translation* has no distinctive character : and, as the author (in his preface) places his chief reliance on the rhetorical embellishments with which he has adorned the sacred text, we are constrained to award a verdict of unqualified condemnation.

The notes which form the Appendix to this volume, are principally selected from English and American writers. They are excerpted indifferently from writers of widely varying creeds......He has introduced many annotations from works not professedly critical. He has elevated some men to the rank of commentators on Scripture, who surely never anticipated that honour. He gives us on the Logos a note from Jefferson, and several of the largest notes are credited to J. Q. Adams, Chancellor Kent and Wirt. The Free Enquirer, an *infidel paper* published at New York, furnishes several short remarks. And there are some original notes, tinged with the translator's usual grandiloquence."—*Am. Monthly Review for March,* 1833, iii, 221, 222, 223.

A correspondent, who has examined this volume, declares it to be "one of the most absurd attempts to improve the authorized version that has ever been attempted."

The following are some of the renderings:

Luke 1:31. And behold, you shall be in a state of gestation.
 38. Behold the handmaid of the Lord; may it be to me in conformity to thy disclosure.
 41. When Elizabeth heard the salutation of Mary, the embryo was joyfully agitated....and Elizabeth was pervaded by the Holy Spirit.
 42. Blessed are you among women! and blessed is your incipient offspring!
 44. When your salutation sounded in my ears, the embryo was enlivened with joy.
John 3: 3. Except a man be reproduced, he cannot realize the reign of God.
 4. Nicodemus says to him, How can a man be produced when he is mature? Can he again pass into a state of embryo, and be produced? &c.
Acts 1:18. And (Judas) falling prostrate, a violent, internal spasm ensued, and all his viscera were emitted.
26:24. Festus declared with a loud voice: Paul you are insane! Multiplied research drives you to distraction.
1 Tim. 4:16. Attend to yourself, and to your doctrine.

2. NEW TESTAMENT: Stereotype edition. Stereotyped by A. Chandler, For the American Bible Society. 1833. (Am. Bib. Soc.)   Sm. Pica, 8.

Pp. 1214; marginal notes in the centre. This seems to be a part of the Bible, No. 7, *supra* p. 222.

3. THE | VILLAGE TESTAMENT: | according to | the Authorized Version, | with | Notes, original and selected; | likewise | Introductions and Concluding Remarks | to each Book, | Polyglott References and Marginal Readings, | Chronological Table, | Geographical Index, | and Maps, | adapted to | Bible Classes and Sunday Schools. | By Rev. William Patton. | Two Volumes in one. | New York: | Published by Conner & Cooke, Franklin Buildings. | 1833. | (Am. Bib. Soc. Lib.)   12.

Title, 1 f.; verso, Names and Order of the Books, Chronol. Order of the Books, Tables of Money, Time, and Length. Notice of copyright by James Conner and William Cooke, 1833, *Stereotyped by Conner & Cooke, New York;* Preface signed W. P., dated New York, Sept., 1833, pp. 3, 4; Introd. pp. 5–12; these form sig. 1. Text: Mat. to Rev. pp. 13–710; Geographical Index, pp. 711–717; Chronol. Index foot of p. 717 and p. 718; sig. 2* to 60^5; a blank leaf completes the last sig.; all in 6s; 3 maps, viz: Map of the Travels of St. Paul; of Canaan adapted to Gospel History; of Canaan, for general purposes. The Text is in paragraphs; the references are on the outer margin; the Notes at the foot of the page. The several pages are within parallel rules.

This Commentary contains much that is found in the Notes upon the New Testament of the Cottage Bible.—*Preface.*

4. NEW TESTAMENT: New-York: Published by Daniel Cooledge, Bookseller, 322 Pearl-Street. 1833. 12.

Rev. ends on p. 321, which contains also, A Table of St. Paul's Apostolic Journeys; Historical Facts in Sacred History; pp. 322–324. There is a wood cut on centre of title page.

5. NEW TESTAMENT: Translated from the Latin Vulgate. Stereotype edition. Utica: Printed by William Williams for the Proprietors. 1833. 12.

This is the Devereux Testament, originally published in 1829. See No. 2, *supra*, p. 198. The error in James, 5 : 17, is continued.

6. NEW TESTAMENT: Stereotype edition. Boston: Lilly, Wait and Company. 1833. (L.) 12.

Pp. 453. Table of Offices, 1 p.

7. THE | ENGLISH VERSION | of the | Polyglott NEW TESTAMENT, | with marginal | readings and references. | Concord, N. H. | Coffin, Roby, Hoag & Co. | 1833. | (L.) 12.

Front. and engr. and printed Title.

8. NEW TESTAMENT: Stereotyped by James Conner, New-York. Concord, N. H.: Printed and Published by Horatio Hill & Co. n. d. 12.

Pp. 226, including Title, in 6^s.

9. NEW TESTAMENT: Stereotyped by Hammond Wallis, New York. Windsor (Vt.), Ide and Goddard's Power Press. n. d. 12.

Same as Ide's New Testament of 1832.

10. NEW TESTAMENT: Hartford: Published by R. White. Stereotyped by L. Johnson, Phila. 1833. 12.

Pp. 259.

11. NEW TESTAMENT: New York: Stereotyped by James Conner, for the American Bible Society. 1833. 16.

43d edition, pp. 226.

12. NEW TESTAMENT: Stereotyped by J. Howe, Philadelphia. Trenton, N. J. Bishop Davenport. 1833. (G. L.) 16.
Pp. 252.

13. NEW TESTAMENT: Stereotyped by Henry Wallis & Luther Roby, Concord, N. H. Published by Coffin, Roby, Hoag & Co. 1833. (L.) 18.

14. NEW TESTAMENT: With the Marginal Readings; and illustrated by Original References, both Parallel and Explanatory, and a Copious Selection, carefully chosen, and newly arranged. With numerous engravings, *and the sterling currency reduced to dollars and cents.* New York: John C. Riker, 15 Ann-Street. Stereotyped by James Conner. 1833. 32.

Engraved title, with Vignette; The Polyglott New Testament, with Marginal Readings, illustrated with numerous engravings. New York: Published by J. C. Riker, Franklin buildings, 1831; Title, 1 f.; verso, Order of the Books; Preface, pp. ii; Text: Mat. to Rev. pp. 3-350; sig. A (which includes T. and Pref.) to I in 8s, K in 2s, then G in 6s, and L in 8s, M in 16s, O to U in 8⁴, V in 5s, followed by T in 3s and W in 8s. The marginal readings are in the centre of the page, between the columns of text, with the sterling currency reduced to dollars and cents.

The illustrations are: The Holy Family, *Front.*; Murder of the Innocents; Christ Blessing Little Children; Prodigal Son; Crucifixion.

Each of the books is headed by a wood engraving, illustrating some portion of the text.

15. KEKITCHEMANITOMENAHN | Gahbemahjeinnunk | Jesus Christ, | Oloashke | Wawweendummahgawin. | Albany: | Packard and Van Benthuysen, printers. | 1833. | (L.) 12.

This is a Translation of the New Testament into the Chippewa language, by Dr. Edwin James, assisted by John Tanner. At the end are the Ten Commandments and a Hymn in the same language.

16. NE RAORIHWADOGENNHTI ne Shongwayaner Yesus Keristus jiniihorihoten ne Royatadogenhti LUKE. New York: Printed by McElrath, Bangs & Herbert, for the Young Men's Bible Society, Methodist Church. 1833. 12.

This is a Translation of the Gospel of St. Luke into the Mohawk language by A. Hill, corrected by J. A. Wilkes, Jr., of Grand River, C. W. The English and Indian are parallel.

1834.

1. HOLY BIBLE: Stereotype edition. New York: Stereotyped by A. Chandler and printed by D. Fanshaw; For the American Bible Society. 1834. (Am. Antiq. Soc., Worcester: Friends' Assoc., Phil.) Pica 4.

Title, 1 f.; verso, Names and Order of the Books; Text: Gen. to Mal., pp. 3-793; verso of 793, Table of Measures, Weights, Time; 2 ff. blank for Fam. Rec. New Test. Title, 1 p.; verso, blank; Text: Mat. to Rev., pp. 797-1043. Sigs. in 4s. References in centre of the page.

2. HOLY BIBLE: With Canne's Marginal references, Key sheet of Questions, &c., &c. By Harvey Wilbur. Text corrected according to the Standard of the American Bible Society. Stereotyped by James Conner, New York. New York: Published by E. & J. White, No. 108 Pearl Street. 1834. (L.) 4.

This is another issue of Wilbur's Reference Bible, *supra* p. 188. The copyright is dated August, 1825, and there are engraved frontispieces to the Old and New Testaments. The imprint to the New Test. is—New York: Published by N. & J. White. E. Sanderson printer, Elizabethtown, N. Jersey, 1837.

3. HOLY BIBLE: Cooperstown, N. Y.: Stereotyped, printed and published by H. & E. Phinney & Co. 1834. (L.) 4.

No wood cuts nor Apocrypha; N. Test. title is dated 1835.

4. HOLY BIBLE: With Apocrypha, Canne's Marginal Notes and References, Index, Tables and Concordance. Philadelphia: Stereotyped and published by C. Alexander & Co., Athenian Buildings, Franklin Place, and sold by all the principal booksellers in the United States. 1834. (L.) 4.

25 Maps and Engravings from M. Carey's worn out plates; some of them dated 1805.

5. HOLY BIBLE: New York: Stereotyped by A. Chandler, for the American Bible Society. 1834. Sm. Pica 8.

With References.

6. HOLY BIBLE: New York: For the Auxiliary New York Bible and Common Prayer Book Society, Depository 46 Lumber street. 1834. 12.

Pp. 1014.

7. HOLY BIBLE: Stereotype edition. New York: Stereotyped by A. Chandler, Printed by D. Fanshaw, For the American Bible Society. 1834. (Am. Antiq. Soc., Worcester; G. L.) 12.

Reference Bible; 1st edition, pp. 984; References in 2 columns, in the centre of the pages.

8. HOLY BIBLE. Stereotype Edition. **Boston**: Published for the Booksellers. 1834. 12.

Title, 1 f.; verso, blank; Names and Order of all the Books, 1 p.; verso, Account of the Dates; Text: Gen. to Rev. pp. 5–805; verso of 605, Tables of Scripture Measures and of Time; followed by one blank leaf for Fam. Rec.; sigs. A^3 to Cc^3; (mock Title), Stereotype Edition. The New Testament, &c., no date 1 p.; verso, blank; Text: Mat. to Rev., pp. 609–792; sigs. Cc^5 to Kk^{12}, all in 12^s.

This edition agrees in every respect (except the mock title and the leaf for Fam. Rec.) with Websters and Skinners' Albany 12mo.

1 Tim. 4:16 is incorrect.

9. THE | HOLY BIBLE, | containing | the Old Testament | and the New, | translated out of | **The Original Tongues**: | and | with former Translations | diligently compared and revised. | The Text of the common Translation is arranged in Paragraphs, | such as the sense requires: The divisions of Chapters and | Verses being noted in the margin, for Reference. | By James Nourse. | Boston: | Perkins, Marvin & Co. | Philadelphia: | Henry Perkins. | 1834. | (L). 12.

Title, 1 f.; verso, Extract of Copyright, dated 1834; Stereotyped by J. Howe, Phil. (This leaf is preceded by an advertisement and followed by) Preface, pp. iii-vii; verso of vii, Names and Order: Text: Gen. to Mal. pp. 9–942, followed by a blank leaf; Title to New Test. 1 f.; verso, Names of Books; Text. Mat. to Rev., pp. 3–322, followed by Recommendations, 2 pp; sigs. 6^s.

The following misprint occurs in this edition: Rom. 4:5—his faith is counted for unrighteousness.

10. HOLY BIBLE: Arranged in Paragraphs and Parallelisms, with philological and explanatory Annotations. By T. W.

Coit, D. D., Rector of Christ Church, Cambridge. Cambridge: Printed by and for Manson & Grant. Boston: Published by William Pierce, and sold by all the Booksellers throughout the United States. 1834. (Boston Athenæum; G. L.) 12.

Title, 1 f.; verso, Notice of Copyright; Preface, dated Nov. 3, 1834, pp. iii–viii; The Translators to the Reader, pp. ix–xix; Table of Jewish Measures, Weights and Coins, pp. xx–xxii; Jewish Modes of Computing Time, pp. xxiii–xxiv; Names and Order of Books, p. xxv; verso of xxv, blank; Text: Gen. to Mal., pp. 1–963; New Test. title, 1 p.; verso, copyright; Books of the New Test.; Table of Dates, 1 p.; Text: Mat. to Rev , pp. 1–230.

This edition is accompanied by brief occasional explanations of verbal difficulties &c., surprisingly condensed, with the Chronology on each page. It has, also, what has never before appeared in any American edition, the original Address of the Translators to the Reader, as it appeared in the first edition of King James' Bible in 1611' Dr. Coit has retained in the inner margin of this edition the number designating the chapters and verses in the common division.—*Amer. Baptist Magazine*, xv, 99.

This work has been reprinted in London in 1838.

11. HOLY BIBLE: Boston: Published by Nathan Hale, Devonshire Street; Cottons and Barnard, Washington Street. 1834. (G. L.) 12.

Pp. 510, 162; 8 wood cut maps.

12. HOLY BIBLE: Stereotyped by B. & J. Collins, New York. Hartford, Ct. Normand Burr. 1834. 12.

The date on the title page is torn off, but the vol. is accompanied by Psalms in Metre, same imprint, with date 1834.

13. HOLY BIBLE: Stereotyped by B. and J. Collins, New York. Pittsburgh (Penn.): Published by Johnston and Stockton. 1834. (L.) 12.

14. THE RIGHT-AIM SCHOOL BIBLE; comprising the Holy Bible of the Old and New Testament, and an Annexment containing the Free-Debt-Rule Petitions, addressed, the first to the Twenty-four States, the Second to the Congress, the Third to the President, of the United States of America, and affixed Memorials; the Fourth Petition to three High

Officers of the Government of England. Also the Declaration of Freedebtism. Rufus Davenport. Stereotype Print. 1834. (Harvard Coll.) 12.

On the subject of Freedom from debt on the surrender of property; on the principle of the petition in the Lord's Prayer, Forgive us &c.

15. **Die Bibel,** | ober | Die ganze | **Heilige Schrift** | des | alten und neun | Testaments. | Nach Dr. Martin Luther's Uebersetzung. | Zwölfte Auflage. | Stereotypirt von J. Howe, Philadelphia. | Philadelphia, | Gedruckt für die Amerikanische Bibel-Gesellschaft, | bey Georg W. Mentz und Sohn, Buchhändler, | Nro. 53, in der Nord-Drittenstraße. | 1834. | (Am. Bib. Soc.) 12.

This is a continuation of No. 14, of 1833, with Testament of 1835.

16. HOLY BIBLE: Stereotyped by J. Howe, Philad. Hartford, Ct. Published by Andrus & Judd. 1834. 12.

17. HOLY BIBLE, containing the Old Testament and the New. Hartford, Ct.: Published by Andrus & Judd. 1834. 24.

Pp. 729, 225.

18. HOLY BIBLE: Amherst, Ms. J. S. & C. Adams. Stereotyped by L. Johnson. 1834. 24.

Pp. 856, 259. There are other copies without date.

19. HOLY BIBLE: Philadelphia: Hogan and Thompson, 139 Market Street. 1834. (L.) 32.

Pp. 819, 256; at end, Psalms in metre, additional. Other copies (without Psalms) have an engraved title page with imprint as above, and a printed title with imprint: Philadelphia, Alexander Towar, also Hogan & Thompson, 139¼ Market street. *Stereotyped by L. Johnson.* 1832.

20. HOLY BIBLE, containing the Old Testament and the New. Stereotyped by Henry Wallis & Luther Roby, Concord, N. H. Concord, N. H.: Published by C. & A. Hoag. 1834. 32.

Pp. 852, 258; engraved title: The Everlasting Gospel. Imprint as above.

21. ISAIAH: A New Translation: With a preliminary Discourse and Notes. By Robert Lowth, D. D., F. R. SS., Lond. and Goet., &c. From the Tenth English Edition. Boston: William Hilliard, 14 Water Street. Cambridge: James Munroe and Company. 1834.   8.
Pp. 423.

22. THE | CHILD'S | BIBLE, | with Plates. | Vignette, a King's head. | By a Lady of Cincinnati. | Stereotyped by J. A. James, No. 1 Baker street, Cincinnati, Ohio. | Philadelphia: | Henry F. Conners. | n. d.   (L.)   142.
Wood cut engravings. Copyright dated 1834; The Text is the same as that of No. 7, of 1811. See *supra*, p. 106.

1. NEW TESTAMENT. Translated from the Latin Vulgat: Philadelphia: Published by Eugene Cummiskey. 1834.
Edition 500 copies.

2. NEW TESTAMENT: | arranged in paragraphs and parallelisms, | with philological and explanatory annotations. | By T. W. Coit, D. D. | Rector of Christ Church, Cambridge. | Cambridge: | Printed by and for Manson & Grant. | Boston: | Published by William Peirce, | and sold by all booksellers throughout the United States. | 1834. | (A. G. J.)   12.
This seems to be the New Test. of the Bible No. 1 *supra*, published separately.

3. THE RIGHT AIM TESTAMENT: comprising the text of the New Testament and an annexment of Free Debt rules. By Rufus Davenport. Boston. 1834.   (L.)   12.
The Testament of Bible No. 14 *supra*, published separately.

4. THE | NEW TESTAMENT | of our | Lord and Saviour | Jesus Christ; | translated out of the | Latin Vulgate, | diligently compared with | the Original Greek, | and first published by | the English College of Rheims, | Anno 1582. | With the | Original Preface, | Arguments and Tables, | Marginal Notes, | and | Annotations. | To which are now added, | An Introductory Essay; | and a | complete Topical and Textual Index. | New York: | Published by Jonathan

Leavitt, | 182 Broadway. | Boston: Crocker and Brewster, | 47 Washington street. | 1834. | (L.; Am. Antiq. Soc. Worcester, Mass.) 8.

Title, 1 f.; verso, Certificate of copyright, dated 1833., John H. Turney's stereotype; Notice, Recommendations and Certificate, pp. iii, iv; Introductory Address to Protestants, pp. 5–8; Preface, pp. 9–23; Books of the New Test. ; Introd. Remarks, pp. 24, 25, Sum of the New Test., foot of p. 25 ; Sum of the Four Gospels, p. 26; Text: Mat. to Apocal. pp. 27–438; Appendix, 1 p.; Explication of certain words, 1 p.; Index, pp. 441–458, in 8s.

This edition is accompanied by a certificate in these words:

" We have compared this New-York edition of the Romish Testament and Annotations with the first publication of that volume, which was issued at Rheims, in 1582; and, after examination, we do hereby certify, that the present reprint is an exact and faithful copy of the original work, without abridgment or addition, except that the Latin of a few phrases which were translated by the annotators, and some unimportant expletive words were undesignedly omitted. The orthography also has been modernized."

The reader can judge for himself how far this is correct, by comparing the few extracts we give below (those marked (F.) being found also in the edition of the Rhemes Testament published in London, and known as *Fulke's Confutation*):

From the RHEMES edition, 1582.	From the NEW YORK edition, 1834.
Preface, p. 1. We haue yet through God's goodnes at length fully finished for thee (most Christian reader) all the New Testament,	*Preface*, p. 9. We have at length fully furnished all the New Testament.
more agreable to God's word and honour or edification of the faithful,	more agreeable to God's word and honour, or edification for faith,
p. 2. the dispensing of Gods mysteries and treasures	the dispensing of God's mysteries, and measures
and George the Patriarch	and Gregory the Patriarch, (F.)
The Slauonians affirme they haue the Scriptures	The Sclavonians assume they have the Scriptures.
p. 7. such as either contemne	p. 12. such as either condemn
p. 11. the same church which the holy Scripture most certainly and euidently sheweth and pointeth vnto.	p. 16. ......which the holy Scripture most certainly and evidently showeth and appointeth unto.
p. 13. one English Bible of the yere 1562, foloweth the errour of the Greeke.	p. 17. one English Bible of the year 1562, following the error of the Greek.
It were infinite to set downe al such places, where the aduersaries, especially Beza, follow the old vulgar Latin	It were difficult to set down all such places, where &c.
as *Mat.* 6 to the end of the *Pater noster*	as Mark 6, to the end of the Paternoster.

p. 13. and reprehendeth Valla Marc 6, 11, these wordes, *Amen I say to you*	p. 17. and reprehendeth *Ulla* Matt. 6, 11; these words: Amen &c.
it is no derogation to the vulgar Latin text.... to disagree from the Greeke	it is no derogation to the vulgar Latin text.... not to disagree from the Greek.
and this the Aduersary himself, their greatest and latest translatour of the Greeke, doth auouch	and this the adversary himself, their greatest and latest translations of the Greek, doth avonch
p. 14. Whereunto the latin translations that faile in any place, must needes yeld. *Li* 2 *de doct. Christ*, c. 15.	whereunto the Latin translations that fail in every place must need yield. *Lib.* 2, *de doct. Christ.* 25.
If these marginal Greeke copies If al Erasmus Greeke copies haue not that which is in the vulgar Latin	p. 18. If these original Greek copies If all Erasmus' Greek copies have not that which is the vulgar Latin.
Gagnele the Frenche Kings preacher; and he that might commannde in al the King's libraries, he found Greeke copies	Gagniez found Greek copies
p. 18. Was Primasius....a Papist, for vsing this text, and al the rest, that haue done the like?	p. 20. Was Primasius....a Papist, for using this text, and all the rest, they have done the like?
p. 22. Fare wel good Reader, and if we profit the any whit by our poor paines.	p. 23. Farewell, reader, and if we profit thee anywhat by our poor pains
Argument of S. Mat. Gospel. Of S. Matthew we haue	p. 27. Of Saint Matthew we hear
Text, p 14. Note to Mat. c. v, 33. as it is most plaine in S. Marke and S. Luke, who leaue out this exception.	p. 32. as it is most plain in Mark and Luke, who leave out this exposition. (F.)
p. 24. Note to c. ix, 21. Where it [the image of Christ] was (as Sozomenus writeth) unto his time.	p. 38. where it was, as Sozonemus writeth, unto this time.
p. 45. Note to c. xvi, 17. for the beleefe and publike profession thereof he [Peter] is counted blessed	p. 49. for the belief and public possession thereof he is counted blessed.
p. 46, l. 27. Which doth expressly stop them of al their vaine evasions.	p. 49. Which doth expressly stop them of all their evasions. (F.)
p. 47, l. 17. Peter....upon whom our Lord built.	p. 50. Peter....upon whom the Lord built. (F.)
p. 61. Note on Mat. xxi, 8. holy church maketh a solemne Procession every yere vpon this day, specially in our Countrie when it was Catholike, with the B. Sacrament,	p. 57. holy church maketh a solemn Procession every year upon this day, with the B. Sacrament

We might add other passages wherein the N. Y. edition varies from the original, but these will suffice. Before taking leave of the subject, however, we can not but express a regret, that "the Latin of a few phrases...... were undesignedly omitted;" as the omission renders obscure, if not wholly unintelligible in the reprint, parts of the Preface which, if printed as in the original, would be clear and therefore appreciated by the Biblical scholar.

5. THE VILLAGE TESTAMENT: | according to | the authorized version, | with | Notes, original and selected; | likewise | Introductions and concluding Remarks | to each Book, | Polyglott References and Marginal Readings, | Geographical Index, | Chronological and other Tables : | adapted to | Bible Classes and Sunday Schools. | By Rev. William Patton. | Second Edition. | New York: | Published by Henry C. Sleight. | Sold by Booksellers generally, throughout the Union. | 1834. | 12.

This is the edition of 1833 with a new Title page ; 3 Maps.

6. NEW TESTAMENT. Stereotype Edition. New York: Stereotyped by James Conner for the American Bible Society. 1834. 12.

49th edition ; pp. 226 ; headings to columns and chapters.

7. NEW TESTAMENT. New York: Stereotyped by A. Chandler for the American Bible Society. 1834. Pearl, 32.

8. NEW TESTAMENT: Concord, N. H. Charles Hoag. 1834. (L.) 32.

With Bible of 1836. q. v.

9. NEW TESTAMENT: Arranged in Paragraphs such as the Sense requires, &c. By James Nourse. Boston: Perkins, Marvin and Co. Philadelphia: Henry Perkins. 1834. (L.) 12.

10. AN EXPOSITION of the Gospels of St. Matthew and St. Mark, and of several other detached parts of Holy Scriptures. By Rev. Richard Watson. New York. 1834. (Doyle's Catalogue.) 8.

The author had contemplated writing Expository Notes on the entire New Testament; but lived only to complete his Commentary on the Gospels of St. Matthew and St. Mark, and on Luke i-xiii, 15, and Romans i-iii, 21.—*Horne.*

11. THE | GENERAL HISTORY | of the | Christian Church, | from | her birth | to | her final triumphant state in Heaven : | Chiefly deduced from the APOCALYPSE of St. John, | the Apostle and Evangelist. | By Sig. Pastorini. | Second American edition. | New York : | Published by J. Doyle, No. 12 Liberty Street. Stereotyped by Conner & Cooke. 1834. (L.) 12.

Pp. 396; with portrait of the Right Rev. Charles Walmesley, the author. He was Catholic Bishop of the Western district, England. The Apocalypse extends from p. 362 to 394 inclusive.

1835.

1. LA BIBLIA | Vulgata Latina | Traducida en Español, | y anotada | conforme al Sentido de los Santos padres | y espositores católicos, | Por el ilustrisimo Señor | Don Felipe Scio de San Miguel, | Provincial que fué del órden de las escuelas pias de Castilla, | Preceptor del Serenisimo Señor Principe de | Asturias, y Obispo de Segovia. | Tomo I. | del Antiguo Testamento. | El Genesis y el Exodo. | Primera Edicion Megicana, | Sacada de la tercera y última de España. | Mégico : | En casa de Cornelio C. Sebring. | 1831. | (Am. Bib. Soc.) 4.

This Work is in Ten Volumes, divided into 20 parts. Vol. I., part i; Engraved Title page—Antiguo | Testamento | (near the top); at foot—Mégico : | Edicion de Sebring. | Then Title as given above, 1 p.; Licencia & Decreto; Nota del Revisar, 1 p.; Advertencia & Nota, pp. 5–9; Disertacion preliminar, pp. 10—part of 33; Dissertacion Segunda, rest of p. 33–46; Introduction, pp. 47—part of 56; Advertencia, rest of p. 56; Los Libros de las Sanctas Escrituras, p. 57; Advertencia al Pentateuchas y al Genesis de Moises, pp. 58–60; El Genesis, pp. 61–343; sigs. (beginning with printed title) 1 to recto of 43^4 in 4^s. Text in two columns ; Notes below. 2d part contains Exodus, pp. 339–563; Advertencia, pp. 339–340; Text (Latin and Spanish) : pp. 341–556; Indice, pp. 557–563; verso of pp. 563, Errata, sigs. 44–71^2.

Vol. II. Title as above, except that from the word " conforme " to " católicos " is one line; Vol. marked, Tomo II. | and after the word " Testamento," | El Levitico, los Números y el Deuteronomio. | 1 p.; verso, blank; Advertencia, 2 pp.; Leviticus, pp. 5–135; p. 136, blank; Advertencia, pp. 137–139; p. 140, blank; Numbers, pp. 141–322; Adver., pp. 323, 324; Deuteronomy, pp. 325–478; Indice, pp. 479–484; sigs. 1–61$_2$.

Vol. III. Title as in Vol. I, except Tomo III. | and after the word " Testamento," Josué, Jueces, Rut y Libro I. II. III. & IV de los Reyes. | 1 p.; verso, blank; Adv. pp. 3, 4; Josué, pp. 5–112; Adv. pp. 113, 114; Jueces, pp. 115–228; Adv. 229; p.

230, blank; Rut, pp. 231-247; p. 248, blank; Adv. pp. 249-251; p. 252, blank; Reyes, pp. 253-148 (*sic.* for 814); Indice, pp. 815-826; sigs. 1-103⁵.

Vol. IV. Title as of Vol. I, except Tomo IV. | after the word "Testamento," Los dos Libros de los Paralipomenos, los dos de Esdras, el de Tobias, | el de Judit y el de Ester. | Imprint, Méjico | En casa de Sebring y West. | 1832. | 1 p.; verso, blank; Adv. pp. 3-5; p. 6 blank; Paral. pp. 7-269: Adv. p. 270; Esdras, pp. 271-372; Adv. pp. 373, 4; Tobias, pp. 317-417; p. 418 blank; Adv. pp. 419-421; p. 422, blank; Judit, pp. 423-475; p. 476 blank; Adv. pp. 477, 478; Ester, pp. 479-530; Indice, pp. 531-539; sigs. pp. 1-682.

Vol. V. Title as in I, except Tomo V. | after "Testamento," El Libro de Job con su paráfrasis, y el de los Salmos. | 1 p.; verso, blank; Adv. pp. 3-6; Job, pp. 7-155; p. 156 blank; Version parafrassica del Libro de Job, pp. 157-214; Adv., 215-223; p. 224, blank; Salmos, pp. 225-632; Indice, pp. 633-644; sigs. pp. 1-81².

Vol. VI. Title as of I, except Tomo VI. | after "Testamento," Version de S. Gerónimo de los Salmos, y la Paráfrasis de todos ellos, | los Proverbos, el Eclesiastes, el Cantar de Cantares y la Sabiduria. | 1 p.; verso, blank; Version des Gerónimo pp. 3-99; p. 100 blank; Parafrasis, pp. 101-265; p. 266 blank; Adv. pp. 267-269; p. 270 blank; Prov. pp. 271-385; p. 386 blank; Adv. pp. 387-388; Eccles. pp. 389-430; Adv. pp. 431-434; El Cantar, pp. 435-495; p. 496 blank; Adv. pp. 497, 498; La Sab. pp. 499-568; Indice, pp. 569-574; sigs. 1-72³.

Vol. VII. Title as of I, except Tomo VII. | after "Testamento," El Libro de Ecclesiástico y la Profecie de Isaias. | Imprint, En casa de Sebring y Compañia. | 1833. | 1 p.; verso, blank; Adv. pp. 3, 4; Ecclesiastico, pp. 5-218; Adv. pp. 219-221; p. 222 blank; Isaias, pp. 223-489; p. 490 blank; Indice, pp. 491-499; p. 500 blank; sigs. 1-63².

Vol. VIII. Title as in I, except Tomo VIII. | after "Testamento," La Profecia y los Trenos de Jeremias, con la Parafrasis, la Profecia | de Baruc y lo de Ezequiel. | Imprint, En casa de Sebring y West. | 1833. | 1 p.; verso, blank; Adv. pp. 3-5; p. 6 blank; Jerem. pp. 7-262; Adv. pp. 263, 264; Trenos, pp. 265-309; p. 310 blank; Adv. pp. 311, 312; Baruc, pp. 313-345; p. 346, blank; Adv. pp. 347, 348; Ezequiel, pp. 349-589; p. 590 blank; Indice, pp. 591-599; sigs. 1-75³.

Vol. IX. Title as of I, except Tomo IX. | after Testamento, La Profecia de Daniel, | los doce Profetas menores y los Libros I. y II. de los Macabeos. | Imprint, En casa de Sebring y West. | 1834. | 1 p.; verso blank; Adv. pp. 3-5; Daniel, pp. 7-97; Adv. pp. 98, 99; Oseas, pp. 100-142; Adv. p. 143; Joel, pp. 144-157; Adv. p. 158; Amos, pp. 159-187; Adv. p. 188; Abdias, pp. 189-193; Adv. p. 194; Jonas, pp. 195-204; Adv. p. 205; Miquéas, pp. 206-228; Adv. p. 229; Naun, pp. 230-240; Adv. p. 241; Habacuc, pp. 242-255; Adv. p. 256; Sosonias, pp. 257-268; Adv. p. 269; Aggeo, pp. 270-277; Adv. p. 278; Zacarias, pp. 279-326; Adv. p. 327; Malaquias, pp. 328-342; Adv. p. 343-346; Macabees, pp. 347-563; p. 564 blank; Indice, pp. 565-575; sigs. 1-72⁴.

Vol. X. being Tomo I, | Del Nuevo Testamento. | San Mateo, San Marcos, San Lucas, San Juan y los Hechos de los Apostoles. | 1834. Title 1 p.; verso, blank; Adv. pp. 3, 4; San. Mat. pp. 5-165; Adv. 166; Marc, pp. 167-246; Adv. pp. 247, 248; Luc, pp. 249-392; Adv p. 393; Juan, pp. 394-519; Adv. pp. 520, 521; Hechos, pp. 522-665; Indice, pp. 666-678; sigs. 1-85³.

Vol. XI. Being Tomo II, | Del Nuevo Testamento. | Las Epistolas de San Pablo, les Epistolas Catolicas, y el Apocolipsis de San Juan. | Imprint, En casa de Cornelio C Sebring | 1835. | Title, 1 p.; verso, blank; Adv. pp. 3-6; Epistol. de S. Pablo, pp. 7-339; Adv. pp. 340-342; Ep. a los Heb. pp. 342-395; Adv. p. 396; Santiago, pp. 397-413; Apoc. ends on p. 560; Tab. Cronologicas, pp 561-629; Indice, pp 630-694; sigs. 1 to 94.

2. THE | HOLY BIBLE: | Containing | The Old Testament; | Translated | out of the Original Hebrew, | and with the | former Translations | diligently compared and revised: | and | the Greek New Testament; | printed from the | Text and with the various readings of | Knapp: | together with | the commonly received | English Translation. | Designed for the Use of Students. | Stereotype Edition. | New York: | Published by Charles Starr. | 1835. | Stereotyped by A. Chandler. | (L.) 4.

This is called the Student's Bible. The text is printed in a small column on the margin of a wide sheet of ruled paper.

3. THE | DEVOTIONAL | FAMILY BIBLE: | with | Practical and Experimental Reflections on each Verse | of the | Old and New Testaments, | and | rich marginal References. | By the | Rev. Alexander Fletcher, D. D. | Author of "A Guide to Family Devotion," etc. | Illustrated with numerous Engravings. | London and New York: | Virtue, Emmins and Company. | n. d. (Conn. Hist. Soc.) 4.

Title, 1 f.; verso, blank; Address, pp. iii, iv; Text: Gen. to Mal., pp. 1-1260; sigs. B to 14S; Fam. Rec., 2 ff. The New Test. title, 1 f; verso, blank; Mat. to Rev. pp. 1261-1622; sigs. 14T to 18R; Names and Order of the Books; List of Orders and Sects; Tables of Measures and Weights and of Time, 2 pp.; sigs. in 2ˢ; References in the centre; Reflections at foot of the pp.

List of Engravings:
Moses with Tables of the Law; Front. to O. T.
Death of Abel...Engraved by *Edwards*.
Abraham and Three Angels.
Departure of Hagar.
Hagar and Ishmael.
Rebecca receiving Isaac's Presents....................................*Armytage*.
Departure of Rebecca..:...*Armytage*.
Arrival of Rebeckah...*Mitchell*.
Jacob's Well at Sychar....... ....*E. W. Topham*.
Jacob's Vision.
Jacob in the house of Laban.. ....*Edwards*.
Meeting of Esau and Jacob.

Joseph sold by his Brethren.
Joseph interpreting Pharaoh's dream..................................*Bannister.*
Joseph presenting his father to Pharaoh..............................*Greatback.*
Finding of Moses...*Armytage.*
Moses in the Land of Midian..*Armytage.*
Departure of the Israelites.............................*Smillie & Hinchelwood.*
Moses Smiting the Rock...*Rogers.*
Moses meeting his Wife and Sons.
The Sun commanded to stand still..................................*John Rogers.*
Jephtha's Return...*Rolph.*
The Sacrifice of Jephtha's Daughter.
Manoah's Sacrifice.
Boaz and Ruth...*Walker.*
Samuel before Eli...*Rogers.*
David playing to Saul...*Rogers.*
Saul presenting his daughter Mirab to David.
Judgment of Solomon..*White.*
Esther before Ahasuerus...*Rogers.*
The Lord gave and the Lord hath taken away, blessed be the Name of the Lord.
Mount Hermon.
Jews' place of wailing, Jerusalem.
The Handwriting on the Wall.
Tombs in the Valley of Jehosaphat...................................*Brandard.*
Ruins of the City of Samaria..........................*Smillie & Henshelwood.*
Bethlehem..*Brandard.*
Scene on the River Nile at Philoe....................................*Cousen.*
Mount of Olives..*Brandard.*
Madonna and Child..*J. Brown*
Christ Stilleth the Storm.
The Blind receiving their Sight.
Mount of Olives and Jerusalem...*Wallis.*
Garden of Gethsamene..*Brandard.*
Vale of Nazareth..*Cousen.*
Raising of Jairus' Daughter..*Perran.*
Christ Blessing Little Children.
Christ taken down from the Cross.
Basilica at Bethlem..*Roberts.*
Holy Family...*Brandard.*
Infant St. John.
Well near Emaus...*Cousen.*
Jesus and the Samaritan.
Lake of Tiberias...*Bentley.*
Church of the Holy Sepulchre...*Challis.*
Peter and John at the Beautiful Gate.
Paul Preaching at Athens.

This work was issued in numbers, and is still in the market. It is sometimes found in 2 volumes.

4. HOLY BIBLE: with Apocrypha, Canne's References, Index, Table, Lives and Martyrdom of the Apostles and Evangelists. Text corrected according to the standard of the American Bible Society. Stereotyped by James Conner, New York. Hartford: Andrus and Judd, Lee Street. 1835. (L.) 4.

This is another issue of Wilbur's Reference Bible. See *supra*, pp. 188, 189. Engraved frontispiece and Title page (Published by Silas Andrus 1835.) and 12 leaves each containing 6 small wood cuts, arranged in two columns.

5. HOLY BIBLE: Cooperstown, N. Y. Stereotyped and published by H. & E. Phinney. 1835. 4.

With New Testament, dated 1836.

6. HOLY BIBLE, translated from the Latin Vulgat: with Annotations, References and Indexes. Philadelphia: Published by Eugene Cummiskey. 1835. 8.

Edition 500.

7. HOLY BIBLE: New York: Published by Robinson, Pratt & Co. 1835. (Conn. Hist. Soc.) 8.

Pp. 773.

8. HOLY BIBLE: Stereotyped by James Conner. | Elizabethtown, N. J.: | Printed and Published by Edward Sanderson. | Sold in New York by N. & J. White, 63 Wall Street and B. & J. Collins | No. 230 Pearl St. | 1835. | (L.) . 8.

Wood cut Frontispiece.

9. HOLY BIBLE: With the References and marginal readings of the Polyglott Bible, and numerous additions from Bagster's Comprehensive Bible. Stereotyped by Conner & Cooke. Boston: Published by George Gaylord. 1835. (L.) 8.

Title, 1 f.; verso, Names and Order, Chronol. Order, Tables of Weights and Measures, Notice of Copyright, 1833; Text: Gen. to Mal., pp. 3–581; 582 blank; sigs. 1_2 to 73_3 in 4^s; Title to N. T., 1 p.; verso, blank; Text: Mat. to Rev., pp. 585–762; sigs. 74_1 to 96^1 in 4^s; References in centre; Wood cut Frontispiece.

10. THE | HOLY BIBLE: | containing the | Old and New Testaments, | according to the | Authorized Version; | with | the references and marginal readings | of the | Polyglott Bible, | with numerous additions from | Bagster's Comprehensive Bible. | New York: | J. P. Peaslee. | 1835. | 12.

<small>This Bible is printed from a duplicate set of Conner & Cooke's plates already described under No. 9, of 1833. As in all Conner & Cooke's plates of this Bible, p. 658 is marked 558. The New Testament title is marked "First Edition" (as in Conner & Cooke's of 1833), with imprint as above. The back of the cover is marked "28 Plates." They are wood cuts, two on a page. The Frontispiece to the N. T. is Jesus Christ (*Ecce Homo*) "engraved by M. Pechonino from a picture by Leslie, after Guido." References in centre of page.

In this copy, p. 351 is omitted, p. 251 being reprinted by mistake in its place.</small>

11. THE ENGLISH VERSION of the POLYGLOTT BIBLE: with Marginal Readings: Together with A Copious and Original Selection of references to parallel and illustrative passages. Exhibited in a manner hitherto unattempted. Stereotyped by L. Johnson. Philadelphia: Published by Desilver, Thomas & Co., No. 247 Market street. 1835.   12.

<small>This volume agrees with the Polyglott published by Key & Meilke, Philadelphia, 1831, and is seemingly from duplicate plates.

Engravings: Destruction of Jerusalem, Front. to O. T., *Ellis*; Repose in Egypt, Front. to N. T., *Ellis*. Engraved titles to O. and N. T.</small>

12. HOLY BIBLE: The text of the common version arranged in paragraphs, such as the sense requires; the divisions of chapters and verses being noted in the margin, for reference. By James Nourse. Boston: Perkins, Marvin & Company. Philadelphia: Henry Perkins. 1835.   12.

<small>A continuation of No. 9, of 1834.</small>

13. HOLY BIBLE: Hartford: Printed by Hudson & Goodwin. 1835.   (B.)   12.

14. HOLY BIBLE: Hartford: Published by Hudson & Skinner. 1835.   (B.)   12.

<small>Same as No. 16 of 1828, *supra* p. 191, except that the present copy has on the verso of the title—The property of   in a border.</small>

15. HOLY BIBLE: Stereotyped by J. Howe, Philad. Hartford, Ct. Published by Andrus & Judd. 1835.   12.
Same as Andrus's 12mo of 1832.

16. HOLY BIBLE: containing the Old Testament and the New. Stereotyped by J. Howe, Philadelphia. Hartford, Ct.: Published by Andrus & Judd. 1835.   24.

17. NETUM EWH OOMAHZENAHEGUN owh Moses, Genesis aszhenekahdaig. Kahahnekahnootahmoobeung owh kahkewaquouaby, ahneshenahba Makahdawekoonahya. Toronto: Printed for the Toronto Auxiliary Bible Society, at the Christian Guardian Office. 1835.   12.
This is a translation of the Book of Genesis into the Chippewa language, by the Rev. Peter Jones, a native clergyman.

1. NEW TESTAMENT: Translated from the Latin Vulgat. Philadelphia: Published by Eugene Cummiskey. 1835.   8.
Edition 500.

2. NEW TESTAMENT: Stereotype edition. New York: Stereotyped by James Conner, for the American Bible Society. 1835.   12.
Pp. 226. 55th edition. Headings to columns and chapters from same plates as edition of 1834.

3. NEW TESTAMENT: Translated from the Latin Vulgat. Utica: Printed by William Williams for the Proprietors. 1835. (L.)   12.
The Devereux Testament. See *supra*, p. 198.

4. NEW TESTAMENT: Stereotype edition. Hartford, Conn. Published by Andrus & Judd, Lee Street. n. d.   12.
Pp. 257.

5. Das | Neue Testament | unsers | Herrn und Heilandes | Jesu Christi. | Nach Dr. Martin Luther's Uebersetzung. | Stereotypert von J. Howe, Philadelphia. | New York, | Herausgegen von der

Amerikanische Bibel= | Gesellschaft. | 1835. | (Amer. Bib. Soc.) 12.

Title, 1 p.; Verzeichniß der Bücher, 1 p.; at top, Erste Ausgabe; below, Gedruckt von D. Fanshaw. |
Collation agrees with New Testament of Philadelphia, 1835, in number of pp, but the sigs. are in Nos. from 36 to recto of 47⁵ in 12ˢ; verso of 47⁵, blank: then follows in this edition, Ueberficht des Inhalts aller Bücher des Alten und Neuen Testaments, pp. 275-288; sigs. 47⁶ to verso of 47¹² in 12ˢ; showing that this Testament forms part of a Bible.

6. 'H | KAINH ΔIAΘHKH | τοῦ | Κυριου και Σωτηρος | 'ημων | Ιησοῦ Χριστοῦ, | μεταφρασθεισα εκ της Παλαιας | εις την | καθ ομιλουμενην | Ελληνικην Διαλεκτον. | Δια Δαπανης της εν | Αμερικη Ιερογραφικης | εταιρειας. | Νεα Υορκ. | Εκ της Τυπογραφιας | Δανιηλ Φανσά, | ετει αωλγ. | 1835. | (Am. Bib. Soc.) 12.

Title, 1 f.; verso, Order of the Books of the New Test. (in Greek); Text: pp. 3-360; sigs. in 12ᵃ.
This is the 2d Edition of the New Testament in modern Greek, printed by the American Bible Society. It appears from the Greek date that the 1st edition was published in 1833.

7. LUTHER'S GERMAN VERSION | of the | Gospel of St. John, | with an | Interlinear English Translation, | for the use of Students. | By Charles Follen, | Professor of the German Language and Literature | in Harvard University. | Cambridge: | James Munroe and Company, | Booksellers to the University. | Boston: | 134, Washington Street. | 1835. | (Gowans.) 12.

Pref., p. 12; Text: pp. 160.

8. NE NE JINIHODIYEREN ne Rodiyatadogenhti, kanijengehaga kaweanondahkon ne tehaweanatennyon ne kenwendeshon nok oni shodigwatagwen ne William Hess and John A. Wilkes, Jr. New-York: Published by the Young Men's Bible Society of New-York, Auxiliary to the Bible Society of the Methodist Episcopal Church. Howe & Bates, Printers. 1835. 12.

On the recto, or opposite page—The Acts of the Apostles in the Mohawk Language, translated by H. A. Hill, with corrections by William Hess and John A. Wilkes, Jr. Imprint as above. With the volume is bound a Translation into the Mohawk language of The EPISTLE of PAUL the Apostle to the ROMANS, by the same gentlemen.

9. NE YEHONYATON ne Royatadogenhti PAUL jinonka ne GALA-
TIANS. New York: Published by Howe & Bates, for the
Young Men's Bible Society of New York, auxiliary to the
Bible Society of the Methodist Episcopal Church. 1835. 12.

This is the Epistle to the Galatians translated into the Mohawk language by William Hess, with corrections by J. A. Wilkes, Jr.

10. THE EPISTLE of ST. PAUL to the Romans: a new translation (with a commentary) by M. Stuart. Second edition.
Andover. 1835. (Archd. Cotton.) 8.

1836.

1. HOLY BIBLE: Cooperstown (N. Y.) Stereotyped, printed
and published by H. & E. Phinney, and sold by them at
their Bookstore, and by the Booksellers generally in the
United States. 1836. 4.

2. HOLY BIBLE, translated from the Latin Vulgat: With Annotations, References and Index. Philadelphia: Published
by Eugene Cummiskey. Stereotyped by J. Howe. 1836.
(L.) 8.

Title, 1 f.; verso blank; Admonition, Letter of Pius VI.; Approbation, Signed †HENRY CONWELL, Bishop of Pennsylvania and dated 13th December, 1824, 1 p.; Trans-lation of the Decree of the Council of Trent and the Order of the Books of the Old Test. p. 4.; Text: Gen. to II Mac. pp. 5–681 (p. 589 is marked incorrectly 389), sigs. A. (which includes Title and prel. leaf) to recto of 4 O^1; Hist. and Chronol. Index to the Old Test. pp. 682–691; verso of 691, blank; sig. verso of 4 O^1 to recto of 4 O^6 all the signatures are in 4^s except 4O, which is in 6^s; Fam. Rec. 2ff; New Test. title (as in edition of 1824), adding after the word " Scriptures " | Approved by Dr. Con-well, Bishop of Philadelphia. | and dated 1836. 1 p. verso, blank; Approb. of Dr. Troy, 1 p.; verso, Approbation of Bishop Conwell, Order of the Books of the New Test., Note ; Text, and following matter to Hist. and Chronol. Index to New Testament inclusive, as in edition of 1824. The engraved frontispiece is torn out in the copy examined.

On comparing this edition with the Cummiskey 8vo of 1824, it will be observed that it differs in having the text of the Old Testament paged continuously from Gen. to Maccabees. In the first edition it was divided into two parts both in the paging and signatures.

The edition consisted of 1000 copies.

3. HOLY BIBLE, translated from the Latin Vulgate: With Annotations, References and Index. Published with the approbation of the Right Rev. John Dubois, Catholic Bishop of New York. New York: Published by John Doyle, No. 294 Pearl Street. Stereotyped by Conner & Cook. 1836. 8.

<small>This is a reprint of the edition of 1833, with merely a new Title page, 3 wood cuts and 1 steel engraving of the Crucifixion. Pearson's name at the end is suppressed. The transposition at page 43 in the edition of 1833, is corrected in this edition. The New Testament is dated 1833.</small>

4. HOLY BIBLE: Stereotype edition. New York: Stereotyped by A. Chandler. Printed by D. Fanshaw, for the American Bible Society. 1836. 12.

<small>With references.</small>

5. HOLY BIBLE: New York: For the Auxiliary New York Bible and Common Prayer Book Society. Depository 46 Lumber Street. 1836. 12.

<small>New Testament title dated 1835. Sigs. in 6s. Pp. 1044.</small>

6. HOLY BIBLE: Philadelphia: Hogan and Thompson. 1836. 12.

<small>Pp. 1098 and 342, in 12s; on foot of verso, Stereotyped by Haswell & Barangton, Philadelphia.</small>

7. HOLY BIBLE: Arranged in Paragraphs, such as the Sense requires. By J. Nourse. Boston: Perkins, Marvin & Company. Philadelphia: Henry Perkins. 1836. 12.

<small>See No. 12, *supra* p. 242.</small>

8. HOLY BIBLE: Stereotyped by J. Howe, Philadelphia. Hartford: Published by Judd, Loomis & Co. 1836. 12.

<small>Pp. 655. Contents, 656–661.</small>

9. HOLY BIBLE: Hartford: Printed by Hudson & Goodwin. 1836. (B.) 12.

10. THE ENGLISH VERSION of the POLYGLOTT BIBLE. Stereotyped by Henry Wallis and L. Roby, Concord, N. H. Concord, N. H.: Published by Roby, Kimball and Merrill. Luther Roby, Printer. 1836. 24.
Pp. viii, 587, 190. Engr. front. and titles to O. and N. T.

11. HOLY BIBLE: Stereotyped by Henry Wallis and Luther Roby, Concord, N. H.: Published by Charles Hoag. 1836. 32.
With engr. front. and title page. New Test., same imprint, but dated 1834.

12. HOLY BIBLE, containing the Old Testament and the New. Stereotyped by Luther Roby, Concord, N. H. Concord, N. H.: Published by Oliver L. Sanborn. 1836. 32.
Allison & Foster, Printers. Pp. 852, 259. Front. to O. and N. T.

13. THE ENGLISH VERSION of the POLYGLOTT BIBLE, with Marginal Readings and References. Woodstock, Vt. J. B. & S. L. Chase & Co. 1836. (L.) 16.
Title, 1 f.; verso, Order of the Books of the O. T.; at foot, Stereotyped by T. G. Wells & Co., Boston. Preface, signed T. C., 2 pp.; Text: Gen. to Mal., pp. 1-856; sig. 1-107; cont. of O. T., pp. 857-864; Table of Weights and Money, Table of Time, p. 866 (*for* 865); Table of Scripture Measures, p. 867 (*for* 866). The Polyglott New Testament, imprint as above, 1 p.; verso, Order of the Books of the N. T.; at foot, name of stereotyper, as above; Text: Mat. to Rev., pp. 3-259; Contents of N. T., pp. 260-262; Discourses, Parables and Miracles of Jesus in Chronol. Order, pp. 263, 264; A Concise Harmony of the Gospels, pp. 265-267; Chronological Table of our Saviour's life, 1 p.; sigs. 1² to 34², all in 4ˢ; References in center of the pages.

Engravings: Eve offering Adam the apple; Front. to O. T.; Adam and Eve quitting Paradise; Death of Abel; Abraham about to sacrifice Isaac; The Flood; Daniel in the Lion's Den; Birth of the Saviour; Front. to N. T.; Murder of the Innocents; Baptism of the Saviour; The Saviour Walking on the Waters; The Last Supper; The Crucifixion.

The running lines on pp. 212 and 213 of the New Test. are transposed; the former having Chap. IV, V, instead of I Timothy, which is incorrectly at the head of p. 213.

14. HOLY BIBLE: Northampton: J. H. Butler. Buffalo: T. & M. Butler. 1836. (Conn. Hist. Soc. Lib.) 16.
Pp. 856, 259.

15. HOLY BIBLE: Amherst, Ms. J. S. & C. Adams. Stereotyped by L. Johnson. 1836. 16.

Pp. 856, 259. The Text of Nos. 13, 14 and 15, seems to be from the same plates. See No. 18, of 1834.

16. HOLY BIBLE: New York: George Dearborn. 1836. 24.

Pp. 726, 221. This is called, on an engraved Title page, "The Diamond Bible." It has a number of etchings.

17. Christology of the Old Testament, and a Commentary on the predictions of the Messiah by the Prophets. By E. W. Hengstenberg, D. D. Professor of Theology in the University of Berlin. Translated from the German by Reuel Keith, D. D. Alexandria, D. C. Vol. I. 1836. 8.

This Volume contains General Introduction, Messianic prophecies in the Pentateuch and Psalms, the Godhead of the Messiah in the Old Testament, the proofs of a suffering and atoning Messiah, &c., and the Messianic prophecies in Isaiah.

1. NEW TESTAMENT: By the American and Massachusetts Bible Societies. Boston: Printed at the New England Institution. 4 vols. 1836. (Cat. Br. and For. Bib. Soc.) 4.

In raised letters, for the Use of the Blind.

2. NEW TESTAMENT: Cooperstown, N. Y. H. & E. Phinney. 1836. 4.

With Bible of 1835.

3. PRONOUNCING TESTAMENT: By Israel Alger. Boston: Crocker and Brewster. 1836. 12.

See No. 4, of 1822, *supra* p. 159.

4. NEW TESTAMENT: Boston: Hilliard, Gray & Co. 1836. (G. L.) 12.

4th edition.

5. NEW TESTAMENT: Arranged in Paragraphs. By James Nourse. Boston: Hilliard, Gray & Co. 1836. (G. L.) 12.

See No. 9 of 1834.

—1837.]   AMERICAN BIBLES.   249

6. NEW TESTAMENT: Published by the Bible Association of Friends in America. Philadelphia. 1836.   18.

7. NEW TESTAMENT: New York: Printed by D. Fanshaw for the American Bible Society. Stereotyped by A. Chandler. 1836.   24.
33d edition.

8. EVANGELICAL HISTORY; | or the Books of | the NEW TESTAMENT; | with a | General Introduction, | a | Preface to each Book, | and Notes explanatory and critical. | In Two Volumes. | By Alden Bradford. Vol. I. | Containing the Four Gospels. | Boston: Joseph Dowe. | 1836. | (G. L.) 12.

9. Ἡ | ΚΑΙΝΗ ΔΙΑΘΗΚΗ | τοῦ | Κυριου και Σωτηρος | ἡμων | Ιησοῦ Χριστοῦ, | μεταφρασθεισα εκ της Παλαιας | εις την | καθ ομιλουμενην | Ἑλληνικην Διαλεκτον. | Δια Δαπανης της εν | Αμερικη Ιερογραφικης | εταιρειας. | Νεα Υορκ. | Εκ της Τυπογραφιας | Δανιηλ Φανσὰ. | 1836. | (Am. Bib. Soc.)   12.
This is the third edition of the American Bible Society's New Testament, in modern Greek. See No. 6 of 1835.

1837.

1. HOLY BIBLE: With Apocrypha, Canne's Marginal References, Index, Tables, Lives of the Apostles, and Concordance. Text corrected according to the Standard of the American Bible Society. Stereotyped by James Conner. New York: Published by T. Mason & G. Lane, for the Methodist Episcopal Church, at the Conference Office, 200 Mulberry street. 1837.   (L.)   4.
Title, 1 f.; Witherspoon's pref., 1 p.; Advertisement, Names and Order, 1 p.; Text: Gen. to Mal., pp. 5–527; sigs. A to 3U⁴, in 4s, including Title and 2 prel. pp.; Stones's Guide to Reading the Scriptures, p. 528; Apocrypha (in smaller type), pp. 1–78; 1 blank leaf; sigs. A to K⁴ in 4s; New Testament, Title, 1 p.; verso, blank; Mat. to Rev., pp. 3–168; sigs. 3X to 4S⁴ in 4s; Index, pp. 1–9; Tables, &c., p. 10; Text of O. T. quoted in the New, pp. 12, 13; Lives and Martyrdom, pp. 14, 15; 1 blank leaf; sigs. A to B⁴ in 4s; Title to Browne's Concordance, Stereotyped by B. & J. Collins, no date, 1 p.;

32

To the Reader, 1 p.; Text, 3-56; sigs. A to G in 4°; Psalms in Metre (no title page), pp. 1-19; Engr. front. to O. and N. Test. The Bible is paged at the bottom; the Concordance and Psalms at the top of the pp.; all the sigs. are in 4°, and sigs. A include the Titles.

The Engravings are: Jacob meeting Rachael; front to O. T., *Balch;* The Ascension; front. to N. T., *J. G. Kellogg.*

The Text seems to be printed from the plates of the Wilbur Reference Bible. See *supra* p. 168.

2. THE | HOLY BIBLE, | containing the | Old and New Testaments; | together with | the Apocrypha | translated from the original tongues, | and | with the former translations diligently compared and revised; | with | Canne's marginal notes and references. | To which are added, | an Index; | an Alphabetical table | of all the names in the Old and New Testaments, with their significations; | Table of Scripture weights, measures, and coins, &c.; | Concordance, and the Psalms of David in metre. | New York: | Nafis and Cornish. | St. Louis: Nafis, Cornish & Co. n. d. (Lib. Legislative Assembly, Canada.) 4.

Title, To the Reader, Names and Order of the Books, Contents of the Books, 4 pp.; Text: Gen. to Rev., pp. 5-829; Apocrypha (paged separately), pp. (i)-(cxlvii); Fam. Rec., 2 ff.; after Revelations follow Index, Table of Time, Chron. Index which ends as follows: "Then the whole sum and Number of Years, from the beginning of the world unto this present year of our Lord God 1833 are" &c.; then Tables of Scripture Measures, Weights and Coins; Judea, Palestine and the Holy Land; Analysis of the Old and New Testaments; Table of the several Passages in the Old Test. quoted in the New; Table of Offices and Conditions of Men; Table of Kindred; Alphabetical Table of Proper Names; pp. *i-xxi;* Title to Brown's Brief Concordance, imprint as above (no date), 1 p.; verso, To the Reader; Text: pp. [1]-[56]; Psalms in Metre, pp. 1-19. All are marked at foot of the pages, except the Psalms, which are paged at top.

List of Engravings:

1. Repentance of Judas, painted by E. Bird, R. A.; *T. Kelly* sc. 2. Pharoah's sorcery. 3. Sampson betrayed. 4. Daniel interpreting for Belshazzar. 5. The Annunciation. 6. Magi offering presents. 7. Judas casting away the pieces of silver. 8. Christ raising the widow's son. 9. Incredulity of Thomas. 10. Vision of the Dragon chained. All except the first, on wood, engraved by Anderson.

This Bible appeared originally in 1833.

3. HOLY BIBLE: Cooperstown (N. Y.), Stereotyped, printed and published by H. & E. Phinney, and sold by them at their Bookstore, and by the Booksellers generally in the United States. 1837. 4.

4. HOLY BIBLE: Stereotype edition. New York: Stereotyped by A. Chandler, for the American Bible Society. 1837. 12.

D. Fanshaw, Printer. Pp. 669. Short headings to col. and chap. Seemingly a copy of the Nonpareil 12mo of 1830. The New Test. title is marked Nonpareil 12mo.

5. THE | HOLY BIBLE | of the Old and New | Testaments. | Boston: | Published by Otis Clapp, | No. 121 Washington Street. | 1837. | (G. L.)   12.

Verso of title, blank; "From the Arcana Cœlestia of Emanuel Swedenborg," 1 p.
This volume contains the books only which Swedenborg indicates as having an internal sense, viz.:

Genesis,	I Samuel,	Lamentations,	Jonah,
Exodus,	II Samuel,	Ezekiel,	Micah,
Leviticus,	I Kings,	Daniel,	Nahum,
Numbers,	II Kings,	Hosea,	Habakkuk,
Deuteronomy,	Psalms,	Joel,	Zephaniah,
Joshua,	Isaiah,	Amos,	Haggai,
Judges,	Jeremiah,	Obadiah,	Zechariah,
			Malachi.

Matthew,   Mark,   Luke,   John,   The Apocalypse.

The Text is that of the common version, and is printed from the plates of a common 12mo Bible, the parts not containing the internal sense being omitted, and the paging is continued as it would be if the whole text were included.

6. THE | HOLY BIBLE, | translated from | the Latin Vulgate: | Diligently compared with | the Hebrew, Greek, and other editions, | in various Languages; | With | Annotations by the Rev. Dr. Challoner; | Together with | References and an Historical and Chronological Index. | With the Approbation of the Provincial Council. | Baltimore: | Published by Fielding Lucas, Jr. | 138 Market Street. | n. d. (L.) 12.

Title (within rules), 1 f.; verso, Approbation of the Provincial Council, dated 22d April, 1837, and Approbation of the University of Doway; Admonition, Letter of Pius VI, and A Prayer, p. 3; verso, Decree of the Council of Trent, and Order of the Books of the Old Test.; Text: Gen. to Mac., pp. 5–808; sigs. A (which includes title and prel. leaf) to verso of $3Y^2$ in 6^s, and 1 to verso of 101^4 in 4^s; A Table of References, pp. 809, 810; sig. A^1 (not marked) and in fig. 102; Title to New Test., 1 p; verso, A Prayer, Approbation of the New Test. by the Univ. of Rheims, The Books of the New Test. and Note; sig. A^2 and 102^2; Text: Mat. to Apocal., pp. 5–214; Tables of all the Epistles and Gospels, 1 p.; verso, blank; sigs. A^3 to recto of S^6 in 6^s; and $102^{3,4}$, then 1 (not marked, which is p. 2) to recto of 27^4 in 4^s.

In Gen. 4:14, the words "and from thy face I shall be hid, and I shall be a vagabond and a fugitive on the earth," are omitted.

7. THE ENGLISH VERSION of the POLYGLOTT BIBLE: Stereotyped by L. Johnson. Philadelphia: Published by Desilver, Thomas & Co., No. 253 Market street. 1837.   12.

<small>With engr. T. and front. Philadelphia: Published by Thomas Cowperthwaite & Co., 253 Market street. See No. 11 of 1835.</small>

8. POCKET REFERENCE BIBLE. | The English Version | of the | Polyglott Bible, | containing the | Old and New Testaments, | with | Original Selections of references to parallel | and illustrative passages; | and | Marginal readings. | Together with other valuable additions: the | whole designed to facilitate the acquisition | of Scripture knowledge | in Bible classes, Sunday schools &c. | Stereotyped by L. Johnson. | Baltimore: | Published by Armstrong & Berry, | No. 134 Market Street. | 1837. | 24.

<small>Engr. titles to O. and N. Testaments, see *supra*, p. 217.</small>

9. HOLY BIBLE, containing the Old Testament and the New: Stereotyped by J. Howe, Philad. Hartford, *Ct.:* Published by Judd, Loomis & Co. 1837.   (G. L)   24.

<small>Contents of the Books of the O. Test, pp. 3–10; Text: pp. 11–729; New Test., pp. 222; Contents, pp. 223–225. Two plates in front of Old Test.
An error occurs in this edition in II. Tim. 3:16, the text reading: "All Scripture is given by inspiration of God, and is profitable......for destruction" instead of, instruction.</small>

10. HOLY BIBLE: Authorised version. With notes, practical and explanatory, by the Rev. Henry Stebbing, A. M., Member of the Royal Society of Literature. London: Allan Bell & Co. Warwick Square, T. Tegg & Son; and H. Washburne, J. K. Herrick, New York. 1837.   32.

<small>Bound in 2 vols. pp. 1084 and 338, with a number of etchings with inscriptions in English and French.
Copies of Stebbing's Diamond Bible had been smuggled for a number of years into the United States. It was finally seized by the revenue officers and its illegal introduction put an end to.</small>

11. A NEW TRANSLATION of the Hebrew Prophets, arranged in Chronological Order. By George R. Noyes. 3 vols. Vol. I, containing Joel, Amos, Hosea, Isaiah, and Micah. Bos-

ton, Charles Bowen. 1838. Vol. II, containing Nahum, Zephaniah, Habakkuk, Obadiah, Jeremiah, Lamentations. Boston: James Munroe and Company. 1837. Vol. III, containing Ezekiel, Daniel, Haggai, Zechariah, Jonah, and Malachi. Boston: James Munroe and Company. 1837. (Harvard Coll.; G. L.) 12.

1. NEW TESTAMENT: New York: Published by N. & J. White. E. Sanderson, Printer, Elizabethtown, N. J. 1837. 4.
With Bible No. 2 of 1834.

2. EXPLANATORY | NOTES | upon the | NEW TESTAMENT. | By John Wesley, M. A. | Late Fellow of Lincoln College, Oxford. | New York: | Published by T. Mason and G. Lane, | for the Methodist Episcopal Church, at the Conference | Office, 200 Mulberry-Street. | J. Collord, Printer. | 1837. | 8.
Pp. 734. The text, which is that of the Common English Translation, with some of Bengel's readings incorporated, is in paragraphs; the number of the chapters and verses being noted in the margin. Many of the notes are borrowed from Bengel's *Gnomon Novi Testamenti*, Heylin's *Theological Lectures*, Guyse and Doddridge.

3. NEW TESTAMENT: New York: American Bible Society. 1837. Pica 8.
Psalms appended.

4. 'Η ΚΑΙΝΗ ΔΙΑΘΗΚΗ. | The | Greek Testament, | with English Notes, | Critical, Philological, and Exegetical, | partly | selected and arranged from the best Commentators, ancient and modern, | but chiefly original. | The whole being specially adapted to the Use of | Academical Students, Candidates for the Sacred office, and Ministers: | though also intended as a Manual Edition for the Use of | Theological Students in general. | By the | Rev. S. T. Bloomfield, D. D., F. S. A. | Vicar of Bisbrooke, Rutland. | First American from the Second London Edition. | In Two Volumes. | Vol I. | Boston: | Published by Perkins and Marvin. | New York: Gould and Newman. |

Philadelphia: Henry Perkins. | 1837. | (Norman C. Stoughton, Albany.) 8.

Title, 1 f. ; verso, Extract of Copyright dated 1836; below, Stereotyped by Folsom, Wells, and Thurston. Perkins and Marvin, Printers; Preface to the American edition, signed, M. Stuart, *Andover Theol. Seminary, October* 1st, 1836, pp. iii, iv, v; verso of v., blank; Dr. Bloomfield's Preface, pp. vii-xx ; Preface to the Second Edition, pp. xxi-xxxi ; verso, Explanation of Characters used in the Work ; sigs. *a* (which includes title p.) to verso of d^4 in 4^s; Text: Mat. to the end of Acts, pp. 1–597; sigs. 1 to recto of 75^3 in 4^s, a blank leaf completing the sig. 2d vol., Title as above, except Vol. II., 1 p.; verso, Extract of Copyright, &c., as in vol. I. Text : Romans to Rev. pp. 3–606, sigs. 1 to verso of 76^3; Index I., pp. 607–616; Index II., pp. 617–631; verso, blank; sigs. 76_4 to recto of 79^4 in 4^s.

The text of this work is formed on the basis of the last edition of Robert Stephens adopted by Mill. In the second edition which is here reprinted, the editor states that he has embodied the results of an attentive study of the reformers, Luther, Calvin and Melancthon. He has also given more regular and copious introductions to all the books of the New Testament.

5. NEW TESTAMENT: Arranged in Historical and Chronological Order; with Copious Notes on the principal Subjects in Theology; the Gospels on the basis of the Harmonies of Lightfoot, Doddridge, Pilkington, Macombe, Michaelis; the account of the Resurrection on the authorities of West, Towson and Cranfield. The Epistles are inserted in their places, and divided according to the Apostle's arguments. By the Rev. George Townsend, M. A., Prebendary of Durham, and Vicar of North Allerton. The whole revised, divided into paragraphs, punctuated according to the best Critical Texts, the Italic words reëxamined, Passages and Words of doubtful authority marked, a choice and copious Selection of parallel passages given &c. By the Rev. T. W. Coit, D. D., late President of Transylvania University. Boston: Published by Perkins and Marvin. Philadelphia: Henry Perkins. 1837. (L.; G. L.) 8.

1st American edition.

6. NEW TESTAMENT: Stereotype edition. Philadelphia: Published by A. J. Dickinson and C. Ward, and for sale by the Booksellers generally. 1837. (L.) 12.

Text: pp. 3–453; Table of Offices, p. 454; sigs. 1 to 38^0, all in 6^s, except sig. 1, which is in 5^s.

7. NEW TESTAMENT: Stereotype Edition. Hartford: Judd, Loomis & Co. 1837.   (L.)   12.

8. THE | NEW TESTAMENT | of our | Lord and Saviour Jesus Christ. | By | William Tyndale, | the Martyr. | The original edition, 1526, | Being the first vernacular translation from the Greek. | With a | Memoir of his life and writings. | To which are annexed, | The essential variations of Coverdale's, Thomas Matthew's, | Cranmer's, the Genevan, and the Bishops' Bibles, | as marginal readings. | By J. P. Dabney. | Andover: | Printed and Published by Gould and Newman: | From the London edition of Bagster. | New York: | Corner of Fulton and Nassau Streets. | MDCCCXXXVII. | (L.; G. L.)   12.

<small>Title, 1 f.; verso, Extract from copy right; Preface, pp. iii–viii, dated Andover, Aug. 9, 1837; Mock title, Memoir, &c., 1 f.; verso, Arms and Pedigree of Tyndale; Text of Memoir, pp. 11–82; List of Books ascribed to Tyndale, pp. 83, 84; Historic notices of the Ante-James Versions; Versions of the Scripture subsequent to that of Tyndale, pp. 65–98; Collations, pp. 99–102; List of distinctive expressions of Tyndale, 103–105; Additions and Corrections, at bottom of 105; verso, blank; Woodcut Title-page to N. T., M.D.XXVI; verso, blank; sigs. in numbers, 1 to 9 in 6s, including this last title; Mat. to Rev., no paging; sigs. A to TT5 in 6s; To the Reader, 2 pp. TT6.

Mr. Lee Wilson is very severe on Dabney's remarks respecting the different versions, and particularly on his ignorance of the number of editions of Tyndale's Testament. Mr. Dabney had not the means of informing himself on this subject, and should have been more modest in his strictures on Mr. Offer.</small>

9. THE | POLYGLOTT | NEW TESTAMENT. | With marginal Readings and References. | Woodstock, Vt. | J. B. & S. L. Chase & Co. | 1837. | -   16.

<small>This is the New Testament of No. 12 of 1836, published separately.</small>

10. NEW TESTAMENT: Philadelphia: McCarty & Davis, 175 Market Street. Stereotyped by L. Johnson. 1837. (L.)   24.

11. EL | NUEVO TESTAMENTO, | traducido al Español | por el R. P. Felipe scio de S. Miguel, | de las Escuelas Pias, Obispo de Segovia. | Nueva York: | Edicion estereotipica por F. F. Ripley, | A costa de la Sociedad Americana de

la Biblia. | Formada en Nueva York, A. D. 1816. | Imprinta de D. Fanshaw. | 1837. | 32.

<small>Text: pp. 1–477; sigs. A to 2G. This is a Catholic Testament, but without notes.</small>

12. THE FOUR GOSPELS, translated from the Original Greek, with preliminary Dissertations and Notes, critical and explanatory. By Rev. George Campbell, Principal of Marischal College and one of the Ministers of Aberdeen. In Two Volumes. Andover: Printed and published by Gould and Newman. New York: corner of Fulton and Nassau St. 1837.   8.

<small>See *supra* pp. 52, 55, 106, for other editions of this work.</small>

13. THE FOUR GOSPELS, with Notes, chiefly explanatory, designed for teachers in Sabbath Schools and Bible Classes, and as an aid to Family Instruction. 2 vols. By Henry I. Ripley. Boston: 1837.   12.

<small>Colored Map.</small>

14. KEY to the REVELATION. By Elkan Smith. Boston: Whipple and Damrell. 1837.   12.

1838.

1. HOLY BIBLE: with Canne's Notes and References, Index, Tables, &c. Hartford: Andrus, Judd & Franklin. 1838. (Am. Bib. Soc.)   Fol.

<small>Same as No. 2 of 1829.</small>

2. HOLY BIBLE: with References and Various Readings. Illustrated with Engravings. In Two Volumes. Vol. I. Baltimore: Lewis & Coleman. John D. Fry, Printer. n. d.   4.

<small>Ornamental Title. (Below, Picture of Solomon's Temple.) Published by Joseph N. Lewis, Baltimore; verso, blank; Printed Title, 1 f.; verso, blank; Names and Order of all the Books, 1 p.; verso, A Guide to regular perusal of the Holy Scriptures, by William Stones. Also, Proper Lessons for Public Worship and Sunday Mornings</small>

throughout the Year. Proper Lessons for particular days. Text: Gen. to close of Solomon's Song, pp. 1-787; end of Vol. I; sigs. D (1st p. of Text) to recto of 5K². Vol. II, Title page, 1 p.; verso, blank; Text: Isaiah to Mal., pp. 3-277; sigs. A to recto of 2M³; Apocrypha (in smaller type), pp. 1-139; sigs. A to recto of S²; Fam. Rec., 2 ff.; Title to New Test.; Imprint as above, 1 p.; verso, blank; Text: Mat. to Rev., pp. 281-600; sigs. 2N to verso of 4F⁴, all in 4s.

This Bible was published in Numbers. An inscription on the cover bears date Jan. 1, 1838. The Old Testament contains 4 plates, the New Testament 13 plates. *H. A. Boardman*, D. D.

3. HOLY BIBLE: New York: Stereotyped by A. Chandler, and Printed by D. Fanshaw, For the American Bible Society. 1838. (L.) Pica 4.

5th edition. Printed previously to the alterations in the new version.

4. HOLY BIBLE: with Canne's Marginal Notes and References. To which are added, An Index, An Alphabetical Table of all the Names in the Old and New Testaments, with their Significations, Tables of Scripture Weights, Measures and Coins &c. Cincinnati: Published by U. P. James, No. 26 Pearl Street; and sold by all the principal Booksellers in the United States. 1838. (L.) 4.

Title, 1 f.; verso, blank; To the Reader, and Advertisement to Alexander's stereotype edition, 1 p.; Names and Order, p. 4; Contents, pp. (5)-(8); Text: Gen. to Mal., pp. 9-632; sigs. B to verso of 4K⁴, in 4s; Apocrypha, in smaller type, pp. (i)-(*cxlvii*); sigs. A* to recto of T*², in 4s, followed by a blank page; Fam. Rec., 2 ff.; New Testament title, same imprint, 1 p.; verso, Account of Dates; Text: Mat. to Rev., pp. 635-829; verso, blank; Index, pp. *i-xi*; Table of Time also on p. *xi*; Index of Years; Tables of Weights &c., pp. *xii*, *xiii*; Account of Judea and Analysis, p. *xiv*; Table of Texts, Offices, Kindred, pp. *xv*, *xvi*; Alphabetical Table, pp. *xvii-xxi*; sigs. (including title) 4L to recto of 5P², in 4s, followed by a blank page; Brown's Concordance: Philadelphia: Printed and published by Charles Alexander & Co., Athenian Buildings, Franklin Place, n. d., 1 p.; verso, To the Reader; Text: pp. [3]-[56]; sigs. A to G₄ in 4s; 5 large woodcuts.

This Bible seems to correspond with that published by Nafis and Cornish, *supra* p. 250. For Alexander's edition, see No. 4 of 1834.

5. HOLY BIBLE: Stereotype edition. New York: Stereotyped by A. Chandler, for the American Bible Society. 1838. (L.) Sm. pica 8.

D. Fanshaw, printer, 117 Nassau street.

6. THE OLD TESTAMENT, arranged in Historical and Chronological order (on the basis of Lightfoot's Chronicles), in such a manner that the Books, Chapters, Psalms, Prophecies, &c. &c., may be read in one connected History, in the words of the authorized Translation. With Notes and Copious Indexes. By the Rev. George Townsend, M. A., Prebendary of Durham, and Vicar of North Allerton. Revised, punctuated, divided into Paragraphs and Parallelisms, Italic words reëxamined, a choice and Copious Selection of references given. By the Rev. T. W. Coit, D. D., late President of Transylvania University. Boston: Published by Perkins and Marvin. Philadelphia: Henry Perkins. 1838. (L.) 8.

1st American Edition, pp. viii, 1168, 24. For the New Testament, see 1837.

7. HOLY BIBLE: according to the commonly received version. London: Imprinted by Robert Barker, 1611. New York: Stereotyped by White & Hagar, for the American and Foreign Bible Society. John Gray, Printer. 1838. (L.) 8.

The Oxford reprint, 1833, is so exactly literatim as to retain even the manifest errors of the press.—*Amer. Bible Soc. Cat.*, p. 9. This American reprint is said to be also full of errors.

8. HOLY BIBLE: New York: Published by T. Mason and G. Lane, for the Methodist Episcopal Church, at the Conference Office, 200 Mulberry street. *J. Collord, Printer.* 1838. 12.

Pp. 510, 162. On verso of New Testament title, Stereotyped at the Boston Type and Stereotype Foundry.

9. HOLY BIBLE: New York: Stereotyped by A. Chandler for the American Bible Society. 1838. Nonp. 12.

11th edition, pp. 669. See Bible No. 4 of 1837.

10. HOLY BIBLE: Imprinted by Robert Barker, 1611. Reprinted by the American Bible Society, New York. 1838. (Am. Bible Soc.) 18.

11. HOLY BIBLE, containing the Old Testament and the New. Stereotyped by J. Howe, Phil. Hartford, Ct.: Andrus, Judd and Franklin. 1838.   24.
   Pp. 729, 222; Contents, 223-225; 16 woodcuts and 4 engravings.

12. HOLY BIBLE: Stereotyped by Henry Wallis and L. Roby, Concord, N. H. Concord, N. H.: Published by Roby, Kimball & Merrell. 1838.   24.

13. THE ENGLISH VERSION of the POLYGLOTT BIBLE. Springfield: Published by G. & C. Merriam. 1838.   24.

14. HOLY BIBLE, containing the Old Testament and the New. New York: Robinson and Franklin, successors to Leavitt, Lord & Co., 180 Broadway. 1838.   32.
   Pp. 852, 259; Contents, 261-263. 2 front. to Old Testament.

15. HOLY BIBLE: New York: Stereotyped by Smith & Valentine, for American Bible Society. 1838.   Diamond 32.

16. HOLY BIBLE: Philadelphia: Hogan & Thompson, No. 30, N. Fourth street. 1838.   32.
   Same as No. 21 of 1832. Imprint to Engraved T.: Philadelphia, Hogan & Thompson, 139 Market street. 1834.

17. JOB. By Geo. R. Noyes. Boston: James Monroe. 1838. (G. L.)   12.

1. NEW TESTAMENT: London, Imprinted by Robert Barker, 1611. New York: Stereotyped by White and Hagar, for American and Foreign Bible Society. John Gray, Printer. 1838.   (L.)   12.
   Pp. 236. A Baptist version.

2. NEW TESTAMENT: | Stereotyped by J. Howe, New-York. | Newark, N. J. | Printed and published by Benjamin Olds. | 1838. | 12.
   Pp. 3-288. Sigs. A to Z in 6s. There is a vignette on wood on the title page: The Good Samaritan. Brief headings to chapters.

1839.

1. HOLY BIBLE: With Apocrypha, marginal Notes and References, Index, Tables, &c. Philadelphia: Published by McCarty and Davis, No. 171 Market street. I. Ashmead & Co., Printers. 1839. (L.) 4.

This is a continuation of the Carey edition. There is no Apocrypha in this copy. It has a large woodcut frontis., and four wood engravings.
Lev 19:12 is incorrect: *the* God for *thy* God.

2. HOLY BIBLE: With Apocrypha, Canne's Marginal Notes and References, Index, Tables &c. Philadelphia: Published and for sale by Hogan & Thompson, No. 30 North Fourth Street. Printed by Jasper Harding, No. 74 South Second Street. 1839. (L.) 4.

The Text of the Old and the New Testaments agrees in sigs. and pagination, with Phinney's Cooperstown 4to (see *supra* pp. 157, 158); that of the Apocrypha, with Alexander's edition, *supra* p. 229, but dated 1838. This volume, has, in addition, Brown's Concordance: Alexander's stereotype edition; imprint, Philadelphia: Printed and Published by Charles Alexander & Co., Athenian Buildings, Franklin place; pp. [3]-[56]; and Psalms in Metre, pp. 19.

3. HOLY BIBLE: Concord, N. H. Roby, Kimball & Merrell. 1839. 4.

4. HOLY BIBLE: Translated from the Latin Vulgat: with Annotations, References, and a Historical and Chronological Index. First Stereotype, from the fifth Dublin edition. Newly revised and corrected according to the Clementin edition of the Scriptures. Philadelphia: Published by Eugene Cummiskey. Stereotyped by J. Howe. 1839. (Rev. Mr. Rooney, Albany.) 8.

This edition agrees with that of 1836, *supra* p. 245. It has, in addition, however, before the printed Title page, Approbations of Archbishop Eccleston of Baltimore; of Bishops Conwell and Kenrick of Philadelphia, and Dr. Hughes, coadjutor Bishop of New York. And an Engraved Title with Vignette, The Finding of Moses.

5. HOLY BIBLE: According to the commonly received version. London: Imprinted by Robert Barker, 1611. New York: Stereotyped by White & Hagar, for the American and Foreign Bible Society. John Gray, Printer. 1839. (L.) 8.

6. THE OLD TESTAMENT, arranged in Historical and Chronological order (on the basis of Lightfoot's Chronicles), &c., &c. With Notes and Copious Indexes. By the Rev. George Townsend, M. A., Prebendary of Durham, and Vicar of North Allerton. Revised, &c. By the Rev. T. W. Coit, D. D., late President of Transylvania University. Boston: Published by Perkins and Marvin. Philadelphia: Henry Perkins. 1839. (G. L.) 8.

A continuation of No. 6, of 1838, with new title page. For the New Testament, see 1837.

7. THE ENGLISH VERSION of the POLYGLOTT BIBLE: with marginal Readings: together with Copious and Original Selection of references to parallel and illustrative passages, exhibited in a manner hitherto unattempted. Stereotyped by L. Johnson. Philadelphia: Thomas, Cowperthwaite & Co. 1839. 12.

Engraved title; Philadelphia; Published by Thomas, Cowperthwaite & Co., No. 253 Market Street, 1 f.; verso, blank; printed title within double rules, 1 p.; verso, Order of the Books of the O. and N. T.; Chronol. Order, p. ii; Preface, pp. iii to viii; Text: Gen. to Mal., pp. 3–587; p. 588, blank; Engr. title to N. Test.; same imprint, 1 f.; verso, blank; Text: Mat. to Rev., pp. 3–190; sigs. in 6^s; Front. to O. T., Samuel and Eli, *J. B. Neagle*; to N. T., The Repose in Egypt, *Ellis*.

8. THE HOLY BIBLE: | With | the References and marginal Readings | of the | Polyglott Bible. | with numerous additions from | Bagster's Comprehensive Bible. | Philadelphia: | Published by Robert P. Desilver, | No. 255, Market Street. | 1839. | 12.

Title, 1 f.; verso, Names and Order; Copyright dated 1833; C. Sherman & Co, Printers. Text: Gen. to Mal., pp. 3–716; sig. 1–60^4; N. T. title, 1 f.; Text: pp. 719–937; sig. 60^4–79^1; Psalms in Metre, pp. 939-982; sig. 79^2–82.

Plates:

Front. Abraham offering up Isaac,................................*F. Kearney.*
Sampson betrayed by Delilah,....................................*Kearney.*
Daniel in the Lion's Den, ...*Kearney.*
Jonah cast into the Sea,.......................................*Kearney.*
Front. Appearance to the Shepherds,............................*Kearney.*
Christ raising the Widow's Son,................................*Kearney.*
Entombing of Christ,...*Kearney.*

Compare with No. 9 of 1833, with which the Text seems to agree.

9. HOLY BIBLE: New York, Stereotyped for the American
Bible Society, by E. & J. White. D. Fanshaw, Printer.
1839. (L.) 12.

10. HOLY BIBLE: New York, Stereotyped by A. Chandler, for
the American Bible Society. D. Fanshaw, Printer. 1839.
(L.) 12.

21st ed. Probably from the same plates as No. 9, of 1829, with new Title pages.

11. HOLY BIBLE: New York, Stereotyped by A. Chandler.
Printed by D. Fanshaw, for the American Bible Society.
1839. (L.) 12.

A Reference Bible. 5th edition.

12. HOLY BIBLE: Stereotyped by J. Howe, Philadelphia. New
York: Robinson and Franklin (successors to Leavitt,
Lord & Co.). 1839. 12.

Text: pp. 655; Contents, pp. 656–660; sigs. in 6s; 2 fronts to O. T., Ruth, and Feast of the Tabernacle, having at foot of each, "Hartford: Andrus & Judd."

13. HOLY BIBLE: Stereotyped by J. Howe, Philadelphia. Hartford: Andrus, Judd & Franklin. 1839. 12.

Pp. 655; sigs. in 6s; several wood engravings.

14. HOLY BIBLE: Middletown, Conn. E. Hunt & Co. 1839.
(B.) 12.

15. HOLY BIBLE: Brattleboro, Vt. 1839. 12.

Engraved title: The | Holy Bible. | (Vignette.) | Published by | The | Brattleboro Bible Company. | Pp. 1003, 321; Front. to O. T.

16. HOLY BIBLE: Baltimore: Armstrong & Berry. M.DCCC-
XXXIX. (L.) 12.

Text: Gen. to Mal., pp. 1003; Cont., pp. 1004–1018. New Test. title, 1 f.; Mat. to Rev., pp. 321; Cont., pp. 322–328.

17. HOLY BIBLE: New York: Robinson & Franklin, successors to Leavitt, Lord & Co., 180 Broadway. 1839.   32.

Pp. 852, 259. Contents, pp. 261-263. Sigs. in 8s. Engravings:
St. Michael,..*Illman & Pilbrow.*
Christ led to Crucifixion,...................................*Illman & Pilbrow.*
Triumph of Mordecai,..*Illman & Pilbrow.*
The Nativity,...*Illman & Pilbrow.*

18. HOLY BIBLE: New York: Charles Wells, 56 Gold street. n. d.   32.

Pp. 726, 221. Front. and engr. title page. The printer occupied the premises above mentioned, from 1836-1843. *N. Y. Directory.*

19. HOLY BIBLE: Stereotyped by Henry Wallis and Luther Roby, Concord, N. H. Portland: Published by O. L. Sanborn. 1839.   (Harvard Coll.)   32.

20. NE KAGHYADONGHSERA ne Royadadokenghdy ne ISAIAH. New York: Printed for the American Bible Society. D. Fanshaw, Printer. 1839.   18.

This is a Mohawk version of the Book of Isaiah.

1. NEW TESTAMENT: Cooperstown, N. Y.: stereotyped, printed and published by H. & E. Phinney, and sold by them at their bookstore, and by the booksellers generally in the United States. 1839.   (L.)   4.

Frontisp. and four woodcuts.

2. THE FAMILY EXPOSITOR, or a Paraphrase and Version of the New Testament, with Critical notes and a Practical Improvement to each section. By Philip Doddridge, D. D. American Edition, with a life of the author, by N. W. Fiske, and an Introductory Essay, by Moses Stuart. Thirteenth edition. Amherst, Mass.: Published by Charles McFarland. 1839.   8.

Portrait and Plates.

3. O NOVO TESTAMENTO: traduzido em Portugues, pelo J. Ferreira A. d'Almeida. Nova York: A custa da Socieda de Americana da Biblia. 1839.   (Am. Bib. Soc. Lib.)   8.

This is a Protestant version.

4. O | Novo Testamento | de | Nosso Senhor | Jesu Christo, | traduzido em Portugues | segundo a Vulgata, | pelo Padre | Antonio Pereira de Figueiredo. | Nova York: | Ediçao estereotipica por J. S. Redfield, | a custa da Socieda de Americana da Biblia, | formada em Nova York, A. D. 1816. | Impresa por D. Fanshaw. | 1839. | (L.)   12.

    Title, 1 f.; verso, Indice and Ed. 1mo; Text: pp. 3–282; sigs. 1 to 12⁹ in 12º, including Title. This is a Catholic Testament.

5. **Das Neue | Testament** | unsers | Herrn und Heilandes | Jesu Christi, | nach der Uebersetzung | Dr. Martin Luthers. | Nebst einer Vollstandigen anweisung | der | Episteln und Evangelein aller Sonn= und Festage | durch ganze Jahr. | Philadelphia, | Herausgegeben von Kimber und Sharpless, Buchhändler | Nro. 8 Sud Dritte= Strasse. | 1839. | Stereotypirt von A. and W. Blumer, Allentown. (L.)   12.

   Pp. 420.

6. The New Testament, | in the | Common Version | with | Amendments of language, | By Noah Webster, LL. D. | New Haven: | Published by S. Babcock. | Stereotyped by J. S. Redfield, New York. | 1839. | (L.)   12.

   See 1833. 1 Tim. 4 : 16 is incorrect.

7. New Testament: New York: S. Colman, 141 Nassau street. 1839.   12.

   Pp. 447.

8. New Testament: New York: Stereotyped ed. J. S. Redfield, for the American Bible Society. 1839. (Rev. Dr. Brigham.)   Brevier 18.

9. New Testament: Philadelphia: Haswell, Barrington & Haswell, No. 293, Market Street. 1839.   24.

   Pp. 318.

1840.

1. HOLY BIBLE: With Apocrypha, Canne's Marginal Notes and References; Index, Alphabetical Table of Names, Tables of Scripture Weights, Measures and Coins, &c. Cooperstown, N. Y.: Published and sold by H. & E. Phinney. Sold also by J. Tiffany, Utica. 1840. (L.) 4.

Title, 1 f.; verso, Names and Order; To the Reader, p. 3; Cont., pp. 4-8, making with Title 1 sig.; Text: Gen. to Mal., pp. 9-594; sig. B to 8W³; Table of Passages, p. 575; Chronolog. Index, Tables of Time and Offices, p. 576 (3W⁴); Fam. Rec., 2 ff.; Apocrypha (in smaller type), pp. 1-99; sig. A to N²; p. 100, blank. New Test. title: Cooperstown (N. Y.), Stereotyped, Printed and published by H. & E. Phinney, and sold by them at their Bookstore, and by the Booksellers generally in the United States. 1839, 1 p.; verso, Account of dates &c.; Text: Mat. to Rev., pp. 579-754; sig. including Title, 3X to 4U¹; Index, Tables, Alphabetical list of proper names, pp. 755-768; sig. 4U² to 4V⁴ in 4ˢ; Brown's Concordance (no title p.), pp. (1)-(35); sig. A to E²; but sig. letters A and B are omitted. Sigs. all in 4ˢ.

Engravings (on wood): Front. and 14 in O. T.; Front. and 4 in N. T.

2. HOLY BIBLE: Translated from the Latin Vulgat: With Annotations, References, and a Historical and Chronological Index. First Stereotype from the Fifth Dublin Edition. 𝕻𝖍𝖎𝖑𝖆𝖉𝖊𝖑𝖕𝖍𝖎𝖆: Published by Eugene Cummiskey. Stereotyped by J. Howe. 1840. (L.) 8.

Front. to O. T., Finding of Moses; to the N. T., The Virgin and Child. Engraved for the Catholic Expositor. James Harris, Engraver, 58 Nassau street. The Approbations in this edition are printed on the verso of the Title page.

This volume agrees with that already given, 1839.

3. HOLY BIBLE: New York: Stereotype edition, by J. S. Redfield, for the American Bible Society. 1840. (Rev. Dr. Brigham.) Long Pr. 8.

4. HOLY BIBLE: New York: Published by the American Bible Society. D. Fanshaw, Printer. Stereotyped by E. & J. White. 1840. 12.

Pp. 832 and 254.

5. HOLY BIBLE: Philadelphia: Hogan & Thompson. 1840. 12.

Pp. 1096, 342.

6. POLYGLOTT FAMILY BIBLE: With marginal readings, references, and parallel passages. Keene, N. H.: I. & I. W. Prentiss. 1840. (L.) 12.

7. HOLY BIBLE: New York: Stereotyped by Richard C. Valentine, for the American Bible Society. Instituted &c. *Printed by D. Fanshaw.* 1840. Ref. Pearl 18.
1st edition.

8. THE ENGLISH VERSION of the POLYGLOTT BIBLE: With marginal Readings: Together with a copious and original Selection of References to parallel and Illustrative passages. Exhibited in a manner hitherto unattempted. Springfield: Published by G. & C. Merriam. 1840. 82.

The Text corresponds with that of Chase's Woodstock edition of 1836, and the headings of pp. 212, 213, are transposed in this also. The vol. has two engraved titles and a few etchings.

9. AN ABSTRACT of the HISTORY of the OLD and NEW TESTAMENTS, divided into Three parts. Part I. From the Creation to the Birth of Christ. Part II. The Life of our Lord Jesus Christ. Part III. The Acts of the Apostles, and the Establishment of the Church throughout the World. By the Ven. and Right Rev. Richard Challoner, D. D., Bishop of Tebra, and V. A. Third American Edition. Revised by the Very Rev. John Power, V. G. with the Approbation of the most rev. Archbishop Ecclison, of Baltimore, and the Rt. Rev. J. Dubois, B-p N. Y. New York: Published by John McSweeny. Stereotyped by Smith & Wright, 216 William St., N. Y. 1840. (Rev. Mr. Rooney, Albany.) 12.

3 plates. A considerable part of the New Testament History consists of portions of the Sacred Text, printed, however, in paragraphs. The dedication is dated 15 February 1834.

1. THE | NEW TESTAMENT | of our | Lord and Saviour Jesus Christ, | translated from the | Latin Vulgate: | Diligently compared with the Original Greek: | and first published by | The English College at Rheims, A. D. 1582. | With

Annotations, References, and an Historical and | Chronological Index. | From the last London and Dublin edition. | Published with the approbation of the Right Rev. Francis Patrick Kenrick, | and the Right Rev. J. Hughes. | Philadelphia : | Eugene Cummiskey, 130 South Sixth St. | Stereotyped by L. Johnson. | 1840. | (L.)   12.

Title, 1 f. ; verso, Approbations, dated 1st October, 1839, Books of the New Test. ; Text: Gen. to Apocal., pp. 3–421; sigs. in figures and letters; 1 to 3 in 6^s, 4 to 51 in 4^s, 52 in 12^s. This sig. is completed with a blank leaf. At p. 25 commence the sig. letters with C, and run to 2N^1 in 6^s; Table of Epist. and Gosp., pp. 422, 423; Table of References, pp. 424–426; Index, pp. 427–429; at foot of p. 429, Table of Time; verso of 2N^1 to 2N^5, a blank leaf completing the sig. The notes and references are at foot of the pp.

The edition consisted of 2750 copies. Some have, at the end, 3 pp. of Eugene Cummiskey's advertisement of Catholic Publications.

2. NEW TESTAMENT: Philadelphia: Wm. S. Young, 173 Race Street. 1840.   (L.)   12.

3. NEW TESTAMENT: Translated from the Latin Vulgate: With annotations to clear up the principal difficulties of Holy Writ, as approved by the Right Reverend John Dubois, Catholic Bishop of New York.   Stereotype edition. Utica: Printed by Thomas Davis, for the Proprietors. 1840.   (L.)   12.

This is the Devereux Testament, with a new Title page merely, the certificate of copyright being omitted. The typographical error in James 5:17, already noted, is continued. See 1829.

4. NEW TESTAMENT: Stereotype edition. Newburyport: Published by John G. Tilton. 1840.   (L.)   12.
Pp. 450.

5. POLYGLOTT FAMILY TESTAMENT. | The | New Testament | of | our Lord and Saviour Jesus Christ : | With the Marginal Readings, | compendious Annotations, | and | Copious References to Parallel and | Illustrative Passages. | Keene, N. H. | J. & J. W. Prentiss. | 1840. | (L.; G. L.)   12.

On reverse of Title, Extract of Copyright, dated 1833, obtained by James Conner & W. R. Cooke, New York. Stereotyped by Conner and Cooke, New York; Text: Mat. to Rev., pp. 3–422; sigs. in 12^s.

6. NEW TESTAMENT: With amendments of the Language. By Noah Webster, LL. D. New Haven: Published by S. Babcock. Stereotyped by J. S. Redfield, New York. 1840. (L.) 12.

7. POLYGLOTT REFERENCE TESTAMENT: New York: G. Wells. 1840. (G. L.) 32.

1841.

1. HOLY BIBLE. (In raised letters for the Blind.) 8 vols. New York. 1841. (L.) 4.

2. HOLY BIBLE: Boston: Munroe & Francis; Hilliard, Gray & Co.; Crocker & Brewster. New Test. Boston: Mathew Hale, Congress Street, and Alex. Price, 228½ Washington street. 1841. (L.) 8.

3. HOLY BIBLE: With the References and marginal Readings of the Polyglott Bible, and numerous additions from Bagster's Comprehensive Bible. Philadelphia: Thomas, Cowperthwaite & Co. 1841. (L.) 8.

With Psalms in metre.

4. HOLY BIBLE: Stereotype edition. Cooperstown, N. Y.: Published by H. & E. Phinney. 1841. (L.) 8.

Title, 1 f.; verso, Names and Order of all the Books; Text: Gen. to Mal., pp. 3–486; sigs. 1 to 31^3 in 8^s; A to X^3 in 12^s, and A to $2R^3$ in 6^s (A to F of these last are not marked); Fam. Rec., 2 ff.; Title to N. Test., 1 f.; verso, Tables of Scripture Measures, Weights and Money, and of Time; Text: Mat. to Rev., pp. 3–162; sigs. 31^5 to 41^4 in 8^s; X^5 to 2D (misprinted L) in 12^s; 2R to 3F in 6^s.

1 front. and 4 engrav. in O. T.; 1 front. and 2 engrav. in N. T., all on wood.

The total number printed of this Bible was 2000; the stereotype plates have been long since destroyed. *E. P.*

5. HOLY BIBLE: New York: Stereotyped by Richard C. Valentine, for the American Bible Society. Instituted in the year 1816. *Printed by D. Fanshaw.* 1841. 12.

6. HOLY BIBLE: Hartford: William Andrus. 1841.   12.
Stereotyped by A. Chandler; pp. 824, 251, with Psalms in Metre, p. 70. Front. and Titles engraved by W. D. Smith.

7. HOLY BIBLE: *Stereotyped by D. & G. Bruce, New York.* Hartford: William Andrus. 1841.   12.
2 engr. front., pp. 837 in 12*. This seems to be the same as Daniel D. Smith's New York 12mo ed. of 1827, with new Titles.

8. THE ENGLISH VERSION of the POLYGLOTT BIBLE: Stereotyped by L. Johnson, Philadelphia: Thomas, Cowperthwaite & Co. 1841.   12.
Pp. 587, 190. Engr. Front. and Title to O. and N. Test.

9. HOLY BIBLE: Philadelphia: Thomas, Cowperthwaite & Co. 253 Market St. 1841.   32.
Engr. titles and front.

10. HOLY BIBLE: in the common version, with amendments of Language by Noah Webster, LL. D.   New Haven: Published by N. Webster.   M.DCCCXLI.   32.

11. HOLY BIBLE, containing the Old Testament and the New. Stereotyped by Henry Wallis and L. Roby, Concord, N. H.   Portland: Sanborn, Sherburne & Co. 1841.   32.
Pp. 852, 259.

1. NEW TESTAMENT: Stereotyped by B. & J. Collins, New York. Boston: Benjamin Adams. 1841. (L.; G. L.) 12.
Pp. 290.

2. NEW TESTAMENT: Translated from the Latin Vulgate. Philadelphia: Published by Eugene Cummiskey. 1841.   8.
Edition 2000.

3. NEW TESTAMENT: Concord, N. H. Roby, Kimball & Merrell. 1841.   12.
Pp. 3-807.

4. NEW TESTAMENT: Stereotype edition. Philadelphia: Published by Crolius & Gladding, No. 341 Market Street, above Ninth, North side. *Printed by King & Baird*, No. 9 George Street. 1841. (L.) 12.
Pp. 453, in 6s.

5. **Das | Neue Testament** | unsers | Herrn und Heilandes | Jesu Christi. | Nach Dr. Martin Luther's Uebersetzung. | Stereotypirt von J. Howe, Philadelphia. | Philadelphia, | Herausgegeben von Georg W. Menz und Sohn, Buchhändler | Nro. 53 in der Nord Dritten Strasse. | 1841. | (L.) 12.
Title, 1 f.; verso, Verzeichniss der Bücher; Text: pp. 3-269; Verzeichniss der Episteln, &c., pp. 670-673 (?), followed by a blank leaf; sigs. *A to *X⁶ in 6s.

6. NEW TESTAMENT: New York: Stereotyped by Smith and Valentine, for the American Bible Society instituted in New York in 1816. Printed by D. Fanshaw. 1841. (L.) 32.

1842.

1. HOLY BIBLE: Stereotyped by James Conner, New York. Hartford: Printed and published by Silas Andrus. 1842. fol.

2. THE HOLY BIBLE: | being | the English Version | of the | Old and New Testament, | made by order of King James I. | carefully revised and amended, | by | several Biblical scholars. | Second Edition. | Philadelphia. | Published for David Bernard. | By J. B. Lippincott, corner of Fourth and Race streets. | Stereotyped by L. Johnson. | 1842. | (L.) 8.
Title, 1 f.; verso, Names and Order, Notice of Copyright, 1842; Kay & Brother, printers; Pref., pp. iii, iv, dated Feb. 1, 1842; Text: Gen. to Mal., 1-629; Passages collated from O. T., 630-631; Table of Script. Measures, &c. of Time, 632, 3C⁴; Fam. Rec., 2 ff.; sig. A to 3G in 6s, and 1 to 79 in 4s. N. Test., same imp., 1 p.; verso, Names and Order; Pref. signed A. C. Kendrick, p. iii; Text: 1-190; Gen. Index, 191, 192; A to Q in 6s, 80 to 103 in 4s.

3. HOLY BIBLE: New York: Printed by D. Fanshaw for the
   Amer. Bible Society. 1842. 33d edition. (L.) Nonp. 12.

4. HOLY BIBLE: New York, Printed by D. Fanshaw "For the
   American Bible Society." 1842. Min. 12.
   41st edition, pp. 852; Family Record; sigs. in 12ˢ; 1 to 36, A to 2N; the last sig. is in 6ˢ.

5. HOLY BIBLE: Hartford: Published by William Andrus.
   1842. (B.) 12.
   Pp 824, 251.

6. HOLY BIBLE: Stereotyped by J. Howe, Phil. Hartford:
   Published by William Andrus. 1842. 12.
   Pp. 655. Contents, 656–681; 12 plates (wood cuts), 2 on a page; Map of Canaan. Page 536 is headed Chap. II. instead of S. Luke.

7. HOLY BIBLE: Greenfield, Mass.: Published by W. & H.
   Merriam. 1842. (L.) 18.
   Four etchings, 2 in each Test., with engr. front. and titles to O. and N. T. "Diamond Bible;" "Diamond New Testament." Greenfield, Mass., Published by W. & H. Merriam. n. d.

8. HOLY BIBLE, containing the Old Testament and the New
   &c. Stereotyped by J. Howe, Philad. Philadelphia: R.
   W. Pomeroy, No. 3 Minor Street. 1842. 32.
   Pp. 819, 256, with Psalms in metre, pp. 83. Front. and engr. title: Hogan & Thompson, 139 Market St. 1834.

9. HOLY BIBLE, containing the Old Testament and the New.
   Philadelphia: John Locken, 311, Market St. 1842. 32.
   Engraved front. and title, "The Everlasting Gospel." See *post* No. 11, of 1843.

10. HOLY BIBLE, containing the Old Testament and the New.
    Stereotyped by J. Howe, Phil. Hartford: Published by
    William Andrus. 1842. 24 (or 32).
    The Text is in double columns, but in paragraphs, several verses being included in one paragraph. Engr. front. and woodcuts. Pp. 615, 192.

11. HOLY BIBLE, containing the Old Testament and the New. Portland: Sanborn and Carter. 1842.   32.
    Engraved Title: "The Everlasting Gospel;" same imprint. Pp. 852, 259.

12. ISAIAH. A Comment on the 23d chapter of the Prophet Isaiah. Springfield: Printed by Wood and Rupp. 1842. (Am. Antiq. Soc., Worcester, Mass.)   8.

1. NEW TESTAMENT: Stereotyped by B. & J. Collins, New York. Philadelphia: Published by Kimber & Sharpless, No. 50 North Fourth Street. n. d.   4.
   Pp. 265. 13 plates, 1 map, and an engraved title. Psalms of David, pp. 18.

2. NEW TESTAMENT: Translated out of the Latin Vulgate: With Annotations to clear up the principal difficulties of Holy Writ. *As approved by the* Right Reverend John Dubois, *Catholic Bishop of New-York.* The law of the Lord is unspotted, converting souls; the testimony of the Lord is faithful, giving wisdom to little ones. *Ps.* xviii. 8. Stereotype edition. New-York: D. & J. Sadlier, Bookbinders and Catholic Booksellers, No. 19 Carmine, corner of Bleecker Streets. 1842.   12.
   This is the 1st edition of Sadlier's Testament, from the plates of the "Devereux Testament," *supra* p. 198, which were purchased by the firm. On the verso of the title page is the original approbation of Bishop Dubois, dated 7th Sept. 1828.
   The error in James 5:17 is continued.

3. NEW TESTAMENT: Stereotype edition. Philadelphia: Published by Griffith & Simon, 188 North Third Street, and 384 North Second Street. 1842.   12.
   On the verso of Title page: King & Baird, Printers, No. 9, George Street, Philadelphia.

4. NEW TESTAMENT: With brief Explanatory Notes. By Jacob & John S. C. Abbott. Boston: Published by Crocker & Brewster, 47 Washington Street. 1842.   8.
   1st edition. Stereotyped by the Boston Type and Stereotype Company. Pp. 566.

5. 'Η | ΚΑΙΝΗ ΔΙΑΘΗΚΗ | του | Κυριου και Σωτηρος | 'ημων | Ιησου Χριστου, | μεταφρασθεισα εκ της Παλαιας | εις την | καθ ομιλουμενην | Ελληνικην Διαλεκτον. | Δια Δαπανης της εν | Αμερικη Ιερογραφικης | εταιρειας. | Νεα Υορκ. | Εκ της Τυπογραφιας | Δανιηλ Φανσά. | 1842. | (N. Y. State Lib.) 12.

5th edition of the Testament, *supra* p. 244.

1843.

1. HOLY BIBLE: With Canne's marginal notes and references, Apocrypha, Index and Tables. Stereotyped by James Conner, New York. Hartford (Conn.): Printed and published by Silas Andrus. 1843. (L.) fol.

A reprint of the edition of 1829. An engr. front. to each Testament.

2. HOLY BIBLE: Cooperstown, N. Y., Stereotyped, Printed and published by H. & E. Phinney, and sold by them at their Bookstore, and by the Booksellers generally in the United States. 1843. 4.

3. PICTORIAL BIBLE: with more than 1000 woodcut Illustrations. Imprint to engraved Title: New York: J. S. Redfield, Clinton Hall, corner of Nassau and Beekman streets. Imprint to printed Title: J. S. Redfield, Clinton Hall. Philadelphia: Thomas, Cowperthwait & Co. Boston: Price & Co. 1843. (L.) 8.

Imprint on the printed title to N. T. is the same as on the engraved titles, but with date 1846. Tables of ancient Chronology and map of Palestine precede the N. Test.

4. HOLY BIBLE: New York: Printed by D. Fanshaw, For "The American Bible Society." 1843. 12.

29th edition; pp. 824, 251; sigs. in 12s.

5. HOLY BIBLE: New York: American Bible Society. 1843. Pearl 18.

With References.

6. HOLY BIBLE: Stereotyped by J. Howe, Philadelphia. Hartford: S. Andrus & Son. 1843. (L.) 12.

Two engraved plates and 20 woodcuts, the latter arranged 2 in a page. Some copies are without dates, but accompanied by Psalms in metre.

7. HOLY BIBLE: Stereotyped by D. & G. Bruce, New York. Hartford: William Andrus. 1843. 12.

Pp. 637, 337.

8. HOLY BIBLE: containing the Old Testament and the New. Hartford: S. Andrus & Son. 1843. 24.

With engr. front. and a number of woodcuts 2 on a page.

9. HOLY BIBLE: Philadelphia: Published by Mentz & Rovoudt, No. 58, North Third Street. 1843. (L.) 24.

Title, 1 f.; verso, Names and Order of the Books; at foot, "*This Edition is published from the most approved Standard Copy of the Holy Bible.*" Text: Gen. to Mal., pp. 3–599; verso of 599, Table of Measures, Weights, Money and Time; Contents of O. T., pp. 601–606; sigs. A to Eee^3 in 6^s, and (A) to (Z) in 12^s; 1 blank leaf. New Testament title, 1 f.; verso, blank; Text: Mat. to Rev., pp. 3–179; p. 180, blank; Cont., pp. 181, 182; sigs. A to Q^1 in 6^s, and (A) to (H)^7 in 12$_s$.

10. HOLY BIBLE: Philadelphia: J. B. Lippincott & Co. MDCCCXLIII. 24.

Pp. 824 and 251. Bound up with Book of Common Prayer.

11. HOLY BIBLE: Philadelphia: John Locken, 311 Market St. 1843. 32.

Engraved titles to O. and N. T. (with vignette of The Finding of Moses to the former); The Everlasting Gospel. J. Locken, Philadelphia. n. d.; pp. 852, 259; Contents, 261–263; Front. to O. T., Daniel in the Lion's Den; to N. T., The Holy Family. Engr., The Repose in Egypt; The Resurrection; Christ blessing Little Children; Christ in the garden with Mary.

This edition accompanies The Book of Common Prayer. Philadelphia: Lippincott & Co. 1842. On comparing, it seems to be from the same plates as Robinson & Franklin's Bible, *supra*, 1839.

12. ENGLISH VERSION of the POLYGLOTT BIBLE. Springfield: Published by G. & C. Merriam. 1843. 32.

Engr. front. and several etchings.

13. THE ENGLISH VERSION of the POLYGLOTT BIBLE, with the Marginal readings: together with a copious and original selection of References to parallel and illustrative passages, exhibited in a manner hitherto unattempted. Boston: Published by R. H. Sherburne. 1843. 32.

Text agrees with Chase's Woodstock ed. of 1836.

1. NEW TESTAMENT: according to the commonly received version. | London, Imprinted by Robert Barker, 1611. | Third edition. | New York: | Stereotyped by White and Hagar, for the | American and Foreign Bible Society. | *John Gray, Printer.* | 1843. | 12.

See 1838.

2. NEW TESTAMENT: Newburyport, Mass., Published by Wm. W. Nason. 1843. 12.

3. NEW TESTAMENT: William Stewart, Hagerstown, Indiana. n. d. (L.) 24.

Annexed is an edition of The Shorter Catechism, with proofs. Hagerstown: Published by William Stewart. Edwin Bell, Printer. 1843.

4. NEW TESTAMENT: Cooperstown: H. & E. Phinney. 1843. 48.

Stereotyped by Richard C. Valentine, 45, Gold-Street, New York; pp. 454; Front. The Agony in the Garden, Engr. by M. Osborne; Engr. Title page; and following plates from the same burin; Christ disputing with the Doctors; Christ and the Woman of Samaria.

5300 copies of this Testament have been issued from the Cooperstown press, from 1832–1848. E. P.

5. NEW TESTAMENT: Hartford: S. Andrus. 1843. 48.

1844.

1. THE | HOLY BIBLE: | containing the | Old and New Testaments: | translated out of | the Original Tongues | and with | the former Translations diligently compared | and revised. | Philadelphia: | J. B. Lippincott & Company. | M.DCCCXLIV. | 4.

Title, 1 f.; verso, blank; Names and Order, p. 2; verso, blank; Text: Gen. to Mal., pp. 3-1098; sigs. A to 6N¹; Fam. Rec., 2 ff.; New Test. title, same imprint, 1 p.; verso, blank; Text: Mat. to Rev., pp. 1101-1440; sigs. 6N³ to 8E in 4ˢ.

This edition is without notes or engraving. The pages are included within double rules; it is a beautiful specimen of typography.

2. HOLY BIBLE: Stereotype edition. | Philadelphia: | Published by | The Bible Association of Friends in America. | No. 50, North Fourth Street, up stairs. | 1844. | 8.

See 1831.

3. HOLY BIBLE, translated from the Latin Vulgate; With Annotations, References, and an Historical and Chronological Index. From the last London and Dublin Editions. The whole revised and diligently compared with the Latin Vulgate. Published with the Approbation of the Right Reverend John Hughes, D. D., Bishop of New York. New York: Published by Edward Dunigan, 151 Fulton Street. 1844.   (L.)   8.

The Text of this edition is from the Stereotype plates of Doyle's Douay Bible, No. 5, *supra*, p. 220, and has been issued in different styles; one called, The Illustrated edition, was published, in parts, with Lithograph titles in Colors (in addition to the printed titles), with engraved frontispiece, St. Patrick's Cathedral, New York. Approbation, dated 27th Jan. 1844, thirteen steel plates, and 4 ff. engraved for Family Record; another copy has the two illuminated titles and *eight* steel plates; another the titles in colors, and *six* steel plates, whilst a fourth was issued with a frontispiece and *nine* engravings on wood in the Old Testament, and a front. on steel to the New Testament.

4. HOLY BIBLE: according to the authorized version. With explanatory Notes, Practical Observations, and Copious Marginal References. By Thomas Scott, Rector, &c. From the latest London Edition, with the author's last Corrections and Improvements. To which is added, a Concordance to the Holy Scriptures of the New and Old Testaments, by the Rev. John Brown of Haddington. New York: W. E. Dear, Printer and publisher, 2 Ann Street. 1844.   (L.)   8.

3 volumes, stereotype edition.

5. HOLY BIBLE: Philadelphia: Published by R. S. H. George. No. 26, South 5th Street. 1844.   (L.)   8.

6. HOLY BIBLE: With Canne's Marginal Notes and References, and a Concise Table of Contents of the books of the Old and New Testaments. Stereotyped by J. Howe, Philadelphia. Hartford: S. Andrus & Son. 1844. (L.) 8.

Title, 1 f.; verso, Names and Order, To the Reader; 2 p.; Contents, pp. 5-10; Text: Gen. to Mal., pp. 11-619; Tables of Measures, &c , p. 620, followed by 2 blank ff. ; sigs. A^6 to 20^8 in 8^s.; Apocrypha, pp. 1-109, followed by a blank leaf; sigs. A* to G*^{8} in 8_s; Fam. Rec., 4ff.; New Test., title (same imprint), 1 p.; verso, Account of Dates and Time; Text: Mat. to Rev., pp. 623-811; verso of 811, blank; sigs. 2P2 to $3A^8$ in 8^s; Brown's Concordance; stereotyped as above; no imprint; title, 1 p.; To the Reader, 1 p.; Text: pp. 3-136; sigs, A to L in 8^s; Psalms in Metre, pp. 1-39; sigs. A to recto of C^4 in 6_s, 2 plates.

7. THE | HOLY BIBLE: | containing the | Old and New Testaments, | according to the | authorized version: | With | the references and marginal readings | of the | Polyglott Bible, | with numerous additions from | Bagster's Comprehensive Bible. | Philadelphia: | Lindsay & Blakiston. | N. W. corner of Fourth and Chestnut streets. | 1844. | 12.

Illuminated title: The | Bible | with | Marginal Readings | and References | 1 p.; Printed Title, 1 f.; verso, Names and Order of all the Books; Notice of Copyright by James Conner and William R. Cooke, 1833, C. Sherman & Co., Printers. The Text corresponds in all respects with that of the Bible Annual, No. 9, *supra* p. 223. Front to O. T., Abraham's Sacrifice; to N. Test., Christ disputing with the Doctors.

Mr. Conner having decided on stereotyping an elegant edition of the Polyglott Bible (12mo), he got up a new size and style of type called Agate, cut in a condensed and compressed manner; the intention being to admit of a certain number of figures and points coming within a given space—the whole included within a center column of notes. Of this Bible he made several sets of plates from the same composition; then took out the references and center column of notes, and completed many sets of an 18mo Bible, and a proportionate number of plates for the New Testament. *N. Y. Printer*, II. 2.

Some copies of Lindsay & Blakiston's edition are without any year on the title page.

9. HOLY BIBLE: From the authorized Oxford edition. Appointed to be read in Churches. Philadelphia: Hogan and Thompson. 1844. 12.

Pp. 1098, 342, in 12^s.

10. ENGLISH VERSION of the POLYGLOTT BIBLE: Stereotyped by L. Johnson. Philadelphia: Thomas, Cowperthwaite & Co. 1844. 12.

With N. Test. of 1843.

8. HOLY BIBLE: Philadelphia: Published by R. S. H. George, No. 26, South Fifth Street, For the Bible Committee of the Society of the Protestant Episcopal Church for the Advancement of Christianity in Pennsylvania. 1844.   12.

Pp. 1044, in 6s. The title p. to the New Test. has after "Revised," the words, "By his Majesty's Special Command, appointed to be read in Churches," with this imprint: Philadelphia: Published by R. S. H. George, 26 South Fifth Street. 1844.

11. HOLY BIBLE: New York: American Bible Society. 1844.
Nonp. 12.
Pp. 669.

12. HOLY BIBLE: New York: Stereotyped by R. C. Valentine, For the American Bible Society. 1844.   Bourg. 12.

1st ed., pp. 1284.

13. HOLY BIBLE: New York: Printed by D. Fanshaw, for the American Bible Society. 1844.   (L.)   Min. 12.

53d Edition. This is from the same plates as the Ed. of 1829, 1830. Full headings to Chapters, &c.

14. HOLY BIBLE: according to the commonly received version. London: 1611. Imprinted by Robert Barker, New York. Stereotyped by White and Hagar, for the American and Foreign Bible Society. Sixth edition. 1844. (N. Y. State Library.)   12.

15. HOLY BIBLE: Stereotype edition. Concord, N. H.: Luther Roby. 1844.   (G. L.)   12.

Pp. 824, 251. Stereotyped at the Boston Type and Stereotype Foundry; no references.

16. ENGLISH VERSION of the POLYGLOTT BIBLE, with Marginal Readings, references &c. Portland: Published by Sanborn & Carter. 1844.   12.

Engr. title and front. to Old and New Test.

17. HOLY BIBLE: Stereotype edition. Hartford: S. Andrus & Son. 1844.   12.

Stereotyped by A. Chandler. Pp. 824, 251. Engr. front. and title to O. T. Other copies have Andrus & Son on imprint.

18. HOLY BIBLE: Stereotyped by D. & G. Bruce, New York. Hartford: S. Andrus & Son. 1844. 12.
Text: pp. 837; Gen. Cont., pp. 656–681. No date to title of New Test. Engr. front. to O. and N. Testaments.

19. HOLY BIBLE: Hartford: S. Andrus and Son. 1844. (L.) 24.
2 Engraved Fronts. and a number of Woodcuts, 2 on a page; pp. 852 and 259. Some copies have Scotch Psalms in Metre, 81 pp. additional.

20. HOLY BIBLE: containing the Old Testament and the New. Philadelphia: Thomas, Cowperthwaite & Co., 253, Market Street. 1844. 24.
Pp. 852, 259; Contents and Psalms in Metre, additional.

21. HOLY BIBLE: containing the Old Testament and the New. Philadelphia: Sorin & Ball, 311 Market St. 1844. 24.
Pp. 852, 259; Contents, pp. 261-263. Psalms in Metre, pp. 81.; sigs. in 8s, with several Engravings and Engraved Titles, "The Everlasting Gospel. J. Locken. Philadelphia."
For Locken's edition, see 1843.

22. HOLY BIBLE: containing the Old Testament and the New. Stereotyped by J. Howe, Phila. Philadelphia: Hogan & Thompson, No. 30, North Fourth Street. 1844. 32.

23. HOLY BIBLE: Philadelphia: R. S. H. George, 26 South Fifth Street. 1844. 32.
T. K. & P. G. Collins, Printers, Philadelphia. Imprint to N. Test., Philadelphia: Sorin & Ball, 1844. Pp. 852 and 259. With Book of Common Prayer, Phil.: J. B. Lippincott. 1842.

24. HOLY BIBLE: containing the Old Testament and the New. Stereotyped by J. Howe, Philad. Hartford, Ct.: Published by Silas Andrus & Son. 1844. 32.
Pp. 729, 222; Contents, pp. 223, 224.

25. HOLY BIBLE: containing the Old Testament and the New. Stereotyped by Henry Wallis and L. Roby, Concord, N. H. Portland: Sanborn & Carter. 1844. 32.

26. ERRATA of the Protestant Bible; or the Truth of the English Translations examined; in a Treatise, showing some of the Errors that are to be found in the English translations of the Sacred Scriptures, used by Protestants, against such points of Religious Doctrine as are the Subject of Controversy between them and the Members of the Catholic Church; in which also, from their mistranslating the twenty-third verse of the fourteenth chapter of the Acts of the Apostles, the consecration of Dr. Matthew Parker the first Protestant Archbishop of Canterbury is occasionally considered. By Thomas Ward, Esq. A new Edition, carefully revised and corrected. To which are added, The celebrated Preface of the Rev. Doctor Lingard, in answer to Ryan's "Analysis," and a Vindication by the Right Rev. Doctor Milner, in Answer to Grier's Reply. Text: Revelations xxii. 18, 19. New York: Published by D. & J. Sadlier, No. 58 Gold Street. 1844. 8.

It contains portions of the Scriptures, in the Rheims, Bishops', and authorized versions. *Archd. Cotton.*

1. NEW TESTAMENT: Stereotyped by R. C. Valentine for the American and Foreign Bible Society. 1844. (N. Y. State Lib.) 8.

Baptist version; pp. 288 and Psalms, pp. 74.

2. NEW TESTAMENT: Translated from the Latin Vulgate. Philadelphia: Published by Eugene Cummiskey. 1844.

Edition 1000.

3. NEW TESTAMENT: With the Book of Psalms. New York: Printed for the American Bible Society. 1844. 12.

4. NEW TESTAMENT: Stereotyped by Luther Roby, Concord, N. H. Concord, N. H.: Published by Luther Roby. 1844. (A. G. J.) 32.

5. NEW TESTAMENT: Translated from the Latin Vulgat: With 𝔄nnotations and 𝔑eferences. Baltimore: Published by Fielding Lucas, Jr., No. 170 Market Street. n. d. 2.
This is Testament No. 10 of 1831, with a New Imprint.

6. LE | NOUVEAU TESTAMENT | de notre Seigneur | Jesus Christ, | revu sur les Originaux | Par David Martin, | Ministre du Saint Evangile à Utrecht. | New-York: | Publié par la Société Biblique Americaine, | Fondée en MDCCCXVI. | 1844. | (Am. Bib. Soc.)   12.
This is a Protestant version.

7. THE | GOSPEL | according to MATTHEW, | and the | ACTS of the APOSTLES; | translated into the | Putawatomic language. | By Johnston Lykins. | Carefully compared with the Greek text. | Published under the patronage of the American and Foreign Bible Society, by the Board of | Managers of the American Indian Mission Asso- | ciation. | Louisville, Ky. | *William C. Buck, Printer.* | 1844.   12.
There is a title in Indian as follows:
Oti ere | Mnoahemowun | Kavnupomk mrto, | epe | Katotmoat nwakanhik | Kaoneperuk e Putrwatmemwun. | O Hanstan Nykens, 1844 Tso Pponkit pe Kanckit | Hesus Knyst. | Pp. 240.

1845.

1. HOLY BIBLE: With Canne's Marginal Notes and References, Apocrypha, Index, and Tables. Stereotyped by James Conner. Hartford: S. Andrus & Son. 1845.   fol.
The collation agrees with the ed. of 1829. q. v.

2. THE | HOLY BIBLE, | translated from | the Latin Vulgate: | Diligently compared with | the Hebrew, Greek, and other Editions | in various languages. | The Old Testament was first published by the English College at Doway, A. D. 1609: | and | the New Testament by the English College at Rhemes, A. D. 1582. | With | Annotations, by the Rev. Dr. Challoner; | together with References, and an | Historical and Chronological ·Index. | Revised and corrected

according to the Clementine edition of the Scriptures. | With the approbation of the Right Rev. Bishop Hughes. | With a number of Steel Engravings. | New York: Published by D. & J. Sadlier, | No. 58 Gold, and 221 Bleecker Street. | n. d. | (L.)   4.

Engr. title with an architectural design and figures of St. Peter and St. Paul, 1 f.; Printed title, within double black lines, 1 f.; verso, blank; Approbation, Translation of the Decree of the Council of Trent, p. 3; Letter of Pope Pius VII, Admonition Prayer, Order of the Books of the Old Testament, p. 4; Text: Gen. to Mac., pp. 5–786; verso, blank; sigs. A (which includes title and 2 prel. pp.) to 5G¹; Index, pp. 787–793; verso, blank; sigs. 5G² to 5H¹; Family Record, 2 leaves; New Test., Engr. title with Vignette, The Adoration of the Shepherds, Engr. by Dick; Printed title (within double rules), 1 f.; verso, blank; Admonition, Letter of Pope Pius VI, Prayer, p. 3; Approbation, The Books of the New Test., p. 4; Text: Mat. to Rev., pp. 5–222; sigs. 5H², (which includes title, and 2 pp. of Mat., 2 prel. pp.; then follow 5I, one leaf; B in 3ˢ, 5K, 1 leaf; C in 3ˢ, 5L, 1 f.; D in 3ˢ, 5M, 1 f.; E in 3ˢ, 5N, 1 f.; F in 3ˢ, and so on alternately to Rev., 6L, 1 f.; and Ee³; Table of Epist. and Gosp., pp. 223, 224, 6M; Table of Ref., pp. 225, 226; Index, pp. 227, 228, followed by a blank leaf; Ff in 3ˢ; Errata of the Protestant Bible; or the Truth of the English Translations examined by Thomas Ward, Esq., a new edition carefully revised and corrected, with preface of the Rev. Doctor Lingard in answer to Ryan's "Analysis," and a Vindication by the Right Rev. Doctor Milner, in answer to Grier's "Reply." New York: Published by D. & J. Sadlier, No. 58 Gold Street. 1844. 1 p.; verso, blank; Dedication, dated 1st July, 1841, 1 p.; Contents, 1 p.; Lingard's Preface, Author's Pref. and Text: pp. 1–118; sig. 1 to 16¹.

Engravings:
1. Rebecca giving Abraham's servant to drink.................................... *Loudon.*
2. Agar in the wilderness.. *Jordon & Halpin.*
3. Lay not thy hand upon the boy... *Jordon & Halpin.*
4. Joseph sold.. *A. L. Dick.*
5. And Boaz said to Ruth: Hear me daughter................................. *Jordon & Halpin.*
6. Ascent of Elijah... *Dick.*
7. Esther petitioning the King... *J. Rogers.*

At the foot is "London: George Virtue:" and on the left corner page 499, which does not correspond with the page of this edition, p. 397.

1. The Redeemer.. *Loudon.*
3. To sit on my right or left hand is not mine to give..................... *Dick.*
4. The Agony in the garden... *G. Parker. Loudon.*
5. The Salutation............. From another of Virtue's London plates. *J. Rogers.*
6. The return of the Prodigal Son.. *Dick.*
7. Thomas putting his finger in the Saviour's side....................... *Dick.*
8. The Angels releasing the Apostles from prison....................... *J. Rogers.*
From another of Virtue's London plates.

Plate No. 6 of the Old Testament, is marked 2d Kings, Chap. 2; Ver. 1–13; instead of 4th Kings. In the text of the Douay Version, the prophet is called "Elias," not Elijah.

3. HOLY BIBLE: Designed for the use of Students. Stereotype Edition. New York: J. C. Riker, 129 Fulton Street. 1845. 4.

Pp. 776, 234, with Latin Glossary at the end, 9 pp. The words " Original Greek " on the title of the New Testament, are followed by these: Printed from the | Text and with the various readings of | Knapp; | Together with | the commonly received English Translation. | Designed for the Use of the Students. | Imprint as above.

4. HOLY BIBLE: New York: Stereotyped by T. B. Smith, for the American and Foreign Bible Society. 1845. Sm. Pica 8.

5. HOLY BIBLE, translated from the Latin Vulgat: With Annotations, References and Indexes. Philadelphia: Published by Eugene Cummiskey. Stereotyped by J. Howe, 1845. 8.

Edition 1000.

6. THE | HOLY BIBLE; | containing the Old and New Testaments, | according to the | Authorized Version; | with | the References and Marginal readings | of the Polyglott Bible, | with numerous additions from | Bagster's Comprehensive Bible. | Cooperstown: | Published by H. & E. Phinney. | 1845. | 8.

Title, 1 f.; verso, Names and Order of the Books of the O. and N. T.; Chronol. Order of the Books of the O. and N. T.; Notice of Copyright by James Conner & William R. Cooke, dated New York, 1833. Stereotyped by Conner & Cooke; Kingsland & Baptist, Print. 1 p.; Text: Gen. to Mal., pp. 3–716; (p. 658 marked 558) sig. 1^2 to 60^4 in 6^s; and A^3 to $2U^6$ in 8^s; N. Test. title, 1 f.; verso, blank; Text. Mat. to Rev., pp. 719–937; sigs. 60^6 to 79^1 in 6^s; $2U^7$ to 31^5 in 8^s; References in centre of the pp.

Front. to O. T.; Sarah requiring Abraham to cast out Hagar and her son. *Gimbrede;* To N. T., The Lord looking on Peter. *Gimbrede.*

Mr. E. Phinney informs me that their firm printed only 1000 copies of this Polyglott Bible. It is at present entirely out of the market, the issues of the Bible Society having rendered its further publication entirely unprofitable. It was from a duplicate set of Conner & Cooke's plates. See 1833.

7. HOLY BIBLE: New York: Stereotyped by D. Fanshaw, for the American Bible Society. 1845. Nonp. 12.

8. HOLY BIBLE: New York: Stereotyped by T. B. Smith, for the American and Foreign Bible Society. 1845. Brev. 12.

9. HOLY BIBLE: The text of the common version arranged in paragraphs, the chapters and verses being noted in the margin. By James Nourse. Hartford: Published by Andrus and Son. Stereotyped by J. Howe, Philadelphia. 1845. (L.) 12.

Engraved front. to N. Test.

10. HOLY BIBLE: Stereotyped by J. Howe, Philadelphia. Hartford: S. Andrus and Son. 1845. 12.

Pp. 681. Front. to O. and N. Test.; at the end, General Contents.

11. THE ENGLISH VERSION of the POLYGLOTT BIBLE. Portland: Sanborn and Carter. 1845. 12.

Pp. 587, 190. Engr. front. and titles to O. and N. Test.

12. HOLY BIBLE: New York: American and Foreign Bible Society. MDCCCXLV. (N. Y. State Lib.) 18.

13. HOLY BIBLE: Philadelphia: Uriah Hunt & Son, 44 North Fourth Street, and for sale by Booksellers generally throughout the United States. 1845. 24.

Pp. 852, 259; Psalms in metre, pp. 81; engraved front. and title, "The Everlasting Gospel."

14. HOLY BIBLE: containing the Old Testament and the New. Philadelphia: Thomas, Cowperthwaite & Co., 253 Market Street. 1845. 24.

Engr. front. to Old and New Test.

15. THE ENGLISH VERSION of the POLYGLOTT BIBLE. Philadelphia: Sorin and Ball, No. 42 North First Street. *Stereotyped by J. C. D. Christman & Co.* 1845. 32.

Engraved front. and title; same imprint.

16. HOLY BIBLE: New York: American Bible Society. Instituted in the year M.D.CCCXVI. 1845. 32.

154th edition.

17. HOLY BIBLE: Troy, N. Y.: Published by W. & H. Merriam. 1845. 32.

Contents of Old Test., pp. 1-8; Text: pp. 726, 221; Contents of N. Test., pp. 222-224; sigs. in 8s; with Book of Common Prayer: Philadelphia, Lippincott & Co., 1842.

1. NEW TESTAMENT: Stereotype edition. Stereotyped by B. & J. Collins, New York. Boston: Benjamin Adams. 1845. (L.) 8.

2. NEW TESTAMENT: New York: Stereotyped by T. B. Smith, for the American and Foreign Bible Society. 1845.
Sm. pica 8.

3. NEW TESTAMENT: New York: Stereotyped by T. B. Smith, for the American and Foreign Bible Society. 1845. Brev. 12.
Pp. 346.

4. NEW TESTAMENT: New York: Stereotyped by T. B. Smith, for the American and Foreign Bible Society. 1845. 16.

This Society published also this year a New Testament—Nonpar. 18mo.

5. NEW TESTAMENT: New York: American Bible Society. 1845. Pica 12.
Psalms appended.

6. NEW TESTAMENT: Translated out of the Latin Vulgate: With Annotations. *As Approved by the* Right Rev. John Hughes, *Catholic Bishop of New York.* New York: D. & J. Sadlier, 58 Gold Street. 1845. (L.) 12.

This is No. 2 of 1842, with a new Title page. The error in James 5:17 is continued.

7. 'Η ΚΑΙΝΗ ΔΙΑΘΗΚΗ | Novum Testamentum Graece | post | Ioh. Aug. Henr. Tittmannum | Olim Prof. Lips. | Ad fidem optimorum Librorum | secundis curis recognovit | Lectionumque varietatem notavit | Augustus Hahn | In Acad. Vratisl. Prof. | Editio Americana Stereotypa | curante | Edvardo Robinson, S. T. D. | Neo-Eboraci: | Sum-

tibus et Typis Leavitt et Trow | Bostoniae: | Apud Crocker
et Brewster. | MDCCCXLV. | 12.

Title, 1 f.; verso, University Press, John F. Trow & Co., 33 Ann St, New York;
Extract of Copyright, dated 1842; Prof. Tittman Lectori, dated 25 Nov. 1819, pp. iii,
iv, v; Prof. Hahn's Preface, dated May, 1840, pp. vi–xii; Advertisement signed E. R.
and dated 10 May, 1842, pp. xiii, xiv; Notices of the Principal Manuscripts and other
Helps for the Criticism of the Greek Text, pp. xv–xxviii; sigs. 1 to 3^2 in 6^s; Text:
pp. 1–508; sigs. 1 to verso of 43^2 in 6^s; at end, Leavitt, Trow & Company's Catalogue.

This edition professes to be a faithful reprint of the text and notes of Hahn, whose
account of the MSS &c. is here translated into English.

8. NEW TESTAMENT: Boston: W. D. Ticknor. 1845.   12.
Pp. 450.

9. NEW TESTAMENT: Translated from the Latin Vulgate:
With Annotations, a Chronological Index, Table of References, etc., etc. Approved by the Right Rev. John
Hughes, D. D., Bishop of New York. New York: Edward Dunigan, 151 Fulton Street, near Broadway. 1845. 18.

Title, 1 f.; verso, Order of the Books; Letter of Pius VI, 1 p.; verso, blank; Text:
pp. 5–349; Index, pp. 350–352; Table of Epist. and Gosp., pp. 352–354; Table of
Ref., pp 354–356.

Mr. Shea says: The text of this Testament is from the plates of a Belfast edition.

10. NEW TESTAMENT: Concord, N. H.: Luther Roby. 1845.
(G. L.)   32.

11. EL NUEVO TESTAMENTO, traducido al Castellano por Cipriano de Valera en 1602. Nuevo York: 1845.   12.

This is a Protestant version, published by the American Bible Society.

12. THE COMPLETE EVANGELIST; comprising The History of
the Life, Actions, Death, Resurrection, Ascension, and
Doctrine, of Jesus Christ. Intended to embrace every
important expression and idea recorded in the Writings
of Matthew, Mark, Luke, and John, in the words of the
authorized Translations. The whole arranged according
to the Order of Time in which the several Transactions
occurred, as nearly as that order can be ascertained. Edit-

ed by William Bolles. New London: Bolles & Williams. 1845. 12.

Title, 1 f.; verso, Copyright, Stereotyped by Redfield & Savage, 13 Chambers street, N. Y.; Pref. 1 f; verso blank; Table of Cont., pp. iii–viii; Text: pp. 7–226; sigs. 1–19 in 6s, the Pref. Cont. and 4 pp. of the Text being included in sig. 1. The Title and subsequent pp. are within rules.

13. THE FOUR GOSPELS. By Rev. George Campbell; and the Epistles by Rev. James McKnight. Hartford: J. Gaylord Wells. 1845. (G. L.) 32.

14. THE | ACTS of the APOSTLES, | in four books: | With | copious notes. | Οὕτω κατὰ κράτος ὁ λόγος τοῦ Κυρίου ηὔξανε καὶ ἴσχυεν. | "So mightily grew the word and was confirmed." | Δεῖ με καὶ Ῥώμην ἰδεῖν. | "I must see Rome also." | Acts. xix. 20, 21. | By the | Rev. Charles Constantine Pise, D. D., | Author of | "Aletheia," "St. Ignatius and his first companions," etc. | n. d. (L.) 4.

Map; then title, 1 p.; verso, Notice of Copyright, dated 1845; Dedication to the Right Rev. J. McCloskey, D. D., Coadjutor of New York, 1 p.; verso, blank; Introduction, 1 p.; verso, blank; Preface, 1 p.; verso, blank; Text: pp. 9–77; verso of p. 77, blank, Appendix, pp. 79, 80; sigs. 1 to verso of 10⁴ in 4s; Text in double columns. 1 plate at p. 81, viz: The release of the Apostles from prison.

15. THE | ACTS of the APOSTLES, | in four books: | With | copious notes. | Οὕτω κατὰ κράτος ὁ λόγος τοῦ Κυρίου ηὔξανε καὶ ἴσχυεν. | "So mightily grew the word, and was confirmed." | Δεῖ με καὶ Ῥώμην ἰδεῖν. | "I must see Rome also." | Acts, xix. 20, 21. | By the | Rev. Charles Constantine Pise, D. D. | Author of "Aletheia," "St. Ignatius and his first | companions," etc., etc. | New York: | Johnson, Fry and Company, | 27 Beekman Street. | n. d. (L.) 4.

Title, 1 f.; verso, Copyright, entered by R. Martin & Co. in the year 1845; Dedication to Right Rev. J. McCloskey, D. D., Coadjutor of NewYork, 1 p.; verso, blank; Introduction, pp. v, vi; Preface, pp. vii–ix; verso, blank; Text: pp. 11–224; Appendix, pp. 225–228; List of Engravings, 1 p; verso, blank; sigs. 1 to 5 in 4s; then 4* in 4s, then 5 to verso of 19⁶ in 6s; a leaf of engravings and a blank leaf additional; pp. 137–168 are printed within a 3 line border; 12 plates; Text in a single column; size 12mo, printed as a quarto.

These editions of the Acts are usually met bound up with Rutter's Life of Christ. The copy containing No. 14, was published in 25 numbers, Dr. Pise's work occupying a part of No. 17, and the whole of Nos. 18 to 24 inclusive; No. 25 contains Family Records.

1846.

1. THE | ILLUMINATED BIBLE, | containing the | Old and New Testaments, | translated out of the Original Tongues, | and with the former Translations diligently compared and revised. | With Marginal Readings, References, and Chronological dates. | Also, | the Apocrypha. | To which are added, | a Chronological Index, | an Index of the Subjects contained in the Old and New Testaments, | Tables of Weights, Coins, Measures, a List of proper Names, | a Concordance &c. | Embellished with sixteen hundred historical Engravings by J. A. Adams, more than fourteen | hundred of which are from original designs, by J. G. Chapman. | New York: | Harper & Brothers, Publishers, | 82 Cliff Street. | 1846. | Entered according to Act of Congress, in the year 1843, by *Harper & Brothers*, in the Clerk's Office of the Southern District of New York. | (L.) 4.

Ornamented presentation leaf, A Sacred Token from   to   , 1 f.; Woodcut frontispiece: The Meeting of Jacob and Joseph; Illuminated Title: The | Holy | Bible. | with Vignette: Abraham about to sacrifice Isaac, 1 f.; printed Title page (within a red border), 1 p.; verso, blank; Names and Order of all the Books, &c., 1 p.; verso, blank; Text: Gen. to Mal., pp. 1-844; sigs. none before p. 65, which is marked I, then K to 50^2; sigs. in 4^s; The | Apocrypha. | With Marginal Readings, References, and Chronological Dates. | Embellished with numerous Engravings, by J. A. Adams, after original designs, by J. G. Chapman. | Imprint, &c., as above (within a red border), 1 p.; verso, blank; Text: (in smaller type), pp. 1-128; sigs. A to 2, in 4^s; Fam. Rec., 3 ff, with illuminated interleaves; Frontispiece, Christ healing Bartimeus; Illuminated title to New Testament with Vignette: Rachel weeping for her children; 1 p.; printed Title page; The | New Testament | of our | Lord and Saviour Jesus Christ, | translated out of the Original Greek, | and with former Translations diligently compared and revised. | With | marginal readings, references, and chronological dates. | Embellished, &c., Imprint as above (within an ornamented border), 1 p.; verso, blank; Text: Mat. to Rev., pp. 1-256; sigs. A to li in 4^s; Alphabetical table of proper names, pp. 1-3; Tables of Weights, Measures, Coins and Time, p. 4; Chronol. Index, pp. 1-8; Index to Subjects, pp. 1-14; A Concordance, pp. 1-34; sigs. in 4^s.

This work was originally announced in 1843, and was issued in about 50 numbers at 25 cents each. The references are in the centre of the page and the text is appropriately illustrated, after the French style, with small woodcuts and initial letters; many of these, with the border pieces around the title page, were electrotyped by Mr. Adams, for whom the credit is claimed of having taken in 1841, the first electrotype in

America from a wood cut. The artists were engaged for more than six years in the preparation of the designs and engravings, and the expense attending the publication amounted, the publishers say, to over twenty thousand dollars.

2. THE | HOLY BIBLE, | containing the | Old and New Testaments: | 𝕮𝖗𝖆𝖓𝖘𝖑𝖆𝖙𝖊𝖉 𝖔𝖚𝖙 𝖔𝖋 𝖙𝖍𝖊 𝕺𝖗𝖎𝖌𝖎𝖓𝖆𝖑 𝕿𝖔𝖓𝖌𝖚𝖊𝖘; | and with the | former Translations diligently compared and revised. | With | Canne's Marginal References. | Together with the | Apocrypha and Concordance. | To which are added | An Index, and References, | and | a Key sheet of Questions, | geographical, historical, practical, and experimental; | accompanied with valuable | Chronological Harmonies of both Testaments, and highly useful Tables of Scripture Names, | Scripture Geography, Scripture Chronology, Scripture References &c. | The text corrected according to the Standard | of the | American Bible Society. | Troy, N. Y.: | Published by W. & H. Merriam. | 1846. | (L.) 4.

Title, 1 f.; verso, List of Books; To the Reader (Collins's Preface), 1 p.; Key, 1 p.; Text: Gen. to Mal., pp. 5-527; p. 528, blank; sigs. A³ to 3U in 4s, 2 to 132 in 2s; Apocrypha, in smaller type, pp. 1-78; sigs. A to K³, in 4s, and 1 to 20 in 2s, a blank leaf completing the sig.; Family Rec., 2 ff.; New Test. title, 1 p.; verso, blank; Text: Mat. to Rev., pp. 3-168; sigs. including title, 3X to 4S in 4s, and 133² to 174 in 2s; Index, Tables of Kindred, of Weights, &c., and of Offices, pp. 1-10; sigs. 4V to 4X1 in 4s, and 177 to 179¹ in 2s; Useful Tables | of | Scripture Names, Scripture Geography, Scripture Chronology, | and | Scripture References. | Including | Valuable Harmonies of the Scriptures, | by the Rev. G. Townsend of Cambridge, England. | Prepared to accompany | the Reference Bible. | By Harvey Wilbur, A. M. | 1 p.; verso, Key to pronunciation of the vowels, by Walker; Text: pp. 13-32; sigs. 4X³ to 4Z in 4s, and 180 to 184 in 2s; Brown's Brief Concordance, stereotyped by C. Alexander & Co., title, 1 p.; verso; To the Reader; Text: pp. [3] to [56], no sigs. Large Woodcut front. and 4 cuts to O. T.; woodcut front. and 6 cuts to N. T.

This Bible, I am informed, was originally stereotyped in Philadelphia; sold to a house in Baltimore and next bought by Homer Merriam of Troy. The stereotype plates were sold by the latter to a house in Dayton, Ohio, which now publishes a Bible from them.

3. HOLY BIBLE: Translated from the Latin Vulgat: With Annotations, References and Indexes. Philadelphia: Published by Eugene Cummiskey. Stereotyped by J. Howe. 1846. 8.

Edition 1000.

4. HOLY BIBLE: Philadelphia: Published by James B. Smith & Co., No. 610 Chestnut Street. 1846. 12.
Pp. 648.

5. HOLY BIBLE: New York: New York Bible and Common Prayer Book Society. Piercy & Reed, Printers. 1846. (Gowans.) 12.
Pp. 798.

6. HOLY BIBLE: New York: American Bible Society. 1846. 12.
With References; 8th ed., pp. 984.

7. HOLY BIBLE: New York: American Bible Society. Instituted in the year MDCCC.XVI. 1846. (Gowans.) 18.
Pp. 974, 304.

8. ENGLISH VERSION of the POLYGLOTT BIBLE: Illustrated with Maps and Engravings. Hartford: Published by S. Andrus & Son. *Stereotyped by J. C. D. Christman & Co., Philada.* 1846. 12.
Pp. 823, 256; Psalms in Metre, pp. 73.

9. HOLY BIBLE: Stereotype edition. Hartford: S. Andrus & Son. 1846. 12.
Pp. 824, 251; Psalms in Metre, pp. 70.

10. HOLY BIBLE: New York: American Bible Society. Instituted in the year MDCCCXVI. 1846. 24.
15th edition, pp. 979.

11. HOLY BIBLE: Hartford: Silas Andrus & Son. *Stereotyped by J. C. D. Christman & Co., Phila.* 1846. 32.
Pp. 932, 292, in 8°; front. to O. T.

12. HOLY BIBLE: Portland: Sanborn and Carter. 1846. 32.
Pp. 852, 250, with Psalms in Metre.

13. תורת האלהים | חומש ראשון | כולל | ספר בראשית | הונה כאתי הקטן | יצחק
בן אורי ז"ל ן' אליעזר | פה פילאדילפיא | כבית ובדפוס של הנביר קננו שרמן |
במצות הממדר | בשנת תּוֹרָה צוה לנו משה לפֹק |

13. The Law of God. | Volume First, | containing | The Book of Genesis. | Edited, | and with former Translations diligently compared and revised, | By Isaac Leeser. | Philadelphia : | Printed by C. Sherman, | For the Editor. | 5605. | Five Volumes.   (L.)   8.

Mock title, | ספר תּוֹרָה The | Pentateuch. | 1 p.; verso, Hebrew Title; English title, 1 p.; verso, Extract of Copyright, dated 1845; Pref., pp. v-x; title, | ספר בראשית ראשון להורת האלהים | יקוף משנבברא העולם עד שכח יוסף אלפים ושלש מאות והשך שנים : | The Law of God. | Vol. I. | The Book of Genesis. | 1 p.; Text: (Heb. and Eng. alternately) pp. 2-130; verso, Addenda to p. 126; then title, | לספר בראשית | הפטרות | סדר | The Haphtoroth | for | The Book of Genesis, | according to the various customs. | 1 p.; then Hebrew and English alternately, pp. 132-175; sigs. 2 to 6, then 2 to 30⁶ in 6ˢ, followed by 2 pp., one of text and another blank. Vol. 2. Hebrew mock title as in Vol. I, 1 p.; verso, תורת האלהים | חומש שני | כולל | ספר שמות | הונה מאתי הקטן | יצחק בן אורי ז"ל ן' אליעזר | פה פילאדיליפיא | בבית ובדפוס של הנביר קנו שרבן | כמצות

הממדר | בשנה. תּוֹרָה צוה לנו משה לפֹק | then English title as in Vol. I, except the lines, Volume Second, | containing | The Book of Exodus. | 1 p.; verso, Certificate of Copyright; then : ספר שמות | שני לתורת אלהים | יקוף משפת יוסף עד שהוקם המשכן מאה וארבעים שנה | The Law of God, | Vol. II. | The Book of Exodus. | 1 p.; verso, the first page of Exodus, followed by pp. 4–113 (English); verso, last page of Hebrew, followed by 1¼ pp. of Hebrew; Exodus ends on p. 113; then title, | לבפר שמות | הפטרות | סדר | The Haphtoroth | for | The Book of Exodus. | According to the various customs. | 1 p.; verso, Hebrew, 1 p.; and pp. 116–168 (English); sigs. 1 to 28⁶ in 6ˢ. Vol. 3. Mock title as above; verso, title, תורת האלהים | חומש שלישי | כולל | ספר ויקרא | הונה מאתי הקטן | יצחק בן אורי ז"ל ן' אליעזר | פה פילאדיליפיא | בבית ובדפוס של הנביר קנו שרבן | כבצות הממדר | בשנת תּוֹרָה צוה לנו משה לפֹק | then English title as above, except Volume Third, | The Book of Leviticus. | 1 p.; verso, Extract of Copyright; title, | ספר ויקרא שלישי להורת האלהים | יקוף משהוקם המשכן בשנה השנית באחר לחרש הראשון | עד אחר לחדש השני | חדשים The Law of God. | Vol. III. | The Book of Leviticus. | 1 p.; verso, first page of Hebrew, then pp. 4–84 (English); verso, last page of Hebrew; then title, | סדר | הפטרות | לספר ויקרא The Haphtoroth | for | The Book of Leviticus. | According to the various customs. | followed by text, pp. 86 (English) to verso of 152. Vol. 4. Mock title as above; verso, תורת האלהים | חומש רביעי | כולל | ספר בבדבר | הונה מאתי הקטן | יצחק בן אורי ז"ל ן' אליעזר | פה פילאדיליפיא | בבית ובדפוס של הנביר קנו שרבן | בכצות הממדר | בשנת תּוֹרָה צוה לנו משה לפֹק | then English title as above, except Volume Fourth. | The Book of Numbers. | 1 p.; verso, Extract of Copyright; title, | ספר בבדבר רביעי להורת אלהים | יקוף מאחר לחדש השני בשנה השנית עד אחד לחרש עשתי | עשר בשנה הארבעים | שלשים ושנה ותשעה חדשים The Law of God. | Vol. IV. | The Book of Numbers. | 1 p.; verso, first page of Hebrew text; then pp. 4 (English) to 117; extract, 1 p.; then title, | סדר | הפטרות | לבפר בבדבר לפי חלופי המנהגים | The Haphtoroth | for | The Book of Numbers. | According to the various customs. | 1 p ; verso, Hebrew text, pp. 19

(English) to 149. Vol. 5. Mock title as before; verso, title, | חומש חמישי | תורת האלהים | כולל | ספר דברים | הונה מאתי הקטן | יצחק בן אורי ז"ל ן' אליעזר | פה פילאדילפיא | בבית ובדפוס של | הנביר קנע שרמן | כמצות הטםדר | כשנת חורה צוה לנו משה לפק | then English title as in Vol. I, except Volume Fifth. | The Book of Deuteronomy. | verso, Extract of Copyright; then title, | ספר דברים | חמישי לתורת אלהים | יקוף | כאחר לחרש העשהו עיקר כשנת הארבעים ער | אשר חצו יצי בכי אבל | כשה בשבעה לחרש הראשון בשנת הארבעים ואחת | שנים חדשים ובבעה ימים | The Law of God. | Vol. V. | The Book of Deuteronomy. | 1 p.; verso, first page of Hebrew; then pp. 4 (English) to verso of 100; then title, | לבפר הרברים | ההפטרות | סרר | The Haphtoroth | for | The Book of Deuteronomy. | According to לפי הלופי הםנהגים | the various customs. | 1 p.; verso, Hebrew and English alternately, pp. 101-135; verso of 135 is, I presume, 10th chapter of Esther, followed by the translation of it on page marked 153 (English); below, "End of the Third Volume;" sig. 26*; verso, blank. This agrees in pagination and sig. with the end of the 3d volume, and has probably been omitted there and added here (for to take away the chapter of Esther referred to above, would take away the last page of English, 135, of this volume, 5); then follow Contents, pp. 136-141; Directions for the Reading of the Law, pp. 142-144; Postscript, pp. 145-147, dated Philadelphia, Jany 8, 1846; sigs. 1 to 23^3 in 6^s; verso of 23^3, Chaldee English Esther X, p. 153; sig. 26*; verso, blank; then sig. 24^{1-6}.

This edition of the Pentateuch was undertaken exclusively for the use of the Jews. It was first announced about the year 1838; the Hebrew has been printed from the text of Rabbi Wolf Heidenheim; as respects the translation, the editor acknowledges to have received the greatest aid from the Pentateuch of Hyman Arnheim, of Glogau, the Bible of Zunz, the Works of Mendelssohn, Hochstratter, Johlson, Heineman, and others. He has not looked at a single work issued by the English Jews, nor borrowed an idea or suggestion from any of them, living or dead.

It is published in two forms, 12mo and 8vo; the former at $10, and the latter at $12, in paper covers.

14. LA SAINTE BIBLE, | qui contient, | le Vieux et le Nouveau Testament; | revue sur les Originaux, | par David Martin, | Ministre du Saint Evangile à Utrecht. | New York: | Société Biblique | Americaine, | établie en MDCCCXVI. | 1846. | 12.

Title, 1 f.; verso, Noms de tous les Livres; Text: pp. 3-819; Fam. Reg., 2 ff.; Title to N. Test., imprint as above, 1 p.; verso, Noms de tous les Livres; Text: pp. 3-261. It is a Protestant version.

15. A Critical Commentary on the Books of GENESIS and PSALMS inclusive, by Bishop Patrick. Philadelphia: Carey & Hart. New York: Wiley & Putnam. 2 vols. 1846. (L.) 8.

The 2d vol. is dated 1844.

16. THE PSALMS: a new version, by Geo. R. Noyes. Boston: James Munroe & Co. 1846. (G. L.) 12.

17. THE PROVERBS, ECCLESIASTES, and the CANTICLES; a New version, with Notes, by G. R. Noyes. Boston: James Munroe & Co. 1846. (G. L.) 12.

1. PICTORIAL TESTAMENT: New York: J. S. Redfield. 1846. (L.) 8.
With Bible of 1843.

2. NEW TESTAMENT: the Text carefully printed from the most correct copies of the present authorized version, including the marginal readings and parallel texts, with a commentary and practical notes by Rev. Adam Clarke. Map. Philadelphia. 1846. 8.

3. THE FAMILY EXPOSITOR. By Philip Doddridge, D. D. Amherst, Mass.: Published by Charles McFarland. 1846. 8.
See 1839.

4. 'H ΚΑΙΝΗ ΔΙΑΘΗΚΗ. The Greek Testament, with English Notes, Critical, Philological, and Exegetical &c. By the Rev. S. T. Bloomfield, D. D., F. S. A., Vicar of Bisbrooke, Rutland. Fifth American from the Second London Edition. In Two Volumes. Boston: Published by Perkins and Marvin. New York: Gould and Newman. Philadelphia: Henry Perkins. 1846. (Am. Bib. Soc.) 8.
See 1837.

5. NEW TESTAMENT: Stereotyped by Baker & Greele, Boston. Cooperstown: Published by H. & E. Phinney. 1846. 12.
Title, 1 f.; verso, Order of the Books; Text: Mat. to Rev., pp. 3–315; sigs. A² to CC⁸; in 12ˢ.
"We printed 1000 of the 12mo Test. and subsequently condemned the plates to metal." *E. P.*

6. NEW TESTAMENT: Auburn: Published by Henry Oliphant. 1846. 12.
Pp. 299; v. 25 of Luke XX, is marked 26; and 1 Tim. 4:16 is incorrect.

7. NEW TESTAMENT: Philadelphia: J. Gladding, No. 341
   Market Street. 1846.   (L.)   12.

8. NEW TESTAMENT: Philadelphia: William S. Young, No.
   173 Race Street, or No. 50 North Sixth Street. 1846.
   (L.)   12.
   Same as the preceding.

9. NEW TESTAMENT: Philadelphia: A. H. Rowand, No. 188
   Callowhill Street, near Fifth, south side. 1846. (L.) 18.
   Text and Table of Kindred, pp. 321; A concise History of the New Testament, pp. 322; Reasons why the Christian Religion is preferable to all others, pp. 323, 324.

10. NEW TESTAMENT: Stereotype edition. Philadelphia: Jesper
    Harding. 1846.   (L.)   12.

11. NEW TESTAMENT: New York: American Bible Society.
    1846.   (G. L.)   24.
    With Psalms.

12. 'Η ΚΑΙΝΗ ΔΙΑΘΗΚΗ. The New Testament: With short explanatory Notes, and numerous references to illustrative and parallel passages, printed in a centre column. *Illustrated with Maps.* New York: Published by A. S. Barnes & Co., No. 51 John Street. 1846.   32.
    The Polymicrian Testament (see 1832), with a frontispiece: The Ascension, and an engraved title in addition to the maps already noted.

13. 'Η ΚΑΙΝΗ ΔΙΑΘΗΚΗ. | Novum Testamentum | ad | Exemplar Millianum, | cum | Emendationibus et Lectionibus Griesbachii, | præcipuis vocibus ellipticis, | Thematibus omnium vocum difficiliorum, | atque locis Scripturæ parallelis | Studio et labore | Gulielmi Greenfield. | Hanc editionem primam Americanam, | summâ curâ recensuit, atque mendis quàm plurimis expurgavit, | Josephus P. Engles, A.M. | Philadelphiæ: | Perkins et Purves. | 1846. | (O. L. Holley.)   32.
    1 Engraved p. containing the Words, The New Testament, in 48 different languages; verso, blank; printed title, 1 f.; verso, The languages in the order in which they are

disposed; below, Ex Officinâ Stereotypâ L. Johnson. Preface to the American edition, pp. 3–5; Abbreviations, p. 6; Text: pp. 7–557; sigs. 1 (which includes Title and 2 prel. ff.), to recto of 35⁷; verso, Το Της Καινης Διαθηκης Τελος. Δοξα μόνῳ τῷ θεῷ. Appendix, pp. 559–571; verso, blank; Ligatures or Abbreviations, 1 p.; verso, blank; The | Polymicrian | Greek Lexicon | to the | New Testament; | in which | The various senses of the words are distinctly | explained in English, and authorized by | References to passages of Scripture. | By W. Greenfield, | editor of "Bagster's Comprehensive Bible." "The Polymicrian Greek | Testament," &c. | ΠΟΛΛΟΙ μεν θνητοις ΓΛΩΤΤΑΙ, μια δ'Αθανατοισιν. | Multæ terricolis linguæ, cœlestibus una | *Earth speaks with many tongues, Heaven knows but one.* | Philadelphia: Perkins and Purves. | 1846. | 1 p.; verso, Principal Abbreviations; below, *Stereotyped by L. Johnson, Philadelphia;* Advertisement, pp. iii, iv; 1 p., recto, blank, verso; Greek Numerals; Text: pp. 1–281; sigs. 1–18, all in 8ˢ; Maps of the Tetrarchies, of St. Paul's Travels; Text in two columns; References, different Readings, present tenses of the most difficult verbs and supplied words, in the centre.

This is called the Polymicrian Greek Testament. Mr. Greenfield, the editor, was originally a bookbinder. He eventually acquired such a knowledge of languages both ancient and modern, as entitled him to rank with the most eminent linguists, and finally became superintendent of translations of the Bible in foreign languages, published under the care of the British and Foreign Bible Society. Mr. Greenfield died in 1831, at the early age of thirty-two. His Polymicrian Greek Testament was originally published in London in 1829.

In the present edition *several hundred* errors have been corrected, which are said to be in the London Edition.

14. THE ANGLO-SAXON VERSION of The Holy GOSPELS, edited by Benjamin Thorpe. New York: Wiley & Putnam. 1846. (L.; G. L.) 12.

15. AN EXAMINATION of the Testimony of the FOUR EVANGELISTS, by the Rules of Evidence administered in Courts of Justice. With an account of the Trial of Jesus. By Simon Greenleaf, LL. D., Royall Professor of Law in Harvard University. Boston: Charles C. Little and James Brown. 1846. (N. Y. State Lib.) 8.

This work contains the Four Gospels as arranged by Archbishop Newcome, with the corrections of Dr. Robinson.

16. THE ACTS of the APOSTLES, arranged for Families and Sunday Schools. With Notes and Questions. By T. B. Fox. Boston: William Crosby and H. P. Nichols, 118 Washington Street. 1846. 12.

1847.

1. <u>Butler's Edition.</u> | THE | HOLY BIBLE: | containing the | Old and New Testaments: | Translated out of | the Original Tongues, | and with the former Translations | diligently compared and revised. | With References and various Readings. | Together with the | Apocrypha. | In Two Volumes. | Vol. I. | Philadelphia: | Published by E. H. Butler & Co. | 1847. | 4.

Colored title, 1 p.; verso, blank; printed title, 1 p.; verso, blank; Names and Order of the Books, 1 p.; verso, blank; Text: Gen. to Song of Solomon, pp. 1-787; verso of 787, blank; sigs. D to recto of 5K^2; Vol. II. Title as above except Vol. II 1 p.; verso, blank; Text: Isaiah to Mal., pp. 3-277; sigs. A (not marked), to recto of 2M^3; verso of 277, blank; Apocrypha, in smaller type, pp. 1-139; verso of 139, blank; sigs. A (not marked) to recto of S^2; Fam. Rec., 2 ff.; New Test. title in colors 1 p.; verso, blank; <u>Butler's edition.</u> | The | New Testament | of our Lord and Saviour | Jesus Christ, | translated out of | the Original Greek, | and with the former Translations | diligently compared and revised. | With References and various Readings. | Imprint as above; 1 p.; verso, blank; Text: Mat. to Rev., pp. 281-600; sigs. 2N to 4F^4, all in 4°.

This Bible was published in 116 numbers; the references are at the foot of the pp. The following are the illustrations in the volumes: Moses with the Tables of the Law; lith. front. to O. T.; The Fall of Babel, *Sartain;* The Exodus, *Sartain;* Ruth gleaning, *J. Sartain*, sc.; Jeremiah, *Sartain*, sc.; Judith and Holofernes, *Sartain*, sc.; Ecce Homo, Front. to N. T. lith. in gold; The Tribute, *Sartain*, sc.; The Agony, *Sartain*, sc.; Christ weeping over Jerusalem, *A. H. Ritchie*, sc.; Martha's Complaint, *Ritchie*, sc.; The Reproof, *Sartain*, sc.

2. HOLY BIBLE, translated from the Latin Vulgat. Philadelphia: Published by Eugene Cummiskey. Stereotyped by J. Howe. 1847.   8.

Edition 500.

3. HOLY BIBLE: New York: American Bible Society. Instituted in the year 1816. 1847.   (L.)   8.

7th and 28th editions; New Testament, 1848; showing amendments by collation since 1839.

4. HOLY BIBLE: Philadelphia: Jesper Harding. 1847.   12.

Stereotyped ed.; pp. 486, 162, including both titles.

5. HOLY BIBLE: Philadelphia: J. B. Lippincott & Co. 1847. 12.
   With Book of Common Prayer, same Imprint, but 1845.

6. HOLY BIBLE: Philadelphia: Hogan and Thompson. 1847. 12.
   Same as the ed. of 1836; with New Testament of 1845.

7. THE ENGLISH VERSION of the POLYGLOTT BIBLE: with a copious and original selection of References to parallel and illustrative passages, exhibited in a manner hitherto unattempted. Stereotyped by Henry Wallis and J. Roby, Concord, N. H. Philadelphia: Published by Grigg, Elliott & Co. 1847. 24.
   Engr. title with Imprint, Portland: Sanborn & Carter, 1845. Imprint to the N. Test., Portland: Hyde, Lord & Duren, 1847. Pref. signed T. C.; pp. 587, 190; References in centre of the pp.; Front. and Vign. to O. and N. T.
   See Thomas, Cowperthwaite & Co's ed., 1839.

8. HOLY BIBLE: Stereotyped by J. Howe, Philadelphia. Hartford: S. Andrus & Son. 1847. 12.
   2 Front. and several Woodcuts in N. T., 3 on a page; with Psalms in Metre; pp. 720.

9. Die Bibel, | oder | Die Ganze | Heilige Schrift | des | alten und neuen | Testaments. | New York, | Herausgegen von der Amerikanischen Bibel= | Gesellschaft. | 1847. | 12.
   20te Auflage, pp. 828, 273. The New Testament title bears date 1848.

10. HOLY BIBLE: containing the Old Testament and the New. Philadelphia: G. Eckendorff, 548 West Market Street. 1847. 24.
    Pp. 852, 259; Contents, pp. 261-263; Psalms in Metre, pp. 81.

11. THE ENGLISH VERSION of the POLYGLOTT BIBLE. New York: Published by the American and Foreign Bible Society. 1847. 32.
    Engr. title and front. to O. and N. Test. 3 plates in the Old, and 1 in New Test. The Imprint on the engr. title is "Springfield, Published by Geo. & Chas. Merriam, Main St.

12. HOLY BIBLE: Troy, N. Y.: Published by Merriam, Moore
& Co. 1847. 24.

This seems to be Dearborn's "Diamond Bible" of 1836, with new titles and Psalms in Metre, pp. 76. It is accompanied by the same engravings.

13. HOLY BIBLE: Portland: Sanborn & Carter. 1847. 32.

Stereotyped by Thurston & Co., Portland, Me.; pp. 817, 259; with Book of Common Prayer—Philadelphia: Lippincott, Grambo & Co. 1850.

14. The Earlier and Later Prophecies of ISAIAH. By Joseph Addison Alexander. 2 vols. New York. 1847. (Doyle's Cat.) 8.

15. HISTORY OF THE BIBLE. Cooperstown: Printed by H. & E. Phinney. 1847. (L.) 142.

Frontispiece, Moses receiving the Law; Text: pp. 11-192; A^6 to M^8 in 8^s. A few woodcuts, and many portraits. It is an exact reprint of the Bible History, 1811.

1. NEW TESTAMENT: Translated out of the Latin Vulgate: With Annotations, to clear up the principal difficulties of Holy Writ. As approved by the Right Reverend John Hughes, Catholic Bishop of New York. Stereotype edition. New York: D. & J. Sadlier, 58 Gold Street. 1847. (L.) 12.

From the plates of the Devereux Testament, see 1820, 1835, 1840, 1845. The error in James 5:17 is continued.

2. NEW TESTAMENT: Auburn: Published by Henry Oliphant. 1847. (B.) 12.

See 1846.

3. NEW TESTAMENT: Cooperstown: H. & E. Phinney. 1847. 16.

Text: pp. 3-340; Contents, pp. 341-344; Stereotyped by R. C. Valentine, 45 Gold street, New York. A steel engraving of the Crucifixion and several woodcuts accompany the Volume.

4. Exposition of the Epistle to the ROMANS; with Remarks on the Commentaries of Dr. Macknight, Professor Moses Stuart, and Professor Tholuck. By Robert Haldane, Esq. From the fifth Edinburgh Edition. New York: Robert Carter, 58 Canal street; and Pittsburgh, 56 Market street. 1847. 8.

1848.

1. HOLY BIBLE: With Canne's Marginal Notes and References. To which are added, An Index; An Alphabetical Table of all the Names in the Old and New Testaments, with their Significations, Table of Scripture Weights, Measures, and Coins, &c.; Philadelphia: Published by Miller & Burlock, Sansom Street, above Eleventh. 1848.   4.

This Bible was issued for the first time in November, 1846, between which date and November, 1859, 33,800 copies have been printed, some with the Apocrypha, Brown's Concordance, and the Psalms in Metre. Those issued since 1851 are without date.

Though represented by the publishers as a "new edition," it is proper to add that it corresponds, in the text and other parts, with the edition of Nafis & Cornish, *supra* p. 250, and with that of Cincinnati, *supra*, p. 257.

2. THE | HOLY BIBLE: | containing the | Old and New Testaments, | translated from the Original Tongues, | and | with the former Translations | diligently compared and revised, | with | Canne's Marginal Notes and References. | To which are added, | An Index; | an Alphabetical Table | of all the Names in the Old and New Testaments, with their Significations; | Table of Scripture Weights, Measures and Coin, &c. | Philadelphia: | Harvey Griffith, No. 384, North Second Street. | 1848. | 4.

This volume agrees, in pagination and signatures, with the preceding, but there is neither Index nor Tables in the copy examined. The text of the New Test. is followed immediately by a Concordance.

3. HOLY BIBLE: With Canne's Marginal Notes and References. Together with the Apocrypha. To which are added, An Index; An Alphabetical Table of all the Names in the Old and New Testaments, with their Significations; also, Tables of Scripture Weights, Measures and Coins, and Concordance. Hartford: Sumner and Goodman. 1848. (L.)   4.

This Bible is identical with that of H. & E. Phinney's Cooperstown edition, *supra* p. 158, *plus* The Apocrypha, which is printed in smaller type and contains pp. 96; and Concordance (in 7 columns), pp. 31.

The Illustrations are; the Dream of Pharaoh, as a front. to the Old Test., and Jesus and the Samaritan, as front. to the New Test.

4. HOLY BIBLE: With | Canne's Marginal Notes and References. | Together with | The Apocrypha. | To which are added | An Index: | An Alphabetical Table of all the Names in the Old and New Testament, | with their Significations; | also, | Table of Scripture Weights, Measures and Coins. | Cooperstown, N. Y. | Published by H. & E. Phinney, | Buffalo, F. W. Breed. | 1848. | 4.

The pagination of this volume corresponds with that of the Cooperstown 4to already described, *supra* p. 158; but the signatures are in 8^s, and run as follows: for the old Test., A (which includes title and 3 prel. ff.), to verso of 2L^8; Fam. Rec., 2 ff.; The Apocrypha (in smaller type). pp. 1–99; sigs. A to G^2 in 8^s; New Test. title, Cooperstown, N. Y. | Published and sold by H. & E. Phinney.... Sold also by I. Tiffany, Utica. | 1848. | sigs. to Text of New Test., 2M to verso of 2X^1, and then for the appended matter 2X^2 to verso of 2X^8; Brown's Concordance (6 columns to a p.), no title; pp. (1)–(35.)

Front. to Old and New Test.; 6 plates to the Old, and 2 to the New Test.; all engraved on wood.

5. POLYGLOTT BIBLE: With Apocrypha, Brown's Concordance, Index, Illustrations, &c. Boston: Phillips & Sampson, 110, Washington Street. 1848.   (L.)   8.

Two titles, one within a border, the other printed; separate title to Concordance; same imprint. Illustrations, 16 large woodcuts, including front. to N. Testament.

6. THE | HOLY BIBLE, | containing | the Old Testament and the New | according to | the commonly received version. | New York: | American and Foreign Bible Society. | Stereotyped by C. Davison & Company, 33 Gold Street. | 1848. | 8.

Pp. 510, 161. Imprint to N. T.: New York: | Stereotyped by C. Davison & Co. for the | American and Foreign Bible Society. | 1848. |

7. HOLY BIBLE: New York: American Bible Society. 1848. 8.
With References used in the recent collation.

8. HOLY BIBLE: New York: American Bible Society. 1848.   Ref. 12.

9. HOLY BIBLE: New York: American Bible Society. Instituted in the year MDCCCXVI. 1848.   18.
Pp. 974, 304.

10. HOLY BIBLE: (Nourse's paragraph edition.) New York: American and Foreign Bible Society. Instituted in the year 1837. 1848. (L.) 12.

On verso of title, extract of Copyright 1834; Perkins, Marvin & Co., Mass., below John J. Reid, Printer, 16 Spruce street. Pp. vii, 942, 322, followed by list of quotations in the New Test. pp. 523-524. Romans, 4:5, correct.

11. HOLY BIBLE: Stereotyped by J. Howe, Philadelphia. Hartford: S. Andrus & Son. 1848. 12.

Front. to O. T.; Front. and a number of small woodcuts (3 on a page), in N. T.; at the end, Gen. Contents and Psalms of David in Metre; pp. 820.

12. THE ENGLISH VERSION of the POLYGLOTT BIBLE: Stereotyped by L. Johnson. Philadelphia: Thomas, Cowperthwaite & Co. 1848. 12.

Pp. 587, 190. Printed by Smith & Peters, Franklin Buildings, Sixth street below Arch, Philadelphia. Engr. Front. and Titles to O. and N. Test.

13. HOLY BIBLE: Portland: Sanborn & Carter. 1848. (L.) 18.

Pp. 1077, 259. With Engraved Title, "The Everlasting Gospel," and engr. front.

14. HOLY BIBLE, containing the Old Testament and the New. Hartford: S. Andrus & Son. 1848. 24.

Pp. 852, 259. Contents, pp. 261-263; Psalms in Metre, pp. 81; Engr. front. and title.

15. HOLY BIBLE: Philadelphia: J. B. Lippincott & Co. 1848. 24.

Pp. 856, 259. Psalms in Metre, pp. 77.

16. HOLY BIBLE: Philadelphia: Published by Jesper Harding, No. 57 South Third Street. 1848. 32.

Pp. 819, 256. Psalms in Metre, pp. 87.

17. HOLY BIBLE: Philadelphia: Thomas, Cowperthwaite & Co. 283 Market Street. 1848. 32.

Engr. front. and title.

18. THE ENGLISH VERSION of the POLYGLOTT BIBLE. Springfield: Published by Merriam, Chapin & Co. 1848. 32.

1. The | New Testament | of our | Lord and Saviour | Jesus Christ, | translated out of | the Original Greek; | and with | the former translations diligently compared and revised. | Philadelphia: | Published by Edward W. Miller, | No. 11 Little George Street. | 1848. | For Sale by S. Snyder, No. 340 North Second Street, and Booksellers generally. | 4.
With Miller & Burlock's Bible.

2. New Testament: Filadelfia: Publict by A. Komstock, M. D., No. 100 Mulberry Street. 1848.   (L.)   8.
Comstock's Phonetic Testament.

3. New Testament: Portland: Jona: Morgan, S. Colesworthy. 1848.   (G. L.)   8.
The Orthography is somewhat curious.

4. New Testament: New York: American Bible Society. 1848.   (L.)   8.
29th edition. Previous to the alteration with Book of Psalms.

5. New Testament: New York: American Bible Society. 1848.   (L.)   12.
With Bible of 1847, shewing amendments by collation since 1839.

6. New Testament: Hartford, Conn. E. Hunt. 1848. (L.) 12.

7. New Testament: New York: American Bible Society. 1848.   (Rev. Dr. Brigham.)   Agate 32.

8. The | New Testament | of | our Lord and Saviour Jesus Christ, | translated into | the Choctaw language. | Pin | Chitokaka pi Okchalinchi Chisvs Klaist | in Testament Himona, | Chahta anumpa Atoshowa hoke. | New York: | American Bible Society, | Instituted in the year MDCCC XVI. | 1848. | 12.
This translation is by the Rev. Alfred Wright; pp. 818.

9. **Das Neue | Testament** | unsers | Herrn und Heilandes | Jesu Christi. | Nach der deutschen Uebersetzung | von Dr. Martin Luther. | Mit Kurzem Inhalt eines jeden Capitels, volstän= | diger anweisung gleichher Schriftstellen, | ünd aller Sonn=und Festäglichen | Evan= gelein und Episteln. | Mit Zwolf Bilden geziert. | Harrisburg, Pa. | Gedruckt und zu haben bei Gustav S. Pieters. | 1848. | (L.) 12.

Text: pp. 5-511; Anweisung, pp. 1-5; sigs. 3 to verso 45⁶ in 6ˢ. The cuts are coarse.

10. HAUH TIBOSA NE LUKE KINENA. The Gospel according to St. Luke, translated into the *Grebo* Tongue by the Rev. John Payne, Missionary of the Protestant Episcopal Church at Cavalla, West Africa. Published by the American Bible Society. 1848. 16.

1849.

1. THE | HOLY BIBLE, | containing the | Old and New Testa- ments: | Together with The Apocrypha: | Translated out of the Original Tongues, | and with | the former Transla- tions diligently compared and revised. | With | Canne's Marginal Notes and References. | To which are added | An Index; | An Alphabetical Table | of all the Names in the Old and New Testaments, with their Significations, | Tables of Scripture Weights, Measures, and Coins, &c. | Buffalo: | Published by Phinney & Co. | New York: | Ivison & Phinney. | 1849. | 4.

After the destruction of H. & E. Phinney's plates by the fire in 1849, Messrs. Phin- ney & Co. of Buffalo purchased the plates on which this Bible is printed, from Sum- ner & Goodman, Hartford, Conn. See No. 3 of 1848.

2. HOLY BIBLE: The text corrected according to the Standard of the American Bible Society. Stereotyped by James Conner, New York. Hartford: S. Andrus & Son. 1849. 4.

With Brown's Concordance and Psalms in Metre; 12 fine plates and maps. See No. 4, *supra* p. 241.

3. HOLY BIBLE: Cincinnati: E. Morgan & Co. 1849. (G. L.) 4.

4. תורה נביאים וכתובים | Seu | Biblia Hebraica | secundum editiones | Jos. Athiæ, Joannis Leusden, | Jo. Simonis aliorumque, | inprimis | Everardi Van der Hooght, | D. Henrici Opitii, et Wolfii Heidenheim, | cum additionibus | Claviquc Masoretica et Rabbinica | Augusti Hahn. | Nunc denuo recognita et emendata ab | Isaaco Leeser, V. D. M. | Synagogæ Mikve Israel, Phila. | et Josepho Jaquett, V. D. M. | Presbyter Prot. Epis. Ecclesiæ, U. S. | Editio Stereotypa. | Novi Eboraci: | Sumptibus Joannis Wiley, | 161 Broadway; et Londini, 13 Paternoster Row. | Philadelphiæ: J. W. Moore. | Typis L. Johnson et Soc. Phila. | 1849. | 8.

Title, 1 f.; verso, blank; Leeser's Preface, dated 7th Sept. 1848; pp. iii, iv; Hahn's Preface, dated Vratislave, 7 Jany. 1839, pp. v, vi; Preface to the 1st edition, dated Leipsic 9 Septr. 1831, pp. vii–xviii; Preface to the 3d edition, dated Leipsic 13th June, 1833, pp. xix, xx; Mock Title, תורה | Quinque libri Mosis. | 1 p.; verso, blank; sigs. A² to B6 in 6ˢ; Text: pp. 1–350; Mock Title, נביאים ראשונים | Prophetæ priores. | &c. 1 p.; Text: pp. 352–660; Mock Title, נביאים אחרונים | Prophetæ posteriores. | &c.. 1 p.; verso, blank; Text: pp. 663–990; Mock Title, כתובים | Hagiographa. | &c., 1 p.; verso, blank; Text: pp. 993–1396; Index and Sectiones Propheticæ, pp. 1397–1400; Clavis, pp. 1401–1416; at foot of last p., Typis Laurentii Johnson et Sociorum, | Philadelphiæ. | sigs. A to verso of 6C⁶ in 6ˢ, and 1 to 177⁴ in 4ˢ.

This is represented to be the first edition of the Hebrew Bible with points printed in América.

5. Holy Bible: New York: American Bible Society. 1849. 8.
17th edition. Pp. 968, 303, 1.

6. Holy Bible: New York: American Bible Society. Instituted in the year M.D.CCCXVI. 1849. (Rev. Dr. Campbell.) 12.
9th edition. Pp. 1282; Contents of N. T., 2 pp.

7. Holy Bible: New York: American Bible Society. Instituted &c. 1849.   12.
17th edition. O. T. pp. 592; Family Rec., 4 pp.; N. T., pp. 184.

8. Holy Bible: New York: American Bible Society. Instituted in the year MDCCCXVI. 1849. (Gowans.) 18.
Pp. 805, 250.

9. Holy Bible: Philadelphia: Published by Jesper Harding. No. 57 South Third Street. 1849.   32.

10. HOLY BIBLE: containing the Old Testament and the New. Philadelphia: Miller and Burlock. n. d.   32.

Pp. 852, 259; Contents, pp. 261-263; Psalms in Metre, pp. 81.

The first edition of this Bible was published in July, 1849. Twenty editions of it have been issued since that time, amounting, in all, as we learn from the publishers, to 61,000 copies.

1. NEW TESTAMENT: (English and Dutch in parallel columns.) New York: American Bible Society. 1849. (Rev. Dr. Brigham.)   Bourg. 12.

2. NEW TESTAMENT: (English and German in parallel columns.) New York: American Bible Society. 1849. (Rev. Dr. Brigham.)   Bourg. 12.

3. NEW TESTAMENT: (English and Danish in parallel columns.) New York: American Bible Society. 1849. (Rev. Dr. Brigham.)   Bourg. 12.

4. NEW TESTAMENT: New York: American Bible Society. - Instituted &c. 1849.   16.

Pp. 349; Contents, pp. 350-352. 19th ed.

5. NEW TESTAMENT: Buffalo: Published by Phinney & Co. 32.

First Buffalo edition.

6. THE FOUR GOSPELS, | translated from the Latin Vulgate, | and diligently compared with the Original Greek Text, | being a revision of the Rhemish Translation, | with Notes, Critical and Explanatory. | By | the Right Rev. Francis Patrick Kenrick, | Bishop of Philadelphia. | "That thou mayst know the certainty of those words in which thou hast been instructed." | *Luke* i. 4. | New York: | Edward Dunigan & Brother, | 151 Fulton Street. | 1849. | (L.) 8.

Title, 1 f.; verso, Notice of Copyright, dated 1849; Dedication, To the Hierarchy of the United States, assembled in the Seventh Provincial Council of Baltimore, dated May 1, 1849, 1 p.; verso, blank; Synopsis of the Gospels (according to the Bible de Vence), pp. 5-14; Explanations, pp. 15, 16; Mock title, The | Four Gospels, | translated from the Latin Vulgate, | diligently compared with the Greek Text; | with | Notes. | By Francis Patrick Kenrick, | Bishop of Philadelphia. | "That thou mayst know the certainty of those words in which thou hast been instructed,"

Luke, i, 4; 1 p.; verso, blank; General Preface, pp. 19-30; Pref. to the Gosp. of St. Matthew, pp. 31, 32; Text of Mat., pp. 33-211; verso of p. 211, blank; Pref. to Gosp. of Mark, 1 p.; Text of Mark, pp. 214-299; verso of 299, blank; Pref. to the Gosp. of St. Luke, 1 p.; Text of Luke, pp. 302-450; Pref. to the Gosp. of John, 1 p.: Text of John, pp. 452-572; sigs. 1 to verso of 30⁶ in 8ˢ. Map of Palestine.

The translation is carefully executed, and the numerous notes are short, clear and often highly instructive. Although the Bishop adheres to the distinctive interpretation of his church, there is not throughout the entire volume a single uncharitable sentiment, nor a harsh and irritating expression towards those of another communion. *Archd. Cotton's Rhemes and Douay.*

7. THE GOOD NEWS of our Lord Jesus, the Anointed, from the critical Greek text of Tillotson. Boston: Published by Joshua V. Himes. 1849. (L.; G. L.) 12.

This is said to be the "Millerite New Testament." The preface is signed N. N. Whiting, Williamsburg, Long Island. Many controverted texts are printed within brackets; "baptize" and "baptism," immerse and immersion. In other respects the variations from the common version are few.

1850.

1. THE | HOLY BIBLE, | translated from | the Latin Vulgate: | diligently compared with the Hebrew, Greek and other editions | in various languages. | Vignette, Moses giving the Law. Published by | Tallis, Willoughby & Co. | London and New York. | n. d. fol.

This is a copy of the engraved title page of an edition of the Douay Bible proposed to be published in thirty parts by the above house, with thirty-one beautiful engravings. In a cross in the centre of the paper cover, the following title was printed: The | Holy Bible | translated from the Latin Vulgate: | diligently compared | With the Hebrew, Greek, | and other editions | in various languages. | With | Annotations, References, and a Historical | and Chronological Index. | The whole revised | by the Rev. George L. Haydock. | The inaccuracies of former Editions are corrected | by the Very Rev. Dr. Hamell, V. G. |

Only six numbers of this edition were issued and, the house having dissolved, the plates were bought by D. & J. Sadlier and suppressed. The edition bore the approbations of the Most Rev. the Archbishop of New York, the Bishops of Albany, Philadelphia, and many other Catholic Divines in the United States.

2. THE | HOLY BIBLE, | containing the | Old and New Testaments: | together with | the Apocrypha: | Translated out of the Original Tongues, | and with | the former Translations diligently compared and revised. | With | Canne's

Marginal Notes and References. | To which are added | An Index; | An Alphabetical Table | of all the Names in the Old and New Testaments, with their Significations; | Tables of Scripture Weights, Measures, and Coins, &c. | Rochester, N. Y.: | Published by Wanzer, Foote & Co. | 1850. | (L.) 4.

This Bible corresponds with H. & E. Phinney's Cooperstown edition, *supra* pp. 157, 158, having, in addition, the Apocrypha, in brevier type, pp. 1-96; sigs. A to M., and Concordance, pp. 1-31; sigs. A to D.; Front. on wood to O. & N. T. and 2 wood engravings to N. T. The references are on the inner and outer margins.

3. HOLY BIBLE: With Canne's Marginal References; Together with the Apocrypha and Concordance. To which are added An Index and References, and a Key Sheet of Questions, Geographical, Historical, Practical, and Experimental; accompanied with valuable Chronological Harmonies of both Testaments, and highly useful Tables of Scripture Names, Scripture Geography, Scripture Chronology, Scripture References, &c. The text corrected according to the Standard of the American Bible Society. Troy, N. Y.: Published by Merriam, Moore & Co. 1850. 4.

This is another issue of the Merriam 4to of 1846. q. v.

4. HOLY BIBLE: With Canne's Marginal References, Index, Tables and Psalms of David in Metre. Philadelphia: Published by John B. Perry, No. 198 Market Street, and for sale by Wm. Holdredge, 140 Fulton Street, New York. W. A. Leary, 138 North Second Street; New York: Nafis & Cornish. 1850. (L.) 4.

The text of this edition corresponds in pagination and signatures with that of Nafis and Cornish, *supra* p. 250, and of the Cincinnati Bible, *supra* p. 257. This copy however wants the Apocrypha and Concordance. The imprint on the title to the New Test. has Perry's name only.

5. HOLY BIBLE: With Apocrypha, Canne's Marginal Notes and References, Index, Tables, Brown's Concordance. Concord, N. H.: Published by Luther Roby. 1850. (L.) 4.

With engr. front. to O. & N. Test. and one plate in each Test. Preface to Collins's ed. prefixed. The text is apparently from duplicate plates of Sumner & Goodman's 4to of 1848.

6. HOLY BIBLE: With Canne's References, Apocrypha, Index, and Tables. Hartford: Published by A. C. Goodman & Co. 1850.   (L.)   4.

   Engr. front. to O. & N. Test.; Collins's advertisement of 1819; Brown's Concordance, stereotyped by B. & J. Collins, and Psalms of David.

7. HOLY BIBLE, translated from the Latin Vulgate. Published with the approbation of the Most Rev. John Hughes, D. D., Archbishop of New York, Most Rev. Samuel Eccleston, D. D., Archbishop of Baltimore, and the Right Rev. Bishop of Boston. With parallel references. New York: Edward Dunigan & Brother, 151 Fulton Street. n. d.   8.

   This is called, The Illustrated Family Edition. It has an illuminated title and 15 plates. It is the edition of 1844, with new titles.

8. HOLY BIBLE, translated from the Latin Vulgat: With Annotations, References, and a Historical and Chronological Index. Philadelphia: Published by Eugene Cummiskey. Stereotyped by J. Howe. 1850.   8.

   Edition 500. With Approbations of Archbishop Eccleston of Baltimore, Bishops Conwell and Kenrick of Philadelphia, and Bishop Hughes of New York. See 1839.

9. HOLY BIBLE: Philadelphia: Published by Hogan and Thompson. 1850.   12.

   Pp. 1098, 342.

10. HOLY BIBLE: Philadelphia: Lippincott, Grambo & Co., Successors to Grigg, Elliot & Co. 1850.   12.

11. HOLY BIBLE: Stereotype edition. Hartford: S. Andrus & Co. 1850.   12.

   Pp. 824, 251; with Psalms in Metre, pp. 92. No date to N. T.

12. HOLY BIBLE: New York: American Bible Society. Instituted in the year M.D.CCCXVI. 1850.   12.

   57th and 61st editions; pp. 592, 184, with Family Record.

13. HOLY BIBLE: New York: American Bible Society. 1850. 12.

   Pp. 1282, 2.

14. HOLY BIBLE: New York: American Bible Society. 1850. 12.
12th ed. pp. 984; References in the centre of the pp. New Test. 1848.

15. **Bibelen** | eller | **Den Hellige Skrift,** | indeholdende det | Gamle og Nye Testamentes | Canoniste Bøger. | New York: | Udgi= vet af det Amerikaniste Bibel=Selskab. | 1850. | (G. L.) 12.
This is the 2d edition of the Bible in the Danish language, published by the American Bible Society, pp. 920, 287.

16. A | BIBLIA SAGRADA, | Contendo | O Velho e O Novo Testamento, | Traduzida em Portuguez | pelo Padre | Joao Ferreira A D'Almeida, | Minestro Pregador do Soncto Evangelho em Batavia. | Nova York: | Sociedade Americana da Biblia. | 1850. | (G. L.) 12.
3d edition. On reverse of title, Index; Old Testament ends on page 836; New Testament, of the date, 1848, pp. 283.
This is a Protestant version. It was originally published at Batavia in 1748-1753.

17. HOLY BIBLE: New York: American Bible Society. 1850. 18.
Pp. 1278. This is called the "Pocket Minion" edition.

18. HOLY BIBLE: Philadelphia: J. B. Lippincott & Co. 1850. 24.
Pp. 824 and 251.

19. HOLY BIBLE: Philadelphia: Published by Jesper Harding, No. 57 South Third Street. 1850. 32.

20. AN | EXPOSITION | of the | Lamentations of the Prophet | Jeremias. | Translated from the French of | Père Berthier, S. J. | By the | Most Rev. Wm. Walsh | Archbishop of Halifax. | New York: | E. Dunigan & Brother, | 151 Fulton Street | n. d. 16.

21. HISTORY OF THE BIBLE. Buffalo: Phinney & Co. 1850. 142.
Front. and 23 woodcuts; sigs. in 8s, A to M. See 1847.

1. THE | NEW TESTAMENT: | of our | Lord and Saviour Jesus Christ, | translated out of | **The Original Greek;** | and with | the former Translations diligently compared and revised. | Philadelphia: | Published by Thomas, Cowperthwait & Co. | 1850. | 4.

2. THE | NEW TESTAMENT | of | our Lord and Saviour | Jesus
Christ, | translated from the | 𝔏𝔞𝔱𝔦𝔫 𝔙𝔲𝔩𝔤𝔞𝔱𝔢 : | and dili-
gently compared with the | 𝔒𝔯𝔦𝔤𝔦𝔫𝔞𝔩 𝔊𝔯𝔢𝔢𝔨. | Newly re-
vised and corrected, | with Annotations, | explanatory of
the most difficult passages. | Illuminated after Original
Drawings. | By W. H. Hewett, Esq. | New York : | Hew-
ett & Spooner, 106 Liberty Street. | John J. Reed, Printer,
16 Spruce-Street. | 1850. | (L.)   8.

 Presentation plate, 1 p.; verso, blank; Letter of Pius VI, 1 p.; verso, blank; Approbations of one Archbishop and six Bishops, dated 1847, 1848, 1 p.; verso, blank;
Family Record, 3 ff.; printed title, 1 f.; verso, blank; Pref. 1 p.; verso, Order of the
Books; Text: Mat. to Apocal., pp. 1–389; verso, blank; Table of Epist. & Gosp., pp.
391, 392; Hist. and Chronol. Index, pp. 393, 394 (marked 294), Table of References,
pp. 395, 396 (marked 296); no sig. marks or letters.
 This is called "The Pictorial Catholic New Testament." It was originally published
in numbers, the first in 1848. It is embellished with nearly 150 fine woodcuts, to
some of which Mr. Hewett's name is appended, who is stated to be "one of the best
wood engravers that this country has produced." The engravings are copied from
original masterpieces of the best artists. There are, in addition, marginal arabesque
ornaments adapted to each page and also several hundred ornamental initial letters,
one of which embellishes the head of each chapter.
 Mr. Shea says, this Testament was edited by the Rev. James McMahon of New York,
who revised it by the Vulgate, and not only made it conform to the division of the
verses in the Clementine edition, but in translating availed himself of the Greek, and
in the Epistles of St. Paul, of the light which Hebrew throws on the Hebraisms of
that Apostle.
 The edition was purchased in 1854 by John Murphy & Co., Baltimore, by whom
the work has since been issued, and the copy before us, though retaining the imprint
of Hewett & Spooner, has "Baltimore, Murphy & Co.," on the back of the cover.

3. NEW TESTAMENT: New York: American Bible Society.
1850.   8.

4. 𝔇𝔞𝔰 𝔑𝔢𝔲𝔢 𝔗𝔢𝔰𝔱𝔞𝔪𝔢𝔫𝔱 | unſers | Herrn und Heilandes | Jeſu
Chriſti. | New York: Amerikaniſche Bibel-Geſellſchaft. | Gegründet
in 1816. | 1850. | (L.)   8.
 29te Ausgabe; pp. 472, in 8s.

5. NEW TESTAMENT: (English and Spanish in parallel columns.)
New York: American Bible Society. 1850.   Bourg. 12.

6. NEW TESTAMENT: Cincinnati: H. S. & J. Applegate. 1850.
(G. L.)   16.

7. NEW TESTAMENT: Translated from the Latin Vulgate: With annotations &c. New York: Edward Dunigan & Brother. 151 Fulton Street. 1850. 18.
A reissue of the N. T. of 1845, with new title page.

8. NEW TESTAMENT: New York: American Bible Society. 1850. (L.) 24.
48th edition.

9. NEW TESTAMENT: Philadelphia: Miller and Burlock. n. d. 32.
With Psalms. The publishers state that since June 1850, they have issued seven editions of this Testament, amounting in the aggregate, to 11,000 copies.

10. EWH | OOMENWAHJEMOOWIN | owh Tawanemenung | Jesus Christ, | kahenahjemoowand egewh newin Manwahjemoojig | owh St. Matthew owh St. Mark owh St. Luke | kuhya owh St. John. | Keahnekuhnootuhbeegahdag | Anwawand egewh Ahneshenahbag Ojibwag anindjig. | Keenahkoonegewaud kuhya ketebahahmahgawaud | egewh Mahyahmahwejegajig | Society for promoting Christian Knowledge, | ewede London Anduhzhetahwaud. | Toronto: | Printed by A. F. Plees, No. 7 King Street. | 1850. 8.
This is a translation of the Gospels into the Chippeway language, by the Rev. Dr. O'Meara, Missionary of the Church of England, at Manitoualin. Pp. 338; sigs. in 4s.

11. The First Book of Moses, called GENESIS, translated into The Grebo Tongue; | by the Rev. John Payne &c. New York: Published by the American Bible Society. 1850. (N. Y. State Lib.) 18.

12. the | book of Psalms | translated out of | the original tongues, | & with the | former translations diligently compared | & revised. | New York: american bible society, | instituted in the year 1816. | 1850. | (N. Y. State Lib.) 4.
Pp. 872-974. This is a portion of the Bible printed in raised letters for the use of the Blind.

13. THE ACTS OF THE APOSTLES, translated into The Arrawack Tongue; By the Rev. Theodore Shultz, in Eighteen Hun-

dred and Two. New York: Published by the American Bible Society. Instituted in the year MDCCCXVI. 1850. (N. Y. State Lib.) 18.

1851.

1. THE | HOLY BIBLE, | containing the | Old and New Testaments: | With | **References and Illustrations,** | an exact Summary of the several Books, | a | Paraphrase on the most obscure or important parts: | an | Analysis of the Contents of each Chapter; | To which are annexed, | an Extensive Introduction, | explanatory Notes and Evangelical Reflections, &c. | By the | Reverend John Brown, | Minister of the Gospel at Haddington. | Embellished with a series of beautiful engravings. | Baltimore: | Published by Joseph Neal. | n. d. fol.

Frontispiece, 1 f.; Engraved title, 1 f.; Printed title (as above), 1 p.; verso, blank; Then the Introduction, Text and appended matter, as in No. 1 of 1822.

Engravings:
1. Christ weeping over Jerusalem............................... Front *Tucker.*
2. Hagar and Ishmael..*Sartain.*
3. Departure of Hagar.. *Kelley.*
4. Rebecca receiving Isaac's presents.......................... *Kelley.*
5. Finding of Moses................................. *J. B. Neagle,* Phil.
6. Departure of the Israelites from Egypt. Published by Samuel Walker, Boston.*Schoff.*
7. Moses with the Law. Boston: Published by S. Walker............... *Kelley.*
8. Belshazzar's feast.. *Kelley.*
9. Destruction of Jerusalem foretold........................... *F. Walker.*
10. Christ appearing to Mary Magdalen .... *John Rogers.*
11. Christ blessing little children.
12. Christ and woman of Samaria................................. *John Rogers.*

The illustrations however occasionally vary. Some copies have plates of, Joseph sold by his brethren; Jacob in the house of Laban; Joshua commanding the Sun; The Deluge; Jerusalem; Samuel before Eli; Jeptha's return; The arrival of Rebecca; and duplicate plates of, Joseph interpreting Pharaoh's dream; in addition to Nos. 1, 2 and 11 of the preceeding.

This is a reissue in numbers of Brown's Self Interpreting Bible, from the old stereotype plates of Walker or Kinnersley of 1820-22 (see *supra* pp. 150, 156), with the original recommendations of that edition, written in 1820, now reprinted on the covers. The present edition has changed hands since it was commenced. The Imprint on the cover of Part 1 is—Published by John Wallace, 3 Rechabite Hall, Fayette street, Baltimore, no date; Parts 2 to 40 have, Baltimore: Published by Joseph Neal

1847. Over this a slip has been pasted—Baltimore: Published by John Cathers & Co., corner of Holiday and Baltimore Streets. MDCCCLI.; the covers of parts 21 to 40 then again have the imprint—Publication Office | No. 3 Rechabite Hall, Fayette Street, | Baltimore. | From "the Printing Office" Sun Iron Building, Balt. | The type is badly worn.

2. HOLY BIBLE: The text conformable to the Standard edition of the American Bible Society. Philadelphia: Published by Lippincott, Grambo & Co., Successors to Grigg, Elliot & Co., No. 14 North Fourth Street. 1851.   (L.)   4.

Title, 1 f.; verso, Names and Order (Apocrypha not included); To the Reader p. 3; Contents, pp. 4-8; Text: Gen. to Mal., pp. 9-574; Table, p. 575; Index, Table and Analysis, pp. 576; Apocrypha (in smaller type), pp. 1-88; Family Record, 2 ff.; New Testament, title, 1 p.; verso, Account of dates and time of writing the books of N. T.; Text: Mat. to Rev., pp. 579-754; Index, pp. 755-762; Account of Judea, Table of Kindred, p. 763; Tables of Measures, p. 764; Table of Proper Names, pp. 765-768; Psalms in Metre, pp. 1-22; Concordance, pp. 1-41. Engr. front. and title to Old Test. and 9 large woodcuts. Some copies are without woodcuts.

By reference to the year 1822, it will be seen that the pagination of the text of this edition agrees with that of the Cooperstown Bible.

3. HOLY BIBLE: With the Apocrypha, Canne's Marginal Notes and References. To which are added An Index; An Alphabetical Table of all the Names in the Old and New Testaments, with their Significations; Table of Scripture Weights, Measures, and Coins, &c., Concordance and Psalms in Metre. Philadelphia: James A. Bill, No. 253 Market Street. n. d.   4.

This is Miller and Burlock's edition (see 1848, No. 1), with the Apocrypha, Brown's Brief Concordance and Psalms. The Imprint to the Concordance is, Philadelphia: Published by Edward W. Miller, Artizan Building, Ransted Place, 1850. 1 p.; verso, To the Reader; Text: pp. [3]-[56]; Psalms in Metre, pp. 1-19.

4. HOLY BIBLE: With References and Various Readings, and Apocrypha. In Two Volumes. Philadelphia: Published by E. H. Butler & Co. 1851.   4.

See No. 1, 1847. This copy has only a front. to Old Test., Ruth gleaning; and one to New Test., Going to the Sepulchre (The Three Maries), both on steel.

5. HOLY BIBLE, translated from the Latin Vulgate: With Annotations by the Right Rev. Dr. Challoner; together with References, and an Historical and Chronological Index, revised and corrected according to the Clementine edition of the Scriptures. With the Approbation of the Most Rev.

John Hughes, D. D., Archbishop of New York. New York: Published by D. & J. Sadlier & Co., 164, William Street. Boston: 128 Federal Street, and 179 Notre Dame Street, Montreal, C. E. 1851.   (L.)   4.

<small>This a continuation of Sadlier's 4to already described at p. 281. The vignette on the engraved title page is, St. John in the Desert. The front. to the New Test. is The Adoration by the Shepherds. The other engravings are as already enumerated; but plate 6 is now: The Ascent of Elias, 4th Kings; and, "London: George Virtue," is erased from the plates which bore that inscription in the edition of 1845. The Imprint to Ward's Errata is, New York: Published by D. & J. Sadlier & Co., No. 164 William street. Boston: 128 Federal street. n. d.</small>

6. HOLY BIBLE: With Apocrypha, Brown's Concordance, and Psalms in Metre. New York: Published by Leavitt and Allen, 27 Dey Street. n. d.   (L.)   4.

<small>This Bible was printed from the plates of an edition published previously by Hogan and Thompson of Philadelphia. The text of the Old and New Testaments corresponds exactly with that of No. 2 of 1839, *supra* p. 260; but the Marginal Notes, References, and the running Contents at the top of the columns of the latter, are omitted in Leavitt and Allen's edition, the text of which is embraced within parallel rules, having only the number of chapters at the top. There is a colored front. to Old Testament. The Apocrypha, pp. 1-96, is in smaller type; it contains also Concordance, pp. 1-36, and Psalms in Metre, pp. 1-28; but the Table of Passages, Chronol. Index, &c., are in front, in place of Witherspoon's Preface and the Table of Contents.</small>

7. HÒLY BIBLE: According to the authorized version; with the marginal references and the usual various readings. Also Notes; reflections; questions; improved readings; improved divisions of chapters; the chronological order; metrical portions distinguished; and various other advantages, without disturbing the usual order of the Books, verses and chapters. By the Rev. Ingram Cobbin, A. M. Illustrated with numerous descriptive engravings. New York: Samuel Hueston, 139 Nassau Street. 1851. (L.) 4.

<small>Ornamented title, "The Illustrated Domestic Bible, by the Rev. Ingram Cobbin, M. A." (no imprint), 1 p.; verso, blank; printed title, 1 p.; verso, blank; Preface, dated Camberwell, Aug. 15, 1847, 2 pp.; Key to this work, 1 p.; verso, blank; Text: Gen. to Mal., pp. 3-999; Historical connexion of the O. & N. Test. p. 1000; sigs. B2 to 6L; Fam. Rec., 2 ff; title to New Test. 1 p.; verso, blank; Text: Mat. to Rev., pp. 5-375; Supplementary illustrations, selected chapters adapted for reading on particular occasions, p. 376 (not marked). sigs. A³ to 3A, all in 4s; Indexes, pp. i-xii.

This volume was published in twenty-five numbers; it has brief Notes and Reflections by the editor, and a Map; woodcut titles precede Pentateuch, Joshua, Job, Isaiah, Gospels and Epistles, and it is profusely embellished with fine woodcut engravings, illustrative of oriental scenery and manners, copied from Cobbin's Pictorial Bible.</small>

8. HOLY BIBLE: With Apocrypha, Canne's Marginal Notes and References; Index, Alphabetical Tables of Names, Scripture Weights, Measures and Coins. Auburn: James M. Alden. 1851. 4.

From duplicate plates of the Cooperstown Bible of 1822, with Apocrypha and Concordance.

9. HOLY BIBLE: With Apocrypha, Canne's Marginal Notes and References, Index, and Tables. Hartford: Published by A. C. Goodman & Co. 1851. (L.) 4.

Engr. front. to O. & N. Test; Advertisement to Collins's stereotyped ed. of 1819; Brown's Concordance; stereotyped by B. & J. Collins; Psalms in Metre. See No. 6 of 1850.

10. HOLY BIBLE: With References and marginal readings of the Polyglott Bible, with numerous additions from Bagster's Comprehensive Bible. New York: Published by Pratt, Woodford & Co. 1851. (L.) 8.

Title and prel. matter, pp. 1–40; Text: Gen. to Mal., pp. 3–581; 1 blank p.; Fam. Rec., 2 ff.; New Test. title, 1 p.; verso, blank; Mat. to Rev., pp. 585–762; Chronol. Index, pp. 763–772; General Table of Psalmody, p. 733.

11. HOLY BIBLE: New York: American Bible Society. 1851. (G. L.) Pica 8.

Revised edition.

12. HOLY BIBLE: New York: American Bible Society. 1851. (G. L.) Sm. pica 8.

23d edition.

13. LA | BIBLIA SAGRADA, | Traducida | en Español. | Version cotegada cuidadosamente con las | Lenguas Antiguas. | Jesus Respondio: *Escudrinad las Escrituras.* S. Juan, cap. V, ver. 39. | Nueva-York. | Edicion Esteriotipica. | 1851. | (G. L.) 8.

2d edition; pp. 926, 294; sigs. in 8ˢ.

14. HOLY BIBLE: New York: American Bible Society. 1851. Nonp. 12.

87th edition.

316   AMERICAN BIBLES.   [1851—

15. HOLY BIBLE: New York: American Bible Society. 1851.
(G. L.)   Minion 12.
75th edition.

16. **Die Bibel,** | oder | Die Ganze | **Heilege Schrift** | des | alten
und neuen | Testaments. | New York, | Herausgegen von der Amerikanischen Bibel- | Gesellschaft. | 1851. | (G. L.)   12.
27te Ausgabe.

17. THE HOLY BIBLE, | containing | The Old and New Testaments: | Translated | out of the Original Tongues, | and | with the former Translations diligently | compared and revised. | Published by Richard & George S. Wood, | New York. | n. d.   12.

Title, 1 f.; verso, The Names and Order; at foot of the page, an Oval on the border of which is printed, Richard & George S. Wood, | Proprietors. New York | ; in the centre, Woodvale | Water-power Press, | Morristown, N. J. | Text: Gen. to Mal., pp. 3-486; sigs. A, not marked, to verso of X³; New Testament, Stereotype edition. Imprint as above, 1 p.; verso, Tables of Scripture Measures, Weights, Money and Time; Text: Mat. to Rev., pp. 3-162; sigs. X⁴ to 2D¹²; sigs. in 12⁴; Brief headings to columns and chapters. 1 Tim. 4:16, incorrect.

18. HOLY BIBLE: Philadelphia: Lippincott, Grambo & Co., Successors to Grigg, Elliot & Co., No. 14, North Front St. 1851.   12.
Pp. 1044.

19. HOLY BIBLE: New York: American Bible Society. 1851.
(G. L.)   Minion 18.
10th edition.

20. THE ENGLISH VERSION of the POLYGLOTT BIBLE. Stereotyped by L. Johnson. Philadelphia: Thomas, Cowperthwaite & Co. 1851.   24.
For collation, see 1839.

21. HOLY BIBLE: New York: American Bible Society. 1851.
(G. L.)   Agate 24.
46th edition.

22. HOLY BIBLE: Philadelphia: Lippincott, Grambo & Co., Successors to Grigg, Elliot & Co., No. 14, North Fourth St. 1851.   32.
Pp. 726, 221; Psalms in Metre, pp. 81.

23. HOLY BIBLE: New York: American Bible Society. 1851.
(G. L.)   Diamond 32.
38th edition.

24. THE LENTEN MANUAL and Companion for Passion Time and Holy Week. Translated and Compiled from Various Sources. By the Right Rev. Dr. Walsh, Bishop of Halifax. New York: Dunigan and Brother, 151 Fulton St. 1851.   16.
From p. 89-262 contains, An Exposition of the Lamentations of the Prophet Jeremias.

25. THE | BOOK OF PSALMS, | translated out of | the Original Hebrew: | and with | the former translations diligently compared | and revised. | New York: | American Bible Society, | Instituted in the Year 1816. | 1851. | 64.
Pp. 100.

1. Family Bible. | THE | NEW TESTAMENT | of | our Lord and Saviour Jesus Christ: | With | brief Notes and Instructions, | designed | to give the results of Critical investigation, and to assist | common readers to understand the meaning of the | Holy Spirit in the inspired word. | Including | the References and Marginal Readings of the Polyglott Bible. | Published by the | American Tract Society. | New York: | 150 Nassau Street. | n. d.   (L.)   8.
Text: pp. 3-425; Map of Palestine in the time of David, and Map of the Countries mentioned in the Bible. The copy before us is accompanied by the Psalms of David marked, pp. 665-766, being a part of the O. T. (*post* 1857) bound in. The copyright of this edition is dated 1851.

2. NEW TESTAMENT: or the Book of the Holy Gospel of our Lord and our God, Jesus, the Messiah. A literal translation from the Syriac Peshitu version, by James Murdock, D. D. New York: Stanford & Swords. 1851.   (L.)   8.
First edition; Portrait.

3. NEW TESTAMENT: New York: American Bible Society. 1851.   (Rev. Dr. Brigham; G. L.)   Pica 8.
Psalms appended.

4. NEW TESTAMENT: (English and Swedish) New York: American Bible Society. 1851. Bourg. 12.

5. The commonly received version of the NEW TESTAMENT &c. with several hundred emendations. Edited by Spencer H. Cone and Wm. H. Wyckoff. I am not ashamed &c. New York: E. H. Tripp, 262 Greenwich Street. 1851. (L.) 12.

<small>Baptist version. The words "baptize" and "baptism" are rendered throughout, Immerse and Immersion.</small>

6. NEW TESTAMENT: Translated out of the Latin Vulgate: With Annotations &c. New York: D. & J. Sadlier, 164 William Street. n. d. 12.

<small>Same as the edition of 1842. The error in James 5 : 17 is continued.</small>

7. NEW TESTAMENT: Translated from the Latin Vulgate; With Annotations, a Chronological Index, Tables of References, etc., etc. Approved by the Most Rev. John Hughes, D. D., Archbishop of New York. New York: Edward Dunigan & Brother, 151 Fulton Street. 1851. (G. L.) 18.

<small>The same as the edition of 1845.</small>

8. NEW TESTAMENT: New York: American Bible Society. Instituted &c. 1851. 32.

<small>129th edition. Pp. 349; Contents, pp. 350, 352.</small>

9. NEW TESTAMENT: New York: American Bible Society. 1851. Agate 32.

10. NEW TESTAMENT: New York: American Bible Society. Instituted &c. 1816. 1851. (Rev. Dr. Brigham.) Diam. 64.

<small>Psalms appended; pp. 384.</small>

11. THE | EPISTLES AND GOSPELS | for the | Sundays | and | Principal Festivals | throughout the year. | Boston: | Patrick Donahoe. | 1851. | (L.) 18.

<small>These are the Epistles and Gospels read at the Mass, according to their order.</small>

12. THE | ACTS OF THE APOSTLES, | the | EPISTLES of St. Paul, | the | CATHOLIC EPISTLES, | and | the APOCALYPSE. | Translated from the Latin Vulgate, and diligently compared with the | Greek text, being a revision of the Rhemish Translation, | with Notes, | critical and explanatory, | By Francis Patrick Kenrick, | Bishop of Philadelphia. | "Beloved, be mindful of the words which were spoken before the Apostles of our Lord Jesus | Christ." JUDE v. 17. | New York: | Edward Dunigan and Brother, | Fulton Street, near Broadway. | 1851. | (L.; G. L.)   8.

Title, 1 f.; verso, Notice of Copyright; Philadelphia: C. Sherman, Printer. Contents, pp. iii, iv; General Introd., pp. ix-xiii; Brief Notice of Manuscripts, Chief versions and Abbreviations, pp. xiv-xvi; Introd. to the Acts, pp. 17, 18; Chronol. Table, p. 19; verso, blank; Text: Acts of the Apostles, pp. 21-161; verso, blank; Gen. Introd. to Ep. of St. Paul, Chron. Table and Introd. to Ep. to Romans, pp. 163-165; Text: pp. 166-239; verso, blank; Introd. to 1 Corinth., pp. 241, 242; Text: pp. 243-308; Introd. to 2 Corinth., p. 309; Text; pp. 310-347; verso, blank; Introd. to Ep. to Galat., pp. 349, 350; Text: pp. 351-374; Introd. to Ephes., pp. 375, 376; Text: pp. 377-398; Introd. to Philip., pp. 399, 400; Text: pp. 401-416; Introd. to Colos., p. 417; Text: pp. 418-430; Introd. to 1 Thess., pp. 431, 432; Text: pp. 433-443; verso, blank; Introd. to 2 Thess., p. 445; Text: pp. 446-452; Introd. to 1 Timothy, pp. 453, 454; Text: pp. 455-472; Introd. to 2 Timothy, pp. 473, 474; Text: pp. 475-485; verso, blank; Introd. to Titus, pp. 487, 488; Text: pp. 489-496; Introd. to Philemon, p. 497, verso; Text: pp. 498-500; Introd. to Hebrews, pp. 501-503; Text: pp. 504-546; Introd. to James, pp. 547, 548; Text: pp. 549-564; Introd. to 1 Peter, pp. 565-566; Text: pp. 567-582; Introd. to 2 Peter, pp. 583-585; Text: pp. 586-595; verso, blank; Introd. to Ep. of John, pp. 597, 598; Text: pp. 599-616; Introd. to Jude, p. 617; Text: pp. 618-622; Introd. to Apocal., pp. 623-626; Text: pp. 627-680; sigs. 1-43 in 8s, except the first and last which are in 4s. The title page and contents, 2 ff., are not included in the signature. Map of the Countries traveled by the Apostles, and a list of Bishop Kenrick's works precede the title.

13. THE ACTS of the APOSTLES, translated into 𝕮𝖍𝖊 𝕲𝖗𝖊𝖇𝖔 𝕮𝖔𝖓𝖌𝖚𝖊; by the Rev. John Payne &c. New York: Published by the American Bible Society. Instituted &c. 1851.   (N. Y. State Lib.)   18.

14. AN ANALYSIS of the 24th Chapter of MATTHEW. By Hiram Carleton. Windsor: Printed at the Chronicle Press. 1851.   (B.)   8.

15. A TRANSLATION and Exposition of the First Epistle of the Apostle PETER. By John T. Demarest, Minister of the

Reformed Dutch Church at Montague, N. J. New York: John Moffet, 311 Broadway. 1851. 8.

16. THE GENERAL HISTORY of the CHRISTIAN CHURCH...... Chiefly deduced from the APOCALYPSE of St. John. By Sig. Pastorini. Published by D. & J. Sadlier & Co., 164 William Street. 1851. 12.

Portrait of Bishop Walmesley. This is No. 11, *supra* p. 237, with a new imprint.

17. EXPOSITION of the APOCALYPSE. By T. Wickes. New York: 1851. 12.

1852.

1. THE | HOLY BIBLE, | translated from | the Latin Vulgate : | Diligently compared | with the Hebrew, Greek, and other editions in divers languages. | The | Old Testament, | first published by the English College at Douay, A. D. 1609. | And | The New Testament, | first published by the English College at Rheims, A. D. 1582. | With | Useful Notes, | critical, historical, controversial, and explanatory, | selected from the most eminent Commentators, and the most able and judicious critics. | By the Rev. George Leo Haydock. | *Haurietis aquas in gaudio de fontibus Salvatoris.* | You shall draw waters with joy from the Saviour's fountains. Isai. xii, 3. | *Da mihi intellectum, et discam mandata tua.* | Give me understanding, and I will learn thy commandments. Ps. cxviii, 73. | New York : | Edward Dunigan and Brother, | 151 Fulton Street, near Broadway. | 1852. | · 4.

Title, 1 f.; verso, Approbation of the Most Rev. Archbishop Hughes, dated 5th May, 1852; Haydock's Dedication, 1 p.; Names and Order of all the Books of the Old and New Test., Note, 1 p.; Advertisement, Approbations of the O. and N. Test., Approb. of the Univ. of Douay, Approb. of the University of Rheims, Approb. of Dr. Challoner's ed., p. 5; Admonition, Letter of Pope Pius VI, A prayer before reading the Scriptures, Translation of the Decree of the Council of Trent, p. 6, and part of p. 7; A short sketch of the principal Epochs, remainder of p. 7; Haydock's Preface, pp. 9-11; A list of the principal Commentators, completing p. 11; verso, blank; making, with the title, sigs. 1 and 2^2; Text: Gen. to Mac., pp. (13)-(1226.) sigs. 2^3 to verso of 54^1. At the end of II Mac. this " *N. B.* The Third and Fourth Book of Machabees, as also the Third and Fourth Book of Esdras (which some call the First and Second

AMERICAN BIBLES.

Book of Esdras), and the Prayer of Manasses, are here omitted, because they have never been received by the Church. Ch." Historical and Chronol. Index, pp. (1227)–(1231), verso, blank; sigs. 154² to 154⁴; Family Record, with engr. headings and borders, 3 ff.; The | New Testament | of | our Lord and Saviour | Jesus Christ; | first published by the English College at Rheims, A. D. 1852. | Translated from | the Latin Vulgate: | Diligently compared | with the Original Text, | and other editions in divers languages. | With Useful Notes, | critical, historical, controversial and explanatory, | selected from the most eminent commentators, and the most able and judicious critics. | Haurietis aquas &c. | Da mihi intellectum &c. | All things that are read in the Holy Scriptures, we must hear with great attention to our instruction and salvation; but those things | especially must be committed to memory, that serve most to confute heretics, whose deceits cease not to circumvent or ensnare all the weaker sort, | and the more negligent persons."—*S. Aug. tract. 2 in epis. Joan.* | New York: | Edward Dunigan and Brother, | 151 Fulton street, near Broadway. | 1854. | 1 p.; verso, blank; Gen. Preface to the New Testament, pp. (1235)–(1245), verso, blank; sigs. 155 to 156³; Text: Mat. to Apocalypse, pp. (1247)–(1657), verso, blank; sigs. 156⁴ to recto of 208¹; Hist. and Chronol. Index to N. T., pp. (1659)–(1660); Tables of Scripture Weights, &c., and Time, p. (1661); Table of References, pp. (1662)–(1666); Table of Epist. & Gosp., p. (1667); Theological History in Miniature, pp. (1668)–(1671); verso, blank; sigs. 208² to recto of 209⁴; sigs. in 4ˢ but printed in 8ˢ. The pages inclosed within double lines.

List of Engravings:
Moses receiving the Tables of the Law. Frontispiece to O. T. Engr. by *J. N. Gimbrede.*
Abraham about to sacrifice Isaac. Vignette to engr. title to O. T. After Murillo.
Agar and Ishmael. After Steinle.
The arrival of Rebecca. Painted by Schopin.
Jacob in the House of Laban. Steinle pinxt.
Joseph sold by his brethren. Overbeck.
Aaron. Dyer pinxt.
The first fruits of Canaan. Steinle.
Moses raises the Brazen Serpent.
David and Abisai in King Saul's tent. Steinle.
Judgment of Solomon...*A. L. Dick.*
Daniel in the Lion's den..*A. L. Dick.*
Jesus Christ. Frontispiece to New Test.................................*Parker.*
Christ carrying the cross. Vignette to engr. title.
The Infant St. John..*Parker.*
Little children brought to Christ......................................*Dick.*
The Three Maries.
The Annunciation...*Gimbrede.*
The Crucifixion. Copyrighted in 1844...................................*Dick.*

This is called, A New Edition of Haydock's Catholic Bible, to distinguish it from that published by Mr. Cummiskey in 1824. It was issued in 38 parts. The Rev. J. R. Bayley, now Bishop of Newark, N. J., edited a few sheets; the Rev J. McMahon, the remainder. The latter gentleman made, says Mr. Shea, many corrections in the text and notes. Many errors in the Old Testament have been overlooked, notwithstanding, and a curious mistake is retained in the original note on Genesis, 1: 16, where light is said to " be nearly 3000 years in coming to us from the remotest star in our *stratum;*"

a palpable misprint, for "system" says Archd. Cotton, which Mr. Haydock had himself detected and removed. The directions to the Binder, at the end of this volume, order "The Preface to the American edition to be inserted in the beginning, between pages 8 and 9." But there is no such preface in the copy before us, nor in any other edition of this Bible that we have seen.

2. HOLY BIBLE, translated from the Latin Vulgate: With Annotations by Dr. Challoner, &c. New York: Published by D. & J. Sadlier & Co., 164 William Street. Boston: 128 Federal Street, and 179 Notre Dame Street, Montreal, C. E. n. d. (L.) 4.

This is the edition of 1851 with new titles; engr. front., engr. title page (an architectural design and figures of Peter and Paul); with the Approbation of the Rt. Revd. Dr. Hughes, Bishop of New York. Published by D. & J. Sadlier, 58 Gold street, New York. 3 plates to Old Test., an engr. front. and 3 plates to New Test. Ward's Errata does not accompany this copy.

3. Die | **Heilige Schrift** | des | alten Testamentes. | Aus der Vulgata | mit Bezug auf den Grundtext neu übersetzt, | von | Dr. Joseph Franz Allioli, | mit | einer Auswahl seiner Anmerkungen. | Herausgegeben von einem Priester der Versammlung des | allerheiligsten Erlösers, | mit | Gutheißung und Approbation des Hochwürdigsten | Bischofs von New-York, Dr. Joannes Hughes. | New-York: | D. & J. Sadlier, No. 58 Gold-Straße. | Boston, No. 72 Federal-Straße. | Stereotypie und Druck von H. Ludwig & Comp., | No. 70 Vesey-Straße. | 1852. | 8.

Title, 1 f.; verso, blank; Vorrede, p. (3); verso, Verzeichniß aller Bücher des alten und neuen Testaments; Text: Gen. to II Mac., pp. 5–891, verso of 891, blank; sigs. 1 (which includes title and 1 prel. leaf) to recto of 56⁶; 2 blank leaves to complete sig. which is in 8ˢ; Fam. Rec., 2 ff.; Die | Heilige | Schrift | des neuen Testamentes. | Aus der Vulgata | mit Bezug auf den Grundtext neu übersetzt, | von | Dr. Joseph Franz Allioli, | mit | einer Auswahl seiner Anmerkungen. | Herausgegeben von einem Priester der Versammlung des | allerheiligsten Erlösers, | mit | Gutheißung und Approbation des Hochwürdigsten | Bischofs von New-York, Dr. Joannes Hughes. | Zu haben bei | D. & J. Sadlier, 164 William-Straße. | 1852. | 1 p.; verso, blank; Vorrede des Herausgebers, p. (3); Vorwort zu den h. Evangelien, p. (4); Text: Mat. to Offenbarung, pp. 5–268; sigs. 1 (which incl. title and 1 prel. f.), to verso of 17⁶; Epistel und Evangelien auf Alle Sonn-und Festage | des Jahres. | 2 pp.; 1 blank leaf to complete sig. in 8ˢ; front. to Old Test., **Abraham und Isaac.**

Dr. Allioli the editor of the original edition of this work, is a canon of the Cathedral of Ratisbon. The American edition was published in two forms; one as above; another in numbers with an engraved title page and 16 plates. It was revised, and Dr. Allioli's notes abridged, by the Rev. Gabriel Rumpeler, one of the Redemptorist Fathers, of New York, who published an edition or two of it and then passed the plates to the

Messrs. Sadlier who sold about 2000 copies. The plates have since been sold to a house in Germany, whence this market is supplied, as there is no Catholic Bible published at present in German in the United States.

The following is a Translation of the Preface prefixed, by Father Rumpeler, to the New Testament:

The reading of the Bible has become, among the Catholic population of the United States of America, a general practice, by what authority we shall not stop to inquire. Suffice it, the universal practice hath created a habit which we do not praise, neither will we absolutely condemn. The actual want, universally perceptible, of a German Catholic Bible approved by the Holy See, up to this time a desideratum in this country, hath induced us rather to transplant into American soil this truly literal Translation of the Holy Scriptures by Dr. FRANZ AILIOLI, which has been received with universal, undivided approbation, is widely dispersed and obtains at present in Germany an almost exclusive circulation, in order thereby to provide against the erroneous understanding of the word of God, often occasioned by the use of Protestant, as well as numerous corrupt Catholic, Bibles, especially that of Van Ess. To facilitate the purchase of this Book, the editor hath thought proper to abridge the often recurring, less necessary, and more abstruse notes in the original work which have been approved by several Bishops; yet so, that the sense thereof has now suffered a change in but very few instances which have been seen and approved by our Most Reverend Bishop Dr. John Hughes. The editor thus hopes to have supplied a pressing want, and to have merited the gratitude, of the public.

The Editor,
P. G. R.

4. HOLY BIBLE, translated from the Latin Vulgate: With Annotations, References, and Index. From the last London and Dublin Editions. Published with the Approbation of the Most Rev. John Hughes, D. D., Archbishop of New York. New York: Published by Edward Dunigan & Brother, No. 151 Fulton Street. 1852. (L.; Georgetown Coll.) 8.

Engraved front.; Engr. Approbation; Colored Title and 2 plates to O. T.; Engr. front.; Colored Title and 4 plates to N. Test. See No. 3 of 1844.

5. HOLY BIBLE, translated from the Latin Vulgate: With Annotations, References and Indexes. Philadelphia: Published by Eugene Cummiskey. Stereotyped by J. Howe. 1852. 8.

Edition 500.

6. THE | HOLY BIBLE, | translated from | the Latin Vulgate: | Diligently compared with | the Hebrew, Greek, and other editions, | in divers languages. | The Old Testament, | first published by | the English College at Doway, A. D.,

1609. | And | the New Testament, | first published by | the English College | at Rheims, A. D. 1582. | With Annotations and References, | and a | Historical and Chronological Index. | Boston: | Patrick Donahoe, 3 Franklin Street. | 1852. | (L.; G. L.)   8.

Title, 1 f.; verso, Approbations of the Archbishop of Baltimore, of the Bishops of Philadelphia and New York, and of the Bishop of Boston, the last dated August 10, 1852; Admonition, Letter of Pius VI, and Bishop Conwell's Approbation of Cummiskey's 4to and 8vo stereotype editions, dated 13th September, 1824, 1 p.; Translation of the Decree of the Council of Trent, p. 4; then the Text and Index as in Cummiskey's 8vo edition of 1834, *supra* p. 245. The New Testament, &c., with Annotations and References, and a Historical and Chronological Index. Imprint as above, 1 p.; verso, The Order of the Books, Note, Approbation of the Bishop of Boston, dated August 10, 1852; Dr. Troy's Approbation of the Irish edition of 1791, 1 p.; verso, blank; Then Text, &c , as in Cummiskey's edition, the plates of which had been purchased by Mr. Lucas of Baltimore, who sold them to Mr. Donahoe.

The volume before us has a lithograph frontispiece to the Old Test. and another to the New Test., viz: Moses, and the Crucifixion. Some copies have 2 leaves of Fam. Rec. preceding the title. The work is advertised as "The Unrivalled dollar edition of the Douay Bible." The copy in the Boston Athenæum is on large paper, with the titles and pages inclosed within parallel rules.

7. LA | BIBLIA SAGRADA, | Traducida | en Español. | Version cotegada cuidadosamente con las | Lenguas Antiguas. | Jesus Respondio: *Escudrinad las Escrituras*. S. Juan, cap. V, ver. 39. | Nueva-York. | Edicion Esteriotipica. | 1852. | 8.

8. HOLY BIBLE: New York: American Bible Society. 1852. (Rev. Dr. Brigham.)   Pica 8.

9. HOLY BIBLE: New York: American Bible Society. Instituted in the year M.DCCCXVI. 1852. (G. L.)   Nonp. 12.
9th and 95th editions; Pp. 592 and 184.

10. LA | SAINTE BIBLE, | qui contient | le Vieux et le Nouveau Testament; | Revue sur les Originaux, | Par David Martin, | Ministre du Saint Evangile à Utrecht. | New York: | Societé Biblique Americaine, | établie en MDCCCXVI. | 1852. | (G. L.)   12.

5th edition, pp. 819, 261. The Rev. Mr. Martin was pastor of the Walloon Church at Utrecht. His revision of the Genevan Version of the French Bible was first printed at Amsterdam in 1707. See 1846 for the 1st N. Y. edition.

11. HOLY BIBLE: New York: Published by the New York Bible and Common Prayer Book Society, No. 20 John Street. 1852. 12.

12. HOLY BIBLE: New York: American Bible Society. 1852. Pearl 18.

13. HOLY BIBLE: Philadelphia: Lippincott, Grambo & Co., Successors to Grigg, Elliot & Co. 1852. 12.

14. HOLY BIBLE: Philadelphia: Thomas, Cowperthwaite & Co. No. 253 Market Street. 1852. 32.
Engr. front. and title, with Contents and Psalms, pp. 852, 259, 3 and 81.

15. THE | BOOKS | of | JOSHUA, JUDGES, and RUTH, | translated into | The Choctaw language. | Choshua, nan apesa Vhlcha Holisso, | Michla Lulh Holisso, | aiena kvt toshowvt | Chahta anumpa Toba hoke. | New York: | American Bible Society, | Instituted in the year MDCCCXVI. | 1852. | 12.
Pp. 151.

16. The | First and Second Books of SAMUEL, | and the first Book of KINGS, | translated into | the Choctaw Language. | Samuel J. Holisso | Vmmona, Atukla Itatuklo, | micha | Miko Vhleha, | isht anumpa Vmmona | aiena kvt Toshowvt | Chahta anumpa Toba hoke. | New-York: | American Bible Society, | Instituted in the year MDCCCXVI. | 1852. | 12.
Pp. 256. The translations 15 and 16 were made with the assistance of the Rev. Cyrus Byington.

1. NEW TESTAMENT: Translated from the Latin Vulgat: With Annotations and References, and a Historical and Chronological Index. Boston: Patrick Donahoe, 3 Franklin Street. 1852. (L.; G. L.) 8.
This is the New Testament portion of the Bible published this year by the same bookseller, bound up separately.

2. THE NEW TESTAMENT expounded and illustrated according to the usual Marginal References in the very words of the Holy Scriptures, with Notes and a Complete Harmony of the Gospels. By Clement Moody, M. A., Magdalen Hall, Oxford; Perpetual Curate of Sebergham. New York: Published by George Lane and Levi Scott, 200 Mulberry Street. Joseph Longking, Printer. 1852.   8.
Pp. 665.

3. Die | **Heilige Schrift** | des | neuen Testamentes. | Aus der Vulgata | mit Bezug auf den Grundtert neu übersetzt, | von | Dr. Joseph Franz Allioli, | mit | einer Auswahl seiner Anmerkungen. | Herausgegeben von einem Priester der Versammlung des | allerheiligsten Erlösers, | mit Gutheißung und Approbation des Hochwürdigsten | Bischofs von New-York, Dr. Joannes Hughes. | Zu haben bei | D. & J. Sadlier, 164 William-Straße. | 1852. | 8.

This is the New Testament of the Bible, *supra* No. 3, printed separately, with Frontispiece—The Flight into Egypt, engraved by *T. Kelley*, below, D. & J. Sadlier, 58 Gold street.

4. NEW TESTAMENT: Auburn: Published by J. M. Alden. 1852.   12.

5. AN | EXPOSITION | of | the New Testament, | or | The New Covenant | of our | Sovereign Saviour. | The Anointed. | Acts 8:30—Do you understand the book which you are reading? | By Hezekiah Woodruff. | Auburn: | Henry Oliphant, Printer, Genesee Street. | 1852. | 16.

The object of the author of this edition has been (he says) to present the rising generation with the Holy Scriptures in an idiom with which they are familiar. Accordingly, the Gospel of St. Matthew (the only one contained in the volume) is entitled, "The Good News of Salvation according to Matthew;" The Acts of the Apostles—"The Doings of the Commissioners;" The Epistles—"The Letter of Paul (a Commissioner), to the Romans," or Corinthians &c. The word, Lord, is turned into "Sovereign;" the proper name of the Saviour is "The Anointed," and the Disciples are called, "Pupils." The following are specimens of the text:

John the Baptist's "food was small animals and vegitable honey." Mat. 3:4.
Happy are they who hunger and thirst for correctness. Ibid 5:6.
Unless your correctness shall exceed the correctness of the clergy. Ibid 5:20.
Whoever shall say to his brother, Silly fellow....and whoever shall say to him Abandoned Wretch, will be in danger of eternal burnings. Ibid 5:22.

Whoever shall divorce his wife except on account of lustful conduct before marriage, not apparent till after marriage. Ibid 5 ; 32.
The Son-of-man maketh his exit. Ibid 26 : 24.
Immediately he [Judas] came to the Saviour, and said, Your most obedient, Preceptor, Ibid 26:49.

6. NEW TESTAMENT: Translated from the Latin Vulgate: With Annotations &c. New York: Edward Dunigan & Brother, 151 Fulton Street. 1852.   (L.)   18.

7. NEW TESTAMENT: New York: Leavitt & Allen, 27 Dey-Street. 1852.   (Gowans.)   18.
Pp. 191.

8. A NEW | HARMONY and Exposition | of | the GOSPELS : | consisting of | A parallel and combined arrangement, | On a New Plan, | of the Narratives of the Four Evangelists, | according to the authorized Translation ; | and | a continuous Commentary, | with | Brief Notes subjoined. | Being the First Period of the Gospel History. | With a Supplement, | containing extended Chronological and Topographical Dissertations, | and a Complete Analytical Index. | By James Strong, A. M. | Illustrated by Maps and Engravings. | New-York : | Published by Carlton & Phillips, | 200 Mulberry-street. | 1852. | (G. L.)   8.

Mock Title, The Gospel History. | A Harmony and Exposition | of the | Christian Scriptures. | Part First. | The Gospels. | 1 p.; verso, blank; Engraved title, The Gospel History. | First Part. | (Antique Profile of Christ, carved on an Emerald obtained from the Turks in the 15th cent.) Arranged | By James Strong, A. M. | New York: | Carlton & Phillips. | 1 f.; Printed title, 1 f.; verso, Notice of Copyright, dated 1852; Pref. signed by the author, dated Flushing, L. I., April, 1852, pp. v-x; Explanation, pp. xi-xii; Contents, 1 p.; verso, blank; Illustrations, pp. xv-xvii, verso, blank; Maps (list of), 1 p.; verso, blank; Textual Index, pp. xxii-xxx; Mock Title, Harmony and Exposition; sigs. A (not marked) and B in 8^s; Text: pp. 1–388; sigs. I to 25^2 in 8^s; Mock title, A Supplement | to the | Harmony and Exposition of the Gospels; | Containing Three Appendices : | I. Tables and Chronological Calculations. | II. On the Topography of Ancient Jerusalem, with Maps. | III. An Analytical and Synoptical Index of the Gospels. | 1 p.; verso, blank; Appendix I, 1 p.; verso, blank; Tables of Measures, Weights, Money, Time and Winds, pp. 5*, 6*; The Time of Christ's Birth, pp. 7*-24*; Comparative Table of different Harmonies, pp. 25*-28*; Mock Title, Appendix II, 1 p.; verso, blank; Topography of Ancient Jerusalem, pp. †3–42†; Mock Title, Appendix III, 1 p.; Analytical and Synoptical Index, pp. 2‡-79‡; the last page having instead of the regular number, "Whole number of pages | of letter press | 579; verso, blank; sigs. 25³ to recto of 34⁵; Catalogue of Books published by Carlton & Phillips, 3 ff. to complete sig.

Illustrations. Ancient Jerusalem: Miss Hartland, *del.*, *J. C. Buttree*, sc.; Key to the View of Ancient Jerusalem: Key to the View of Modern Jerusalem: Modern Jerusalem; Ulric Halbreeter; *James Smillie:* Modern Jerusalem, from the North, wood engrav., *Roberts:* Modern Nazareth, wood engrav., *Lossing–Barritt:* The River Jordan, Colored Lith: Jacob's Well, The Valley of Schechem, 2 wood engrav. (on 1 page), *Roberts:* Modern Nain, Colored Lith.: The Sea of Galilee, Colored Lith.: Mount Hermon, Colored Lith.: The Pool of Siloam, Colored Lith.: Modern Bethany, wood engrav., *Lossing–Barritt:* The enclosure of the Harem at Jerusalem, The Jews wailing place at Jerusalem, wood engrav. 2 on a page, *Roberts:* The Garden of Gethsemane, Colored Lith.: The Mount of Olives, wood engr., *Lossing-Barritt:* A New Map of Ancient Jerusalem before its destruction by the Romans: Modern Jerusalem according to the late English military survey: Ground Plan of the Temple at Jerusalem: Detailed Plan of the Modern Temple area at Jerusalem.

There is another issue of this volume with the imprint: 𝔑𝔢𝔴 𝔜𝔬𝔯𝔨: | Published by Lane & Scott, | 200 Mulberry-street. | Joseph Longking, printer. | 1852. |

9. The Gospel according to ST. JOHN, translated into 𝔗𝔥𝔢 𝔐𝔭𝔴𝔬𝔫𝔤𝔴𝔢 𝔏𝔞𝔫𝔤𝔲𝔞𝔤𝔢; by Missionaries of the American Board of Commissioners for Foreign Missions, Gaboon, Western Africa. New York: Published by the American Bible Society, instituted in the year MDCCCXVI. 1852. (N. Y. State Lib.) 18.

1853.

1. HOLY BIBLE: With Canne's Notes, Apocrypha, An Index and Tables. Stereotyped by James Conner, New York. Hartford (Conn.): Silas Andrus & Son. n. d. fol.

A reprint in all respects of the edition of 1829. q. v.

2. THE | HOLY BIBLE, | 𝔗𝔯𝔞𝔫𝔰𝔩𝔞𝔱𝔢𝔡 𝔣𝔯𝔬𝔪 𝔱𝔥𝔢 𝔏𝔞𝔱𝔦𝔫 𝔙𝔲𝔩𝔤𝔞𝔱𝔢: | diligently compared with the | Hebrew, Greek, and other editions in divers Languages. | The | Old Testament, | first published by the English College at | Douay, A. D. 1609. | And | The New Testament, | first published by the English College at | Rheims, A. D. 1582. | With | Useful Notes, Critical, Historical, Controversial, and Explanatory, | selected from the most eminent Commentators, and the most able and judicious Critics, | By the late Rev. Geo. Leo Haydock, | and other Divines. | The Text carefully collated with that of the original edition, | and the Anno-

tations abridged, | By the Very Rev. F. C. Husenbeth, D. D. V. G., | Canon of the English Chapter. | Haurietis aquas &c.; | Da mihi intellectum &c. | New York: | George Virtue, 26 John Street. | n. d.   (L.; Georgetown Coll.)   4.

Illuminated title; Engr. Title; Printed Title (as above), 1 f.; verso, blank; Ded. 1 f.; verso, Dr. Husenbeth's Notice, dated Sept. 27th, 1850; Approbation of 3 Amer. Archbishops, and 7 Bishops, 2 pp.; Approb. of the Bishops of the Catholic Church in Eng., 2 pp.; Names and Order of all the Books of O. and N. Test., note, 1 p. marked 354 at foot; verso, blank; making sig. A of the Eng. plates; exclusive of the leaf of Approb. of the Amer. Hierarchy which was stereotyped in this country; Text: Gen. to Psalms, pp. 1-692; sigs. B to verso of 4T^2; Engraved Title " The Holy Bible," with Vignette of the Resurrection: Text: Proverbs to II Mac., pp. 1-381; verso of 381, blank; sigs. B to recto of 3C^3; each sig. marked also Vol. II; Index, pp. 383-386; sigs. 3C^4 to recto of 3D^2; Family Record, 2 ff.; The New Testament, Imprint: London and New York: Virtue, Emmins and Roberts, 1 p; verso, blank; Pref. &c., pp. iii-x; sig. b.; Text: Mat. to Apocalypse, pp. 1-346; sigs. B to verso of 2Y^1; Index to N. T., pp. 347, 348; Tab. of Ref., pp. 349-353; verso of 353, blank; Table of Epist. and Gospels, pp. 355, 356; 2Y^2 to verso of 2Z^2, all in 4s; each page is included within double rules and each sig. of the New Testament is marked also, N. T.

There are in the Old Testament: 28 engravings.

Joseph presenting his father to Pharaoh, Front. to O. T.; Death of Abel; Hagar and Ishmael; Rebecca receiving Isaac's presents; Departure of Rebecca; Arrival of Rebecca; Jacob in the house of Laban; Joseph sold; Joseph interpreting Pharaoh's dream; Moses in the land of Midian; Moses smiting the rock; Moses meeting his wife and sons; Joshua commands the sun to stand still; Jael and Sisera; Boaz and Ruth; Samuel before Heli; David playing to Saul; Saul presenting his daughter to David; The Judgment of Solomon; Solomon did evil in the sight of the Lord; The Ascent of Elijah; Jezrahel, Mount Gilboa, and Bethsan; The Captives in Babylon; Judith with the head of Holofernes; Death of the Blessed Virgin, Frontispiece; The Resurrection, Vignette to Vol. II.; Susanna and the Elders; Tombs in the Valley of Jehosophat; Ruins in the city of Samaria.

In the New Testament: 16.

Madonna and Child; The Repose in the way; Christ stilleth the storm; The Mount of Olives and Jerusalem; The Raising of Jairus's Daughter; The Transfiguration; Christ taken down from the Cross; Cavern where the Holy Cross was found; Shrine of the Nativity, Bethlehem; The Holy Family; The Infant St. John; Our Blessed Redeemer; Jesus and the Samaritan; The Good Shepherd; Fields of Bethania; Peter and John at the Beautiful Gate.

This work was printed originally at Bungay in Suffolk, Eng., and published in London in 1853, in two volumes, with 51 engravings. The plates were afterwards imported into this country and the work is issued in New York in 36 numbers.

In regard to the *Notes*, I am inclined to think (says Archd. Cotton) from an inspection of the first two chapters of Genesis only, that the "abridgment" has been made carelessly, and in a manner more calculated to obscure the sense than illustrate it. For instance, in a note on Genesis, 1:19, Haydock spoke of "the remotest star in our stratum " (a misprint for "system") "beyond which are others immensely distant,"

&c. Dr. Husenbeth leaves out the words, "in our stratum," and by doing so contrives to give the sentence rather an ambiguous turn, "the remotest star, beyond which are others" &c. Again, in a note on Genesis, 2:2, Haydock speaking of the seventh day observed, "This day was commanded, Ex. xx, 8. to be kept holy by the Jews, as it had probably been from the beginning. Philo says, it is the festival of the Universe, and Josephus asserts, there is no town which does not acknowledge the religion of the sabbath. But this point is controverted" &c. Dr. Husenbeth omits the whole of the passage from "Philo" to "Sabbath" inclusive yet goes on, "But this point is controverted" &c. Apart from the Notes the text abounds with errors which we have no room to indicate.

3. HOLY BIBLE, translated from the Latin Vulgat: With Useful Notes, critical, historical, controversial, and explanatory, selected from the most eminent commentators, and the most able and judicious critics. By the Rev. Geo. Leo Haydock. (Texts of Scripture.) New York: Edward Dunigan and Brother, 151 Fulton Street. 1853.   4.
A revised edition of the Bible of 1852. Not seen.

4. HOLY BIBLE, translated from the Latin Vulgate: With Annotations by Dr. Challoner &c. New York: Published by D. & J. Sadlier & Co., 164 William Street. Boston: 128 Federal Street. Montreal, C. E.: corner of Notre Dame and St. Francis Xavier's Streets. 1853.   (L.)   4.
Engr. frontisp. and title page (John the Baptist), and 7 plates; Printed title followed by a leaf, containing an engr. Vignette and approb. of 6 Archbishops and Bishops; The text of each page is embraced within a border of two lines. The New Test. has an engr. front., title page, and 12 plates; Imprint as above, with date 1857. Ward's Errata accompanies the volume. The text is probably from the same stereotype plates as the edition of 1851 and 1852.

5. תורה נביאים וכתובים | The | Twenty-four Books | of the | Holy Scriptures: | carefully translated | according to the Masoretic Text, on the Basis of the | English Version, | after the best Jewish Authorities; | and supplied with | short Explanatory Notes. | By | Isaac Leeser. | כי לא תשכח מפי זרעו | "For it shall not be forgotten out of the mouth of his seed." Deut. xxxi, 21. | Philadelphia: | Published at 371 Walnut Street. | 5614. | (L.)   4.
Title, 1 f.; verso, Extract of Copyright, dated 1853; Stereotyped by L. Johnson & Co., Philadelphia; Pref. dated Philadelphia, Sept. 20, 1853, pp. iii, iv; Mock title to the Pentateuch in Heb and Eng.; The Holy Scriptures, Part First, 1 p.; verso, blank; Text: Gen. to Deut., pp. 3–254; Mock title, as above, Part 2, Division 1st.

Joshua to 2 Kings, 1 p.; verso, blank; Text: pp. 257-458; Title, as above, Part Second, Division II. Isaiah to Malachi., 1 p.; verso, blank; Text. pp. 461-710; Title as above, Part Third, Psalms, Job, Ruth, Eccles., Daniel, Nehemiah, Proverbs, Song of Songs, Lamentations, Esther, Ezra 1st and 2d, Chronicles; Text: pp. 713 to 1011, verso, blank. There is no sig. mark from title to p. 8 incl. 6 ff.; then on p. 9 sigs. B to 6B² in 4ˢ; Fam. Rec., 2 ff.; Text: printed in double columns, with notes at the bottom of the page.

The Text is in English, printed in double columns. Mr. Leeser the translator "is an Israelite in faith in the full sense of the word." In style he has endeavored to adhere to that of the ordinary English Version, whilst he has taken so much care to avoid its faults, that this may be called a new Version especially as regards the Prophets, Psalms and Job. No individual has been questioned as to the meaning of any word, and Bagster's Bible is the only English book that has been consulted in the progress of the translation, which occupied occasionally more than fifteen years.

6. ANNOTATED PARAGRAPH BIBLE: New York: C. B. Norton. 1853.   (G. L.)   8.

7. HOLY BIBLE: With Apocrypha, Canne's Marginal Notes and References, Index, Titles, Tables, Concordance and Psalms in Metre. Philadelphia: Jesper Harding. 1853. (L.) 4.

Engr. front., colored title and 10 large woodcuts to O. T.; Engr. front. and 8 large woodcuts to N. Test.

In an early edition of Harding's 4to Bible, a curious mistake, it is said, occurred in 1 Kings, 1 : 21, wherein the text—" the king shail † sleep with his fathers," was printed "the king shall dagger sleep with his fathers." The error was soon discovered and corrected.

8. HOLY BIBLE: Philadelphia: Lippincott, Grambo & Co., Successors to Grigg, Elliot & Co., No. 14 North Front Street. 1853.   (L.)   8.

Each page of the Text is included within double lines.

9. THE SELF EXPLANATORY REFERENCE BIBLE: With Marginal Readings and original and selected parallel References, printed at length. New York: R. Carter and Brothers. 1853.   8.

The References, &c., are printed in full in two small columns in the centre of the page.

10. HOLY BIBLE: New York: American Bible Society. 1853.
Bourgeois 8.
With references.

11. FAMILY BIBLE: With brief Notes and Instructions. By the Rev. Justin Edwards, D. D., including the References and Marginal readings of the Polyglott Bible. Vol. I. Genesis to Job. New York: 150 Nassau Street. 1853.   8.
Pp. 664.

12. HOLY BIBLE: New York: American Bible Society. 1853.
Nonp. ref. 12.

13. HOLY BIBLE: New York: American Bible Society. 1853.
Brevier 12.

14. HOLY BIBLE: New York: American Bible Society. Instituted &c. 1853.   18.
Pp. 974, 304.

15. HOLY BIBLE: New York: American Bible Society. 1853.
Agate 24.

16. ENGLISH VERSION of the POLYGLOTT BIBLE: With Marginal Readings &c. Illustrated with Maps and Engravings. Philadelphia: Lippincott, Grambo & Co. 1853.   12.
Pp. 824, 256. Psalms in Metre, pp. 77; References in the centre of pp.

17. HOLY BIBLE: Philadelphia: Thomas, Cowperthwaite & Co. 1853.   (Mr. McAllister.)   12.

18. HOLY BIBLE: Philadelphia: Miller & Burlock. 1853. (Mr. McAllister.)   16.

19. HOLY BIBLE: Northampton, Mass.: Hopkins, Bridgman & Co. 1853.   32.
Engr. front. and title to O. and N. Test.; Contents and Psalms. On verso of printed title, Printed by Smith and Peters, Franklin Buildings, Sixth street, below Arch, Philadelphia, pp. 852, 259, 3, and 81. Apparently from duplicate plates of Cowperthwaite's edition.

20. HOLY BIBLE: containing the Old Testament and the New. Portland: Sanborn & Carter. 1853.   32.
Engr. front. and title with N. Test., dated 1851; Psalms in Metre.

21. EXPOSITION of the LAMENTATIONS of the Prophet Jeremiah. Translated from the French, By the Most Rev. Wm. Walsh, D. D., Archbishop of Halifax, N. S. New York: Edward Dunigan and Brother. 1853. 16.

22. THE BIBLE MANUAL; comprising Selections of Scripture, arranged for occasions of private and public worship, both special and ordinary. Together with Scripture expressions of Prayer, abridged from Matthew Henry, with an Appendix consisting of a copious classification of Scripture Text, presenting a systematic view of the doctrines and duties of Revelation. By W. W. Everts, pastor of Laight street Church, New York. Third Edition. New York: Lewis Colby & Co. 1853. 12.

Copyright dated 1846; Introduction dated April 1846; Stereotyped by Vincent L. Dill, 128 Fulton St., Sun building, N. Y. Pp. xii, 324; 3 maps.

23. THE SCRIPTURE TEXT BOOK. Scripture texts arranged for the Use of Ministers, S. S. Teachers, and Families. Search the Scriptures. Fifth Edition. New York: Lewis Colby & Co. 1853. 12.
Pp. 154.

1. NEW TESTAMENT: Translated from the Latin Vulgate: With Annotations by the Right Rev. R. Challoner, D. D.; Together with References, and an Historical and Chronological Index. Revised and corrected according to the Clementine edition of the Scriptures. New York: Published by D. & J. Sadlier & Co., 164 William Street. Boston: 128 Federal Street. Montreal, C. E.: corner of Notre Dame and St. Francis Streets. 1853. 4.

This is the New Testament of the Sadlier 4to Bible, printed separately. It contains the following fine engravings:
The Redeemer. Painted by Carlo Dolce. Frontispiece.
The Adoration of the Shepherds. Vignette to Engr. title. Painted by Ant Raphael Mengs;..................engraved by.....................*A. L. Dick.*
The Redeemer of the World. Ary Scheffer......................*S. Hollyer*, N. Y.
Zebedee's Children............................ ....*R. Thew*, sc.
Our Saviour in the Garden. Matt. 26:39. Carlo Dolci.. ....*G. Parker.*

Jerusalem. W. H. Bartlett..*A. L. Dick.*
Ecce Homo. Vandyke..*S. Hollyer,* N. Y.
The Salutation of the Virgin. Murillo............................*J. Rogers.*
Jesus in the midst of the Doctors. De Caisne...................*S. Hollyer,* N. Y.
The Prodigal Son
The Descent from the Cross. Rubens........................*H. B. Hall.*
The Good Shepherd.
Incredulity of St. Thomas.
The Angel releasing the Apostles from prison. Kirk.........*J. Rogers.*

2. NEW TESTAMENT: (English and French.) New York: American Bible Society. 1853. (Rev. Dr. Brigham.)
Bourg. 12.

3. NEW TESTAMENT: New York: American Bible Society. Instituted &c. 1853. 32.
Pp. 354.

4. EL | NUEVO TESTAMENTO | de | Nuestro Señor y Salvador | Jesu-Christo, | nuevamente traducido de la Vulgata latina al español, | aclarado el sentido de algunas lugares, con la luz que dan los tex- | tos originales hebréo y griego, é ilustrado con várias notas, sacadas de los santos padres y ex- | positores sagrados, | por | el exmo. Sr. Dn. Felix Torres Amat, | obispo de Astorga. | Lleva añadidas algunas notas tomadas del P. Scio y otros calificados | interpretes, | con la aprobacion del | illmo. fr. José S. Alemany, | obispo de Monterey, California. | Primera edicion conforme a la segunda del obispo Amat. | Nueva York: | Eduardo Dunigan y hermano, | Calle de Fulton, No. 151. | 1853. | 12.

Title, 1 f.; verso, Imprimatur. Neo Eboraci die xxx. Mar. 1853. †Joannes, Archiep. Neo Ebor., and copyright; Indice, 1 p.; Introduccion, pp. 5-6; Text: pp. 503; sigs. 1 to 21.

5. MANUAL of the GOSPELS, being an Abridgment of the Author's "Harmony and Exposition of the Gospels;" for the use of Sunday Schools, Bible Classes and Families. By James Strong, A. M. Edited by Daniel P. Kidder. New York: Published by Carlton & Phillips, 200 Mulberry Street. 1853. 12.

6. THE GOSPEL | according to Saint MATTHEW, | in the Micmac Language. | Printed | for the Use of the Micmac Mission | by the British and Foreign | Bible Society. | Charlottetown: | Printed by G. T. Haszard. | 1853. (Hon. Joseph Howe, Halifax, N. S.) 12.

The Phonetic Alphabet is used in this volume, which consists of pp. 118. At the end is Psalm 23, in Indian metre, and a Hymn, "In de Dark Wood, no Indian nigh," also in Micmac.

1854.

1. THE | COMPREHENSIVE BIBLE, | containing the | Old and New Testament, | according to | the authorized Version, | with | the various readings and marginal notes usually printed therewith; | a general Introduction | containing Disquisitions on the genuineness, authenticity, and inspiration of the Holy Scriptures, various divisions and | marks of distinction in the sacred writings; ancient versions; coins, weights, and measures; | various sects among the Jews; | Introductory and Concluding Remarks to each Book: | The parallel Passages | contained in Canne's Bible; Dr. Adam Clarke's Commentary, 7 vols.; Rev. John Brown's Self-Interpreting Bible, 2 vols.; Dr. Blayney's Bible; | Bishop Wilson's Bible, edited by Crutwell; Rev. T. Scott's Commentary, 6 vols.; and the | English Version of Bagster's Polyglott Bible, systematically arranged: | Philological and explanatory Notes: | A Table of Contents, arranged in Historical Order: | An Analysis and Compendium of the Holy Scriptures: | A Chronological Index, | interspersed with Synchronisms of the most important Epochs and Events in profane History; | An Index of Subjects contained in the Old and New Testaments | and | an Index to the Notes, Introduction, and concluding Remarks. | Multæ terricolis lingua, &c. | Philadelphia: | Lippincott, Grambo & Co. (successors to Grigg, Elliot & Co.), No. 14 North Fourth Street. | 1854. | (L.)   4.

Title, 1 f.; verso, Names and Order; Editor's Preface, dated December, 1826; pp. 3, 4; General Contents, pp. 5, 6; Translators to the Readers, pp. 7-16; Contents, 17-21; Second Contents, pp. 22-52; Introd., pp. 53-92; sigs. (title incl.) 1 to 12²; Text: Gen. to Mal., pp. 93-1090; sigs. 12³ to 137¹; Gen. Outline, pp. 1091-1094;

sigs. 1372 to 1373[3]; Fam. Record, 2 ff.; New Test. title, 1 f.; verso, blank; Text: Mat. to Rev., pp. 1097-1430; sigs. 138 to 179[3]; Indexes, pp. 1431-1460; sigs. 179[4] to 183[2]; At the end of Index, Multa terricolis lingua, &c., Psalms in Metre, pp. 1-24; sigs. in 4s; Engr. front. and title to O. T. only; Marginal Notes in centre of the pp.

This Bible was published originally in London in 1827, and reprinted in 1846; it contains 4000 notes, which by a simple Index are made to illustrate 40,000 passages. They comprise illustrations of Jewish manners, customs, rites, and ceremonies. *Bohn's Lowndes.* The editor was William Greenfield. *Horne.*

2. HOLY BIBLE: With Apocrypha, Canne's Marginal Notes and References, Index, Tables, Concordance, and Psalms in Metre. Philadelphia: Jesper Harding. 1854. (L.) 4.

Colored front. and 12 large woodcuts to O. Test.; and Colored front. and 8 colored large woodcuts to N. Test.

3. Butler's Edition. HOLY BIBLE: With references and various readings, together with the Apocrypha. Philadelphia: Published by E. H. Butler & Co. 1854. (L.) Pica 4.

A stereotype edition on tinted paper. Front. colored title page; printed ditto and 4 engr. plates to O. T.; Front. colored and printed title page and 2 engravings to New Test. Pp. 1213.

4. HOLY BIBLE: Syracuse: Mills, Hopkins & Co. 1854. 4.

Pp. 1148. Plates.

5. HOLY BIBLE: Philadelphia: Printed for the American and Foreign Bible Society, by the Bible Association of Friends in America. 1854. (L.) 8.

Stereotyped edition; no Apocrypha; no change in Version; Brown's Concordance.

6. HOLY BIBLE, translated from the Latin Vulgate: With Annotations, References, Index, &c. New York: Published by Edward Dunigan & Bro., No. 151 Fulton Street. 1854. (L.) 8.

Same as 1844; woodcut front. to O. T.

7. HOLY BIBLE: New York: Printed by the New York Bible and Common Prayer Book Society. 1854. 8.

8. HOLY BIBLE: New York: American Bible Society. Instituted &c. 1854. (L.) 8.

The new version, with alterations.

9. HOLY BIBLE: New York: American Bible Society. Instituted in the year MDCCCXVI. 1854. (L.) Bourg. 12.
   19th edition. Printed previously to the new version. Contents at end.

10. HOLY BIBLE: New York: American Bible Society. Instituted in the year MDCCCXVI. 1854. Nonp. 12.
    36th and 37th editions; pp. 767.

11. LA SAINTE BIBLE, | qui contient | le Vieux et le Nouveau Testament; | Revue sur les Originaux, | Par David Martin, | Ministre du Saint Evangile à Utrecht. | New York: | Société Biblique Americaine, | établie en MDCCCXVI. | 1854. | (G. L.) 12.

12. ENGLISH VERSION of the POLYGLOTT BIBLE. Illustrated with Maps and Engravings. Philadelphia: Lippincott, Grambo & Co. 1854. 12.
    Same as the ed. of 1853.

13. HOLY BIBLE: Philadelphia: Lippincott, Grambo & Co. 1854. 32.
    On verso of title, Printed by C. Sherman. Pp. 725 and 221. Psalms in Metre, pp. 81.

14. HOLY BIBLE: New York: American Bible Society. Diamond edition. 1854. 32.

15. THE | GOSPEL BY MOSES, | in the Book of Genesis; | or the Old Testament Unveiled. | By C. H. Putnam. | "And not as Moses, *which* put a vail over his face, that the children of Israel could not stedfastly look to the end | of that which is abolished: | But their minds were blinded: for until this day remaineth the same vail untaken away in the reading of the old | testament; which *vail* is done away in Christ." 2 Cor. iii, 13, 14. | New York: | Edward H. Fletcher, Nassau Street. | 1854. | 8.
    Preface, pp. v-xi; Text: pp. 3-480; Errata, 1 p.; Appendix, pp. 483-486; sigs. in 8s.

1. Butler's Edition. NEW TESTAMENT: With References and various Readings. Philadelphia: Published by E. H. Butler & Co. 1854. Pica 4.

2. NEW TESTAMENT: Philadelphia: Thomas Davis's edition. Stereotyped by John Howe. n. d. 8.

3. 'Η ΚΑΙΝΗ ΔΙΑΘΗΚΗ. IL NUOVO TESTAMENTO: Traduzione del Greco par cura Dr. G. Achille. New York: American Bible Union. 1854. 8.

Pp. 343, with an Introduction by W. H. Wickoff.

4. NEW TESTAMENT: (English and German in parallel columns.) New York: American Bible Society. Instituted in the year MDCCCXVI. 1854. 12.

Pp. 670.

5. LE | NOUVEAU TESTAMENT | de | Notre Seigneur Jesus-Christ | d'apres la Version revue par | J. F. Ostervald. | New York: | Société Bibliqué (*sic*) Américaine | instituée en MDCCCXVI. | 1854. | (N. Y. State Lib.) 12.

3d edition. French and English in parallel columns.

6. NEW TESTAMENT: Translated from the Latin Vulgate: New York: Edward Dunigan & Brother. 151 Fulton Street. 1854. 18.

Same as the edition of 1854, with engr. front. and a title with Vignette of John the Baptist. The printed title within rules has a small vignette also of an angel with the motto, Excelsior.

7. A NEW HARMONY and Exposition of the GOSPELS. By James Strong, A. M. Illustrated by Maps and Engravings. New York: Published by Carlton and Phillips, 200 Mulberry Street. 1854. 8.

8. THE | HISTORY OF CHRIST, | according to Inspiration; | Chronologically arranged in one consecutive | narrative. | With the References. | Boston: | Heath and Graves, | 79 Cornhill. | 1844. | (L.) 12.

Verso of title, Ex. of Copyright, 1854; Asa Wilbur, Mass | Stereotyped by | Hobart & Robins. | New England Type and Stereotype Foundry. | Boston : | Damrell & Moore, Printers, Boston. | Preface, 2 pp.; Contents, pp. v-xiv; sigs. in 6^s, including title page and 4 pp. of Contents, viz: sig. 2 includes from last leaf of Contents to 14 of text; Text: pp. 5-251; sigs. 3 (commencing on page 15) to 22^b in 6^s.

This is a Harmony of the Gospels by Asa Wilbur.

9. The Second Epistle of PETER, the Epistles of John and Jude, and the Revelation, translated from the Greek on the basis of the common English version, with Notes. New York: American Bible Union. 1854.   (L.)   4.

Title and 10 prel. pp.; Errata, 1 f.; Text: pp. 253. This is a Baptist version. The translation is by Rev. Dr. Lillie.

1855.

1. THE | HOLY BIBLE, | containing | the Old and New Testaments : | Translated out of the Original Tongues : | and with the former Translations diligently compared and revised. | With marginal Readings, References, and Chronological dates. | Auburn : | William J. Moses, and Miller, Orton & Mulligan. | New York : | Miller, Orton & Mulligan, 25 Park row. | 1855. | 4.

Engraved title: The | Old Testament | illustrated with Engravings | from the designs of | Richard Westall, Esq., | R. A. | Vignette, Moses receiving the Law, all within an ornamental border; 1 f.; verso, blank; Printed title, 1 f.; verso, blank; A brief account of the authorized version of the Scriptures, extracted from Clark's General Preface, pp. iii, iv; Fletcher's Divine Authority, pp. v-vii; Contents, pp. viii-xii; sigs. A to B^2 in 4^s; Table of Measures &c., Table of Offices, p. 1; Order of the Books, p. 2; Text: Gen. to Mal., pp. 3-797; sigs. A (which includes 2 pp. of prel. matter) to 3D^7 in 8^s, and in sig. 1 to 100^3 in 4^s; Fam. Rec., 2 ff.; 1 leaf blank; Apocrypha in small type, pp. 1-120; sigs. A to H^4 in 8^s, and (1) to (15) in 4^s; New Test., Engr. title with Vignette; Angel appearing to Shepherds, 1 p.; verso, blank; printed half title, 1 p.; verso, blank; Text: Mat. to Rev , pp. 3-253; sigs A^2 to Q^6 in 8^s, (1) to (32^3), in 4^s; The Discourses, Parables and Miracles of Jesus, p. 254; Contents, pp. 255, 256; remainder of sig. Q; Psalms in Metre, pp. 1-23; verso, blank; Concordance, pp. 1-39; sigs. 1-5^4 in 4^s.

Front. Isaac blessing Jacob instead of Esau, *W. D. Smith;* David and Bathsheba, *Smith.*

2. HOLY BIBLE: Auburn and Rochester: Alden & Beardsley. 1855.   4.

With illustrations.

3. COMPREHENSIVE BIBLE: Philadelphia: Lippincott, Grambo
& Company. 1855. (L.) 4.

From the same stereotype plates as the edition of 1854; engraved front. and colored title page to Old. Test., and engr. front. to New Test.; Psalms in Metre at the end, without separate title.

4. HOLY BIBLE: Philadelphia: Lippincott, Grambo & Co.
1855. 4.

The same as No. 1 of 1844. Chromo. Lith. front. to Old Test.; 1 engraving in Old and 1 in New Test.

5. Standard Imperial Quarto Bible. | Printed from stereo-copper plates. | THE | HOLY BIBLE: | containing the | Old and New Testaments: | Translated out of | the Original Tongues, | and with the former Translations diligently compared and revised. | With | An Index of Subjects, the Harmony of the Four Evangelists, | and Tables of Measures, Weights, and Coins. | Philadelphia: | Published by H. C. Peck & Theo. Bliss. | 1855. | 4.

Title, 1 f.; verso, Names and Order of Books at foot, Electro-Stereotyped by L. Johnson & Co. Philadelphia: Printed by C. Sherman & Co., Text: Gen. to Mal., pp. 3–1130; sigs. A (which includes title) to 6R^1; Family Record, 4 ff.; New Testament: title, 1 f.; verso, blank: Text: Mat. to Rev., pp. 3–356; sigs. 1 to 45^2; Index, pp. 357–381; Harmony, pp. 381, 382: at foot of p. 382, Tables of Measures; sigs. 45^3 to 68, a blank leaf completing this sig.; all in 4^a except 6R.

6. HOLY BIBLE: Philadelphia: Published by John B. Perry, 198 Market Street; Leary & Getz, No. 138 North Second Street. Baltimore: Walker & Medairy, John Cushing & Co., and Cushing & Baily. 1855. (L.) 4.

With Index, Tables, Concordance and Psalms in Metre, but no Apocrypha; woodcut front. to both Test.; that to the New has a cut in the centre and smaller ones around it. The imprint to the New Test. has Perry's name only, and is without date. Text conformable to the standard of American Bible Society before the changes.

7. THE | HOLY BIBLE; | containing the | Old and New Testaments: | Translated out of the Original Tongues, | and | with the former Translations diligently compared and revised. | With | Canne's marginal notes and references. | To which are added, | An Index; | An Alphabetical Table of all the Names in the Old and New Testaments, with their significations; | Tables of Scripture weights, mea-

sures, and coins, &c. | New York: | Sheldon, Lamport &
Blakeman. | 115 Nassau Street. | 1855. | (L.)   4.

Front. and 1 engraving in Old Test.; Front. and 3 engr. in New Test., all on wood.
The paging and signatures of this volume agree with Phinney's editions, *supra* pp.
157, 158, 265, *less* Index and Tables all which are omitted, except those on p. 576.
The references are printed on the inner and outer margins of the text.

8. HOLY BIBLE, translated from the Latin Vulgate: with Useful Notes &c. By the Rev. George Leo Haydock. New York: Edward Dunigan and Brother, 151 Fulton Street, near Broadway. 1855.   (L.)   4.

The edition of 1852, revised. Before the title is a leaf, on recto of which is a handsomely engraved copy of a letter accompanying a gold medal sent by the Pope to the publishers, dated Rome, July 6, 1853; printed title, 1 p.; verso, blank; Approbation of Archbishop Hughes, 1 p.; verso, Haydock's Dedication; Names and Order of all the Books, 1 p.; verso, Advertisement, Approbations of the Old and New Test., Approb. of the Univ. of Douay, Approb. of the Univ. of Rheims, Approb. of Dr. Challoner's edition; Admonition; Letter of Pius VI; A Prayer, Translation of the Decree of the Council of Trent, pp. 7 and part of 8; A Short Sketch of the principal Epochs, remainder of p. 8; Haydock's Preface, p. 9 to a part of p. 12; List of the principal Commentators, completing p. 12. The text, plates, &c., as described under 1852; no directions to the binder.

9. HOLY BIBLE: New York: American Bible Society. 1855. (Rev. Dr. Brigham.)   English type.   Imp. 4.
With references.

10. HOLY BIBLE: Troy: Merriam, Moore & Co. 1855. (L.) 4.
12 large woodcuts including frontis. to Old and New Test. See 1850.

11. THE | HOLY BIBLE, | containing the | Old and New Testaments, | together with the | Apocrypha; | Translated out of the Original Tongues, | and | with the former Translations diligently compared and revised. | To which is appended, | A Concordance, the Psalms of David in Metre. | The Text conformable to the Standard of the American Bible Society. | Cincinnati: | More, Wilstach, Keys & Overend. | 1855.   (Gowans.)   4.
Pp. 576, 96, 192, 41, 22.

12. A COMPREHENSIVE COMMENTARY on the HOLY BIBLE; containing the Text according to the Authorized Version,

with marginal References; Matthew Henry's Commentary; the Practical Observations of the Rev. Thomas Scott; with extensive Explanatory, Critical, and Philological Notes, selected from Scott, Doddridge, Clarke, Gill, Patrick, Lowth, Calmet, Stuart, Bush, &c., &c.; the whole designed to be a Digest of the best Bible Commentaries, &c.; conveniently arranged for Family Reading, Bible Classes, &c. Embellished with numerous Wood Engravings. Edited by the Rev. William Jenks, D. D. 5 volumes. Including Supplement, containing a Concordance, Biographical Notices, an Index to the Bible, Chronological Tables, &c., and an Index to the Commentary. Philadelphia: 1855. 8.

Pp. 5044. This work was published originally at Brattleboro, Vermont, in 1834–1838. Dr. Jenks was assisted in the preparation of it by the Rev. L. J. Hoadley and J. W. Jenks, M. A.

13. HOLY BIBLE, translated from the Latin Vulgate: With Annotations, References, and Index. Published with the approbation of the Most Reverend John Hughes, D. D., &c. New York: Published by Edward Dunigan & Brother, No. 151 Fulton-Street. 1855. 8.

Engr. front. to O. T.; Moses with the Tables of the Law, *Gimbrede;* Engr. Approb. dated 27th Jany. 1844 and notice of Copyright, 1844 (Prud'homme), all surmounted by an engraving of St. Patrick's Cathedral, New York; 2 plates to O. T.; Judgment of Solomon after Rubens, engr. by *Dick;* Daniel in the Lion's den, *Dick;* Engr. Family Record, 4 ff.; Front to N. T.; Jesus Christ, engr. by *Parker;* The Crucifixion, *Dick;* Little Children brought to Christ, *Dick;* The Annunciation, *Gimbrede;* The Infant St. John, *Parker;* Two of these were engr. for the American edition of 1844; each page is within double lines; other copies have only 2 front. and 2 plates.

Text the same as No. 3, *supra* p. 276. For collation see 1833.

14. HOLY BIBLE: New York: American Bible Society. 1855. (G. L.) Sm. pica 8.

2d edition revised. A remarkable error occurs in Mark 5:3, which reads: Who had his dwelling among the *lambs,* instead of, *tombs.*

15. HOLY BIBLE: Auburn and Rochester, N. Y.: Alden & Beardsley. 1855. (L.) 12.

Engr. front. and title to O. T.; Printed titles to O. and N. Test. Stereotype edition.

16. HOLY BIBLE: Philadelphia: Lippincott, Grambo & Co. 1855.   12.

17. HOLY BIBLE: From the authorized Oxford Edition. Appointed to be read in Churches. Philadelphia: Wm. S. & Alfred Martien. 1855.   16.
Pp. 1098, 342. No Apocrypha.

18. POLYGLOTT BIBLE: Stereotype edition. New York: Published by John F. Trow, 49 Ann Street. 1855. (L.)   16.

19. HOLY BIBLE: Philadelphia: Lippincott, Grambo & Co. 1855.   24.
Pp. 824, 251; Psalms in Metre, pp. 77.

20. THE PRONOUNCING BIBLE. By Israel Alger Junr. Philadelphia: W. S. Young. 1855. (Mr. McAllister.)   12.
See No. 5, *supra* p. 173.

21. THE | HISTORY OF | JOB; | A Tale, | illustrative of the dispensations of | the Almighty; | Reconstructed in the English Language | to accord with the long-lost Arabic. | With brief comments and explanations. | Published by Samuel Reeve of Washington City, D. C. | Edited and for sale by L. M. Arnold, Poughkeepsie, N. Y. | 1855. | (B.)   8.
Pp. 94. The Publisher's Preface says, "The author chooses not to be announced."

1. NEW TESTAMENT: A literal translation from the Syriac Peschitu Version. By James Murdock, D. D. New York: Published by Stanford & Swords, 637 Broadway. 1855. (L.)   8.
Portrait; pp. 526. See 1851.

2. NEW TESTAMENT: Translated from the Latin Vulgate: New York: Published by Edw. Dunigan & Brother, 151 Fulton Street. 1855. (L.)   8.
With Bible of 1856.

3. NEW TESTAMENT: New York: Robert R. Collins, No. 254 Pearl Street. 1855. 8.

4. NEW TESTAMENT: New York: American Bible Society. Instituted &c. 1855. 8.
   37th edition; pp. 3–447; with Book of Psalms, same imprint; pp. 3–112.

5. NEW TESTAMENT: (English and Welsh) New York: American Bible Society. 1855. (Rev. Dr. Brigham.) Bourg. 12.

6. NEW TESTAMENT: New York: Edward Dunigan & Brother, 151 Fulton Street. 1855. 18.

7. A | Translation | of | THE GOSPELS, | with Notes. | By Andrew Norton. | 2 vols. | Boston: | Little, Brown & Co. | 1855. (Gowans; G. L.) 8.
   This is a Unitarian version. Vol. I, contains the Text, pp. 450; Vol II, the Notes, pp. 571.

8. THE GOSPELS; with Moral Reflections on each Verse. By Pasquier Quesnel. With an Introductory Essay by the Rev. Daniel Wilson, D. D., Bishop of Calcutta. Revised by the Rev. Henry A. Boardman, D. D. Philadelphia: Parry & McMillan. 1855. 2 vols. 8.

1856.

1. HOLY BIBLE, translated from the Latin Vulgate: With Useful Notes, critical, historical, and explanatory, Selected... by the Rev. George Leo Haydock. New York: Edward Dunigan & Brother, 151 Fulton Street, near Broadway. 1856. 4.
   Before the Engraved Title is a leaf, on the recto of which is an engraved copy of the Pope's Letter to the Publishers, with a Gold Medal as in the edition of 1855, 1 f.; Engraved Title, 1 f.; Printed Title, 1 f.; verso, blank; Approbation of Archbishop Hughes, 1 p.; verso, Haydock's Dedication; Fac-similes of the Approbations of 6 Archbishops and 26 Bishops of the United States and British N. A. Provinces, 4 ff. Some copies have a fac-simile of a Letter from Cardinal Wiseman. The arrange-

ment of these preliminary pages differs, in several copies, according to the pleasure of the binder. Names and order, 1 p.; verso, Advertisement, Approb. of the Univ. of Douay, of the Univ. of Rheims, and of Dr. Challoner's ed., 1 p.; Admonition, Letter of Pius VI, A prayer, Translation of the Decree of the Council of Trent, 1 p. and part of p. 8; A short sketch of the principal events, remainder of p. 8; Preface, pp. 9 to a part of 12; List of the principal commentators, remainder of p. 12; then Text &c., as in the edition of 1852. The date to the title of the New Testament in one of the copies examined, is 1855. The engravings are the same as in the edition of 1852, but there are only two (Mary Magdalen and the Three Maries), in the New Testament of the date of 1855.

The following errors are noted in this edition:

Exodus 8 : 22, The words "wherein my people is" are omitted.
 35 : 23, The words "fine linen and goats hair, rams' skins dyed" are omitted.
 36 : 34, The words "casting for them sockets of silver," are omitted.
Josue 7 : 17, The words, "Zare, Bringing that also by the houses, he found it *to be*" are omitted.

2. [Cambridge Edition.] HOLY BIBLE: With Canne's marginal Notes and References. Together with the Apocrypha. To which are added An Index, and an Alphabetical Table of all the Names in the Old and New Testaments, with their significations. Also, Tables of Scripture Weights, Measures and Coins. New York: A. S. Barnes & Co., 51 John-Street. 1856.   4.

The stereotype plates from which the above volume was printed are very badly worn; they seem to have been originally cast for Collins's 4to Bible, see *supra* 1821, with which this edition agrees in every respect. The Psalms in Metre, pp. 1-22 are, however, an addition.

Engravings: The Commandments, *R. Martin, New York;* Front. to O. T., Death of Achin, *James Bannister;* Riches of Ophir, *J. C. Buttre;* Pool of Siloame, *James D. Smillie;* Front. to N. T., Mount of Olives, *J. D. Smillie;* Sea of Tiberias, *J. Bannister*

3. HOLY BIBLE, translated from the Latin Vulgat: With Annotations, by the Rev. Dr. Challoner; together with References, and an Historical and Chronological Index. Revised and corrected according to the Clementine edition of the Scriptures. With the approbation of the Most Rev. John Hughes, Archbishop of New York. New York: Published by D. & J. Sadlier & Co., 164 William Street. Boston: 128 Federal Street, and 179 Notre Dame Street, Montreal, C. E. 1856.   4.

This edition is from the same stereotype plates as Sadlier's 4tos already noted, 1845, 1851, and the subjects of the engravings are the same as enumerated in that of 1845, with the addition of "*Das Urthiel Salomon*, The Judgment of Solomon," in the O. T. But the plates seem to have been retouched, and different borders and new inscriptions have been added in most instances. The names of the artists are omitted except in a few of the plates.

4. THE | HOLY BIBLE, | containing the | Old and New Testaments: | Translated out of | The Original Tongues, | and with | the former Translations diligently compared | and revised. | New York: | American Bible Society, | instituted in the year MDCCCXVI. | 1856. | (L.; N. Y. State Lib.)   Imp. 4.

1st edition. Title, 1 f.; verso, blank; Names and Order, 1 p.; at foot, 1st edition; verso, blank; Text: Gen to Rev., pp. 1163, sigs. (including title and 1 prel. p.), 1 to recto of 146^2 in 4^s. The 2d edition of this Bible is called "The Royal copy," because several in rich binding were sent to different royal personages.

These Bibles contain the alterations and corrections of the ed. of 1811, adopted by the American Bible Society, which gave rise to the controversy in 1857.

5. THE | HOLY BIBLE, | containing the | Old and New Testaments, | together with the Apocrypha: | Translated out of the Original Tongues, | and | with the former Translations diligently compared and revised. | To which is appended, | A Concordance, the Psalms of David in Metre, | An Index; Tables and other useful matters. | The Text conformable the the standard of the American Bible Society. | Philadelphia: | Published by T. K. Collins, Jr. | No. 8, North Sixth Street. | 1856. | (L.)   4.

This edition agrees with that of Lippincott, Grambo & Co.'s No. 2 of 1851. The references are arranged in two columns in the centre of the page. The imprint on the title page of the New Testament is, Philadelphia: | J. B. Lippincott & Company. | 1856. | On the verso, Account of Dates and Times; below, Stereotyped by L. Johnson & Co. | Printed by T. K. & P. G. Collins | No. 1 Lodge Alley, Philadelphia. | The appended matter is: Account of Judea and Table of Kindred, p. 763; Tables of Measures &c., pp. 764 and half of 765; Alphabetical Table of proper Names, remainder of pp. 765-768. The Apocrypha, Concordance and Psalms in Metre do not accompany the volume before us. The illustrations are 6 large woodcuts within borders, viz: Frontis. and 1 in the Old, and front. and 3 in the New Test.

6. HOLY BIBLE: With | Canne's marginal Notes and References. | To which are added, | an Index, | an Alphabetical Table | of all the Names in the Old and New Testaments,

with their significations; | Tables of Weights, Measures and Coins, etc. | Philadelphia: | Jesper Harding, No. 57 S. Third St. | 1856. | (L.) 4.

Title, 1 f.; verso, blank; To the Reader, p. 3; Names and Order, including Apocrypha, p. 4; Contents, pp. (5)-(6); p. 5 is marked, sig. 2; Text: Gen. to Mal., pp. 5-570; sigs. 2^2 to verso of 72^4 in 4^s; Family Record, 2 ff.; No Apocrypha; Title to New Testament, 1 p.; Imprint as above, 1 p.; verso, Account of dates or time, &c.; Text: Mat. to Rev., pp. 573-748; Index, pp. 749 to part of 760; Table of time and Chronol. Index, remainder of p. 760; Tables of Measures, Weights and Coins, Analysis of Old and New Testament, and Tables of Kindred, pp. 761, 762; Account of Judea, p. 763; Alphabet. Table, pp. 764-768; Table of Passages—quoted by Christ and the Apostles, Table of Offices, pp. 769, 770; sigs. 73^2 to verso of 97^4 in 4^s; Psalms in Metre, no separate title, pp. 1-22; sigs. 1 to verso of 3^3 in 4^s; Marginal References in the inner and outer margins; columns of text divided by a double rule.

2 woodcuts in the Old Test: The church comforted, *Isaiah*, 4:7; Jonah preaching to the Ninevites, *Josiah*, 3:4.

2 woodcuts in the New Test.: Judas casting away the pieces of silver, *Mat.*, 27:5; Christ raiseth Lazareth, *John*, 11:43, 44.

7. HOLY BIBLE: Philadelphia: Published by John B. Perry, 198, Market Street; Leary & Getz, 138, North Second Street. Baltimore: Walker and Medairy, John Cushing & Co. and Cushing & Bailey. n. d. (L.) 4.

With Apocrypha, colored front. and 19 large woodcuts including front. to N. T. Many of the cuts are surrounded by 16 small ones from subjects of the N. T. Text conformable to the standard of the American Bible Society before the changes. See 1855.

8. HOLY BIBLE: With Index, Harmony of the four Evangelists and Tables of Measures &c. Philadelphia: Published by .H. C. Peck and Theo. Bliss. n. d. (L.) Imp. 4.

This is the Bible No. 4 of 1855, without date. The text and accessories are amended according to the version of the American Bible Society. The frontispiece and 14 plates are from designs by Raphael, Rubens, Vernet and Overbeck.

9. HOLY BIBLE; Philadelphia; Charles Desilver, 251 Market Street. 1856. 4.

2 colored lithographs and numerous engravings.

10. THE | HOLY BIBLE, | containing | The Old and New Testaments: | Translated out of the Original Tongues: | And with the former Translations diligently compared and re-

vised. | With | marginal Readings, References, and chronological dates. | Auburn : | William J. Moses. | 1856. | 4.

<small>This Bible was published in two forms; one with Psalms, Concordance and Record, pp. 1130; the other, with Apocrypha added, pp. 1250. The copies are embellished some with six, some with eight and others with ten engravings, and are sold at prices varying from four to twelve dollars. The references are printed in the centre of the page, between the columns of the text.</small>

11. HOLY BIBLE, translated from the Latin Vulgate : With Annotations, References, Index &c. New York : Published by Edward Dunigan & Bro., No. 151 Fulton Street. 1856. (L.) 8.

<small>New Test. dated 1855.</small>

12. HOLY BIBLE: New York: Electrotyped by the American Bible Society. 1856. Gt. Pr. 8.

<small>Psalms appended.</small>

13. HOLY BIBLE: Philadelphia: Printed for the American and Foreign Bible Association. By the Bible Association of Friends in America. 1856. (L.) 8.

<small>Baptist version, with Brown's Concordance but no Apocrypha.</small>

14. HOLY BIBLE: Philadelphia: Lindsay and Blakiston. 1856. (L.) 8.

<small>Pp. 1282. On the top of the title page are the words: Crown octavo Oxford edition.</small>

15. LA | BIBLIA SAGRADA, | traducida | en Espanol. | Version cotijada cuidadosamente con las | Lenguas antiguas. | Jesus respondio :˜Escudrinad das Escrituras. S. Juan, cap V, Ver 39. | Neuva-York. | Edicion Esteriotipica. | 1856. | (N. Y. State Lib.) 8.

<small>6th edition. This is called Spanish 12mo; but the sigs. are in 8s.</small>

16. LA | SAINTE BIBLE, | qui contient | le Vieux et le Nouveau Testament; | revue sur les Originaux, | par David Martin, | Ministre du Saint Evangile à Utrecht | New York: | Société Bibliqué (*sic*) Américaine, | établie en MDCCCXVI. | 1856. | (N. Y. State Lib.) 12

<small>7th edition.</small>

17. ENGLISH VERSION of the POLYGLOTT BIBLE. Stereotyped by L. Johnson. Philadelphia: Charles Desilver, No. 253 Market Street. 1856. 12.
Pp. 587, 180; Psalms in Metre, same imprint, pp. 64. Compare Mielke's ed. 1832.

18. HOLY BIBLE: (Polyglott.) Philadelphia: J. B. Lippincott & Co. 1856. 12.

19. HOLY BIBLE: Philadelphia: J. B. Lippincott & Co. 1856. (L.) 18.
With Scotch Psalms in Metre.

20. HOLY BIBLE: New York: American Bible Society. 1856.
Agate 18.
13th edition.

21. HOLY BIBLE: New York: American Bible Society. 1856.
Pearl Ref. 18.
43d edition.

22. THE | BOOK OF JOB; | the | Common English Version, the Hebrew Text, | and the | Revised Version | of the | American Bible Union, | with | critical and philological Notes. | New York: | American Bible Union. | Louisville: Bible Revision Association. Cincinnati: American Christian Bible Society. | London: Trübner & Co., No. 12 Paternoster row. | 1856. | (L.; G. L.) 4.

Title, 1 f.; verso, Notice of Copyright, dated 1856; at foot, Thomas Holman, Printer and Stereotyper, corner Centre and White Sts. N. Y.; Mock title, Book of Job. | Part first. | The Common English Version, the Hebrew Text | and the Revised Version, | with critical and philological Notes. | 1 p; verso, blank; Introduction, pp. v-xxx; 1 blank leaf; no sig. mark; Mock title, as above, 1 p.; verso, Notice of Copyright, dated 1855; at foot, Millar & Holman, Printers and stereotypers N. Y.; Text: pp. 3-165; p. 166 blank; sig. 1 to 21³ in 4s, some of the sig. numbers, however, are not marked.

This Vol. contains King James's Version, the Hebrew text and the revised version (Baptist), in parallel columns and notes at the foot of each page.

23. THE | BOOK OF JOB. | A translation | from the Original Hebrew | on the basis of | The common and earlier English versions. | For the American Bible Union | by Thomas

J. Conant D. D. | Professor of Sacred Literature in Rochester Theological Seminary. | New York: | American Bible Union. | Louisville, Ky.: Bible Revision Association. London: Trübner & Co., Paternoster row. | 1856. | 4.

<small>Title, 1 f.; verso, Notice of Copyright, 1856, Holman, Printer and stereotyper, New York: Text: pp. 3–52.
The revised version and marginal readings are reprinted here alone without the notes.</small>

24. THE PROPHETS of the RESTORATION; or Haggai, Zechariah and Malachi. A New Translation, with Notes, by Rev. T. V. Moore, D. D. New York. 1856. 8.
Pp. 408.

1. HET | NIEUWE TESTAMENT, | of | alle de Boeken des Nieuwen Verbonds | van onzen Heer | Jezus Christus; | op last van de Hoog-Mog. Heeren | Staten Generaal ber Vereenigde Nederlanden, | en volgens het besluit van de Synode Nationaal | gehouden te Dordrecht in de jaren MDCXVIII en MDCXIX, | uit de oorspronkelijke (Grieksche) taal | in onze Nederlansche getrouwelijk overgezet. | Gedrukt bij het | Amerikaansche Bijbelgenootschap, | te Nieuw York. | 1856. | (N. Y. State Lib.) 12.
<small>The New Testament in Dutch and English, on opposite columns. 4th edition.</small>

2. EL | NUEVO TESTAMENTO | de Nuestro Señor | Jesu-Christo. | Version cotejada cuidadosamente con las | antiguas Traducciones | y revisada con areglo al original Griego | por la | Sociedad Americana de la Biblia. | Jesus respondio: Escudrinad las Escrituras. S. Juan, Cap. V, Ver. 39. | Edicion Esteriotipica. | Nueva-York. | 1856. | (N. Y. State Lib.) 12.
<small>Spanish and English in parallel columns. 4th edition.</small>

3. Iu | Otoshki-kikindiuin | au | Tebeniminvng gaie bemajünvng | Jesus Christ: | ima | Ojibue inuemning giizhitong. | The | New Testament | of | our Lord and Saviour Jesus Christ: | Translated into the language | of the | Ojibwa Indians. | New York: | American Bible Society, | instituted in the year MDCCCXVI. | 1856. | (N. Y. State Lib.) 12.

4. NEW TESTAMENT: New York: Electrotyped by the American Bible Society. 1856. (Rev. Dr. Brigham.) Agate 32.
Pp. 306.

5. NEW TESTAMENT: Buffalo: Phinney & Co. 1856.   32.
Pp. 340. Cont., pp. 341 to 344. First published by H. & E. Phinney, Cooperstown, in 1832, between which time and 1848, they sold rising 200,000 copies, chiefly for Sunday Schools. *E. P.*

6. TRANSLATION of the GOSPELS, with Notes. By Andrew Norton. 2 vols. Boston: Little, Brown & Co. 1856.   8.

7. Commentary on the FOUR GOSPELS. By S. H. Tyng, D. D. New York. 1856.   8.
Fine Engravings.

8. Notes on the ACTS of the APOSTLES, designed for Sunday Schools &c. By the Rev. Bradford K. Pierce. New York: Carlton and Porter, Sunday School Union, 200 Mulberry Street. 1856.   12.
Copyrighted 1848.

9. THE | EPISTLES OF PAUL | to | the THESSALONIANS: | 𝔗𝔯𝔞𝔫𝔰𝔩𝔞𝔱𝔢𝔡 𝔣𝔯𝔬𝔪 𝔱𝔥𝔢 𝔊𝔯𝔢𝔢𝔨, | on the basis of the common English version, | with Notes, | by | the Translator of II Peter — Revelation. | New York: | American Bible Union. | London: Trübner & Co., No. 12 Paternoster row. | 1856. | (L.; G. L.)   4.
Title, 1 f.; verso, Circular, Notice of Copyright, both dated 1856; at foot, Holman, Printer and Stereotyper, New York; Introd., List of Abbreviations and works cited, pp. iii-viii; no sigs.; Text: pp. 3-73; verso, blank; sigs. 1 to 10^1 in 4^s; 1 blank leaf.
This Vol. contains King James's version, the Greek text and revised (Baptist) version in parallel columns, followed by the revised version in paragraphs. The translation is by Rev. Dr. Lillie.

10. The | Epistle to the GALATIANS, | in Greek and English. | With an Analysis and Exegetical Commentary. | By | Samuel H. Turner, D. D., | Professor, &c. | New York: | Dana and Company, 381 Broadway. | 1856. | (L.)   8.

1st edition. Title, 1 f.; Contents, pp. iii–iv; Preface, pp. v to vii; Introduction, pp. ix to xiii; Analysis, pp. 1 to 10; Text arranged as above, pp. 11 to 94; Questions on the preceding Exposition, pp. 95 to 98; List of Works by Dr. Turner, 4 pages.

11. The Last of the EPISTLES: a Commentary upon the Epistle of ST. JUDE, designed for the General reader, as well as for the Exegetical Student. By Frederick Gardinier, M. A. Boston. 1856.   8.

Pp. 276.

12. THE DIVINE LIBRARY; or Cyclopedia of Inspiration. The Gospel of our Lord and Savior Jesus Christ, according to St. Matthew. Received version in paragraph form. Baltimore: T. H. Stockton, No. 68 Lexington St. 1856. (Rev. Dr. Campbell.)   12.

Stereotyped by L. Johnson & Co., Philadelphia: Printed by T. K. & P. G. Collins. Text: pp. 3–123, p. 124 blank; Index, pp. 125–130, 1 blank leaf; Appendix, 1 p.; verso, Notes; the text conformable to the standard of the American Bible Society, no head lines, The Paragraphs corrected with Bagster's Critical N. T. Literary Apparatus 1 p.; verso, blank; Horne's Introduction to the Gospel of St. Matthew, tenth edition, revised &c., by Samuel Prideaux Tregelles, LL. D. First American edition, unabridged. Philadelphia: T. H. Stockton, 1857; 1 p.; verso, Notes by the Author and Editor; Contents. 1 p.; verso, blank; Text: pp. 3–57; verso, blank; Pictorial Apparatus, 1 p.; verso, Explanation; List of Engravings; Map of Jerusalem; View of Jerusalem, colored; Mount of Olives.

1857.

1. THE | PICTORIAL BIBLE, | being | the Old and New Testaments | according to | the authorized version: | Illustrated with more than | one thousand engravings, | representing | the Historical events, | after celebrated pictures; | the Landscapes Scenes, | from original drawings, or from authentic engravings; | and the subjects of | Natural History, costume, and antiquities, | from the best sources. | New York: | Published by Robert Sears, 181 William Street. | 1857. | 4.

Title, 1 f.; verso, The Names and Order of the Books; at foot, C. A. Alvord, Printer, | No. 15 Vandewater St., N. Y. | List of Illustrations to O. T.; pp. i–vi; Text: Gen. to Mal., pp. 3–1102; sigs. 1^2 to 138^3; Ancient Chronology, | comprising | the

Epochs and years, | with | the Genealogies and History | of | the Holy Bible, | from | the Creation of the World to the end of the seventy weeks of Daniel | Extracted from the | "Chronicum Biblicum," | by Abraham Calovius, | President of the University of Wittemberg. | Translated for the Pictorial Bible. | 1 p. (1103); verso, blank; Notice, p. 1105; Profitable reading of the Scriptures of Truth, p. 1106; Summary of the Whole Scripture, pp. 1107, 1108; Ancient Chronology, pp. 1109, 1110; Chronological Tables, pp. 1111–1119; Books of O. & N. T., pp. 1120; Genealogical Tables, pp. 1121–1124; sigs. 138^4 to 141^2; Family Register, 4 ff.; Map of Palestine; Title to the New Testament, 1 p.; verso, Table of Scripture Measures &c., Table of Time; Text: Mat. to Rev., pp. 3–348; sig. 1^2 to 44^2; List of Illustrations to N. T., pp. i, ii; sigs. in 4^s.

Colored ornamental titles to O. & N. T. The engravings are on wood and printed with the text.

2. HOLY BIBLE, translated from the Latin Vulgate: With Haydock's Notes &c. New York: Published by Edw. Dunigan and Brother, 371 Broadway. 1857.   4.

Many corrections were made in the stereotype plates previous to printing this edition.

3. HOLY BIBLE: With Apocrypha. 𝔗𝔥𝔢 𝔱𝔢𝔵𝔱 𝔠𝔬𝔫𝔣𝔬𝔯𝔪𝔞𝔟𝔩𝔢 𝔱𝔬 𝔱𝔥𝔢 𝔖𝔱𝔞𝔫𝔡𝔞𝔯𝔡 𝔬𝔣 𝔱𝔥𝔢 𝔄𝔪𝔢𝔯𝔦𝔠𝔞𝔫 𝔅𝔦𝔟𝔩𝔢 𝔖𝔬𝔠𝔦𝔢𝔱𝔶. Philadelphia: Published by John B. Perry, 534 (formerly 198) Market Street. Baltimore: Medairy & Musselman; and Whiting, Cushing and Comstock. 1857.   4.

Title, 1 f.; verso, Names and Order of Books; To the Reader (Witherspoon's Preface), p. 3; Contents, pp. 4–8; Text: Gen. to Mal., pp. 9–574; Table of Passages, &c., pp. 575, 576; Apocrypha (in smaller type), pp. 1–88; Family Record, 2 ff.; N. Testament title, Imprint: Philadelphia: Published by John B. Perry, 198 Market street; Stereotyped by L. Johnson & Co., n. d.; 1 p.; verso, Account of dates; Text: Mat. to Rev., pp. 579–754; Index, pp. 755–762; Judea; Table of Kindred; Table of Scripture Measures &c., pp. 763, 764; Table of Names, pp. 765–768; Concordance, pp. 1–41; Psalms in Metre, pp. 1–22; Woodcut front. to Old and New Test. Compare No. 2 of 1851.

4. HOLY BIBLE: With Apocrypha, Concordance, Psalms in Metre, Index, Tables and other useful matters. Text conformable to the Standard of the American Bible Society. Philadelphia: J. B. Lippincott & Company. 1857.   4.

Same as No. 2 of 1851. Front. to O. & N. T.

5. COMPREHENSIVE BIBLE. Philadelphia: J. B. Lippincott & Company. 1857.   4.

Engr. front. and title; Plates; Psalms in Metre, see No. 1 of 1854.

6. HOLY BIBLE: With Apocrypha, Concordance, Psalms in Metre, Index, Tables and other useful matters. The Text conformable to the Standard of the American Bible Society. Philadelphia: Whilt & Yost, Family Bible publishers and general Bookbinders, 805 Market Street, above Eighth St. 1857. 4.

This edition corresponds with No. 3, *supra*.

Embellishments: Titles to O. and N. Test. in Colors with Vignettes; Moses with Table of the Law; Joseph sold by his brethren; Tamar receiving Judah's pledge; Caleb and Joshua (Chromo. Lithograph); Christ blessing little children; Prodigal Son; Descent from the Cross; Burial of Christ (Chromo. Lith.).

7. THE | HOLY BIBLE, | containing the | Old and New Testaments, | translated out of the Original Tongues, | together with the | Apocrypha, Concordance and Psalms, | and | with the former Translations diligently compared and revised. | The Text conformable to the Oxford Edition of the Year of our Lord 1610, | And the American Bible Society's Original Standard Edition of 1816. | "If any man shall add unto these things, God shall add unto him the plagues that are written in this book: If any man shall take away | from the words of the book of this prophecy, God shall take away his part out of the book of life, and out of the | holy city, and *from* the things which are written in this book."—Rev. xxii, 18, 19. | Philadelphia: | Jesper Harding & Son. | 1857. (L.) 4.

Title, 1 f.; verso, blank; Names and Order, 1 p.; at foot, Stereotyped by Jesper Harding & Son; | verso, blank; To the Reader, (Witherspoon's Pref.), p. 3; Contents, pp. 4-8; these 4 ff. are sig. A not marked; Text: Gen. to Mal., pp. 9-574; sigs. *B* to verso of 3W^3; Tables and Analysis, pp. 575, 576; sig. 3W^4 in 4ª; and 1 to 367 in 8ª; Apocrypha, in smaller type, pp. 1 to 116; sigs. A (not marked) to verso of P^2 in 4ª; Fam. Rec., 2 ff.; The | New Testament | of our | Lord and Saviour Jesus Christ, | translated out of | the Original Greek; | and with | the former Translations diligently compared and revised. | Philadelphia: | Jesper Harding & Son. | 1856; | 1 p.; verso, Account of the dates; at foot, Stereotyped by | Jesper Harding & Son, | No. 57 South Third Street, Philadelphia, | Text: Mat. to Rev., pp. 579-754; Index, pp. 755-762; Account of Judea, Tables of Time &c., Alphabetical Table, pp. 763-768; sigs. (including title page), 3X to verso of 4V^4 in 4ª, and 37 to 488 in 8ª; Concordance (no title page), pp. 1-31; sigs. A to recto of F^1 in 4ª; verso, blank; Psalms in Metre, pp. 1-22; sigs. F^2 to verso of H^4 in 4ª.

Woodcut front. to Old and New Testament, and 4 woodcuts in the Old Testament. References in the centre of the columns; none in the Apocrypha.

This Bible is published in different styles: With and without Apocrypha, Concordance and Psalms, or with any one of these; also with more or less plates; some copies having as many as 20 engravings. The text is that of the American Bible Society, before the alterations.

8. HOLY BIBLE: Together with the Apocrypha, Concordance and Psalms, and with the former Translations diligently compared and revised. The Text conformable to the Oxford Edition of the Year of our Lord 1610, And the American Bible Society's Original Standard Edition of 1816. Two verses of Rev. Philadelphia: Jesper Harding & Son. 1857. 4.

Vol. I. Title, 1 f.; verso, blank; Text: Gen. to Song of Solomon, pp. 1-787; sigs. B to recto of 5K²; verso, blank; Vol. II. title repeated with date 1858, 1 p.; verso, blank; Text: Isaiah to Mal., pp. 3-277; sigs. A (not marked) to recto 2M³; verso, blank; Apocrypha in smaller type, pp. 1-116; sigs. A to verso of P², Fam. Rec., with engraved headings, 3ff.; New Testament, imprint as above but dated 1858, 1 p.; verso, blank; Text: Mat. to Rev., pp. 281-600; sigs. 2N to recto of 4F⁴ in 4ˢ; Concordance (without separate title), pp. 1-41; Psalms in Metre, pp. 1-22; sigs. A (not marked) to verso of H⁴ in 4ˢ; References at foot of the pages; each page is embraced within double rules; columns divided by a double rule.

This Bible is printed in English type, and was published in 50 numbers: it is issued in divers styles, some without plates, others with illuminated titles and from 8 to 16 steel engravings. It is called Harding's superfine or extra superfine edition. The text is according to the standard of the American Bible Society, before the alterations.

9. HOLY BIBLE: Together with the Apocrypha, Concordance and Psalms, and with the former Translations diligently compared and revised. The Text conformable to the Oxford Edition of the Year of our Lord 1610, And the American Bible Society's Original Standard Edition of 1816. Two verses of Rev. Philadelphia: Jesper Harding & Son. 1857. 4.

Title, 1 p.; verso, blank; Names and Order, 1 p.; at foot, Stereotyped by Jesper Harding & Son, No. 57 South Third Street, Philadelphia; verso, blank; To the Reader p. 3; Contents, pp. 4-8; being sig. A not marked; Text: Gen. to Mal., pp. 9-772; sigs. B to recto of 4F³; Table of passages, p. 772; Chron. Index, Table of Time, Table of Offices, Analysis of the Old and New Test., pp. 774; sigs. 4V⁴ in 4ˢ; Apocrypha, pp. 1-116; sigs. A (not marked) to verso of P² in 4ˢ; illuminated Fam. Rec., 2 ff.; Title to the New Testament, imprint as above, 1 p.; verso, Account of dates; at foot, Stereotyped by | Jesper Harding & Son, | 57 South Third Street, Philadelphia. | Text : Mat. to Rev., pp. 777-1017; sigs. 4X to recto of 6C¹, verso, blank; Index, pp. 1019-1026; Judea, Table of Kindred, p. 1027; Table of Scripture Weights &c., p.

1028 and part of 1029; Alphabetical Table, pp. 1029-1032; sigs. 6C² to verso of 6D¹ in 4º, and in figures 1 to verso of 65⁴ in 8º; Concordance (without title page), pp. 1-41 and Psalms in Metre, pp. 1-22; References in centre of the columns; columns separated by parallel rules.

This is called Harding's Royal Quarto; it is printed in small pica type leaded, and is published with 8 or 10 steel engravings.

These three Bibles, Nos. 7, 8, 9, are issued annually, with new title pages, and altered date.

10. HOLY BIBLE: With References and various Readings. Philadelphia: Published by E. & H. Butler & Co. 1857. (L.)   4.

Front. and engr. titles to Old and New Test.; 4 engr. to O. T. and Apocr. and 6 to N. T.; all colored, printed titles to Old Test.; the Prophets and New Test.; Apocrypha in smaller type.

11. HOLY BIBLE: With Marginal Notes and References, Apocrypha, Concordance, Psalms in Metre, and Paraphrases. Auburn & Buffalo: John E. Beardsley. n. d.   4.

Pp. 1250. This edition is advertised with 7 steel plates, 3 maps; steel titles and records; also with 18 steel plates, 3 maps, colored and illuminated frontis. titles and records.

12. HOLY BIBLE: With Canne's Marginal Notes and References, Apocrypha, Index, Alphabetical Table of Names, Table of Weights, Measures and Coins, &c., with Brown's Concordance, and Psalms in Metre. Auburn and Buffalo: John E. Beardsley. n. d.   4.

Title, 1 f.; verso, blank; Books of O. & N. T., Account of Dates, 1 p.; verso, blank; the paging of the text then corresponds with that of Collins & Co.'s 4to, New York: 1821, but the sigs. of the Old and New Test. of this edition are marked by figures 2-126, in 4ˢ; those of the Apocrypha, by letters sigs. A to S¹, also in 4ˢ; at the end, Brown's Concordance, stereotyped by J. Howe; Title, 1 p.; verso, to the Reader; Text: pp. 3-54; Psalms in Metre, pp. 1-18; sig. 98² to 106 [shewing that they belonged to some other book;] Paraphrases of various passages of Scripture, pp. 1-6.

Engravings: Murder of Abel, Front. to O. T., *F. Kearney;* Map of Journeyings; Map of Canaan; Peaceable Kingdom of the Branch, *Tanner, Vallance, Kearney & Co.*; Vision of the Heroes, *Chas. Heath;* Tobias and the Angel, *Tanner, Vallance, Kearney & Co.;* Thomas's Incredulity, Front. to N. T., *Haines;* Last Supper, *J. B. Neagle;* Adoration of the Shepherds, *Chas. Heath;* Map of St. Paul's Travels.

13. HOLY BIBLE: Together with The Apocrypha; with Canne's Marginal Notes and References, to which are added An

Index: An Alphabetical Table of all the Names in the Old and New Testaments, with their Significations, Tables of Scripture Weights, Measures, and Coins, &c. Buffalo: Published by Phinney & Co. New York: Ivison & Phinney. 1857. (Gowans.) 4.

_{Old Test.; pp. 576; Apocrypha, pp. 96; New Test., pp. 192; Psalms in Metre, pp. 28; Paraphrase in verse, pp. 6.}

14. THE | HOLY BIBLE: | containing the | Old and New Testaments, | 𝕋ranslated out of the 𝕆riginal 𝕋ongues : | And with the former Translations diligently compared and revised. With | Canne's Marginal References. | Together with the | Apocrypha and Concordance. | To which are added, | An Index, and Reference, | and | A Key Sheet of Questions, | geographical, historical, practical, and experimental ; | accompanied with valuable | Chronological Harmonies of both Testaments, and highly useful tables of Scripture Names, | Scripture Geography, Scripture Chronology, Scripture References &c. | The Text corrected according to the Standard | of the | American Bible Society. | Dayton, Ohio : | E. A. & T. T. More. | 1857. | (L.) 4.

_{This is Wilbur's Reference Bible printed, apparently, from the plates of the Merriam edition No. 2 of 1846. q. v. With Psalms in Metre, pp. 1 to 24; sigs. A to C.}

_{The References in O. and N. T. are in the centre of the pp. In the Apocrypha also in the centre, but in some of the pages they do not extend down the entire page, so that a part of these pages are without any references, and here the columns of the text come close together.}

_{This volume has been issued with different sets of engravings. In one, an ornamental title colored; the frontispiece to O. T. is, The sending away of Hagar; Plates: 1. Joseph sold by his brethren, no engr's name; 2. Moses smiting the rock, no engr's name; 3. Boaz and Ruth, engr. by *Bartas P. Newman*, at J. M. Butler's establishment, Jayne's Building, Philadelphia; Front. to N. Test., The Holy Family, engraved by *McGoffin*, printed by J. M. Butler; 1. Taking down from the Cross, after Rubens.}

_{In the other, same front. to O. T.; plates: 1. Abraham and Hagar, a different design in oval; small front. to N. T.; Holy Family, a different design in oval; Plate 1. John the Baptist after Raphael, in oval; 2. Maries at the Sepulchre, oval; 3. Sea of Tiberias; 4. Athens from the Ilissus.}

15. THE | FAMILY BIBLE; | containing | the Old and New Testaments: | with | brief Notes and Instructions, | designed | to give the results of Critical Investigation, and to assist |

358   AMERICAN BIBLES.   [1857—

Common Readers to understand the meaning of the | Holy Spirit in the inspired Word. | Including | the References and Marginal Readings of the | Polyglott Bible. | Published by the | American Tract Society. | New York: | 15 Nassau Street. | Boston: 28 Cornhill. | n. d. (L.; G. L.) 8.

<small>Title, 1 f.; verso, Notice of Copyright, dated 1857; Names and Order of Books, 1 p.; verso, blank; The Bible God's Gift, pp. 5, 6; signed J[ustin] E[dwards]; Harmony of the Holy Scriptures, signed T. C. [Thomas Coit], pp. 7–12; Text: Gen. to Mal., pp. 1–1166; sig. 1–745; Fam. Reo., 2 ff.; The | New Testament | of | our Lord and Saviour Jesus Christ: | With | brief Notes and Instructions: | Containing | the References and Marginal Readings | of the Polyglott Bible. | Imprint as above; 1 f.; verso, blank; Mat. to Rev., pp. 3–425; sig. 74^2 to 101^2; Synopsis of Robinson's Harmony of the Gosp., pp. 426–431; Index and Tables, pp. 432–441; sig. 101^2 to 102^2; Notes at foot of the pp.; sigs. in 8^s, worked in 4^s; Maps of Palestine, Holy Land, Countries mentioned in the Bible, Jerusalem.</small>

16. COTTAGE BIBLE and Family Expositor: With practical expositions and explanatory Notes. By Thomas Williams. To which are added, the References and marginal Readings of the Polyglott Bible, with Original Notes, Selections and Index. Revised and corrected. Edited by Rev. Wm. Patton. 2 vols. Hartford: Printed and published by Case, Tiffany & Co. 1857.   (L.)   8.

<small>1st Vol., 8 plates and 2 Maps; 2d Vol., 6 plates and 3 Maps. See p. 221 *supra*, for description of this work.</small>

17. HOLY BIBLE: Translated from the Latin Vulgate: With Annotations, &c., from the last London and Dublin editions. New York: Edward Dunigan & Brother (James B. Kirker), 371 Broadway. 1857.   (L.)   8.

<small>No. 3 of 1844, continued; engraved front.</small>

18. HOLY BIBLE: New York: American Bible Society. 1857. (L.)   8.

<small>This edition (the 55th), was issued in 1855, *before* the alterations, but *now* with a new title page only.</small>

19. HOLY BIBLE: New York: American Bible Society. 1857. (L.)   8.

<small>With alterations and corrections, as already noted sub anno 1856. q. v.</small>

20. HOLY BIBLE: New York: American Bible Society. Instituted &c. 1857. Nonp. ref. 12.
18th ed.; pp. 984.

21. A | BIBLIA SAGRADA, | contendo | O Velho e o Novo Testamento, | traduzida em Portugues | pelo Padre Joao Ferreira A d' Almeida, | Ministro pregador do Sancto Evangelho em Batavia. | Nova York: | Sociedade Americana da Biblia. | 1857. | (N. Y. State Lib.) 12.
6th edition; pp. 886, 283 (see No. 16 of 1850). On the title to the New Testament after " Batavia," follows the line: Reimpresso da Edicao de 1693, revista e emendada.

22. HOLY BIBLE: New York: American Bible Society. 1857. (Rev. Dr. Brigham.) Diamond 16.
Electrotyped edition, with references.

23. HOLY BIBLE: New York: American Bible Society. 1857. 24.

24. HOLY BIBLE: New York: American Bible Society. Instituted, &c. 1857. Diamond 32.
1st edition.

25. THE ENGLISH VERSION of the POLYGLOTT BIBLE: With marginal Readings and References. Illustrated with Maps and Engravings. Philadelphia: J. B. Lippincott & Co. 1857. 12.
Same as No. 16 of 1853.

26. HOLY BIBLE: Philadelphia: J. B. Lippincott & Co. 1857. 32.
Pp. 3-726; 3-221; p. 222 blank; Psalms in Metre, pp. 1-81; sigs. in 8ˢ. From the same plates as the edition of 1851.

27. HOLY BIBLE: Auburn and Buffalo: John E. Beardsley. 1857. 24.
Stereotype edition; pp. 824, 251.

28. THE | BOOK OF JOB. | A translation | from the Original Hebrew | on the basis of | The Common and earlier English Versions. | With an Introduction and explanatory

Notes | for the | English Reader. | For the American Bible Union | by Thomas J. Conant D. D. | Professor of Sacred Literature in Rochester Theological Seminary. | New York: | American Bible Union. | Louisville, Ky.: | Bible Revision Association. London: Trübner & Co., Paternoster row. | 1857. | (L.; G. L.) 4.

Title, 1 f.; verso, Notice of Copyright, dated 1856. At foot, Thomas Holman, Printer and Stereotyper, corner of Centre and White Sts., N. Y. The Book of Job, | with | Explanatory Notes for the English Reader. | 1 p.; verso, Notice of the Plan of the Work; Introduction, pp. v-xix; p. xx; verso, blank; Text: pp. 5-85.

This is the revised (Baptist) version reprinted, the numbering of chapters and verses, marginal readings, statements of contents, &c. being separated from the text, with Notes at foot of each page.

29. THE | PSALMS, | BOOKS OF WISDOM, | and | CANTICLE of CANTICLES. | Translated from the Latin Vulgate; diligently compared with the Hebrew | and Greek, being a revised and corrected edition of the Douay Version, | with Notes critical and explanatory, | by Francis Patrick Kenrick, | Archbishop of Baltimore. | Sing praises to our God, sing ye: Sing praises to our King, sing ye. | For God is King of all the earth: sing ye wisely.—*Ps.* xlvi. | Baltimore: | Lucas Brothers, Publishers. | n. d. (L.) 8.

Title, 1 f.; verso, Notice of Copyright, dated 1857; Dedication, dated January 1857, 1 p.; verso, blank; Gen. Introd., pp. v-xi; verso of xi, Errata; Abridgments, 1 p.; verso, blank; Index, 1 p.; verso, blank; Mock title, The Psalms, 1 p.; verso, blank; Introd., pp. 19-24; Text: pp. 25-262; Mock title, The Proverbs, 1 p.; verso, blank; Introd., pp. 265, 266; Text: pp 267-349; verso, blank; Mock title, Ecclesiastes, 1 p.; verso, blank; Introd., pp. 353, 354; Text: pp. 355-379; verso, blank; Mock title, The Canticle, 1 p.; verso, blank; Introd., pp. 383, 384; Text: pp. 385-400; Mock title, Wisdom, 1 p.; verso, blank; Introd., pp. 403, 404; Text: pp. 405-445; Mock title, Ecclesiasticus, 1 p ; verso, blank; Introd., pp. 449-450; The Prologue, 1 p.; Text: pp. 452-584; sigs. 1 (not marked), to verso of 37⁴ in 8^s.

This is the 3d portion of Archbishop Kenrick's revision of the Douay and Rheims Testaments. See *supra* pp. 305, 319.

1. NEW TESTAMENT: New York: Published by D. & J. Sadlier & Co., 164 William Street. Boston: 128 Federal Street. Montreal, C. E.: corner of Notre Dame and St. Francis Streets. 1857. 4.

With Bible of 1853.

2. NEW TESTAMENT: The text carefully printed from the most correct copies of the present authorized version, including the marginal readings and parallel texts, with a Commentary and critical Notes. Designed as a help to a better Understanding of the Sacred Writings. By Adam Clarke, LL. D., F. S. A., M. R. I. A. New edition improved. Complete in One Volume. Philadelphia: Charles Desilver, No. 253 Market-Street. 1857. 8.

3. THE FAMILY EXPOSITOR; or, a Paraphrase and Version of the New Testament: with Critical Notes, and a Practical Improvement to each Section. By Philip Doddridge, D. D. New York: Robert Carter & Brothers, No. 530 Broadway. 1857. Royal 8.

Copyrighted in March 1833, by J. S & C. Adams and L. Boltwood. Stereotyped at the Boston Type and Stereotype Foundry.

4. NEW TESTAMENT: New York: American Bible Society. 1857. (L.) Gr. Pr. 8.

2d edition, divided into 5 parts with Psalms.

5. NEW TESTAMENT: New York: American Bible Society. 1857. Pica 8.

52d edition, with Book of Psalms.

6. NEW TESTAMENT: New York: American Bible Society. 1857. Bourg. 12.

Electrotyped edition.

7. NEW TESTAMENT: Revised by Cone and W. H. Wyckoff. New York: E. H. Tripp. 1857. (G. L.) 12.

A Baptist edition. See No. 5, p. 318.

8. Ke | Kauoha hou | a ko kakou | Haku e ola'i a Iesu Kristo: | ua unuhiia | mai ka olelo Helene; | a | ua Hooponopono hou ia. | Nu Yoka: | Ua paiia no ko Amerika poe Hoolaha, | i hookumuia i ka makahiki MDCCCXVI. | 1857. | (N. Y. State Lib.) 12.

The New Testament in Hawaiian and English in parallel columns; References in the centre.

9. Η ΚΑΙΝΗ ΔΙΑΘΗΚΗ | Novum Testamentum | Graece | Post | Ioh. Aug. Henr. Tittmannum | Olim Prof. Lips. | Ad fidem optimorum Librorum | secundis curis recognovit. | Lectionumque varietatem notavit | Augustus Hahn | In Acad. Vratisl. Prof. | Editio Americana stereotypa | curante | Edvardo Robinson, S. T. D. | New York: | Leavitt & Allen. | 379 Broadway. | 1857. | 12.

This is a reissue of Mr. Robinson's edition of Hahn's Greek Testament, *supra* p. 285. The doxology is printed within [ ] as "verba suspecta," or "words and passages not supported by the best authorities." In Matt. xxiii, the following verses are numbered, 12, 14, 13, with a note. "Transposuerint G. K. S.," viz; Griesbach, Knapp and Scholz. The transposition occurs originally in the Codex Alexandrinus. Some copies of this volume are published without date.

10. NEW TESTAMENT: New York: American Bible Society. Instituted &c. 1857.   (L.)   Brev. 18.
10th edition, with Book of Psalms.

11. NEW TESTAMENT: Translated from the Latin Vulgate: New York: Edward Dunigan & Bro. (James B. Kirker), 371 Broadway. 1857.   18.

12. NEW TESTAMENT: Printed by authority. T. Nelson & Sons, London, Edinburgh and New York. MDCCCLVII. 48.
2 maps.

13. An Exposition of the 1st Epistle to the CORINTHIANS. By Charles Hodge, D. D., Professor in the Theological Seminary, Princeton. London: James Nisbet and Co., 21 Bemers Street. 1857.   (L.)   12.
From American plates.

14. THE EPISTLE OF PAUL to the THESSALONIANS: Translated from the Greek, on the basis of the common English version, with Notes by the Translator of the II. Peter to Revelation. New York: American Bible Union. 1857.   4.
Baptist version, pp. 78.

15. THE | EPISTLE TO THE EPHESIANS. | 𝕮𝖗𝖆𝖓𝖘𝖑𝖆𝖙𝖊𝖉 𝖋𝖗𝖔𝖒 𝖙𝖍𝖊 𝕲𝖗𝖊𝖊𝖐, | on the basis of the common English version. |

With Notes. | New York: | American Bible Union. | Louisville: Bible Revision Association. Cincinnati: American Christian Bible Society. | London: Trübner & Co. No. 12, Paternoster row. | 1857. | (L.)   4.

Title, 1 p.; verso, Notice of Copyright, dated 1857. At foot, Printed and stereotyped by Thos. Holman, cor. Elm and White Sts., N. Y. Preface and authorities, pp. iii-vi; Text: pp. 1-31; p. 32 blank; The Revised Version of the Epistle to the Ephesians, with Marginal Readings, 1 p.; verso, blank; Text of the revised version (repeated), pp. 35-39; p. 40 blank.

This volume contains the King James Version, the Greek text and revised (Baptist) version in parallel columns, followed by the revised version in paragraphs.

16. THE | EPISTLE TO THE HEBREWS. | 𝔗𝔯𝔞𝔫𝔰𝔩𝔞𝔱𝔢𝔡 from the 𝔊𝔯𝔢𝔢𝔨, | on the basis of the common English version. | With Notes. | New York: | American Bible Union. | Louisville: Bible Revision Association. Cincinnati: American Christian Bible Society. | London: Trübner & Co., No. 12 Paternoster row. | 1857. | (L.; G. L.)   4.

Title, 1 p.; verso, Notice of Copyright, dated 1857. At foot, Miller & Holman, printers and stereotypers, New York. Errata, 1 p.; verso, blank; Introd., pp. iii, iv; Authorities noticed, pp. v, vi; Text: pp. 1-77; p. 78 blank; The Revised Version of the Epistle to the Hebrews; with Marginal Readings, 1 p.; verso, blank; Text of Revised Version (repeated), pp. 81-99; no sigs.; 1 blank leaf.

This volume contains the Royal Version, the Greek text and Revised (Baptist) version, in parallel columns, followed by the revised version in paragraphs.

1858.

1. THE | HOLY BIBLE: | With a | perpetual Genealogical Family Register | entirely new and original. | 𝔑𝔢𝔴 𝔜𝔬𝔯𝔨 𝔞𝔫𝔡 𝔑𝔞𝔰𝔥𝔳𝔦𝔩𝔩𝔢: | Richard Abbey. | 1858. |

Published by R. C. Root, Anthony & Co., 16 Nassau St., | New York. | Sold by the Southern Methodist & Publishing House | Nashville. | (L.)   Imp. 4.

Title, 1 f.; verso, Extract of Copyright, dated 1858; A presentation leaf, engraved in colors, 1 f.; verso, blank; Prefatory note, signed, The Editor, and dated Nashville, August 1858, 2 pp.; Names and Order (no Apocrypha), 1 p.; verso, blank; Text: Gen. to Mal., sigs. A to verso of L3 in 4^s; title to New Test., Imprint as above, 1 p.; verso, blank; Text: Mat. to Rev., sigs. 60 to verso of $7Z^2$ in 4^s; Explanatory Note, 1 p.; verso, blank; Ornamental title: Genealogical | Family | Register | 1 p.; verso, blank; followed by 50 leaves, each page containing blank Certificates of Marriage, Births and Deaths, within a colored ornamental border.

2. The | Holy Bible; | containing | The Old and New Testaments: | Translated out of the Original Tongues: | and with the former translations diligently compared and revised | with | Marginal Readings, References, and Chronological Dates. | Auburn: | William J. Moses. | 1858. | 4.

See 1856.

3. The Pictorial Bible. New York: Published by Robert Sears, 181 William Street. 1858. (L). 4.

See No. 1 of 1857.

4. Holy Bible: With the Apocrypha; A Concordance, the Psalms of David in Metre, an Index, Tables, and other useful matters. The Text conformable to the Standard of the American Bible Society. Philadelphia: J. B. Lippincott & Company. 1858. 4.

Same as No. 2 of 1851.

5. Holy Bible: With Apocrypha. The text conformable to the Standard of the American Bible Society Philadelphia: Published by John B. Perry, 534 (formerly 198) Market Street. Baltimore: Medairy & Musselman; and Whiting, Cushing and Comstock. 1858. 4.

Same as No. 3 of 1857.

6. Holy Bible: With Apocrypha, Concordance, Psalms in Metre, Index, Tables and other useful Matters. The Text conformable to the Standard of the American Bible Society. Philadelphia: Whilt & Yost, Family Bible publishers and general Bookbinders, 805 Market Street, above Eighth Street. 1858. 4.

This edition corresponds with that of Perry, immediately preceding. See also No. 6 of 1857.

7. Holy Bible: With Apocrypha, Concordance and Psalms in Metre &c. The text conformable to the Oxford edition of 1610, And to the American Bible Society's edition of 1816. Philadelphia: Jesper Harding. 1858. 4.

Same as No. 7 of 1857.

8. THE | HOLY BIBLE: | Translated from | the Latin Vulgate: | With Annotations | by the Rev. Dr. Challoner; | Together with References, and an Historical and Chronological Index. | Revised and corrected according to the Clementine edition of the Scriptures. | New York: | Published by D. & J. Sadlier & Co., 164 William Street. | Boston: 128 Federal Street. | Montreal, C. E.: corner of Notre Dame and St. Francis Xavier Streets. | 1858. | 4.

Engr. title with Vignette (St. John in the wilderness); Printed title, 1 f.; verso, blank; Approbation of 3 Archbishops and 3 Bishops, surmounted by an escutcheon, containing the arms of the Holy See, supported by a shield &c., on each side, that on the right bearing the words *Pax vobis*, on the left, *Sacra Congregatio de propaganda fide*, 1 inserted leaf; Engraved title to N. Test. with Vignette (The Adoration by the Shepherds), Printed title with Approb. of the Most Rev. John Hughes, Archbishop of New York; Imprint as above, but date 1857; Ward's Errata at the end of the book. The text and other matter as already described, sub anno 1845.

The following are the engravings in this volume.

IN OLD TESTAMENT.
1. Abraham and Isaac. front.
2. Hagar and Ishmael.
3. Rebecca giving to drink.
4. Joseph and his brethern.
5. Boaz and Ruth.
6. Judgment of Solomon, with the title also in German.
7. Ascent of Elias.
8. Esther petitioning.

IN NEW TESTAMENT.
1. The Redeemer. front.
2. Adoration of the Shepherds. Vign.
3. Redeemer of the World. *S. Hollyer*. N. Y.
4. Zebedee's children.
5. Christ in the Garden.
6. Jerusalem. *Dick*.
7. Ecce Homo. *S. Hollyer*.
8. The Angelic Salutation.
9. Jesus in the Temple. *S. Hollyer*.
10. Prodigal Son.
11. Descent from the Cross. *H. B. Hall*.
12. The Good Shepherd.
13. Incredulity of St. Thomas.
14. The Angel releasing the Apostles.

The plates with the engravers' names are new. In No. 3 of that in New Testament, a Negro Slave in chains is introduced.

9. HOLY BIBLE, translated from the Latin Vulgate: With Useful Notes, critical, historical, controversial, and explanatory, selected from the most eminent commentators, and the most able and judicious critics. By the Rev. George Leo. Haydock. New York: Edward Dunigan & Brother (James B. Kirker), 371 Broadway. 1858.   4.

This is the 3d edition of Dunigan's Haydock. Several errors in the preceding editions are now corrected. In this copy the Approbation page is replaced by an inserted sheet of eight pages of facsimiles of the Approbation of Archbishop Hughes, a letter of Pope Pius IX, and facsimiles of letters of commendation from Cardinal Wiseman, Archbishops Bedini, Purcell, Romilli, Turgeon, Blanc, Alemany, P. R. Kenrick, F. P. Kenrick, Bishops Charbonnel, Martin, O'Connor, Demers, O'Regan, Rappe, Bayley, Blanchet, Lefevere, Whelan, Spalding, Vandevelde, de St. Palais, Odin, Reynolds, Bacon, Baraga, McCloskey, Henni, Fitzpatrick, Portier, de Goesbriand, Carrell, Cretin, Loras, Miles, Loughlin, Timon and Young. *Shea's Bib. of Cath Bibles.*

List of engravings:
Letter of Pope Pius IX, engraved title (Abraham's Sacrifice); Moses with the Tables of the Law; Agar and Ishmael; Arrival of Rebecca; Jacob in the House of Laban; Joseph sold to his brethren; Aaron the High Priest; The first fruits of Canaan; Moses raises the Brazen Serpent; David and Abisai in Saul's tent; The Judgment of Solomon; Daniel in the Lion's Den; Jesus Christ the Redeemer; Jesus carrying his Cross; The infant St. John; Mary Magdalen; Christ blessing little children; The Three Marys; The Annunciation; The Crucifixion; Family Record.

10. HOLY BIBLE: Together with The Apocrypha; with Canne's Marginal Notes and References, to which are added An Index: An Alphabetical Table of all the Names in the Old and New Testaments, with their Significations, Tables of Scripture Weights, Measures, and Coins, &c. Buffalo: Published by Phinney & Co. New York: Ivison & Phinney. 1858. 4.

11. HOLY BIBLE, translated from the Latin Vulgate: With Annotations, References and Index. New York: Edward Dunigan & Brother (James B. Kirker), 371 Broadway. 1858. 8.

With frontispiece of "Jesus Christ" engraved on steel by Parker. See No. 3 of 1844.

12. HOLY BIBLE, translated from the Latin Vulgate: With Annotations and References, and a Historical and Chronological Index. Boston: Patrick Donahoe, 23 Franklin Street. 1858. 8.

The same as the edition of 1852, by the same publisher. In the copy before us pp. 3 and 4 are transposed.

13. HOLY BIBLE: New York: American Bible Society. 1858.
Bourg. 12.

23d edition.

14. HOLY BIBLE: (in Welsh.) New York: American Bible Society. 1858. (L.) Nonp. 12.

15. HOLY BIBLE: New York: American Bible Society. Instituted in the year MDCCCXVI. 1858. (G. L.) Brevier 12.

29th edition. Two errors occur in this edition, in Psalms 29 : 3, which reads: The Voice of the Lord is upon the Laters [for Waters]; the God of glory thundereth; the Word [Lord] is upon many waters.

16. HOLY BIBLE: New York: American Bible Society. 1858.
Nonp. 12.
22d edition.

17. HOLY BIBLE: New York: American Bible Society. 1858.
Minion 18.
32d edition.

18. HOLY BIBLE: New York: American Bible Society. Instituted in the year MDCCCXVI. 1858. Agate 18.

19. HOLY BIBLE: New York: American Bible Society. 1858.
Diamond ref. 18.
2d edition.

20. THE ENGLISH VERSION of the POLYGLOTT BIBLE. With Marginal Readings and References. Illustrated with Maps and Engravings. Philadelphia: J. B. Lippincott & Co. 1858. 12.

Pp. 824, 256; Psalms in Metre, pp. 77; Preface signed T. C.

1. NEW TESTAMENT: New York: Collins & Brother, publishers, 82 Warren Street. n. d. 8.

Title, 1 f.; verso, Stereotyped by T. B. Smith & Son, 84 Beekman St., N. Y. Printed by C. A. Alvord, 15 Vandewater St. To the Reader, 1 p.; Contents 1 p.; Text: Mat. to Rev., pp. 1–511; verso, blank; Index, pp. 513–548.

In this edition which is styled, a Paragraph New Testament, the divisions into chapters and verses are omitted, but the chapter and verse with which each page commences are given at the head of the page. The text of the authorised English version according to Bagster, Eyre and Spottiswood, is followed, except that quotation points are introduced to mark distinct speeches and conversations. The Index of subjects is from Bagster's edition.

2. NEW TESTAMENT: Translated from the Latin Vulgate: Philadelphia: Published by E. Cummiskey. 1858. 8.

Edition 500.

3. NEW TESTAMENT: Revised version in Paragraph form, with Horne's Introduction, revised &c. by Samuel Prideaux Tregelles, and Student's Memorandum Book. 4 vols. Philadelphia: T. H. Stockton. 1858. 12·

Each book is separately paged.

4. Η ΚΑΙΝΉ ΔΙΑΘΉΚΗ. | Novum | Testamentum, | cum versione Latina | Ariæ Montani, | in quo tum selecti Versiculi 1900, quibus omnes Novi Testamenti voces | continentur, Astericis notantur; | Tum omnes et singulæ voces, semel vel sæpius occurrentes peculiari notâ | distinguuntur. | Auctore | Johanne Leusden, | professore. | Philadelphia: | J. B. Lippincott & Co. | 1858. | 12.

Title, 1 f.; verso, blank; Text: pp. 3–755; sigs. A (which includes title) to recto of 125 in 12s; Text in Greek and Latin in parallel columns. The running titles at the top of the pages are in Latin. Verses 13 : 14 of Mat. 23, are transposed.

This is a stereotype edition and is still in the market with the dates of imprint altered according to the year of publication.

5. 'Η ΚΑΙΝΗ ΔΙΑΘΗΚΗ. | Novum | Testamentum | Græcum. | Ad exemplar | Roberti Stephani accuratissime editum. | Cura P. Wilson, LL. D. | Coll. Columb. Neo. Eboracen. Prof. Emer. | Stereotypis Hammondi Wallis, Novi Eboraci. | Philadelphia: | J. B. Lippincott & Co. | 1858. | 12.

The same as No. 9 of 1828, *supra* p. 186; but the type is pretty badly worn. In Mat. 23 : 15, 14, the order of the verses is inverted.

6. THE | NEW TESTAMENT, | translated from the Original Greek, with Chronological | Arrangement of the Sacred Books and improved | Divisions of Chapters and Verses. | By | Leicester Ambrose Sawyer. | Boston: | John P. Jewett and Company. | Cleveland, Ohio: | Henry P. B. Jewett. | London: Sampson Low, Son and Company. | 1858. | (L.; G.L.) 12.

Title 1 f.; verso, Notice of Copyright, lithotyped by Cowles and Company. | 17 Washington St., Boston. | Press of Allen & Farnham. | Pref., pp. iii-xi; p. xii, blank; Text: Mat. to Rev., pp. 13–423; sig. 2–36^2 in 6^s.

7. NEW TESTAMENT: Translated from the Latin Vulgate: New York: Edward Dunigan & Bro. (James B. Kirker), 371 Broadway. 1858. 12.

7. NEW TESTAMENT: New York: American Bible Society.
   1858.   12.
   2d edition.

8. NEW TESTAMENT: New York: American Bible Society.
   1858.   Brevier 18.
   Electrotyped edition; Psalms appended.

9. NEW TESTAMENT: New York: American Bible Society.
   1858.   Agate 82.

10. NEW TESTAMENT: New York: American Bible Society.
    1858.   Diamond 64.

11. NEW TESTAMENT: A literal translation from the Syriac
    Peschitu Version. By James Murdock, D. D. New
    York: Robert Carter & Brothers. 1858.   (L.)   8.
    This is the 3d edition of this work. See *supra* pp. 317, 343.

12. THE | GOSPEL according to MATTHEW | chapters I, II, III. |
    Translated from the Greek, | on the basis of the common
    English version. | With Notes. | New York: | American
    Bible Union. | Louisville: | Bible Revision Association. |
    London: Trübner & Co., No. 60 Paternoster Row. |
    1858. | (L.)   4.
    Title, 1 f.; verso, Notice of Copyright; To the Reader, 1 p.; verso, blank; Text:
    pp.1-50; The text is printed, first in 3 columns; King James's version, the Greek
    and the revised version, with the notes below, and then the revised version by itself
    in paragraphs, pp. 51, 52. It is a Baptist version.

13. THE | GOSPEL according to MARK. | 𝕮𝖗𝖆𝖓𝖘𝖑𝖆𝖙𝖊𝖉 𝖋𝖗𝖔𝖒 𝖙𝖍𝖊
    𝕲𝖗𝖊𝖊𝖐, | on the basis of the common English version. |
    With Notes. | New York: American Bible Union. | Louis-
    ville: Bible Revision Association. | London: Trübner &
    Co., No. 60 Paternoster row. | 1858.   (L.)   4.
    Title, 1 f.; verso, Notice of Copyright, dated 1858. At foot, Thomas Holman,
    Printer and Stereotyper, New York. Introd., pp. iii, iv; Authorities quoted, pp. v.
    vi; Text: pp. pp. 1-112. The Revised version of the Gospel according to Mark,
    with Marginal Readings, 1 p.; verso, blank; Text of revised version (repeated), pp.
    115-134; no sigs.; 1 blank leaf.
    This vol. contains King James's version, the Greek text and revised (Baptist) version
    in parallel columns, followed by the revised version in paragraphs.

14. Expository Thoughts on the GOSPELS. For Family and private Use. With the Text complete. By the Rev. J. C. Ryle, B. A., Christ Church, Oxford. Rector of Helmingham, Suffolk. Author of "Living and Dead" &c., &c., &c. St. Matthew and St. Mark. Two Volumes. New York: Robert Carter and Brothers, 530 Broadway. 1858.
12.

15. Poetical Expression | of | THE GOSPELS. | By William J. Knowles, | Boston: | Published by the Author. | 1858. | (L.)   12.

A very prosaic epitome in rhyme of the Four Gospels, with woodcuts.

16. ACTS of the APOSTLES. | 𝕿𝖗𝖆𝖓𝖘𝖑𝖆𝖙𝖊𝖉 𝖋𝖗𝖔𝖒 𝖙𝖍𝖊 𝕲𝖗𝖊𝖊𝖐, | on the basis of the Common English Version. | With Notes. | New York: American Bible Union. | Louisville: Bible Revision Association. | London: Trübner & Co., No. 60 Paternoster Row. | 1858. | (L.)   4.

Title, 1 f.; verso, Notice of Copyright, dated 1858. At foot, Thomas Holman, Printer and Stereotyper, New York. Advertisement, pp. iii, iv; Text: pp. 1-190; 1 blank leaf; Acts of the Apostles. | Revised version | arranged in paragraphs. | 1 p.; verso, blank; Text of revised version (repeated), pp. 193-224; no sigs. Revised English Scriptures etc., published and for sale by the American Bible Union, 1 page.

This vol. contains King James's version, the Greek text and revised (Baptist) version in parallel columns, followed by the revised version in paragraphs.

17. An Exposition of the First Epistle to the CORINTHIANS. By Charles Hodge, D. D., Professor in the Theological Seminary, Princeton, N. J. New York: Robert Carter and Brothers, 530 Broadway. 1858.   12.

18. An Exposition of the APOCALPYSE of St. John the Apostle. By a Secular Priest. Boston: Published by Patrick Donahoe, No. 23 Franklin Street. 1858.   (L.)   8.

The Rev. Edward Putnam of North Whitefield, Maine, is the author of this volume.

19. The GENERAL HISTORY of the CHRISTIAN CHURCH from her birth to her final triumphant State in Heaven, chiefly deduced from the Apocalypse of St. John, the Apostle and Evangelist. By Sig. Pastorini. Fifth American Edition.

New York: D. & J. Sadlier & Co., 164 William Street. Boston: 128 Federal Street. Montreal: cor. Notre Dame and Francis Xavier Sts. 1858. 12.

This seems to be from the stereotype plates of Doyle's edition of 1834, q. v. It has a portrait of the Right Rev. Dr. Walmesley, the author.

1859.

1. THE | SELF-INTERPRETING BIBLE, | containing | The Old and New Testaments | according to | The Authorized Version; | with | An Introduction: Marginal References and Illustrations; a Summary of the several Books; | an Analysis of each Chapter; a Paraphrase, and Evangelical Reflections upon | the most important Passages; and numerous explanatory notes; | By the | Rev. John Brown, D. D. | A New edition | in which the text is more fully elucidated by upwards of eight thousand explanatory and critical notes and concluding | observations on each book. | By the Rev. Henry Cooke, D. D., LL. D. | Embellished with numerous highly finished steel engravings | from paintings by the most eminent artists. | New York: | Johnson, Fry and Company, | 27 Beckman Street. | n. d. (L.) fol.

Title, 1 f.; verso, blank; Brown's Preface, p. (iii); Names and Order, &c., Table of Offices, &c., p. (iv); Introduction, p. (v), to half of p. (xvi); Appendix, rest of pp. (xvi) and (xvii); verso, blank; Text: Genesis to Malachi, pp. (1) to (741); verso, blank; Outline of the principal prophetic Kingdoms of the Earth, pp. (743) and (744); sig. 1 to verso of 98⁴ in 4ˢ; Preface to the Apocryphal Books, p. (1); Text: pp. (2) to (122); sig. A to verso of Q¹ in 4ˢ. At the bottom of page (122), Billin and Brother, Printers and Stereotypers, XX North William Street, New York; Engraved leaf of Family Records, verso, blank; The | New Test. | of our | Lord and Saviour, Jesus Christ, | to which are annexed many references and illustrations, | an exact summary of the several Books: | a Paraphrase | on the | most obscure or important Books, and an Analysis of the | Contents of each Chapter, | together with | explanatory Notes and evangelical Reflections. | By the Rev. John Brown, D. D. | A new edition | in which the text is more fully elucidated by several thousand explanatory and critical Notes and including Observations | on each book. | By the Rev. Henry Cooke, D. D., LL. D., | &c., as in Old Test., 1 p.; verso, blank; Text: Mat. to Rev , pp. (747) to (1030); sigs. 94 (*etc.*) to verso of 129₂ in 4ˢ.

With engraved frontispiece to Old Testament; vignette title to Old Testament and 72 plates, making 74 in all, the greater part are marked R. Martin, and Johnson, Fry & Co. A great many of the plates are the same as in Johnson & Co's edition of

Rutter's life of Christ. This Bible was published in parts, and is just finished. It forms a thick folio in large type, and includes matter from the Commentaries of Scott, D'Oyly, Mant and others.

2. ILLUMINATED BIBLE. New York: Harper & Brothers. 1859. (L.) 4.

This is a mere reprint of the 1st edition. *See* 1846. The ornamental presentation leaf however, in the copy examined, follows the printed title, and the supplemental matter following the text is paged consecutively, 1–60.

3. HOLY BIBLE: With Canne's marginal Notes and References, Index and Tables. New York: Published by Cornish, Lamport & Co., No. 8 Park Place. n. d. (L.) 4.

Title, 1 f.; verso, blank; To the Reader, 1 p.; Names and Order of Books, 1 p.; Contents, pp. 5–8; Text: Gen. to Mal., pp. 9–632; Fam. Rec., 2 ff.; New Test., title, 1 p.; verso, Account of dates or time of writing New Testament; Mat. to Rev., pp. 635–829; 2 woodcut front. There is no Apocrypha, though it is among the names and order of books; neither is there any index or tables.

4. THE | HOLY BIBLE, | containing the | Old and New Testaments: | Translated out of | the Original Tongues, | and with the former Translations | diligently compared and revised. | From the authorized Oxford edition. | Together with the | Apocrypha. | New York: | Published by Leavitt and Allen. | n. d. (L.) 4.

Title, 1 f.; verso, blank; Text: Gen. to Mal., pp. 5–1004; sigs. 2 to verso of 126⁴ in 4ˢ; Apocrypha, in smaller type, pp. 1005–1120; sigs. 127 to verso of 141² in 4ˢ; Family Record, 3 ff.; The | New Testament | of | our Lord and Saviour | Jesus Christ, | translated out of | the Original Greek, | and with the former Translations | diligently compared and revised | From the authorized Oxford edition. | New York: | Published by Leavitt and Allen. | n. d. 1 p.; verso, blank; Text: Mat. to Rev., pp. 1123–1431; sigs. 141⁴ to recto of 180² in 4ˢ (last sig. 180 not marked.)

Engr. front.; Moses with the Tables of the Law; Vignette title, Holy Family; 4 plates in the Old and 4 in the New Test., from the same plates as Johnson & Fry's Family Bible. The titles and each page are embraced within a single rule.

This edition was, we are informed, stereotyped about 12 years ago for Hogan & Thompson who printed 500 copies, and sold the plates to Brown of Boston. They, without printing any, sold the plates to Leavitt and Allen, who printed the above edition from them in the summer of 1859.

5. HOLY BIBLE; With Apocrypha, Concordance and Psalms in Metre. New York: Published by Leavitt & Allen, 379 Broadway. n. d. 4.

Same as the edition No. 6, of 1851. Type badly worn.

6. COLLATERAL BIBLE: Philadelphia: John Laval and S. F. Bradford. 3 vols.   (Mr. McAllister.)   4.
See No 3 of 1826, *supra* p. 177.

7. HOLY BIBLE: With Apocrypha, Concordance and Psalms in Metre. Philadelphia: Jesper Harding and Son. 1859.   4.
From the same plates as No. 7 of 1857; Apocrypha, pp. 1-116, in smaller type; Colored titles to Old and New Test.; on verso of the title to New Test., Stereotyped by Jesper Harding & Son, No. 57 South Third street, Philadelphia. The engravings are, Belshazzar's feast, front.; 2. Departure of Hagar; 3. Finding of Moses; 4. The Lord gave and the Lord hath taken away; 5. Captives of Babylon; 6. Christ blessing little children; 7. Warning to Joseph (Chromo. Lithographs); 8. Christ weeping over Jerusalem.

8. HOLY BIBLE: Philadelphia: J. B. Lippincott & Company. 1859.   4.
The pagination and matter are the same as No. 2 of 1851. The illustrations are, Moses striking the rock and a number of woodcuts.

9. HOLY BIBLE: Philadelphia: Jesper Harding & Son. 1859.   12.
Pp. 499, 156.

10. HOLY BIBLE: New York: Delisser & Procter, 508 Broadway (Successors to Stanford & Swords). 1859. (L.) 18.
Pp. 932, 292.

11. The Pocket Paragraph Bible. | THE | HOLY BIBLE: containing the | Old and New Testaments; | according to the | Authentic Version | arranged in Paragraphs and Parallelisms. | With an entirely new selection of References to Parallels, | And illustrative Passages, Prefaces to the Several Books, and Numerous Notes. | New York: | George E. Eyre and William Spottiswood. | M.DCCC.LIX. | 18.
Pp. 705. Two Maps.
Although this Bible has a New York imprint, still it must have been published in London. Indeed, the New Testament has a London title; besides, everything else, Maps, paper and binding, goes to show that it is an English book. *Gowans.*

12. HOLY BIBLE: Philadelphia: Jesper Harding & Son. 1859.   32.

13. HOLY BIBLE: Philadelphia: J. B. Lippincott & Co. 1859. 32.
With Psalms.

14. Proverbs of SOLOMON illustrated. With Preface by James Hamilton, D. D. New York: Robert Carter & Brothers, 530 Broadway. 1859. 8.
With Plates.

15. THE | BOOK OF JOB, | and the | Prophets. | Translated from the Vulgate, | and diligently compared with the | original text, being a revised edition of the Douay Version, | with Notes, critical and explanatory, | by Francis Patrick Kenrick, | Archbishop of Baltimore. | Prophecy came not at any time by the will of man, &c., 2 Peter 1:21. | Baltimore: | Kelley, Hedian & Piet. | 1859. | (L.)   8.

Mock title, 1 f.; verso, blank; Title, 1 f.; verso, Notice of Copyright; General Introd., pp. v, vi; Abbreviations, 1 p.; verso, blank; Index, pp. ix, x; Job, 1 p.; verso, blank; Introduction, pp. xiii-xv; verso of xv, blank; Text: pp. 17-106; Gen. Introd. to the Prophets, pp. 107-112; Isaiah, 1 p.; verso, blank; Introd., pp. 115, 116; Text: pp. 117, 275; verso of 275, blank; Jeremiah, 1 p.; verso, blank; Introd., pp. 279, 280; Text: pp. 281-425; verso of 425, blank; The Lamentations of Jeremiah, pp. 427-441; verso of 441, blank; Baruch, 1 p.; verso, blank; Introd , pp. 445, 446; Text: pp. 447-464; Ezekiel, 1 p.; verso, blank; Introd., pp. 467, 468; Text: pp. 469-590; Daniel, 1 p.; verso, blank; Introd , pp. 593-595; verso of 595, blank; Text: pp. 597-647; verso of 647, blank; The | Minor Prophets. | 1 p.; verso, blank; Introd., pp. 651, 652; Text: pp. 653-799; verso of 689, 709, 721, 737, being blank; sigs. 1 to 50 in 8s.

This is the *fourth* part of Archbishop Kenrick's revised edition of the Douay and Rheims Testaments. The work has recently been completed by the publication of the following volumes:

16. THE | PENTATEUCH. | Translated from the Vulgate, | and diligently compared with the Original Text, | being a revised edition of the Douay Version. | With Notes, critical and explanatory. | By | Francis Patrick Kenrick, | Archbishop of Baltimore. | "If ye did believe in Moses, ye would believe Me also: for he wrote of Me." JOHN, 5:46. | Baltimore: | Kelley, Hedian & Piet. | 1860. | 8.
Pp. 559.

17. THE | HISTORICAL BOOKS | of the OLD TESTAMENT. | Translated from the Latin Vulgate, | diligently compared with the Original Text, being a revised | edition of the Douay Version. | With Notes, critical and explanatory. | By | Francis Patrick Kenrick, | Archbishop of Baltimore. | " Whatever things were written, were written for our instruction, that through patience, | and the consolation of Scriptures, we may have hope." ROM. 15 : 4. | Baltimore: | Kelley, Hedian and Piet. | 1860. | 8.

Pp. 897.

Archbishop Kenrick's revision of the Douay Version is an immense labor, and one which has as yet been hardly appreciated according to its merits. It is a work on which has been bestowed a vast amount of rare and valuable learning, every text, every word seems to have been the object of diligent study, and of careful comparison with the original text. Few persons, till they compare the two, will suspect its very great superiority over our common Douay Bibles, either in accuracy or elegance. *Brownson's Review.*

1. CODEX VATICANUS. | H KAINH ΔIAΘHKH. | Novum Testamentum | Graece | ex antiquissimo Codice Vaticano | edidit | Angelus Maius | S. R. E. Card. | Ad fidem Editionis Romanae accuratius impressum. | New York: | D. Appleton and Co., 346 and 348 Broadway. | MDCCCLIX. | (N. Y. State Lib.; L.)   8.

Title, 1 p.; verso, blank; The Publishers' Advertisement, pp. i–iv ; these 3 ff. are without any sig. mark ; Text: pp. 1–498; sigs. 1 to verso of 32^1; Antiquae Collationis Codicis Comparatio cum nova, pp. 499–502; Elenchos, 1 p. ; sigs. 32^2 to recto of 324; sigs. in 8^s.

This volume was published in London by Williams & Norgate and D. Nutt, and an edition imported with the name of the New York firm on the title page. It was printed in whole or in part, in Leipsic. The London edition has a table of Errata, which is not in this copy.

2. THE | GREEK TESTAMENT: | With a critically revised Text: A Digest of | Various Readings: Marginal References to Verbal and | Idiomatic Usage : Prolegomena : | And a Critical and Exegetical Commentary. | For the Use of Theological Students and Ministers. | By Henry Alford, B. D. | Minister of Quebec Chapel, London, | and late Fellow of Trinity College, Cambridge. | In Four Volumes. | Vol. I. | Containing | The Four Gospels. | New York: |

Harper & Brothers, Publishers, | Franklin Square. | 1859. |
(N. Y. State Lib.; L.)   8.

Mock title, The Greek Testament. | Vol. I. | The Four Gospels. | 1 p.; verso, ἵνα ἐπιγνῷς περὶ ὧν κατηχήθης λόγων τὴν ἀσφάλειαν. | LUKE, i, 4. | Title, 1 p.; verso, blank; Advertisement to the 3d edition, 1 p.; verso, Advertisement to the 2d edition, Contents of the Prolegomena, pp. vii, viii; 4 ff. or half sig. not marked; Prolegomena, pp. 1]-100], marked at foot; sigs. a to verso g² in 8ˢ; Text: pp. 1-835; sigs. A to recto of Ggg² in 8ˢ.

The matter of the Prolegomena, digest of various readings and notes are from Meyer's and Olshausen's Commentaries on the Gospels, Stier's Reden Jesu, Tischendorf's 2d Leipsic edition of the Greek Testament, De Wette's Handbuch and Luthardt's recent work on St. John's Gospel.

This is a reprint of the 1st volume only of the third edition of Dr. Alford's Greek Testament. A fourth edition of the original work has since been published in London, in which the digest of various readings has been rewritten and the body of marginal references much revised and enlarged. In common with all the most ancient authorities, it omits the doxology at the end of Mat. 6:13, "on every ground of sound criticism" (*Note*, p. 55); and with the Codex Vaticanus, v. 14 of Mat. 23, which it pronounces "interpolated" in *Note*, p. 211.

3. The COTTAGE POLYGLOTT TESTAMENT, according to the Authorized Version, with Notes, Original and Selected, likewise introductory and concluding Remarks to each Book, Polyglott References, and marginal Readings, Chronological Tables, Geographical Index and Maps. Adapted to Bible Classes, Sunday Schools and Christians generally, by William Patton, D. D. New York: Published by J. S. Gilman, 82 Beekman Street. 1859. Sm. 12.

This is the Village Testament of 1833, with new imprint.

4. Η ΚΑΙΝΗ ΔΙΑΘΗΚΗ. | The Four Gospels and Acts of the Apostles, | in Greek. | With English Notes, critical, philological, and exe- | getical; Maps, Indexes, etc. | Together with the Epistles and Apocalypse. | The whole forming the complete Text of | 𝕮𝖍𝖊 𝕹𝖊𝖜 𝕮𝖊𝖘𝖙𝖆𝖒𝖊𝖓𝖙, | For the Use of Schools, Colleges, and Theological Seminaries. | By Rev. J. A. Spencer, A. M. | Author of | "The Christian instructed," "History of the English Reformation," etc. | τὸ καλὸν καγαθον. | New York: | Harper & Brother, Publishers, | 329 & 331 Pearl Street, | Franklin Square. | 1859. | 12.

Title, 1 f.; verso, Notice of Copyright, dated 1847; Preface, dated New York, September 1847, pp. iii–viii; Introductory remarks on the Language of the New Testament, pp. ix–xii; sig. 4; Mock title, το κατα Ματθαιον | Ευαγγελιον. | 1 p.; verso, Argument to St. Matthew's Gospel; Text: pp. 3–595; verso, blank; sigs. A (which includes Mock title) to recto of Bb^{10}; Index, I. Greek words and Phrases; II. Matters; pp. 597–611; sigs. Bb^{11} to recto of Cc^6; Mock titles and arguments precede each Gospel, the Acts and Epistles; sigs. in 12s.

The text of this edition is that of Dr. Mill, printed at Oxford in 1707, and finally under the care of Dr. Burton of that University in 1831. The division into verses however, has been followed "at the urgent request of the publishers, though contrary to the preference of the editor." The doxology is retained, but in the note is said "to be rejected by many editors as an interpolation." Verses 13, 14, of Matthew, chap. 23; are transposed.

A Map of the Countries mentioned in the New Testament, showing the routes of St. Paul, accompanies the volume.

5. NEW TESTAMENT: Philadelphia: Jesper Harding & Son. 1859. 12.

This is the Testament of No. 7, *supra*, published separately; pp. 156; with Contents, and Psalms of David, pp. 66.

6. NEW TESTAMENT: Philadelphia: Published by James B. Smith & Co., No. 610 Chestnut Street. 1859. 12.

7. NEW TESTAMENT: New York: Delisser & Procter, 508 Broadway (Successors to Stanford & Swords.) 1859. (Gowans.) 18.

Pp. 292.

8. NEW TESTAMENT: Philadelphia: Published by James B. Smith & Co., No. 610 Chestnut Street. 1859. 18.

9. NEW TESTAMENT: Philadelphia: Published by James B. Smith & Co., No. 610 Chestnut Street. 1859. 32.

Pp. 354.

10. The FOUR GOSPELS, according to the Authorized Version, with the original and selected Parallel references and Marginal readings, and an original and copious Critical and Explanatory Commentary. By Rev. David Brown, D. D., Professor, Free Church College, Aberdeen. Philadelphia: William & Alfred Martien, No. 606 Chestnut Street. 1859. 8.

11. The | Epistles to the HEBREWS, | in | Greek and English, | With an Analysis and Exegetical Commentary. | By | Samuel H. Turner, D. D., | Professor of Biblical Learning, &c., in the General Theological Seminary, &c. | Revised and corrected. | New York: | Anson D. F. Randolph, 683 Broadway. | 1859. | (L.)   8.

Title, 1 f.; Introduction, pp. iii-viii, and blank leaf; Analysis, pp. 1-16; Text, Greek and English, in parallel columns, and Commentary below, pp. 17-166; blank leaf; title to Appendix, 1 f.; Note dated Dec., 1853, 1 p.; verso, blank; Appendix, containing Questions in the preceding Exposition, pp. 169-200.
Originally published by Stanford and Swords, in 1852, and republished in 1858.

12. The Epistles to the ROMANS, in Greek and English, &c., by Samuel H. Turner, D. D., &c., Revised and corrected. | New York: | Anson D. F. Randolph, 683 Broadway. | 1859. | (L.)   8.

Title, 1 f.; Order dated August, 1853, 1 p.; verso, blank; Contents, pp. vii, viii; Introduction, pp. ix-xvi; Analysis, pp. 1-17; 18 blank; Text, pp. 19-234; Appendix title, 2 pp.; Note, 1 p., dated Dec., 1853; Appendix, Questions, &c., pp. 237-252. Published originally in 1853.

13. Expository Thoughts on the GOSPELS, with the Text complete. By the Rev. J. C. Ryle. New York: Robert Carter & Brothers. 4 vols.   (L.)   12.

Matthew, Mark, 1 vol. each, and Luke, 1st vol., 1859. Luke, 2d vol., 1860, to be continued; printed in England in parts. See No. 14, p. 370.

ADDENDA.

1770–1774.

1. THE | GARDEN OF THE SOUL: | or, a | Manual | of | Spiritual Exercises | and | Instructions | for | Christians, who | living in the World | aspire to devotion. | The seventh edition, corrected. | London: Printed. | Philadelphia: reprinted, | By Joseph Crukshank in Market | Street, between Second and Third Streets. | n. d.   **18.**

<small>36 pp; woodcut Crucifixion facing title, pp. 14–20; Bible texts; p. 104, Benedicite, Dan. iii; p. 105, Ps. xciv; p. 106, Ps. xcix; p. 107, Ps. cli; p. 109, Ps. cxvi, cxxxvii; p. 110, Ps. cxlviii; p. 111, Ps. cl; Benedictus, Luke, p. 124–136, Vespers (Latin and English); pp. 144–150, Complin English; pp. 157–167, Seven Penitential Psalms. This is said to be the *first* Catholic Prayer printed in this country. *J. G. S.*</small>

1784.

1. THE | HISTORY | of the | Old and New | Testaments, | interspersed with | moral and instructive | reflections, | chiefly taken from | the Holy Fathers. | From the French. | By J. Reeve. | The third edition. | Philadelphia: | Printed by M. Steiner, in Race Street, | for C. Talbot, late of Dublin, Printer and Bookseller. | 1784. | **8.**

<small>Title and Preface, pp. i–vi; Subscribers names, 2 pp; Text: pp. 1–536 (rectius 436) sigs. a–z, aa–zz, aaa–iii. The | History | of the | New Testament, | interspersed with | instructive and moral | reflections, | chiefly taken from the Holy Fathers. | From the French. | By J. Reeve. | Philadelphia: | Printed for C. Talbot, late of Dublin, Printer and Bookseller. | p 295; verso, blank. *J. G. S.*</small>

1792.

1. A | Commentary | on the | Book of Psalms. | In which | Their Literal or Historical Sense, as they relate to King David, and | the People of Israel, is Illustrated, | And their application to Messiah, to the Church, and to Individuals, | as members thereof, is pointed out: | With a view to render the use of the Psalter Pleasing and Profitable | to all Orders and Degrees of Christians. | The First American, from the Fourth British | Edition. | By George, Lord Bishop of Norwich, and President of Magdalen College, Oxford. | *All things must be fulfilled, which were written in the Psalms concerning me."* Luke xxiv, 44. | *I will sing with the spirit, and I will sing with the understanding also.* 1 Cor. xiv, 15. | *They sing the song of Moses, and the song of the Lamb.* Rev. xv, 3. | Vol. I. | Philadelphia: Printed by William Young, Bookseller, No. 52. Second-Street. | The Corner of Chesnut-street | M.DCC,XCII. | 8.

Title, 1 f.; verso, blank; then a second title, A | Commentary | &c. as above, except that the line and word "edition," after British, is omitted. Vol. I. omitted, and on the imprint the line ends Second- | street. The Pref. (iii)-xxxiv ; Table of Psalms, 1 p.; verso, blank; A Commentary, 1-268 (in. Ps. 78); sigs. B to Pp complete. The Vol. II. has a title like that of Vol. I., with Vol. II.; verso, blank; pp. 269-554, beginning "made to Abraham;" sigs. Qq to verso of Eeee². *J. G. S.*

1797.

1. A | Catholic Liturgy, | or | Forms of Prayer. | Christians of all Denominations may unite in | these Prayers, as they allude to no Doctrines, | but such as are universally professed by all who | call themselves Christians. | Printed by Samuel Hall, No. 53, Cornhill, Boston. | 1797. | 8.

Title, 1 f.; verso, blank; p. 3-44; sig. B (p. 9) to F (p. 41); facing p. 44 is a page headed "Catholic Lecture, at Concert Hall," signed "Nathan Davies" Boston, March 25, 1797.

This volume contains: p. 20, Ps. xxxiv; p. 21, Ps. li; p. 22, Ps. lxvii; p. 23, Ps. ciii; p. 24, Ps. cxvi; p. 25, Ps. cxxxix; p. 26, Mat. v, 1-20; p. 28, Mat. vi, 19-34; p. 29, Mat. vii, 1-12; p. 10, Rom. xii; p. 32, Colos. iii; p. 33-5, James i. *J. G. S.*

1804.

1. HOLY BIBLE: Boston: | Printed for Thomas & Andrews, | By J. T. Buckingham, | sold wholesale and retail at their Bookstore, No. 45, New- | bury-Street, and by by (*sic*) the principal Book- | sellers in the United States. | 1804. | (Gowans.)   12.

See No. 5 of 1804.

1812.

1. THE | HOLY BIBLE, | containing the | Old and New | Testaments. | Translated out of | 𝕿𝖍𝖊 𝕺𝖗𝖎𝖌𝖎𝖓𝖆𝖑 𝕿𝖔𝖓𝖌𝖚𝖊𝖘, | and with | the former translations diligently | compared and revised. | Printed for the New York Bible | Society. | Hartford, Connecticut. | Printed by | Hudson & Goodwin. | 1812. | (L.)   12.

The same as No. 5, of 1809, with a variation in the imprint.

1813.

1. A | Commentary | on | The BOOK OF PSALMS. | In which | their literal or historical sense, | as they relate to | King David, and the people of Israel | is illustrated ; | and their application to | Messiah, to the Church, and to individuals, | as members thereof, is pointed out; | with a view to render the | use of the Psalter pleasing and profitable | to all orders and degrees of Christians. | By George, Lord Bishop of Norwich, | and President of Magdalen College, Oxford. | All things....me. Luke xxiv, 44. | I will.... also. 1 Cor. xiv, 15. | They sing....Lamb. Rev. xv, 3. | New York: | Published by Griffin & Rudd, 189 Greenwich-street. | Paul and Thomas, Printers. | 1813. | (N. Y. Soc. Lib.)   8.

Title, 1 f.; verso, blank; Pref. (iii)-xxxviii; Table, 1 p.; verso, blank; Comment., (41)-620; sigs. B to 4F²; with portrait lettered "Dʳ Geo : Horne | Late Bishop of Norwich. | Pubᵈ by Griffin & Rudd. NYork. | Underneath the head, T. Gimbrede, sc. NY. J. G. S.

2. **Das Neue | Testament** | unsers | Herrn und Heilandes | Jesu Christi, | nach der Deutschen Übersetzung | D Martin Luthers. | Mit kurzem | Inhalt eines jeden Capitels, | und | vollständiger Anweisung gleicher Schriftstellen. | Wie auch | aller Sonn- und Festtägigen | Evangelien und Episteln. | Philadelphia: | Gedruckt für Philipp H. Ricklin. | 1813. | (L.) 12.

Title, 1 f.; verso, blank; Verzeichniß der Bücher, 1 p.; verso, blank; Text: pp. 5 to 537; Anweisung der Episteln, 5 pages not numbered; sig. A⁴ to verso of Z3¹ in 6ˢ, followed by a blank leaf.

1819.

1. HOLY BIBLE: Boston: Printed by John H. A. Frost, Congress Street, for West, Richardson and Lord, No. 75 Cornhill. 1819. 12.

Stereotype edition. Many large editions were printed from these stereotype plates in succeeding years. *Melvin Lord.*

1820.

1. NEW TESTAMENT. Boston: Published by Richardson & Lord. 1820. 12.

Large numbers were continued to be printed from the stereotype plates of this edition. *Melvin Lord.*

1822.

1. THE | COLUMBIAN FAMILY AND PULPIT BIBLE: | Being a corrected and improved American edition of the | Popular English | Family Bible; | With concise Notes and Annotations, | Theological, Historical, Chronological, Critical, Practical, Moral and Explanatory. | From | Poole, Brown, Doctors A. Clarke, Coke, Scott, Doddridge, &c. | With numerous Additions, in the present Work, from those | distinguished modern Biblical Critics, | Michaelis, Lowth, Newcome, Blaney, Horsley, Campbell, Gerard, Macknight, &c. | Containing also, | sundry important received various Readings, from | the most ancient Hebrew and Greek Manuscripts, | and | the most celebrated Versions of Scripture. | Also, sundry corrections and improvements, of our excellent English Version (generally admitted by learned

Christians | of every name), with References to Authors, Versions and Manuscripts. | Also, an | Illustrative Argument | prefixed to each Sacred Book or Epistle, from the first Authorities. | Together with | A valuable Appendix, or Supplement. | First American Edition, | embellished with Engravings. | *Search the Scriptures; for in them ye think ye have eternal life: and they are they which testify of me. . . . John v, 39.* | *These were more noble than those of Thessalonica, in that they received the word with all readiness of mind, and searched the Scriptures* | *daily, whether those things were so. . . . Acts xvii, 11.* | Boston: | Published by Joseph Teal, | Printed by J. H. A. Frost, opposite U. S. Bank, Congress Street. | 1822. | (G. L.)   fol.

Engraved Title, The Complete | Family Bible, | Containing the Sacred Text | of the | Old and New Testaments, | with the | Apocrypha at Large, | *illustrated with* | Notes and Annotations | Selected | *From the Writings of* | Scott, Poole, Henry, Brown, Clarke, and Wesley. | Embellished with numerous engravings. | Vignette, Adam and Eve in Paradise, Shepperson, del. *J. Chorley*, sculp. Boston. Published by Joseph Teal. | 1 f.; verso, blank; Printed title, 1 p.; verso, blank; Preface by the American Editor, dated September 21, 1822, 2 pp.; Introduction, 2 pp, and part of the 3d; verso of 3d page, Names and Order of all the Books (including those of the Apocrypha, which, however, are not in this volume); These 4 prel. ff. compose sig. A in 4^s; Text: Gen. to Mal., sigs. A to verso of $E10^2$; No title to the New Testament; Text: Mat. to Rev., sigs. F10 to verso of $A13^2$; A Chronological Index, 1 p.; A Geographical Index, 1 p.; A Table of Offices and conditions of Men, 1 p.; Tables of Scripture Measures, &c., 1 p.; sig. B13 ^{1} and ^{2}, all in 2^s; there are sig. figures in addition, sigs. A and B are each marked 1; then no figures until S2 and T2, each of which are marked 21, and so on to verso of $B13^2$ which is 139^4, all in 4^s.

Engravings:

The High Priest. Frontispiece to O. Test . . . . *J. Chorley*, sculp.
Adam and Eve. Gen. C 3, V 6. At top, Engraved for Fowler's Family Bible.
The Deluge.
Noah's Ark. At foot, Engraved for J. Teal's Edition. . . . . *Kelly*. sc.
Noah's Sacrifice. At foot, Engraved for J. Teal's Edition.. . . . . *Kelly*, sculpt.
Tower of Babel. At foot, Engraved for Teal's Edition . . . . *I. Chorley*, sc.
The Angel appearing to Hagar. At the top, ΘΕΟΣ.
Abraham's Faith   At top, Engraved for Fowler's Family Bible. . . . . *Gregory*, sc.
Jacob's Dream. At top, Engraved for Fowler's Family Bible. . . . . *Gregory*, sc.
Joseph cast into the Pit. At foot, Engraved for Teal's Edition. Craig, del. *I. Chorley*, sc.
The Finding of Moses. At foot, Engraved for J. Teal's Edition. W. M. Craig, del.
    Kelley, sc.
Pharaoh and his host drowned. At foot, Teal's Edition. . . . . *I. Chorley*, sc.
*Map of the Country from Suez to Mount Sinai.
Moses delivering the Law. At foot, Engraved for Teal's Edition. W. M. Craig, del.
    I. Chorley, sc.

Death of Abimelech. At foot, Teal's Edition. Graig, del............*I. Chorley*, sc.
Jepthah's rash vow..J. V. N. T., sc.
Sampson slaying the lion.......................................*I. Chorley*, sculp.
David before Saul ....*I. Chorley*, sc.
Solomon's Temple.
The Shunamite's son restored.
The Triumph of Mordecai. At foot, Engraved for J. Teal's Edition. W. M. Craig, del. *T. Kelly*, sc.
The Rock smitten. At foot, Engraved for J. Teal's Edition...............*Kelly*, sc.
Zechariah's Vision. At top, Engraved for Fowler's Family Bible........*Gregory*, sc.
The Annunciation.
Virgin Mary and Child. At foot, Teal's Edition. Raphael............*I. Chorley*, sc.
The Wise Men's offering. At foot, Teal's Edition.
The Maries at the Sepulchre. B. West, F. R. A. Pinxt.....*O. H. Throop*, sc. Boston.
*Geographical Illustrations of Scripture Histories, particularly Journeys.
Raising the Widow's Son. W. M. Craig, del.....................*I. Chorley*, sculp.
Christ's Agony. At foot, Engraved for Teal's Edition. W. M. Craig, del..*I. Chorley*, sculp.
*Jerusalem and places adjacent. At foot, *Charlestown, Mass. Published by S Etheridge junr.*, 1813.
Christ and the Woman of Samaria. At foot, Engraved for J. Teal's Edition. Monsiau, delt... ....*T. Kelly*, sc.
The Crucifixion. At foot, Engraved for J. Teal's Edition. Vandyke pinxt. *T. Kelly*, sculp.
St. Paul at Melita. At foot, Engraved for J. Teal's Edition............*T. Kelly*, sc.
Paul reproving Peter...*A. Bowen*, sc.
Hebrews Ch. 1 v. 6...................................*I. Chorley*, sculp. Boston.
Death on the pale Horse. At foot, Engraved for Teal's Edition. W. M. Craig, del. *I. Chorley*, sculp. Brattro. Vt.

The Maps marked with a * appeared previously in an edition of Calmet's Dictionary of the Bible, published in Boston by Etheridge, in 4 vols. 4to.

The Columbian Family Bible was published in numbers; the subscription amounted to upwards of 3000. It is without Marginal References. MR. TEAL the publisher, came to America about the year 1820, as book agent for an English house, and afterwards went into business on his own account, when he undertook to republish, by subscription, an English Family Bible, but whose edition is not stated. Calling on the Rev. JONATHAN HOMER, D. D., of Newtown, Mass., that clergyman learned that no person had been engaged to see to the correctness of the work, and thereupon undertook that responsibility. (*Melvin Lord.*) He accordingly revised the Practical Observatious; condensed many of the Notes of the original edition, those especially from the commencement of the Prophets being new; almost wholly rewrote the Arguments prefixed to the Books from the beginning of Isaiah, and corrected the dates of writing those of the New Testament. (*Preface.*) The work was printed or set up in the establishment of Richardson & Lord, Boston, and on account of the conductor of the Office, J. H. A. Frost. (*Mr. Lord.*) Dr. Homer was a graduate of Harvard College; possessed a collection of rare Bibles and was quite a critic. He died 11th August, 1843, having been fifty years in the ministry.

2. A Commentary on THE BOOK OF PSLAMS. By George, Lord Bishop of Norwich, and President of Magdalen College, Oxford. To which is prefixed, A Memoir of the Life of the Author. Philadelphia: 1822. (Mass. Hist. Soc.) 8.

1823.

1. THE | HOLY BIBLE, | containing | the Old and New Testaments, | and | the Apocrypha. | Translated out of the Original Tongues, | and with | the former Translations diligently compared and revised, | By the Special Command of King James I. of England. | New York: | Printed and Published by T. and J. Swords, | No. 99 Pearl-street. | 1823. | (L.) 4.

Title, 1 f.; verso, blank; Dedication to King James, 1 p.; Names and Order, 1 p.; Text: Gen. to Mal., sig. 1 to recto of 93² in 4s; Apocrypha, in smaller type, verso of 93² to recto 111³ in 4s; a blank page; Family Record, 2 leaves; Title to New Testament; The | New Testament | of our | Lord and Saviour | Jesus Christ. | Translated out of | the Original Greek; | and with | the former translations diligently compared and revised. | By the special command of King James I of England. | New York: | Printed and published by T. and J. Swords, | No. 99 Pearl Street, | 1822 | verso, blank; Text: Mat. to Rev., sig. 112 to recto of 140² in 4s; followed by a blank page; Index, 14 leaves; sig. 140³ & ⁴ then 141 to verso of 145 in 2s; Table of Measures and Appendix 3 pp.; Table of Offices and Time, 1 p.; Table of Kindred, 1 p.; sig. 145² to recto of 146², followed by a blank page.

2. HOLY BIBLE: with Apocrypha, Marginal Notes and References, Index, Tables, &c. Philadelphia: H. C. Carey & I. Lea, Chesnut Street. 1823. 4.

A reissue of Carey's 4to Bible of 1812. See No. 3, *supra* p. 172

3. Stereotype edition. NEW TESTAMENT: with references and a key sheet of questions — Historical, Doctrinal, and Practical: designed to Facilitate the Acquisition of Scriptural Knowledge, in Bible Classes, Sunday Schools, Common Schools, and private Families. By Hervey Wilbur, A. M. Boston: Published by R. Bannister, and sold by the principal Booksellers in the United States. Stereotyped by T. H. Carter & Co. 1823. (Gowans.) 12.

Pp. 321.

1824.

1. LE | NOUVEAU TESTAMENT | de | notre Seigneur Jésus Christ. | Imprimé sur la dernière édition de Paris. | Revue et corrigée avec soin | d'après le texte Grec. | A Boston : | Chez J. H. A. Frost. | 1824. | (Melvin Lord.) 12.

This edition of the New Testament was printed by J. H. A. Frost, especially for and by order of Richardson & Lord, in their office, of which he was Superintendent.

1825.

Some thirty-five years ago, say about 1825, there was published at Boston, by the Company of Booksellers, a handsome octavo Bible; and also, by the same, about the same period, an edition of a size a little less than Octavo, on a minion type, and called The Minion Bible. *Melvin Lord.*

2. NEW TESTAMENT: Boston: Published by Richardson and Lord. 1825. 18.

This edition was designed for the use of Schools. It was edited by Renselaer Bentley, and contained a Vocabulary of all the words used in the book, alphabetically arranged, with their division, accentuation, part of speech, and definition; also, a list of all the proper names embraced in it, accented and pronounced. *Melvin Lord.*

1826.

1. LA | BIBLIA SAGRADA, | a saber: | El Antiguo y el Nuevo Testamento, | traducidos de la | Vulgata Latina | en Español, | por el Rmo. P. Felipe Scio de S. Miguel, | Obispo electo de Segovia. | Nueva Edicion, | a costa de la Sociedad Americana de la Biblia, | conforme à la Segunda, que revista y corregida publicó su misno traductor | el Año de 1797 en Madrid. | Jesus respondió: *Escudriñad las Escrituras.* | S. Juan, cap. v. ver. 39. | Nueva-York : | Edicion estereotipica por A. Chandler. | 1826. | 8.

3d edition, from the same plates as edition of 1824. See No. 5, *supra* p. 166.

1827.

1. NEW TESTAMENT: Boston: Richardson & Lord. 1827. 12.
Pp. 312. *Melvin Lord.*

1828.

1. THE | HOLY BIBLE, | containing the | Old and New Testaments; | together with | the Apocalypse. | Translated out of the Original Tongues, | and with | the former Translations diligently compared | and revised. | (Imprint torn off.) 4.

Title, 1 p.; verso, blank; Names and Order, 1 p.; Contents, pp. 4–8; Text with double rule between columns, no marginal references; Gen. to Mal., pp. 9–574; Chronol. Index and Tables of Time and Offices, p. 575; verso, blank; sigs. B to 3W⁴ in 4ˢ; Apoc. in smaller type, pp. 1 to 96; sigs. A to verso of M⁴ in 4ˢ; Title, The | New Testament | of our | Lord and Saviour | Jesus Christ. | Translated out of | the Original Greek, | and with | the former translations diligently compared | and revised. | New York: | Elam Bliss, | Broadway. | 1828. | 1 p ; verso, Account of dates, &c. | Text: Mat. to 20 Ch. of Rev., pp. 579–752; 1 leaf wanting; Table of Weights, &c., Analysis of Old and New Testament; Table of Kindred, pp. 755, 756; sigs. including title, 3X to 4U² or 4V² in 4ˢ.

1831.

1. REFERENCE BIBLE: By Harvey Wilbur. Boston: Carter Hendee & Co. 1831. Small 12.

Pp. 321. The references not being found very useful, were stricken from the plates, and the volume subsequently published without them. *Melvin Lord.*

1832.

1. NEW TESTAMENT: Stereotyped by James Conner, New York. Utica: Printed and published by William Williams. 1832. 18.

Title, 1 f.; verso, Names and Order of the Books; Text: pp. 3–237; verso, A Table of Time, and Account of Dates; sigs. 1 (including title), to verso of 20⁵; followed by a blank leaf; sigs. in 6ˢ; brief headings to columns and chapters. A school edition, common version.

1833.

1. A Commentary on The BOOK OF PSALMS &c. By George, Lord Bishop of Norwich, and President of Magdalen College, Oxford. To which is prefixed, A Memoir of the Life of the Author. Philadelphia: Alexander Towar, 19 St. James Street; Hogan & Thompson, 139 Market Street. New York: Swords, Standford, & Co. Pittsburg: David M. Hogan. Tuscaloosa, Ala.: D. Woodruff. 1833. 8.

Title, 1 f.; verso, blank; Advertisement, 1 p.; verso, blank; Memoir, pp. 5-12; Preface, pp. 13-35; Table of Psalms, p. 36; Text: pp. 37-425; sigs. 1 to recto of 36³ in 6s.

1834.

1. HOLY BIBLE: Pittsburg: Cook & Schoyer. 1834. (Mr. McAllister.) 18.

1835.

1. A | Commentary | on the | Epistle to the ROMANS, | designed for | Students of the English Bible. | By | Charles Hodge, | Professor of Biblical Literature at the Theological Seminary | at Princeton. | Philadelphia. | Published by Grigg & Elliot, | No. 9 North Fourth Street. | 1835. | (L.) 8.
Pp. 588; 1st edition.

1836.

1. HOLY BIBLE: Philadelphia: Desilver, Thomas & Co. 1836. (Mr. McAllister.) 18.

2. A Commentary on the Epistle to the ROMANS. By Charles Hodge, Professor, &c. Abridged by the author for the use of Sunday Schools and Bible Classes. Philadelphia: Henry Perkins, 134 Chesnut Street. Boston: Perkins & Marvin, 114 Washington Street. 1836. (L.) 12.

1838.

1. HOLY BIBLE: New York: Published by Robinson, Pratt & Co. 1838. (Mr. McAllister.) 8.
See No. 7 of 1835.

1846.

1. HOLY BIBLE: Hartford: S. Andrus & Son. 1846. 24.
Pp. 726, 324; 4 plates.

2. The | Earlier Prophecies | of | ISAIAH. | By | Rev. Addison Alexander, | Professor in the Theological Seminary, Princeton, New Jersey. | New York and London : | Wiley and Putnam. | 1846. | (L.) 8.
Pp. lxxi, and 652; first edition.

3. LE | NOUVEAU TESTAMENT | de | Notre-Seigneur Jesus-Christ, | Traduit en Francais, | avec le | Commentaire Litteral | Du Pere de Carrières dans le texte, | Et des notes explicatives, morales et dogmatiques, pour | en Faciliter l'Intelligence. | Publié avec l'approbation de | monseigneur L'Archevêque de Quebec. | A Quebec : | Chez J.-Bte. Frechette, Pere, | Imprimeur-Libraire, No. 13, Rue Lamontagne. | M.DCCC.XLVI. | (L.) 8.
Pp. 752. This is the only edition of the Scriptures that has been published in Canada East.

1847.

1. Das | Neue Testament | unsers | Herrn und Heilandes | Jesu Christi. | New York: | Amerikanische Bibel-Gesellschaft. | Gegrundet in 1816. | 1847. | (L.) 8.
Title within rules, 1 p.; verso, 19te Ausgabe, Verzeichniß, &c., 1 p.; Text: pp. 3-467; Verzeichniß der Sonn-und Festäglichen Episteln, also on pp. 467-471; Verzeichniß des Episteln &c. der Aposteltage &c., p. 472; sigs. including title, 1 to verso of 30⁴ in 8°.

1849.

1. HOLY BIBLE, containing the Old Testament and the New. Portland: Sanborn & Carter. 1849.   18.

With engraved title, The Everlasting Gospel. Portland, Me.: Sanborn & Carter. 1847. See No. 13 of 1848, *supra* p. 301.

1853.

1. **Die Bibel,** | oder | Die ganze | **Heilige Schrift** | des | alten und neun | Testaments. | Nach Dr. Martin Luther's Uebersetzung. | Stereotypirt von J. Howe, Philadelphia. | Philadelphia, | Gedruckt fur die Aur. Bibel-Gesellschaft | bey Georg B. Mentz und Sohn, | Buchhändler, | Nro. 53, in der Nord-Drittenstrasse. | 1853. | (L.)   12.

12th edition. See No. 15 of 1834, *supra* p. 232.

2. HENRY'S EXPOSITION of the Old and New Testament. First American Edition. Philadelphia: A. Towar and Hogan & Thompson. 6 vols. (Mr. McAllister.)

See No. 22, *supra* p. 134.

1848.

1. NOVUM | TESTAMENTUM | Domini Nostri | Jesu Christi. | Interprete Theodoro Beza. | Philadelphia: | Geo. S. Appleton, 148 | Chestnut street. | New York: | D. Appleton & Co., 200 Broadway. | 1848. | 12.

Pp. 291. This is a stereotyped school edition.

MANUSCRIPTS.

1. A Manuscript Translation of the Scriptures into the English Language, made by some former Member of Princeton College, N. J.   n. d.   fol.

This title is taken from the Catalogue of Books contained in the Library of the American Bible Society. New York, 1855, p. At our request the manuscript has been examined by J. G. SHEA, Esq., the well known biblical scholar, who describes it as a set of foolscap sheets numbered from 33 to 306, of what is technically called *copy*, having the usual marks of the printer and having already passed through the press. It includes from Psalms 22 : 20, to the end of that book, Proverbs, Ecclesiastes, Solomon's Song, Esaias, Jeremias, Jonas, Micha, Nahum, Habbakkuk, Sophonrias, Haggai, Zacharias and Malachi. On comparing it with CHARLES THOMSON's edition of the Septuagint and with his handwriting, it is found to be undoubtedly a portion of the autograph translation of that work. The ascribed authorship in the Catalogue is therefore erroneous.

2. THE GOSPELS, written in the Negro Patois of English with Arabic characters, by London, a Mandingo Slave in Georgia.

This manuscript is in the possession of W. B. Hodgson, Esq., of Savannah, into whose hands it came some time after London's death. The manuscript has the vowel points correctly used. He apparently got some one to read the Bible for him and he wrote it phonetically, using Arabic letters. Mr. Hodgson in a paper on it read before the Ethnological Society in 1857, gave the following as a specimen :

Fas chapta ab jon,
Inde beginnen wasde wad;
Ande Wad waswid Gad,
Ande wad was Gad.   *J. G. S.*

AMERICAN BIBLES.

Titles received too late for classification.

1816.

1. NEW TESTAMENT: Newburyport: Published by Wm. B. Allen & Co. 1816. 32.

It is bound up with a copy of a New Testament Dictionary by Elias Smith. Philadelphia, 1812, pp. 384, who probably was the editor, as it seems to have been got up to match with his Dictionary. *Rev. Elias Nason.*

1830.

1. NEW TESTAMENT: Exeter, N. H. Published by Andrew Poor and James Derby, for the Proprietors. C. Morris, printer. Stereotyped by the Publishers. 1830. 8.

Two volumes marked V. VI. of Scott's Commentary, and containing pp. 828 and 872. *Rev. Elias Nason.*

1833.

1. A | HARMONY | OF | THE FOUR GOSPELS. | Founded on the arrangement of the Harmonia | Evangelica, by the Rev. Edward | Greswell. | With the Practical Reflections | of Dr. Doddridge. | Designed for the use of Families and Schools, and for | private Education. | By the Rev. E. | Bickersteth. | Rector of Walton, Herts. | Philadelphia: | Published by Key & Biddle, Minor-Street. | 1833. | 12.

Title, 1 p; verso, R. & G. S. Wood, printers, New York. Preface, dated Walton Rectory, Oct. 1, 1832, pp. iii, iv; Introduction, pp. v–x; Contents, pp. xi–xvi; Mock Title, 1 f.; Text. pp. 3–414; Table of the Sections and Chapters, pp. 415–420; sigs. in 6ˢ.

INDEX.

Abbey, Richard, 363.
Abbott, Jacob and John S. C., Notes on the New Testament, 272.
Abridgment of the Bible, Sellon's, 115. See *Bible abridged.*
Abstract of the History of the Old and New Testaments, Challoner's, 266.
Accompt, a further, of the progress of the Gospel amongst the Indians in New England, a rare tract, 3.
Achilli, G., Italian Testament, 338.
Acts, Baptist version of the, 370.
   in Cherokee, 219.
   Fox's, 295.
   in Grebo, 319.
   Kenrick's, 319.
   in Mohawk, 244.
   Pierce on the, 351.
   Pise's edition, 287.
   of the days of the Son of Man, 92.
Adams, J. A., 223.
Adams, Benjamin, 260, 285.
   Henry, 193.
   J. S. & C., 192, 232, 248.
Addenda, 379.
Address of Carey, Stewart & Co., soliciting subscriptions for their Doway Bible, xxvii; of the translators of King James's Bible to the reader, published for the first time in America, 231.
Aitken, Jane, 91.
   Robert, publishes an edition of the Testament, xx, 30; report on his petition to Congress, xxi; his Bible recommended by Congress, xxii; is nearly ruined by the speculation, xxiii; vote of the Philadelphia Synod in favor of, ibid; description of his edition, 31.

Albany, 48, 116, 134, 139, 144, 158, 167, 175, 228.
Alden, James M., 315, 326.
   & Beardsley, 339, 342.
Alemany, José S., Spanish Testament, 334.
Alexander, Joseph Addison, writes a preface for Henry's Commentary, 195; on Isaiah, 298, 389.
   C. & Co., 229.
Alexandria (D. C.), 248.
Alford, Henry, Greek Testament, 375.
Algor, Israel, Pronouncing Testament, 159, 163, 192, 248.
   Pronouncing Bible, 173, 178, 343.
Allan, John, owns a copy of Eliot's Indian Bible, 9, 12.
Allen, Dr., a copy of Eliot's Bible owned by, 18.
   Edward, his correspondence, relative to the patent to John Baskett, xvi, xvii.
   James, signs the Imprimatur of Eliot's Harmony, 12.
   & Co., 122, 126.
Allioli, Joseph Franz, his German Catholic Bible, 322; Testament, 326.
Allison, Burgiss, a Baptist clergyman, xxxi.
   Patrick, chaplain to Congress, urges the American government to print an edition of the Bible, xix; report to Congress on his memorial, xx; authorized to obtain subscriptions for Collins's Bible, xxx.
Almeida, J. Fereira A. d', Testament in Portuguese, 263; Bible, 309, 359.
America, first Bible printed in, vi, 6.
American Antiquarian Society, copy of a rare tract in, vii; owns copies of Eliot's Bible, 12, 18.

INDEX.

American Bible Society, 135, 138, 140, 144, 147, 148, 149, 150, 151, 152, 153, 154, 159, 161, 163, 164, 166, 168, 176, 179, 181, 183, 184, 186, 190, 192, 196, 197, 200, 201, 202, 203, 206, 209, 213, 216, 218, 222, 224, 226, 227, 229, 230, 232, 236, 243, 244, 246, 249, 251, 253, 255, 257, 258, 259, 262, 263, 264, 265, 266, 268, 270, 271, 273, 278, 280, 281, 283, 284, 285, 286, 290, 292, 294, 296, 297, 300, 302, 303, 304, 305, 308, 309, 310, 311, 312, 315, 316, 317, 318, 319, 324, 325, 328, 331, 332, 334, 336, 337, 338, 341, 342, 344, 346, 348, 349, 350, 351, 358, 359, 361, 362, 366, 367, 369, 389.
    quartos, 229, 257, 341, 346 ; part of the MS. of Charles Thomson's translation of the Septuagint, in the library of, 391.
    Bible Union, 338, 339, 349, 350, 351, 360, 362, 363, 369, 370.
    and Foreign Bible Society, 258, 259, 260, 275, 278, 280, 281, 283, 284, 285, 297, 300, 301.
    Philosophical Society, copies of Eliot's Bibles in, 12, 18.
    Sunday School Union, 190, 192.
    Tract Society, 317, 358.
Amherst (Mass.), 192, 232, 248, 263, 293.
Anderson, A., 51, 57, 87, 113, 250.
Andover, 122, 194, 245, 255, 256.
    Theological Seminary owns a copy of Eliot's Bible, 18.
Andrews, F. & J., 187.
Andrews, William, a portion of Genesis translated into Mohawk under the direction of, 21, 27.
Andrus, Silas, folio Bible, 194, 270, 273, 281, 328.
    duodecimo Bible, 167, 179, 184, 191, 197, 210, 216.
    eighteenmo Bible, 184.
    twenty-fourmo Bible, 191, 204, 217.
    Testament, 169, 180, 186, 200, 212.
    S. & Co., 308.
    William, 269, 271, 274.
    & Judd, 224, 232, 241, 243.
    Judd & Franklin, 256, 259, 262.
    & Son, 274, 277, 278, 279, 281, 284, 290, 297, 301, 303, 328, 389.
Anglo-Saxon Gospels, Thorpe's, 295.
Annotated Paragraph Bible, 331.
Annotations on the New Testament, J. P. Dabney's, 201.
Annual, The Bible, 223.
Apocalypse, Croly on the, 187.
    Putnam on the, 370.
    Walmesley on the, 90, 237, 320, 370.
    Winthrop's translation of the, 50.
    See *Revelation*.

Appendix to the New Testament, Winthrop's, 98.
Applegate, H. S. & J., 310.
Appleton, George S., 390.
    & Co., 375.
Arawak, editions in, 56, 311.
Arian edition of the Gospels, 200.
Armstrong, James F., clerk of the General Presbyterian Assembly, xxx, xxxi.
    Samuel T., 127, 134, 143, 182.
    & Berry, 252, 262.
    & Plaskitt, 212, 217.
Arnold, L. M., History of Job, 343.
Ashton, John, a Catholic clergyman of Maryland, xxv.
Ashurst, Mr., copies of Eliot's Indian Testament sent to, 4.
Association of Congregational Ministers in Boston urged to have an edition of the Bible printed, xx ; their reasons for declining to comply with that request, xxi.
Atwood, Moses G., 210, 216.
Auburn (N. Y.), 293, 298, 315, 326, 348, 364.
    and Buffalo, 356, 359.
    and Rochester, 339, 342.
Austin, David, Burkett's Notes, 49.
    Samuel, revises Thomas's folio Bible, 40.
Auxiliary New York Bible and Common Prayer Book Society, 190, 195, 209, 230, 246.
Avery, Joseph, revises Thomas's quarto Bible, 41.

Babcock, John, 55.
    S., 264, 268.
Backus, E. F., 184.
Bailey, Francis, 30.
    J. & Dickson, 53.
Baisch, Ernst Ludwig, German Bible imported in sheets by, 28.
Balch, ——, 250.
Balch, Hezekiah, xxx.
Baldwin, Josiah B., 169.
Ballard, J. A., 215.
Baltimore (Md.), 92, 101, 106, 110, 201, 211, 212, 213, 214, 217, 251, 252, 256, 262, 281, 312, 352, 360, 374, 375.
    Bible Society, imports stereotype plates from London, and sells them to the American Bible Society, 209.
Bancroft, Aaron, revises Thomas's edition of the Bible, 40.
    George, his opinion respecting the edition of the Bible said to have been printed in Boston in 1752, xv.
Bannister, James, 345.

INDEX. 395

Bannister, R., 385.
Baptist Associations recommend Isaac Collins's Bible, xxxi; call on Congress to adopt measures to prevent the publication of inaccurate editions of the Bible, xli. versions, 259, 280, 318, 339, 349, 351, 359, 360, 362, 368, 369, 370.
Barclay, Henry, superintends translation of a portion of scripture into Mohawk, 27.
Barker, Christopher, where a copy of his patent is to be found, xvii.
Robert, Bible, 258, 260, 278; Testament, 250, 275.
Barnard, John, new version of the Psalms of David, 24.
Barnard (Vt.), 115.
Barnes & Co., 294, 345.
Bär, Johann, 146.
Barritt, ——, 328.
Bartram, A., 55.
Baskett, John, unsuccessful attempt to procure a copy of the letters patent issued to, xvi; where recited, xvii.
Mark, Bible said to have been printed in Boston with the imprint of, xlii; Bibles with the imprint of, xvi.
Thomas, Bibles with the imprint of, xv.
Bayley, J. R., edits a portion of Haydock's Bible, 321.
Beach, Lazarus, 61.
Beardsley, John E., 356, 359.
Bedell, Gregory T., assists in editing the Collateral Bible, 177.
Bedlington, Timothy, 193.
Beeston, Francis, a Catholic clergyman in Philadelphia, xxv.
Belchertown, 199.
Belfast (Ire.), a Testament printed from plates imported from, 286.
Belknap & Hall, 50.
Belsham, Thomas, Introduction and Notes to a Socinian New Testament, 97.
Bemis, James D., 149.
Benson, Egbert, Apostolic Epistles translated by, 206.
Bentley, Renselaer, a New Testament, edited by, 386.
Bernard, David, 270.
Berriman & Co., 51.
Berthier, Père, Lamentations, 309.
Bethany (Va.), 193, 206.
Beza, Theodore, Latin Testament, 390.
Bible, causes that prevented its publication in the colonies, v; price of the, in England in the last century, ibid; said to have been printed in English in Boston in 1752,

xiii; types or paper for an edition of the, not to be had in the United States, xx, nor in Boston, xxi; Congress called on to establish a censorship over the printing of the, xxxix; the first printed in America, 6; in a European language, 22; imported in sheets, 28; the first in English, with an American imprint, 31; the first quarto in English, 34; the first folio, 38; imported in type, 46; first printed in the United States from stereotype plates, 110; first printed from American stereotype plates, 125; first folio edition stereotyped in the United States, 195; first octavo printed by the American Bible Society with headings and full contents, 209.
Bible abridged, 31, 36, 105, 115.
Alger's Pronouncing, 173, 178, 343.
Annual, The, 223.
Association of Friends. See *Friends*.
Barker's, 258, 260, 278.
for the Blind, 268.
Class Book, Wilbur's, 163.
Collateral, 177.
and Common Prayer Book Society, 209, 325, 336 See *Auxiliary*.
Comprehensive, 335, 340.
Congress. See *Congress*.
Danish, 309.
Douay. See *Douay Bible*.
Eliot's Indian, 6, 8, 13; errors in, 7; varieties of, 9, 17; some particulars respecting, ibid; names of persons and libraries having copies of, 12, 18.
French. See *French Bible*.
German, Allioli's, 322.
American Bible Society's, 297.
Bär's, 146.
Goeb's, 114.
imported in sheets, 28.
Jungmann's, 78.
Kimber & Sharpless's, 181.
Mentz's, 204, 224, 232, 390.
Saur's, 22, 25, 29.
Hebrew, prospectus issued for printing a, xlviii, 101. 'See *Biblia Hebraica*; *Hebrew*.
Hieroglyphic, 33, 47, 145.
History, 106, 309. See *Power; Reeve*.
Jewish, 330.
Manual, 333.
Mexican, 237.
Noah Webster's, 222, 269.
Paragraph. See *Paragraph*.
Portuguese. See *Portuguese*.
Right aim or free debt, 231.
Self-Interpreting. See *Brown, John*.

396   INDEX.

Bible Society, Baltimore, sell a set of London stereotype plates to the American Bible Society, 209.
    New York, 126, 135, 381. See *American Bible Society*.
    Philadelphia, 110, 136.
    Spanish. See *Spanish*.
    Thomas's prospectus of, xxxiii. See *Thomas, Isaiah*.
    Townsend's, 254, 258, 261.
    Wilbur's Reference. See *Wilbur*.
Bibles, used for cartridge paper and horse litter, xiii, 29; scarcity of in America, xix; Congress resolves to import 20,000, xx; imported from Holland, xxi; wheat, rye, Indian corn, butter, pork, taken in part payment for, xxxiii; smuggled into the United States, 252.
Biblia Americana, viz prospectus of, vii; title of, 19.
    Hebraica, 120, 304.
Biblical Catechism, Wilbur's, 139;
Bill, James A., 313.
Billings, Thomas, 187.
Billmeyer, G. & D., 128.
    Michael, 50, 71, 88, 150, 161.
Blind, Testament for the, 248; Bible for the, 268; Psalms for the, 311;
Bliss, Elam, 186, 387.
    & White, 158.
Bloomfield, S. T., Greek Testament, 253, 293.
Boardman, Henry A., Quesnel's Gospels, 344.
Boarman, John, a Catholic clergyman of Maryland, xxv.
Bolles, William, Complete Evangelist, 286.
    & Williams, 287.
Bonifacius, An Essay by Cotton Mather, title of, vi.
Bonsal & Niles, 75.
Book trade in the colonies, previous to the revolutionary war, depressed state of, xix.
Borrenstein, D. A., 186.
Boston, unsuccessful attempt of Cotton Mather to print his Biblia Americana in, vi; a Bible said to have been printed in 1752 in, xiii; prospectus to reprint Clark's Family Bible issued in, xvii; the association of Congregational Ministers of, are of opinion that there are not types and paper sufficient in that town for an edition of the Bible, xxi.
    editions printed in, 12, 18, 21, 22, 23, 24, 25, 26, 27, 28, 32, 33, 48, 49, 50, 54, 60, 71, 74, 84, 88, 92, 95, 96, 97, 101, 102, 103, 105, 106, 110, 115, 116, 117, 119, 121, 122, 126, 127, 134, 139, 143, 144, 145, 148, 151, 159, 160, 163, 164, 169, 174, 175, 176, 177, 178, 179, 180, 182, 185, 187, 192, 193, 197, 204, 205, 207, 208, 210, 211, 215, 218, 225, 227, 230, 231, 233, 236, 241, 242, 246, 248, 251, 252, 253, 254, 258, 259, 261, 268, 269, 272, 275, 285, 286, 292, 293, 295, 300, 318, 324, 325, 338, 344, 351, 352, 366, 368, 370, 380, 381, 382, 383, 385, 386, 387.
Boston Athenæum, copies of Eliot's Indian Bible in, 12, 18.
    Daily Advertiser, 192.
Boudinot, E. See *Worcester, S. A.*
Bowden, 384.
Bowdoin College, a copy of Eliot's Bible in, 18.
Bowen, A., 384.
Bowen, Charles, 253.
Bower, J., 76, 107, 118, 119, 123, 130, 190.
Boyd, ——, 118, 129, 138, 153.
    & *Maverick*, 129, 153, 162.
Boyle, Robert, John Eliot writes to, 16; dedication of the second edition of the Indian Bible to, 17.
Bradford, Alden, Evangelical History, 116, 249.
    Samuel F., 84, 85, 177.
    William, 21.
    & Read, 117.
Brant's translation of the Gospel of St. Mark, 201.
Brattleborough (Vt.), 144, 184, 187, 189, 190, 220, 262, 342.
Bridgeport, 169.
Brinley, George, copy of Eliot's Indian Bible owned by, 18.
Brookfield, B. F., 218.
Brookfield (Mass.), 102, 124. See *Merriam & Co.*
Brown, T., 157.
Brown, David, Four Gospels, 377.
    Hori, 151.
    John, Self-Interpreting Bible, proposals for printing, xxxvi; various editions of, 43, 82, 150, 156, 176, 194, 219, 312; Cooke's edition, 371. Concordance, when first printed in America, 42.
    John Carter, owns copies of Eliot's Indian Bible, 12, 18.
    University, a copy of Eliot's Indian Bible in, 12.
    William, Jeremiah Goodrich borrows observations from a Testament, published by, 176.
Bruce, D. & G., print the first Bible from American stereotype plates, 126; their editions, 125, 149, 153, 155. See *Holbrook & Fessenden; Mercein*.

INDEX. 397

Brynberg, Peter, 65, 81.
Buckingham, J. T., 102, 127.
Buffalo (N. Y.), 303, 305, 309, 351, 356, 357, 360.
Bulkley, Peter, signs dedication of Eliot's Indian Bible, 17.
Bunce, G. F., 206.
Burder and Hughes, Henry's Commentary edited by, 195.
Burkett, William, Expository Notes, 49, 52, 55.
Burr, Normand, 231.
Burtis, James A., 155.
Butler, E. H., quarto Bibles, 206, 313, 336, 356; Testament, 338.
    J. B., 210.
    J. H., 247.
    William, 64, 71.
Butter taken in part payment for Bibles, xxxiii.
Buttre, J. C., 328, 345.
Buzby, Benjamin C., 106.
Byington, Cyrus, translations into Choctaw, 325.

Calmet's Dictionary of the Bible, S. Etheridge publishes an edition of, 384.
Cambridge (Eng.), errors in editions of, xliv, xlv, xlvii.
    (Mass.), Psalms in Hebrew, published at, xlviii; editions printed in, 1, 6, 9, 13, 96, 97, 98, 151, 185, 201, 231, 233, 244.
Campbell, Alexander, Testament, 193, 206; particulars of, 194.
    George, Four Gospels, 52, 55, 106, 256, 287.
Campbell, R., 178.
Canada, editions in, xlix, 389.
Canandaigua, 149.
Canfield, P., his information respecting Hudson & Goodwin's Bible, 96.
Canne's References, modern, full of errors, 87.
Canticles, Noyes, 293.
Carey, Mathew, issues proposals for publishing a Doway Bible, xxiv; advertisements respecting that edition, xxvi; address to the subscribers and to the Protestants of the United States in behalf of it, xxvii; when completed, xxviii; publishes a quarto King James Bible, xlii; his account of his standing editions, ibid; purchases the standing types of the Hugh Gaine Bible, xlviii, 70.
    Doway Bible, 34, 75, 76.
    quarto Bibles (King James), 57, 59, 62, 65, 67, 72, 76, 78, 82, 91, 93, 94, 98, 103, 107, 112, 118, 123, 124, 130, 131, 132, 133, 134 (see *McCarty & Davis*); errors in, 58, 63, 66, 108, 118; one of the editions made up of odd signatures, 68; various styles of, 95, 132, 133.
Carey, Mathew, Rheims Testament, 80, 106, 136.
    quarto Testament (King James), 84, 87, 88.
    duodecimo Bibles, 70, 83, 87, 92, 100, 105, 110, 111, 119, 135, 136, 139; error in, 92; duodecimo Testament, 136.
    & Hart, 292.
    & Lea, quarto Testament, 142, 159; quarto Bible, 172, 385; duodecimo Bible, 167.
    & Son, quarto Bible, 141, 142, 147.
    Stewart & Co., their address in favor of the Doway Bible, xxvii; their edition, 34.
Carlton & Phillips, 327, 334, 338.
    & Porter, 351.
Carleton, Hiram, 319.
Carrières, Père du, French Testament with notes of, 389.
Carroll, John, Bishop of Baltimore, authorized to receive subscriptions for Carey's Doway Bible, xxiv, xxv.
Carter, Robert, 298.
    & Brothers, 331, 361, 369, 370, 374, 378.
    Hendee & Co., 387.
Carvill, G. & C., 186.
Case, Lockwood & Co., purchase the Cottage Bible, 222.
    Tiffany & Co., 358.
Catechism of the Bible, Menzies Rayner, 145.
    short Biblical, Harvey Wilbur, 139.
Catholic Bible. See *Carey; Cummiskey; Donahoe; Doway; Doyle; Dunnigan; Kenrick; Lucas.*
    Lecture, Nathan Davies, 380.
    Liturgy, the, 54, 380.
Censorship of the Biblical press, attempt to establish a, xxxix, xl, xli.
Challoner, Dr., Bible reprinted in America, 35, 281; History of the Old and New Testaments, 266.
Chandler, A., 200.
Chapman, Ezekiel, J., Notes on New Testament, 148; on Scripture, 213.
Charles II, dedication of Eliot's Indian Testament to, 4; of Eliot's Indian Bible to, 10.
Charlestown (Mass.), 69, 71, 80, 113.
Charlottetown (P. E. I.), 335.
Chase & Co., 247, 255.
Chauncey, Charles, his letter to Dr. Lyman on the feasibility of printing an edition of the Bible in Boston, xxi.
Cherokee, Gospel of St. Matthew and Acts in, 219.

INDEX.

Cheverus, Bishop, approves a French Testament, published in Boston, xlviii, 102.
Child's Book, 233.
Chippewa, Genesis in, 243; Testament in, 228; the Gospels in, 311.
Choctaw, editions in, 302, 325.
Chorley, ——, 383, 384.
Christian's, The, New and Complete Family Bible, xxiv, 35; Dr. Wright, author of, 62.
Christians of every denomination, Isaiah Thomas's address to, xxxiv.
Christology, Hengstenberg's, 248.
Cincinnati, 257, 303, 310, 341.
Cist, Charles, 55, 56.
Claesse, Lawrence, translates a portion of the Scriptures into the Mohawk language, 21.
Clapp, Otis, 251.
Claremont (N. H.), 204, 213.
Clarendon, Earl, a copy of Eliot's Indian Testament sent to, 4.
Clark, George, 210.
Clarke, Adam, Commentary, 104; on the New Testament, 293, 361.
    Samuel, proposals issued for reprinting his edition of the Bible, xvii, 27.
Clergy, Isaiah Thomas's address to the, xxxiv.
Cobbin, Ingram, Pictorial Bible, 314.
Cochrane, Jesse, 136.
Codex Alexandrinus, transposition in Matthew, c. 23 in the, 362.
    Vaticanus, 375.
Coffin, Langdon, 207.
    Roby, Hoag & Co., 227, 228.
Coit, T. W., Paragraph Bible, 230; Paragraph Testament by, 233; Townsend's Testament, 254, 258, 261.
Colby & Co., 333.
Collateral Bible, 177, 373.
Collins, Isaac, publishes a New Testament, xxviii; his proposals for a quarto Bible, xxix; recommendations of his edition, xxx, xxxi; date of its publication, xxxii; his quarto Bible, 42 (see *Collins, Perkins & Co.*); octavo Bible, 47; Testaments, 33, 49.
    Robert R., 344.
    T. K., 346.
    & Brother, 367.
    & Co., quarto Bible, 117, 124; quarto Testament, 121; stereotype quarto Bible, 128, 137, 147, 152; varieties of, 129; duodecimo Bible, 138; other editions printed from their plates, 164, 207, 345.
    & Hannay, 138, 144, 154, 215.
    Perkins & Co., 86.
Colman, S., 264.

Colton & Seely, 205.
Columbian and Family Pulpit Bible, 382; edited by Rev. Dr. Homer, 384.
Compendium of the Bible, by Rodolphus Dickinson, 120.
Complete Evangelist, the, 286.
Comprehensive Bible, Greenfield's, 335, 340, 353.
Conant, Thomas J., Translation of Job, 349, 350.
Concord (N. H.), 163, 200, 210, 216, 227, 228, 232, 236, 247, 259, 260, 269, 278, 280, 286, 297, 307.
Cone, Spencer H., and W. H. Wyckoff, revised Testament, 318, 361.
Congregational Library Association, own a copy of Eliot's Indian Bible, 18.
    Ministers, Boston Association of. See *Association*.
Congress, Continental, urged to print an edition of the Bible, xix; resolve to import 20,000 Bibles, xx; Robert Aitken petitions, respecting his edition of the Bible, ibid; report thereon, xxi; their resolution approving that undertaking, xxii; called "The Bible of Congress," xxiii.
    (United States) requested to establish a censorship over the Biblical press, xxxix; order the petition to lie on the table, xli.
Connecticut votes in favor of importing 20,000 copies of the Bible, xx; first Testament printed in, 86; first Bible in, 95.
Conner & Cooke, 222, 223.
Conners, Henry F., 233.
Convention, Congregational (Mass.), petition Congress to establish a censorship over the biblical press, xxxix; invite the coöperation of other religious denominations therein, xl; their petition laid on the table, xli; decline appointing a committee to revise Isaiah Thomas's editions, xlii.
    Protestant Episcopal, recommend Isaac Collins's Bible, xxxi.
Cook & Schoyer, 388.
Cooke, Henry, edits Brown's Self-Interpreting Bible, 371.
    J. & Co., 101.
    & Hale, 145.
    & Sons, 145, 187.
Cooledge, Daniel, 227.
Cooper, Robert, member of the Presbyterian Assembly of Pennsylvania, xxx.
Cooperstown, 158, 165, 189, 195, 202, 208, 215, 218, 229, 241, 245, 248, 250, 263, 265, 268, 273, 275, 283, 293, 298, 300.

INDEX. 399

Corinthians, Hodge on, 362, 370.
Cornish, Lamport & Co., 372.
Correspondence respecting the patent issued to John Baskett, xvi, xvii.
Cottage Bible, Williams's, 221, 358.
Polyglott Testament, 376. See *Village Testament.*
Cotton, John, revises Eliot's Indian Bible, 14.
Coverly, Nathaniel, 32.
Crocker & Brewster, 248, 272.
Crolius & Gladding, 270.
Croly, George, Apocalypse, 187.
Crosby & Nichols, 295.
Cruikshank, Joseph, 32, 379.
Cummings, J. A., Testament with notes, 121, 185, 218.
   & Hilliard, 121.
   Hilliard & Co., 163, 169, 176, 179, 180.
Cummiskey, Eugene, folio Bible, 170.
   quarto Bible, 171, 176.
   octavo Bible, 165, 166, 183, 190, 208, 215, 241, 245, 260, 265, 283, 289, 296, 308, 323.
   Testament, 168, 193, 199, 210, 211, 233, 243, 266, 269, 280, 367.
   Ward's errata, 168.
   sells his stereotype plates to Fielding Lucas of Baltimore, 211, 213, 214.
Cunningham, James, 169.
Currency, sterling, reduced to dollars and cents, in an edition of the New Testament, 228.
Cushing, Edmund, 174, 179, 187, 195, 208.

Dabney, J. P., Annotations on the New Testament, 201; Tyndale's Testament, 255.
Dana & Co., 351.
Daniel, remarks on, 48.
Danish Bible, 309.
Davenport, Bishop, 228.
   Rufus, Free Debt Bible, 232, and Testament, 233.
Davies, Nathan, Catholic Lecture by, 380.
Davis, M. L. & W. A., 59.
   Thomas, 267, 338.
Davison, G. M., 125, 220.
Day, Mills, issues a prospectus of a Hebrew Bible, 101.
Dayton (O.), 357.
Dear, W. E., 276.
Dearborn, George, 248, 298.
Debt, a Bible in support of freedom from, 231, and Testament, 233.
Dedication to Eliot's Indian Testament, 4; to Eliot's Indian Bible, 10, 17.
Definition Testament, Goodrich's, 175.

Delaplaine & Murray propose to republish Macklin's edition of the Bible, 111.
Parker, Kimber & Richardson issue proposals for publishing a Bible, 117.
Delaware, votes against importing Bibles, xx.
   Indian, Epistles of John in, 146; Lieberkuhn's Harmony in, 155.
Delisser & Procter, 373, 377.
Demarest, John T., on Peter, 319.
Dencke, C. F., Epistles of St. John in Delaware, 146.
Denio, John, 80, 106.
   & Phelps, 140.
Derby, James, 213.
Desilver, Charles, 347, 349, 361.
   Robert P., 261.
   Thomas, 136.
   & Co., 242, 252, 388.
Devens, Richard, metrical paraphrase of Job, 50.
Devereux Testament, 199, 227, 243, 267; similarity between it and the Lucas duodecimo, 211; Sadlier's, a continuation of the, 272.
Devotional Family Bible, Fletcher's, 239.
Diamond Bible, The, 248, 252, 298; Testament, 271.
Diary, Cotton Mather's, extract from, 20.
Dick, ——, 223, 321, 342, 365; A. L., 282, 333, 334.
Dickinson, Rodolphus, compendium of the Bible, 120; New Testament, 225; peculiarities of his translation, 226.
   & Ward, 254.
Dictionary of the Bible, 101.
   Calmet's, published in Boston, 384.
Diggs, Thomas, a Catholic clergyman of Maryland, xxv.
Divine Library, 352.
Dix, Joseph, 115.
Dobson, J., 32.
   Thomas, 52, 56, 61; publishes a Hebrew Bible, 120.
Dodd & Rumsey, 84.
Doddrige, Philip, Family Expositor, 88, 263, 293, 361; a congregationalist, 194.
   Family Expositor abridged, 90.
Dodge & Sayre, 119.
Donahoe, Patrick, 318; Doway Bible, 324, 366; purchases Cummiskey's plates, 324; Testament, 325; Putnam's Apocalypse, 370.
Doolittle, A., 40, 44, 45, 51, 61, 70, 123.
Dornin, Bernard, 90; proposes to publish an edition of the Doway Bible, 159.

INDEX.

Doway Bible, proposals for publishing a, xxiv; names of clergymen authorized to receive subscriptions for, xxv; advertisement announcing the first number, xxvi; address of the publishers soliciting subscriptions for, xxvii; completed, xxviii.
    editions of the, 34, 75, 76, 165, 166, 170, 171, 176, 183, 190, 208, 215, 220, 241, 245, 246, 251, 260, 265, 276, 281, 283, 289, 296, 306, 308, 313, 320, 322, 323, 328, 330, 336, 341, 342, 344, 345, 348, 353, 358, 365, 366, 374, 375.
    Archbishop Kenrick's revised edition of. See *Kenrick*.
Dowe, Joseph, 249.
Doyle, ——, a Catholic clergyman of Maryland, xxv.
    John, Doway Bible, 220, 246; Dunigan purchases the plates of, 276; Pastorini, 237; plates of Pastorini sold to Sadlier, 371.
D'Oyley and Mant's Bible with Notes by Dr. Hobart, 142.
Doxology, the, its correctness questioned, 362, 376, 377.
Draper, ——, 67.
Drenker, John, xxx.
Duane, James, chairman of the committee in Congress to whom Robert Aitken's petition was referred, xxi; his letter to the chaplains of Congress thereon, xxii; chairman of the committee in the New York Senate to whom Hodge, Allen and Campbell's petition was referred, xxxvii.
Dudley, Joseph, signs dedication of Eliot's Indian Bible, 17.
Duffield, George, chaplain of Congress, recommends Robert Aitken's edition of the Bible, xxii; to obtain subscriptions for Collins's Bible, xxx.
Duffy, W., 140; proposes to publish a Doway Bible, 141.
Dunigan, Edward, publishes Kenrick's revision of the Acts, 319.
    Haydock's quarto, 320, 330, 341, 344, 353, 365.
    octavo Bible, 276, 308, 323, 336, 342, 348, 358, 366; various styles of, 276.
    Lamentations, 309, 373.
    Lenten Manual, 317.
    Rheims Testament, 286, 311, 318, 327, 338, 343, 344, 362, 368.
    Spanish Testament, 334.
Dunning & Hyer, 52.
Duponceau, Mr., his opinion of the value of Eliot's Indian Bible, 17.
Durell, William, 57, 60, 61; error in his folio Bible, 57.

Durrie & Peck, 222.
Dutch Testament, 350.
Duyckinck, Evert, 81, 88, 92, 111, 112, 116, 125; errors in his duodecimo Testament, 81.

Ecclesiastes, Noyes on, 293.
Eckendorff, G., 297.
Eddy, ——, 225.
    Isaac, 109.
Edes & Gill, 26.
    & Sons, 32.
Edwards, Justin, Family Bible, 332, 357; Family Testament, 317.
Edwin, D., 118.
    & Maverick, 129.
Electrotyped engravings introduced in America, 288; editions, 348, 351, 369.
Eliot, John, his the first Bible printed in America, v, vi, xiii; particulars respecting his translations of the Scriptures, 3, 6, 10, 16, 17.
    Indian Bible, 6, 8, 13; errors in, 7, 14, 15, 16; facsimile of title pages of, between 8, 9; varieties of, 9, 16; dedications of, 10, 17; who own copies of, 12, 18.
    Testament, 1, 13; errors in, 2; two varieties of, 9; facsimile of title pages of, 1.
    Harmony, 12.
Elizabethtown, 34, 181, 200, 218, 224, 241.
Ellis, G. B., 171, 242, 261.
Ely, Ezra Styles, assists in editing the Collateral Bible, 177.
Endicott, Gov., announces the completion of Eliot's translation of the Bible into the Indian language, 3.
Engles, Joseph P., his revised edition of Greenfield's Greek Testament, 294.
English editions with American imprints, 85, 239, 252, 329, 362, 373, 375, 378.
Engravers' names are printed in this index in italic, q. v.
Ephesians, Baptist translation of, 362.
Epistles, Apostolic, Judge Benson's translation of the, 206.
    of St. John in Delaware, 146.
    and Gospels in German, 30.
    and Gospels throughout the year, 318.
Errata in English editions of the Bible, xliii, xliv.
    Ward's, of the Protestant Bible, 168, 280.
Errors in American editions of the Scriptures, 2, 3, 7, 14, 15, 16, 30, 31, 32, 34, 36, 37, 43, 53, 55, 57, 58, 64, 66, 70, 71, 81, 92, 95, 96, 101, 102, 106, 108, 130, 143, 144, 152, 154, 164, 167, 172, 174, 179, 180, 191, 197, 198, 199, 207, 208, 210, 214, 220, 221, 223, 227, 230, 242,

251, 252, 260, 272, 293, 298, 318, 321, 331, 342, 345, 367.
Errors in Leavitt's reprint of the original edition of the Rheims Testament, 234, 235.
Essay upon the good that is to be devised and designed, title of, vi.
Etheridge, Samuel, 69, 71, 80, 88, 113, 384; errors in his edition, 70.
Evangelical History, Alden Bradford's, 116, 249.
Evangelists, Greenleaf's examination of the Testimony of, 295.
Thomson's Synopsis of the, 128.
Everett, Edward, 12, 18.
Everts, W. W., Bible Manual, 333.
Ewer, Charles, 197.
& Bedlington, 164, 182, 187; republish Collins & Co.'s Bible, 165.
Examination of the Testimony of the four Evangelists, Greenleaf's, 295.
Exeter (N. H.), 187, 213, 392.
Exposition of the Apocalypse, Putnam's, 370.
of the Lamentations, translations of Père Berthier's, 309, 333.
of the Old Testament, Orton's, 80.
of St. Luke, Sumner's, 219.
of St. Matthew and Mark, Watson's, 236.
of Peter, Demarest's, 319.
Expositor, Doddridge's Family, 88, 263, 293, 361; abridged, 90.
Expository Notes, Burkitt's, 49, 52, 55.
Thoughts on the Gospels, Ryle's, 370.
Eyre & Spottiswood, 373.

Faber, Johan Gotlieb, writes a preface to an edition of Luther's German Bible, 28.
Fairman, G., 87.
& *Maverick*, 129, 162.
Family Bible, Scott's, 73, 99, 100.
Edwards's, 332, 357.
Family Expositor, Doddridge's, 88, 263, 293, 361; abridged, 90.
Fanshaw, Daniel, 155.
Felch, Cheever, chaplain United States Navy, sets up part of the Walpole Bible, 125.
Figueiredo, Antonia Pereira de, Portuguese Testament, 264.
Finley, James, xxx.
Fischer, Joh. Jac. Gottlob, his translation of the Passion, Resurrection, &c., of the Saviour, into Arawak, 56.
Fiske, N. W., Life of Doddridge, 263.
Flagg & Gould, 122.
& Gray, 145.
Fleet, Thomas, 22.
Fleming, John, issues proposals for reprinting Rev. Samuel Clarke's Bible, xvii, 27.

Fletcher, Alexander, Devotional Family Bible, 239.
Edward H., 337.
Follen, Charles, Luther's version of St. John's Gospel, 244.
Foster, Benjamin, a Baptist clergyman, xxxi.
John, 12.
Fowles, W. B, 163.
Foz, Gilbert, 57.
Fox, T. B., Acts, 295.
Frankfort on the Main, inscription in a copy of Saur's edition of the Bible found in, 23.
Frechette, J. B., 389.
F. I. L., 130, 131, 141; *Frederick, J. L.*, 131, 190.
Freedom from debt, a Bible in support of, 231; Testament, 233.
French Bible, 126, 151, 292, 324, 337, 348.
Testament, xlviii, 102, 181, 213, 281, 338, 389.
Friederici, E., St. John's Gospel in Greek and English, 206.
Friends, the, recommend Isaac Collins's quarto Bible, xxx.
Bible Association of, 208, 211, 249, 276, 336, 348.
Frost, J. H. A., 151, 175, 382, 384, 386.
Furman, ———, 118.

Gaine, Hugh, Testament, xxxvi, 36; duodecimo Bible, xxxviii, 46; Mathew Carey purchases the stereotypes of his Bible, xxxix, 70; Duyckinck copies his Testament, 81.
Galatians, in Mohawk, 245.
Turner on, 351.
Garden of the Soul, 379.
Gardinier, Frederick, on St. Jude, 352.
Gardner, John G., owns a copy of Eliot's Bible, 12.
Gaylord, George, 241.
& Wells, 287.
Geddes, W. F., 205.
General Court of Massachusetts, not disposed to print an edition of the Bible, xxi.
Genesis, a portion of, printed as a specimen, 27, 34, 101.
in Chippewa, 243.
in Grebo, 311.
in Mohawk, 21, 26.
Patrick on, 292.
Gentleman, Robert, edits Orton's Exposition, 80.
George, R. S. II., 276, 278, 279.
Georgetown (D. C.), 140.
Georgia votes in favor of importing 20,000 Bibles, xx.
the Gospels in patois, by a slave of, 391.

German, editions in, 22, 24, 25, 27, 28, 29, 30, 32, 50, 71, 78, 88, 111, 114, 122, 127, 146, 150, 161, 181, 193, 204, 205, 224, 232, 243, 264, 270, 297, 303, 310, 316, 322, 326, 382, 389, 390.
    Catholic Bible, Allioli's, 322.
    edition with American imprint, 28.
Germantown, 22, 24, 25, 27, 28, 29, 30, 50, 71, 88, 150, 161.
Geschichte von der Marterwoche, &c., unsers herrn....Jesu Christi, in Arawak, 56.
Gilman, J. S., 376.
    & McKillip, 224.
Gimbrede, J. N., 321, 342.
    T., 137, 153, 162, 283.
Gladding, J., 294.
Godwin, A., 44.
Goeb, Friedrich, publishes the first edition of the Bible in Western Pennsylvania, 114; also, a Testament, 122.
Gomez, Benjamin, 60.
Goodman & Co., 308, 315.
Goodrich, Jeremiah, Definition Testament, 175.
    Samuel G., 144, 145, 149, 155.
Goodwin, George, 164.
    & Sons, 141, 154, 160.
Gospel, Mark's, in Mohawk, 201.
    Matthew's, in Mohawk, 21, 27, 214; portions of, 26, 27, 28; Baptist version of three chapters of, 369; in Micmac, 335; in Putawatomie, 281.
    Luke's, in Seneca, 201; in Mohawk, 228; in Grebo, 303.
    John's, Mayhew's translation of, 18; in Greek and English, 206; in Mohawk, 146; Luther's version, 244.
Gospels, in Anglo-Saxon, 295.
    and Epistles in the Mexican dialect, xlix.
    Bickersteth's Harmony, 392.
    Brown on the, 377.
    Campbell's, 52, 55, 106, 256, 287.
    in Chippewa, 311.
    in Greek, 176, 376.
    Greenleaf's examination of the Testimony of the, 295.
    Kenrick's, 305.
    Knowles's Poetical expression of, 370.
    in Negro patois, 391.
    Newcome's Harmony of the, 98, 122.
    Norton's, 344.
    Quesnel's, 344.
    Ripley on the, 256.
    Ryle's Expository Thoughts on, 370, 378.
    Strong's Harmony of the, 327, 338.
    Thomson's Synopsis of the, 128.
    Tyng on the, 351.
    Wilbur's Harmony of the, 339.

Gould & Newman, 255, 256.
Graessel, Lawrence, a Catholic clergyman in Philadelphia, xxv.
Gray & Bowen, 205, 208.
Grebo, Gospel of Luke in, 303; Genesis, 311; Acts, 319.
Greek, New Testament translated by St. Jerome from the, li.
    Galatians in English and, 351.
    Gospels in, 122, 176, 376.
    Testaments, xlviii, 56, 84, 85, 97, 122, 160, 186, 253, 285, 293, 294, 362, 368, 375, 376; modern, 244, 249, 273. See *Codex Vaticanus.*
Green, B., 18.
    Samuel, 18.
    Bushell & Allen, 23.
    & Johnson, 1, 6, 9.
Greenfield, William, 219; Greek Testament, 219, 294; Comprehensive Bible, 335, 340, 353.
Greenfield (Mass.), 80, 106, 120, 140, 271.
Greenleaf, Simon, examination of the Testimony of the Four Evangelists by, 295.
Greenleaf's press, 49.
Greenough, William, 154.
    & Son, 179.
    & Stebbins, 95, 101; error in, 95.
Gregory, ——, 383, 384.
Gridley, E. J., 70.
Griesbach, Jo. Jac., Four Gospels, 176; Greek Testament, 97, 160; English Testament conformable to the text of, 192, 205.
Griffin & Rudd, 381.
Griffith, Harvey, 209.
    & Simon, 272.
Grigg & Elliot, 388.
    Elliott & Co., 297.
G[uild], B[enjamin], Paragraph Testament published at the expense of, 185.

Hagerstown (Indiana), 275.
Hagerty, John, 101, 105, 110; error, 101.
Hahn, Augustus, Greek Testament, 285, 362.
Haines, ——, 162, 356.
Haldane, Robert, Exposition of Romans, 298.
Hale, Mervin, 181.
    Nathan, 215, 231.
    & Hosmer, 115.
Hall, H. B., 384, 365.
Hall, Samuel, 50, 380.
    & Sellers, 31.
Hamell, Dr., a few numbers of his edition of Haydock's Doway Bible published, 306.
Hamilton, James, Proverbs of Solomon, 374.
    Wilhelm, 111.
Hamm, P. E., 171.

INDEX. 403

Hancock, Governor, said to possess a copy of the Bible, printed in Boston in 1752, xiii.
John, leaves a legacy for the gratuitous distribution of the New Testament, &c., 97.
Hansard's Typographia contains copies of the patents issued to Christopher Barker and others, as King's printers, xvii.
Harding, Jesper, Kimber & Sharpless sell the plates of their quarto Bible to, 162; quarto Bibles, 331, 336, 346, 347, 354, 355, 364; curious error in, 331; duodecimo Bibles, 296, 373; thirty-twomo Bibles, 301, 304, 300; duodecimo Testament, 294.
& Son, 373.
Hare, Francis, Psalms in Hebrew, 96.
Harmony, Bickersteth's, 392.
Bradford's, 116, 249.
Eliot's, vi, 12.
Fisher's, 56.
Lieberkuhn's, 155.
Merrell's, of the Kings and Prophets, 218.
Moody's, 326.
Muenscher's, 194.
Newcome's, 98; Greek, 122.
Strong's, 327, 338.
Thomson's, 128.
Wilbur's, 338.
Zentler's, 92.
Harper & Brothers, 288, 372, 376.
Harris, James, 265.
Harris, T. S., St. Luke's Gospel in Seneca, 202.
Harrisburg, 303.
Harrison, Charles T., 156.
W., 66, 67, 77, 83, 118, 129.
Hart, Joshua, a Presbyterian clergyman, appointed to obtain subscriptions for Collins's Bible, xxx.
Oliver, a Baptist clergyman, xxxi.
Hartford, 55, 84, 90, 95, 101, 110, 115, 119, 126, 127, 134, 136, 139, 141, 144, 145, 148, 149, 154, 155, 158, 160, 164, 167, 169, 179, 180, 184, 186, 187, 191, 194, 197, 200, 204, 210, 212, 216, 217, 224, 232, 241, 242, 243, 246, 252, 255, 256, 259, 262, 269, 270, 271, 273, 274, 275, 277, 278, 279, 281, 284, 287, 290, 297, 299, 301, 302, 303, 308, 315, 358, 381, 388.
Harvard University, copies of Eliot's Indian Bibles in, 12, 18.
Haswell, Barrington & Haswell, 264.
Haszard, G. T., 335.
Hatch, George W., 208.
Hatfield (Mass.), Rev. Dr. Lyman of, recommends the printing of an edition of the Bible, xx.
Haven, J. P., 182, 183.

Hawaiian Testament, 361.
Haydock, George Leo, Doway Bible, 170, 320, 328, 330, 341, 344, 353, 365; errors in, 321; a few numbers published of Dr. Hamell's edition of, 306.
Heath & Graves, 338.
Heath, ——, 162; *Charles*, 187, 188, 356.
Hebrew, books of the Old Testament translated by St. Jerome, from the, li.
Bible, 120; with points, 304; Leeser's translation, 330.
part of Genesis in, 101.
Pentateuch, 291.
Psalms in, 96.
Hebrews, Stuart on, 194; Baptist revision of, 363; Turner on, 378.
Henchman, D., alleged edition of the Bible printed for, xiii; and Testament, xiv; mentioned, 21, 22, 23.
Hengstenberg, E. W., Christology, 248.
Henry, J., 147.
Henry's Commentary, 134, 195, 390.
Heptinstall's Imperial quarto Bible, the plates in Durell's folio edition are copied from, 57.
Hess, William, corrects the Mohawk translation of the Acts, 244; translates the Epistle to the Galatians into Mohawk, 245.
Heuston, Samuel, 314.
Hewett, W. H., Pictorial Catholic New Testament, 310.
Hieroglyphick (Hieroglyphical) Bible, 33, 47, 145.
Hill, James, 70.
Samuel, 39, 61, 94.
Hill, A., Gospel of Luke in Mohawk, 228.
H. A., Acts in Mohawk, 244; St. Paul's Epistle to the Romans in Mohawk, 244.
& Co., 200, 227.
Hilliard, William, 233.
& Brown, 185, 201.
& Metcalf, 98, 151.
Gray & Co., 248.
Little & Wilkins, 178, 185, 218.
Hills, David, 185.
Himes, Joshua V., 306.
Hinckley, Thomas, signs dedication of Eliot's Indian Bible, 17.
Historical Books of the Old and New Testament, Kenrick, 375.
History of the Latin Vulgate, li.
of the Bible, 121, 298, 309, 379.
of Christ, Asa Wilbur's, 338.
of the Old and New Testament, Power's edition of Challoner's, 266.
Hitt & Paul, 104.
Hoadley, L. J., assists in preparing Jenks' Commentary on the Bible, 342.

404   INDEX.

Hoag, Charles, 236, 247.
   C. & A., 232, 236.
Hobart, John Henry, edits D'Oyley and Mant's Bible, 142.
Hodge, Charles, Exposition of the first epistle to the Corinthians, 362, 370; on Romans, 388.
   Robert, 82.
   & Campbell, 44, 45.
   Allen & Campbell, their proposals for publishing Brown's Self-Interpreting Bible, xxxvi; petition the New York legislature to recommend their edition of Brown's Self-Interpreting Bible, xxxvii; Bible abridged, 36.
Hodgson, W. B., owns a version of the Gospels in Negro patois, 391.
Hogan & Thompson, quarto Bibles, 260; duodecimo, 246, 265, 277, 297, 308; thirty-twomo, 217, 232, 224, 259, 279.
   & Towars, 134.
Hoge, Moses, xxx.
Holbrook & Fessenden, 184, 187, 189, 190.
Holbrooke, J., 144.
Holdship & Son, 210.
Holland, Congress recommended to import Bibles from, xx; Bibles imported from, xxi.
Hollyer, S., 333, 334, 365.
Holmes, Abiel, his error in regard to the first quarto Bible issued from the American press, xiii.
Homer, Jonathan, edits the Columbian Family Bible, 384.
Hoogland, ——, 183.
Hooker, ——, 129, 137, 138, 153.
Hopkins, Bridgman & Co., 332.
Horne on the Psalms, 380, 381, 385, 388.
Horwitz, Mr., proposes to publish a Hebrew Bible, 120.
Hosford, E. & E., 158.
Hot pressed Bible, the first, 54.
Howard, Simeon, of the committee to obtain a law establishing a censorship over the biblical press, xxxix.
Howe & Bates, 245.
Huchenson, Mr., copies of Eliot's Testament sent to, 4.
Hudson & Goodwin, 95, 101, 110, 115, 119, 126, 127, 134, 139, 144, 148, 154, 158, 167, 180, 191, 197, 204, 210, 217, 242, 246, 381; errors in, 96, 127; particulars respecting their edition, 96.
   & Skinner, 191, 197, 204, 210, 217, 224, 242.
Hunt, E., 302.
   & Co., 262.
   & Son, 284.
Hyde, Lord & Duren, 297.

Ide, Simeon, 137, 181, 192, 218.
   & Goddard, 227.
Illman & Pilbrow, 263.
Illuminated Bible, Harper's, 288, 372; expense of publishing, 289.
Illustrated Domestic Bible, 314.
   Family Doway Bible, 308.
Imprimatur to Eliot's Harmony, 12.
Indian corn taken in pay for Bibles, xxxiii.
Indian languages, editions of the Scriptures in, xlix; 1, 6, 8, 13, 18, 21, 26, 27, 56, 146, 155, 201, 202, 228, 243, 244, 245, 263, 302, 303, 325, 328, 335, 350, 361.
Ingraham & Putnam, 185.
Inscription on a copy of a Saur Bible at Frankfort, 23.
Introduction, v.
Isaiah, xxxvi, 48, 50, 64, 71, 127, 233, 272, 298; in Mohawk, 263.
Italian Testament, Achilli, 338.

James, Edwin, New Testament in Chippewa, 228.
   U. P., 257.
Jenkins, Augustus, a Catholic clergyman of Maryland, xxv.
Jenks, William, Commentary on the Bible, 341.
   J. W., assists in the preparation of the Commentary on the Bible, 342.
Jerome prepares the Latin Vulgate, li.
Jesus, Trial of, 295.
Jewett & Co., 368.
Jewish Bible, Leeser's, 330.
Job, Conant's translation, 349, 359.
   Devens' Metrical Paraphrase on, 50.
   History of, 343.
   Kenrick's translation, 374.
   Noyes' version, 185, 259.
   Rowley's version, 175.
John, Gospel of, in Indian and English, vi, 18.
   in Greek and English, 206.
   Luther's Version of, 244.
   in Mohawk, 146.
   in Mpongwe, 328.
Johnson, Benjamin, 64, 74, 97, 115.
   Jacob, 87.
   Marmaduke, 1, 4, 6, 9.
   Fry & Co., 287, 371.
   & Warner, 93.
Johnston & Stockton, 231.
Johnstone & Van Norden, 164.
Jones, ——, 77.
Jones, ——, a member of the Protestant Episcopal Convention, xxxi.
   Peter, Genesis in Chippewa, 243.
   Samuel, a Baptist clergyman, xxxi.
Jordon & Halpin, 282.
Joseph, Macgowan's Life of, 80.

INDEX. 405

Joshua, Judges, Ruth, Samuel and Kings, in Choctaw, 325.
Judd, Mr., xxx.
  Loomis & Co., 246, 252, 255; error in, 252.
Jude, Gardinier on, 352.
Jungman, Gottlob, 79.

Kearney, F., 118, 129, 153, 162, 223, 261, 356; & Maverick, 129, 153.
Keating, Thomas, a Catholic clergyman of Philadelphia, xxv.
Keenan, W., 223.
Keene (N. H.), 146, 266, 267.
Keith, Reuel, Hengstenberg's Christology, 248.
Kelley, Hedian & Piet, 374, 375.
Kellogg, J. G., 204, 250.
Kelly, T., 157, 171, 178, 250, 312, 326, 383, 384.
Kendall, Charles, finishes the Walpole Bible, 125; his statement respecting the second Vermont Bible, 189.
Kennicott, Benjamin, Psalms from the Hebrew Bible of, 96.
Kenrick, Francis Patrick, publishes a new edition of the Doway Bible, liii; Four Gospels, 305; Acts, 319; Psalms &c., 360; Job, 374; Pentateuch, 374; Historical Books of the Old Testament, 375.
Kentucky Auxiliary Bible Society, 148.
  & Meilke, 209, 242.
Key & Biddle, 392.
  Meilke & Biddle, 216.
Kidder, Daniel P., Abridgment of Strong's Harmony of the Gospels, 334.
Kimber & Conrad, 87, 94, 98.
  & Sharpless, 154; quarto Bible, 161, 195; sell the plates of their quarto Bible to Jesper Harding, 162; German Bible, 181; German Testament, 264; English Testament, 272.
Kings, a Commentary on the Book of, published at Lima, xlix.
Kinnersley, T., 156, 176, 194, 219. See Neal.
Kirk, T., 81.
Kittery (Me.), 218.
Kneeland, Abner, New Testament in Greek and English, 160; Greek Testament, 160; English Testament, 163.
  D., 27.
  D. & J., 25, 26.
  S., 21.
  & Adams, 26.
  & Green, particulars of an alleged edition of the Bible, printed by them in 1752, xiii.
Knowles, William J., Poetical expression of the Gospels, 370.
Kollock, Shepard, 34.

Lamentations, 309, 317, 333.
Lancaster, 53, 111, 146.
Lane & Scott, 326.
Larkin, E., 115.
Latin Vulgate, History of the, li.
  Testament, Beza's, 390.
Laval & Bradford, 373.
Lawson, ——, 54.
Leavitt, Jonathan, 234.
  & Allen, 314, 327, 362, 372.
Leeser, Isaac, The Pentateuch, 201; Hebrew Bible, 304; the twenty-four Books of the Holy Scriptures, in English, 330.
Leicester, 151.
Leney, W. S., 87.
Lenox, James, title of a rare Tract in his collection, 3; owns copies of the Eliot Bible, 12, 18.
Lenten Manual, 317.
Lessons from the Scriptures, 154, 163.
Leusden, John, Greek Testament, 84, 85, 368.
Levey, ——, 87.
Lewis & Coleman, 256.
Lexington (Ky.), 148.
Lieberkuhn, Samuel, Harmony in Delaware, 155.
Life of Christ, by Valverdis, xlix; by Paul Wright, 61.
  of Joseph, Macgowan's, 80.
Lillie, Dr., second Epistle of Peter, Epistles of John, Jude, and Revelations, 339; Thessalonians, 351, 362.
Lilly, Colman & Holden, 225.
  Wait & Co., 227.
Lima, Scriptural Works printed at, xlix.
Lincoln & Edmands, 134, 139, 148, 151, 159, 163, 174, 178, 192, 205.
  & Gleason, 84, 90.
Lindsay & Blakiston, 277, 348.
Lippincott, J. B. & Co., quarto Bible, 275, 353, 364, 373; octavo, 270; duodecimo, 349, 359, 367; eighteenmo, 349; twenty-fourmo, 274, 301, 309; thirty-twomo, 359, 374; Greek Testament, 368.
  Grambo & Co., quarto Bibles, 313, 335, 340; octavo, 331; duodecimo, 297, 308, 316, 325, 332, 337, 343; twenty-fourmo, 309, 343; thirty-twomo, 316, 337.
Little & Brown, 295.
  Brown & Co., 344, 351.
Livermore, George, owns copies of Eliot's Indian Bible, 12, 18; calls attention to the dedication to the second edition of that work, 17.
Livingston, William, governor of New Jersey, his opinion of Isaac Collins's work, xxix.
Locken, John, 271, 274, 279.

Loganian Library, 12.
London, a negro slave, the Gospels by, 391.
London editions, errors in, xliv; with American imprints, 252, 362, 373, 375.
Longacre, ——, 223.
Loomis & Co., 212.
Lord's prayer, Samuel Mather's version of the, 26.
Lossing, ——, 328.
Loudon, ——, 282.
Louisville (Ky.), 281.
Love, G., 93, 94.
Lowell (Mass.), 187.
Lowth, Bishop, Isaiah, 48, 127, 233.
Lucas, Fielding, quarto Doway Bible, 214; duodecimo Bible, 251; sells the plates to P. Donahoe, 324; duodecimo Testament, 211, 281; it corresponds with the Devereux Testament, 211; thirty-twomo Testament, 213.
    Brothers, 360.
Lucian the Martyr, the Psalms in the Vulgate from the version of, li.
Luke, Gospel of, in Seneca, 201; in Mohawk, 228; Sumner's Exposition of, 219; in Grebo, 303.
Lunenburg (Mass.), 154, 174, 179, 187, 195, 208.
Luther's version of the Gospel of St. John, 244.
Lykins, Johnston, Gospel of Matthew in Putawatomie, 281.
Lyman, William Joseph, recommends that an edition of the Bible be printed, xx.

McAlpine, William, 27, 28.
McCarty & Davis, 189, 205, 207, 214, 255, 260.
McCaulle, Thomas, xxx.
McCorkle, William, Collateral Bible, 177.
McCullock, John, 43.
McCullogh, William, 128.
McDonald, John, New Testament, 116, 149.
McElrath & Bangs, 201, 214.
    & Herbert, 228.
McFarland, Charles, 263, 293.
McGoffin, ——, 357.
Macgowan, John, Life of Joseph, by, 80.
McKean, Mr., one of the committee of Congress to which Robert Aitken's petition was referred, xxi.
McKee, James, xxx.
Macklin's edition of the Bible, proposed to be republished, 111.
Macknight, James, Epistles, 103, 287.
McMahon, James, revises the Rheims Testament, 310; and Haydock's Doway Bible, 321.

McSweeney, John, 266.
McWhorter, Alexander, xxx.
Mai, Cardinal, Codex Vaticanus, 375.
Mann & Douglas, 79.
Manson & Grant, 231, 233.
Manual, Judge Benson's, 206; of the Gospels, Strong's, 334.
Manuscripts, 19, 391.
Mark, Gospel of, in Mohawk, 201; Baptist translation of, 369.
Marks, Samuel, 181.
Martin, David, French Testament, 281; French Bible, 292, 324, 337, 348.
Martin, R., 345.
Martien, W. S. & Alfred, 343, 377.
Maryland votes against importing Bibles, xx.
Mason, John, Spiritual Songs, 22.
    & Lane, 249, 253, 258.
Massachusetts votes in favor of importing 20,000 Bibles, xx; would not be at the expense of printing an edition of the Bible, xxi.
    Historical Society, copy of a rare tract in, vi; the Biblia Americana in, xii, 20; owns copies of Eliot's Indian Bibles, 12, 18.
Mather, Cotton, prepares his Biblia Americana, vi, 19; his prospectus, vii; unpublished, xii; his enthusiasm at sight of Eliot's Indian Bible, 7; extract from his journal, 20.
    Increase, 12.
    Samuel, his version of the Lord's Prayer, 26.
Matthew, Gospel of, in Cherokee, 219.
    in Mohawk, 21, 27, 214.
    portions of, 26, 27, 28, 33, 54.
    in Putawatomie, 281.
    Analysis of the 24th chapters of, 319.
    in Micmac, 335.
    transposition in the 23d chapter of, 362.
    Baptist translation of three chapters of, 369.
Matthews, Ignatius, a Catholic clergyman of Maryland, xxv.
Maverick, ——, 36, 44.
    Peter, 87, 100, 118, 129, 153, 162.
Mayhew, Experience, translates the Gospel of St. John into Indian, 18.
Meilke, Edward C., 216.
Mentz, G. W., 193, 205.
    & Son, English Bibles, 203, 209; German Bible, 204, 224, 232, 300; German Testaments, 270.
    & Rovoudt, 274.
Mercein, W., 135.
Merrell, Stephen, Harmony of the Kings and Prophets, 218.
Merriam, Ebenezer, notice of, 124.
    & Co., error in their Brookfield Tes-

INDEX. 407

tament, 102; some particulars respecting their Bible, 124.
Merriam, G. & C., 259, 266, 274, 297.
   W. & H., 271, 285; their quarto Bible, 289.
   Chapin & Co., 301.
   Moore & Co., 298, 307, 341.
Merrifield & Cochran, 108.
Methodist Book Concern, 191.
Mexican Bible, 237.
Mexico, Epistles and Gospels in the Indian dialect of, xlix.
Micmac, Gospel of St. Matthew in, 335.
Middletown (Conn.), 216, 262.
Mill, John, Greek Testament, 56, 122, 294.
Miller, Edward, W., 302.
   Samuel, his statement respecting the condition of the book trade previous to the Revolutionary War, xix; his mistake in regard to Isaac Collins's Bible, xxxii.
   & Burlock, 299, 305, 311, 313, 332.
   & Hutchens, 155.
Millerite Testament, 306.
Mills, Hopkins & Co., 336.
Mixteca (New Sp.), Epistles and Gospels in the dialect of, xlix.
Moffet, John, 320.
Mohawk, part of Genesis in, 26.
   Gospel of St. John in, 146.
   St. Mark in, 201.
   St. Matthew in, 214.
   St. Luke in, 228.
   Acts in, 244.
   Romans in, 244.
   Galatians in, 245.
   Isaiah in, 263.
Molyneux, Robert, a Catholic clergyman of Maryland, xxv.
Monotessaron, John S. Thompson, 200.
Monroe, James, 259.
Moody, Clement, New Testament, 326.
Moore, J. W., 304.
   T. V., Prophets of the Restoration, 350.
More, E. & T. T., 357.
   Wilstach, Keys & Overend, 341.
Morgan, Jonathan, 302.
   & Co., 303.
Morrison & Co., 146.
Morristown, 79.
Morse, Abel, 36, 49.
   Jedediah, one of the committee to obtain a law establishing a censorship over the press, xxxix.
Moses, the Gospel by. E. H. Putnam, 337.
Moses, William J., 339, 348, 364.
Mpongwe, Gospel of St. John in, 328.
Muenscher, Joseph, Harmony, 104.
Munroe & Co., 244, 253, 292, 293.
   & Francis, 268.

Munroe, Francis, & Parker, 126.
Murdock, James, Syriac Peshitu Testament, 317, 343, 369.
Murphy, Henry C., owns a copy of the Eliot Bible, 12.
   & Co., purchase the Pictorial Catholic Testament, 310.
Mycall, John, 43.

Nafis & Cornish, 250.
Names of Institutions and persons owning copies of Eliot's Indian Bible, 12, 18.
Nashville (Ky.), 363.
Nason, William W., 275.
Natick, the Bible translated into the language of the Indians of, 3; town of, owns a copy of that Bible, 18.
Neagle, J. or J. B., 156, 157, 162, 171, 178, 207, 208, 261, 312, 356.
Neal, Joseph, 312.
Neale, L., a Catholic clergyman of Maryland, xxv.
Neall, Daniel, 200.
Negalle, ——, 93.
Negro, the Gospels in patois by London, an American, 301.
Nelson & Sons, 362.
Newark (N. J.), 259.
Newbury (Vt.), 176.
Newburyport, 43, 61, 122, 126, 267, 275, 392.
Newcome's New Testament, Unitarian edition of, 96; Harmony, 98, 122.
New Echota, 219.
New England, the Bible translated into the language of the Indians of, 3.
   Library, 18.
New Hampshire votes in favor of importing 20,000 Bibles, xx.
New Haven, 36, 49, 53, 55, 101, 145, 222, 264, 268, 269.
New Ipswich, 137.
New Jersey votes in favor of importing 20,000 copies of the Bible, xx; first Testament printed in, 33; first Bible in, 42.
New London, 287.
Newman, Bartas P., 357.
Newman, Dr., engaged on a new English version of the Latin Vulgate, liii.
Newport (R. I.), a copy of Eliot's Indian Bible in the Library of the Congregational Church at, 12.
New Testament. See *Testament*.
New York, state, votes against Congress importing Bibles, xx; resolution of the legislature of, in favor of Brown's Self-Interpreting Bible, xxxvii.
   city, first Bible printed in, xxxvi, 44; editions printed in, 21, 36, 44, 45, 46, 49, 52, 57, 59, 60, 61,

408   INDEX.

68, 81, 82, 85, 86, 88, 90, 92, 99, 100, 102, 104, 106, 109, 111, 112, 113, 114, 116, 117, 119, 121, 124, 125, 126, 128, 135, 137, 138, 140, 143, 144, 147, 148, 150, 151, 152, 153, 154. 155, 156, 157, 158, 159, 161, 163, 164, 166, 169, 173, 176, 181, 182, 183, 184, 186, 187, 190, 191, 192, 194, 195, 196, 197, 200, 201, 202, 203, 206, 209, 212, 213, 214, 215, 217, 219, 220, 222, 226, 227, 228, 229, 230, 233, 236, 237, 239, 241, 242, 243, 244, 245, 246, 248, 249, 251, 252, 253, 255, 257, 258, 259, 260, 262, 263, 264, 265, 266, 268, 270, 271, 272, 273, 275, 276, 278, 280, 281, 282, 283, 284, 285, 286, 287, 288, 290, 292, 293, 294, 295, 296, 297, 298, 300, 301, 302, 303, 304, 305, 308, 309, 310, 311, 312, 314, 315, 316, 317, 318, 319, 320, 323, 324, 325, 326, 327, 328, 329, 330, 331, 332, 333, 334, 336, 337, 338, 339, 341, 342, 343, 344, 345, 346, 348, 349, 350, 351, 353, 358, 359, 360, 361, 362, 363, 364, 365, 366, 367, 368, 369, 370, 371, 372, 373, 374, 375, 376, 377, 378, 381, 385, 386, 389.

New York Bible Society, 127, 135, 381. See *American Bible Society.*
Bible and Common Prayer Book Society, 135, 195, 200, 230, 246, 290, 325, 336.
Historical Society, copy of Eliot's Indian Bible in, 18.
State Library, a copy of Eliot's Indian Bible in, 18.
Nicklin, Philip H., 382,
Niles, William N., 216.
Norman, J., 39, 40, 93, 94.
Norman, John, 33.
William, 48.
Northampton, 64, 71, 194, 247, 332.
North Carolina votes against importing Bibles, xx.
Norton, Andrew, The Gospels with Notes, 344, 351.
C. B., 381.
Norwich, bishop of. See *Horne.*
Notes on New Testament, Abbotts', 272; Chapman's, 148; Wesley's, 253; on Scripture, 213.
Nourse, James, Bible, 230, 242, 246, 284, 301; error in, 230.
Paragraph Testament, 186, 198, 236, 248.
Noyes, George P., Job, 185, 259; Prophets, 252; Psalms, 292; Proverbs, Ecclesiastes and Canticles, 293.

Oakes, Urian, 12.
O'Brien, Edward, 53; Tiebout &, 55.

O'Brien, Mr., a Catholic clergyman in New York, xxv.
Offer, Mr., J. P. Dabney reproved for his strictures on, 255.
Oglivie, John, superintends translation of portion of Scripture into Mohawk, 27.
Ohio, the first Bible in, 357.
Ojibwa, see *Chippewa.*
Olds, Benjamin, 259.
Old Testament, Archbishop Kenrick's translation of the Historical Books of the, 375.
and New Testaments digested, 92.
Oliphant, Henry, 293, 294, 298, 326.
Olney, J., New Testament, 211, 212.
O'Meara, Gospels in Ojibway, 311.
Orton, Job, Exposition of the Old Testament, 80.
Osborne, M., 275.
Ostervald, J. F., Bibles with Observations of, 112; French Testament, 338.
Owen, John, CXXXth Psalm, 84.
Oxford Bible, errors in, xliv.

Packard & Van Benthuysen, 228.
Palfrey, J. Gorham, Testament conformable to Griesbach, 192, 205.
Palmer, J., 157.
Palmer, S., Doddridge's Family Expositor, abridged, 90.
Paragraph Bible, Andrus's edition, 271.
Annotated, 331.
Coit's, 230.
Nourse's, 230, 242, 246, 284, 301.
Pocket, 373.
Smith's edition, 191.
Testaments, 169, 185, 186, 198, 211, 233, 236, 248, 253, 367, 368.
Parker, G., 282, 321, 333, 342, 366.
Parker, Samuel, letter of the Massachusetts Congregational ministers to, xl.
& Robinson, 61.
Parry & McMillan, 344.
Pastorini's History of the Church, 90, 237, 320, 370.
Patrick, Bishop, Genesis and Psalms, 292.
Patton, William, Cottage Bible, 222, 358; Village Testament, 226, 236; published under the name of the Cottage Polyglott Testament, 376.
Payne, John, translation of the Gospel of St. Luke into Grebo, 303; of Genesis, 311; of the Acts, 319.
Payson, Phillip, one of the committee to procure the establishment of a censorship over the biblical press, xxxix.
S., superintends the publication of a New Testament, 137.
Peaslee, J. P., 242.

Peck & Bliss, 340, 347.
& Wood, 220.
Pellentz, James, a Catholic clergyman in Pennsylvania, xxv.
Pelton, C., 191.
Pennsylvania votes in favor of importing 20,000 Bibles, xx.
Western, first Bible in, 114.
Pentateuch, Kenrick's, 374.
Leeser's, 291.
Perkins, Henry, 388.
& Marvin, 253, 254, 258, 261, 293.
Marvin & Co., 230, 236, 242, 246.
& Purves, 294.
Perry, John B., quarto Bible, 340, 347, 307, 353, 364.
Peter, Demarest's Exposition of the first Epistle of, 319.
Lillie's translation of the second Epistle of, 339.
Philadelphia editions, 28, 30, 31, 32, 33, 34, 35, 42, 43, 46, 51, 52, 54, 55, 56, 57, 59, 61, 62, 64, 65, 67, 70, 71, 72, 73, 74, 75, 76, 77, 78, 80, 82, 83, 84, 85, 87, 88, 91, 92, 93, 94, 97, 98, 100, 103, 105, 106, 107, 110, 111, 112, 114, 115, 116, 118, 119, 120, 123, 124, 127, 128, 130, 131-134, 135, 136, 139, 141, 142, 143, 147, 148, 152, 154, 159, 160, 161, 162, 164, 165, 166, 167, 168, 170, 172, 173, 174, 176, 177, 181, 183, 189, 190, 192, 193, 195, 197, 198, 199, 200, 202, 203, 204, 205, 207, 208, 209, 210, 211, 214, 215, 216, 217, 218, 229, 232, 233, 241, 242, 243, 245, 249, 252, 254, 255, 259, 260, 261, 264, 265, 267, 268, 269, 270, 271, 272, 274, 275, 276, 277, 278, 279, 280, 283, 284, 289, 290, 291, 292, 294, 296, 297, 299, 301, 302, 304, 305, 307, 308, 309, 311, 313, 316, 323, 325, 330, 331, 332, 335, 336, 337, 338, 340, 342, 343, 344, 346, 347, 348, 349, 353, 354, 355, 356, 359, 361, 364, 367, 368, 372, 373, 374, 377, 379, 380, 382, 385, 388, 390, 392.
Bible Society, print the Bible for the first time from stereotype plates, 110. See *Bible Society, Philadelphia.*
Library owns a copy of Eliot's Bible, 18.
Names of Catholic clergymen in 1790 in, xxv.
Synod recommend Robert Aitken's Bible, xxiii.
Phillips & Sampson, 300.
Phinney, H. & E., 158, 165, 189, 195, 202, 208, 215, 218, 229, 241, 245, 248, 250, 263, 265, 268, 273, 275, 283, 293, 298, 300.

Phinney & Co., Buffalo, quarto Bible, 303, 357, 366.
thirty-twomo Testament, 305, 351.
Phonetic Testament, 302.
Pictorial Bible, 273, 352, 364; Testament, 293.
Pictorial Catholic Testament, 310.
Pierce, Bradford K., on the Acts, 351.
Pieters, Gustav S., 303.
Pile, Henry, a Catholic clergyman in Maryland, xxv.
Pise, Charles Constantine. Acts, 287.
Pittsburgh (Pa.), 210, 212, 231, 388.
Plees, A. F., 311.
Plocher, ——, 129.
Plymouth (Mass.), John Cotton, minister at, 14.
Polyglott Bible, English version of, 174, 209, 217, 241, 242, 247, 252, 259, 261, 266, 269, 274, 275, 277, 278, 284, 290, 297, 301, 316, 332, 337, 343, 349, 359, 367.
Testament, 213, 227, 255, 267, 268.
Polymicrian English Testament, 219, 294.
Greek Testament, 294.
Pomeroy, R. W., 218, 271.
Poor & Derby, 392.
Pork taken in payment for Bibles, xxxii.
Portland (Me.), 263, 269, 272, 278, 280, 284, 290, 298, 301, 302, 332, 390.
Portuguese Testament, 263, 264.
Bible, 309, 350.
Pounder, Jonathan, 116.
Poupard, James, 66.
Power, John, History of the Old and New Testament, 266; Testament, 169.
Pratt, G. W., owns copy of Eliot's Indian Bible, 18.
Woodford & Co., 315.
Prentiss, J. & J. W., 266, 267.
Presbyterian General Assembly, recommend Isaac Collins's Bible, xxx.
Price of Bibles in England in the last century, v; of Carey's Doway Bible, xxvi; of Isaac Collins's quarto Bible, xxix, 129, 130, ; of Carey's quarto Bibles, 131, 134; of Cummiskey's folio, 171.
Prichard & Hall, 33.
Prime, Mr., his error in regard to the first quarto Bible printed in America, xxviii.
Prince, Thomas, peculiarity in his copy of the Eliot Bible, 17.
Printer, J., an Indian, employed on Eliot's Bible, 17; and on other works, 18.
Proctor, N., 26.
Pronouncing Bible, Alger's, 173, 178, 343; Testament, Alger's, 159, 162, 193, 205, 248.

410   INDEX.

Prophets of the Restoration, 350.
Proposals of John Fleming, for printing Clark's Family Bible, xvii; of Carey's Doway Bible, xxiv; of Isaac Collins's quarto Bible, xxix; for publishing Thomas's Bible, xxxiii; for publishing Brown's Self-Interpreting Bible, xxxvi.
Proverbs, 25, 26, 27, 32, 33, 101.
  illustrated, Hamilton, 374.
  Noyes, 293.
Providence (R. I.), 155.
Psalm, 130th, Owen, 84.
Psalms, in the Vulgate, whence translated, li.
  in Indian metre, printed, 10, 14.
  for the Blind, 311.
  in Hebrew, 96.
  Horne on, 380, 381, 385.
  Noyes, 292.
  Patrick on, 292.
  Wisdom, Canticles, Kenrick's translation, 360.
Psalterium Americanum, portions of Scripture in, 21.
Putawatomie, the Gospel of Matthew, and the Acts in, 281.
Putnam, C. H., the Gospel by Moses, 337.
  Edward, Exposition of the Apocalypse, 370.

Quakers. See *Friends.*
Quebec, 389.
Quesnel, Pasquier, Gospels, 344.

Randolph, Anson D. F., 378.
Ratliffe, John, objects to the low price he is paid for binding Eliot's Indian Bible, 10.
Rayner, Menzies, Catechism of the Bible, 145.
Reading, 79.
Redfield, J. S., 273, 293.
Reeve, J., History of the Bible, 121, 379.
  Samuel, 343.
Reeves, John, his edition of the Bible referred to, 185.
  Eyre & Strahan, King's printers, where a copy of their patent is to be found, xvii.
Reference Bible, 179, 188, 217, 220, 229, 241, 250, 252, 357, 387.
  Self-explanatory, 331.
  Testament, 180, 185, 192, 199, 212, 268, 385.
Reid, Thomas, xxx.
Resolution of the Continental Congress, to import 20,000 Bibles, xx; recommending Robert Aitken's Bible, xxii; of the Philadelphia Synod to the same effect, xxiii; of the Quakers, and of the Presbyterian General Assembly, in favor of Isaac Collins's Bible, xxx; of the Protestant Episcopal Convention, to the same effect, xxxi.
Revelation, Remarks on, 48; Smith's Key to, 256.
Rheims, the Catholic Testament translated at, lii.
  Testaments, 80, 106, 136, 140, 168, 193, 198, 199, 210, 211, 213, 227, 233, 243, 266, 267, 269, 272, 280, 281, 285, 286, 298, 310, 311, 318, 325, 327, 333, 338, 343, 362, 367, 368.
  Testament of 1582, New York edition of, 233; discrepancies and errors in, 234, 235.
Rhode Island votes in favor of importing 20,000 copies of the Bible, xx.
Rice, David, xxx.
Richardson & Lord, 382, 386, 387; Columbian Family and Pulpit Bible set up in their establishment, 384.
  Lord & Holbrook, 204.
Right Aim Bible, 231; Testament, 233.
Riker, J. C., 213, 228, 283.
Ripley, Henry I., Notes on the Gospels, 256.
Ritchie, A. H., 296.
Roberts, ——, 328.
Robinson, ——, 129, 131.
Robinson, D. F., purchases the Cottage Bible, 222.
  Edward, his edition of Tittman's Greek Testament, 285, 362.
  & Franklin, 259, 262, 263.
  Pratt & Co., 241, 380.
Roby, Luther, 163, 278, 280, 286, 307.
  Kimball & Merrell, 247, 259, 260, 269.
Rochester (N. Y.), 207.
Rodriguez, Louis, translates the Proverbs of Solomon into the Mexican dialect, xlix.
Rogers, J., 282, 312, 334.
Rogers, William, recommends Macgowan's Life of Joseph, 80.
  & Fowle, said to have printed a Testament in Boston about 1752, xiv.
Rollin, M., suggests the publication of Selections from the Scriptures, 33.
Rollinson, ——, 44, 45, 51.
Romans, in Mohawk, 244; Stuart on, 245; Haldane's Exposition, 298; Turner's 378; Hodge on, 388.
Rowand, A. H., 294.
Rowley, Abraham, Ten Chapters of Job, 175.
Roxbury, John Eliot minister at, 3, 12.
Royal copy of the Bible, 346.

Royaumont, Sieur de, M. de Sacy writes under the pseudonym of, 121.
Rumpeler, Gabriel, edits Allioli's German Bible, 322; his preface, 323.
Rye taken in part payment for Bibles, xxxiii.
Ryle, J. C., Expository Thoughts on the Gospels, 370, 378.

Sacred Extracts, 96.
Sacy, Louis Isaac Le Maistre de, his Testament republished, 102; wrote under the pseudonym of Sieur de Royaumont, 121.
Sadlier's quarto Bibles, 281, 313, 322, 330, 345, 365.
— suppress Tallis, Willoughby & Co.'s edition of the Doway Bible, 306.
— Testament, 272, 285, 298, 318, 333, 360.
— German Bible, 322; German Testament, 326.
— Pastorini, 320, 371.
— Ward's Errata, 280.
Sage & Clough, 68, 82.
Sainte Bible, le. See *French*.
Salem (N. Y.), 84.
Samuel and Kings, in Choctaw, 325.
Sanborn, Oliver L., 247, 263.
— Sherburne & Co., 269.
— & Carter, 272, 278, 280, 284, 290, 298, 301, 332, 390.
Sta. Maria, Didacus de, translates the Epistles and Gospels into the Mexican tongue, xlix.
Sanderson, Edward, 224, 241, 253.
— J., 200.
Saratoga Springs, 220.
Sargeant, Ezra, 104.
Sartain, J., 296, 312.
Saur, Christopher, biographical notice of, xii; commences printing his German Bible, xiii; Bible printed by, 22, 25, 28, 29; inscription in a copy of one of his Bibles in Frankfort, 23; Testament, 24, 25, 27, 28, 29; Gospels and Epistles, 30.
Sawyer, Leicester Ambrose, Testament, 368.
Schoff, ——, 312.
Schoyer, R., 212.
Scientia Biblica, 177.
Scio de St. Migeul, Felipe, Spanish Bible, 166, 197, 216, 237, 386; books suppressed in, 198, 203; Testament, 150, 161, 213, 255.
Scoles, ——, 57, 61, 87, 113.
Scotland, Congress recommended to import Bibles from, xx.
Scott's Family Bible, 73, 99, 100, 105, 114, 119, 134, 143, 182, 208, 215, 276; number of editions and copies of, published from 1800-1819, in the United States, 183.
Scripture Lessons, 154, 163.
— Text Book, 333.
Sears, Robert, 352, 364.
Sebring, C., 237.
Selectœ e Vetere Testamento, 33, 75.
Self-Interpreting Bible, Brown's, proposals for publishing, xxxvi; editions of, 43, 82, 150, 156, 176, 219, 312; Cooke's edition, 371.
Sellon's Abridgement of the Bible, 115.
Seneca, the Gospel of St. Luke translated into, 201. See *Sermon*.
Septuagint, Thomson's translation of the, 91; part of the MS. of the translation discovered, 391.
Sermon on the Mount, 26, 27, 32, 33; in Seneca, 202.
Sewell, Charles, a Catholic clergyman, xxv.
Seymour, J., 121.
Seymour, Joseph, 39, 40, 61, 93, 94.
— *J. H.*, 39, 40, 93, 94.
Shallus, F., 51, 66, 77, 107, 108, 123.
Shaw, S., 175.
Shea, J. G., his report on the manuscript of Charles Thomson's Septuagint, 391.
Sheldon & Goodrich, 136, 141.
— Lamport & Blakeman, 341.
Sherburne, R. H., 275.
Sherman, C., 291.
Shultz, Theodore, Acts in Arrawack by, 311.
Slave, the Gospels by London, a Negro, 391.
Sleight, Henry C., 188, 192, 196, 236.
Smillie, James, 208, 223, 328.
— *J. D.*, 345.
Smith, *Wm. D.*, 173, 221, 269, 339.
— Smith, Daniel D., Bible, 157, 167, 173, 183, 191, 215; Testament, 175.
— Elias, New Testament Dictionary, 392.
— Elkan, Key to Revelation, 256.
— James B. & Co., 216, 218, 290, 377.
— John, Treatise on the Prophets, 48.
— John Blair, member of the General Presbyterian Assembly, xxx.
Smuggling Bibles into the United States, 252.
Socinianism, modern, editions in support of, 97, 344.
Solomon's Proverbs, in the Mexican tongue, xlix.
— illustrated, Hamilton, 374.
Solomon's Song, editions of, 22, 23, 71.
Somerset (Pa.), 114, 122.
Song of Songs, see *Solomon's*.
Sorin & Ball, 279, 284.

South Carolina votes against importing Bibles, xx.
Southwick, H. C., 116.
Spanish Bibles, 166, 197, 203, 216, 287, 315, 324, 348, 386; Testaments, 150, 161, 213, 255, 286, 334, 350.
Spencer, J. A., Greek Gospels and Acts, 376.
Springfield (Mass.), 259, 266, 272, 274, 301.
Standing editions of the Bible, Carey's, 73.
 Gaine's, 46.
 Hudson and Goodwin's, 96.
 Luther's, xlvii.
 Thomas', 53.
Stanford & Swords, 317, 343.
Starr, Charles, 239.
Stebbing, Henry, Diamond Bible, 252.
Steiner, Melchior, 32, 379.
Stephens, Robert, Greek Testament, 186, 368.
Stereotype Bible, first in America, 110; the first from American plates, 125; first quarto, 128; the art first introduced, 129; first folio, 194.
Stewart, William, 275.
Stimpson & Clapp, 211.
Stockton, T. H., 352, 368.
Stoughton, William, signs the dedication of the 2d edition of Eliot's Indian Bible, 17.
Strong, James, Harmony of the Gospels, 327, 338; abridged, 334.
Stuart, Moses, Bloomfield's Greek Testament, 254.
 Essay on Doddridge Family Expositor, 263.
 Newcome's Harmony, 122; St. Paul to the Hebrews, by, 194; to the Romans, 245.
Student's Bible, 239, 283.
Sumner, John Bird, Exposition of the Gospel of Luke, 219.
Mr., purchases the plates of the Cottage Bible, 222.
 & Goodman, 299; sell their plates to Phinney & Co., 303.
Sunday School Union, 198. See *American Sunday School Union.*
Swan & Allinson, 85.
Swedenborg Bible, 251.
Swords, T. & J., 143, 385.
Synopsis of the Gospels, Charles Thomson, 128.
Syracuse, 386.
Syriac Peshitu Testament, translation of, 317, 343, 369.

Talbot, C., 379.
Tallis, Willoughby & Co., 306.

Tanner, B., 58, 67, 76, 78, 83, 87, 107, 108, 119, 129, 131, 137, 153, 162.
 & *Levey,* 87.
 D., 162.
Tanner, John, assists in the translation of the New Testament into the Chippewa language, 228.
Tanner, Vallance, Kearney & Co., 137, 162, 356.
Taylor, William, proposes to publish a Doway Bible, 149.
Teal, Joseph, 383; some particulars of, 384.
Testament, said to have been printed in English, in Boston in 1752, xiv; revised by St. Jerome, li; the first printed in English with an American imprint, xx, 30.
 Alger's Pronouncing. See *Pronouncing.*
 Barker's, 259, 275.
 Bentley's, 386.
 Beza's Latin, 390.
 for the Blind, 248.
 with Clarke's Notes, 293.
 Cottage Polyglott, 376.
 Cumming's, 121, 185, 218.
 Dabney's Annotations on the, 201.
 Dickinson's, 225.
 in English and Danish, 305.
  and Dutch, 305, 350.
  and French, 334, 338. See *French.*
  and German, 305, 338.
  and Haiwaiian, 361.
  and Spanish, 350.
  and Swedish, 318.
  and Welsh, 344.
 German, 24, 25, 27, 28, 29, 32, 50, 71, 88, 111, 122, 127, 150, 161, 193, 205, 243, 264, 270, 303, 310, 382, 389.
 Greek. See *Greek.*
 Guild's, 185.
 Indian, 1, 228, 302, 350.
 Italian, 338.
 Latin, Beza's, 390.
 Millerite, 306.
 Nourse's. See *Nourse.*
 Ojibway. See *Chippewa.*
 Olney's, 211, 212.
 J. Gorham Palfrey's, 192, 205.
 Phonetic, 302.
 Polymicrian, 210.
 Portuguese, 263, 264.
 Power's, 169.
 Revised, 169.
 Rheims. See *Rheims.*
 Spanish. See *Spanish.*
 Townsend's, 254.
 Tyndale's, 255.
 Unitarian, 96, 344.

INDEX. 413

Testament, Village, 226, 236.
  Wakefield's, 151.
  Webster's, 264, 268.
  Wesley's, 258.
  Winthrop's Appendix to the, 98.
  Woodruff's, 326.
Testaments, Old and New, digested, 92.
Thacher, Thomas, signs the imprimatur for Eliot's Harmony, 12.
Thatcher, Peter, one of the Committee to obtain a Censorship over the Biblical Press, xxxix.
Thessalonians, Lillie's translation of, 351, 362.
Thew, R., 333.
Thomas, Isaiah, his account of a Bible said to have been printed at Boston in 1752, xiii; Mr. Bancroft's opinion thereof, xv; mistake of, in regard to Collins's octavo Bible, xxxii; mistake of, in regard to the dedication of Eliot's Indian Testament, 4; various editions, 33, 34, 50; folio Bible, 38; quarto, 40; varieties of, 41; octavo, 46, 63; errors in, 64; duodecimo Bibles, 53, 54, 55, 64; errors in, 53, 55; Testament, 61.
  Isaiah, junior, 56, 65, 10, 122.
  & Andrews, 60, 71, 74, 80, 84, 92, 105, 110, 115, 116, 119, 381; error in, 60, 71, 74, 105; error on title page, 381.
  Son & Thomas, 52.
  Cowperthwaite & Co., 261, 268, 269, 277, 279, 284, 301, 309, 316, 325, 332.
Thompson, John S. Monotessaron, 200.
  Mr., author of the Hieroglyphical Bible, 48.
  & Small, 54.
Thomson, Charles, translation of the Greek Septuagint, 91; part of the MS. of it discovered, 391; Synopsis of the Gospels, 128.
Thorpe, Benjamin, Anglo-Saxon Gospels, 295.
Throop, O. H., 384.
Thumb Bible, 26.
Ticknor, W. D., 286.
Tiebout, C., 44, 51, 58, 67, 73, 76, 77, 78, 83, 87, 98, 99, 108, 119, 131.
  & Maverick, 129, 162.
Tiebout & O'Brien, 55.
Tilton, John G., 267.
Tittman's Greek Testament, 285, 362.
Toronto (C. W.), 243, 311; English Bible printed in, xlix.
Towar, Alexander, 217, 218, 388, 390.
  & Hogan, 192, 195, 197, 202, 203, 217.

Townsend, George, New Testament in Chronological order, 254; Old Testament, 258, 261.
Translators of King James's Bible, their Address to the Reader, published for the first time in America, 231.
Tregelles, Samuel Prideaux, Paragraph Testament, with Horne's Introduction, revised, 352, 368.
Trent, Council of, declares the Latin Vulgate authentic, lii.
Trenton, 34, 42, 47, 49, 228.
Trial of Jesus, Greenleaf on the, 295.
Tripp, E. H., 318, 361.
Trow, John F., 348.
Troy, Dr., first American edition of his Bible, 76.
Troy (N. Y.), 285, 289, 298, 307, 341.
Trumbull, ——, makes honorable mention of Maverick, the engraver, 36.
Tucker, ——, 312.
Turner, Samuel H., Galatians, 351.
  on Hebrews; on Romans, 378.
Twenty-four books of Scriptures, Leeser's, 330.
Tyndale, William, Testament, 255.
Tyng, S. H., on the Gospels, 351.

Unitarianism. See *Socinianism*.
United States of Columbia Bibles, 53, 54, 55.
Unrivaled Dollar Edition of the Doway Bible, 324.
Usher, Mr., 4.
Utica, 149, 155, 160, 182, 198, 213, 227, 243, 267, 387.

Valera, Cipriano de, Spanish Testament, 286.
Valverde, Ferdinand de, Life of Christ, xlix.
Van der Hooght, Hebrew Bible, 120.
Van Ess's Bible, said to be corrupt, 323.
Van Horne, William, clerk of the Baptist Association, xxxii.
Van Ness, Mr., one of the Committee in the N. Y. Senate, to whom the petition in favor of Brown's Self-Interpreting Bible was referred, xxxvii.
Vera, Ludovicus de, of Lima, author of a Commentary on the Book of Kings, xlviii.
Verbum Sempiternum, 26.
Vermont, 108, 115, 189.
Village Testament, 226, 236.
Virginia votes against importing Bibles, xx.
Virtue, George, 329.
  Emmins & Company, 239.
Vote in the Continental Congress on the question of importing Bibles, xx.

Vulgate, Latin, History of the, li; translated into English, lii.

Wait & Co., 96, 97, 103.
Waitt & Dow, 210.
Wakefield, Gilbert, Testament translated by, 151.
Walker, F., 312.
Walker, S., 150, 177.
Walmesley, Charles. See *Pastorini.*
Walpole (N. H.), an account of the Bible printed there, 125.
Walsh, William, Exposition of the Lamentations, 309, 383; Lenten Manual, 317.
Walton, James, a Catholic clergyman in Maryland, xxv.
Wanzer, Foote & Co., 307.
Ward, Thomas, Errata of the Protestant Bible, 168, 280.
Wardle, Thomas, 174.
Warnick, ——, 131, 142.
Washington, George, heads the subscription list for Brown's Self-Interpreting Bible, 44.
Washington city, 343.
Watson, Richard, Exposition of the Gospels of St. Matthew and St. Mark, 236.
Watts, John, Leusden's Greek Testament, 84, 85.
— introduces the art of stereotyping into the United States, 129.
Webster, C. R. & G., 48.
— Noah, Bible, 222, 269; Testament, 264, 268.
Websters and Skinners, 139, 144, 167.
Wells, Charles, 263.
— G., 268.
— J. Gaylord, 287.
— W., 103, 106.
— & Hilliard, 97.
Welsh Testament, 344; Bible, 366.
Wesley, John, Notes on the New Testament, 253.
West & Richardson, 145.
— Richardson & Lord, 151, 382.
Weston, Henry W., 66, 77.
Wharton & Bowes, 25, 26.
Wheat taken in payment for Bibles, xxiii.
Whilt & Yost, 354, 364.
Whipple, Anson, 125.
— & Damrell, 256.
White, E. & J., 229.
— N. & J., 217, 220, 224, 229, 253.
— R., 227.
— William, Chaplain of Congress, recommends Robert Aitken's edition of the Bible, xxii.
— Gallaher & White, 184, 217.
— & Reed, 176.

Whitehall, 64, 92.
Whiting, N. N., Millerite Testament, 306.
— & Watson, 100, 111, 113, 114.
Wiatt, Solomon, 97.
Wickes, T., 320.
Wilbur, Asa, History of Christ, 338.
— Hervey, Short Biblical Catechism, 139; Bible Class Book, 163.
— quarto Reference Bible, 188, 220, 229, 241, 250, 357.
— duodecimo Reference Bible, 179, 387.
— Reference Testament, 163, 180, 185, 192, 199, 385.
Wiley, John, 304.
— & Putnam, 295, 389.
Wilkes, John A., junior, assists in translating portions of the Scriptures into Mohawk, 228, 244, 245.
Wilkins, J. H., Revised Testament, 169.
Willard, Joseph, one of the committee to petition Congress to establish a censorship over the Biblical press, xxxix.
Williams, J. & B., 187.
— R. P. & C., 144, 145.
— T., Solomon's Song, 71.
— Thomas, Cottage Bible, 221, 358.
— William, 140, 155, 160, 387; publishes an edition of Phinney's Bible, 182, and the Devereux Testament, 198, 227, 243, 267.
— & Whiting, 99, 100, 102.
Wilmington (Del.), 65, 75, 81.
Wilson, C. P., Greek Testament, 186, 368.
— Matthew, a Presbyterian clergyman, xxx.
— S., 190.
Windsor (Vt.), 108, 136, 181, 192, 218, 227, 319.
Winthrop, James, Apocalypse, 50; appendix to New Testament, 98.
Wisdom in Miniature, 101.
Wiseman, Cardinal, his opinion of the modern Doway Bible, lii.
Witherspoon, John, one of the committee of Congress to whom Robert Aitken's petition was referred, xxi; writes an address for Collins's Bible, 42.
Wood, Richard & George S., 316.
— S., 106.
— & Rupp, 272.
Woodhouse, William, 35.
Woodruff, Hezekiah, Testament, 326.
Woodruff, W., 171.
Woodstock (Vt.), 205, 247, 255.
Woodward, W., 73.
— W. W., 53, 71, 83, 100, 105, 106, 114, 119, 127, 135, 148.
Worcester, S. A. & E. Boudinot, translate part of the New Testament into Cherokee, 219.

INDEX. 415

Worcester (Mass.), 33, 34, 38, 41, 46, 50, 52, 53, 54, 55, 56, 61, 63, 65.
Wright, Alfred, Choctaw Testament, 302.
    James, his letter in answer to an inquiry for the patent issued to John Baskett, xvii.
    Paul, 35; Life of Christ, 61; author of the Christian's Family Bible, 62.
Wyckoff, W. H., writes an introduction to Achilli's Italian Testament, 338. See *Cone*.

Yale College owns copy of Eliot's Bible, 18.
Y. J. or *Yeager J.*, 123, 130, 131.
Young, William, 35, 42, 46, 64, 92, 380.
    William J., 380.
    William S., 267, 343.
    & Minns, 49.

Zeisberger, David, his translation of Lieberkuhn's Harmony, 155.
Zentler, Conrad, 92.

www.ingramcontent.com/pod-product-compliance
Lightning Source LLC
Chambersburg PA
CBHW051844300426
44117CB00006B/265